GLOBAL GENTRIFICATIONS

Uneven development and displacement

Edited by Loretta Lees, Hyun Bang Shin and Ernesto López-Morales

First published in Great Britain in 2015 by

Policy Press
University of Bristol
1-9 Old Park Hill
Bristol BS2 8BB
UK
t: +44 (0)117 954 5940
pp-info@bristol.ac.uk
www.policypress.co.uk

North America office:
Policy Press
c/o The University of Chicago Press
1427 East 60th Street
Chicago, IL 60637, USA
t: +1 773 702 7700
f: +1 773-702-9756
sales@press.uchicago.edu
www.press.uchicago.edu

British Library Cataloguing in Publication Data
A catalogue record for this book is available from the British Library.

Library of Congress Cataloging-in-Publication Data
A catalog record for this book has been requested.

ISBN 978 1 44731 347 2 hardcover
ISBN 978 1 44731 348 9 paperback

Cover design by Qube Design Associates, Bristol
Front cover: image kindly supplied by Ernesto López-Morales
Printed and bound in Great Britain by Hobbs, Southampton
Policy Press uses environmentally responsible print partners

Contents

List of figures and tables

Figures

Tables

Notes on the editors

Loretta Lees is Professor of Human Geography at the University of Leicester. She is an international expert on gentrification, urban regeneration, urban policy, urban public space and urban community. She has co-authored and co-edited a number of books on gentrification: *Global gentrifications and comparative urbanisms* (Polity, forthcoming, with Shin and López-Morales), *Gentrification* (Routledge, 2008), *The gentrification reader* (Routledge, 2010), *Mixed communities: gentrification by stealth?* (Policy Press/University of Chicago Press, 2011). She has recently published *An Anti-Gentrification Toolkit for Council Tenants in London (2014)* with The London Tenants Federation, Just Space and Southwark Notes Archive Group.

Hyun Bang Shin is Associate Professor of Geography and Urban Studies at the London School of Economics and Political Science. His main research interests lie in the critical analysis of the political economic dynamics of urban (re-)development. He has written widely on Asian urbanisation, speculative urbanisation, the politics of displacement and urban spectacles. He is currently working on a number of book projects including (with Lees and López-Morales) *Global gentrifications and comparative urbanisms* (Polity, forthcoming), *Making China urban*, and a co-edited volume *Contesting urban space in East Asia*.

Ernesto López-Morales is an Associate Professor in Urban Planning in the Faculty of Architecture and Urbanism at the University of Chile. He is principal researcher in the CONTESTED CITIES international network, where he focuses on gentrification, neoliberal urbanism and housing in Chile and Ibero-American cities. He has recently authored an ebook: *Urbanismo proempresarial y destrucción creativa* (Redalyc, 2013), co-authored *Chile Urbano hacia el Siglo XXI* (Editorial Universitaria, 2013), and is about to publish (with Lees and Shin) *Global gentrifications and comparative urbanisms* (Polity, forthcoming). He is the author of several articles on gentrification and neoliberalism.

Notes on the contributors

Georgia Alexandri is a researcher at the National Social Research Centre in Greece. She holds a bachelor's degree in Economics from the Athens University of Economics and Business, a Master of Science in Sustainability and Planning, with distinction, from Cardiff University and a PhD from Harokopio University. Her research interests focus on gentrification, Athens, southern Europe, crisis, social and spatial justice, social movements and fear of the 'other'.

Eduardo Ascensão is a researcher at Centro de Estudos Geográficos, University of Lisbon (CEG-UL). An anthropologist and urban geographer, his research interests are in urban theory, the geographies of architecture, housing, migration and post-colonialism, with a special focus on the informal city in Portuguese-speaking countries. His current research combines an ethnographic look at the architects of the informal city, that is, slum dwellers, with an analysis of the socio-technological and policy milieu that underpins urban informality. His publications include the article 'Following engineers and architects through slums' in *Análise Social* (2013) vol 206, no xlviii, pp 2182-999, awarded the Bengt Turner Award 2012 for best European paper by the European Network for Housing Research.

Surajit Chakravarty is an Assistant Professor of Urban Planning at ALHOSN University in Abu Dhabi. He has a PhD from the University of Southern California and his research focuses on community planning, primarily affordable housing, civic engagement and planning in multicultural societies. Surajit is also interested in the processes of urbanisation in developing countries.

Eric Clark is Professor of Geography at Lund University in Sweden. He has researched the political economy of space in terms of land rent, gentrification and accumulation by dispossession, especially in the Swedish context. He is currently working on two large research programmes with Lund University Centre of Excellence for the Integration of Social and Natural Dimensions of Sustainability

Jake Cummings holds a Master in Urban Planning from the Harvard Graduate School of Design and a Bachelor of Science in civil and environmental engineering from Cornell University. His studies in urban planning have focused on the city of Rio de Janeiro, Brazil, examined through the lenses of housing policy, neighbourhood and community development, and social innovation. He is an ongoing collaborator with Catalytic Communities, a social enterprise in Rio de Janeiro dedicated to the empowerment of informal settlements and their residents.

Christiaan De Beukelaer is a PhD researcher and teaching assistant at the Institute of Communications Studies, University of Leeds. His research primarily focuses on the role of culture and cultural industries in international development. He serves on the Management Committee of European Science Foundation-funded European Cooperation in Science and Technology (COST) Action 'Investigating Cultural Sustainability', and is winner of the 2012 Cultural Policy Research Award, granted by the European Cultural Foundation and Riksbankens Jubileumsfond (in collaboration with the European network on Cultural Management and Cultural Policy education).

María Mercedes Di Virgilio is an Associate Professor in the School of Social Sciences, University of Buenos Aires. From 2004 to 2008, she coordinated the Urban Studies Area of the Gino Germani Research Institute, University of Buenos Aires. She is a sociologist interested in different dimensions of the urban social question, as well as public policies that manage cities. She has been a consultant for public and international organisations on issues related to public policy management. She was recently (in 2013) awarded a Mobility Scholarship to work in Paris on the project 'Processes and practices of residential and daily mobility within the context of Latin American cities'.

Sapana Doshi is an Assistant Professor in the School of Geography and Development at the University of Arizona, where she teaches critical development studies, urban geography, feminist theory and political geography. Her most recent research focuses social mobilisation around urban displacement and the political economy and cultural politics of slum redevelopment in Mumbai, India. She has published several book chapters and articles in journals including *Antipode: A Radical Journal of Geography* and *Geopolitics*.

Mohamed Elshahed is a Cairo-based scholar and researcher currently completing his doctoral dissertation in the Middle East Studies Department at New York University. His dissertation, 'Revolutionary modernism? Architecture and the politics of transition in Egypt, 1936–1967', focuses on architecture and urban planning in Egypt during the period of political transition around the 1952 coup d'état. Mohamed has a Bachelor of Architecture degree from the New Jersey Institute of Technology and a Masters in Architecture Studies from the Massachusetts Institute of Technology.

Amiram Gonen is Emeritus Professor in the Geography Department, Hebrew University of Jerusalem. He has been researching gentrification processes in Israel for the last three decades. Much of his research focuses on the relationship between gentrification in Israel and the political and social circumstances of the country. His research has been published in several academic journals, as well as in his book, *Between city and suburb: urban residential processes and patterns* (Avebury, 1995).

Seong-Kyu Ha is Professor of Urban Planning and Housing Policy in the Department of Urban Planning and Real Estate at Chung-Ang University, Seoul, South Korea. He received a Masters in City and Regional Planning from the London School of Economics, and a doctorate in Urban Planning from University College London. He was Vice President of Chung-Ang University (2008–10). He also served as President of the Korea Housing Policy Association and the Korea Regional Development Association; he is now a member of the board of directors of the Korea Housing Institute. He has written extensively on housing and urban issues in Korea and elsewhere in Asia, including on low-income housing policy and urban renewal.

Arif Hasan is an architect planner in private practice in Karachi. He is a Visiting Professor of Architecture and Planning at NED University, Karachi; the chairperson of the Orangi Pilot Project and the Karachi Urban Resource Centre; and a founding member of the Asian Coalition for Housing Rights, Bangkok. His research and activism relates primarily to land, housing and community involvement in city planning in Asia in general and in Karachi in particular. He is the author of several books and book chapters on planning and development.

Hilda María Herzer (1943–2012) was Professor of Urban Theory at the School of Social Sciences, University of Buenos Aires. She held a PhD in Political Sociology from New York University and was an important initiator and pacesetter in the field of urban and environmental studies, both in Argentina and in Latin America. From 1989 to 1990, she was the Gino Germani Institute's director; in 2000, she assumed public office in the State Secretariat for Science and Technology, where she established the guidelines of the Programme Red de Argentinos Investigadores y Cientificos en el Exterior (RAICES) to repatriate scientists living abroad. During her academic career she produced a vast corpus of research and publications on environmental and urban issues that received national and international recognition.

Liling Huang is Associate Professor in the Graduate Institute of Building and Planning, National Taiwan University. Her research focuses on the governance of global cities; she teaches classes on community planning, social housing and globalising cities in Asia. She is also one of the founding members of Organization of Urban Re-s (OURS), a non-governmental organisation working on public participation, social justice and urban policies in Taiwan.

Tolga İslam is Associate Professor in the Urban Planning Department of Yildiz Technical University. As a researcher, he has been working on different aspects of gentrification in Istanbul for the past 10 years. He has edited a book and published several articles on gentrification in Istanbul.

Michael Janoschka is the Ramón y Cajal Research Professor at the Department of Political Science and International Relations, Universidad Autónoma de Madrid. He is the scientific coordinator of the research network CONTESTED CITIES (2012–16, financed by the European Commission), the project

CIUDAD Y CRISIS (2013–15, financed by the Spanish Ministry of Economy and Competitiveness) and an interdisciplinary research group that focuses on: (i) processes of gentrification, displacement and social exclusion in the neoliberal city; (ii) struggles for housing, the right to the city and geographies of counter-hegemonic social movements; and (iii) the transformation of public space and the politics of symbolic appropriation of space.

Gareth Jones is Professor in Urban Geography at the London School of Economics and Political Science. His recent research is centred on issues of violence, access to space and livelihood, gated estates and identities, and representations of the 'slum' in the popular media in Mexico, Brazil, South Africa, Ghana and India. He is co-editor (with Dennis Rodgers) of *Youth violence in Latin America: gangs and juvenile justice in perspective* (Palgrave Macmillan, 2009).

Marieke Krijnen is a PhD student in the Department of Conflict and Development Studies at Ghent University. Her research focuses on processes of urban transformation in Beirut, their potential contribution to a more cosmopolitan, post-colonial urban studies, and their implications for critical theories of globalisation processes, neoliberalism and space; especially in relation to notions of global and local, whose reification she seeks to unsettle.

Marianne Millstein is a researcher at the Nordic Africa Institute, Uppsala, Sweden. She holds a PhD in human geography from the University of Oslo, Norway. She has done extensive research on the politics of urban governance and community organising in Cape Town, South Africa. She draws on a broad range of theoretical perspectives on urban governance and democratisation, state–civil society relations, and citizenship. In her most recent research, she explores the governance and everyday experiences of temporary relocations in Cape Town.

Chinwe Nwanna is a Senior Lecturer in the Department of Sociology, University of Lagos, Nigeria. Her teaching concerns urbanisation, the sociology of urban life and rural to urban labour migration. She has extensively researched urban problems and urban management in Lagos State, Nigeria.

Abdellatif Qamhaieh is an Assistant Professor in the Urban Planning Department at ALHOSN University, Abu Dhabi. His research interests include housing and community development, crime prevention planning, and urban design. Since moving to the United Arab Emirates three years ago, he has been interested in the rapid growth taking place in the Gulf Cooperation Council (GCC) countries and in the impact this growth has had on the region's cities and their residents.

Julie Ren is a researcher in urban geography at the Humboldt University Berlin, researching art spaces and issues of transnational mobility in Berlin and Beijing with support from the Research Institute for Urban and Regional Development.

She was formerly a Fulbright Fellow, having studied at the Hertie School of Governance and Wesleyan University.

María Carla Rodríguez is a sociologist at the University of Buenos Aires. She is a militant of the Movement of Occupants and Tenants (MOI) and of Workers Central Argentina (CTA). Her research is on urban and housing policies, the social production of habitat, social movements, and transnationality. Her most recent publications include *La cuestión urbana interrogada. Transformaciones urbanas, ambientales y políticas públicas en la Argentina* (with Hilda Herzer, María Gabriela Merlinsky and María Mercedes Di Virgilio) (2011, Buenos Aires: Café de las Ciudades) and *Caleidoscopio de las políticas territoriales. Un rompecabezas para armar* (with María Mercedes Di Virgilio) (PROMETEO LIBROS, 2011).

Bahar Sakızlıoğlu is a researcher at the Urban and Regional Research Center, University of Utrecht, The Netherlands. Among her main research interests are accumulation by dispossession, gentrification and displacement. She has published papers on the politics of gentrification and displacement experiences of disadvantaged groups in restructuring neighbourhoods. She has just completed her PhD on residents' displacement experiences in the cities of Amsterdam and Istanbul.

Elke Schlack is an architect and holds a PhD in Urban Development from the Technische Universität Berlin. She is an Assistant Professor at the Centro de Investigaciones Territoriales y Urbanas (CITU) at Andres Bello University, Chile, and at the School of Architecture of the Catholic University of Chile. Her research focuses on theory, design patterns, public policies and urban regulations related to urban renewal and public space. Her research has been published mostly in Spanish-language journals and in English and German in book chapters. She is currently editing the book *POPS – el uso público en el espacio urbano.*

Jorge Sequera has a PhD in Sociology from the Universidad Complutense de Madrid and is currently a postdoctoral researcher in the Department of Political Science and International Relations, Universidad Autónoma de Madrid. He is part of the research network CONTESTED CITIES (funded by the European Commission) and is developing studies about micro-resistance in gentrifying neighbourhoods in Buenos Aires, as well as a comparativist study of gentrification and resistance in different Latin American cities.

Yannick Sudermann holds a master's degree in Geography and Political Science from the University of Erlangen-Nuremberg and a PhD in Geography from the University of Edinburgh. His research interests lie within the fields of urban studies, critical geography and comparative politics, with a particular focus on gentrification in authoritarian states. His doctoral research scrutinises the interplay between gentrification, heritage conservation and authoritarian governance in the historic centre of the Syrian capital of Damascus prior to the civil war. Yannick has presented his work at several international conferences and is co-author (with Balsam Ahmad) of *Syria's contrasting neighbourhoods: gentrification and informal settlements juxtaposed* (St Andrews: University of St Andrews Centre for Syrian Studies, 2012).

Annika Teppo is an Associate Professor and the head of the Urban Dynamics cluster at the Nordic Africa Institute, Uppsala, Sweden. She holds a PhD in Social and Cultural Anthropology and the title of Docent in Urban Studies from the University of Helsinki, Finland. Essentially an anthropologist drawing from a multidisciplinary theoretical background, she has carried out a number of ethnographic research projects on race, class, spirituality and public space in post-apartheid cities.

Neil Turnbull is a qualified architect and graduate of the Edinburgh College of Art. He works as a researcher and lecturer at the Centro de Investigaciones Territoriales y Urbanas (CITU) at the University Andres Bello, Chile, and lectures at the Faculty of Architecture and Urbanism at the University of Chile. He has led research projects and co-authored published work on the transformation of the city and its impact on social sustainability, with an emphasis on the role of public policy, urban legislation and public participation.

Foreword

This book grew out of a 2012 international seminar series co-organised by the editors, entitled 'Towards an Emerging Geography of Gentrification in the Global South'. We thank the Urban Studies Foundation and the *Urban Studies* journal who funded the two workshops in London and Santiago de Chile. A special thank you to all those who took part and were willing to try and think outside the 'gentrification box'. In addition, our thanks to Alison Shaw and Laura Vickers at Policy Press and an anonymous reviewer for all their work in supporting this book.

This collection is in memory of two distinguished professors who researched and wrote about gentrification: the sociologist **Hilda María Herzer,** who was a co-investigator on the seminar series that underpinned this book but who very sadly passed away in 2012; and the geographer **Neil Smith**, who also very sadly passed away in 2012, whose assertions about gentrification as the leading edge of global urbanism also underpinned, and indeed continue to underpin, this book.

Hilda, Neil, this book is for you both.

ONE

Introduction: 'gentrification' – a global urban process?

Loretta Lees, Hyun Bang Shin and Ernesto López-Morales

> To what extent is gentrification a global phenomenon, with diverse causes and characteristics, or a phenomenon of globalisation, conceived as a process of capital expansion, uneven urban development and neighbourhood changes in 'new' cities? (Atkinson and Bridge, 2005, p 2)

Introduction: moving beyond the usual gentrification suspects

Gentrification has been a major focus of several (inter)disciplinary literatures for many years, including but not limited to geography, sociology, urban studies, urban planning, anthropology, political science and economics, but its theoretical and conceptual framing has, to date, been constrained by an Anglo-American lens. This collection responds directly and forcefully to address the limitations of this gentrification lens in ways that have not been attempted before. In so doing, it critically assesses the meaning and significance of gentrification in cities outside of the usual suspects: a large number of the book's chapters are located outside of the Global North in post-colonial and, in some cases, non-white urban contexts that are increasingly confronted by global as well as local (re)development pressures. In addition, some of the chapters focus on cities that sit awkwardly between the so-called Global North and South (eg Lisbon in Portugal) and the Global West and East (eg Istanbul in Turkey). The collection delivers on promises made by other gentrification scholars, for example, Atkinson and Bridge (2005), who outlined the need for a truly cosmopolitan, global, view of gentrification, even if we recognise that such a cosmopolitan view is not easy to obtain. A cosmopolitan view is worldly wise, well-travelled, urbane, refined and aware, but in this collection, we aspire to a 'cosmopolitan prospect' rather than 'view', for 'prospect' conjures up a more forward-looking cosmopolitanism, one with aspect, perspective and outlook at its heart. In this book, we seek to move the gentrification literature in the direction of a properly global urban studies, we discuss the extent to which 'gentrification' is a global process and, in so doing, highlight the injustices, the uneven developments and displacements that this process is yielding globally.

For decades, authors and experts on gentrification have espoused the global nature of gentrification, at the same time asking for a more global investigation into the process. Many of these references to the globalisation of gentrification were in nations and cities linked to the Global North (eg, on the Australian rent gap, see Badcock, 1989; on the functional gap in Prague, see Sykora, 1993), but some began to emerge from the Global South itself (eg, on Puebla, Mexico, see Jones and Varley, 1999). Then, as the process moved into the 21st century, the late Neil Smith (2002; see also Smith and Derksen, 2002) talked about 'gentrification going global', 'gentrification generalised' and gentrification as a 'global urban strategy', connecting with debates on globalism, neoliberalism and the changing role of the state. Sometime earlier, Smith (1996) had looked for gentrification battlefields around the world, but Clark (2005) warned that some places experiencing gentrification did so differently, the dealings with gentrification in Sweden, for example, were less violent. Kovács and Wiessner (1999) also argued in sharp contrast to Smith (1996) – who used Budapest to demonstrate gentrification in post-communist Europe – that gentrification was not occurring in Budapest in the West European and North American sense of the word. While there have been a few academic journal articles that have attempted a more cosmopolitan view of gentrification (eg Harris, 2008), there has not been a sustained engagement with serious conversations across different contexts. Porter and Shaw's (2008) edited book features great case studies from Europe, North and South America, Asia, South Africa, the Middle East, and Australia; it develops a comparative analysis of regeneration/gentrification strategies, their effects and efforts to resist them, but it does not pay enough attention to the issues of developmentalism, universalism and categorisation in comparative urbanism (Lees, 2012, 2014).

This book provides exactly that kind of dialogue and theoretical/empirical learning from/with the Global South and the Global North. Such an endeavour necessitates hard empirical and conceptual work and a lot of collaboration with specialist authors working in/on cities across the globe. To that end, we have assembled a team of collaborators who are, for the most part, beyond the usual suspects in gentrification authorship, a number of these are young scholars who have entered gentrification studies and are asking many of the same questions that we ask in this book, others are more mature scholars who are reflecting back on, and beyond, their previous writings on gentrification. Some of the contributors were selected from a group of invited researchers who took part in the international seminar series we co-organised, entitled 'Towards an Emerging Geography of Gentrification in the Global South', held in London and Santiago de Chile; others were approached separately in the knowledge that they had written on, or were researching, gentrification or related urban processes in diverse parts of the globe. The contributors were encouraged to challenge theoretical and epistemological perspectives that have been based on Northern/Western experiences of gentrification, perspectives that have become hegemonic in the international gentrification literature.

We have worked to formulate a genuinely collaborative project enabling learning about gentrification from outside the comfort zone of the Global North. Given the differences between the various authors in terms of languages spoken, stage of career, academic discipline, educational training and so on, we do not apologise for the fact that the individual chapters are quite mixed – some of them theoretically and conceptually dense, others fairly accessible; some very versed in the gentrification literature, others less so. Some actively engage their academic work with anti-gentrification activism or support grassroots movements (for whom there seems to be little doubt that gentrification is actually taking place in their cities), while others reflect from purely scholarly analysis. Of course, as Robinson (2011, p 2) has pointed out, collections of case studies from different places do not simply constitute a comparative analysis. She is right, and during the editing process for this book, we have taken a more interventionist role: we have pushed authors to 'unlearn' how we/they think about gentrification, its practices and ideologies, even to abandon or parochialise the term 'gentrification' itself; and we have gone back and forth with authors pushing them to directly address as a series of questions (see Figure 1.1).

Figure 1.1: The questions asked of the contributors and ourselves

- What is the complex geographical contingency to gentrification?
- How is gentrification framed and defined in their context?
- What are its causes and consequences?
- Is the concept of 'gentrification' really suitable for denoting the processes of restructuring being experienced in inner-city or peripheral areas in the cities outside the Global North?
- Are there endogenous processes that would be better captured by concepts other than gentrification?
- How useful is the literature on gentrification from the Global North in theorising or conceptualising what is going on in the countries and cities they write about?
- What does the (Western) gentrification concept do analytically that other concepts cannot do better?

In doing this, a number of the chapters achieve a real critical edge, albeit to a varying degree. Getting the authors and their chapters to speak to each other, as Robinson (2011) suggests, is much more difficult when nearly all of these authors have a language other than English as their first language and when they are already pushing themselves to think beyond the confines of the gentrification literature to date. As such, in the conclusion to this book (see Chapter Twenty-two), we do the work of speaking across and through all the chapters ourselves (the fact that we three editors have expertise from/on different parts of the globe has helped this process), pulling together what we (and the contributors) have learned. Juxtaposing diverse cases of urban development outside the Global North and beyond the usual suspects has not only moved us beyond overgeneralising on gentrification processes (which hide other processes at work), but also enabled us to (re)discover the important generalities and specificities associated with the process of gentrification globally.

Gentrification in comparative perspective

In the 1980s, 1990s and, indeed, into the 2000s, the internationally comparative work that was being undertaken on gentrification predominantly compared Western cities.[1] Research in gentrification outside of the usual suspects also viewed gentrification through an Anglo-American gentrification lens, for example, Badcock's (1989) emulation of Marxist rent gap theory in Adelaide and Cybriwsky's (1998) account of gentrification in Tokyo, even if some offered much more critical and contextual accounts, for example, Sykora's (1993) 'functional gap' in post-socialist Prague. New work on gentrification informed by post-colonial writings also tended to view the process through an Anglo-American lens, for example, Shaw's (2000) 'Harleminising' aborigines in Sydney's Redfern neighbourhood. Atkinson and Bridge's (2005) collection, *Gentrification in a global context*, offered a much wider view of gentrification around the globe, which it evoked well through the phase 'new urban colonialism', but it failed to undertake a thorough comparative urbanism. However, if one delves deeply into the chapters in that book, from outside of the usual suspects, one can find comparative grievances, comparative urbanisms and concerns that their cases do not quite fit with the Anglo-American norm. Petsimeris (2005), for example, wonders why Southern European cities have been all but ignored in the gentrification literature, and points readers towards a significant literature on the structure and evolution of the Southern European city as different to Northern European cities. He argues: 'Southern European cities are highly heterogeneous and complex, and the processes of gentrification are for this reason very different in terms of its temporality and spatiality' (Petsimeris, 2005, p 242). He concludes that the root causes and intensity of gentrification in Southern European cities are not the same as in Britain and North America, but his comparator remains the Global North. Rubino (2005) questions if there might be a specifically Latin American gentrification by revisiting the Chicago School. Krase (2005) compares a Polish–American neighbourhood in New York with one in Krakow, attempting an interesting comparison across time, space and transnational ethnic connections using image-based research. He argues that although the causes of gentrification are different in the two neighbourhoods, the aesthetic practice (style, taste) of gentrification is similar. He states:

> If we were to suspend our ideological beliefs for a moment we might find some gross historical similarities between Greenpoint, Brooklyn, United States and post-socialist Krakow, Poland. For one they are both places that have suffered extensive physical deterioration in the 1970s and 1980s only to find themselves desirable destinations for higher status migrants at the turn of the century. (Krase, 2005, p 205)

However, should we really ignore contextual, ideological differences? Sykora (2005, p 90, emphases added) is uncomfortable in his assertions of gentrification in post-communist cities:

> it is increasingly clear that the implementation of market reforms in Eastern European 'post-communist' cities has often led to pronounced urban restructuring and neighbourhood changes that are, *to some extent*, similar to transformations mapped out for cities in the west.... In conclusion we point to the specificities of gentrification in post-communist cities that *might* have some relevance for the general discussion of the process and its trajectories under differing systemic conditions.

He concludes that 'Gentrification is not generally a major factor in the transformations of post-communist cities' (Sykora, 2005, p 104), arguing that there has been no pioneer phase for post-communist gentrification with a *desire* for inner-city living; instead, the process is more utilitarian, driven by demand for housing in pleasant locations near to the places of work of the professional classes (Sykora, 2005, p 105). However, Sykora does not go so far as to state that the processes at work in post-communist cities are not gentrification, but something else.

Debating the epistemological limits of 'gentrification'

Over the years, there has been anxiety on and off about the term 'gentrification' being stretched beyond its limits. Bondi (1999, p 255) warned researchers not to overload the concept of gentrification with reconceptualisations: 'the more researchers have attempted to pin it down the more burdens the concept has had to carry'; nevertheless, she also argued that 'creative approaches to the production of academic knowledge entail cyclical processes of conceptualisation and reconceptualisation'. This book attempts that creative approach; by way of contrast, not only did Bondi (1999) want gentrification research to be allowed to 'disintegrate under the weight of these burdens', but she herself disintegrated under the weight of these burdens and withdrew from researching gentrification itself. A couple of years later, Lambert and Boddy (2002) argued quite forcefully that new-build developments in British city centres should not be categorised as 'gentrification', but rather as 're-urbanisation' (see Davidson and Lees, 2005; Lees et al, 2008, pp 138–141). In contrast, in his discussion of aggressive new-build redevelopments in central Tokyo under the Japanese *dokken kokka* (construction state), where office buildings, high-rise luxury apartments, upmarket retailing and arts facilities were being built for the wealthy, Cybriwsky (2011, p 243) argues: 'Yes, of course it is gentrification, without a doubt!' The key to this process is the unevenness in the ways in which Tokyo was seeing the rise of such new investments. Butler (2007, p 167) has also mulled over the epistemology of gentrification but expressed concern 'not that [the gentrification] concept has become "diluted" but rather that there is now an expectation of what we should expect to find which blinds us to the continued diversity of consequences'. He makes a good point, although there is hardly a single 'we' given an increasingly diversified global academia facing the diverse emergences and consequences of gentrification and other processes in different, complex urban systems around the world. More than preserving and 'patrolling' the use of the 'gentrification' concept (to quote Ananya Roy's [2009] call for a truly post-colonial theorisation), what is needed now is proper global debate among scholars from the South, North, West and East, as is the main goal of this book.

More recently, Maloutas (2012) has asked whether the use of the Anglo-American term 'gentrification' facilitates or impedes understanding of processes of urban restructuring in different contexts. Like in this book, he invites scholars to discuss some of the epistemological limits of current urban theorisations on gentrification. However, his arguments are somewhat confused and based on a rather circumscribed review of the gentrification literature.[2] For one, he ignores the fact that there was significant debate in the 1990s about the contextual nature of gentrification, when a number of authors claimed terminological diversity for the same process, for example, 'embourgeoisement', 'aburguesamiento', 'elitización', 'urban reconquest' and so on (this debate was especially strong in Spain, see, for instance, García-Herrera, 2001). Indeed, this terminological debate led to the withdrawal of some scholars from gentrification studies altogether. Maloutas (2012) argues: that we need to pay more attention to context in gentrification studies; that gentrification research needs to be brought into new contexts in an attempt to explain specific processes that may look dissimilar; and that we need stronger and deeper evidence on the causal mechanisms of gentrification. Yet, confusingly, he also argues that 'looking for gentrification in increasingly varied contexts displaces emphasis from causal mechanisms and processes to similarities in outcomes across contexts, and leads to a loss of analytical rigour' (Maloutas, 2012, p 34). Like Atkinson (2008), he argues that gentrification researchers have tended to label too many kinds of neighbourhood change as gentrification and that this elasticity has reduced the bite of critical studies of its localised appearance, diminishing policymaker interest as a result. We agree that a poor theorisation of gentrification may lead to faulty accounts of cases of urban change labelled incorrectly as gentrification; however, on the other hand, we believe that a large number of well-analysed cases help extract the global regularities of the causes of gentrification. In fact, Maloutas (2012) is recalling an epistemological problem that has been around since Popper (1998) about the empirical nature of theorisation and the extent to which a theory can inductively emerge from certain empirical evidence. The whole debate about case-oriented analysis has been drawn on the assumption that it is possible to induce regularities from a distinct number of different cases and that this is, in fact, a good way to create knowledge (see Ragin, 1987; Flyvbjerg, 2006). To consider gentrification as 'a mid-range theory' (see Butler, 2010) is not necessarily wrong if it is accepted that this mid-range theory will help consolidate and articulate empirical regularities that would otherwise appear disarticulated. Without a gentrification theory that serves as an 'umbrella' (see Davidson and Lees, 2005), the debate we are holding now in this book would probably not exist, neither would most of the gentrification debates held hitherto by scholars in different contexts, and nor would urban activists around the world be able to identify the different types of redevelopment-led displacement that are in many ways part of the same repertoire of class restructuring in global capitalism.

Maloutas (2012) argues that three key reference points are necessary conditions for gentrification: gentrification aesthetics; the presence of a middle class (as a particularly well-defined social segment); and post-industrialisation. He argues that through these, we can assess whether gentrification is really a different or only vaguely related phenomenon in different places. This is too simplistic an idea about gentrification, or, worse, a reification of contextual epiphenomena, such as the way gentrification has looked, smelled or tasted in some specific (North American and West European) contexts at very specific times. Maloutas (2012) seems to be trapped in a 'dilution' (see Butler, 2007), as he never defines gentrification but nevertheless makes claims about what gentrification should *not* be, based on three necessary conditions for the process. However, gentrification aesthetics are just an effect of gentrification; the middle classes depend on historical socio-cultural particularities[3] that do not exist in many cases where gentrification is 'allowed' to exist; and, finally, there are post-industrial cities that do not have gentrification and, likewise, cities that have gentrification but have not experienced deindustrialisation and a move to post-industrialisation (see Lees, 2014).

Maloutas (2012) claims that there is an 'attachment' of gentrification to the Anglo-American metropolis. We agree, but his argument is epistemologically blurry. First, does that 'attachment' come from the fact that those metropolises were the places where gentrification was first studied scientifically, and, if so, why? Or, is this an attachment that responds to certain conditions that only Anglo-American cities have in common or that only Maloutas sees? In fact, the gentrification literature has been clear that West European and North American cities are different from each other (see the section on gentrification in comparative perspective earlier; see also Lees, 2012). As a good example of this, the different nature of gentrification experienced in the US compared with that in Canada made the early 1980s' dispute between Neil Smith and David Ley something much more interesting than the ideological quarrel that it has long been reported as (on the quarrel, see Lees et al, 2008) because this dispute was also fundamentally about the very different nature of the cases they were researching (see Lees, 2000). However, at that time, no one dared to deny that both were cases of gentrification. As such, Maloutas's (2012) argument about the contextual attachment of gentrification seems as problematic as arguing that Marx's notion of the working class equals only the physical and psychological attributes that Engels described for the British and German proletariat in the mid-1800s. What Maloutas (2012) has contributed is a fossilisation, rather than contextualisation, of the concepts by confining them to the particular geographical and historical specificities that generated them.

We claim (of course, the elephant in the room is who should define where the limits of a concept should be), like most of the authors in this book, that there are more relevant and necessary conditions for gentrification to exist: the class polarisation that lies beneath the appearances of gentrifying urban areas across the globe; the noticeable increase in investment put into the economic circuits of urban 'regeneration' (or the secondary circuit of the built environment, as David Harvey or Henri Lefebvre would call it); and different forms of displacement – direct displacement, indirect displacement, exclusionary displacement, displacement pressure, social exclusion and so on (see also Davidson and Lees, 2005; Slater, 2009; Marcuse, 2010; Aalbers, 2011). On the contrary, there seems to be an 'epistemological' temptation to see gentrification as deeply context-dependent because the particularities observed in a specific number of gentrification cases in the Global North are apparently hard to replicate elsewhere. We think that it is time to reconsider the regularities that lie behind those processes, and consider what is central to the process of gentrification itself insofar as a large number of cases can illuminate this reflection.

More recently, Ley and Teo (2014) have explored the epistemological argument raised by Maloutas (2012) in considering the identification and naming (or absence of naming) of gentrification in Hong Kong. They, too, are concerned about the 'conceptual overreach' of 'gentrification' from the Anglo-American heartland to the cities of the Asia-Pacific and specifically Hong Kong. However, they conclude that just because the word 'gentrification' is missing from public and academic discourse in Hong Kong, it does not mean that gentrification is not happening: 'It is only the critical view of gentrification in Euro-America compared with the neutral or even affirmative view of urban redevelopment in Hong Kong that confounds the global symmetry' (Ley and Teo, 2014). They argue that the ideological consensus about the role of property in upward social mobility, a set of values that have been hitherto unquestioned, is becoming seen as socially unjust.

These fears that 'gentrification' has become a 'regulating fiction', 'a self-fulfilling prophesy', deserve our attention. We must consider, as do Ley and Teo (2014), if use of the term/concept 'gentrification' outside of Euro-America represents a 'false rupture (a severing from its source region) and false universalisation (uncritically universalizing it)' (Bourdieu and Wacquant, 1999, p 43). This is something that this book seeks to do.

Questioning a global gentrification

The overall aim of this book is to put the concept of gentrification into question globally, recognising that this might contribute to dislocating existing conceptualisations of gentrification and could potentially allow for the development of new lines of analysis of urban change. To that end, we draw *conceptually* on the 'new' literatures on comparative urbanism and policy mobilities and *practically* on the knowledge of gentrification researchers working on/in the Global South and in other atypical contexts. We do not seek to be 'comparative' in a structured or traditional fashion (ie flattening cases through a limited number of factors or categories), but rather 'exploratory' and, in many ways, unstructured (following McFarlane and Robinson, 2012). As such, the book offers a much-needed 'deep' and case-oriented empirical lens through which to view the comparative urbanism of gentrification in the Global South and beyond the usual suspects, revealing multiple translations throughout the world. The 'new' comparative urbanism (see Robinson, 2006) asserts that urban theory as it has developed is colonial, hegemonic and based on a selective number of cities, a situation that has been fuelled by the global and world cities debates. As McFarlane (2010) argues, claims about the city (and, here, we could insert 'gentrification') as a category are too often made with implicitly the Global North in mind. As such, we have made significant strides to bring into the debate a large number of cases from the Global South and East. However, as this book shows, it is very difficult to break this hegemony and, in fact, the comparison remains an important one – we should not throw the baby out with the bathwater. Robinson (2006, 2011) argues that contemporary urban theory has pushed to the side some cities, especially those deemed to be non-modern, even primitive. The result is different literatures: urban geography tends to focus on wealthier cities that have become universalised and development geographers on poorer cities contributing to the development geography literature. Following Robinson's (2006) plea for a post-colonial urban theory that acknowledges the potential of learning from the experiences and accounts of urban life in different cities, we have tried hard in this book to look beyond the usual suspects. We offer here a 'comparative gesture' (see Robinson, 2011) as a first step towards a properly comparative global gentrification studies that can lead the way in undermining the hegemony of gentrification as a model for the development of cities everywhere. However, in so doing, we stand aside from other comparative urbanists in our belief that to flatten the globe and its multiple urban hierarchies so as to appreciate difference hides social injustices and neglects important power relations.

Ward (2010) discusses how the 1970s and 1980s did produce a comparative urban studies, mainly inspired by a Marxist perspective that sought regularities and patterns through a grand and overarching theoretical lens providing a cross-national comparative perspective. Nevertheless, he argues that these studies were hampered by an understanding of cities as bounded and discrete units, and of geographical scales as fixed and pre-given. These, of course, are shortcomings that both post-colonial and post-structuralist theory have identified, the question, then, becomes whether a truly comparative urban studies can be undertaken. According to Ward, the answer is 'Yes', as long as we are informed by past work and theorise back from empirical accounts of various cities. Ward (like Robinson) provides no methodological framework for how this might be done. 'Doing' comparative urbanism scientifically remains a rather open question, it remains a field of inquiry that aims to develop 'knowledge, understanding and generalization at a level between what is true for all cities and what is true for one city at a given point in time' (Nijman, 2007, p 1).

The 'new' comparative urbanism's goal to decentre urban studies from the Global North implies that social-scientific research methods, especially those usually associated with positivism, should be replaced by 'academic impressionism'. There are, of course, lots of problems with this. Various issues emerge, for example, if we are not to classify cities to compare differences in performance between cities because that would always imply a hierarchy, and if we are to stick to the idea that they are all a category of one, then what can we actually do? It is not surprising that scholars who have argued for a 'new' approach to comparative urban studies concern themselves with city government, governance and the travelling of policies.[4] After all, the themes and research questions that can be formulated around these do not need to reflect very much on the ideas that cities are not bounded, self-enclosed objects and that scales are not self-evident; furthermore, their plea for relational understandings is easy to live up to because such topics are primarily about how cities are actors that communicate and connect to other places. However, it is a little more complicated when, for example, one has to engage with questions that constitute what we still consider to be the core of urban studies, for example, the understanding of processes and mechanisms that produce durable urban inequalities and their spatial expressions. All in all, it is important to bear in mind Ananya Roy's (2009) call to reinforce:

> the distinctive experiences of the cities of the global South [to] generate productive and provocative theoretical frameworks for all cities. [However, on the other hand, the] critique of the EuroAmerican hegemony of urban theory is thus not an argument about the inapplicability of the EuroAmerican ideas to the cities of the global South. It is not worthwhile to police the borders across which ideas, policies, and practices flow and mutate. The concern is the limited sites at which theoretical production is currently theorized and with the failure of imagination and epistemology that is thus engendered. It is time to blast open theoretical geographies, to produce a new set of concepts, in the crucible of a new repertoire of cities. (Roy, 2009, p 820)

Overview of the book

We have organised the book chapters into alphabetical order of author surname. We have done this deliberately to mix up the chapters randomly, in part to play to the comparative urbanism agenda and to flatten any regional or city hierarchies that might emerge, but more so to allow us to pull out emerging themes and lessons that are not then forced to conform to a synthetic structure. Some readers might have liked us to have organised the chapters loosely by region, but it is not easy to fit these cases into regions, for example: despite Cairo being long theorised as a Middle Eastern city and the intellectual capital of the Islamic world, it is in

Africa; Istanbul tends to be theorised as a Middle Eastern city, yet it is straddles East (Asia) and West (Europe); Lisbon is in Europe (the Global North) but shares a lot in common with the Global South; and South and East Asian cities, like those in Pakistan, India, China and Taiwan, are very different. A number of Latin American researchers have asserted a specifically 'Latin American gentrification' (see Janoschka et al, 2013), but we believe that theoretical or conceptual insight does not always follow regional lines, even if we recognise that there are: Latin American urbanisms that might be linked with urbanisms in Spain and Portugal; Middle Eastern gentrifications in for example Israel, Syria and Lebanon that might be related to conflicts and population migrations as a result of conflicts in that region; and East Asian gentrifications where the role of the state is more prominent than elsewhere in facilitating real estate development.

We have designed the book to speak to different levels of readership. For more advanced readers, the book demonstrates both the complexities and difficulties of undertaking comparative urban analysis, but also the fruitions. For more junior readers (eg undergraduates and master's students), the range of empirical case studies provides them with a good grasp of the theoretical debates and also useful case studies to flesh out these academic debates. Following on from this introduction, in Chapter Two, Georgia Alexandri shows how gentrification is rising like a phoenix from the ashes of inner-city 'crisis' in Athens like in New York City in the 1970s and 1980s. For now, gentrification dynamics in Athens are seen to operate at the micro-scale and enmesh in a complex way with urban fears about illegal immigrants, drug users and the homeless.

In Chapter Three, Eduardo Ascensão discusses slum gentrification in Lisbon, Portugal, focusing in particular on Quinta da Serra. His detailed ethnographic work reveals the injustices in this process, the reality of displacement and attempts to resist. He reveals the institutional imaginings and governmentalities that are part of 'gentrification' as the building of a modern, European and multicultural Portugal over the past 35 years.

In Chapter Four, Surajit Chakravarty and Abdellatif Qamhaieh examine the policies causing the gentrification of Abu Dhabi's city centre that are displacing segments of the population. They argue that although there are stark differences between the planning cultures of Abu Dhabi and those of cities in Western Europe or North America, there are similarities in how the 'spatial fix' is administered.

In Chapter Five, Jake Cummings focuses on the development of 'favela chic' and 'favela gentrification' in Rio de Janeiro, Brazil, related to aggressive state-led securitisation policies and housing relocation programmes, plus local and global real estate powers campaigning for favela renovation. Favela residents' and gentrifying newcomers' discourses are compared, showing 'sub-gentrification' trends (fostered by thriving informal property markets and indigenous land-owners consolidating their wealth by capitalising on their properties) and a second trend of hyper-mobile international newcomers that lie at the vanguard of the gentrification of favelas in touristic areas.

In Chapter Six, Sapana Doshi critically engages with theories of gentrification through the prism of Indian cities and highlights four key factors shaping Indian urban transformation: (1) informal regimes of urban development, settlement and governance; (2) new state formations consolidating urban elite and middle-class power; (3) the contradictory desires and fragmented subjectivities shaping subaltern mobilisations; and (4) the role of identity-based violence and exclusion in displacement politics. Significantly, she argues against staging an Indian ideal-type of gentrification and calls for more attention to the diverse extra-economic processes that produce Indian cities. She also claims that in the context of elite world-class making and the prevalence of identity politics, the anti-capitalist 'right to the city' may not be the best rallying cry for anti-gentrification activities in Indian cities.

In Chapter Seven, Mohamed Elshahed discusses gentrification in Cairo in the context of a city where the wealthy are opting for new gated developments. He argues that the recent interest in investing in downtown is akin to more conventional processes of gentrification; however, the conditions in Cairo make these prospects for gentrification difficult to realise – gentrification limited.

In Chapter Eight, Amiram Gonen, following Atkinson (2003), discusses gentrification in Israel as middle-class resettlement amenable to a range of locational and social qualities, inner city, suburban and rural. He discusses the diversity and widespread nature of gentrification in Israel. The factors behind gentrification are different to those in Anglo-American cities, for, like in Paris, the middle classes opted predominantly for inner-urban living and lower-class populations lived on the fringes of cities, hence his attempt to introduce the Hebrew term *hitbargenoot* following the French term *embourgeoisement*.

In Chapter Nine, Seong-Kyu Ha discusses the endogenous dynamics of urban renewal in Seoul, South Korea, as what he terms 'renewal-induced gentrification'. He asserts that Seoul has been witnessing one of the world's most aggressive residential renewal programmes, for large-scale redevelopment programmes, such as 'joint redevelopment' and 'new town in town', have focused on maximising landlord profits rather than on improving the housing welfare of low-income residents who have been displaced from their neighbourhoods. He also discusses the likelihood of anti-gentrification struggles in South Korea with reference to a community-based cooperative approach in Seoul.

In Chapter Ten, Arif Hasan demonstrates how processes of gentrification in Karachi, Pakistan, are linked to networks with differing spatial reaches. Not only are those behind an emerging historic preservation movement in Karachi trained in the West, but the money and design ideas behind the proposed large-scale developments on Karachi's coast are from Dubai-based companies. Perhaps most importantly, however, most of these redevelopment plans were shelved due in large part to civil society resistance to gentrification, demonstrating that anti-gentrification resistance can be successful in the Global South.

In Chapter Eleven, Hilda Herzer, María Mercedes Di Virgilio and María Carla Rodríguez seek to increase the 'evidence base' on gentrification in Latin

American cities through a longitudinal study of the La Boca, San Telmo and Barracas quarters in Buenos Aires. Interestingly, gentrification in Buenos Aires is first and foremost about providing cultural, touristic, educational, commercial and so on services for high-income groups, and only after that about housing for higher-income groups.

In Chapter Twelve, Liling Huang stresses the role of the high percentage of public lands located in the city centre and in strategic areas and their influence on gentrification in Taipei, Taiwan. She discusses how, due to deregulation, a large number of public housing units became upscale commodities on the real estate market, as the state sold them into gentrification, turned them into enclaves for the wealthy and elite professionals, and also pushed up housing prices in the surrounding areas.

In Chapter Thirteen, Tolga İslam and Bahar Sakızlıoğlu argue for a grounded approach to researching different geographies of gentrification that understands local political contexts and actually existing neoliberalisms in different cities/regions/countries, including the role and power of the state, elite coalitions and so on that give rise to urban policies promoting gentrification. Comparing Sulukule and Tarlabasi in central Istanbul, neighbourhoods that have been transformed based on the same renewal law, they show how even in two seemingly similar cases within the same city, the making of, and resistance to, gentrification can take quite different forms.

In Chapter Fourteen, Gareth Jones revisits the city of Puebla in Mexico, which he wrote about in the 1990s with Ann Varley, looking again at gentrification but in the new context of Mexico having fully embraced neoliberalism. He looks at representations of culture and especially ethnicity in the Paseo project, which set out to establish a cultural, tourist and business district across 27 city blocks in the historic centre, covering a number of 'barrios'. Here, the Mexican state has underwritten real estate speculation, facilitating a bolder intervention to promote the interests of corporate capital in urban centres.

In Chapter Fifteen, Marieke Krijnen and Christiaan De Beukelaer show how much processes of gentrification diverge in a single city – Beirut – with different networks of capital formation and visions of the urban future reflecting Lebanon's history of conflict and the various ways in which neighbourhoods and social groups are linked to regional and global circuits of capital.

In Chapter Sixteen, Chinwe Nwanna looks at two cases of gentrification in Lagos Mega City – one an example of slum gentrification, the other the gentrification of government-owned housing, with both seeing the forcible eviction of tenants. She also discusses the revanchist acts of Governor Fashola, who moved the destitute and mentally ill off the streets of Lagos with a view to world-city status.

In Chapter Seventeen, Julie Ren examines whether gentrification is an effective means to describe the changes that urban China is undergoing, showing the descriptive limits of the gentrification lens. She discusses both the strategic reasons for studying 'gentrification' in China and the potential shortcomings.

She is especially concerned that 'gentrification' research in China may obscure a more contextually relevant understanding of urban inequality and that rebalancing the equation towards 'the particular' might isolate Chinese urbanism in its own parochial frame.

In Chapter Eighteen, Elke Schlack and Neil Turnbull review the 'Latin American gentrification' literature, which was interested in the 1990s in the consequences of gentrification for low-income populations in traditional historical centres, but moved on in the 2000s to look at the production of gentrification rooted in land policies and housing markets in neoliberalised contexts. They step aside from the bulk of the work on gentrification in Chile, which has focused to date on the latter, for example, new-build gentrification (see López-Morales, 2010, 2011), and look instead at the rehabilitation of existing structures in inner-city Santiago. In so doing, they look at the commercial gentrifications that are putting pressure on residential neighbourhoods and making profit through the exploitation of distinctive neighbourhood cultural attributes.

In Chapter Nineteen, Jorge Sequera and Michael Janoschka deliberately step aside from the iconic examples of Barcelona and Bilbao in Spain and discuss Madrid. They compare two different neighbourhoods in the historic core – Lavapiés and Triball – and show how different dispositifs are used in the production of gentrification, and also how gentrification is limited not just by the Spanish housing crisis, but also by non-European immigrants, a counterculture, escalating struggles for the right to housing as a response to the social and economic crisis, and new residents that do not fit the profile of the desired neighbourhood.

In Chapter Twenty, Yannick Sudermann demonstrates the relationship between Syrian middle-class professionals, regime cronies and their changing consumer preferences, and the process of gentrification. He argues that the production of gentrification in the Syrian capital followed the logics of the market but also depended on an authoritarian state that used gentrification in order to secure its power at the local scale.

In Chapter Twenty-one, Annika Teppo and Marianne Millstein discuss the place that the notion of gentrification occupies in the South African context, using examples from Cape Town. They argue that the public justifications of, discussions and disputes about, and material and social conditions related to gentrification processes differ in South Africa from those in the Global North. They show why those defending gentrification appeal to a moral post-colonial racial discourse.

In Chapter Twenty-two, the conclusion, we pull out the main lessons that we have learned from reading these chapters altogether. Here, we begin the 'comparative urbanism' that gentrification studies now demands; however, this is but a first step, a foray, for that project needs to be longer, deeper and more sustained than can be achieved here.

Finally, at the end of the book, Eric Clark, an American who lives and writes about gentrification in Sweden but who has begun to look at gentrification in East Asia, has been invited to write the Afterword.

Notes

[1] For example: across Canadian inner cities, see Smith and Williams (1986) and Ley (1986); on London and New York City, see Lees (1994); on London, Paris and New York City, see Carpenter and Lees (1995); on New York City and Toronto, see Slater (2002); and on Brussels and Montreal, see Van Criekingen and Decroly (2003).

[2] Maloutas's scepticism about the applicability of gentrification theory outside the North/West is not based on enough evidence. His article itself is confined to the Northern/Western literature: it presents 101 references, of which only 11 come from contexts outside of the North Atlantic, and seven of those are chapters from the same book (Atkinson and Bridge, 2005). Only four of his references are accounts outside of Europe or North America, and he missed a number of significant papers on gentrification in Latin America, Africa and East Asia.

[3] For example, Lemanski and Lama-Rewal (2010) have critiqued and deconstructed Indian class categorisations with respect to urban governance issues in Delhi, arguing that the new middle class is a small elite and that, numerically, the large lower-middle class is much more significant in urban populations. In Latin America, the ascending urban middle classes of the 1930s–1960s were hinges for the modernisation of Latin American states and pushed for more redistributive policies (Hardoy, 1975), differing from middle-class constructions in North Atlantic cases. Furthermore, Wang and Lau (2009) have written about gentrification and Shanghai's new middle class, concluding that '[t]he seemingly familiar (with Western conceptualizations) outputs are actually the result of different mechanisms occurring through different historical pathways' (Wang and Lau, 2009, p 65).

[4] This critique developed out of a 2011 Deutscher Akademischer Austausch Dienst (DAAD)-funded workshop in London and Berlin on comparative urbanism co-organised by Tim Butler, Loretta Lees, Talja Blokland and Isle Helbrecht. Thanks to all who attended for their input, which is summarised here.

References

Aalbers, M. (2011) *Place, exclusion and mortgage markets*, Chichester: John Wiley and Sons.

Atkinson, R. (2003) 'Introduction: misunderstood saviour or vengeful wrecker? The many meanings and problems of gentrification', *Urban Studies*, vol 20, no 12, pp 2343–50.

Atkinson, R. (2008) 'Gentrification, segregation and the vocabulary of affluent residential choice', *Urban Studies*, vol 45, no 12, pp 2626–36.

Atkinson, R. and Bridge, G. (eds) (2005) *Gentrification in a global context: the new urban colonialism*, London: Routledge.

Badcock, B. (1989) 'An Australian view of the rent gap hypothesis', *Annals of the Association of American Geographers*, vol 79, no 1, pp 125–45.

Bondi, L. (1999) 'Between the woof and the weft: a response to Loretta Lees', *Environment and Planning D: Society and Space*, vol 17, no 3, pp 253–5.

Bourdieu, P. and Wacquant, L. (1999) 'On the cunning of imperialist reason', *Theory, Culture and Society*, vol 16, no 1, pp 41–58.

Butler, T. (2007) 'For gentrification?', *Environment and Planning A*, vol 39, pp 162–81.

Butler, T. (2010) 'Gentrification and globalization: the emergence of a middle range theory?'. Available at: http://blogs.sciences-po.fr/recherche-villes/files/2010/01/cahier_ville_0514.pdf

Carpenter, J. and Lees, L. (1995) 'Gentrification in New York, London and Paris: an international comparison', *International Journal of Urban and Regional Research*, vol 19, no 2, pp 286–303.

Clark, E. (2005) 'The order and simplicity of gentrification – a political challenge', in R. Atkinson and G. Bridge (eds) *Gentrification in a global context: the new urban colonialism*, London: Routledge, pp 256–64.

Cybriwsky, R. (1998) *Tokyo: the Shogun's city at the twenty-first century*, Chichester: John Wiley and Sons.

Cybriwsky, R. (2011) *Roppongi Crosing: the demise of a Tokyo nightclub district and the reshaping of a global city*, Athens, GA: University of Georgia Press.

Davidson, M. and Lees, L. (2005) 'New build "gentrification" and London's riverside renaissance', *Environment and Planning A*, vol 37, no 7, pp 1165–90.

Flyvberg, B. (2006) 'Five misunderstandings about case study research', *Qualitative Inquiry*, vol 12, no 2, pp 219–45.

García-Herrera, L.M. (2001) 'Elitización: propuesta en español para el término Gentrificación, Biblio 3W', *Revista Bibliográfica de Geografía y Ciencias Sociales*, vol 6, p 332.

Hardoy, J.E. (1975) 'Two thousand years of Latin American urbanization', in J.E. Hardoy (ed) *Urbanization in Latin America: approaches and issues*, New York, NY: Anchor Books, pp 3–56.

Harris, A. (2008) 'From London to Mumbai and back again: gentrification and public policy in comparative perspective', *Urban Studies*, vol 45, no 12, pp 2407–28.

Janoschka, M., Sequera, J. and Salinas, L. (2013) 'Gentrification in Spain and Latin America – a critical dialogue', *International Journal of Urban and Regional Research*, vol 38, no 4, pp 1234-65.

Jones, G. and Varley, A. (1999) 'The reconquest of the historic center: urban conservation and gentrification in Puebla, Mexico', *Environment and Planning A*, vol 31, pp 1547–66.

Kovács, Z. and Wiessner, R. (1999) *Stadt- und Wohnungsmarketentwiclung in Budapest. Zur Entwicklung der inner stadtischen Wohnquartiere im Transformationsprozess*, Beitrage zur Regionalen Geographie 48, Leipzig: Institut fur Landerkunde.

Krase, J. (2005) 'Poland and Polonia: migration, and the re-incorporation of ethnic aesthetic practice in the taste of luxury', in R. Atkinson and G. Bridge (eds) *Gentrification in a global context: the new urban colonialism*, London: Routledge, pp 185–208.

Lambert, C. and Boddy, M. (2002) 'Transforming the city: post-recession gentrification and re-urbanisation', paper presented at 'Upward neighbourhood trajectories: gentrification in the new century', 26–27 September, University of Glasgow, UK.

Lees, L. (1994) 'Gentrification in London and New York: an Atlantic gap?', *Housing Studies*, vol 9, no 2, pp 199–217.

Lees, L. (2000) 'A re-appraisal of gentrification: towards a "geography of gentrification"', *Progress in Human Geography*, vol 24, no 3, pp 389–408.

Lees, L. (2012) 'The geography of gentrification: thinking through comparative urbanism', *Progress in Human Geography*, vol 36, no 2, pp 155–71.

Lees, L. (2014) 'Gentrification in the global South?', in S. Parnell and S. Oldfield (eds) *The Routledge handbook on cities of the Global South*, Routledge: New York, pp 506-21.

Lees, L., Slater, T. and Wyly, E. (2008) *Gentrification*, New York, NY: Routledge.

Lemanski, C. and Lama-Rewal, S.T. (2010) 'The "missing middle": participatory urban governance in Delhi's unauthorized colonies'. Available at: www2.warwick.ac.uk/fac/soc/wbs/projects/orthodoxies/conference2010/papers/101202_lemanski_c.pdf

Ley, D. (1986) 'Alternative explanations for inner-city gentrification: a Canadian assessment', *Annals of the Association of American Geographers*, vol 76, no 4, pp 521–35.

Ley, D. and Teo, S.-Y. (2014) 'Gentrification in Hong Kong? Epistemology vs. ontology', *International Journal of Urban and Regional Research*, vol 38, no 4, pp 1286-303.

López-Morales, E. (2010) 'Real estate market, urban policy and entrepreneurial ideology in the "gentrification by ground rent dispossession" of Santiago de Chile', *Journal of Latin American Geography*, vol 9, no 1, pp 145–73.

López-Morales, E. (2011) 'Gentrification by ground rent dispossession: the shadows cast by large scale urban renewal in Santiago de Chile', *International Journal of Urban and Regional Research*, vol 35, no 2, pp 1–28.

Maloutas, T. (2012) 'Contextual diversity in gentrification research', *Critical Sociology*, vol 38, no 1, pp 33–48.

Marcuse, P. (2010) 'A note from Peter Marcuse', *City*, vol 14, no 1, pp 187–8.

McFarlane, C. (2010) 'The comparative city: knowledge, learning, urbanism', *International Journal of Urban and Regional Research*, vol 34, pp 725–42.

McFarlane, C. and Robinson, J. (2012) 'Experiments in comparative urbanism', *Urban Geography*, vol 33, no 6, pp 765–73.

Nijman, J. (2007) 'Introduction – comparative urbanism', *Urban Geography*, vol 28, pp 1–6.

Petsimeris, P. (2005) 'Out of squalor and towards another urban renaissance? Gentrification and neighbourhood transformations in Southern Europe', in R. Atkinson and G. Bridge (eds) *Gentrification in a global context: the new urban colonialism*, London: Routledge, pp 240–55.

Popper, K. (1998) 'The problem of induction', in M. Curd and J.A. Cover (eds) *Philosophy of science: the central issues*, New York, NY, and London: W.W. Norton, pp 426–31.

Porter, L. and Shaw, K. (eds) (2008) *Whose urban renaissance? An international comparison of urban regeneration strategies*, London: Routledge.

Ragin, C. (1987) *The comparative method*, Berkeley, CA: University of California Press.

Robinson, J. (2006) *Ordinary cities: between modernity and development*, London: Routledge.

Robinson, J. (2011) 'Cities in a world of cities: the comparative gesture', *International Journal of Urban and Regional Research*, vol 35, no 1, pp 1–23.

Roy, A. (2009) 'The 21st century metropolis: new geographies of theory', *Regional Studies*, vol 43, no 6, pp 819–30.

Rubino, S. (2005) 'A curious blend? City revitalization, gentrification and commodification in Brazil', in R. Atkinson and G. Bridge (eds) *Gentrification in a global context: the new urban colonialism*, London: Routledge, pp 225–39.

Shaw, W. (2000) 'Ways of whiteness: Harlemising Sydney's aboriginal Redfern', *Australian Geographical Studies*, vol 38, no 3, pp 291–305.

Slater, T. (2002) 'Looking at the "North American City" through the lens of gentrification discourse', *Urban Geography*, vol 23, no 2, pp 131–53.

Slater, T. (2009) 'Missing Marcuse: on gentrification and displacement', *City*, vol 13, no 2, pp 292–311.

Smith, N. (1996) *The new urban frontier: gentrification and the revanchist city*, London and New York, NY: Routledge.

Smith, N. (2002) 'New globalism, new urbanism: gentrification as global urban strategy', *Antipode*, vol 34, no 3, pp 427–50.

Smith, N. and Derksen, J. (2002) 'Urban regeneration: gentrification as global urban strategy', in R. Shier (ed) *Stan Douglas: every block on 100 West Hastings*, Vancouver: Contemporary Art Gallery, pp 62–95.

Smith, N. and Williams, P. (eds) (1986) *Gentrification of the city*, London: Allen & Unwin.

Sykora, L. (1993) 'City in transition: the role of the rent gap in Prague's revitalization', *Tijdschrift voor Economisce en Sociale Geografie*, vol 84, no 4, pp 281–93.

Sykora, L. (2005) 'Gentrification in post-communist cities', in R. Atkinson and G. Bridge (eds) *gentrification in a global context: the new urban colonialism*, London: Routledge, pp 90–105.

Van Criekingen, M. and Decroly, J. (2003) 'Revisiting the diversity of gentrification: neighbourhood renewal processes in Brussels and Montreal', *Urban Studies*, vol 40, no 12, pp 2451–68.

Wang, J. and Lau, S.S.Y. (2009) 'Gentrification and Shanghai's new middle class: another reflection on the cultural consumption thesis', *Cities*, vol 26, no 2, pp 57–66.

Ward, K. (2010) 'Towards a relational comparative approach to the study of cities', *Progress in Human Geography*, vol 34, pp 471–87.

TWO

Unravelling the yarn of gentrification trends in the contested inner city of Athens

Georgia Alexandri

Introduction

Gentrification as a word per se does not exist in the Greek language. The word εξευγενισμός (*exevgenismós*) is used in order to describe the process of gentrification. This word is actually the outcome of academic efforts to transfer/translate the word gentrification into the Greek vocabulary. The meaning of this word is rather confusing; in Greek ευγενικός (*evgenikós*), means 'gentle'. Gentle is related to ευγενής (*evgenís*), which refers to nobility and/or 'being noble'. Hence, the Greek term could be understood as 'a gentle process of the gentry'. As there is nothing gentle to the gentrification process, I prefer to use the English word 'gentrification', which is highly political (see Davidson and Lees, 2005; Slater, 2006), instead of the neutral Greek equivalent. The Greek media and academics use both the English and the Greek words. Activists and artists use mostly the English 'gentrification' rather than the Greek term, while local Athenians, although very well informed about the process, use none of these words. They prefer verbal combinations, like urban regeneration or renovation; however, they are surprised when it is explained that there is an English word that underlines the social injustice of the process.

There is one well-documented case of gentrification in Athens – that is, the neighbourhood called Plaka, which is situated at the foot of the Acropolis (Sarigiannis, 2000; Kaftantzoglou, 2001). In the late 1980s, the Ministry of Culture appropriated properties to preserve their cultural heritage and the Ministry of Planning simultaneously proceeded to pedestrianise the area, impose planning restrictions and prohibit vehicle circulation. Land prices increased, the former impoverished residents were evicted and the new land uses were mostly related to the tourist industry. Nowadays, the new residential clientele mostly consists of the upper-middle classes and every visitor to Athens is invited to walk through the picturesque streets of Plaka. In this chapter, I argue that there are other cases of gentrification in Athens. By the end of the 1990s and beginning of the 2000s, the rent gap expansion through underutilisation, as characterised by Shin (2009a) when researching gentrification in South Korea, provided prime opportunities for commercial gentrification in Athens. The entertainment industry invaded the neighbourhood of Psiri and the area of Gazi (see Figure 2.1), adjacent to Plaka, and displaced impoverished households, turning the districts into 24-hour playgrounds of entertainment (Alexandri, 2005; Tzirtzilaki, 2009). There are some authors currently arguing that residential incidences of gentrification can hardly take place in Athens, as the housing stock in central areas is the outcome of 'antiparochi'[1] practices; thus, the reproduction patterns of the middle classes are different to the ones discussed in the dominant Western contexts (Maloutas et al, 2012). By way of contrast, I argue that gentrification in Athens, in both residential and commercial terms, can be identified at least at the micro-scale.

Figure 2.1: Metaxourgio in Athens

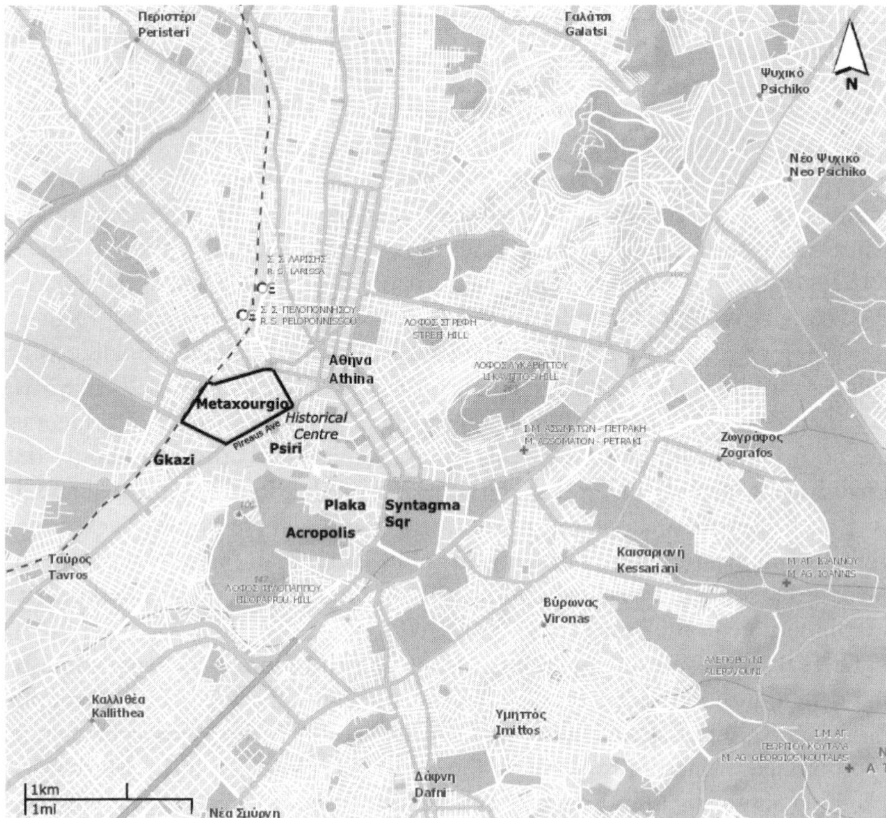

Source: www.xo.gr/map/

Gentrification in Athens?

After the Second World War, the housing stock in the densely built city centre of Athens was the outcome of speculation via the system of antiparochi. As public housing for the deprived urban population was not on the political agenda, housing was provided by private market mechanisms via this system. In central areas, its implementation led to the demolition of the majority of low-rise housing and its replacement by high-rise and dense blocks of flats. This system further resulted in high numbers of small homeowners and a vertical social differentiation pattern, where the richer households resided in the upper floors and the lower strata on the ground floors and in basements (Maloutas and Karadimitriou, 2001).

By the mid-1970s, the deterioration of the inner-city built environment led to the suburbanisation of the middle classes and to significant vacancy numbers in the inner-city housing stock (Maloutas et al, 2012). The inflow of immigrant populations after the 1990s, especially from Eastern European countries (Kandylis et al, 2012), was oriented towards these declining central areas, in the affordable floors of the private housing stock produced by the system of antiparochi. The vertical segregation pattern of the inner city was sustained, though it encompassed the new ethnic/immigrant variable, that is, the variable of the 'other'. Feelings of discomfort escalated especially after the 2000s, with the arrival of the most recent immigrant populations from African and other Arab countries who were undocumented and roamed the public spaces of the city, getting victimised by the mafia and/or police surveillance (Kandylis et al, 2012). By the mid-2000s, 10% of the Athenian population of around 4 million people consisted of immigrants (Arapoglou, 2006), though the actual number was/is greater as undocumented immigrants' numbers cannot be captured in statistics (Kandylis et al, 2012). The middle classes in the city centre began to feel trapped in the deteriorating urban conditions and turned against the immigrant 'others'.

From the end of the 2000s, the urban crisis reinforced the fearful actions of the middle classes against the immigrant 'others'. With the rise of neo-fascist discourse, the immigrant population was held responsible for the socio-economic disasters of the country. The high unemployment rates were related to the increasing numbers of the immigrant population, especially in recent years, when the unemployment rate in Greece became the highest of the European Union (EU) member states (in August 2013, it was 27.6%; see Eurostat, 2013). Undocumented immigrants were blamed for the images of homelessness in the city centre. Although there is no official number of homeless, non-governmental organisations (NGOs) claim that there are more than 20,000 homeless people for whom there is no shelter or housing provision (Klimaka, 2013). As fear lies at the core of a new racism (Koskela, 2010), policies and initiatives launched in the current 'phobopolis' (Lopes de Souza, 2009, cited in Janoschka et al, 2013) of Athens reflect the fear of the middle classes, while a rise in neo-Nazi practices is responsible for dozens of immigrant assassinations in inner-city areas.

Driven by a general despair for the urban condition, the social-democrat Mayor of Athens decided to remove the benches in public spaces so that homeless people would have nowhere to sit, and to remove the rubbish bins from central squares so that the poor cannot search for food in popular public spaces and demonstrators cannot set bins on fire. The mayor has declared that he is willing 'to "restart" Athens', even if this means coming into conflict with pre-existing interests' (Kaminis, 2013), referring to his recent collaboration with the Minister of Public Order and Citizen Protection (POCP). The Mayor noted that 'the image of the city will change decisively only when citizens and businesses return to the centre' (Kaminis, 2012b). Since the end of 2012, squats in the city centre were sealed in order to create a good business climate (Vradis, 2013). The Mayor has been clear that 'we have to increase the levels of security … to renovate deteriorated inner areas' (Kaminis, 2012a); hence, he is engaging in a regeneration project called 'Re-launch Athens', aiming to create more appropriate inner-city conditions for the middle classes. In the summer of 2012, the POCP launched the 'Hospitable Zeus' project, which focuses on the arrest of undocumented immigrants in the centre of Athens. So far, 4,000 people have been arrested and transferred to special concentration camps (Karatziou, 2013). It is not surprising that this socio-spatial cleansing project is especially noticeable in inner-city areas with gentrification potential.

Since the late 1990s, a neoliberal shift in city planning and labour policies related to the preparation of the city for the Olympic Games of 2004 created prime opportunities for gentrification in some derelict inner-city areas (eg Shin, 2009b, 2012). The beautification of the city consisted of regeneration schemes, pedestrianisations, inner-city metro stations and the unification of archaeological sites. Regeneration tactics were accompanied by surveillance policies, and the projects launched for the Olympic Games changed the land use patterns and values of the city (Vaiou, 2002). Since then, in the axis towards the port of Piraeus, where minor industrial activities were located (Leontidou, 1989), symbolic economies related to culture and nightlife entertainment have emerged (Souliotis, 2009). Regeneration plans denoted the clustering of cultural uses in former industrial spaces, important museums relocated themselves and luxurious hotels and restaurants opened to service the Olympic Games clientele and more affluent, future tourists. At the entrance to the Piraeus axis lies a newly hyped area of the city, the neighbourhood of Metaxourgio, which this chapter will now focus on.

The case of Metaxourgio

Metaxourgio is a former working-class area in close proximity to the main squares of the city and to important archaeological sites such as the Acropolis (see Figure 2.1). The area is named after the first silk[2] factory to function at the end of 19th century. The district was not that affected by the system of antiparochi, as anticipated profit could not be raised due to small industrial usage and the related pollution that kept the land prices low. Nowadays, the housing stock in the area mostly consists of low-storey houses, some of neoclassical architecture. After the 1970s, prostitutes started gathering in the area, and in the 1980s, the gypsy community was given incentives to reside in Metaxourgio as it was one of the cheapest parts of the city centre at that time. These factors pushed the better-off residents to the suburbs; those who remained in the area did not have the economic power to relocate themselves. After the 1990s, many immigrants found shelter in the area's abandoned housing stock, and after the 2000s, the Chinese population created residential and commercial clusters there. Due to its close proximity to the city centre, the area experiences all the inner-city phenomena (deterioration, delinquency, otherness) that make Athenians and the Mayor feel insecure.

Despite this, on 6 January 2011, Catherin Drake (2011) reported in *Time* magazine: 'The best place to take the pulse of the new Athens is Keramikos-Metaxourgio,[3] a bustling quarter where Chinese merchants, North African immigrants, gallery owners and the café set exist side by side with the city's demimonde'. Also, in April 2011, *Air France Magazine* urged its passengers to visit Athens' creative surge in: 'Metaxourgio a working class district ... the new hip gallery spot' (*Air France Magazine*, 2011, p 126). So, what are these new micro-geographies of hipness that have arisen in a time of crisis in Metaxourgio? Are they gentrification? Can we really talk about gentrification in Athens, a city where the basics for gentrification, like interesting inner-city building stock and the expansion of new middle classes, seem not to be there, and, moreover, a city in a period of extreme economic, social and cultural crisis?

For researchers of/from the non-anglophone world, researching gentrification-like processes is a difficult task. There is a constant need to compare the implicit contextual assumptions against the contextual realities of the process (Maloutas, 2012). Gentrification as a concept has been stretched to embrace divergent urban processes (Kalantides, 2007; Maloutas, 2012); hence, gentrification researchers need be very conscious about their research criteria. However, at the core of gentrification research lies the identification of social and spatial injustice via the appropriation of space by the middle classes and the displacement of impoverished households (Lees et al, 2008).

In this chapter, I investigate four elements of gentrification, as suggested by Davidson and Lees (2005), to make my case for the gentrification of Metaxourgio: capital reinvestment; change in the urban landscape; social upgrading by incoming higher-income groups; and the direct or indirect displacement of low-income groups. The research itself was qualitative and consisted of in situ observation, photographs, the collection of planning proposals, newspaper and magazine articles, and research on blogs. In addition, a total of 74 semi-structured, open-ended interviews were conducted with gentrifiers (26), lifelong residents (15), immigrants (13), planners (3), politicians (4), developers (2), local entrepreneurs (10) and school teachers (1).

I argue that gentrification is evident in Metaxourgio at the micro-scale and takes a specific spatial form, reflecting the Athenian socio-economic context. Renovated spaces lie next to spaces of deterioration (see Figure 2.2) and new middle-class people share the neighbourhood space with the deprived population. The process can be characterised as *punctuated* (identified at the street level, in buildings or apartments) and *scattered* in space (gentrification enclaves in several parts of the district).

Figure 2.2: Punctuated gentrification in Metaxourgio: renovated buildings next to derelict ones

Note: Photograph taken by Georgia Alexandri in the year 2010.

Gentrification in Metaxourgio has mostly been privately led, with the initiatives mostly undertaken by individuals. Houses have been renovated by a new upper-middle-class population. In the mid-1990s, the renovations typically cost around €150,000 (the properties themselves only cost around €55,000 at that time); this slipped to approximately €140,000 in 2007. The gentrifiers, characterised by cultural rather than economic capital, used sweat equity to renovate their houses or flats (see Zukin, 1989). Since 2009, GEK TERNA S.A., a real estate company, has also erected a secluded development, a small-scale gated edifice consisting of four multi-storey buildings fenced in with concrete and endowed with security systems, an inner courtyard, a private pool and parking lot, at a charge of €4,000 per square metre.

In fact, the state has not been totally absent from capital reinvestment in Metaxourgio, for in the 1980s, the local government pedestrianised several streets in the area (see Figure 2.3) and developed regeneration plans; although these were never applied, they created expectations that the neighbourhood would soon be regenerated. In addition, for the 2004 Olympic Games, a touristic pedestrian-walk was introduced by the Unification of Archeological Sites Enterprise, uniting important archaeological sites with the area of Metaxourgio. In this way, expectation about the regeneration of the area was encouraged and members of the middle classes began to buy properties in the 1990s and into the 2000s so as to take advantage of the low prices before the widening of the rent gap (Smith and Williams, 1986). Additionally, in 2010, prior to the municipal elections, the former silk factory was transformed into the municipal gallery of the city. Also, in 2011, the area was designated as a 'zone of special regeneration', providing economic incentives related to building restoration and reuse that mainly have to do with tax reductions.

Figure 2.3: Gentrification on the back of the 1980s' pedestrianisation

Note: Photograph taken by Georgia Alexandri in 2012.

In terms of land values, prices 'had gone crazy till 2008' (interview with a local realtor, 2011); landlords were asking the same amount of money per square metre as in the affluent suburbs of the city.[4] Due to the real estate crisis, the emergent rent gap froze, and after the 2008 economic crisis, prices began to decline. Real estate newspapers claim that the emergent gentrification in the neighbourhood has kept the local prices and rents higher compared to neighbouring ones (Rousanoglou, 2012). Nevertheless, the freezing of the rent gap has provided more bohemian gentrifiers, especially artists, with more time and space to gentrify. Rent decreases have made possible the opening of more performance studios and artistic spaces.

Land use changes have also been related to capital reinvestment. New land uses have mushroomed in the area, including theatres, galleries, a new wave of *kafeneia*,[5] expensive gourmet restaurants, bars, fashion/clothes shops and a shop with organic products. The area's nightlife and artistic-ness is hyped in newspapers and lifestyle magazines such as *Vogue*. Those entrepreneurs that decide to open up businesses in Metaxourgio bear the cost of the building improvements and renovations. For example, with respect to new artistic spaces, the agreement with the landlord is that artists would renovate the building – where a gypsy family used to live – and they would not pay rent for two years as recompense. From the beginning of the 2000s, the property developer Jason Tsakonas, through his real estate company 'Oliaros Properties', bought 65 properties in the area, that is, 4% of the housing stock. His general plan was to turn them into residential spaces or workshops for creative activities in the city centre (Tsilimidou, 2012). So far, the properties are provided for free to artists or are used every two years for the Remap Art Exhibition. In this exhibition, the area is actually 'remapped', as artists from all parts of the world are invited to display their creations, and visitors are provided with maps of the area indicating the topos of the exhibits. Additionally, Tsakonas has co-established with middle-class gentrifiers in the area the KM-Protypi Geitonia[6] Network, which has collaborated with European schools of architecture, organising workshops for the area, and he is working with local and foreign architectural offices over regeneration schemes for the area. Indeed, he has launched two architectural competitions: one for students' residences in one of his properties; and the other for the renovation of four of his buildings. This is a quite strategic way to raise money to be able to gentrify in a period of extreme austerity.

The gentrifiers identified in the research were middle class and were categorised into two groups. Bohemian gentrifiers were characterised by more cultural than economic capital, rented houses or flats, were related to the alternative artistic scene (actors, musicians, performers) and earned less than €1,000 per month. The other category of gentrifiers was characterised by economic capital and consisted mostly of homeowners. As stated in many interviews, they moved from more affluent areas of the city (either central or suburban) because they were attracted by the urban village feel or the energies therein due to the immediacy to the archaeological sites. They mostly worked in the private sector as architects, lawyers and economists, and their monthly household income was around €3,000–€5,000. There was strong evidence from the interviews that middle-class gentrifiers studied or worked in Western cities where gentrification has already taken place. Having already experienced gentrification elsewhere, they located themselves in Metaxourgio believing that the future outcome of the neighbourhood would be similar to gentrified ones in New York, London or Paris. It is interesting that these gentrifiers have made their way to Metaxourgio hoping for the same experience of gentrification that they had in other cities outside Greece; hence, in this case, the topological imagination (Robinson, 2011) transferred to Athens becomes a gentrification driver. As expressed by a gentrifier:

> 'we are people that have travelled a lot ... we know what Soho means and we identified the process in New York with the restorations of old buildings, the loft living and everything ... all of us who have gathered here we decided to do so, since we already knew and we were influenced by what goes on in inner-city underdeveloped areas ... by this aesthetic of deprivation ... and the first people to rehabilitate these areas were artists.' (Interview with a singer, 8 February 2010)

This inflow of people was accompanied by the outflow of 'other' people. Those who were evicted belonged to the most underprivileged groups – the gypsy population and the migrant and undocumented migrant populations. Two cases of evictions of lifelong household residents and one case of a bohemian gentrifier were identified in the research. Displacement has been indirect via rental increases after renting leases expired, especially if the property was claimed for a new land use, such as a bar or a *kafeneio*, which would provide the landlord with a much higher profit. More direct forms of displacement were also identified in that the power and water supplies, especially of the gypsy population, had been cut off. As indicated in one interview:

> 'there were many gypsy families living in these old houses that share the same yard[7] ... at that time, nobody wanted to live in these houses and the gypsy families rented them with very little money ... it has been three years now that realtors have expressed interest in the area ... so they bought the houses and evicted the families.' (Interview with a gentrifier, set designer, 28 March 2011)

Apart from the gypsy community, no other mass eviction has taken place, which might explain the non-existence of anti-gentrification activism in the area. Then again, any anti-gentrification resistance would suffer from the weak social networks and relations among the different groups in this neighbourhood.

The everyday realities of gentrification in Metaxourgio: living in fear and isolation

In the gentrifying Metaxourgio, the same 'social tectonics' identified in areas of gentrification in London (Butler and Robson, 2001) are apparent. Although sharing the same neighbourhood, the different groups of people experience parallel lives, mostly mixing with people of the same socio-economic status and cultural profile. They might both visit *kafeneia* or tavernas but, nonetheless, the social interaction among gentrifiers, lifelong residents and immigrants is quite superficial. The immigrants, in particular, prefer to socialise outside the area in different parts of the city; the lifelong residents, especially men, hang out in one traditional *kafeneio*; while the gentrifier population is more apparent in the new land uses that have conquered the public spaces of the area. The notion of social cohesion stands only among people of the same class or cultural disposition (Ley, 1996); by contrast, inter-social relations are pervaded by fearful syndromes:

> 'this is a working-class area, and when they see me walking my dog on the street, they call me names such as faggot and stuff ... in the building that I live, there is a cocktail of ethnicities ... we have different timetables ... when should we meet? For an afternoon drink? [Ironic

> question] ... I only know the person who lives upstairs – he is a famous actor.' (Interview with a gentrifier, cloth designer, 8 March 2010)

Here, we see that the gentrifier does not want to mix with the older residents of the area, be they working-class Greeks or the immigrant population. His sense of belonging is in line with the artists and the new 'not mainstream' people in the area, that can "*bring about change*", as he claims in a latter part of the interview. He expresses a sense of irony at his difference to his neighbours, though this could be a reaction to the verbal abuse he has suffered in the public spaces of the neighbourhood (on the fear that arises from oppression or harassment, see Zizek, 2008). By way of contrast, the artistic scene provides him with the shelter of social cohesion.

Many of the gentrifiers in Metaxourgio expressed real fear of the non-gentrifier 'other':

> 'I am not a racist ... never will I be, but sometimes I am afraid. When I see someone and he is a drug addict, or an immigrant, whatever ... when I return home at night and there are two or three tall dark guys in front of my doorstep, I am afraid.' (Interview with a gentrifier, waitress/teacher, 17 April 2010)

Those deemed to cause this new 'fear' were/are, like in Smith's (1996) revanchist New York City, the immigrant, the homeless, the poor or the drug user, that is, the 'other' population. In Metaxourgio, gentrification dynamics have capitalised on the broader middle-class phobias against the immigrant population, future instability and the deterioration of the city centre. In gentrifying places, in times of crisis, the ostracism of the 'other' deepens the urban frontier. The punishing of the poor by the iron fist of the penal state (Wacquant, 2009) is celebrated by gentrifiers, who call for the further socio-spatial cleansing of the city centre and, thus, of this contested neighbourhood. Gentrifiers are satisfied with the increased policing of the public space of the area (memo, 5 March 2011) and, thus, with the sealing of buildings where undocumented immigrants reside (memo, 13 June 2013). However, it is not just the middle classes expressing this fear, long-term residents and, indeed, some immigrants themselves have turned against the unwelcome 'other'.

Lifelong residents in Metaxourgio blame the immigrants for the deterioration of the neighbourhood. They feel more secure with the arrival of wealthier residents and the new land uses that "*put lights in the streets*"; thus, they sound relieved about the displacement of the gypsy population. As one old-timer said in an interview: "some years ago, I was ashamed to confess that I live in Metaxourgio, but now I am proud of it". The gentrifiers seem to have developed deeper fears related to their somewhat risky economic investments in rehabilitating property in the area. In times of liquidity, individuals bear the consequences of their initial 'free choices' (Bauman, 2007), and whenever there is a suspicion that things may change, but not according to our preferences, anger arises (Arendt, 1970): 'I want to leave my flat and go to the theatre, there is this homeless man outside the door, and I feel trapped' (gentrifier of the GEK TERNA complex, judge, memo, 7 March 2011).

The immigrants or the homeless who disturb middle-class aesthetics have to be displaced, for they create feelings of insecurity. The presence of immigrants and the homeless reproduce images of violence (dirt, Muslim, dark skin, terrorism, war) that disrupt the tranquillity of middle-class life. Displacement can take place either by punitive policies, such as the current socio-spatial cleansing police project, or by acts that are the free will of the gentrifiers. In neoliberalism, as freedom is projected as a virtue for every individual (Harvey, 2007a), the prevalence of individual initiatives in gentrifying spaces broadens the horizon of gentrification. Defensive homeownership strategies associated with the neoliberal rationale which dictates that self-determined people can affect social contexts through personal practices (Maloutas and Pantelidou-Malouta, 2004) end up legitimising displacement and reinforcing gentrification.

Jason and *Argonautica*[8] in Metaxourgio

In Athens, gentrifiers, as they accuse the 'other', have put concerted pressure on the state to undertake schemes that will protect them and their homes so as to tame the wild (inner) city (Smith, 1996) and cleanse it of those 'others' that are supposedly creating the insecurity. In fact, a coalition of inner-city entrepreneurs and residents sent a letter to the municipality and other related urban affairs ministries urging 'the need to follow the methods used successfully in the upgrading of city centres in other European cities' (Coalition of Active Citizens for the City Centre, 2011). In essence, they were advocating the same neoliberal policies of social control that have purified other European cities of unwelcome uses and users, while honouring social cohesion, safety and urban sustainability. Of course, such spatial and social control policies facilitate the circulation of capital in the built environment, for the desire to purify urban spaces from any behaviour that provokes anxieties is related to investment opportunities (Bannister and Fyfe, 2001) or particular political processes (Coleman, 2004).

The main investor in Metaxourgio, J. Tsakonas, along with the KM-Protypi Geitoneia network of middle-class gentrifiers and the support of some new entrepreneurs, has engaged in practices that have been heavily publicised in the press as the 'positive activism' of city-centre residents, as good 'bottom-up' approaches. The group presented a regeneration proposal to the municipal council and a meeting took place with the head of the Attica region police department, the main request was the securitisation of the area, especially via police street patrols. In order to improve the real or perceived safety of some groups, policies are being launched at the expense of 'other' groups (Pain, 2001), for the newly formed DIAS[9] motorcycle police are now present in several parts of the area, and it is currently arresting undocumented immigrants under the framework of the 'Hospitable Zeus' project.

In other defensive homeownership strategies, the network of gentrifiers has 'adopted' three empty private plots, which were transformed into temporary urban gardens; by now, the vegetation in these gardens is dead and two of the 'gardens' remain fenced in, hence protected from the 'others'. A 'temporary' playground was also erected on a plot belonging to a public agency, which also remains closed and fenced. Furthermore, a plot that accommodates the ancient graveyard of Keramikos, called Public Sign, which consists of the tombs of important ancient Greek politicians and warriors, has been revitalised and turned into a small 'park'; this initiative was planned by famous architectural offices and sponsored by private companies such as IKEA. One week prior to this revitalisation, the plot was being cleaned by municipal services. The first birthday of the Public Sign 'park' was celebrated by six hours of live radio shows.

Popular artists with political connections have also managed to get the local police force to watch over their homes, beyond the already installed CCTV cameras. These initiatives illustrate a revanchist, defensive reaction against urban fears. When such actions take place in a gentrifying area, another form of urban frontier seems to be established – a frontier that builds on urban fears, on phobias of 'the other' and on anxieties about the future of a contested (reinvested) space. The gentrifers' strategies outlined here can be regarded as defensive homeownership strategies (Atkinson, 2006). Such tactics also act as gentrification drivers as they advertise the area and strengthen the spatial conquest on behalf of the middle classes. The underlying logic inside the gentrifers' Trojan Horse is to transform the area into an inner-city playground '*for people like them*' and attract uses that tally with their cultural dispositions.

Tsakonas set a six-month deadline for the authorities, provoking them to regenerate the area. In his declarations, he asserts that after years of active engagement with the neighbourhood, it is '*now or never*' for his regeneration vision to take place. After bidding for EU financing through the Joint European Support for Sustainable Investment in City Areas (JESSICA)[10] programme (Tsilimidou, 2012), his regeneration proposal, consisting of a street market in place of the red-light district and the clustering of creative uses and specialised residences, has already been approved by the local authority and it is up to the National Bank to agree on its final approval. Moreover, the Mayor declared that his biggest challenge lay in the uplifting of inner-city areas, especially of Metaxourgio (Palaiologos, 2013). While applauding Tsakonas's gentrification proposal, the municipality of Athens wants to rethink regeneration/gentrification in the centre of Athens.

Conclusion

The 'Rethink Athens' project, which seeks to pedestrianise a major axis in the city centre, is another prime example of attempts to create the ground for more gentrification (Davidson, 2012). In times of crisis, regeneration schemes and surveillance projects aiming to cleanse the city elicit creative destruction (Harvey, 2007b) in actually existing neoliberalism (Brenner and Theodore, 2002). The rolling out of the state is accompanied by the shrinking of the 'left hand' (welfare, employment), while the 'right hand' takes its most punitive form (Bourdieu, 2008). It seems that, like in New York City in the 1970s and 1980s, gentrification is rising like a phoenix from the ashes of inner-city 'crisis' Athens.

Well hidden behind the 'rethink', 'relaunch', 'restart' of 'remap' Athens projects, via regenerations and revitalisation projects, and/or art exhibitions, lies the notion of gentrification (Lees, 2008). Investments in the built environment are projected as the way out of the urban crisis; hence, gentrification initiatives are praised as the noble acts of inner-city investors/saviours and risky residents/gentrifiers. The punitive policies that target the 'other', like police projects and the removal of public furniture, capitalise on the fear of the middle classes, legitimise displacement and desire overall social and spatial control (see Davis, 2006). The 'right hand' of the state helps to establish gentrification and works in tandem with individual desires for inner-city social cleansing.

Gentrification dynamics in Athens have, so far, arisen at the micro-scale. This is not to suggest that the process is less violent, but to underpin the fact that it is identified at the core of a city whose basic characteristics suggest that gentrification can hardly take place. Processes identified at the micro-scale are related to broader city dynamics and, thus, reflect the way that everyday realities and social and spatial practices shape future dynamics (Lefebvre, 1991). This micro-geography of gentrification in Athens suggests that gentrification enmeshes with urban fears (Alexandri, forthcoming). Gentrifiers trapped in the turmoil of the urban crisis feel threatened by the undesirable 'other'. In order to secure their investments and thus their safety, they engage in defensive strategies and create networks that push for the full gentrification of their areas and, thus, the eviction of 'people not like them'. The 'other', that is, the immigrant without papers, the drug user or the homeless person, is a threat to their investment; hence, it has to be displaced. Fear of the 'other' thus becomes the main driver of gentrification.

The case of Athens, as outlined in this chapter, suggests the need for a broader conceptualisation of the way gentrification enmeshes with urban fears. There are some similarities, as argued, with Smith's (1996) revanchist city, but there are some significant contextual differences too. In New York, the collaboration of the municipality, the police department and the realtors was more effective: the zero tolerance dogma turned against the unwanted others and cleansed the central areas where investors were reluctant to undertake risks. In the case of Athens in crisis, where the state is proven ineffective, the future outcome of the pursuits of gentrifiers is not guaranteed. The middle classes turn against the 'other' while undertaking initiatives to attract better-off uses and users. In the meantime, displacement and anxiety characterise the process, in particular, in neighbourhoods like Metaxourgio. The case of Athens suggests that gentrification is driven by middle-class desires and fears. Further and deeper research on gentrification is needed in order to shed light on the specific contextualities in each case, which will enrich research, boost the academic dialogue and help us to claim our rights in the (inner) city.

Notes

[1] Antiparochi refers to the system where housing is co-created by small owners and small construction firms in ad hoc joint ventures to produce small condominiums.

[2] Silk in Greek is μετξι (*metáxi*); hence, the area was named Metaxourgio (Metax-ourgio) after its silk factory.

[3] Keramikos is the ancient Greek name for the southern part of the neighbourhood related to the graveyard of important politicians and dead warriors of the Peloponnesian war (431–404 BC), called Public Sign.

[4] Approximately €1,700 per square metre.

[5] Traditionally, a *kafeneio* used to be a place where working-class men would spend their leisure time drinking coffee or local spirits with *meze*, that is, a variety of local appetisers at very low prices. New entrepreneurs, inspired by the idea of the traditional *kafeneio*, have established *neo-kafeneia*, which cater to young people, both men and women.

[6] 'Protypi Geitonia' means exemplar/ideal neighbourhood.

[7] Many low-storey working-class Athenian houses developed around a common inner yard. In this yard, sanitary facilities were installed, as the houses did not have lavatory spaces.

[8] The *Argonautica* is an ancient Greek epic poem about the myth of the voyage of Jason and the Argonauts to retrieve the Golden Fleece from Colchis.

[9] The DIAS police force is a highly equipped motorcycle unit formed after the December 2008 riots in order to be able to circulate fast in the city.

[10] The JESSICA programme is a European Commission project in cooperation with the European Investment Bank (EIB) and the Council of Europe Development Bank (CEB).

References

Air France Magazine (2011) April issue.

Alexandri, G. (2005) 'The Gas district gentrification story', unpublished MSc thesis, School of City and Regional Planning, Cardiff University, UK.

Alexandri, G. (forthcoming) 'Read between the lines; gentrification tendencies and issues of urban fear in the midst of Athens' crisis', *Urban Studies.*

Arapoglou, V.P. (2006) 'Immigration, segregation and urban development in Athens: the relevance of the LA debate for southern metropolises', *The Greek Review of Social Research*, vol 121, no 1, pp 11–38.

Arendt, H. (1970) *On violence*, San Diego, CA, New York, NY, and London: A Harvest Book, Harcourt Brace and Company.

Atkinson, R. (2006) 'Padding the bunker: strategies of middle-class disaffiliation and colonisation in the city', *Urban Studies*, vol 43, no 4, pp 819–32.

Bannister, J. and Fyfe, N.R. (2001) 'Fear and the city', *Urban Studies*, vol 38, nos 5/6, pp 807–13.

Bauman, Z. (2007) *Liquid times; living in an age of uncertainty*, Cambridge and Malden, MA: Polity Press.

Bourdieu, P. (2008) 'The left hand and the right hand of the state', *The Variant*, vol 32, no 2, pp 3–4.

Brenner, N. and Theodore, N. (2002) 'Cities and the geographies of "actually existing neoliberalism"', *Antipode*, vol 34, no 3, pp 349–79.

Butler, T. and Robson, G. (2001) 'Social capital, gentrification and neighbourhood change in London: a comparison of three South London neighbourhoods', *Urban Studies*, vol 38, no 12, pp 2145–62.

Coalition of Active Citizens for the City Centre (2011) 'From the historic centre to the historic ghetto', letter to the Prime Minister, the Attica Region Governor and the Mayor of Athens, 27 April. Available at: http://www.kmprotypigeitonia.org/?p=news&id=letteristorikoghetto (accessed 30 April 2011).

Coleman, R. (2004) 'Images from a neoliberal city; the state, surveillance and social control', *Critical Criminology*, vol 12, no 1, pp 21–42.

Davidson, M. (2012) 'Critical commentary. Gentrification in crisis: towards consensus or disagreement?', *Urban Studies*, vol 48, no 10, pp 1987–96.

Davidson, M. and Lees, L. (2005) 'New build gentrification and London's riverside renaissance', *Environment and Planning D*, vol 37, pp 1165–90.

Davis, M. (2006) *City of quartz: excavating the future in Los Angeles*, London and New York, NY: Verso.

Drake, C. (2011) 'Next time you are in Athens', *Time*, 6 January. Available at: http://www.time.com/time/travel/article/0,31542,2040981,00.html (accessed 10 February 2011).

Eurostat (2013) 'Eurostat news release Euro indicators, 126/2013', released 30 August. Available at: epp.eurostat.ec.europa.eu/cache/...30082013.../3-30082013-AP-EN.PDF (accessed 29 September 2013).

Harvey, D. (2007a) *A brief story of neoliberalism*, Oxford and New York, NY: Oxford University Press.

Harvey, D. (2007b) 'Neoliberalism as creative destruction', *The Annals of the American Academy*, vol 610, no 1, pp 22–45.

Janoschka, M., Sequera, J. and Salinas, L. (2014) 'Gentrification in Spain and Latin America – a critical dialogue', *International Journal of Urban and Regional Research*, vol 38, no 4, pp 1234-65.

Kaftantzoglou, R. (2001) *In the shade of the Holy Rock*, Athens: Greek Letters, National Centre of Social Research (in Greek).

Kalantides, A. (2007) 'For a more rigorous use of the term gentrification', *Geographies*, vol 13, pp 158–72 (in Greek).

Kaminis, G. (2012a) 'The mayor's speech to the conference on criminality, policing and (in)security in the commercial district of Athens'. Available at: http://www.cityofathens.gr/node/19862 (accessed 14 March 2012) (in Greek).

Kaminis, G. (2012b) 'There is no place in the city centre where I feel safe to walk alone', Newsit. Available at: http://news247.gr/eidiseis/synentefxeis/kaminhs_den_yparxei_shmeio_ths_athhnas_poy_fovamai_na_perpathsw.1741137.html (accessed 20 April 2012).

Kaminis, G. (2013) 'Historical centre of Athens; amongst obsolescence and hope', *Ermis*, special tribute, 25 January (in Greek).

Kandylis, G., Maloutas, T. and Sayas, J. (2012) 'Immigration, inequality and diversity: socio-ethnic hierarchy and spatial organization in Athens, Greece', *European Urban and Regional Studies*, vol 19, no 30, pp 267–86.

Karatziou, N. (2013) 'Getting closer Kaminis and Dendias', *Eleftherotypia*, 24 February. Available at: http://www.enet.gr/?i=news.el.article&id=345866 (accessed 15 March 2013).

Klimaka (2013) 'Project for the support of homeless people'. Available at: http://www.klimaka.org.gr/newsite/index.htm (accessed 18 February 2013).

Koskela, H. (2010) 'Fear and its others', in S. Smith, R. Pain, S. Marston and J.P. Jones (eds) *The Sage handbook of social geographies*, London, Thousand Oaks, CA, and New Delhi: Sage, pp 389–408.

Lees, L. (2008) 'Gentrification and social mixing: towards an inclusive urban renaissance?', *Urban Studies*, vol 45, no 12, pp 2449–70.

Lees, L., Slater, T. and Wyly, E. (2008) *Gentrification*, New York, NY, and London: Routledge, Taylor and Francis.

Lefebvre, H. (1991) *Critique of everyday life* (vol 1), London and New York, NY: Verso.

Leontidou, L. (1989) *Cities of silence: working class colonization of Athens and Piraeus, 1909–1940*, Athens: Cultural and Technological Foundation ETVA (in Greek).

Ley, D. (1996) *The new middle class and the remaking of the central city*, Oxford and New York, NY: Oxford University Press.

Lopes de Souza, M. (2009) 'Social movements in the face of criminal power', *City*, vol 13, no 1, pp 26-52.

Maloutas, T. (2012) 'Contextual diversity in gentrification research', *Critical Sociology*, vol 38, no 10, pp 33–48.

Maloutas, T. and Karadimitriou, N. (2001) 'Vertical social differentiation in Athens: alternative or complement to community segregation?', *International Journal of Urban and Regional Research*, vol 25, no 4, pp 699–716.

Maloutas, T. and Pantelidou-Malouta, M. (2004) 'The glass menagerie of urban governance and social cohesion: concepts and stakes, concepts as stakes', *International Journal of Urban and Regional Research*, vol 28, no 2, pp 449–65.

Maloutas, T., Arapoglou, V., Kandylis, G. and Sayas, J. (2012) 'Social polarisation and de-segregation in Athens', in T. Maloutas and K. Fujita (eds) *Residential segregation in comparative perspective; making sense of contextual diversity*, Surrey and Burlington, VT: Ashgate, pp 257–85.

Pain, R. (2001) 'Gender, race, age and fear in the city', *Urban Studies*, vol 38, nos 5/6, pp 899–913.

Palaiologos, Y. (2013) 'The Mayor of Athens: a sober voice in a world of extremes', *Time*, 12 July. Available at: http://world.time.com/2013/07/12/the-mayor-of-athens-a-sober-voice-in-a-world-of-extremes/#ixzz2ZIRmnZyX (accessed 13 August 2013).

Robinson, J. (2011) 'Cities in a world of cities: the comparative gesture', *International Journal of Urban and Regional Research*, vol 35, no 1, pp 1–23.
Rousanoglou, N. (2012) 'Vertical fall in real estate prices', *Kathimerini*, Economic Section, 18 March, p 5 (in Greek).
Sarigiannis, G. (2000) *Athens, 1830–2000*, Athens: Summetria (in Greek).
Shin, H.B. (2009a) 'Property-based redevelopment and gentrification: the case of Seoul, South Korea', *Geoforum*, vol 40, no 5, pp 906–17.
Shin, H.B. (2009b) 'Life in the shadow of mega-events: Beijing Summer Olympiad and its impact on housing', *Journal of Asian Public Policy*, vol 2, no 2, pp 122–41.
Shin, H.B. (2012) 'Unequal cities of spectacle and mega-events in China', *City: Analysis of Urban Trends, Culture, Theory, Policy, Action*, vol 16, no 6, pp 728–44.
Slater, T. (2006) 'Eviction of critical perspectives from gentrification research', *International Journal of Urban and Regional Research*, vol 30, no 4, pp 737–57.
Smith, N. (1996) *The new urban frontier: gentrification and the revanchist city*, London and New York, NY: Routledge.
Smith, N. and Williams, P. (1986) *Gentrification of the city*, London: Allen and Unwin.
Souliotis, N. (2009) 'Expansion of the common, sophistication of discrimination: the social construction of demand in the Athenian symbolic economy from the mid 70's to date', in D. Emmanuel, E. Zakopoulou, I. Maloutas, R. Kaftantzoglou and M. Hatzigiannis (eds) *Social and spatial transformations in 21st-century Athens*, Athens: National Centre of Social Research, pp 279–320 (in Greek).
Tsilimidou, M. (2012) 'Keramikos-Metaxourgio; a vision for a new neighbourhood in the city, Passpartout', *Ependytis*, 8 December.
Tzirtzilaki E. (2009) *Dis-placed, urban nomads in the metropolis: contemporary issues concerning movement, the city and space*, Athens: Nissos Academic Publishing (in Greek).
Vaiou, D. (2002) 'Milestones in the urban history of Athens', *Treballs de la Societat Catalana de Geografia*, vols 53/54, no 1, pp 209–26.
Vradis, A. (2013) 'A crisis of presence: the war on Greek cities', *Open Democracy: free thinking of the world*. Available at: http://www.opendemocracy.net/opensecurity/antonis-vradis/crisis-of-presence-war-on-greek-cities (accessed 19 September 2013).
Wacquant, L. (2009) *Punishing the poor: the neoliberal government of social insecurity*, Durham, NC, and London: Duke University Press.
Zizek, S. (2008) *Violence: six sideways reflections*, New York, NY: Picador.
Zukin, S. (1989) *Loft living: culture and capital in urban change*, New Brunswick, NJ: Rutgers University Press.

THREE

Slum gentrification in Lisbon, Portugal: displacement and the imagined futures of an informal settlement

Eduardo Ascensão

Introduction

When Lisbon is presented in touristic and official discourses, it is often the city's post-imperial culture that comes to the forefront. The city and its monuments are associated with the history of its Navigators and with the Portuguese Empire, and many elements are presented as 'remnants of empire'. The city centre contains different historical layers (such as a 13th-century Moor neighbourhood, elements of the 16th-century maritime world or late-18th-century rationalist urban design; see França, 2008) but the one thing linking five centuries of history together is the reference to empire. Heroic navigation, scientific expeditions, settlement colonialism and miscegenation, all are summoned to describe the undercurrent of the nation's and of the city's history.

Today, several parts of the city centre are undergoing a rapid process of regeneration and/or gentrification, and these historical themes are often deployed in narrations that legitimate the city's *embourgeoisement*. In the central areas of Avenida da Liberdade, Chiado and Princípe Real, transnational property-led developer gentrification is flourishing – windows are awash with CB Richard Ellis and Sotheby's real estate agents' billboards in both the residential and commercial areas – and is directed at the (national and foreign) affluent populations that, in the past three decades, have fled to the better-off suburbs along the Cascais train line. This is academically referred to as nobilisation (*nobilitação*), in a way, a nuance of the label gentrification given that these areas have always been the more aristocratic ones. Since 2011, this process has been accelerated with the forced 'devaluation of everything' (salaries, labour rights, rent controls, tenant rights) except for the currency (the Euro), under the structural adjustment programme signed with the International Monetary Fund (IMF), the European Commission and the European Central Bank. The recession-inducing remedies (poison) of irrational one-direction austerity (strict conditionality for countries; unconditionality for the finance sector) have created the perfect storm for a revanchist takeover by the upper-middle and upper classes of Lisbon's historical centre.

Even in the face of this, housing and urban studies academics in Portugal tend to minimise the relevance of the concept of gentrification for the case of Lisbon – implying that it belongs exclusively to the repertoire of the Anglo-American city. Exceptions go back to the early 1990s, but were mostly student dissertations (eg Branco, 1992). During the late 1990s and early 2000s, the functional regional planning literature (eg Costa, 2007) aligned itself with the 'creative industries' discourse being proposed by local governments and, oblivious to its critique by, for example, Peck (2005), still suggested that gentrification was benign urban change. For both groups, gentrification simply meant the arrival of pioneer gentrifiers and artists into disused areas or, at most, the marketing of a historical neighbourhood as a nightlife or cultural district. The issues of displacement and the right to the city were put aside. In any case, up until very recently, the number of academic publications on gentrification was miniscule.

Lately, other authors have started to address more seriously the social and spatial implications of gentrification (Rodrigues, 2010; Malheiros et al, 2012; Mendes, 2012), with empirical evidence from the private-led gentrification of the nightlife district of Bairro Alto (Mendes, 2006) or the local government-led initiative revitalising the old 'Moor' quarter, Mouraria (Malheiros et al, 2012). The latter investigated the importance of 'marginal (pioneer) gentrifiers' but also argued that the gentrifiers' social relations were detached from the ageing urban poor who already lived there and the poor immigrants (from Bangladesh, Pakistan, Senegal and China) who had settled there over the past 15 years. They suggest a process that Butler and Robson (2003) term 'tectonic social relations', but, as stated earlier, in this case as well as in others, a domesticated idea of post-colonial multiculturalism serves a strong gentrification agenda (Oliveira, 2013).

These imaginations brand Lisbon's city centre as post-colonial and cosmopolitan in order to appeal to a 'back to the city' movement for the more affluent segments of society, but what they fail to acknowledge is that Lisbon's most relevant post-imperial or post-colonial characteristic in the last three decades has been its relationship with the post-colonial immigrants that settled in informal settlements on the outskirts of the city after the fall of Salazar and Caetano's fascist dictatorship in 1974, and the independence of former colonies such as Angola, Mozambique, Cape Verde or Guinea-Bissau.

Post-colonial migration and the geography of informal settlements in Lisbon

Throughout the 1980s and 1990s, Lisbon's urban expansion was peppered with the informal settlements that these migrants – priced out of the housing market and ineligible for the scarce pool of public housing stock (to this day, the national pool of publically owned dwellings is not bigger than 120,000 dwellings [Carreiras et al, 2011; based on INE, 2001; IHRU, 2007]) – built. These settlements were located in places with a proximity to jobs (Salgueiro, 1977) and, just as importantly, with a certain administrative invisibility that allowed for the illegal occupation and development of medium-sized plots of land that, by then, were neither profitable for agriculture nor likely – at the time – to be legally developed into urban space (Rodrigues, 1989). As a result, a sort of invisible infra-city with infra-citizens left to their own devices grew during this period; at its peak in the late 1980s, the scattered pockets of slums and shanty towns were estimated to be inhabited by 150,000 to 200,000 people (Númena, 2003, p 143).[1]

Shanties coexisted with a different type of housing stock, *clandestinos* – today referred to by an acronym, *AUGI* (*Áreas Urbanas de Génese Ilegal*; *Urban Areas of Illegal Genesis*) – which consist of 'canonical' housing typologies, usually the single-family detached house or the two-storey building, built without planning permission on legally owned agricultural land. *Clandestinos* share many features with other illegal typologies in Southern Europe, such as *viviendas marginales* in Spain, *borghetti* in Italy or *afthereta* in Greece (eg Leontidou, 1990, p 20). Because of the inability of the state to provide housing in sufficient numbers, *clandestinos* as well as *barracas* (shanties) were in effect tacitly accepted by the state (Gaspar, 1989, p 82). This brief mention of *clandestinos* is crucial in understanding how 'slums' began. In fact, if to oversimplify a little, many shanty towns in Lisbon started out as *clandestinos*, but whereas some of the latter were subsequently legalised and provided with infrastructure and municipal services such as rubbish removal, others began to deteriorate into slums. Where land was owned by its inhabitants and illegally built upon, political trade-offs between local authorities and populations with a view to legalisation *a posteriori* could occur. Where land was not owned by inhabitants, nor was it public, it was subject to predatory urban capital, which, because the city was expanding, bought individual plots and consolidated them into larger areas with a view to building new residential developments.[2] Land tenure, class, race and the ability to bargain with local politicians were the key factors in this division between improving and deteriorating neighbourhoods. This evidence supports Roy's (2005, p 149) argument that:

> [urban] informality must be understood not as the object of state regulation but rather as produced by the state itself.... The planning and legal apparatus of the state has the power ... to determine what is informal and what is not, and to determine which forms of informality will thrive and which will disappear.

Mutatis mutandis, in Lisbon, the settlements with the worst conditions did not disappear, they continued and expanded exponentially in the 1980s with post-colonial immigrants.[3] It was this second layer of illegal settlement that formed the constellation of shanty towns mentioned earlier, and this relation between post-colonial migration and settlements of shanty-like dwellings is what makes them somewhat unique, in Europe and worldwide. In terms of historical comparison, the relevance of migration waves immediately after decolonisation becoming integral to the urban growth of 'post-imperial' cities, as is the case in Lisbon, can be accurately compared to Algerian or other Maghreb immigrants settling in Paris's *bidonvilles* in the 1950s–60s (Sayad and Dupuy, 1995), which curiously were to integrate many poor Portuguese immigrants into France in the 1960s (Volovitch-Tavares, 1995). However, in terms of architectural form, for the past 40 years, informality in Europe has tended not to translate into shanty-like dwellings (at least not of a permanent nature).

In 1993, the Portuguese state devised a Special Rehousing Programme (*Plano Especial de Realojamento*; from now on, PER) to rehouse these populations. It involved a substantial financial effort from the state – between at least €1.2 billion, consisting of €600 million in direct subsidies and €600 million in credit lines for municipalities recorded for the period 1994–2004 (IHRU, 2007, pp 142–5), and the more recent figure of €3 billion (*Lusa*, 2013) – to demolish the 30,000 shanties (*barracas*) surveyed at the time (AML, 1997, p 15) and build public housing estates for its inhabitants. The political rationale for the enactment of the programme was connected to the fact that: when Portugal held the European Economic Community (EEC) presidency for the first time in 1992, Lisbon was the only European capital with slums; the city was also going to be the European Capital of Culture in 1994; and it would host the World Fair (Expo 98) in 1998. However, the programme also responded to the long process of internal and post-colonial migration that had happened hand in hand with informal urbanisation.

The programme involved both in situ rehousing, with new buildings either on site or in the immediate vicinities of the previous informal settlements – for instance Casal Ventoso (Chaves, 1999) or Curraleira in the Lisbon municipality; Quinta da Vitória in Loures (Cachado, 2012) – or more complex options, such as the in situ upgrading of the illegal concrete dwellings of Cova da Moura in Amadora (Ascensão, 2013a), and clearance and rehousing in far-away, underserviced areas (without commerce, transport, etc) in municipalities' hinterlands. Examples of the latter include: the transfer of people from the Fontaínhas shanty town to the Casal da Boba estate; from Azinhaga dos Besouros to Casal da Mira in the Amadora municipality; from Pedreira dos Húngaros to the Moínho das Rolas estate in Porto Salvo, municipality of Oeiras; or from Marianas to the Adroana estate in Cascais. All four shanty towns were relatively well located, with great views, proximity to jobs and adjacent to middle-class areas; all four estates are amid agricultural land, isolated and completely segregated. The programme was part of a contradictory class project because, while acknowledging the need to provide decent housing for slum dwellers, in the latter cases, it further segregated them, as if trying to solve a problem by hiding it. Clearance and rehousing was opted for because: the land on which the slums were located increased in value; there was a lack of public land nearby, as was forewarned by Pereira (1993); and local governments were reluctant to expropriate the land from its private owners – who had initially left it vacant and disused but were now looking to make considerable profit from the implementation of the programme, in a type of speculation by absence.

As implementation developed, another facet of the programme started to emerge: the issue of governmentality. One of the programme's principal tenets was that everyone would be rehoused but that no more shanties would be tolerated. This was operationalised through, first, census-like surveying (assessing how many people inhabited these settlements) and, second, categorisation (assessing who was eligible for the programmes). In the process, these slum populations were rendered increasingly visible to the state, becoming part of numeric governmentality (Porter, 1995; Scott, 1998). However, the state encountered many problems. The slum surveys had a 'fixed' date in 1993 and the programme's slow implementation did not factor well with the high turnover of residents in each settlement. Then, using the classic procedures of displacement/gentrification, that is, an un-negotiated administrative notice posted on house doors stating 'Your house will be razed by the government on date x. Please move' (for such a procedure as the mark of gentrification, see Anderson, 1964, cited in Lees et al, 2010, p 318), did not set a good platform for engagement with the slum dwellers. Furthermore, the displacement was in many cases a result of the municipality's financial frailties, which meant that they were open to being captured by predatory urban capital. Finally, the displacement was hidden by the local government and mainstream media's discursive manipulations, which Crozat (2003) described in the case of the settlement of Pedreira dos Húngaros.[4]

So, what we have had in Lisbon over the past decade and a half is a situation of dual gentrification: the gentrification of the city centre, as mentioned earlier, and that of some of the sites where informal settlements once stood. In this chapter, I focus on the gentrification of one informal settlement in particular, the neighbourhood of Quinta da Serra. Drawing on ethnographic research as well as on the excavation of municipal intermediate archives,[5] I discuss the complex intersection of post-coloniality, informality and displacement-gentrification present in the PER programme. The protracted implementation at PER site #44, unjust and disheartening to residents, allowed for the examination of the 'scaffolding' of the production of urban space along class and race lines (Ascensão, 2013b). I begin this case study through the eyes of the residents of the settlement as it was undergoing demolition – when I also engage in 'heterodox comparisons' with the similar experiences of slum dwellers in the Global South – and only then do I look in detail at the institutional imaginings and political economy of the relocation process. I end by describing what is 'actually existing' on the site today, which is a type of low-fi survival that followed the interruption of these institutional imaginings.

In this chapter, I argue that this process involved gentrification through a mechanism not unlike gentrification by ground rent dispossession (López-Morales, 2011; see also Shin, 2008, 2009), state-led but private-profit-protecting. We could label it as 'area gentrification' (akin to urban renewal) in the strict sense of the word 'area', that is, the gentrification of a privileged location (and respective land rights), in an area cleared and earmarked for residential development for white Portuguese middle-class populations by way of a public programme and the state's more forceful instruments that carry out demolitions and evictions, which displaced an incumbent population of mainly black post-colonial poor immigrants who were rehoused in a scattered way to sites much further away, or simply evicted and left homeless if they were found not to be eligible for the programme.

The case I show, exemplary but not unique in Lisbon, thus sits between slum clearance, displacement and evictions – a situation that over the past few decades has mostly been associated with cities of the Global South and their urban poor (eg Mukhija, 2003; Du Plessis, 2006). However, here, it is located in a European capital, revealing a process of gentrification usually associated with the displacement of incumbent populations from either dilapidated central areas or from supposedly obsolete but well-located public housing estates in the Global North (eg Lees, 2014), but here related to a previously disused (thus, squatted) agricultural location, which was then re-zoned and more recently appreciated following the infrastructural investments related to urban mega-events and urban renewal initiatives.

Gentrification and displacement in Quinta da Serra

Quinta da Serra was a small informal settlement built on private land in the late 1970s–early 1980s, located in the Parish Council of Prior Velho in the municipality of Loures, in Lisbon. From a population of around 100 people in the late 1970s (FFH, 1975), mostly white Portuguese rural migrants, it expanded in the late 1980s to between 3,000 and 4,000 people, the majority of whom were immigrants from Portuguese-speaking African countries (PALOPs). Its population declined after that to around 1,500 people during the 2000s. When I conducted research there in 2008, around 50% were Cape Verdean or of Cape-Verdean descent, 30% to 35% were from Guinea-Bissau, around 10% were from Angola and São Tomé and Príncipe, and the few White Portuguese and Gypsies still living there made up 5% (for more, see CML, 2005).

The population of Quinta da Serra was relocated/resettled in the period 2008–12. Different schemes within the PER programme either rehoused eligible households to council housing within the Loures municipality (to estates such as Apelação, viewed as problematic or violent by many inhabitants of Quinta da Serra) or, through the PER Famílias update, subsidised homeownership for them in any part of the country (but with the property price limit set well below market value for the area).[6] However, 35% to 40% of the 1,500 inhabitants were not registered in the 1993 housing programme survey that served as the eligibility document for this resettlement. These residents were simply evicted, as I show later.[7] The neighbourhood underwent a slow process of clearance and will be replaced by upper-middle-class residential buildings within the next two to three years.[8]

During my fieldwork in the neighbourhood, the threat of demolition was ever-present for individual households, and a number of irregular situations arose. For example, since 1993, some PER-eligible individuals had illegally sold their shack upon relocation to other places (either when rehoused by the state or when they moved out by their own means). Selling their shack was possible when the structure was not immediately demolished; indeed, this was a common mistake by the state in the early days of the PER programme. The seller often led the buyer (newly arrived and in need of shelter) to believe that their residence would lead him/her to get a new house in the future too. This was, of course, false and misleading. Shacks had been numbered and granted 'administrative existence' but they were not the (formal, legal or actual) recipient of state help. That recipient had always been the household living inside the shack. However, as is easily imaginable, newly arrived migrants often *preferred* to believe the version they were told even if they suspected it to be false, they accepted the illusion of a better future in order to cope with the present.

A more altruistic logic can be exemplified by the case of an elderly woman who sublet rooms to three young men. She was PER-eligible and they were not. At the time of my fieldwork, she was very reluctant to join any of the relocation schemes because, on the one hand, she would lose income from the rents they paid and, on the other, because she felt responsible for them, in the sense that they would lose a place to live when she moved out (interview, September 2008). The seemingly contradictory terms of, one, pecuniary self-interest and, two, honest feelings of responsibility towards her 'tenants' joined up to explain her reluctance. This is a common feature in complex situations like this, what a city council worker referred to as *negócios de pobreza* (transactions of poverty) (interview, June 2007). Behind the illegal and exploitative practices lay complex individual decisions, in the words of a different city council official:

> 'This is happening American-style now. You have an area in decay, a real estate fund comes in, pushes people out … but that problem will resurface somewhere else.… So what you have is people jumping from a shanty into a brick wall slum. Spaces under stairs are being rented, and so on.' (Interview, October 2008)

Frail resistance: the power of not leaving

For a different resident, it was the PER-eligibility mismatch between him (who is eligible) and his two older sons (who are not PER-eligible because they were over 18 years old when they arrived in 1994) that made him refuse to accept a quick solution after a visit from the landowner's legal representative:

> 'I will only move out once my two sons' situation is resolved. What do they think? I would sign [the compensation agreement] on a Tuesday, on Wednesday they would say "the money is in your account", by Thursday or Friday the shacks would go down. That I don't want.… I will go back home, but only after their situation is secured. [My sons] are not going from here to another piece of rubbish.' (Interview, January 2008)

In the penultimate sentence, he was referring to the option of straight compensation for the shack and moving back to Cape Verde. He preferred this option as his working career was over, he thought that rehousing in Apelação would be a nightmare and a move under the PER-Famílias did not suit his wishes. Whatever he did, however, would have an immediate impact on his sons, who were likely to be left without a home. In addition, he mentioned the implicit value in the choice of compensation over the other options: this way he would 'cost less' to the state – 15% of the average price of a new dwelling, or, indeed, nothing, given that it would be funded by the landowner – so he wanted that goodwill to be, in principle if not in exact value, reverted to his sons. He knew the logic behind this argument was too individualised to be taken on board by the authorities, yet he used it nonetheless. It was a 'family logic': he was willing to move to Cape Verde if that meant his sons could 'collect' something of his housing entitlement. His refusal to leave is a personalised illustration of what Scott (1998) calls the silent resistance to numerical forms of governmentality, and he was using the only power he had left – 'to stay put'. He was familiar with the Apelação council estate that constituted his first option as an eligible individual, but disliked the place. Apart from the conflicting relationship between 'Gypsies' and 'Africans', which led to shootings in the summer of 2008, he had other worries about the move:

> 'It's far away, and … Here, I can go to a store and people know who I am, if I don't have money, they know I am good for my word. At my age, moving to a place where I know almost no one.' (Interview, January 2008)

There was an anticipated sorrow at the loss of his community network, and his concern over his small credit at local stores was a metaphor for all the aspects of familiarity with a place he had lived in for 26 of his 31 years in Portugal. Finally, this resident's concern about the rapid unfolding of events if he were to sign the compensation papers also exposes the different rhythms of state operations regarding informal settlements. Whereas the provision of makeshift infrastructure or setting up collective solutions for relocation were prolonged processes that took years, once a resident formally entered the scheme, the speed of events increased. Procedures started to happen fast, and with a sense that the state wanted demolition to proceed as quickly as possible. The speed was terrifying to residents.

Disassembling the shack: the rights and duties of the Special Rehousing Programme

'D' was the head of a PER household of a house demolished on 15 January 2008. He had in the previous months been consigned to the category of 'absent', allegedly for moving abroad to France; thus, speedy demolition of his house was required. D was PER-eligible but as he failed to reply to the first official notice, he was taken off the list. He contested the second demolition notice, but by that time, it was too late. In any case, he was clearly not residing in the house at the time. In his place was a young couple with a child, allegedly related to him. None of them were PER-eligible. The situation appeared to be one where D had moved out some years earlier but had 'kept his shack' with a view to rehousing when the PER rehousing would happen.[9] In the meantime, he either lent it or sold it to the couple, instructing them to cite a family relationship if asked. Although aware of the scheduled date for demolition, they had not removed their belongings, mostly because they did not have another place to go to. A secondary reason for this was the common hope among residents in similar cases that refusing to leave the house might cancel, suspend or delay demolition.

That morning, the young couple refused to leave when the demolition team arrived. They alerted D, and friends soon joined them. A very tense stand-off arose between them and the city council surveyors. Riot police (*Polícia de Intervenção*) were called to the scene. On one side were the town surveyor, the landowner's representative, the police forces and the subcontracted team, all trying to carry out the demolition. On the other were D, the young couple and their friends, protesting and refusing at first, but later moving out the belongings (furniture, domestic appliances, etc) so that they were not damaged (see Figures 3.1a, 3.1b and 3.1c).

What this case shows – besides the fact these residents tried to play a game they ultimately lost – is how the categorisation of individuals as either eligible or not eligible for relocation shaped their actions. For individuals on one side of the divide, the PER-eligible, this was a customary part of what agents of the state consider the 'abuses' of the relocation scheme, that is, illegal practices or false statements with a view to personal gain from the scheme when they no longer needed it. In the words of a person present that day, referring to D's loss of PER status, "they know very well their rights, not so much their duties or obligations" (field notes, January 2008). On the other side of the divide, false statements among non-PER individuals (such as the pretence of a family connection in this case) were a common strategy to prevent demolition of their only shelter at the time.

Figure 3.1a: Demolition day. Centre, while the demolition team works, a friend of the non-PER young couple residing there removes a television set

Figure 3.1b: The workings of demolition. It is carefully carried out by workers, monitored by the city council and by the police. On the right, a neighbour makes sure an adjacent wall belonging to another structure is not brought down

Figure 3.1c: The aftermath

Note: Photographs by Eduardo Ascensão.

Here, we see the constitution of a way of living based on duplicity and deception, in the sense of deception as a central strategy of the urban poor. This is a topic that different authors have studied in different city peripheries in developing countries (eg De Boeck and Plissart, 2004; Simone, 2004; see also Robinson, 2011, p 18) but it is not something that the gentrification studies literature has discussed in terms of resistance to or fighting gentrification. Such a heterodox comparison between slum dwellers in Africa and African slum dwellers in a European capital may seem overstretched at first glance, but it is only so if we do not count the latter as part of the slum dwellers worldwide, which they clearly are. In many parts of the world, slum dwellers are faced to varying degrees with problems related to population surveys, land tenure insecurity and its connection to lack of housing entitlements (Du Plessis, 2006; Datta, 2012). People's reactions, resistance and circumvention of such problems tends to place them within a frame of rule-breaking, disobedience and deception – something that is ultimately detrimental to themselves individually, but often inevitable given the conditions of exclusion and breach of general social trust. Given the new literature emerging on the gentrification of slums in the Global South (for a summary, see Lees, 2014a), it is imperative that these strategies of the urban poor in the face of such processes are attended to.

These problems of deception can only be fully understood in the case of Quinta da Serra if we lift our gaze upwards from the field and towards the institutional agents, the instruments of implementation and the wider political economy of the place, that is, if we examine the institutional arrangements and interests involved in planning and policy for the area and how they have played out over time.

Institutional imaginings and gentrification

Imagined future 1: intransigent infrastructure and profit margins

The situation described in the previous section, one of prolonged precarity, could have been different; it could have been averted. Between 1997 and the early 2000s, plans to redevelop the area into residential medium-rise apartment blocks, with the population rehoused *in situ*, were very nearly set in motion. Following initial work in 1991, by 1997, the revision of the detailed urban plan (*plano de pormenor*) for the Prior Velho Parish Council, in effect since 1972, was ready; complete with official property records (CML and DPU, 1997; see also the masterplan, CML, 1994). Quinta da Serra was categorised as agricultural land in 1972, but by 1997, had been rezoned as residential land. The proposed plan for the area was medium-rise apartment blocks with an estimated residential capacity of 592 dwellings for 1,954 people. The document estimated a 'present population' of 859 people and 232 shacks (CML, 1994, sheet 46). These figures were from 1990 and they underestimated the population, likely in 1990 to be three or four times higher, and in 1997, at least two times.

The masterplan, designed by the city council planning division, made suggestions that the city council acquire the land, either by negotiating with the owners, by using the preferential buying option available to municipalities or by expropriation (CML, 1994, 2/8, p 15). It mentioned the need for sociological surveys in order to develop allocation criteria for the families to be rehoused, as well as the need to 'involve' the population from the early stages of the process, whether in the design of the new neighbourhood or, later, in its management and conservation, so that it could be well 'appropriated' by residents. It was suggested that regulations allowing for the future acquisition of dwellings by tenants could also contribute to this. This was the clear, intelligent and progressive planning assessment for the area.

At this time, the owners of the land were still *pessoas singulares*, that is, individuals not companies – despite some of them being referred to as mandating or being mandated by a third party (CML and DPU, 1997, sheet 5.1). From this date onwards, the public-listed construction company Somague, with many developments in Loures, became interested and bought these plots of land with a view to future development (Loures Ordnance Survey, 2010).[10] Proximity to the Expo 1998 site then under regeneration, a location allowing for good accessibility to the road system and potential good views of the Tagus River, made it an attractive site. The scheme would be mixed use, with the population rehoused in some of the blocks and the remainder sold on the open market.

The plan presumed a two- or three-stage operation. The first stage comprised clearance of around half the dwellings and temporary accommodation for the residents affected. The second comprised the building of the medium-rise buildings where the entire population would be rehoused and the relocation concluded. The third would then see the clearance of the remaining area and the building of apartment blocks for the open market. If implemented, it could have led to a later situation of gentrification by stealth (see Bridge et al, 2011), but by the people living in shanties, it was regarded as a good solution. Furthermore, this was a similar operation to one Somague was developing in nearby Quinta do Mocho, another PER informal settlement. The necessary trade-off in both cases was that the developer was given planning permission to build in the remaining land for the open market. Mukhija (2003) argues that this type of extra land value should always revert to the original slum dwellers, but a compromise had to be arrived at, one where such additional land value was to revert to the owner, otherwise the company would not be interested.

It must be noted that although Somague would implement the operation, the scheme would still be substantially, if not fully, financed by public money under the PER – typically, the central government would subsidise 50% of the costs and the local government could access credit lines to cover the remaining 50%. A strong commitment from the National Housing Institute (INH at the time) can be seen by the 'voluntary mortgage' Somague put in place on the land at the date at which it became full owner (9 January 2003). The company constituted this mortgage with the INH, not with a banking institution, at the value of €992, 946 (Loures Ordnance Survey, 2010).

Somague developed the plans but was to eventually abandon them. What appears to have happened is that the company became increasingly aware that rehousing all of the population (more people than those initially estimated; again, we see problems with surveys) would mean that the scheme would not be profitable. To back away from these plans, the company used 'technical' reasons, explaining that the terrain was too steep to allow for the two- or three-stage operation. Furthermore, any earthworks would clash with the power lines that pass through the area, as well as with a main water collector that serves Lisbon. Overcoming these technical obstacles to implement any plans would have required the 'unbundling' of relatively stable, 'fixed' network infrastructure systems (Graham and Marvin, 2001). An entirely new technical solution would have had to be deployed by the municipality and the water and electricity companies involved, respectively, *Empresa Pública de Águas Livres* (*EPAL*) (water; 100% publically owned) and *Electridade de Portugal* (*EDP*) (electricity; private with state participation until

2011). That would involve massive earthworks, burying overground power lines and ensuring that the water main was not interfered with.

Like in a game of Mikado, things and people would have to be carefully removed in the correct order before any new construction could begin. Infrastructure thus acted as an impediment to the Somague operation, what Collier (2004) describes as 'intransigent infrastructure'. However, intransigency of the infrastructure was not so significant as to preclude other plans to develop the area some years afterwards, as I show next.

Imagined future 2: eco-imaginations and secretive decision-making

In the following years, cross-participation between Somague and another construction company-developer, Obriverca, saw the latter take on the ownership of the site. In 2007, the city mayor directed the city council's planning division to nominate the area of Prior Velho, an area with disused industrial buildings immediately south of Quinta da Serra, as a site for Europan 9, a European competition for young architects and urban design professionals that tries to help 'cities and developers who have provided sites to find innovative architectural and urban solutions' (Europan, 2007).

The impact the shanty town had on the architects explains why most of the proposals went beyond the area designated for intervention and included the shanty part – Quinta da Serra (interview, October 2008). The brief indicated a population of 322 inhabitants for the area of intervention (8.67 ha) and no specific figures for the study area (15.02 ha). It stated that the plan should include a small hotel (120 rooms), social facilities and housing rehabilitation (Europan, 2008b, p 277). In the initial bid to Europan, the city council had stated the need for 'an innovative housing framework that addresses both the need to relocate (*relocalizar*[11]) the population presently living in precarious housing in the perimeter of the intervention and the establishment of free-market housing' (CML and DPU, 2006, sheets 35-31, p 5). In other planning documents later circulated to the applicants, this was expressed in more precise terms: for the 'study area' (Quinta da Serra), 280 residential units in buildings of up to five storeys, all dedicated to rehouse the population living in *barracas* (CML and DPU, 2006, sheet 20, p 4); for the 'intervention area', 248 units, of which 129 were to rehouse the people whose houses had to be demolished (one infers the 322 inhabitants stated in Europan, 2008a). Finally, an indicative €35 million was given as the total cost of the operation (CML and DPU, 2006, sheet 20, p 8).

The winning proposal by architects Tiago Tomás and Djamila Flor (see Figure 3.2) included a 'green belt' of vegetation walls tied to elevated fences to separate Quinta da Serra and Prior Velho from the dense traffic of the A1 motorway and the overpasses that connect it to the inner regional circular, the CRIL (Circular Regional Interna de Lisboa). The proposal placed the hotel and the better-off residential dwellings inside the intervention area, thus sticking to the brief, but proposed the continuation of the scheme into Quinta da Serra.

However, as in 1997, the proposal was not implemented. The primary reason is that when presented with it, the landowner preferred to develop the area according to a 'similar basic program but using its own architectural team' (CML, 2008). Details of the owner's plan are unknown to the public or to the other stakeholders involved, including the municipal planning division. It can therefore only be speculated, but it is likely that these plans included the highest possible density within that 'basic programme', that is, to accommodate as many middle-class residential units as possible while avoiding the onus of rehousing the entire population on the site.

Figure 3.2: The winning proposal of Europan 9 for the Prior Velho site, by Tiago Tomás and Djamila Flor (Portugal)

Source: Tiago Tomás Architects.

What we see is that the progressive recommendations in the *Plano de pormenor* and in the Europan bid suggest a strong commitment by planners to the ideals of social justice concerning the population of Quinta da Serra; yet, again and again, they ran into other factors such as the owner's interests or the weak finances of the municipality. Although Europan-winning projects are usually built, they are still a purely indicative, non-binding instrument. The owner was consequently under no legal obligation to implement the winning project. Notwithstanding, its rejection of the proposals was a surprise to different stakeholders, in particular, the Europan offices in Lisbon, which had been assured by the city council that the *Plano de pormenor* would take the winning proposals into account (Europan, 2008c).

High-level bureaucracy and secretive decision-making

Importantly, the municipal division responsible for the application to Europan was not contacted by the landowner. High-level bureaucracy was at play, whereby negotiations or bargaining between the landowner and the city council happened only with the mayor and town councillors and were not transparently explained to the departments that were supposed to implement them. Despite the allocation of considerable human resources and money (€32,000 for an abandoned plan), decision-making is mostly secret. The Europan competition was yet another missed opportunity to solve the housing predicament of Quinta da Serra.[12]

In these two proposals, the local government effectively put itself in the position of the public arm of private interests. Unintentionally or not, the institutional arrangement of relocation has seen 'virtuoso social actors' (Flyvbjerg, 2001) such as the city council instituting a complicated framework and a discursive regime that emphasises the 'impossibility' of just solutions for the population, rather than attempting options that would be less profitable for the owner but fairer for the population.

The gentrification of slum areas is becoming a worldwide phenomenon, sometimes conducted by the state (eg Shin, 2009; López-Morales, 2012), and sometimes by the state being co-opted by the dynamics of urban capitalism, as is the case of Quinta da Serra. In both cases, for slum dwellers, the urban renewal of the sites where they live has more often than not become a process they are excluded from. Even as urban planning paradigms shift towards the idea of the 'negotiated city' (Bourdin, 2009), slum dwellers are left out of negotiation platforms and any potential gains they could make are denied from the onset. Displacement wins because it guarantees that the accentuated processes of urban capital accumulation – here, seen in small detail – are not disrupted, and are, indeed, maximised.

In 2008, as the houses in Quinta da Serra began to be demolished, residents tried to allay the disheartening effect by using the cleared sites for (symbolic) productive use (see Figure 3.3) by setting up individual clothes lines on vacant plots. Given that there was not really a lack of space to hang clothes around their still-standing houses, one wonders if this was not a humble mental strategy to fill in the void left by those already displaced, a consolation.

In 2012, at the very end of the process, some of the individuals who were displaced or simply evicted returned and did urban gardening on the site where

Figure 3.3: October 2008 (left) and June 2012 (right)

Note: Photographs by Eduardo Ascensão.

their shack or house once stood (for the same behaviours, see also Batchelor, 2012, p 27; Lees, 2014b).

Conclusion

The gentrification of the slum areas in Lisbon's periphery, like Quinta da Serra, is a pebble in the shoe of a history of urban growth that fits into the broader social process of building a modern, European and then multicultural Portugal over the last 35 years. This situation questions the labelling of Lisbon as a post-colonial/ post-imperial city since the term contradicts the conditions of access to urban space that the mainly black post-colonial immigrants in these slums had/have. This broad assumption is illustrated by their problematic access to public or private housing, which initially led to them erecting informal settlements, and by the fact that despite the honest efforts of the state, including the latter enactment of the de-segregating PER Famílias update reminiscent of the mixed communities paradigm (see Bridge et al, 2011) but which resulted in what I have labelled 'area gentrification', housing inequalities for these populations persist. This is clearly illustrated by the fact that even with the PER and PER Famílias, migrants from PALOP were still over-represented in slum or overcrowded dwellings in the 2001 Census (INE, 2001; see also Malheiros and Vala, 2004, p 1084; Arbaci and Malheiros, 2010, pp 246–7), and have remained so in the 2011 one (INE, 2012).

Atypical as this case might seem at first – slum clearance and 'area gentrification' on the periphery of a European capital – I would conclude by arguing that it belongs to the same global process described in the following:

> Nowadays, *neo-Haussmannization* is a process that ... integrates financial, corporate and state interests, yet tears into the whole globe and seizes land through forcible slum clearance and a handy vehicle for dispossession known as 'eminent domain', wherein the public sector expropriates land and then gives it away for upscale private reappropriation, letting private economic interests cash in on what is legalized looting. (Merrifield, 2013, p 31)

The only difference in the case described, it seems to me, is that the state did not even have to expropriate, it merely sat idle and complicit while urban capital played its game. In the meantime, the population lived (and some still live) under an urban condition of precarity and infra-citizenship, something they unfortunately share with many slum dwellers around the world.

Notes

[1] Initial estimates from 1993 indicated a total of 48,391 dwelling units necessary to rehouse 162,103 people nationwide, with the Lisbon Metropolitan Area (LMA) needing 33,390 dwelling units (Númena, 2003, p 143). In later estimates, this figure was reduced to 29,223 surveyed shacks or slum houses (AML, 1997, p 16), but as I show in the following,

these surveys often failed to count all the residents. In any case, 30,000 dwellings can be conservatively extrapolated to mean around 150,000–180,000 people (five to six inhabitants per dwelling).

[2] This – the extraction by private developers of the added values allowed by unregulated, unchecked and often corrupt changes in zoning (from agricultural to urban) – was 'the business' in Lisbon for over 20 years. It was fuelled at the macroeconomic level by, again, unregulated and unchecked levels of private credit debt (Bingre, 2011). Of course, this was not a localised event: trans-European economic policy and global financial incentives were also partly responsible for similar stories in Spain and Ireland, only with minor variations.

[3] This situation was part of a generalised housing crisis that had developed since the early 1980s, which was not helped by the previous agreement between the IMF and Portugal in 1983, after which the Portuguese government cut public and cooperative housing provision and redirected policy to general supply, leaving large fringes of the population priced out of the market (Ferreira, 1988, p 60; Númena, 2003, p 16).

[4] Artists, though, paid attention to it, for example: the rehousing process of Fontaínhas to the Casal da Boba estate appears in Pedro Costa's celebrated film *Juventude em Marcha* (*Colossal Youth*), from 2006; and the forced evictions of non-PER individuals in Azinhaga dos Besouros (the PER-eligible were rehoused in the Casal da Mira estate) featured in Nathalie Mansoux's *Via de Acesso* (*Access Way*), from 2008.

[5] The ethnographic research (2007–08) involved 42 interviews, 15 of which were life-story interviews with residents, and several follow-up visits up until 2012. Archives consulted included those of the National Housing Institute (today, the Instituto para a Habitação e Reabilitação Urbana [IHRU]), the Loures City Council and the university research centre CET/ISCTE.

[6] For instance, a three-bedroom apartment under this option involves a maximum subsidy of €72,543 for a property that cannot exceed 150% of this subsidy (thus, with a maximum price of around €100,000), whereas such a place is currently being transacted at €140,000–€180,000.

[7] This situation repeated itself in 2013 in the case of the Santa Filomena settlement, where evictions of non-PER individuals were carried out by the Amadora municipality and the police.

[8] The public organisations involved were the Loures City Council, which oversees all aspects of municipal administration, and the IHRU, which is the governmental body that sets out the overarching procedures for the relocation process. The private owner of the land, real estate investment fund Tavfer (possibly linked to construction company-developer Obriverca; see more later), and its legal representatives pursued bilateral agreements with residents within the relocation framework as a means to speed up the process.

[9] Clarification of D's history was not possible. He appeared on the morning of demolition and we arranged for an interview at a later date. He then left. The interview never happened as he never answered his telephone subsequently.

[10] National property records only show Somague as provisional owner by 2002 and full owner by 2003, but given these records are based on a morose cycle of information

sharing from different bureaucracies, it is highly likely that the actual negotiations and change of ownership dated to a few years before.

[11] *Relocalizar* (relocalise) is different than *realojar* (rehouse, relodge). Whereas the latter verb can encompass *in situ* rehousing, *relocalizar* clearly points to displacement.

[12] In March 2009, Obriverca sold the land to *Tavfer – Fundo de Investimento Imobiliário*, a real estate fund with €37 million of capital and a mortgage placed with *Banco Espírito Santo* (Loures Ordnance Survey, 2010). In the contract signed in September 2009 by the fund with the city council to elaborate a new *Plano de pormenor*, no figures are given for rehousing and no information on building indexes is provided (CML, 2009). Since 2010, we can classify the site as being in a state of fallow ground for capital. With construction companies hit hard by the recession, delays in the circuit of capital have been common. However, all indications are that this is a just a pause in the process – that gentrification will shortly resume.

References

AML (Área Metropolitana de Lisboa) (1997) *Caracterização do Programa Especial de Realojamento na Área Metropolitana de Lisboa*, Lisboa: AML.

Anderson, M. (1964) *The federal bulldozer: a critical analysis of urban renewal, 1949–1962*, Cambridge, MA: M.I.T. Press.

Arbaci, S. and Malheiros, J. (2010) 'De-segregation, peripheralisation and the social exclusion of immigrants: Southern European cities in the 1990s', *Journal of Ethnic and Migration Studies*, vol 36, no 2, pp 227–55.

Ascensão, E. (2013a) 'Following engineers and architects through slums: the technoscience of slum intervention in the Portuguese-speaking landscape', *Análise Social*, vol 206, no 1, pp 154–80.

Ascensão, E. (2013b) 'A barraca pós-colonial: materialidade, memória e afecto na arquitectura informal', in N. Domingos and E. Peralta (eds) *A Cidade e o Colonial*, Lisboa: Edições 70, pp 425–73.

Batchelor, A. (2012) 'Imaging change, changing imaginations: the instrumentalisation of images in the revision of social and spatial identity at the Elephant and Castle', MSc Dissertation, London School of Economics and Political Science, London, UK.

Bingre, P. (2011) *Análise das relações da política de solos com o sistema económico: estudo de enquadramento para a preparação da Nova Lei do Solo*, Lisboa: DGOTDU (Direcção-Geral de Ordenamento do Território e Desenvolvimento urbano).

Bourdin, A. (2009) *L'Urbanisme d'après crise*, Paris: Éditions de l'Aube.

Branco, I. (1992) 'O Fenómeno 'Gentrification'na Cidade de Lisboa – O Caso do Bairro da Mouraria', graduate dissertation, ISCTE-IUL, Lisbon, Portugal.

Bridge, G., Butler, T. and Lees, L. (2011) *Mixed communities: gentrification by stealth*, Bristol: The Policy Press.

Butler, T. and Robson, G. (2003) *London calling: the middle classes and the remaking of inner London*, Oxford: Berg.

Cachado, R. (2012) 'Realojamento em zonas de fronteira urbana. O caso da quinta da vitória, Loures', *Forum Sociológico*, no 2, pp 23–31.

Carreiras, M., Amílcar, A., Ferreira, B. and Malheiros, J. (2011) 'Notas sobre a situação da habitação social em Portugal', conference proceedings of the 8th Congress of Portuguese Geography.

Chaves, M. (1999) *Casal Ventoso: da gandaia ao narcotráfico – marginalidade económica e dominação simbólica em Lisboa*, Lisboa: Instituto de Ciências Sociais.

CML (Câmara Municipal de Loures) (1994) *PDM – Plano Director Municipal de Loures – Projecto de Plano, Habitação e Emprego* (vol 2, tome 8), Loures: CML.

CML (2005) *Estudo Sociológico da população Residente nos Núcleos PER – Quinta da Serra, Quinta das Mós e Talude Militar*, Loures: CML/DMH/Grupo de Estudos Sociais.

CML (2008) 'Letter from town councillor João Pedro Rodrigues to Europan', 27/6/2008, ref CML 030254.

CML (2009) 'Minuta do Contrato para a Elaboração do Plano de pormenor do Prior Velho, Proposta 803/2009', contract between the Loures City Council and Tavfer to design a new detailed plan.

CML and DPU (Departamento de Planeamento e Urbanismo) (1997) 'Revisão do Plano de Urbanização do Prior Velho/Sacavém, Cadastro de Propriedade', detailed plan, file DPU/7242.

CML and DPU (2006) 'Candidatura a local alvo do concurso Europan 9', file DPU/50.079, sheet 35-31.

Collier, S. (2004) 'Pipes', in S. Harrison, S. Pile and N. Thrift (eds) *Patterned ground – entanglements of nature and culture*, London: Reaktion, pp 50–2.

Costa, P. (2007) *A cultura em Lisboa: competitividade e desenvolvimento territorial*, Lisboa: Instituto de Ciências Sociais.

Crozat, D. (2003) 'Enjeux de la manipulation de l'image d'un bidonville (Pedreira dos Hungaros a Lisbonne)', *Travaux de l'Institut de Geographie de Reims*, no 115, pp 163–82.

Datta, A. (2012) *The illegal city: space, law and gender in a Delhi squatter settlement*, Farnham: Ashgate.

De Boeck, F. and Plissart, M.-F. (2004) *Kinshasa: tales of the invisible city*, Ghent: Ludion.

Du Plessis, J (2006) 'Forced evictions, development and the need for community-based, locally appropriate alternatives: lessons and challenges from South Africa, Ghana and Thaïland', in M. Huchzermeyer and A. Karam (eds) *Informal settlements: a perpetual challenge*, Cape Town: UCT Press, pp 180–206.

Europan (2007) 'Europan 9'. Available at: http://www.europan-europe.com

Europan (2008a) *Europan # 9 Portugal. Urbanidade Europeia: Cidade Sustentável e Novos Espaços Públicos*, Lisbon: Europan. Available at: http://www.europanportugal.pt/ and http://www.arquitectos.pt/ (Portuguese catalogue).

Europan (2008b) *Europan # 9. European urbanity: sustainable city and new public spaces* (International catalogue), NAI Publishers.

Europan (2008c) 'Letter from architect Pedro Brandão to town councillor Ângela Ferreira', ref. Europan 499/2008.

Ferreira, A.F. (1988) 'Política(s) de habitação em Portugal', *Sociedade e Território*, no 6, pp 54–62.

FFH (Fundo de Fomento à Habitação) (1975) 'Document to the Loures City Council, subject *'Expropriação de terrenos e realização de um programa de habitação social', pelo F.F.H., na zona do Prior Velho*', dated 20 October.

Flyvbjerg, B. (2001) *Making social science matter: why social inquiry fails and how it can succeed again*, Cambridge: Cambridge University Press.

França, J.-A. (2008) *Lisboa, História Física e Moral*, Lisboa: Livros Horizonte.

Gaspar, J. (1989) 'Aspectos da urbanização ilegal nos países mediterrâneos da O.C.D.E.', in C. Rodrigues, I. Guerra and J. Cabral (eds) *Clandestinos em Portugal – Leituras*, Lisboa: Livros Horizonte, pp 82–91.

Graham, S. and Marvin, S. (2001) *Splintering urbanism: networked infrastructures, technological mobilities and the urban condition*, London: Routledge.

IHRU (Instituto para a Habitação e Reabilitação Urbana) (2007) *Atlas da Habitação de Portugal*, Lisboa: IHRU.

INE (Instituto Nacional de Estatística) (2001) *National Census – Portugal 2001*, Lisbon: INE.

INE (2012) *National Census – Portugal 2011, Initial Results*, Lisbon: INE.

Lees, L. (2014a) 'Gentrification in the Global South?', in S. Parnell and S. Oldfield (eds) *The Routledge handbook on cities of the Global South*, Routledge: New York, pp 506-21.

Lees, L. (2014b) 'The death of sustainable communities in London?', in R. Imrie and L. Lees (eds) *Sustainable London? The future of a global city*, Bristol: Policy Press, pp 149-72.

Lees, L. (2014c) 'The urban injustices of New Labour's "new urban renewal": the case of the Aylesbury Estate in London', *Antipode*, vol 46, no 4, pp 921-47.

Lees, L., Slater, T. and Wyly, E. (eds) (2010) *The gentrification reader*, London: Routledge.

Leontidou, L. (1990) *The Mediterranean city in transition: social change and urban development*, Cambridge: Cambridge University Press.

López-Morales, E. (2011) 'Gentrification by ground rent dispossession: the shadows cast by large-scale urban renewal in Santiago de Chile', *International Journal of Urban and Regional Research*, vol 35, no 2, pp 330–57.

López-Morales, E. (2012) 'Insurgency and institutionalized social participation in local-level urban planning: the case of the PAC *comuna*, Santiago de Chile, 2003–5', in T. Samara, S. He and G. Chen (eds) *Locating right to the city in the Global South*, London: Routledge, pp 221–46.

Loures Ordnance Survey (2010) 'Registo Predial de Loures', file 2312/20020521 (larger original plot under file 690/19880331).

Lusa (2013) 'PER: Plano ficou "muito aquém das metas" na integração social-Junta Metropolitana de Lisboa', *Lusa*, 5 May.

Malheiros, J. and Vala, F. (2004) 'Immigration and city change: the region of Lisbon in the turn of the 20th century', *Journal of Ethnic and Migration Studies*, vol 30, no 6, pp 1065–86.

Malheiros, J., Carvalho, R. and Mendes, L. (2012) 'Etnicização residencial e nobilitação urbana marginal: processo de ajustamento ou prática emancipatória num bairro do centro histórico de Lisboa?', *Imigração, diversidade e convivência cultural*, no 97, pp 97-128.

Mendes, L. (2006) 'A nobilitaçao urbana no Bairro Alto: análise de um processo de recomposiçao sócio-espacial', *Finisterra: Revista portuguesa de geografia*, vol 41, no 81, pp 57–82.

Mendes, L. (2012) 'Nobilitação urbana marginal enquanto prática emancipatória: alternativa ao discurso hegemónico da cidade criativa?', *Revista Crítica de Ciências Sociais*, no 99, pp 51–72.

Merrifield, A. (2013) 'Citizen's Agora: the new urban question', *Radical Philosophy*, no 179, pp 31–5.

Mukhija, V. (2003) *Squatters as developers? Slum redevelopment in Mumbai*, Aldershot: Ashgate.

Númena (2003) *National analytical study on housing – RAXEN focal point for Portugal*, report for European Monitoring Center on Racism and Xenophobia (EUMC), Lisboa: Númena.

Oliveira, N. (2013) 'A *Scenescape* da Mouraria: a governança da diversidade cultural na cidade pós-colonial', in N. Domingos and E. Peralta (eds) *A Cidade e o Colonial*, Lisboa: Edições 70.

Peck, J. (2005) 'Struggling with the creative class', *International Journal of Urban and Regional Research*, vol 29, no 4, pp 740–70.

Pereira, N.T. (1993) 'Finalmente, a habitação', *Público*, 20 March, p 17.

Porter, T.M. (1995) *Trust in numbers: the pursuit of objectivity in science and public life*, Princeton, NJ: Princeton University Press.

Robinson, J. (2011) 'Cities in a world of cities: the comparative gesture', *International Journal of Urban and Regional Research*, vol 35, no 1, pp 1–23.

Rodrigues, C. (1989) 'Eficiência e equidade na produção de espaço clandestino', in C. Rodrigues (ed) *Clandestinos em Portugal – Leituras*, Lisboa: Livros Horizonte.

Rodrigues, W. (2010) *Cidade em Transição: Nobilitação urbana, Estilos de Vida e Reurbanização em Lisboa*, Lisboa: Celta Editora.

Roy, A. (2005) 'Urban informality: toward an epistemology of planning', *Journal of the American Planning Association*, vol 71, no 2, pp 147–58.

Salgueiro, T.B. (1977) 'Bairros clandestinos na periferia de Lisboa', *Finisterra – Revista portuguesa de geografia*, vol 12, no 23, pp 28–55.

Sayad, A. and Dupuy, E. (1995) *Un Nanterre Algérien: terre de bidonvilles*, Paris: Autrement.

Scott, J. (1998) *Seeing like a state: how certain schemes to improve the human condition have failed*, New Haven, CT, and London: Yale University Press.

Shin, H.B. (2008) 'Living on the edge: financing post-displacement housing in urban redevelopment projects in Seoul', *Environment and Urbanization*, vol 20, no 2, pp 411–26.

Shin, H.B. (2009) 'Property-based redevelopment and gentrification: the case of Seoul, South Korea', *Geoforum*, vol 40, no 5, pp 906–17.

Simone, A. (2004) 'People as infrastructure: intersecting fragments in Johannesburg', *Public Culture*, vol 16, no 3, pp 407–29.

Volovitch-Tavares, M.-C. (1995) *Portugais à Champigny, le temps des baraques*, Paris: Autrement.

Filmography

Juventude em Marcha (*Colossal Youth*), Pedro Costa, Fiction, 150', Contracosta/Pandora/Ventura, 2006.

Via de Acesso (*Access Way*), Nathalie Mansoux, Documentary, 82', Terratreme, 2008.

FOUR

City upgraded: redesigning and disciplining downtown Abu Dhabi

Surajit Chakravarty and Abdellatif Qamhaieh

Introduction

Gentrification generated by successive investment cycles is a commonplace occurrence in cities today. Social displacement and loss of housing options often follows attempts to redevelop neighbourhoods. Scholars in the field of urban planning have long recognised and critiqued this trend. Brenner and Theodore (2005), MacLeod (2002), Harvey (1978, 2006, 2010) and Smith (1982, 1996, 2010), among others, have argued that gentrification is not merely a by-product of neoliberal planning, but rather a quintessential part of it – a strategy for successive cycles of investment and accumulation. Few studies, though, have examined gentrification in the emerging cities of the Arabian/Persian Gulf region. Urban planning in Abu Dhabi is reconfiguring the city, and, in the process, displacing some segments of the population.

This chapter examines recent policies causing the gentrification of Abu Dhabi's city centre. These include a Revitalisation Plan, together with policies regulating the spatial practices and housing options of the low-income population. Given a paucity of options, the displaced low-income groups are likely to become isolated in remote locations. Although there are stark differences between the planning cultures of Abu Dhabi and those of cities in Western Europe or North America, there are similarities in how the 'spatial fix' is administered. This study sheds light on the causes of the housing affordability problem in Abu Dhabi, and through an analysis of current policies and realities on the ground, it is argued that ongoing development plans are likely to lead to a significant demographic change in the city centre and further squeeze the housing options for the city's less wealthy residents.

Understanding the Abu Dhabi housing market

Rapid social and economic change

Abu Dhabi, the capital of the United Arab Emirates (UAE), has expanded dramatically in terms of wealth, urban growth and infrastructure development over the course of a relatively short history of urbanisation. Located on the Arabian/Persian Gulf, the city grew from a small port on the trade routes passing through the Suez Canal (as late as the 1960s) to a million-plus metropolis, supported by oil wealth and littered with mega-projects. The Urban Structure Framework Plan, a part of Abu Dhabi's plan for the year 2030, promulgated by the Urban Planning Council (UPC), projects that the 'city's population may grow to three million or it may exceed five million by 2030' (UPC, 2007). The figure of 3 million is quoted widely in subsequent UPC documents.

Although Dubai gets most of the attention for its remarkable skyline and the speed with which it has gone up, it is Abu Dhabi, with 90% of the country's oil reserves, that holds the economic and political influence (Parsa et al, 2002; Davidson, 2007). The head of Abu Dhabi's ruling family serves as the president of the UAE. The government has spared no effort in making the city an attractive destination for large corporations and professionals alike.

Abu Dhabi (like other cities in the country) is home to a very large number of expatriates, constituting almost 90% of the city's 1.5 million inhabitants (SCAD, 2011). Rents are very high and disproportionate to incomes, even those of most white-collar employees, who depend on housing allowances to be able to rent accommodation in the city. The burden is greatest for low-wage workers, who constitute almost 50% of the population. Those employed in large groups, and working for corporations, usually live in 'labour housing' projects, commonly known as 'worker residential villages' or 'labour villages'. These dormitories have already earned much notoriety for the poor quality of life most of them offer, though progress has been made in recent years in the quality of facilities. For the low-wage workers, who are employed individually and work for small businesses in the city, rents are an enormous burden, forcing many to share apartments illegally (*Gulf News*, 2005a, 2007a). In many instances, 10 to 12 people may share one-bedroom apartments (*Khaleej Times*, 2006).

Stable political structure, growing economy

A number of factors are important in understanding the specific conditions of the Abu Dhabi housing market. To begin with, Abu Dhabi enjoys a growing economy and stable political system. As Abu Dhabi continues to expand, it remains a favourable destination for large corporations, especially those in the oil and gas, banking and finance, and construction and real estate industries. Incomes are high, both because of the oil-backed economy and in order to remain competitive in global labour recruitment. The competitiveness of the economy, backed by secure oil exports, continuously attracts new employees to the city and sustains high housing demand. Recent political instability in other parts of the Arab world have boosted the UAE's image, and that of Abu Dhabi in particular (in view of Dubai's real estate crash of 2008), as a safe haven for investment and an attractive place to live and work.

The renters' market is currently growing, as rents have stabilised after a recent dip (Jones Lang Lassalle, 2012). The supply of rental housing is expected to increase in the near future with the completion of various large-scale projects. Some of the older housing stock is expected to become available in the mid-range rent category. Yet, rent prices remain significantly inflated, and a large shortage of good-quality mid- and lower-range rental apartments remains persistent. This is confirmed by the UPC's own analyses: 'The residential sector for end-users is currently under-supplied particularly for lower and mid market income brackets' (UPC, 2010a, p 16). Further, '[g]iven the limited new supply that will actually materialise over the next few years and the additional demand that is expected to be realised as rents decline, the residential market is expected to remain under-supplied between 2009 and 2013' (UPC, 2010a, p 16).

Property ownership

In Abu Dhabi, real estate ownership is an exclusive right of the country's nationals. Non-nationals are not eligible to own land. According to a law passed in 2005, non-nationals may own 'floors without land' (ie apartments or offices) in designated 'investment areas', on a 99-year lease basis (Department of Municipal Affairs, 2010). Similar relaxations have helped Dubai attract significant foreign investment in its real estate market (although its over-reliance on real estate also made it vulnerable to the crisis in 2008).

Most nationals own their own houses, usually in the form of a residential villa. The practice of distributing plots to nationals free of charge was initiated by Sheikh Zayed himself (the first president of the country). The wait for a built house is usually a long one and could range from five to 15 years depending on availability. Alternatively, a citizen could elect to receive a plot of land and a long-term interest-free loan to help build their own residence.

Further, restrictions on ownership of property mean that the rent payments from the hundreds of thousands of expatriate residents in the city, through each of their individual lease contracts, ultimately reach the property-owners, who are invariably local citizens. It is worth noting here that the annual rent amount is typically paid as one lump-sum payment at the beginning of the lease period. One can conclude that the system amounts to recurring annual benefits to citizen property-owners, many of whom own multiple properties. Thus, there is an in-built incentive for maintaining high rents, even if they are disconnected from income levels. The high rents are further supported by the limited availability of land in Abu Dhabi due to its island geography.

Developers as an extension of the state

In addition to ownership of land, the work of development and housing construction is also concentrated in the hands of a small number of major developers (prominently, Aldar, Tamouh, Sorouh, Mubadala and a few others).

Moreover, the public and private sectors are deeply intertwined. According to Christopher Davidson (2009, p 72):

> only a few master developers control the main zones and are responsible for the necessary real-estate infrastructure. These master developers are all either majority-owned by parastatals or have such close ties to key members of the ruling family that they are effectively under the government's control.

Major sites marked for development are carved up and distributed to these developers. Those in public positions might also be stakeholders in corporations working in the construction and development sectors. Some of the 'private sector' developers could be considered an extension of the state and of private interests embedded within the state. This fuzzy line between public and private entities is not uncommon in the overall region and applies to various sectors of the economy (notably, telecommunications, aviation and energy).

Unusual demographic composition and housing needs

Much like other countries in the Gulf region, but unique in comparison with other parts of the world, the UAE's demographic composition is characterised by very low numbers of locals (citizens) and a massive expatriate population. The word 'expatriate' is used (instead of, say, 'immigrant') because *all* of the foreign workers and their families must leave the country at the time of termination of their employment. As of 2011, the Emirati nationals represented only 22.05% of the total population of the country (National Bureau of Statistics, 2011). The resultant demographic composition and the concomitant divisions within society create a peculiar set of housing needs.

Generally speaking, Abu Dhabi society can be categorised into three segments: high-net-worth locals and expatriates; middle-class expatriate workers; and blue-collar low-wage expatriate workers. These categories, their subcategories and the corresponding housing arrangements are explained in the following. At the outset, it is important to clarify that this 'categorisation' serves only to describe broad trends. It is based on observations made over three years (from 2010 until 2013) and a degree of inaccuracy is implicit in drawing lines around such categories. It is not possible to provide all the details and the full range of wage categories and housing options, nor is it crucial to the arguments presented here.

The first category, at the top of the income pyramid, is the Emirati nationals. Abu Dhabi has one of the highest figures of per capita gross domestic product (GDP) in the world (AED315,300/USD85,000) (SCAD, 2012b). The nationals, especially those of influential families, are the most likely to benefit from these figures, with very high income levels in some cases. Also, the government's land and property distribution mechanisms and job placement programmes ensure a comfortable living for most nationals, though access is not uniform across the board. A very small number of business families from other parts of the world share this class of income and status. Locals usually live in 'villas' – detached houses, typically of two floors, built on large plots (sometimes more than 1 hectare each). The government has ambitious plans to increase the number of high-quality options within this category, and mega-projects are being arranged so as to maximise the value of villa properties that will be handed over to citizens in due course.

The second category, ranked by income, is that of the expatriate white-collar professionals. This group comprises about 30–35% of the total population. Most of the employees in this 'middle class' are paid globally competitive wages. Contracts for these employees usually include housing allowances. Those at the higher end of the 'middle class' in terms of salary (middle and upper management, professionals, consultants, etc) have the option of renting entire villas or spacious apartments in new buildings and in attractive locations. Most of the new housing stock serves this rent range (annual rent of AED120,000–180,000, ie approximately USD32,000–50,000). Usually built as multiple skyscrapers, this kind of development offers a highly profitable investment opportunity for developers because of both the high rent and the bulk of construction. These apartments, mostly owned by nationals, only become affordable to the 'upper-middle-class' employee through housing allowances. Those at the lower end of the 'middle-class' category usually rent apartments in older buildings or in less desirable locations. These apartments are also usually rented through housing allowances, though more modest compared to the previous group. As explained earlier, without the allowances, housing costs would be prohibitively high and would significantly hurt the city's attractiveness in recruiting expatriate workers.

Further, periodically, policies are introduced to help maintain the profitability of the housing market, preventing its crash. For example, a government decree from September 2012 makes it mandatory for those employed by the Abu Dhabi government to live in Abu Dhabi. The policy aims to bring back to the city's housing market about 10,000 commuting employees and their families who avail of housing allowances provided by one of the Abu Dhabi government agencies but live 120 km away in Dubai (*Emirates 24/7*, 2013). The policy also aims at reducing traffic and enhancing public safety. It is safe to say that the housing needs of the middle class are well taken care of, with the exception of high-quality options for singles looking for studios or one-bedroom apartments.

The final category, which is also the category with the largest number of individuals, is that of blue-collar workers. This group consists mostly of workers from South Asian countries. These individuals can further be categorised as (i) construction workers and (ii) other low-wage workers. The 'construction' industry alone accounts for almost 32% of all workers in Abu Dhabi (SCAD, 2012a). These workers (discussed at length later) are usually categorised as 'bachelors' – a euphemism not necessarily related to their marital status, but rather to their being in the country without their families.

The low-wage, blue-collar group resides in two major housing categories: (a) housing for those employed in groups (ie employed through an employment agency, by, say, a construction company to work on a project or by a private taxi company to drive taxis); and (b) housing for those employed individually (ie sponsored by small business-owners to work in tea shops, in restaurants, in corner stores, as personal assistants, etc).

Those employed in groups through employment agencies (but sometimes also through references) usually live in specially constructed 'worker housing' or 'labour villages'. For these workers, housing arrangements are the responsibility of the employer, as required by the law. The quality of labour villages has improved significantly in recent years. One of the newest models of worker housing, the Industrial City of Abu Dhabi (ICAD) development located in the Musaffah Industrial Area, is highly appreciated by those living there, especially by those who have earlier lived in other dormitory accommodations in the UAE. This has been confirmed by the authors, both on visits to the site and through informal interviews with taxi drivers. Despite improved comfort and convenience, this kind of housing model does create all-male social groups where individuals are stressed by their economic conditions: there are limited options for growth; they are distant from their families and hometowns; and they live far removed from the city (Figure 4.1 shows Musaffah in Abu Dhabi).

Those employed individually usually work and live in the city. For these individuals, rent could be eight or 10 times their salaries. They are either housed in shops, lofts, attics, 'mezzanine' floors or storerooms (illegally, facing frequent campaigns to crack down on employers), or in shared apartments, with as many as 20 people sharing a two-bedroom apartment. The shared apartments could be in old crumbling apartment buildings or, less frequently, in houses in the older suburbs of the city. Most of these shared accommodations are of low quality

Figure 4.1: Musaffah, Abu Dhabi

and display signs of deterioration. They also represent certain dangers to their inhabitants as the buildings are often very old and fire-code and safety violations are widespread.

As recently as 2005, the municipality used categories such as 'low-cost house', 'part of low-cost house', 'shed', 'caravan' and 'shack/box/tent' in official statistics on housing units (see Table 4.1). These data classify housing units and not the number of residents. Therefore, they do not capture the phenomenon of overcrowding. The data also do not cover other informal arrangements, like workers sleeping on shop floors, in storage areas and so on. The typology is no longer used in official publications.

Table 4.1: Number of housing units by type, Abu Dhabi, 2005

Type of building	Abu Dhabi
Total	**137,857**
Flat	96,237
Villa	8,693
Part of villa	3,141
One-storey house	3,325
Low-cost house	11,935
Part of low-cost house	3,089
Separate room	6,841
Shed	1,157
Caravan	1,117
Shack/box/tent	284
Others	2,038

Source: SCAD (2011).

Skewed rent structure

As already discussed, housing costs are so high in Abu Dhabi that upper-middle-class professionals with competitive salaries need an extra allowance to be able to afford housing. On the other hand, low-wage workers have to live in abject conditions. Meanwhile, the benefits of annual rent on all properties (with few exceptions) accrue to the locals. This situation represents a skewed rent structure and helps facilitate capital formation for locals, profitable projects for developers and attractive housing options for the wealthier expatriates. Half of the population falls outside this system.

It is the skewed social composition – including (i) a high proportion of non-nationals not allowed to buy property and (ii) the inordinately large number of urban poor with miniscule incomes compared to prevalent rents – that causes the city to have irrationally high rents. Rationalising the rents (ie making them consistent with real incomes, facilities and quality of life) would radically lower them. This would have two direct effects. First, it would make housing affordable to the low-income population, prompting them, in ever-larger numbers, to live in the city. The second impact of rationalised rents would be to decimate the rental incomes of property-owners, which could be politically highly undesirable.

In this situation, where foreign workers have little influence, the 'logic of capital' (Harvey, 2006, 2010) has the freedom to operate with few social justice concerns. Further, public sector investment in the real estate sector skews the priorities of planners. Given the rent gaps to be realised from valuable land in the 'downtown' area of Abu Dhabi, gentrification is well under way. Through concerted policies and governance practices, the city centre is being (i) redesigned and (ii) disciplined.

Disciplining downtown Abu Dhabi

Reports from the US and Western Europe have shown that conditions of 'blight' in urban neighbourhoods, typically in the inner city, precipitate new rounds of investment to capture the 'rent gap', that is, the difference between the highest realisable rent from any given property and the actual rent being derived from it (Weber, 2002; Slater, 2004; Lees et al, 2008; for non-Western contexts, see also Shin, 2009a; López-Morales, 2010). In an environment where cities are competing for investment (based on assumed benefits in terms of tax revenues, economic development, job creation, etc), the state supports redevelopment by 'disciplining' (Smith, 1996; MacLeod, 2002) unwanted populations (such as the homeless) 'so that the enhancement of a city's image is not compromised by the visible presence of those very marginalized groups' (MacLeod, 2002, p 602).

The political-economic situation in Abu Dhabi is a little different. Even so, the case provides support for the idea that the logic of capital creates similar tendencies, even in widely different contexts. Beyond the obvious matter of the country being an absolute monarchy, with a single main source of wealth, there are three main differences in Abu Dhabi that are relevant to this discussion. First, unlike small town city centres in, say, the post-industrial US, downtown Abu Dhabi is not in 'blight' or even in 'decline'. Some of the buildings are certainly in a poor condition, having been built with modest materials and technologies in the 1970s and 1980s, and having since then withstood many summers of extreme climatic conditions and neglect. Most of these buildings are occupied by low-income workers. The area as a whole is dense (though not *over*crowded), diverse, active and economically versatile and self-sustaining. It is not in need of overhaul from either an economic or a physical perspective. Further, the neighbourhood in question is the city centre of Abu Dhabi, a prospering city with little need for an economic push.

Second, the concern over the 'image' of Abu Dhabi is not about a homeless population (as it was in New York City), but rather the 'bachelor' population. Just as homelessness in Western society is a reflection of its inequalities, the 'bachelor' population is a product of the imbalances in Abu Dhabi. The term 'bachelor' has a specific meaning in Abu Dhabi, referring to the male, not necessarily unmarried (but in the city without their family), low-wage workers usually engaged in labour-intensive jobs like construction and maintenance. They are often blamed for concerns over security (especially the security of women), privacy, health and cleanliness, and other social problems. This group makes up a large number of the low-wage renters in the downtown area.

According to Mohammad and Sidaway (2012), 52% of Abu Dhabi's population are South Asian men. Since South Asians are massively over-represented in the low-wage sector, one can safely *estimate* (in the absence of reliable data) that at least 80% of the 'bachelors' are South Asians. The presence of this large segment of the population (approximately 40% of the total) – 'single' men from South Asia – is one of the defining characteristics of urbanism in the Abu Dhabi city centre, as is their seamless mixing with others from less wealthy Arab and Asian countries. In a city dominated by shopping malls, gated communities and faraway dormitory towns, the 'city centre' is perhaps the only remaining place where people share space with Others, and also the only place where a low-income lifestyle coexists with luxury hotels and middle- to higher-end apartment buildings. Emanating mostly from small towns or villages in Pakistan, India and Bangladesh (with smaller numbers from Sri Lanka and Nepal, and a few from the Philippines and other countries), these men occupy the interstitial spaces of the city centre, particularly in the evening. It is this low-income population (not homeless, but often illegally housed) that is perceived as a liability to the image of Abu Dhabi, particularly in the city centre. The incidence of crime in the city centre is low by all accounts, yet the urbanism they create, bearing traces of the informality typical in South Asian cities, is not considered healthy and orderly. Moreover, most professionals in the field of urban planning and urban design are educated in Western traditions and bring a set of values to the city that is often incongruous with the habitus of a vast majority of the foreign workers.

Third, in terms of citizenship and residency regulations, Abu Dhabi is markedly different from what we find in, say, Western Europe or the US. All of the people being dislocated or having their lives disrupted by the redevelopment of the city centre are non-citizens living on employment-tied visas. Their vulnerability is compounded by their financial woes. While property-owners (citizens) do get a share of the windfall, these low-wage workers and small business operators are left with few options. Despite occasional reports that housing for low-income residents is in the works (*Gulf News*, 2005b, 2007b), not much seems to have changed for this group (*Gulf News*, 2008a, 2009; *The National*, 2010).

Redesigning Abu Dhabi: city centre revitalisation

Construction of the city centre began with modest building in the 1970s and 1980s (the first wave of construction). More contemporary skyscrapers have been added rapidly since the 1990s. The relatively short history of the city has meant that entire blocks or neighbourhoods (with few exceptions) do not share the same character, and vary greatly in terms of building ages, styles and conditions. Very expensive structures are often found right next to old (in some cases, decaying) buildings, exerting obvious economic pressure to redevelop. Figure 4.2 shows examples of old buildings in the city centre that now find themselves surrounded by modern structures demanding high rents.

Figure 4.2: Old buildings in the city centre surrounded by modern structures

In addition, 'downtown revitalisation' in Abu Dhabi city and in other neighbouring communities has been a stated objective of the UPC since at least 2007, when it was mentioned as one of the 'building blocks' in the Urban Structure Framework Plan (UPC, 2007, pp 130–1). It was elaborated upon in subsequent documents:

> A key objective for the UPC is to revitalize the existing communities of Abu Dhabi Emirate. The developments of the revitalization strategies are well underway for both downtown areas of Abu Dhabi City and Al Ain City. The revitalization strategy will infuse the Wasat Madinat, which means 'downtown' in Arabic, of both Abu Dhabi City and Al Ain City with better transport connections and greater pedestrian connectivity, along with high quality community facilities and more sustainable housing options. The revitalization of Wasat Madinat Abu Dhabi and Wasat Madinat Al Ain, includes long-term plans to develop new sports and leisure facilities, cycle routes, underground car parks and the building of new schools.
>
> The construction of a tram system and an underground metro network is another long-term priority for Wasat Madinat Abu Dhabi that will vastly improve connections both downtown and with other parts of the city. (UPC, 2009, p 20)

The language used in the context of 'revitalisation' is worth a closer look. The UPC seems to define 'downtown revitalisation' primarily as 'better transport connections and greater pedestrian connectivity, along with high quality community facilities and more sustainable housing options' and also 'new sports and leisure facilities, cycle routes, underground car parks and the building of new schools' (UPC, 2009). Clearly, the focus is on urban design interventions and improved social infrastructure. There is no mention of job creation, economic development or community building. This raises a question regarding the need for 'revitalisation' in the first place. The downtown area, after all, is highly vital, socially active and economically vibrant. The only 'problem' is that a large number of people occupying this prime real estate are not of the affluent groups who could afford to rent expensive apartments and shop in high-end shopping malls.

The demolition of these buildings will leave no housing options for people of this income group. They will most likely find themselves in labour camps in Musaffah, an industrial wasteland, and one of the remote sites where labour camps are located. Further, paradoxically, the new regulations might precipitate decline in the city centre. Demographic change will fundamentally alter spatial practices, affecting businesses that cater to the needs of the low-income people. One Iranian-origin businessman (born and raised in the UAE), who runs his own apparel store, complained of the lack of business because of the demolition of buildings around this store: "On Friday, after the prayers, people used to come here for shopping. I would sell 60 [pairs of] jeans in one evening. Now I sell three or four." Not only will the city centre lose many businesses like his, but it will also lose the busy street life they nurture.

The downtown revitalisation plan for Abu Dhabi has been prepared with help from international consultancies. Otak's corporate website has a page dedicated to the 'Wasat Madina Abu Dhabi' project. The plan aims to provide 'solutions for congestion, parking, public realm improvements and community facility needs' (Otak, no date). Renderings of the conceived future of the city centre are particularly informative. We see a Hausmannian approach to creating open space, ostensibly to promote 'connectivity'. The new open spaces are also intended to foster a new kind of urbanism. Characterised by low intensity of use, shaded walking areas, bicycle routes, fresh fruit stalls and sidewalk cafes, this vision represents a departure from the spaces created by the current users of the city centre, many of whom cannot afford casual consumption. For these groups, socialising does not happen in cafes and shopping centres, but rather on street corners, in alleys, on the steps outside buildings entrances or on grassy patches *outside* shopping centres or on sidewalks. These spaces of alterity are invested with meaning by the low-wage residents of the city. For many of them, these spaces are the only options for participating in the city. The important local characteristics and social functions of these spaces seem to have been overlooked by planners and designers in an effort to duplicate the urbanism of other places through the transfer of design principles.

Urban design improvements and infrastructure provision dominate almost every plan prepared by the UPC. The most significant new term in the downtown revitalisation plan, camouflaged by the rest of the narrative, is 'more sustainable housing options'. It is hard to fathom what it means – what kind of housing is considered sustainable, and for whom it is intended? One might safely assume, though, that the UPC supports the 'revitalisation' of downtown, and also that it is not overly concerned with the social implications of such improvements.

The law in Abu Dhabi requires property-owners to give six months' notice to occupants when requesting renegotiation of contract terms or termination of the contract. Further, pursuant to Islamic principles, which strongly discourage the waste of land, Article 23 (Chapter 7) of the UAE federal law number 20 of 2006 requires property-owners to act on their stated intentions after obtaining demolition permits. Failure to demolish the building within one year (initial period of six months, with a possibility of a six-month extension) can lead to fines (up to one year's rent) and permission for evicted tenants to reoccupy the property in question. Similarly, eviction of tenants for the purpose of occupying one's own property and then failing to occupy it for over three months can also attract fines, along with the possibility of the tenants being given the choice to move back. The owner must not have another property in Abu Dhabi, and must live in the vacated property at all times (ie without lengthy absences).

The government deserves credit for both its interpretation of Shari'a and for writing laws to curb the fickle eviction of tenants and speculative practices with vacated properties. Property-owners are sometimes eager to have their properties vacated, but not as keen to sell or redevelop, preferring to wait for a bigger windfall. So, a lot of older buildings in the downtown area have been emptied by a combination of ultimatums, pay-offs, avoiding repairs and renovations, and helping occupants find alternative accommodations. However, the ground floors of many of these empty buildings continue to be used by small business establishments (often owned by the owner of the rest of the property) as proof that the building is still under use. This loophole allows property-owners to wait indefinitely for an acceptable deal. Figure 4.3 shows a vacant building where a commercial establishment, a salon, is operating on the ground floor.

Figure 4.3: Salon operating from the ground floor of an empty building

Table 4.2 shows the numbers of building and demolition permits issued by the Abu Dhabi Municipality in recent years. From 2009 to 2011, 478 demolition permits were issued. The locations of these demolitions are not public information. Considering, however, that there are hardly any demolitions in outlying areas, one can assume that most of the buildings earmarked for demolition are in the downtown area. The intensity of building activity in all of Abu Dhabi can be gauged from Table 4.3, which shows that more than 27,000 building construction permits were issued between 2009 and 2011, of which more than half were for residential buildings.

Table 4.2: Number of building demolition permits issued by usage in Abu Dhabi, 2009, 2010 and 2011

Usage	2009	2010	2011
Total[a]	**264**	**89**	**125**
Residential	70	68	92
Commercial	69	11	24
Industrial	77	10	9
Public utilities	48	0	0
Agricultural	0	0	0

Note: [a] Does not include 'renewals or amendments', 'additions and decorations' and temporary permits and others.

Source: SCAD (2012b).

Table 4.3: Number of building construction permits issued – Abu Dhabi and Western Region, 2005–08, and Abu Dhabi, 2009–11

Type of Permit	2005	2006	2007	2008	2009	2010	2011
Total	**5,947**	**6,055**	**3,316**	**4,129**	**8,819**	**7,268**	**11,293**
Commercial	67	67	134	222	388	968	2,272
Residential	705	907	852	1,401	3,718	4,473	6,267
Industry	169	192	252	229	338	638	1,095
Annex of low-cost house	1,566	957	889	174	–	–	–
Public utilities	278	250	240	335	424	3	11
Temporary permits[a]	3,162	3,682	949	1,768	3,629	279	0
Agricultural	–	–	–	–	0	80	84
Residential and commercial	–	–	–	–	296	6	0
Others	–	–	–	–	26	821	1,564

Note: [a] Includes temporary building permits, such as caravans in construction sites.

Source: SCAD (2011, 2012b).

As Abu Dhabi brands itself as a 'world city' and a destination for workers, tourists and investment, the creation of a dedicated urban planning body (the UPC) has brought significant changes to the city. A number of high-end residential developments have been commissioned, especially on nearby developments on Reem Island and Raha Beach. The land available for the city's expansion has been expanded by developing nearby islands, and new entertainment and cultural venues have either been completed or are in the works. The future vision for the city includes a new central business district (separate from the current downtown) and new satellite centres in the suburbs.

The issue of housing affordability has also been of concern to the authorities. A few attempts to find suitable solutions have been initiated, with the latest attempt represented in the Middle-income Housing Policy (UPC, 2011). This policy, however, targets white-collar professionals, who are beneficiaries of housing allowances. While more choices would be appreciated and would serve to keep rents in check, the real issue is finding proper solutions for the people for whom rents are six or eight times their salaries. Moreover, some of the planning and regulatory initiatives attempting to achieve the world-city vision have been producing even more negative impacts on affordability, and are exacerbating the gentrifying problem. For example, a new plan for 'beach development' will create:

> [a] new array of affordable, quality retail and food & beverage outlets [that] will offer choices of local and international flavours and will be easily accessible all along the public beach and the Corniche gardens along with new outdoor decks, which will provide breathtaking views of the waterfront where people will be able to lounge and dine as well. (UPC, 2009)

Other features of the plan include a public beach and boardwalk, an array of activities, rentable cabanas, additional parking facilities, and so on. The improvements attempt to reconstitute the waterfront as a space of entertainment and retail, but, in the process, could end up excluding those without the means to participate in these consumption rituals.

Municipal fines: helping 'clean' the inner city

Apart from the physical redevelopment of the city centre area, other measures are being used to discipline the space and the users. One of the rules being enforced with gusto is the minimum requirement of 30 square metres to operate a business establishment. Many businesses, such as dry cleaners, bakers, tea shops, convenience stores, salons and so on, have been operating for decades in units of about 15–20 square metres. This configuration was the outcome of the affordability of space, in turn, controlled by (a) the clients' ability to pay and (b) the high rents in the city centre. With the new rules in place, many of these businesses in the city centre area will have to close down (commercial/retail displacement/gentrification), as they cannot turn a profit after paying rent for 30 square metres.

Health code-based fines are also on the up (*The National*, 2012a). These, too, disproportionately affect the businesses operating out of small spaces, as they cannot help having packed storage spaces. New fines have also been initiated for hanging laundry on balconies (*The National*, 2012c), not complying with regulations for signage boards (*The National*, 2013a) and displaying cooked food outdoors (*The National*, 2013b). Clearly, those residing in small accommodations and those operating small businesses will be disproportionately affected by these fines.

The minimum space policy is being implemented in conjunction with an effort to remove all instances of workers living in non-residential spaces within the commercial establishment, inside storage spaces or on 'mezzanine' floors. This is supposed to protect the workers' rights to proper housing. There is, however, a lack of consistency in this compassion, as thousands of workers continue to live in storage containers in the Musaffah industrial city (mentioned earlier). When considered together with the 'revitalisation' drive in the city centre and on the Corniche, one can see an organised plan to 'cleanse' (MacLeod, 2002) the inner city, and make it ready for the next round of speculative investment.

Sharing is inefficient: the ban on divided villas and shared apartments

Large villas built on plots of 2,000 square metres or more are common in large parts of Abu Dhabi, starting immediately outside the city centre. In many cases, villas were divided into smaller apartments, or rooms within them were leased out separately. It is not always easy to find lessees who need entire villas for long terms. Thus, owners found that dividing the property was an efficient way of maximising the rent potential of the property and keeping it occupied. The municipality has outlawed this practice, citing fire-code and health violations.

The law is being implemented in successive waves. Owners are fined severely if such accommodations are found, especially within Abu Dhabi's main island (*Gulf News*, 2006, 2007c, 2008b; *Khaleej Times*, 2008a, 2008b, 2008c, 2009, 2012; *The National*, 2012b).

In addition, to deal with the phenomenon of shared apartments, the municipality has made a new rule limiting the number of people sharing an apartment to three (*Emirates 24/7*, 2012). In effect, this policy means that in order to share an apartment, a person must be willing to pay at least AED1,500–2,000 monthly (approximately USD400–550), which, in most cases, is more than twice the person's monthly salary, and about three or four times what they are able to pay after considering other costs and the need to save money and send it home (to justify the whole endeavour). Clearly, sharing apartments is viewed as inefficient, suppressing housing demand *and* hurting the city's image. These measures are killing the only truly affordable housing solution in Abu Dhabi, especially with the absence of formal policies. This is not to suggest that the go-to solution of building more 'labour villages' in remote areas ought to be considered a valid policy option.

There is no evidence that people in low-income groups in Abu Dhabi have displayed criminal behaviour disproportionate to their population (except perhaps in the very labour camps that are seen as the solution to the problem). They deserve a place *in* the city and the dignity of living normal lives in the company of other members of society. Abu Dhabi's planners need to urgently rethink their priorities and develop policy options for imposing quotas for affordable housing on developers, reserving floors in high-rise buildings for shared accommodation and allowing subdivision with necessary health regulations and standards.

A new system of property registration, *Tawtheeq*, has been installed, at least in part, to support the work of eliminating the practice of sharing villas and apartments. The electronic system standardises lease contracts, keeps a record of all residents, issues unique identity numbers to residents and ties these to the residents' annual visa renewal process. Of course, there are real benefits from this system, primarily in terms of modernising property record-keeping and lowering the risks of conflict between lessors and lessees. However, considering the timing of its implementation, and its being tied to the visa process, *Tawtheeq* appears to support the objectives of controlling the housing practices of low-wage residents and boosting housing demand.

Conclusions

Urban planning efforts in Abu Dhabi, particularly those in the downtown area, are trying to 'upgrade' the city (UPC, 2010b). The emphasis appears to be on creating an upscale 'ideal' metropolis that is 'worthy' of Abu Dhabi's economic status and aspirations. Most of the new developments focus on bringing high-end residential, commercial and entertainment developments back towards the urban core and towards the waterfront. The new developments, especially the grand residential towers and large residential villas, are far beyond the economic means of the middle class. The new plans appear to be reversing the older trend, where the most affluent lived in the suburbs, and it is effectively bringing them back into the higher-density areas. In advance of the filtering-up effect in the city centre, the middle- and lower-income segments of society are being coerced out of the city centre by regulatory measures and economic limitations.

As in many cities in developed countries, these policies are creating population movements in opposite directions. While the elite are 'reclaiming' the centre, low-income populations are being cornered into locations of low-quality housing, with environmental liabilities or limited mobility. The case is complicated further by the use of *speculative* real estate as a tool for generating wealth. As Dubai found out in 2008–09, relying on real estate to generate surplus can be a risky policy.

Gentrification in Abu Dhabi might not mean exactly the same as it does in the UK or North America – certainly, the institutional context that influences the planning and execution of all kinds of urbanisation projects is quite different in the UAE – but the economic rationale for redevelopment-led gentrification is very similar, and so are the social impacts and overall welfare effects (see Lees, 2014). Smith (2002) has argued that gentrification may be seen as a 'global urban strategy'. As Smith (2002, p 427) puts it, 'the impulse behind gentrification is now generalized; its incidence is global'. In Abu Dhabi, as elsewhere, capital in circulation in need of surplus-generating activity seeks out opportunities by exploiting rent gaps, and with the help of the state (differences in political economy notwithstanding), removes the inefficiencies obstructing the extraction of the highest possible rent. Needless to say, in a country that makes no claims to democratic process, 'the right to stay put' (Hartman, 1984; Newman and Wyly, 2006; for the case of mainland China, see also Shin, 2013) is a non-starter.

In this study, we have reported the peculiarities of the Abu Dhabi housing market and the processes that are making it difficult for low-income residents of the city to find proper accommodation. Several important lessons emerge. First, developers in Abu Dhabi are not completely separate from the government. Public and private interests share a considerable overlap in construction companies (among other sectors of the economy). What would normally constitute a conflict-of-interest situation in the Western context (even though 'revolving doors' do exist between the public sector and large corporations) is quite normal in this region, as in many other developing countries (see Haila, 2000; Hamilton-Hart, 2000; Shin, 2009b).

Second, planners seem to have assumed, based on conventional wisdom, that a rise in supply will ease the increase in rents. This is certainly true to some extent. However, rent levels are already far too unaffordable for lower- and lower-middle-income groups. Housing options for these groups are getting further reduced with the demolition and reconstruction of older buildings. Workers in these income categories are getting squeezed in an expensive rental market where most of the new supply is coming in to serve the upper end. This will not result in improved access to affordable housing. Rather, the result is likely to be more displacement and crowding in areas farther out from the city centre.

Third, the lowest income groups – those who work in manual labour-intensive jobs – are fortunate in that their housing needs are provided for by their employers. However, that 'solution' is not without significant social issues as it leads to their exclusion from the city and to rather unpleasant conditions within their residential spaces (even though some progress has been made on access to civic infrastructure). As the 'labour village' model becomes more affordable, efficient and acceptable to employers and international observers, it is likely to become the first choice for housing low-wage workers. Although no such policy has been announced, the concentration of 'bachelors' in the suburbs, especially the Musaffah Industrial Area, appears to be a growing trend. Certainly, such an approach is 'efficient' on various counts. Not only does it meet the 'standards' (understood in terms of square feet per person, cleaning schedules, etc), but it also eliminates the low-end consumer base from the city centre, thus allowing land to be used for uses that yield higher rents. Further, from the perspective of city image and branding, it removes an under-consuming (and image-compromising) demographic from the public spaces in the city centre.

The processes of the re-appropriation of space for investment and the consequent displacement of communities are neither new nor unique to Abu Dhabi. The intensification of these trends in cities around the world, however, is impressive, not least because of the vastly divergent social and political contexts where the logic of speculative real estate development has found favour. As cities become spatially polarised (Sassen, 2005), in addition to asking whom we plan for, we are forced to confront new inquiries. What are the functions of cities? Is there any role for urban planning beyond urban design and real estate development?

References

Brenner, N. and Theodore, N. (2005) 'Neoliberalism and the urban condition', *City*, vol 9, no 1, pp 101–7.

Davidson, C. (2007) 'The Emirates of Abu Dhabi and Dubai: contrasting roles in the international system', *Asian Affairs*, vol 38, no 1, pp 33–48.

Davidson, C. (2009) 'Abu Dhabi's new economy: oil, investment and domestic development', *Middle East Policy*, vol 16, no 2, pp 59–79.

Department of Municipal Affairs (2010) 'Law 19 of 2005 concerning real estate property'. Available at: http://dma.abudhabi.ae/en/articles/law.no.nintin.of.twothousandfive.concerning.real.estate.property.aspx (accessed 25 November 2013).

Emirates 24/7 (2012) 'New Abu Dhabi tenant law: more than 3 men cannot share room', 15 October. Available at: http://www.emirates247.com/news/emirates/new-abu-dhabi-tenant-law-more-than-3-men-cannot-share-room-2012-10-15-1.478943 (accessed 27 March 2013).

Emirates 24/7 (2013) '10,000 government staff travel Dubai–Abu Dhabi daily', 29 August. Available at: http://www.emirates247.com/news/emirates/10-000-govt-staff-travel-dubai-abu-dhabi-daily-2013-08-29-1.519211 (accessed 30 October 2013).

Gulf News (2005a) 'High rents force bachelors to stay illegally in shared apartments', 26 January. Available at: http://gulfnews.com/news/gulf/uae/housing-property/high-rents-force-bachelors-to-stay-illegally-in-shared-apartments-1.275100 (accessed 27 March 2013).

Gulf News (2005b) 'More housing units for bachelors in Abu Dhabi', 31 January. Available at: http://gulfnews.com/news/gulf/uae/housing-property/more-housing-units-for-bachelors-in-abu-dhabi-1.275646 (accessed 27 March 2013).

Gulf News (2006) 'Civic body cuts power supply to villas housing bachelors', 4 September. Available at: http://gulfnews.com/news/gulf/uae/general/civic-body-cuts-power-supply-to-villas-housing-bachelors-1.194723 (accessed 27 March 2013).

Gulf News (2007a) '"Bachelors" of a building say rent has increased by 500%', 25 May. Available at: http://gulfnews.com/news/gulf/uae/housing-property/bachelors-of-a-building-say-rent-has-increased-by-500-1.83089 (accessed 27 March 2013).

Gulf News (2007b) 'Low cost housing for bachelors in Abu Dhabi', 20 July. Available at: http://gulfnews.com/news/gulf/uae/housing-property/low-cost-housing-for-bachelors-in-abu-dhabi-1.83090 (accessed 27 March 2013).

Gulf News (2007c) 'Realtors renting villas to bachelors to lose license', 8 August. Available at: http://gulfnews.com/news/gulf/uae/housing-property/realtors-renting-villas-to-bachelors-to-lose-licence-1.107150 (accessed 27 March 2013).

Gulf News (2008a) 'Bachelors say they have no place to call home', 4 February. Available at: http://gulfnews.com/news/gulf/uae/housing-property/bachelors-say-they-have-no-place-to-call-home-1.83092 (accessed 27 March 2013).

Gulf News (2008b) 'Workers barred from areas housing families', 23 May. Available at: http://gulfnews.com/news/gulf/uae/housing-property/workers-barred-from-areas-housing-families-1.106660 (accessed 27 March 2013).

Gulf News (2009) 'Bachelors unhappy with segregated housing plans', 3 May. Available at: http://gulfnews.com/news/gulf/uae/housing-property/bachelors-unhappy-with-segregated-housing-plans-1.83091 (accessed 27 March 2013).

Haila, A. (2000) 'Real estate in global cities: Singapore and Hong Kong as property states', *Urban Studies*, vol 37, pp 2241–56.

Hamilton-Hart, N. (2000) 'The Singapore state revisited', *The Pacific Review*, vol 13, no 2, pp 195–216.

Hartman, C. (1984) 'Right to stay put', in C.C. Geisler and J. Popper (eds) *Land reform, American style*, Totowa, NJ: Rowman and Allanheld.

Harvey, D. (1978) 'On planning the ideology of planning', in R. Burchell and G. Sternlieb (eds) *Planning theory in the 1980s*, New Brunswick, NJ: CUPR, pp 213–33.

Harvey, D. (2006) *The limits to capital*, London and New York, NY: Verso.

Harvey, D. (2010) *The enigma of capital and the crises of capitalism*, London: Profile Books.

Jones Lang Lassalle (2012) 'Abu Dhabi real estate overview Q2 2012', Abu Dhabi, UAE. Available at: http://www.joneslanglasalle-mena.com/mena/en-gb/pages/researchdetails.aspx?itemid=9106 (accessed 25 March 2012).

Khaleej Times (2006) 'Bachelors cry foul over eviction from apartments in Abu Dhabi', 5 September. Available at: http://www.khaleejtimes.com/kt-article-display-1.asp?xfile=data/theuae/2006/September/theuae_September122.xml§ion=theuae (accessed 27 March 2013).

Khaleej Times (2008a) 'Housing woes refuse to go', 21 March. Available at: http://www.khaleejtimes.com/kt-article-display-1.asp?xfile=data/theuae/2008/March/theuae_March666.xml§ion=theuae (accessed 2 May 2013).

Khaleej Times (2008b) 'Life is a misery for "married bachelors"', 16 August. Available at: http://www.khaleejtimes.com/DisplayArticle.asp?xfile=/data/theuae/2008/August/theuae_August307.xml§ion=theuae (accessed 2 May 2013).

Khaleej Times (2008c) 'Abu Dhabi takes tough stand on villa-sharing', 28 October. Available at: http://www.khaleejtimes.com/DisplayArticle08.asp?xfile=data/theuae/2008/October/theuae_October647.xml§ion=theuae (accessed 2 May 2013).

Khaleej Times (2009) 'Housing inspections from tomorrow', 31 January. Available at: http://www.khaleejtimes.com/darticlen.asp?xfile=data/theuae/2009/January/theuae_January610.xml§ion=theuae (accessed 2 May 2013).

Khaleej Times (2012) 'Crackdown on bachelors' housing units', 15 October. Available at: http://article.wn.com/view/2012/10/15/Crackdown_on_bachelors_housing_units/ (accessed 27 March 2013).

Lees, L. (2014) 'The urban injustices of New Labour's "new urban renewal": the case of the Aylesbury Estate in London', *Antipode*, vol 46, no 4, pp 921-47.

Lees, L., Slater, T. and Wyly, E. (2008) *Gentrification*, London: Routledge.

Lopez-Morales, E. (2010) 'Gentrification by ground rent dispossession: the shadows cast by large-scale urban renewal in Santiago de Chile', *International Journal of Urban and Regional Research*, vol 35, no 2, pp 330–57.

MacLeod, G. (2002) 'From urban entrepreneurialism to a "revanchist city"? On the spatial injustices of Glasgow's renaissance', *Antipode*, vol 34, no 3, pp 602–24.

Mohammad, R. and Sidaway, J. (2012) 'Spectacular urbanization amidst variegated geographies of globalization: learning from Abu Dhabi's trajectory through the lives of South Asian men', *International Journal of Urban and Regional Research*, vol 36, no 3, pp 606–27.

National Bureau of Statistics (2011) 'UAE in figures 2011'. Available at: http://www.uaestatistics.gov.ae/ReportDetailsEnglish/tabid/121/Default.aspx?ItemId=2100&PTID=187&MenuId=2 (accessed 25 March 2013).

Newman, K. and Wyly, E.K. (2006) 'The right to stay put, revisited: gentrification and resistance to displacement in New York City', *Urban Studies*, vol 43, no 1, pp 23–57.

Otak (no date) 'Wasat Al Madina revitalization study: Abu Dhabi'. Available at: http://www.otak.com/portfolio/masterplanninglanddevelopment/wasat-al-madina-revitalization-study/ (accessed 15 May 2013).

Parsa, A., Keivani, R., Loo, L.S., Seow, E.O. and Younis, B. (2002) 'Emerging global cities: comparison of Singapore and the city of the United Arab Emirates', *Journal of Real Estate Portfolio Management*, vol 8, no 4, pp 95–101.

Sassen, S. (2005) 'The global city: introducing a concept', *Brown Journal of World Affairs*, vol 12, no 2, pp 27–43.

SCAD (Statistics Centre Abu Dhabi) (2011) *Statistical yearbook of Abu Dhabi 2011*, Abu Dhabi: Statistics Centre.

SCAD (2012a) 'Statistical yearbook of Abu Dhabi 2012: employed by economic activity'. Available at: http://www.scad.ae/en/statistics/Pages/Statistics.aspx?ThemeID=5&TopicID=21&SubTopicID=122&PublicationID=296 (accessed 30 October 2013).

SCAD (2012b) *Abu Dhabi in figures 2011*, Abu Dhabi, UAE: Statistics Centre. Available at: http://www.scad.ae/en/statistics/Pages/Statistics.aspx?ThemeID=4&TopicID=14&SubTopicID=54&PublicationID=58 (accessed 25 March 2013).

Shin, H.B. (2009a) 'Property-based redevelopment and gentrification: the case of Seoul', *Geoforum*, vol 40, no 5, pp 906–17.

Shin, H.B. (2009b) 'Residential redevelopment and entrepreneurial local state: the implications of Beijing's shifting emphasis on urban redevelopment policies', *Urban Studies*, vol 46, no 13, pp 2815–39.

Shin, H.B. (2013) 'The right to the city and critical reflections on China's property rights activism', *Antipode*, vol 45, no 5, pp 1167–89.

Slater, T. (2004) 'North American gentrification/revanchist and emancipatory perspective explored', *Environment and Planning A*, vol 36, no 7, pp 1191–213.

Smith, N. (1982) 'Gentrification and uneven development', *Economic Geography*, vol 58, no 2, pp 139–55.

Smith, N. (1996) *The new urban frontier: gentrification and the revanchist city*, London and New York, NY: Routledge.

Smith, N. (2002) 'New globalism, new urbanism: gentrification as global urban strategy', *Antipode*, vol 34, no 3, pp 427–50.

Smith, N. (2010) 'After Tompkins Square Park: degentrification and the revanchist city', in G. Bridge and S. Watson (eds) *The Blackwell city reader* (2nd edn), Maldon, MA: Wiley-Blackwell.

The National (2010) 'Where can bachelors go now?', 26 March. Available at: http://www.thenational.ae/news/uae-news/where-can-bachelors-go-now (accessed 2 May 2013).

The National (2012a) '187 shops fined for poor health and safety', 20 June. Available at: http://www.thenational.ae/news/uae-news/187-shops-fined-for-poor-health-and-safety (accessed 30 October 2013).

The National (2012b) 'Crowded houses face fines of Dh100,000', 27 October. Available at: http://www.thenational.ae/news/uae-news/crowded-houses-face-fines-of-dh100-000 (accessed 27 March 2013).

The National (2012c) 'Abu Dhabi sets Dh1,000 fine for hanging laundry on your balconies', 7 August. Available at: http://www.thenational.ae/news/uae-news/abu-dhabi-sets-dh1-000-fine-for-hanging-laundry-on-your-balconies (accessed 30 October 2013).

The National (2013a) 'Abu Dhabi businesses have 3 months to change signboards or face fines', 23 April. Available at: http://www.thenational.ae/news/uae-news/abu-dhabi-businesses-have-3-months-to-change-signboards-or-face-fines (accessed 30 October 2013).

The National (2013b) 'Owners face fine if cooked food is displayed outdoors in Abu Dhabi', 12 July. Available at: http://www.thenational.ae/news/uae-news/owners-risk-fines-if-cooked-food-is-displayed-outdoors-in-abu-dhabi (accessed 30 October 2013).

UPC (Urban Planning Council) (2007) 'Plan Abu Dhabi 2030: urban structure framework plan', Abu Dhabi, UAE. Available at: http://www.upc.gov.ae/template/upc/pdf/Capital-2030-en.pdf (accessed 25 March 2013).

UPC (2009) 'Abu Dhabi Urban Planning Council unveils Corniche public beach development plan', Abu Dhabi, UAE. Available at: http://www.upc.gov.ae/media-center/press-releases/abu-dhabi-urban-planning-council-unveils-corniche-public-beach-development-plan.aspx?lang=en-US (accessed 1 August 2013).

UPC (2010a) 'Abu Dhabi real estate market forecast', Abu Dhabi, UAE. Available at: http://www.upc.gov.ae/abu-dhabi-real-estate-market-forecasts.aspx?lang=en-US (accessed 25 March 2013).

UPC (2010b) 'Upgrading downtown', *Vision Magazine*, Issue 2, August.

UPC (2011) 'Middle income rental housing', Abu Dhabi, UAE. Available at: http://www.upc.gov.ae/mirh.aspx?lang=en-US (accessed 25 March 2013).

Weber, R. (2002) 'Extracting value from the city: neoliberalism and urban redevelopment', *Antipode*, vol 34, no 3, pp 519–40.

FIVE

Confronting favela chic: the gentrification of informal settlements in Rio de Janeiro, Brazil

Jake Cummings

Introduction

On the iconic promenade of Copacabana beach, in Rio de Janeiro, Brazil, is an outdoor market selling clothing, artwork and various *tchotchkes* to tourists. Embodied in these wares is Rio's cultivated visual vocabulary in miniature: Christ the Redeemer shelf ornaments, Sugarloaf Mountain key chains, artwork inspired by the city's natural splendour, and other commodifications of the images that have long attracted Brazilians and foreign tourists to this city. However, contemporarily, a new image has joined the jumble: paintings of the haphazard *favelas* on Rio's hillsides are on offer next to those depicting the city's natural splendour and cultural iconography. The Brazilian favela – historically stigmatised as an urban slum and a national embarrassment of poverty and marginalisation incarnate – has begun to be admitted, at least on canvas, to the city's esteemed milieu.

Favelas themselves have come a long way over their 100 years of existence as an informal style of habitation. At one time, these scattered settlements comprised wood or wattle-and-daub shacks, housing economic migrants from other regions of Brazil. Now, no longer properly termed a 'squatter settlement' or a 'slum', favelas have evolved, through the organic process of accretion and collective community building, into consolidated urban villages built of masonry and reinforced concrete. Levels of income, investment and condition vary widely, but households with sufficient means have improved their homes with modern interiors and furnishings. Utilities and other services can be procured informally and recently, in some cases, through formalised relationships with suppliers. Tenurial security is codified in a patchwork of legislation and constitutional guarantees, and informal property markets are robust.

Social attitudes towards favelas in the Brazilian mainstream are also becoming less crudely formed. Political majorities in this class-stratified society are warming to the idea of the social inclusion of the marginalised and the dispossessed, and a set of ongoing policy initiatives at the municipal, state and federal levels, promoted under the theme of 'social integration', aim to introduce new regimes of security, connective infrastructure and/or urban services to some of these informal neighbourhoods. Piloted in the 1990s and intensified in anticipation of

Brazil's hosting of two mega-events – the FIFA World Cup soccer tournament in 2014 and the Summer Olympic Games in 2016 – these programmes reassert state sovereignty over what was once generally assumed to be provisional but ultimately irredeemable typologies of habitation.

Now, after decades of suffering from social stigma, neglect and outright violence, the favelas' historical narrative has reached a plot twist: in many cases, the promise of 'social integration' has triggered just the opposite effect – land speculation, newcomer residents and the transition to the socio-economic exclusivity of gentrification. This chapter tackles this emergent problem, locating 'favela gentrification' (see Figure 5.1) within the larger forces of state-led socio-economic restructuring, and then laying out the economic, social and cultural consequences of these structural forces. The research leading to these conclusions is mainly ethnographic; indeed, quantitative data on informal markets and spatial mobility are scarce. Findings are based primarily on structured, open-ended interviews, at the core of which are interviews with long-time favela residents, business-owners and in-migrants. The last group was composed exclusively of non-Brazilian residents, whose tenure in their respective communities ranged from six months to more than 10 years. These core interviews were supplemented with interviews of professional architects and community organisers working directly with the development of favelas, as well as my own experience of consulting with community leaders on development issues related to favelas. The research focuses, though not exclusively, on two cases in particular: Rocinha, one of Rio's most populous favelas, with between 100,000 and 200,000 inhabitants; and nearby Vidigal, with approximately 20,000 to 40,000 residents.[1] These favelas are situated on opposite sides of the Dois Irmãos mountain, a fixture of Rio's rugged landscape, in the heavily touristic South Zone and in proximity to some of the highest-priced real estate in the formal city.

Favela gentrification

Since approximately 2007, Rio's political and economic environment has created increasing demand pressures on its housing supply and infrastructure. After struggling for decades from dictatorship and hyper-inflation, Brazil's economy experienced rapid growth in the first decade of the 21st century. The selection of Brazil to host the World Cup in 2014 and of Rio de Janeiro to host the Summer Olympic Games in 2016 has prompted investments in urban infrastructure and tourism, creating new opportunities for land speculation and commercial development. These factors have combined to send housing costs growing at a faster rate than incomes within the city of Rio de Janeiro. Between 2008 and 2012, the formal housing sector saw prices double.[2] Demand pressure on real estate in the formal city has, in turn, cascaded into informal markets (Neri, 2011).

Figure 5.1: Favela gentrification in Rocinha on Estrada da Gávea, the main commercial spine. The subheading of the sign for the 'Because' fashion clothing shop reads, 'New York | Paris | Milão | Rocinha'. Newly built floors await tenants

Note: Photograph taken by the author.

In the urban history of Rio de Janeiro, the year 2013 may well be remembered as the year in which the term *gentrificação* entered the common lexicon. During that year, and in the latter half of 2012, articles about the gentrification of favelas sprang up in the international mainstream press: among UK outlets, the BBC and *The Guardian* reported on the phenomenon, while National Public Radio and *The Huffington Post* ran similar stories in the US. Rio's own daily newspaper, *O Globo*, also got in on the act, with periodic articles spotlighting cases where escalating housing costs, real estate speculation and a pioneering set of foreign nationals were all headed to favelas. One story featured a particular section entitled 'O que é gentrificação?' ('What is gentrification?') (*O Globo*, no date).

So, what is gentrification in a Brazilian context, and is it even conceivable that favelas there could be deemed 'gentrified'? The *O Globo* feature attempting to introduce gentrification to a Brazilian audience made do with imported concepts from global neoliberalism or otherwise originating in the Global North. These included 'the entrepreneurial city', the 'branding' of cities and *New York Times* columnist David Brooks's notion of the 'bourgeois bohemian' as a connoisseur of place. Understood along these lines, the idea that favelas could undergo gentrification as an outcome of globalisation and shifting consumer tastes would, indeed, appear novel, given ongoing social stigmatisation, the pervasive reign of drug-trafficking gangs and their violent imprint, and the crowded and substandard conditions that persist in many favelas today.

However, in fact, the socio-spatial pressures that underlie the process of gentrification, as described by recent media reports, are not novel at all. Rather, the practical effect of dislocating favela residents and replacing them with middle-class households, capital enterprise or even nominally 'public' facilities is as old as the favelas themselves. Here, etymology is a guide. While the neologism *gentrificação* was seldom encountered until recently, other terms that have historically been used include *enobrecimento urbano* ('urban ennobling') and the more critical *remoção branca* ('white removal'), *higienização social* ('social hygiene') and *limpeza social* ('social cleansing'). This terminology reflects a rhetoric of opposition to more than 100 years of forced evictions at the behest of the state and real estate capital (also reflecting the racialised power relations left over from Brazil's history of slavery and white supremacy).

In short, Rio's in situ gentrification of today is a contemporary feature of a very old process of urban expansion and beautification at the expense of the poor and landless – what Smith (1996) called 'revanchism' or 'gentrification generalised' (Smith, 1996, 2002). This more generalised process of gentrification in Rio has three components: first, through a pattern of favela removal, usually inhumane and unjustified by any public purpose; second, (ironically) through social integration programmes of security and urbanisation; and, third, through the 'favela chic' phenomenon, wherein a class of newcomers, as consumers of place, is migrating to select favela communities.

Forced removals

During most of the 20th century, the eradication of favelas was official state policy. Employing mega-events as a pretext for removing the poor dates back to 1922, when Rio de Janeiro (then capital of the Republic) hosted international dignitaries for its Centennial of Independence. The urban remaking and 'beautification' leading up to the event included a programme of razing hills located in the city centre, areas where thousands had been living in informal and popular housing (Brandão, 2006; Gonçalves, 2013). By then, turn-of-the-century reforms, cued by Baron Haussmann in Paris, had already sliced broad boulevards through the colonial urban fabric in a 'Belle Epoque Carioca'. In that process, 3,000 people living in tenements were displaced (Brandão, 2006, p 39).

Under Brazil's military dictatorship, which lasted from 1964 to 1985, slum clearance was institutionalised. Official policy was not only to target communities proximate to high-income areas, but also to separate households into different developments based on income, thereby destroying community integrity (Perlman, 2010, p 271). The effect of these actions was to exacerbate spatial sorting by income, not only among relocated favela communities, but also because the relocations generally pushed the poor from the inner city to peripheral ghettos where land was cheap.

In Brazil's democratic era, political institutions have been reformed, but urban outcomes are slow to follow. Particularly in its Constitution, Brazil the democracy is more committed to social justice and equity, and in using urban policy as a tool to advance those goals, than was Brazil the dictatorship. However, in the high-stakes environment of mega-event development, its system of constitutional enforcement can become frayed. Rio's municipal government and its Olympic-planning bodies have not necessarily aligned themselves with the letter and spirit of the federal Constitution and related legislation, which are particularly progressive in their view of urban land as a collective asset. While legal protections for favelas are meant to protect their residents from removals not justified by the public good or environmental risk, these protections have, in fact, been manipulated by the resourceful and sophisticated capitalist and political classes in order to evict politically unsophisticated favela dwellers.[3]

Concurrent with this pattern is the inexorable march of Brazil's national low-income housing programme, Minha Casa Minha Vida (My House My Life). As the public subsidies coming from Minha Casa Minha Vida are targeted at developers to deliver low-cost housing subdivisions and estates, these profit-seeking enterprises are constructing homes where land is cheap – far out on the urban periphery and poorly connected to public transit. As of the end of 2012, 80 percent of permitted housing units for the lowest income strata (zero to three minimum wages) were to be located in the far western reaches of Rio, hours from the city's job centres in the Central and South Zones (Veríssimo, 2012; see also Figure 5.2). While the poor are already being induced to move to these areas through the manipulation of housing supply, forced evictions exacerbate this trend, where replacement housing is generally offered in the form of a dwelling in a newly built Minha Casa Minha Vida development. By the start of the Olympics in 2016, tens of thousands of informal households will have been relocated in this manner (Veríssimo, 2012).

'Social integration'

Rio's efforts at the social integration of favelas – not technically triggered by mega-event planning, but coinciding closely with their announcements – come in two main institutional forms: pacification and urbanisation. 'Pacification' amounts to a reassertion of state sovereignty over favela territories controlled by outlaw organisations, principally the violent gangs of narcotics traffickers for which Rio's favelas are notorious (although it should be stressed that these gangs do not operate exclusively in favelas and not all favelas are ruled by them). Urbanisation programmes, meanwhile, purport to incorporate favela communities into Rio's formal urban systems, such as those relating to utilities, land tenure, social services, circulation and open space networks and standards.

Figure 5.2: Minha Casa Minha Vida developments are from the list of licensed developments as of 2012, published by the Municipal Secretariat of Urbanism

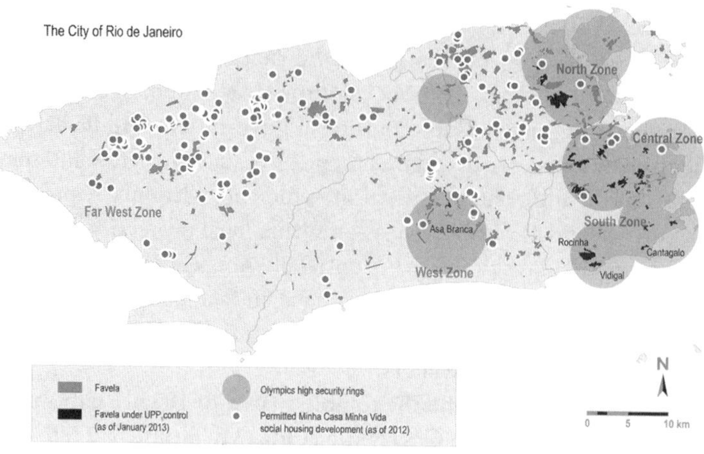

Of these two prongs of social integration, the pacification programme has been more widely applied and consequential to the daily lives of favela residents and their environments. Under the programme, newly trained, military-style Police Pacification Units (UPPs) have been installed as a permanent presence in select favelas to vanquish drug-trafficking networks[4] and to enforce security and state sovereignty. While the first pacifying unit was installed in 2008, one year prior to Rio's selection as the host city for the Olympics, as of the end of 2012, 28 UPPs were in operation in favela territories, all within the Olympic high-security buffer zones designated by the municipal government (see Figure 5.2). A number of studies have shown pacification to have exerted upward pressures on housing costs in favelas. A study by the Fundaçao Getulio Vargas found that the presence of a UPP increased rents by 7 per cent above and beyond their baseline trajectory (the study was performed prior to the pacification of either Rocinha or Vidigal) (Neri, 2011).

The geography of urbanisation has been similar to that of pacification. Physical upgrades under the national government's Growth Acceleration Program (PAC) have focused on high-expense, high-profile connective infrastructure. An aerial gondola linking a complex of informal communities within view of the elevated highway that runs between Rio's international airport and its downtown cost the public R$210 million (USD100 million). The Mirante da Paz, a 23-storey elevator and sky bridge connection, connects Ipanema, one of Rio's most exclusive neighbourhoods, with the favela Cantagalo. In addition, the 2010 launch of the R$8 billion (USD4.0 billion) Morar Carioca programme came with promises to urbanise, relocate or otherwise contend with all of Rio's approximately 1,000 irregular settlements, though implementation of this programme has been politically stalled (Osborn, 2013). Although upgrades were designed on paper to be comprehensive and participatory, by and large, they have been neither – placing emphasis on politicians' pet projects and the activation of land markets in and around favelas, while upgrades that serve the most vulnerable, such as sanitation systems, schools and health services, are delayed into oblivion.

A case in point is the Morro da Providência favela in the central city, on a hill rising above an expansive port redevelopment project known as Porto Maravilha, under the aegis of Olympic-related reforms. Providência is sometimes called Rio's oldest favela (although this is disputed), having survived repeated demolition threats since its founding at the end of the 19th century. In 2010, the UPP arrived; shortly thereafter, construction on another gondola system was begun, branded as 'Morar Carioca', to connect Rio's Central train station with the Porto Maravilha development, overtop Providência's hill. The physical interventions, along with condemnation for 'environmental risk', were to raze over 30 per cent of informal housing in the area. Construction of replacement housing fell behind schedule and court battles ensued over the lack of public participation: 'Actually what they want to do is remove as many people as possible because a favela doesn't fit with the grand plans for the port', was how one community activist perceived the reforms (Assefa, 2012).

In fact, the language of Smith's (1996) revanchism pervades neighbourhood opposition to redevelopment projects in and around favelas – the *remoção branca* of the Belle Epoque Carioca and thereafter. The city's 'Shock of Order' policy, one product of former New York Mayor Rudolph Guiliani's professional consulting with the city, was designed to crack down on petty crime and informal economies as a strategy for securing the city's touristic appeal.

The aggregate effect of these 'social integration' initiatives has been, and will be: intensified flows of capital and newcomers into favelas; the subtraction of affordable housing stock around mega-event development hubs and their respective transportation connections; and new spaces of marginality set up in peripheral, disconnected housing projects. In short, 'social integration' does not equal 'social inclusion'.

Favela chic

With regard to consumer tastes, which are increasingly globalised, a 'favela chic' phenomenon has emerged, with Rio's favelas gaining international attention in recent years. The elevation of favela culture through its associations with samba and *funk carioca* musical styles, as well as the 2002 international hit film *City of God*, have helped to glamorise the favela among young artists and international adventure-seekers. In the wake of *City of God*, an origin story depicting the formation of Rio's violent drug trade in the midst of its marginalised counterculture, well-heeled nightclubs with the name 'Favela Chic' opened their doors in London and Paris, emulating the aesthetic of favelas by using material elements such as masonry, corrugated sheet metal and graffiti as visual tropes (for a similar appropriation in San Francisco, California, see Figure 5.3).

In Rio itself, favela tours for foreign visitors are common, particularly in Rocinha. Hostels catering to young foreigners have opened in the more desirable beachside settlements of Babilônia, Vidigal and Cantagalo – these favelas are relatively accessible (and increasingly more so thanks to urban interventions) from South Zone neighbourhoods already popular with tourists. In these particular places, 'touristification' (the marketing of a neighbourhood as a touristic product) is building steam. However, the term 'touristification' now has more in common with the term 'gentrification' than the process of touristifying. Combined with wide press coverage of the novelty of expatriates taking up residence in favelas – even the US rap artist Kanye West has reportedly expressed interest in setting up a recording studio in Vidigal – the public face of 'favela gentrification' in Rio de Janeiro is now an international one.

Figure 5.3: A flier for a club event in San Francisco, California, appropriating the aesthetic of favelas

In Vidigal in particular, first-hand accounts of rapid rises in foreign investment and the cost of housing abound. Four months after I interviewed her, 'Susan', a 25-year-old English make-up artist and blogger, wrote to tell me that her rent had increased from R$300 to R$500. 'Kate', a 25-year-old American married to a Brazilian local, had likewise noticed property-owners capitalising on increased interest from foreigners:

> 'Since I've been here, a lot more community members are interested in gringos being here, and they're seeing it as a way to make money – to market their own neighbourhood.... [My husband and I] were looking at buying a house last year, and in one year, prices have doubled. Houses that would sell for R$25,000 are now R$50,000 or maybe even R$100,000. People are buying them, from France, from Switzerland, from Germany.'

The clear evidence of housing price inflation in some favelas does not translate to equally clear evidence of resident displacement, though my interviews with residents of Vidigal revealed cases of it. Interviewees articulated examples of direct economic displacement – Susan perceived that "the house owners are able to gain a lot by selling, but all the people renting have to leave or pay more with no rise in income" – as well as what Marcuse (1985) referred to as 'exclusionary displacement'; according to Kate, "People who have lived here because they had no other choice are having to leave because their children will have no way to buy a house." The latter is a version of displacement that differs from the usual concern for renters who can no longer keep up with rising rents, Vidigal being typical of favelas in its high level of homeownership (estimated by community organisers at between 80 and 90 per cent). Private homeownership, however, does not always provide a bulwark against exclusionary or intergenerational displacement, and proximity to extended families and social networks is a key socially empowering feature of favelas. By contrast, no one I spoke with in Rocinha had heard of cases of displacement. 'Pablo', a 32-year-old student and local community organiser, testified to hearing complaints about high rents in Rocinha, but he felt that homes could generally be found in other parts of the favela – a form of 'intra-favela displacement'.

In the introduction to their anthology *Gentrification in a global context*, Atkinson and Bridge (2005) raise the question of whether gentrification of environments that are majority non-white, less developed or located in the Global South follows a model of neocolonialism. Such a framework plausibly describes the contours of other development patterns in Brazil: the creation of a tourist bubble in the colonial neighbourhood of Pelourinho in Salvador da Bahia; the rejection of a Guggenheim museum franchise in Rio on cultural nativist grounds; and Rio's own neighbourhood of Santa Teresa – a corridor of upscale coffee shops, arts festivals and dilapidated pre-modern homes in the formal city frequently occupied by residents from the Global North. However, the wider sweep of urban restructuring outside of Rio's South Zone shows us that the global consumer widely identified with gentrification constitutes only part of the demand side of the equation there. While the supply of land occupied by favelas is shrinking due mainly to removals,[5] official census figures indicate the proportion of the population living in favelas is growing, from 19 per cent of the city in 2000 to 22 per cent in 2010.[6] In addition to migrants from outside Rio, and generational growth, other classes of gentrifiers are placing pressure on informal housing demand. Native Brazilian households from the formal city are entering favelas in search of cheaper housing, though this movement is dampened by the enduring stigmas favelas bear. Perhaps more significantly, inter-favela migration is occurring within their active informal property markets. Favela dwellers who are able to accumulate a small pool of capital can move to better neighbourhoods and redevelop their plots into rental housing for the poorest members of the community.[7] In fact, there is wide variability around the relative desirability of favela communities – residents in neighbourhoods with lower levels of urban accessibility or those governed by outlaw organisations may try to trade up to more accessible or more democratic neighbourhoods free of organised crime. Perhaps 'sub-gentrification' is the appropriate term for low-income households replacing even lower-income households, a mirror image of Lees' (2003) 'super-gentrification' theory applied to Brooklyn Heights in New York City.

The case for empowering favelas

The argument against gentrification, as it tends to manifest in favelas, is concerned not so much with favela 'preservation', as it is often pejoratively termed in the debate over urban restructuring, but rather with a certain kind of legitimation, inclusion and empowerment. Favelas are not static neighbourhoods, and, in fact, they are remarkably evolutionary and adaptive. So, what about them is worth preserving? Given that they appear to be gentrifying, what exactly is at stake?

Here, I identify three key urban roles that favelas perform, thus warranting continued support and investment. The first is economic: favelas are an irreplaceable source of affordable housing in the inner city. The second is social: favelas are an organic, highly configurable and flexible community typology that promotes cooperation and social stability. The third is cultural: favelas are the primary incubators of Rio's defining cultural features. Beyond whatever social injustice exists from the displacing forces of gentrification – severing a community's ties to a particular place to which that community stakes a non-economic claim – responses to gentrification should be responses that retain and empower these three functions of the favela.

At 22 per cent of domiciles, favelas represent by far Rio's most significant supply of affordable housing. Furthermore, despite the best efforts of past projects of eradication and segregation, their geographical dispersion continues to contribute to socio-economic diversity in the public sphere. At the same time, this social interspersion is being kept in check by the strong boundaries resulting from physical walls, de facto security regimes, the material shift in environments between the formal and informal cities, the change in elevation associated with hillside settlements, and the psychological divides created by marginalisation and stigma.

Informal, self-built or incremental housing creates well-known inefficiencies and challenges for urban planners and managers, such as the difficulty in retrofitting utility systems to spontaneous settlements that were not designed for them. However, history suggests that planned settlements for low-income people in Rio fare much worse. Brazil's national system of housing finance, for example, has never successfully penetrated to the lower economic strata of society, where 66 per cent of the population lacks a bank account (Eloy, 2010, p 20). Attempts at social housing programmes since the 1960s have also been largely underfunded and ineffectual (Valença and Bonates, 2010). The notorious City of God, inspiring the novel and movie by the same name, while typically referred to as a favela, was originally an isolated public housing development built for favela evictees. The Minha Casa Minha Vida developments threaten to reproduce this cycle of marginalisation, leading to dysfunction in Rio's latest wave of peripheral relocation.

Thus, the main problem with the valorisation of centrally located favelas is a long-term housing problem. While instances of acute economic displacement in the short term have not yet emerged en masse, unchecked rises in property values threaten the stock of affordable housing in the inner city. Thus far, state-sponsored efforts, while modestly successful in increasing housing stock overall, have been mostly unsuccessful in addressing Rio de Janeiro's problems of efficiency and spatial imbalance. Furthermore, while arguments for attenuating the growth of irregular settlements citywide are well-founded, preserving favelas as a store of accessible housing will be necessary to mitigate the continual process of socio-spatial segregation that is warehousing the poor on the margins of the city.

These public housing developments lack many of the organic advantages of favelas. Consider some of the more vivid design principles that spring forth from that manifesto of the new urbanists, the Charter of the New Urbanism (www.cnu.org/charter): 'neighborhoods should be compact, pedestrian-friendly, and mixed-use'; 'concentrations of civic, institutional, and commercial activity should be embedded'; 'architecture and landscape design should grow from local climate, topography, history, and building practice'; and 'streets and squares should ... encourage walking and enable neighbors to know each other and protect their communities'. Such ideals of traditional neighbourhood design were inspired by the village idylls of Jane Jacobs' Greenwich Village or a typical town centre in the pre-industrialised US or Europe. However, they are also apt descriptors of the typical favela. It may be counter-intuitive to reconcile the dystopian forces that have shaped impoverished, gang-controlled favelas with the utopia of a new urbanist village. However, even as a violent drug trade filled a governance vacuum in most favelas, beneath this authoritarian regime was/is a neighbourhood typology that typically expresses the ideals of walkability, active street life, low-rise density and a mix of uses that nurture the social and ecological sustainability and self-help ethos so prized by the movement.

In fact, community cohesion may be even more of a consistent feature of favelas than gang rule. The West Zone favela Asa Branca, for example, enjoys high levels of employment and school attendance and remains free of any discernible gang activity or drug trade (Faigan, 2010). In its founding during Rio's dark days of drug trafficking and violent gang activity of the 1980s, the village was designed with no routes of egress on three of its edges. This was done with the specific intention to make the community inhospitable to drug traffickers, who need escape routes. Now in the shadow of one of the planned clusters of Olympics venues, Asa Branca's local economy is becoming less communitarian and more transactional. Land plots that normally would have housed owner-occupiers and their families have been converted into efficiency rentals – a case of 'sub-gentrification' dividing the settlement into landlords and tenants. Traditions of collective construction and maintenance of private housing and public works have weakened, forcing the community to turn to the city government to provide a formalised upgrade of its utilities (Cummings, 2011).

The efficiencies of scale associated with the standardisation and mass production of dwellings, so common to urban development, are well-established. Less commonly recognised are the efficiencies of the micro-scale: social connections and bartering, flexibility in use and construction, and incremental development allow residents with modest means to meet their needs as they arise and divest from their assets more easily. These needs are often difficult to anticipate with centralised programmes of popular housing in the socio-political context in Rio. For example, the innovation of a physical plan for a village layout inhospitable to organised gang members is one of many variables not taken into account in the design and management of the housing estates under the Minha Casa Minha Vida programme. As a result, a number of Minha Casa Minha Vida developments constructed over the last five years have already become ruled by vigilante militias (*O Globo*, 2011).

Aside from their function as a space of social solidarity, favela settlements lie at the heart of Rio's cultural identity. Rio's samba schools, which contribute to the city's fame and populate the annual Carnival festivities with performers, are generally rooted in favelas and favela culture. For example, the Mangueira samba school, one of Rio's most famous, is so named for the favela in which its members train. Other musical styles and cultural movements – *pagode*, *funk carioca* and *capoeira*, for example – have been developed or evolved in such marginalised urban spaces. In these spaces, settlers from Brazil's mosaic of regional and ethnic heritages have established themselves and have formed realms of distinct cultural experience. Rio's expressions of culture are a draw for tourists and are often performed in formal spaces of affluence, tourism and leisure, but, generally speaking, the most notable ones tend to be innovated in favelas.

Irrespective of their origins, to approach the subject of preserving a cultural continuity in the face of favela gentrification is to contend with the imprint of criminality. While by no means is the cultural expression of favelas wholly a product of criminality, and neither are all favelas governed (or have been governed) by outlaw regimes, the drug trafficking and violent vigilante gangs have left inextricable marks on favela cultures and identities. In fact, innovative cultural movements in Brazil themselves often follow a trajectory from marginalisation, and even criminalisation, proceeding to mainstream acceptance, and finally attaining status as celebrated markers of Brazilian identity. This is the case with *capoeira*, a martial art originating with enslaved African peoples and migrating to the urban margins in the shadows of a prohibition against a range of Afro-Brazilian cultural traditions in effect until 1937. The current front in Rio's culture wars surrounds the *bailes funk*: dance parties typically sponsored by the drug gangs and featuring the libidinous *funk carioca* musical style. Government proscription of certain events and subgenres of *funk* represents the contemporary chapter of this conflicted cultural history, particularly Afro-Brazilian cultural history. Meanwhile, the hard-edged glamour and eroticism of *bailes funk* and its associations with gang life create an allure for adventure tourists.

While favelas are notorious for *funk carioca* music, this is hardly a defining feature for them. All the same, the legally fraught circumstances of *funk carioca* and its *bailes* present a dilemma for those who would seek to preserve this element of culture. At the time of my interviews, shortly after the pacification of Rocinha and Vidigal, the local *baile funk* events had been shut down in Vidigal and were being supervised by the military police in Rocinha. Banning or regulating the *bailes* and imposing regulations and curfews on other events is a standard part of pacification, or 'de-funkification' (as it has become known), as police view these events as harbouring criminal elements. 'Marcelo', a 49-year-old disc jockey and local tour guide, complained about the lack of activity post-pacification: "The soul has died", he lamented.

In Vidigal, the gentrifying conditions brought about by the pacification police and the rise in property values had effectively replaced the *bailes* with more formalised forms of entertainment. One case of this is Alto Vidigal, a guesthouse opened in 2009 by an Austrian engineer who paid USD10,000 for a dilapidated structure with a sweeping view of Rio's urban shoreline (see Figure 5.4). At the time, Alto Vidigal was a curiosity – a well-heeled gringo abandoning the high cost of apartments in the exclusive neighbourhoods of Ipanema and Leblon and throwing in his lot with the favela. However, party events at Alto Vidigal soon became a regular draw for Vidigal's residents, as well as for Brazilians and expatriates from outside the community. By the time the *bailes funk*, along with the drug trade, were shut down, Alto Vidigal had become firmly part of the tourist circuit of trendy nightlife.

Figure 5.4: The view from the guesthouse, Alto Vidigal

Note: Photograph by the author.

What have such outposts of globalised culture done to Vidigal's cultural authenticity? In her seminal work on the authenticity of gentrifying neighbourhoods, Sharon Zukin (2010, p 20) explains:

> We can see 'authentic' spaces only from outside them. Mobility gives us the distance to view a neighborhood as connoisseurs, to compare it to an absolute standard of urban experience, to judge its character apart from our personal history or intimate social relationships.

For the hyper-mobile class of internationalists that settle into the favela, Zukin's (2010) conception of authenticity is only intensified. Kate explained that "a lot of gringos come in here and it becomes a competition of who knows the favela more.... A lot of people become fanatical about how 'awesome' the favela is." Where Brown-Saracino's (2009) gentrifiers recognise authenticity by particular identity groups that produce it, foreign newcomers tend to associate authenticity by particular qualities and practices that distinguish the favela from mainstream society. For example, the 'sense of community' that foreigners say is lacking in formal South Zone neighbourhoods was cited by seven of the 11 non-Brazilian interviewees.

More fraught dimensions of authenticity are ascribed to the social problems that Rio's favelas are known for. When I contacted 'Hunter', an Australian living in the pacified favela of Cantagalo, about scheduling an interview, he invited me to a party being held in a different part of town. "How would you like to go to a *real* favela?" he asked me, referring to an unpacified settlement in the North Zone, notorious for its drug trade and violence. *Baile funk* parties are signatures of this illicit authenticity. As the arrival of the military police in Vidigal had made gang-sponsored *bailes* a thing of the past, Susan was pestering my research assistant to escort her to his neighbourhood, where *bailes* hosted by the traffickers were still weekly events. 'Cristine', a 40-year-old photographer and social worker, told me flat out: "I don't do post-pacification *bailes*", referring to the events in Rocinha now regulated by the police. The association of favelas with crippling poverty is also implicit in assessments of authenticity. Pablo told me that he often hears the 'myth' that Rocinha is more privileged than other favelas and is therefore not a 'real' favela: "No. Rocinha is a real favela with some of the most serious problems in Brazil", he explained, citing its unparalleled tuberculosis rates and low human development index.

To newcomers, the favelas' authenticity, whether prized or grimly acknowledged, is rooted in a counterculture spawned by marginalisation and a collectivism born of necessity. This is the dilemma of favela authenticity: the very things most favela dwellers desperately need – freedom from violence and equal access to the services and opportunities that the middle class enjoy – are the very things that threaten their 'authenticity'. This transitory version of the concept echoes Jane Jacobs' idealised urban neighbourhoods, the Greenwich Village and the Boston North End of the 1950s, which Herbert Gans (1968/1991) later elaborated as primarily a social product of particular ethnic groups responding to their socio-economic conditions at a certain moment in time.

Conclusion

In this chapter, I have taken a deeper look into Rio de Janeiro's emergent phenomenon of favela gentrification, as conveyed in media reports and in popular discourses. While the term 'gentrification' is mostly applied to the touristic South Zone neighbourhoods, the markers of gentrification – rising property values, greater dominance of the logic of markets, long-term class displacement, the entry of globalised and homogenising cultural and social forces, and so on – are a metro-wide phenomenon.

Cases of gentrification in the Global North generally involve a confluence of forces, and past debates have focused on whether the dominant force driving it lies in shifting consumer tastes (Ley, 1996) or shifting capital flows (Smith, 1996). Gentrification in Rio's favelas does clearly have demand- and supply-side components: it is partly a function of the tastes of a globalised consumer class, partly of Rio's economic growth, and partly of public policy. However, in the midst of this perfect storm, state-led urban restructuring, above all else, is what has flung open the door to tangible signs of gentrification. These urban reforms have enabled a pre-existing demand phenomenon, the 'favela chic', to take hold, most notably, through the effective reconfiguration of security infrastructure by Rio's pacification programme. Other upgrading actions also hold sway: while the Morar Carioca programme has been slow to launch comprehensively, upgrading projects do occur, emphasising connective infrastructure and land regularisation while neglecting sanitation and social services – political priorities that enable property speculation. Alternatives to freehold titling, such as 'right of use' certification, the regulation of the built form, use and individual property rights, have been presented as an alternative and more likely to lead to 'socio-economic sustainability' (Roy, 2005; Handzic, 2010; Fernandes, 2011).[8] However, under Rio's current neoliberal approach, including the formalisation of services such as electricity and the internet, the cost of living in these communities is rising further out of reach for the poor.

While threats to the neighbourhood integrity of favelas in Rio de Janeiro from gentrification are very real, particular attributes of favela communities can and do serve as a bulwark against wholesale displacement in the short term (on gentrification limited, see Ley and Dobson, 2008). High rates of homeownership mean that fewer renters are vulnerable to displacement (although with increasing commodification of informal property, renting is on the rise). The real problem of economic displacement will be experienced over the longer term, as centrally located favelas become middle-class enclaves. Without access to these expanding territories of privilege, the bottom classes will end up even further out on the periphery of the metropolis, worsening the existing problem of socio-economic segregation in Rio de Janeiro. Thus far, policymakers have been unwilling or unable to formulate an effective strategy to address this trend.

The informality and flexibility of favelas also contribute to community stability, as expansion through accretion is a key strength of favela urbanism. In addition to its utility for maintaining the cohesion of extended families, the relatively unregulated incremental building in favelas slows housing inflation because it implies a higher price elasticity of supply than would be experienced in the formal city. Further protecting the affordability of housing for some families are the selective markets at work – sellers in favelas tend to discriminate between buyers, preferring to sell their properties to their families and friends, even in an environment where outsiders are offering higher prices. This behaviour effectively creates two markets for properties: an insider market and an outsider market, where insiders receive prices below the market equilibrium while outsider demand goes unmet.[9]

Despite these mitigating factors, the overwhelming pressures created by Rio's runaway housing market and infrastructure development, combined with evictions and social integration measures, are resulting in signs of economic, cultural and social transition, most intensely in Rio's South Zone, where property is most at a premium. Further research is necessary to measure the extent of these effects, even as media accounts often describe the new, globalised face of South Zone favelas as a foregone conclusion – the new reality. While not yet, in fact, the prevailing reality, the prospects of homogenisation are real: whole neighbourhoods cashing in on their potential in the tourism and leisure economy in the short term while eroding Rio de Janeiro's cultural richness over the long term.

Whatever features of favelas contribute to their resilience and solidarity, the particular vulnerability of favelas' residents to displacement stems from Brazilian society's ongoing transition to democracy. While favelas express strong traditions of collective action outside the purview of the state, most communities are still in the process of building capacity as effective actors on the political scene in advancing community goals. Curiously, the foreign newcomers normally identified as 'gentrifiers' in most press accounts may well play a role in developing this organisational capacity. Not only do the newcomers that I have interviewed from the Global North express an interest in upholding the integrity of favelas as communities, but they also bring to these communities a sense of entitlement: to urban services, to rights of citizenship, to claims to urban space. In communities where the psychology of marginalisation runs deep, foreigners' sense of entitlement could be pivotal for the future of their new neighbourhoods. Indeed, following my study, some of my interviewees are taking action to forge these alliances. The open question is, however, whether these mobilisations of pioneer favela gentrifiers will be enough to counteract the newer waves of newcomers entering, groups who do not necessarily share this empowerment ideology.

Notes

[1] While the official 2010 census performed by the Brazilian Institute of Geography and Statistics (IBGE) lists the population of Rocinha and Vidigal at 69,000 and 13,000, respectively, most professionals with experience with these neighbourhoods estimate their populations to be far higher. An updated census performed as part of the Growth Acceleration Program raised Rocinha's population estimate to 101,000.

[2] From data compiled by ZAP Imóveis. Available at: http://www.zap.com.br/imoveis/fipe-zap/

[3] Examples can be found in a number of alternative journalism sources, including RioOnWatch.org, HBO's documentary *Witness: Rio* and in a feature by *The Nation*, 'Letter from Rio: save Armando's house from the Olympics' (Zirin, 2012). For example, plans for the Olympic Park, in an area of active land speculation, have met with resistance from a legally entitled but inconveniently located favela therein.

[4] Compare with Operation Pressure Point in the Lower East Side of New York City, where the city sought to cleanse drug gangs from the neighbourhood to facilitate gentrification (see Smith, 1996).

[5] 'Favelas Cariocas: Comparação das Áreas Ocupadas 2004–2011', Pereira Passos Municipal Institute of Urbanism.

[6] Data from IBGE.

[7] This is happening, for example, in the favela Asa Branca, according to the president of its residents' association. This neighbourhood in the West Zone still remains far removed from the tourist gaze, but is adjacent to the planned Olympic Park development.

[8] A number of informal neighbourhoods have been designated as 'Special Areas of Social Interest' ('AEIS'), which are a zoning instrument meant to ward off certain kinds of developments and uses, but these laws can be selectively enforced.

[9] The Residents' Association of Vidigal recently told the daily newspaper *Folha de São Paulo* that it was receiving a major increase in foreigners and other outsiders inquiring about available rentals and sales, but not nearly enough stock has been available.

References

Assefa, H. (2012) 'Providência: 115 years of struggle' (video documentary). Available at: http://www.youtube.com/watch?v=it-bdOXxqI4

Atkinson, R. and Bridge, G. (eds) (2005) *Gentrification in a global context: the new urban colonialism*, London: Routledge.

Brandão, Z. (2006) 'Urban planning in Rio de Janeiro: a critical review of the urban design practice in the twentieth century', Centro de Estudos Avançados da Conservação. Available at: http://www.ct.ceci-br.org/ceci/en.html

Brown-Saracino, J. (2009) *A neighborhood that never changes: gentrification, social preservation, and the search for authenticity*, Chicago, IL: University of Chicago Press.

Cummings, J. (2011) 'Preparing for the Olympics: a tale of two favelas', *ReVista, the Harvard Review of Latin America*, vol 11, no 3, pp 81-3.

Eloy, C.M. (2010) 'The revitalisation of Brazil's Housing finance system', *Housing Finance International*, vol 24, no 4, pp 18–21.

Faigan, S. (2010) 'A fresh view of Asa Branca'. Available at: http://rioonwatch.org/?p=356

Fernandes, E. (2011) 'Regularization of informal settlements in Latin America', Policy Focus Report, Lincoln Institute of Land Policy.

Gans, H.J. (1968/1991) *People, plans, and policies: essays on poverty, racism, and other national urban problems*, New York, NY: Columbia University Press.

Gonçalves, R.S. (2013) *Favelas do Rio de Janeiro: História e Direito*, Rio de Janeiro: Pallas.

Handzic, K. (2010) 'Is legalized land tenure necessary in slum upgrading? Learning from Rio's land tenure policies in the Favela Bairro Program', *Habitat International*, vol 34, no 1, pp 11–17.

Lees, L. (2003) 'Super-gentrification: the case of Brooklyn Heights, New York City', in J. Brown- Saracino (ed) *The gentrification debates*, New York, NY: Routledge, pp 113–17.

Lees, L. (2014) 'The urban injustices of New Labour's "new urban renewal": the case of the Aylesbury estate in London', *Antipode*, vol 46, no 4, pp 921-47.

Ley, D. (1996) *The new middle class and the remaking of the central city*, Oxford Geographical and Environmental Studies, Oxford and New York, NY: Oxford University Press.

Ley, D. and Dobson, C. (2008) 'Are there limits to gentrification? The contexts of impeded gentrification in Vancouver', *Urban Studies*, vol 45, no 12, pp 2471–98.

Marcuse, P. (1985) 'Gentrification, abandonment and displacement: connections, causes and policy responses in New York City', *Journal of Urban and Contemporary Law*, vol 28, pp 195–240.

Neri, M.C. (2011) 'UPP2 e a Economia da Rocinha e do Alemão: Do Choque de Ordem ao de Progresso', Fundação Getulio Vargas.

O Globo (no date) 'Cidade em transe'. Available at: http://oglobo.globo.com/infograficos/gentrificacao-cidade-em-transe/

O Globo (2011) 'Minha Casa, Minha Vida is already under the domination of a West Zone militia', June.

Osborn, C. (2013) 'A history of favela upgrades part III: Morar Carioca in vision and practice (2008–present)'. Available at: http://rioonwatch.org/?p=8136

Perlman, J.E. (2010) *Favela: four decades of living on the edge in Rio de Janeiro*, New York, NY: Oxford University Press.

Roy, A. (2005) 'Urban informality', *Journal of the American Planning Association*, vol 71, no 2, pp 147–58.

Smith, N. (1996) *The new urban frontier: gentrification and the revanchist city*, New York, NY: Routledge.

Smith, N. (2002) 'New globalism, new urbanism: gentrification as global urban strategy', *Antipode*, vol 34, no 3, pp 427–50.

Valença, M.M. and Bonates, M.F. (2010) 'The trajectory of social housing policy in Brazil: from the National Housing Bank to the Ministry of Cities', *Habitat International*, vol 34, pp 165–73.

Veríssimo, A.A. (2012) 'Habitação, Emprego e mobilidade: subsídios para o debate sobre a localização da HIS na Cidade do Rio de Janeiro'. Available at: http://abeiradourbanismo.blogspot.com.br/2012/02/habitacao-emprego-e-mobilidade.html

Zirin, D. (2012) 'Letter from Rio: save Armando's house from the Olympics', *The Nation*, 17 September.

Zukin, S. (2010) *Naked city: the death and life of authentic urban places*, New York, NY: Oxford University Press.

SIX

Rethinking gentrification in India: displacement, dispossession and the spectre of development

Sapana Doshi

Introduction

Over the last decade, a surge in scholarship on the displacement of the urban poor in Indian cities has highlighted the need for post-colonial engagement with theories of gentrification. While urban projects and *en masse* displacement warrant the kind of political concern that a globally minded gentrification studies offers (see Smith, 2002), this chapter follows others (see Lees, 2012) in arguing for the need to push the boundaries of theories derived from political-economic processes in Euro-American cities. Although some studies demonstrate the existence of rent gaps (Whitehead and More, 2007) and post-industrial gentrification processes that resemble Northern urban processes (Harris, 2008), most elite usurpations of land in Indian cities have unfolded through a set of market and extra-economic processes and conditions that require distinct if complementary framings. Indeed, the term 'gentrification' is rarely used in vernacular speech and academic writing, which refer instead to slum demolition and resettlement, peri-urban land grabs, and state-led development. Factors influencing urban change in India include informal practices of land settlement and governance, legal and extra-legal modes of land and resource enclosure, and developmentalist interventions of the Indian state, non-governmental organisations (NGOs) and transnational agencies. Some scholars have used the rubric of 'accumulation by dispossession' (Harvey, 2003; Banerjee-Guha, 2010) or the notion of 'enclosure' of various kinds of 'urban commons' (Gidwani and Baviskar, 2011) as an alternative way to conceptualise the extra-economic mechanisms of displacement and dispossession. Another similar perspective posits the Lefebvrian notion of 'urban revolution' as a more appropriate framework than gentrification, because the latter presumes the transformation of already capitalised spaces whereas most newly developing areas of Indian cities are undergoing first-time spatial privatisation (Ghertner, 2014). I stress the need to think of such concepts as complementary to (rather than interchangeable with) gentrification as there is a danger of subsuming process to outcome when deploying any singular framework.

Processual analysis is also especially necessary for understanding the political opportunities and limits circumscribed by complex and uneven forms of displacement and dispossession in Indian cities. Elite-biased urban development is often enacted and negotiated through illegible, illiberal and flexible means (Hansen and Stepputat, 2006; Roy, 2009). Through a variety of development interventions and opaque planning processes in peri-urban and central city areas, slum residents, farmers and informal business-owners experience state and non-state force in different ways and engage with authorities and intermediaries on highly uneven terms. Furthermore, hybrid state agencies and NGOs displace and compensate groups differently based on ambiguous and politicised tenure regularisation regimes, as well as ethnicity, caste, language, gender and location. These distinctions shape how subaltern groups mobilise to contest, advance or rework urban transformation – a scenario that I have elsewhere called 'accumulation by differentiated displacement' (Doshi, 2013a). In this way, Indian cities highlight the blurring of political-economic aspects of urban development and governance with meaning-making socio-spatial practices normally analysed under the separate domain of cultural politics.

Developmentalist, speculative and legal displacement mechanisms, and informal modalities of land occupation and governance manifest in geographically distinct ways across urban India. The following sections engage city-specific literatures to highlight five factors shaping unequal urban transformations: (1) developmentalist urban policies; (2) informal regimes of land development, settlement and governance; (3) new state formations consolidating urban elite and middle-class power; (4) contradictory desires and fragmented experiences and subjectivities shaping subaltern claims to space; and (5) identity-based violence and exclusion in displacement processes. The first section surveys the major development agents and national policies that have advanced a financialised form of urbanisation, causing large-scale displacement in and around cities. The second discusses how informality and ambiguity operates as a system for governing cities that offers states the flexibility to allow *de facto* tenure and compensation to the urban poor while also facilitating slum clearances for (often illegal) world-city development projects. The third section examines how changing articulations of elite and middle-class mobilisation and participation infuse governing regimes with new mechanisms and logics of enclosure. The next section follows De Angelis's (2004) proposition that social mobilisations to counter or mitigate the effects of dispossession are part and parcel of the ongoing character of primitive accumulation. Here, I address how diverse subaltern mobilisations and desires and uneven accommodations made by states and other entities play a critical role in trajectories of urban transformation. Finally, I examine the ways that xenophobic identity politics and social differentiation among the poor serve to legitimise and enable the most severe forms of displacement and dispossession. Vasudevan, McFarlane and Jeffrey's (2008) 'spaces of enclosure' framework is useful for understanding all of these aspects of urbanisation by shifting the focus from systemic over-accumulation, crisis and dispossession to 'the multiple ways in which "enclosure" has been and continues to be implemented and resisted' (Vasudevan et al, 2008, p 1642). This attention to the relationship between dispossession and subjectification makes visible the 'differential consequences of enclosure for different social groups' (Vasudevan et al, 2008, p 1643), as well as the critical new convergences of governance, territoriality and subjectivity that shape urban transformation in India.

Urban policy: post-colonial developmentalism and financialisation

In the domain of recent national policy, urban developmentalism – much like rural interventions – operates through large-scale projects that are increasingly debt-financed. For instance, the Jawaharlal Nehru National Urban Renewal Mission (JNNURM), inaugurated by Prime Minister Manmohan Singh in 2005, aimed to leverage billions of dollars in public and private finance to help Indian cities modernise their urban infrastructure to world-class standards. JNNURM introduced an urban territorial dimension to the economic liberalisation policies launched in the early 1990s. Through JNNURM, the World Bank and other international finance institutions and firms provided supplemental financing of over USD11 billion to over USD20 billion in central government funding. Such high-priority, debt-financed projects often entail large-scale displacements of subaltern groups in order to beautify cities and make room for infrastructure and land uses geared to the elites and upper-middle classes. They have supported a broad range of 'world-class' city building ambitions aimed at promoting key globally connected industries, elite recreation and consumption centres, high-end commercial and residential real estate, and the infrastructural services (roads, airports, water, power, etc) to support them (Baindur and Kamath, 2009). This national agenda for urban development has had different trajectories and political lives across Indian cities.

For instance, in India's densely populated finance capital, Mumbai, world-class roads and bridges, railways, clustered and piecemeal slum redevelopment projects, and environmental preservation schemes mean big business in a city known for extremely expensive and volatile land markets. Here, slum occupants, developers, international finance institutions, corporations, NGOs and a variety of state agents both struggle and collaborate with each other, leading to highly uneven trajectories of development, displacement and dispossession. In Bangalore, as Goldman (2011) has argued, world-city projects amount to a frenzy of state-supported speculative activity entailing the displacement of large numbers of rural inhabitants who cannot prove clear ownership or are pressured to sell their land for a small fraction of its market value. As India's self-proclaimed 'Silicon Valley', Bangalore's information technology (IT) industry has served as the main impetus and justification for government land acquisition in the rural periphery (Nair, 2005; Goldman, 2011). Ironically, Bangalore's IT-focused world-city development projects have also undercut a vast informal economy (including food processing, textiles, manufacturing and services) that employs the majority of the city's population and provides 50–75% of its gross domestic product (GDP) (Benjamin,

2000, 2004). Calcutta and medium-sized cities like Chennai have also adopted mini-Silicon Valley ambitions that have justified peri-urban land grabs. Urban transformation in and around Delhi includes lucrative sprawling developments of business complexes and high-class residential and consumption spaces, as well as special priority projects like those linked to the Commonwealth Games (Dupont, 2011). However, world-class city-making in Delhi also confounds economistic readings of urban change by advancing displacement-inducing projects that do not accrue direct gains for specific groups (Dupont, 2008), but rather support an elite-biased world-class urban aesthetic (Ghertner, 2010).

Aside from direct state-backed land usurpation, there are a number of other indirect ways that investment (and speculation) on infrastructure and real estate can cause the displacement of lower-income groups. For instance, many projects (whether financed through public or private sources) have accompanied mandatory liberalisation reforms that have dovetailed with and reinforced long-standing recommendations and loan conditionalities made by the World Bank and Asian Development Bank (Baindur and Kamath, 2009). Although the emphasis of restructuring and reform has varied across cities, they have broadly included the liberalisation of land markets through the rollback of laws controlling rent and concentration of land ownership, public–private partnerships, property tax reform, and the aggressive leveraging of private finance. These reforms have unleashed formal and informal land and housing markets in ways that threaten lower-income groups' capacity to stay in their neighbourhoods. Another indirect means of displacement that resembles gentrification is ironically through slum upgrading and the provision of basic services and infrastructure for low-income residents. While these meagre pro-poor urban programmes are much needed, Desai and Loftus (2013) remind us of the dangers of 'speculating on slums' and the under-studied phenomenon of informal renting and landlordism. They argue that infrastructural improvements in slums may cause the displacement of the poorest renters, who are squeezed out by relatively better-off lower-middle-class residents offering higher rents or purchasing prices for housing in physically improved settlements. As the first phase of JNNURM comes to a close, a number of new national initiatives are under way that promise both urban services and housing for the poor and world-class infrastructure and commercial and residential development for wealthier classes – a flip-flopping paradigm of 'deliberate policy confusion' according to Mahadevia (2011). In this way, development institutions and policies have been refashioned in the service of capital accumulation in Indian cities but also remain flexible enough to meet political pressures across class constituencies. Such political scenarios suggest the need to go beyond formal policy to address the crucial role of informality and flexible governance as key constitutive elements of development and displacement.

Informality and flexible governance

In Indian cities, like in post-colonial cities around the world, urban neighbourhoods are settled informally and recognised and administered through hybrid, contradictory and ambiguous sets of legal mechanisms and state practices. Informal slum settlement is most often understood to originate with development-induced poverty and migration from the countryside to peripheral urban lands. Residents make incremental improvements to their neighbourhoods through their own investments and through political arrangements with local officials. Slum residents obtain informal and formal access to vital services, as well as temporary de facto tenure arrangements that are, of course, never completely guaranteed. The politics of negotiating needs and contesting evictions in informal settlements has produced strong neighbourhood-based movements and organisations. However, it is a mistake to see informality as limited to spaces occupied by the poor or as a simple vestige of inefficiency that might be overturned by formalisation and titling, as scholars like De Soto (2003) have famously argued. Rather, Roy and Alsayyad (2004) posit that informality is better understood as a 'way of life' – a zone of flexibility and negotiation (especially in terms of land use and access) for all classes, albeit on unequal terms. Developers, elite and middle-class groups, and even state agencies have been known to subvert existing laws to build illegal structures that are subsequently regularised by authorities. Indeed, in the arena of urban redevelopment, wealthier classes have claimed and developed lands with the tacit approval and active assistance of state agents, often breaking zoning regulations with impunity (Ghertner, 2008). State agents and developers also often undertake projects with the support of organised crime syndicates (Weinstein, 2008).

These complex cross-class politics are the focus of several theories of flexible urban governance and critiques of the rubric of 'planning' that are relevant to understanding elite-biased urban transformations in India. For instance, Gururani's (2013) study of the city of Gurgaon, a business and elite enclave on the outskirts of Delhi, reveals the ways that planners and power brokers engage in sanctioned illegality to create bourgeois (neo)liberal urban space in India. Focusing on the dubious processes of land acquisition for development, she writes:

> flexible planning encompasses a range of political techniques through which exemptions are routinely made, plans redrawn, compromises made, and brute force executed. It is not a random act but has a cultural logic that offers access to material and discursive maneuvers of state power, legal and extra-legal networks, and relations of influence. (Gururani, 2013, p 121)

Similarly, Nair (2013) shows how the 'pliability of law' has meant that political struggles to 'regularise' extra-legally settled areas is a principal, albeit contradictory, job of planning authorities in Bangalore. This work refutes the culturalist cliche that India is somehow incapable of 'getting it right' in relation to planning.

Rather, these examples corroborate Roy's (2009) contention that planning is structurally impossible because informality operates as a deregulated – rather than an unregulated – system. Here, ambiguous and shifting land tenure arrangements allow for a flexible 'mode of regulation' through which, for example, state authorities tacitly encourage squatting in exchange for electoral support and also usurp land for developmental purposes. Thus, informality is not simply an exploitative or a subversive domain inhabited and suffered by the urban poor. Rather, states and elites participate and make use of informal land systems for their own developmental agendas, what Roy calls 'informality from above' (Roy, 2009, p 84). This does not mean that all groups experience informality on the same terms. To the extent that informality is an arena of negotiated livelihood and social reproduction, it is also fundamentally constitutive of class and other axes of differentiation, dispossession and marginalisation in Indian cities. The terms of engaging informal systems are shaped by the relative political and economic capacity to legitimate competing land claims under both the law and extra-legal domains. This means that sometimes developmentalist projects are also thwarted by a variety of mobilisations in popular neighbourhoods. In other words, urban power relations are ultimately expressed through uneven positionings within a political terrain contoured by informal property and labour regimes, but not categorically defined by them. Thus, while governments, international development agents and slum residents themselves espouse formalised housing, legal strategies may not actually solve the problem of marginalisation and may, in fact, deepen inequalities across and within classes. In this way, deregulated governance is one important key to understanding how elite and middle-class power to usurp urban space is secured in and beyond the state, a topic to which I will now turn.

World-class cities, upper-class states

A number of studies on Indian cities indicate that the character of local governance has shifted as state agencies facilitate world-city projects and land enclosures. Avenues for elite and middle-class participation have increased alongside the declining power of locally elected municipal bodies, which the working classes primarily utilise to access their needs. Indian urban politics has long corroborated Castells's (1983) classic theory on struggles for 'collective consumption', which demarcated how the urban poor living in informal settlements in Latin American cities negotiated for state provision of temporary tenure security and services in exchange for *en masse* vote delivery. Such patronage-based relationships between local officials and the urban poor enabled working-class influence in urban governance, albeit on less than democratic terms. In recent years, however, these arenas of popular participation have been sidelined by a number of hybrid elite-driven institutions and mechanisms for redevelopment. Modalities of gentrified governance vary across and within Indian cities, ranging from new legal mechanisms and fast-track access to state bodies for developers, corporate and financial elites, and middle-class residential groups to highly centralised bureaucratic urban development agencies. They represent a convergence of two processes: (1) a neoliberal state developmentalism geared towards promoting cities as globally integrated 'growth engines' of the nation (as addressed in the previous section); and (2) new citizen demands to improve urban environments through the enclosing of public lands and removing of the urban poor. The later phenomenon is rooted in the rising power of India's 'new middle classes', who continue to benefit from the economic liberalisation policies launched in the 1990s (Corbridge and Harriss, 2000). These urban consumer-citizens have attained visibility in both national and local political discourse as vanguards of a liberalising India, often positioning themselves as the new 'common man' in opposition to the kind of populist politics associated with post-independence development (Fernandes, 2004; Ray and Katzenstein, 2005). Along with non-resident Indians (NRIs) living abroad, they have fuelled urban real estate development through demands for world-class infrastructure and recreational, residential and consumption spaces. Elite and middle-class power in the state is manifest through a number of different mechanisms.

For instance, in Delhi, the juridical arm of the state has superseded planning agencies and municipal bodies by increasingly ruling in favour of upper-class demands for slum clearance in recent years. One lynchpin legal mechanism that has translated upper- and middle-class interests into court rulings is the Public Interest Litigation (PIL). Bhan (2009, p 133, emphasis added) argues that:

> PILs opened up the door to 'ordinary citizens' to approach the highest courts of the land in matters of public interest either to '... *espouse the cause of the poor and oppressed (representative standing) or to [seek] enforce[ment] [of] performance of public duties (citizen standing)*'.

Despite the gesture to empower 'poor and oppressed' groups, it is middle-class residents' associations that have filed the vast majority of such litigations. Middle-class activism and desires for 'green and slum-free' cities constitute what Baviskar (2003) has called 'bourgeois environmentalism'. Courts have followed suit in upholding their demands for rapid and large-scale slum clearance on grounds of environmental pollution and nuisance (Ghertner, 2008). Throughout Indian cities, including Chennai, Mumbai and Ahmedabad, judicial bodies and other state agencies have also ordered slum clearances along urban waterways and river basins based on dubious environmental logics (Coelho and Raman, 2010; Desai, 2012a; Doshi, 2013b). These forms of juridified slum clearance have eroded meagre protections for slum residents exemplified by the Olga Tellis vs Bombay Municipal Corporation case of 1985. In this case, the Supreme Court ruled that slum demolitions infringed the fundamental right to life protected by the Indian constitution because people lived in slums in order to be near their livelihoods.

Enclosure has also been facilitated by newly empowered 'parastatal' agencies that have taken up the helm of eminent domain for various world-city schemes. Harkening back to expert-driven developmental state bureaucracies, parastatals are quasi-public agencies made up of planning, engineering or finance professionals who have been appointed by state government ministers to raise capital and implement major urban infrastructure projects. Parastatals retain the privilege of being shielded from the vagaries of electoral politics because their heads are directly appointed by state-level ministers for high-priority urban projects. Parastatal entities' increasing involvement in urban real estate and development processes has marginalised elected bodies and other relatively more accountable forms of local government. For instance, in Bangalore, powerful internationally and nationally financed parastatal agencies represent the prime movers and shakers overseeing the city's 'Comprehensive Development Plan' and negotiating land acquisitions for projects. This extra-democratic power is evidenced by the fact that even as Bangalore's city limits have tripled to include seven peripheral towns and 103 villages, municipal elections were suspended between 2006 and 2010 (Goldman, 2011). Other institutions bestowed with the privilege of bypassing the electoral system in Bangalore include expert commissions and taskforces made up of representatives from middle-class citizen action groups, chief executive officers (CEOs) from IT and biotech industries, NGO leaders, and senior government officials. Such groups privilege the upper classes with fast-tracked, exclusive access to key state agents in the planning and implementation process to ensure that projects meet their needs.

In Mumbai, the governing structures of redevelopment projects are similarly designed to bypass political obstacles posed by the urban poor through delimiting the role of the municipal corporation. For instance, Dharavi – a vast area of prime real estate in Mumbai infamously known as 'Asia's largest slum' – has been designated as a high-priority 'clustered redevelopment' project and relegated to an entirely separate governance structure under the auspices of a Mumbai-born developer residing in Long Island, New York. Furthermore, groups like 'Bombay First' – a city-boosting advocacy group made up of Mumbai's top corporate leaders and developers – attained exclusive influence in state planning processes by contracting the transnational consulting firm McKinsey to produce a comprehensive city development plan called 'Vision Mumbai' (Bombay First and McKinsey, 2003). This remarkably thin document introduced little new to the development agenda but was nonetheless adopted in its entirety by the state of Maharashtra as the new city development plan in 2004. In so doing, the state legitimated the role of such groups in urban planning. Elite narratives praise this manner of halting 'vote bank politics', which is despised for delaying and thwarting world-city projects. Even as the channels of the state are increasingly usurped by privileged classes in these ways, subaltern groups have also mobilised through NGOs, social movements and lower-level state agents to resist, negotiate or accommodate to developmental urban transformations, with highly uneven outcomes.

The politics of the displaced

Questions about the agency of the urban poor in the space of informal slum settlements are the subject of a rich and influential body of work in Indian city contexts. By demanding paradigm shifts in understandings of urban democracy and popular politics, studies of subaltern mobilisation are significant to the post-colonial analysis of Indian urbanisation. These analyses go beyond simplistic understandings of resistance against displacement and dispossession to explore less overt 'everyday' forms of negotiation and subversion, as well as thorny questions of desire, accommodation and consent to uneven development. Two authors drawing on Foucaultian framings, Appadurai (2001) and Chatterjee (2004), demonstrate how groups of slum residents and their representatives deploy governmental categories and technologies to access critical needs, including resettlement compensation. Chatterjee has coined the term 'political society' to demarcate these kinds of relationships among states, NGOs and slum dwellers in gentrifying Calcutta. The 'politics of the governed', Chatterjee cautions us, operates very differently from bourgeois-dominated civil society. The property-less urban poor, he argues, do not make claims to land and resources as rights-bearing citizens of a modern nation because they live outside of the purview of the law in informal settlements. Therefore, they must access needs by leveraging informal relationships, creating community solidarity and making moral appeals to development and welfare agencies. The urban poor draw on variety of categories – slum dweller, project affected person and so on – that demarcate them as governable 'vulnerable populations' rather than as citizens. He argues that these 'rumblings of the street' fuse the 'demands of electoral mobilization, on the one hand, and the logic of welfare distribution, on the other' (Chatterjee, 2004, p 135). Thus, these mobilisations of slum residents facing eviction are political, according to Chatterjee, but not in the same way as bourgeois civil society actions (including PLIs) because they do not originate from modern rights claims. Numerous studies of mobilisation in Indian cities corroborate and challenge the political society framework for understanding popular urban politics. For instance, some scholars critique the idea that subaltern subjects necessarily practise a singular politics shaped solely by their illegal conditions of life, while others point to the myriad ways that the ostensibly 'civil' bourgeoisie regularly violate laws and use political networks to accomplish their goals (see Baviskar and Sundar, 2008). Research on slum redevelopment in Mumbai reveals how slum residents have acquiesced and sometimes even embraced slum clearance in exchange for the promise of improved living and legitimacy offered by resettlement into formalised tenements. These studies indicate the need to rework Chatterjee's framework to address the diverse 'bourgeois-like' aspirations and modalities of the politics of subaltern groups and their representatives (Anand and Rademacher, 2011; Doshi, 2013a).

In this regard, Appadurai (2001) celebrates social mobilisations in Mumbai that have gone beyond limited patron–client relations with political parties to offer concrete 'bottom-up' solutions for and by the poor. Appadurai examines the work of the Society for the Promotion of Area Resource Centres (SPARC) Alliance – a world-renowned group consisting of an NGO and two grassroots organisations of current and former slum-dwelling women and men – through the optimistic lens of 'deep democracy' and governmentality 'from below'. He argues that SPARC has produced long-lasting and substantive changes through a slow and steady approach of non-confrontational participation – what he calls 'the politics of patience' – to counter the processes of invisibilisation, party-based clientelism and eviction. These organised groups of slum residents are characterised by the active and extensive participation of women. They work with middle-class NGO staff to collect data about slums through self-enumeration and participatory mapping activities to ensure that state agencies meet their needs for slum-based amenities and resettlement. SPARC leaders have also forged transnational linkages with both development agencies and shack dwellers' groups around the world, which Appadurai (2001) interprets as a horizontal form of globalisation. Despite their differences, both Chatterjee and Appadurai posit that subaltern engagement with governmental welfare and development institutions operates most effectively through intermediaries with close organic ties in morally constituted communities of slum dwellers. Yet, such practices of mobilisation and accommodation have also allowed for a deeper penetration of market forces, as neoliberal slum redevelopment policies and partnerships have yielded substantially to the interests of developers and financiers.

Furthermore, as I have argued elsewhere (Doshi, 2012, 2013a), such contradictions of market-based inclusion reveal a blind spot in both Chatterjee's and Appadurai's readings of slum mobilisations and governance that has to do with a lack of sufficient critical attention to the neoliberal development politics of gendered and identity-based difference. In Mumbai, for instance, women's participation in SPARC Alliance resettlement activities has drawn on naturalised roles of women as non-confrontational community caretakers – based on both feminised participatory development discourse and cultural ideals of womanhood linked to their social reproductive roles as 'mothers' and 'housewives'. These forms of gendered neoliberal participation have silenced men and women slum dwellers' discontent and dissent in relation to difficult off-site resettlement. Ironically, while women have benefitted from resettlement housing and sanitation, those who must work outside of the home have suffered the serious repercussions of increasing commute times and job loss. Thus, while Appadurai (2001) celebrates the role of women as the 'moral core' of the 'politics of patience', it is also true that such practices have facilitated cooperation with elite-biased development and obscured deepening class-, gender- and identity-based inequalities and exclusions embedded in market-oriented processes. Partial and feminised notions of women's needs and participation and gendered disciplining have resulted in new forms of dispossession throughout the urban landscape (Doshi, 2012, 2013a). Such processes indicate the need to link urban studies in India to post-colonial development literatures that have critiqued strategies of empowerment through gendered participation. A number of other conflicts have exposed similar contradictions of market-oriented practices of ostensibly inclusionary development and compensation. For instance, efforts to turn the famed Dharavi slum into an upscale residential and commercial complex in the heart of Mumbai have been vigorously contested due to the project's lack of attention to working-class livelihood concerns and the problem of uneven or inadequate compensation (Weinstein, 2009).

Even in less outwardly participatory state-driven slum clearance and development projects, the politics of the displaced remains a significant, though problematic, force. For instance, in Ahmedabad, as Desai (2012a) explains, a river basin slum clearance project was advanced through a 'politics of cooptation by inclusion' (Desai, 2012a, p 52), whereby state agents advanced an elite-biased project while also accommodating the needs of some affected slum residents through flexible governing mechanisms. Although the project began with promises of environmental improvements and protection from flooding through resettlement for all displaced groups, it ended up benefitting only a portion of project-affected people with onsite resettlement compensation. Key to the process was a flexible governing regime characterised by multiple and shifting terrains of compensation, fragmentary evictions, and piecemeal resettlement. 'In this manner', Desai (2012a, p 55) argues, 'state authorities pursued an ambivalent approach vis-à-vis the urban poor, engaging in multiple and competing practices as well as shifting practices according to their own changing calculations and in response to changing external pressures'.

Benjamin (2008) offers yet another alternative rubric, which he calls 'occupancy urbanism', to address the less visible ways that the urban poor challenge displacement. Occupancy urbanism is defined as a mode of subaltern politics that subverts developmental state programmes that delimit poverty alleviation to 'basic needs' in order to secure elite-biased projects through the depoliticised permissible spaces of inclusion demarcated by NGOs. He takes issue with positions that dismiss 'vote bank' politics – practices ill-defined as 'patron–clientelism' through which poor groups lay 'claim to public investments in basic infrastructure and services via a ground-up process focused on land and economy in return for guaranteed access to voter lists in municipal elections' (Benjamin, 2008, p 719). Benjamin argues that, instead, occupancy urbanism places ethnographic focus on land as an arena of 'stealth-like and quiet, but extensive forms of political consciousness' (Benjamin, 2008, p 720). Drawing on specific land histories from Mumbai, Delhi and Bangalore, Benjamin (2008) argues that elite development projects are consistently subverted as subaltern groups forge connections with state agents (police, middle- and lower-level bureaucrats, municipal politicians, etc) to encroach on land designated for 'world-class' projects, going as far as to reoccupy eviction sites. In this way, occupancy urbanism eschews the notion that gentrified urban developmentalism is a foregone conclusion.

Goldman (2011) offers an additional, less hopeful, concept of speculative citizenship emerging as (soon-to-be) displaced slum residents, farmers and other groups in Bangalore are forced to wager on when and how to sell their land to a flurry of brokers offering meagre resettlement packages or lower-than-market value for their property. Similarly, in Mumbai, redevelopment schemes have brought developers and elected officials (acting as brokers) into negotiations with slum leaders to relinquish their homes in exchange for high-rise resettlement compensation (sometimes on-site for the lucky few, but most often in distant peripheral localities). The privileging of market imperatives has meant that slums must go, but only some displaced slum dwellers gain access to adequate, nearby resettlement. Such forms of speculative citizenship mean that slum dwellers live in state of anxiety, not knowing whether brokers will deliver on the benefits they promise or if they will be swindled. As skewed as this power dynamic of 'public–private partnerships' is (slum dwellers are regularly strong-armed into signing consent forms), those receiving compensation are relatively privileged over the many thousands of evictees excluded via eligibility criteria, loopholes and discriminatory practices embedded within policy frameworks and in everyday city life. Thus, although the category of slum dwellers demarcates class-based spatial differentiation, subaltern groups do not experience and engage with urban transformation homogeneously. The (imperfect) promise of inclusive development is also undergirded by a more sinister politics of community marked by identity-based violence and xenophobic exclusion.

Dispossession through difference

Urban transformation in India has been characterised by the convergence of political-economic processes of development and the cultural politics of identity-based violence, dispossession and socio-spatial marginalisation. Although modern South Asian history has long been marked by elite Hindu movements, economic liberalisation in the 1990s has been associated with an eruption of Hindu nationalist politics and increasing ethno-religious communal tensions in cities throughout India (Corbridge and Harriss, 2000). In the early 1990s, a slew of urban riots were set off by events in the distant northern Indian town of Ayodhya, where militant Hindu nationalist groups embarked on the demolition of the famed Babri mosque in an effort to reclaim the supposed birth site of a Hindu god. The event articulated with already-existing communal tensions, as well as pressures to reclaim land for world-city projects, resulting in large-scale damage and suffering, particularly in low-income Muslim neighbourhoods. Thousands were killed and raped and many more were displaced by the destruction of businesses and residential property. Since then, enduring discrimination, periodic riots and targeted evictions in minority communities has compounded ethno-religious segregation across Indian cities in a number of ways. Muslims throughout Indian cities have especially faced formidable challenges in finding both housing and employment. They routinely experience housing discrimination in desirable central city locations due to a variety of barriers, ranging from linguistic restrictions to false-pretence vegetarian-only mandates imposed by Hindu-majority housing societies. With successive bouts of rioting, Muslim residents have also voluntarily moved into ethnic enclave neighbourhoods as a measure of protection. Self-selected segregation is especially prevalent in slum resettlement colonies where formerly diverse neighbourhoods have chosen to sort themselves into buildings by religion and caste (Gupte, 2012). Ghettoised neighbourhoods have, in turn, experienced even greater vulnerability to disinvestment and neglect by government authorities that represent ethno-religious or linguistic majorities. Regionalist, ethnic and Hindu nationalist politics have territorialised in distinct ways throughout Indian cities, as I discuss later.

In Ahmedabad, the state-sanctioned anti-Muslim pogroms of 2002 and their aftermaths have reconfigured the city and given way to a new Hindu nationalist, regionalist and developmental urban imaginary. Desai's (2012b) discussion of the emergence of entrepreneurial strategies of city imagineering and place-making in Ahmedabad illustrates how boosters have attempted to distance the city from its reputation as a violent and unsafe place. These projects of redevelopment and rehabilitation of the region have drawn on majority citizens' sentiments of Hindu identity, nationalism and Gujarati and civic urban pride to bolster a sense of economic and cultural vibrancy. A flurry of unleashed projects has caused extensive material dispossession and displacement of Muslims from coveted central city spaces. The symbolic erasure of the presence of the Muslim body in the new urban imaginary of Ahmedabad has gone hand in hand with material dispossession and displacement. These processes have also served to legitimate the very dictatorial regime that has perpetuated past and ongoing anti-Muslim violence and exclusion.

In Mumbai, the political economy of urban deindustrialisation, economic liberalisation and redevelopment has also articulated with xenophobic violence to produce both the symbolic and material erasure of Muslim (and, more recently, ethnic North Indian) bodies from urban space. In particular, the Shiv Sena – a grassroots regionalist and Hindu nationalist movement cum political party that defies simple characterisation – played a central role in Mumbai's 1993 communal riots that led to the loss of thousands of lives and untold economic damage in poor and Muslim neighbourhoods throughout the city (Hansen, 2001; Chatterji and Mehta, 2007). Appadurai (2000) has cogently argued that the Shiv Sena 'sutured a specific form of regional chauvinism with a national message about Hindu power through the deployment of the figure of the Muslim as the archetype of the invader, the stranger, and the traitor' (Appadurai, 2000, p 646). From media campaigns to neighbourhood-based organising, the Shiv Sena and more recent spin-off parties regularly conflate Muslims, North Indians and slum dwellers as predatory invaders. These violent discourses of scapegoating outsiders have been both supple and powerful enough to rally hegemonic support among diverse audiences (Masselos and Patel, 2005). The work of Shiv Sena has been to rewrite urban struggles over space and the city itself as a Hindu nationalist geographical imaginary, the ethnically cleansed dream space of a global India writ large on the city. Elsewhere, I have argued (Doshi, 2013a) that this articulation of land and housing struggles with xenophobic identity politics has entailed the embedding of ethno-nationalist ideologies of belonging into neoliberal slum redevelopment policy and practice. This is markedly evident in the implementation of market-based resettlement projects based on a seemingly 'win–win' model, where developers provide resettlement high-rise flats in exchange for rights to build commercial-rate residences on prime real estate. However, compensation eligibility is restricted through policy mechanisms such as the 'cut-off date' – which in the case of Mumbai excludes 'illegal' slum residents and structures that cannot furnish proof of existence prior to 1 January 1995. The cut-off date invokes a practically useful and symbolically powerful distinction between legal and illegal (read: legitimate and illegitimate) slums, allowing states and developers to evade the responsibility for compensating all who are displaced by redevelopment projects. Although exclusions are linked to a variety of factors beyond ethno-religious identity, the logics of rightful belonging to the space of the city *qua* nation has served to justify both targeted evictions in minority settlements and unevenly distributed resettlement compensation.

Even in Calcutta – long thought of as a secular city in which Hindus and Muslims live in relative harmony – aspects of communalism also shape access to urban space. Sanyal (2014) describes a scenario of 'Hindu hegemony' in Calcutta, whereby Hindus drawing on simplified narratives of migration linked to the post-independence partition of India and East and West Pakistan imagine having rights to Muslim-occupied spaces in the city. She argues that 'emptying areas of Muslim inhabitants meant that those who were being displaced by incoming refugees had to go "elsewhere"' (Sanyal, 2014). This process constitutes a scenario of 'double displacement', where those who are displaced go on to displace others. Such battles over citizenship and space complicate singular class-based analyses and suggest the need to attend to the cultural politics and fragmented subjectivities that shape and challenge efforts to advance more just cities.

Conclusion: whither the 'right to the city'?

This chapter has offered a complement to theories of gentrification through the prism of Indian cities by focusing on distinct processes of development, displacement and dispossession. Examples from scholarship on Indian cities show how post-colonial modalities of urban rule and subjectivity shape capitalist accumulation and displacement. In particular, they reveal how developmentalism, informality and flexible governance, elite power in state apparatuses, subaltern desires and political participation, and xenophobic politics fundamentally contour processes of urban transformation. In this way, I have argued that understanding socio-spatial transformation in Indian cities requires a processual analysis of *how* public space is enclosed rather than simply the outcome of class-based displacement. Indeed, most studies of urban transformation in India use concepts other than 'gentrification' because urban transformation in India has advanced through a different set of extra-economic processes and conditions. As such, this chapter endeavours to address dispossessing urbanisation and displacement in Indian cities without offering a new Indian ideal-type of gentrification. Resisting the notion of an Indian-style gentrification is crucial not only for more accurate analyses, but also for effective political practice. In post-colonial India, the 'right to the city' may not adequately serve as a universal rallying cry because of the complex and uneven political entanglements of elite world-class city-making practices and the politics of subaltern groups who embrace, resist and rework projects in diverse ways. Here, the (often broken) promise of development and enduring 'will to improve' (Li, 2007) maintains a political stronghold across class. For instance, some groups aspiring to more than 'the right to the slum' wager on the risky possibility of improved living through resettlement, despite the unequal and elite-biased terms upon which such compensation may be delivered. In this way, subaltern claims may target the 'right to benefit from city development plans' (Arputham and Patel, 2010) rather than an anti-capitalist 'right to the city'. These contradictory mobilisations complicate notions of resistance and suggest that insurgency does not necessarily lead to more just cities (Roy, 2009), as many continue to be severely excluded and dispossessed by violent state and non-state forces. Nonetheless, in response to popular discontent over the vastly inadequate government attention to affordable urban housing, a new national policy, the Rajiv Awas Yojana, promises to channel resources for services, resettlement and *in situ* slum-upgrading projects. Despite these pro-poor gestures, there remains the danger that concessions like resettlement or slum 'regularisation' (a recognition of settlements that allows legal access to services and compensation) 'constantly appear as a favor bestowed on violators rather than as a right demanded from the state' (Nair, 2013, p 54). Thus, the accommodation politics of the poor and their representatives may support and perpetuate dispossessing regimes of rule and enduring inequalities. Under these conditions, questions remain as to how extensively new governmental programmes targeting the poor will deliver on progressive urban change.

The aspects of urban transformation outlined in this chapter can also serve to re-engage with (and rethink) the more-than-economic aspects of gentrification in the Global North. For instance, my discussion of dispossession through difference in Indian cities demonstrates outcomes similar to whitening or even the incidence of 'marginal gentrifiers' (see Lees et al, 2010), even if they operate through different modalities of extra-economic force and formal and informal sovereignty (Hansen and Stepputat, 2006) in India. Indeed, the post-colonial politics of nation and belonging are as alive and well in London's redevelopment as they are in Mumbai's, as Jacobs (2002) reminds us. Recent work on redevelopment in US cities, in turn, points to new ways of conceiving 'race-class' (Brahinsky, 2013) as co-constitutive processes that may prove useful to scholarship on urban India. The flexible and ambiguous regimes of governance characteristic of Indian cities can also speak to the contradictory and opaque strategies of both encouraging and persecuting undocumented labour forces deemed as illegal. That these groups are attacked in and displaced from their residences and other spaces of social reproduction present key concerns to theories of gentrification and rights to the city (see Varsanyi, 2008). Furthermore, and finally, much like the participatory speculative development schemes of the South (Goldman, 2011; Doshi, 2013a), the sub-prime mortgage crisis in the US attests to how the enrolment of lower-income groups and people of colour into neoliberal housing markets can deepen and expand inequality and dispossession (Wyly et al, 2006).

There is also a need for further research into some under-studied aspects of unequal urbanisation within India. For instance, most of the scholarly literature is on India's mega-cities but emerging demographic dynamics point to the need for more attention to rapidly growing small- and medium-sized cities and towns. These urban spaces often have less capacity to generate development support funds from government sources like JNNURM and continue to have high levels of poverty (Kundu and Sarangi, 2007). Studies of Indian urbanisation and urbanism must also connect more intensively to questions of employment as world-class city-building, the destruction not only of centrally located housing, but also vital economic activities that provide livelihoods and low-cost goods and services for working-class urban citizens. This happens through the criminalisation of informal street vendors (Anjaria, 2009), as well as through slum clearances that demolish the factories and micro-businesses that serve and employ the urban poor in informal settlements (Benjamin, 2000). Struggles over livelihoods and the need to nurture pro-poor economies represent an important silence in programmes that focus only on housing and services for the poor. These are some of the contentious fault lines that will likely push the 'right to benefit from city development plans' into new and hopefully more just and emancipatory terrains.

References

Anand, N. and Rademacher, A. (2011) 'Housing in the urban age: inequality and aspiration in Mumbai', *Antipode*, vol 43, pp 1748–72.

Anjaria, J.S. (2009) 'Guardians of the bourgeois city: citizenship, public space, and middle-class activism in Mumbai', *City and Community*, vol 8, pp 391–406.

Appadurai, A. (2000) 'Spectral housing and urban cleansing: notes on millennial Mumbai', *Public Culture*, vol 12, pp 627–51.

Appadurai, A. (2001) 'Deep democracy: urban governmentality and the horizon of politics', *Environment and Urbanization*, vol 13, pp 23–43.

Arputham, J. and Patel, S. (2010) 'Recent developments in plans for Dharavi and for the airport slums in Mumbai', *Environment and Urbanization*, vol 22, pp 501–4.

Baindur, V. and Kamath, L. (2009) *Reengineering urban infrastructure: how the World Bank and Asian Development Bank shape urban infrastructure finance and governance in India*, Mumbai: Bank Information Centre South Asia.

Banerjee-Guha, S. (ed) (2010) *Accumulation by dispossession: transformative cities in the new global order*, New Delhi: Sage.

Baviskar, A. (2003) 'Between violence and desire: space, power, and identity in the making of metropolitan Delhi', *International Social Science Journal*, vol 55, pp 89–98.

Baviskar, A. and Sundar, N. (2008) 'Democracy versus economic transformation?', *Economic and Political Weekly*, vol 43, pp 87–9.

Benjamin, S. (2000) 'Governance, economic settings and poverty in Bangalore', *Environment and Urbanization*, vol 12, pp 35–56.

Benjamin, S. (2004) 'Urban land transformation for pro-poor economies', *Geoforum*, vol 35, pp 177–87.

Benjamin, S. (2008) 'Occupancy urbanism: radicalizing politics and economy beyond policy and programs', *International Journal of Urban and Regional Research*, vol 32, pp 719–29.

Bhan, G. (2009) '"This is no longer the city I once knew": evictions, the urban poor and the right to the city in millennial Delhi', *Environment and Urbanization*, vol 21, pp 127–42.

Bombay First and McKinsey (2003) *Vision Mumbai: transforming Mumbai into a world class city by 2013*, Mumbai: Bombay First and McKinsey Corporation.

Brahinsky, R. (2013) 'Race and the making of Southeast San Francisco: towards a theory of race-class', *Antipode*, online, DOI: 10.1111/anti.12050/abstract.

Castells, M. (1983) *The city and the grassroots: a cross-cultural theory of urban social movements*, Berkeley, CA: University of California Press.

Chatterjee, P. (2004) *The politics of the governed: reflections on popular politics in most of the world*, New York, NY: Columbia University Press.

Chatterji, R. and Mehta, D. (2007) *Living with violence: an anthropology of events and everyday life*, New Delhi: Routledge.

Coelho, K. and Raman, N. (2010) 'Salvaging and scapegoating: slum evictions on Chennai's waterways', *Economic and Political Weekly*, vol 45, pp 19–23.

Corbridge, S. and Harriss, J. (2000) *Reinventing India: liberalization, Hindu nationalism and popular democracy*, Cambridge: Polity Press.

De Angelis, M. (2004) 'Separating the doing and the deed: capital and the continuous character of enclosures', *Historical Materialism*, vol 12, pp 57–87.

Desai, R. (2012a) 'Governing the urban poor: riverfront development, slum resettlement and the politics of inclusion in Ahmedabad', *Economic and Political Weekly*, vol 47, pp 49–56.

Desai, R. (2012b) 'Entrepreneurial urbanism in the time of Hindutva: city imagineering, place marketing, and citizenship in Ahmedabad', in R. Desai and R. Sanyal (eds) *Urbanizing citizenship: contested spaces in Indian cities*, New Delhi: Sage, pp 31–57.

Desai, V. and Loftus, A. (2013) 'Speculating on slums: infrastructural fixes in informal housing in the Global South', *Antipode*, vol 45, pp 789–808.

De Soto, H. (2003) *The mystery of capital: why capitalism triumphs in the West and fails everywhere else* (reprint edn), New York, NY: Basic Books.

Doshi, S. (2012) 'The politics of persuasion: gendered slum citizenship in neoliberal Mumbai', in R. Desai and R. Sanyal (eds) *Urbanising citizenship: perspectives on contested spaces in Indian cities*, New Delhi: Sage, pp 82–108.

Doshi, S. (2013a) 'The politics of the evicted: redevelopment, subjectivity, and difference in Mumbai's slum frontier', *Antipode*, vol 45, pp 844–65.

Doshi, S. (2013b) 'Resettlement ecologies: environmental subjectivity and graduated citizenship in Mumbai', in A. Rademacher and K. Sivaramakrishnan (eds) *Ecologies of urbanism in India: metropolitan civility and sustainability*, Hong Kong: Hong Kong University Press, pp 225–48.

Dupont, V. (2008) 'Slum demolitions in Delhi since the 1990s: an appraisal', *Economic and Political Weekly*, vol 43, pp 79–87.

Dupont, V. (2011) 'The dream of Delhi as a global city', *International Journal of Urban and Regional Research*, vol 35, pp 533–54.

Fernandes, L. (2004) 'The politics of forgetting: class politics, state power and the restructuring of urban space in India', *Urban Studies*, vol 41, pp 2415–30.

Ghertner, D.A. (2008) 'Analysis of new legal discourse behind Delhi's slum demolitions', *Economic and Political Weekly*, vol 43, pp 57–66.

Ghertner, D.A. (2010) 'Calculating without numbers: aesthetic governmentality in Delhi's slums', *Economy and Society*, vol 39, pp 185–217.

Ghertner, D.A. (2014) 'India's urban revolution: geographies of displacement beyond gentrification', *Environment and Planning A*, vol 46, no 7, pp 1554-71.

Gidwani, V. and Baviskar, A. (2011) 'Urban commons', *Economic and Political Weekly*, vol 46, pp 42–3.

Goldman, M. (2011) 'Speculative urbanism and the making of the next world city', *International Journal of Urban and Regional Research*, vol 35, pp 555–81.

Gupte, J. (2012) 'Linking urban vulnerability, extralegal security, and civil violence: the case of the urban dispossessed in Mumbai', in R. Desai and R. Sanyal (eds) *Urbanizing citizenship: contested spaces in Indian cities*, New Delhi: Sage, pp 190–211.

Gururani, S. (2013) 'Flexible planning: the making of India's "Millennium City," Gurgaon', in A. Rademacher and K. Sivaramakrishnan (eds) *Ecologies of urbanism in India: metropolitan civility and sustainability*, Hong Kong: Hong Kong University Press, pp 119–44.

Hansen, T.B. (2001) *Wages of violence: naming and identity in postcolonial Bombay*, Princeton, NJ: Princeton University Press.

Hansen, T.B. and Stepputat, F. (2006) 'Sovereignty revisited', *Annual Review of Anthropology*, vol 35, pp 295–315.

Harris, A. (2008) 'From London to Mumbai and back again: gentrification and public policy in comparative perspective', *Urban Studies*, vol 45, pp 2407–28.

Harvey, D. (2003) *The new imperialism*, Oxford: Oxford University Press.

Jacobs, J.M. (2002) *Edge of empire: postcolonialism and the city*, London and New York, NY: Routledge.

Kundu, A. and Sarangi, N. (2007) 'Migration, employment status and poverty: an analysis across urban centres', *Economic and Political Weekly*, vol 42, pp 299–306.

Lees, L. (2012) 'The geography of gentrification: thinking through comparative urbanism', *Progress in Human Geography*, vol 36, pp 155–71.

Lees, L., Slater, T. and Wyly, E.K. (2010) *The gentrification reader*, London and New York, NY: Routledge.

Li, T.M. (2007) *The will to improve: governmentality, development, and the practice of politics*, Durham, NC: Duke University Press.

Mahadevia, D. (2011) 'Branded and renewed? Policies, politics and processes of urban development in the reform era', *Economic and Political Weekly*, vol 46, pp 56–64.

Masselos, J.C. and Patel, S. (2005) *Bombay and Mumbai: the city in transition*, New Delhi: Oxford University Press.

Nair, J. (2005) *The promise of the metropolis: Bangalore's 20th century*, New Delhi: Oxford University Press.

Nair, J. (2013) 'Is there an "Indian" urbanism?', in A.M. Rademacher and K. Sivaramakrishnan (eds) *Ecologies of urbanism in India: metropolitan civility and sustainability*, Hong Kong: Hong Kong University Press, pp 43–70.

Ray, R. and Katzenstein, M.F. (2005) *Social movements in India: poverty, power, and politics*, New York, NY: Rowman and Littlefield.

Roy, A. (2009) 'Why India cannot plan its cities: informality, insurgence and the idiom of urbanization', *Planning Theory*, vol 8, pp 76–87.

Roy, A. and AlSayyad, N. (2004) *Urban informality: transnational perspectives from the Middle East, Latin America, and South Asia*, Boulder, CO: Lexington Books.

Sanyal, R. (2014) 'Hindu space: urban dislocations in post-partition Calcutta', *Transactions of the Institute of British Geographers*, vol 39, no 1, pp 38-49.

Smith, N. (2002) 'New globalism, new urbanism: gentrification as global urban strategy', *Antipode*, vol 34, pp 427–50.

Varsanyi, M. (2008) 'Immigration policing through the backdoor: city ordinances, the "right to the city," and the exclusion of undocumented day laborers', *Urban Geography*, vol 29, pp 29–52.

Vasudevan, A., McFarlane, C. and Jeffrey, A. (2008) 'Spaces of enclosure', *Geoforum*, vol 39, pp 1641–6.

Weinstein, L. (2008) 'Mumbai's development mafias: globalization, organized crime and land development', *International Journal of Urban and Regional Research*, vol 32, pp 22–39.

Weinstein, L. (2009) 'Democracy in the globalizing Indian city: engagements of political society and the state in globalizing Mumbai', *Politics and Society*, vol 37, pp 397–427.

Whitehead, J. and More, N. (2007) 'Revanchism in Mumbai? Political economy of rent gaps and urban restructuring in a global city', *Economic and Political Weekly*, vol 42, pp 2428–34.

Wyly, E.K., Atia, M., Foxcroft, H., Hammel, D.J. and Phillips-Watts, K. (2006) 'American home: predatory mortgage capital and neighbourhood spaces of race and class exploitation in the United States', *Geografiska Annaler: Series B, Human Geography*, vol 88, pp 105–32.

SEVEN

The prospects of gentrification in downtown Cairo: artists, private investment and the neglectful state

Mohamed Elshahed

In December 2012, the Goethe Institute in downtown Cairo hosted a panel discussion titled 'Artists as Urban Catalysts in Downtown Cairo'. The event was organised by Beth Stryker and Omar Nagati, founders of the Cairo Laboratory for Urban Studies, Training and Environmental Research (CLUSTER). Invited panellists represented two types of stakeholders in downtown: property-owners (Karim Shafei, chief executive officer [CEO] of Al Ismaelia Real Estate Development; and Bruce Ferguson, Dean of the School of Humanities, representing the American University in Cairo [AUC]); and representatives of cultural organisations (Heba Farid, founding member of the Contemporary Image Collective; Ania Szremski, Townhouse Gallery curator; and Tamer El Said, filmmaker and co-founder of Cimatheque). The panel was moderated by the author of this chapter, who was selected by the organisers as the founder of Cairobserver.com, a blog dedicated to Cairo's urban affairs. The panel aimed to bring together the earlier-mentioned stakeholders in a public discussion to re-examine what the organisers called 'the classic appropriation of artists as catalysts for urban regeneration by real-estate developers seeking future gentrification', asking how things might play out differently in Cairo.[1]

Cairo does not offer an example of the emergence of state-led gentrification in the Global South; however, some aspects of conventional gentrification are present in the city but they have yet to produce the kinds of shifts in the urban community that have typically been considered in gentrification studies.[2] Prior to, and after, the 2011 revolution, the state has been focused on transforming the desert peripheries of Egyptian cities across the country into new urban developments where real estate speculation is made possible. Desert land, typically owned by the military, is given value by way of direct sale operations with private investors, who acquire large swathes of land previously unavailable on the market. Policymakers and private capital functioning within the formal economy have abandoned urban cores across Egypt and focused on the gated, privatised, suburban market.[3] The state has led expansionist-urbanising operations that build on policies of neglect governing the urban core, including the Egyptian capital's downtown. Despite the lack of policy or vision for its management or rehabilitation, downtown has attracted individuals including artists and activists, in addition to a few investors interested in urban regeneration and profit. However, because of the particular conditions in Cairo, which do not encourage conventional processes of gentrification, attempts to rehabilitate, renovate and restore otherwise underutilised or neglected spaces within the urban core come at a high cost and test the limits of processes of gentrification in the absence of state concessions and a clear municipal development vision.

Downtown Cairo's services, public spaces and infrastructure have deteriorated, in addition to the exodus of the district's original inhabitants. Rent control laws and accumulated legal battles between owners and inheritors have impeded the development potential of downtown properties (Sims, 2010, p 54; see also Figure 7.1).[4] In addition to municipal deterioration and the degradation of the urban environment in general, downtown Cairo suffers due to the ambiguous heritage status of 19th- and 20th-century architecture in Egypt. In the meantime, since the 1990s, artist spaces have taken root in downtown due to the district's central location, affordability of rent-controlled spaces, availability of space and the presence of potential audiences (writers, leftists and intellectuals who frequent long-established downtown cafes and bars). The presence of artists combined with the heritage value, scale and quality of downtown properties have attracted the attention of private investment aiming to capitalise on downtown's potential as a revived cultural, business and residential centre.

This chapter will investigate the dynamics of urban renewal in the context of a deteriorating Cairo where suburban development continues to boom. First, I will present the physical context of downtown in relation to the rest of Cairo. Second, I will present a historical context to the significance of downtown Cairo

Figure 7.1: Occupancy rates in downtown apartments are low and continue to decline as current rental policies and legal battles over inheritance fuel depopulation

and its place within the Egyptian state's conception of heritage. Third, I will shift the focus onto recent developments regarding the relationship between artists and real estate investment. I will argue that the presence of artists and their spaces is not part of a conventional gentrification process. The recent investment interest in downtown, mostly Egyptian and Gulf capital, aims to follow more conventional processes of gentrification; however, the conditions in Cairo explored in this chapter make these prospects for gentrification difficult to realise. In Cairo, local and indigenous variations resulting from particular political, historical and economic specificities have emerged in recent years and beg for a rethinking or expansion of theories of gentrification.

Placing downtown Cairo within its urban context

Contemporary Cairo (see Figure 7.2) is a decentred city, with its downtown area no longer serving the functions of a city centre. While some businesses remain, such as banks and insurance companies, in addition to some government ministries nearby, downtown has lost several of its main tenants, such as the AUC and the soon-to-be relocated Egyptian Museum, both having moved to the urban periphery. During the past several decades, downtown has also undergone processes of depopulation, which have been coupled with the draining of services that once catered to residents, such as small grocery shops and laundrettes. Yet, the district has been resilient as a place of shopping and a centre for independent and alternative arts and culture. Commercial activity has been homogenised, with entire streets, such as Talaat Harb, once the spine of downtown lined with cinemas and a diverse commercial life, transformed into a shopping strip dominated by two commodities: shoes and casual wear. While the transformation of downtown Cairo is considered by the city's bourgeoisie as downgrading and is perceived to be catering to lower classes, in fact, downtown's commercial activities are not affordable to the masses. However, downtown's transformation has not corresponded with dominating bourgeois aesthetics. The bourgeois who continue to live within the core of the city, as opposed to the new desert gated communities, have been concentrated into five districts, each functioning as an urban centre for the surrounding areas: Zamalek, Mohandeseen, Heliopolis, Madinet Nasr and Maadi. Large shopping malls cater for the bourgeois class living in those areas. In this context, downtown Cairo is a place of past glories that is no longer necessary to visit for commercial or entertainment purposes by the class that once dominated this part of the city (Abaza, 2006, p 193).

Cairo's downtown is located at the geographical centre of the city on the east bank of the Nile, extending east to the edge of the pre-19th century historic core. Ramsis Street and an elevated highway known as the 6th of October Bridge define the northern limits of the district. The area of Tahrir Square, with the Egyptian Museum and the former Nile Hilton, form the western edge. The southern and eastern edges are not as clearly defined, but they roughly fall at Gomhoriya Street to the east and Tahrir Street to the south. The physical area of downtown is not

Figure 7.2: Built-up area of Cairo in 1950 compared to 2009

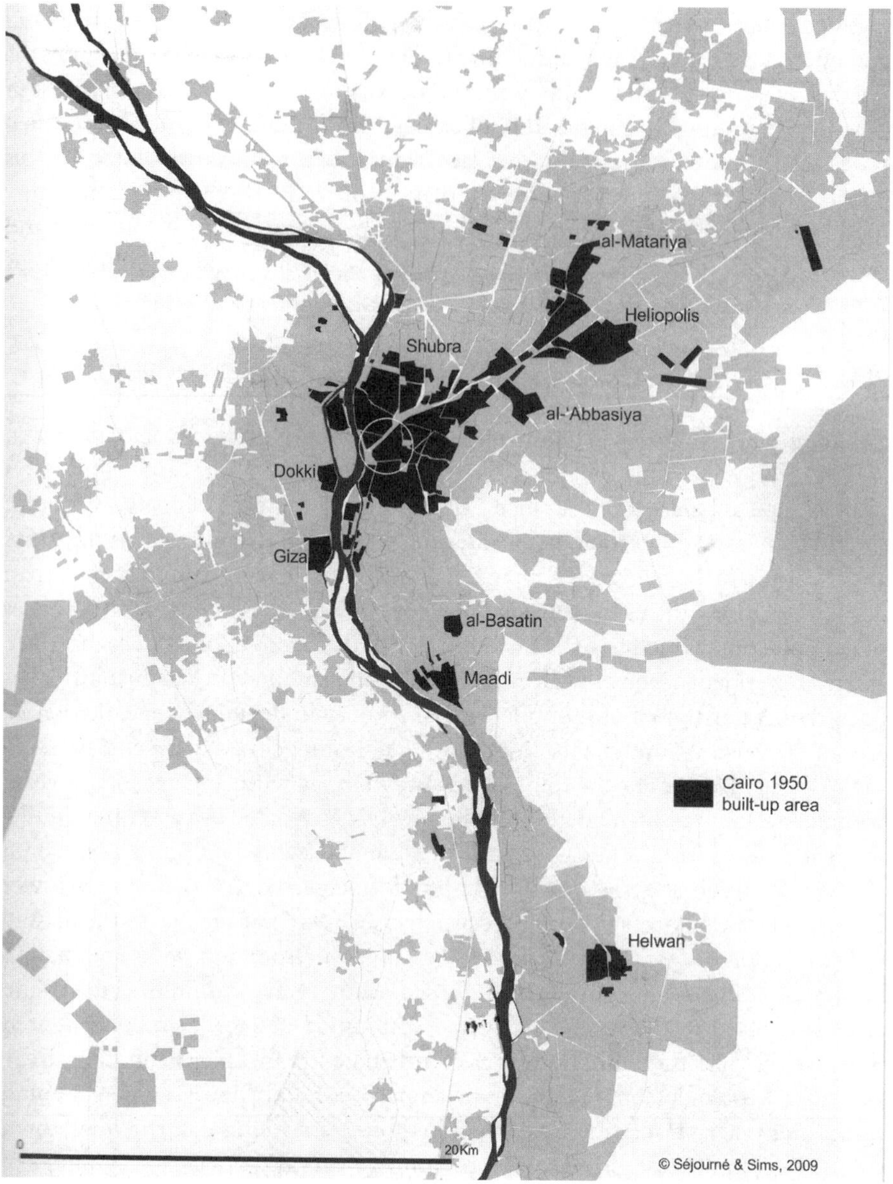

Note: Map courtesy of David Sims.

vast, with the longest distance east to west at about 1,500 metres and the longest distance north to south at about 2,000 metres. This relatively compact zone is surrounded by a rich variety of working-class neighbourhoods, such as Sabtiyyah and Bulaq to the north, Bab el-Shariyah to the east, Abdeen to the south, and Mounira to the south, where many government offices are located. Also south of downtown is Garden City, a residential enclave developed at the dawn of the

20th century, with residential architecture that matches downtown's architectural landscape, though this area was exclusively residential, unlike downtown's mixed-use spaces. Downtown is also served by many amenities at varying degrees of upkeep, such as the city's efficient metro system, with six stations and three lines dotting the district, the capital's main train station is accessible at the northern tip of the district and the city's historic central park of Azbakiyya is at the district's eastern edge.[5]

However, downtown's gentrification potential is limited due to its location in a city where real estate investment is directed towards the desert periphery, where suburban developments are mushrooming. State policy and infrastructure since the late 1990s have been directed towards encouraging the transfer of private wealth to the edge of the urban core: a kind of wealth dispersion, ghettoisation and isolation, perhaps to allow a controlled flourishing of private capital without allowing for the formation of a moneyed urban political entity that may exert pressure on the authoritarian political system (Sims, 2010, p 192). Parts of the city where relatively well-off 'old money' families continue to live, such as Zamalek and Maadi, suffer from deteriorated municipal services, unmaintained streets and sidewalks, uncollected waste, and deteriorating infrastructure. However, such services are available in the privatised gated communities at the periphery, often with subsidised state infrastructure. Potential gentrifiers, young couples, are often unable to borrow from banks (red lining) to buy and restore apartments in the decaying urban core, such as downtown. However, borrowing for the purchase of real estate in new desert communities is facilitated.

The combination of a decaying urban core and an exclusive and isolated suburban alternative has led to the massive expansion of speculation and urbanisation within the informal economy, which functions mainly at the immediate edge of the city, encroaching on agricultural land.[6] This unofficial process of urbanisation led by construction contractors also occurs in pockets within the urban core by purchasing dilapidated, sometimes listed, heritage buildings only to demolish them and replace them with tall high-density apartment blocks. This occurs mainly due to the emergence of a rent gap in the inner city resulting from skyrocketing land values with properties of limited investment return due to the legal complications mentioned earlier. This process significantly raises the market value of property, transforms the physical character of these neighbourhoods and brings in new residents typically from outside the area. However, these kinds of developments, while they could be seen as indigenous forms of gentrification, do not subscribe to the more conventional aesthetic regime of gentrification led by young urban professionals in North-Atlantic cities. These new apartments are often for families, often with remittances from the Gulf countries as the main source of income. This process is often illegal; however, authorities and municipal employees are compensated for their compliance.[7]

In the months following the revolution of 2011, these processes have accelerated at an unprecedented rate, physically transforming the character of the urban core, particularly in working-class districts such as Abbasiyya and Sayyeda Zeynab, as well as in the historic core, such as Darb el-Ahmar, the heart of medieval Cairo. These neighbourhoods have been experiencing drastic transformations, such as increasing densification, loss of architectural heritage and widening rent gaps. In the meantime, the state is continuing to push forth its development schemes for other neighbourhoods that will result in the forced eviction of thousands of families, such as the plan to build a central business district in an area known as the Maspero Triangle just north of downtown. Despite these two trends – one driven by the market and by the construction mafia functioning within the informal economy, and the other led by state officials with ties to international corporations – neither of these trends has made an impact on the transformation of downtown. I would argue that this is partly due to the district's unique set of stakeholders and property-owners but also due to the particular place of downtown within the city's memory.

Historical context: downtown Cairo's transformation and the emergence of its heritage value

Understanding the prospects for gentrification in downtown Cairo requires recognising the district's symbolic and historic significance. Since the late 1990s, there has been a resurgence of interest by self-identifying 'cultured' individuals, such as writers and academics, in downtown as a bohemian bourgeois enclave. This interest was reflected in nostalgic views and reductive understandings of this part of the city, as demonstrated in several works of literature and film.[8] The nostalgia linked to downtown has particular political ingredients. This space of the city has been recorded in collective memory as part of an era that abruptly ended with the 1952 coup d'état/revolution, after which architecture was plain, modernist, socialist and, most importantly, unworthy of remembrance. For example, consider this excerpt from 'A piece of Europe' by Radwa Ashour (2010, p 64):

> We were in Cairo, living in a four-story building on Qasr al-Nil Street, when Farouk boarded al-Mahrusa in Alexandria in July 1952. The building is still there. I sometimes walk past it. I raise my head to look at its balconies: the small, crescent-like balconies that look like jewels surrounding the tall French windows, and the long rectangular ones that are more spacious. Each one is adorned with corrugated iron, intricate designs that come together in floral motifs. I cross the street in order to have the necessary distance to view the entire building. I cross again to steal a quick look at one of the entrances. I recall myself alone or with my mother or father or siblings on the balcony. Baehlar Passage is across the street with its arches. To our right extends Qasr al-Nil Street towards Mustafa Kamel Square. To our left is Sulayman Pasha Square; we can see part of it, with the bronze statue in the center, and two out of four intersections, and the Groppi building, and the

> entrance to the shop with a sign that reads 'Groppi 1924,' and another sign written in Latin letters followed by 'confiserie de la maison royale.'

Nostalgia ignited interest within certain state institutions to revamp or pedestrianise parts of the district.[9] However, these attempts were poorly conceived, lacked long-term vision, were unresponsive to the legal, political and economic dimensions of urban transformation, did not produce a municipal policy that encourages gentrification, and, most importantly, did not engage with the question of municipal governance. The National Organization for Urban Harmony (NOUH) and the Cairo municipality implemented superficial interventions, culminating in painting facades (see Figure 7.3) with a single colour, a yellow-tinted beige, and closing several streets to vehicular traffic. These efforts did not result from rigorous study and research, and the design elements added, such as street lighting, were cheaply constructed and badly designed. Most importantly, these efforts did not involve the local community and local businesses and did not result in a municipal management system to maintain the district with the involvement of residents. A decade later, following the failure of public institutions in rehabilitating downtown, private interests have presented visions for the district that aim to reclaim this once-affluent part of the city. Such plans intend to inject high-end spaces back into an urban context that has economically and physically deteriorated due to government policies of neglect over the past six decades.

Downtown Cairo has been at the centre of several overlapping myths regarding its place in Egyptian urban history. These myths – that downtown signifies a colonial architectural heritage, and that it was the product of an attempt to emulate Paris – have been alienating to the Egyptian public. By framing downtown as exceptional, as colonial, as borrowed in its architecture and inspiration, these narratives have contributed to the increased negligence around this part of the city and have elided the nuances present in its historical development that research has revealed (El Kadi, 2012; see also Edwards, 2002). Furthermore, it is important to consider downtown, as part of modern urban heritage, within the context of Egyptian state institutions that focus on heritage as ancient and medieval, with little attention to the modern. Downtown's buildings are residential and commercial and continue to be part of everyday life in the city, making them challenging for Egypt's archaic heritage structure, which only focuses on historic monuments such as palaces, churches, mosques and funerary architecture that are typically taken out of everyday life, fenced off and often put on tourist itineraries.

According to the accepted narrative of the history of modern Cairo, what is known today as downtown was part of a modernising scheme by Khedive Ismail, ruler of Egypt during 1863–82 (Abu Lughod, 1971, p 96). The plan was part of an effort to make Egypt part of Europe rather than Africa; hence, it was a conscious effort to emulate European contemporary planning, as exemplified in Haussmann's Paris. According to the accepted narrative, this plan turned its back on the existing historic city and expanded westward towards the Nile, creating a dual city, with an oriental Islamic one to the east and a Western European one

Figure 7.3: View of July 26 Street, one of the main boulevards in downtown Cairo connecting Azbakeya to the High Court building. These facades were painted the same colour by the municipality in a half-hearted attempt at urban renewal.

to the west (Abu Lughod, 1965). Recent scholarship has debunked this accepted narrative and has shown that the development of 19th-century Cairo was not merely an effort to visually emulate the urbanity of the contemporary urban West. Rather, it was part of a larger modernising scheme that incorporated aspects of modern planning, such as street lighting, sewage systems and drinking water, as well as the straight boulevard, aspects that were seen in modernising cities across the world from Latin America, to Asia and across Europe. These transformations were part of the spirit of the time and were driven by local concerns for public health and commercial interests.[10] Contrary to the dual city narrative, which claims that Cairo was split into two unequal halves following modern urban expansion, 19th-century infrastructural changes were implemented in both new and old parts of the city, with varying difficulty and speed for obvious reasons (Fahmy, 2002).

Only a small percentage of the urban plan was actually built by 1882, when the British colonised Egypt. Much of the building fabric was filled in during a building boom at the turn of the century from 1897 to 1907, and again in the 1920s following the 1919 Revolution and the founding of Egyptian financial institutions such as Bank Misr. Another period of building commenced in the 1940s as the economy recovered after the end of the Second World War. On 26 January 1952, dozens of downtown buildings were damaged or burned in political protests triggered by a British massacre of Egyptian police a day earlier (Reynolds, 2012).

The rebuilding of such properties ignited yet another development phase in the district that lasted a decade. While British military presence in Cairo continued until 1947, that presence cannot be credited with the city's architectural and urban development during the period from 1882 to 1947. British occupation in Egypt, unlike in India for example, did not invest in urban development (Mitchell, 1988). The private capital of both Egyptian and foreign residents was the driving force behind the various waves of building development and speculation. These processes extended into surrounding neighbourhoods, including middle- and working-class areas such as Sayyeda Zeynab, Abdeen, Shubra and Faggala.

The expression 'Paris along the Nile' is popular among nostalgists and Orientalists alike (Myntii, 1999). It has gained currency among a growing bourgeoisie, who view contemporary Cairo with discontent and find a fragment of its imagined past to be a redeeming escape only because it may be referenced via Paris, the 'capital of modernity' (Harvey, 2006). The dominant narrative about modern Cairo from the 19th century has marked today's downtown area as exceptional, thus severing it from the surrounding areas that developed during that time. That narrative has also presented downtown Cairo in ways that elide the significance of local actors, architects, entrepreneurs and builders who built this part of the city. At the core of the faulty narrative of 'Paris along the Nile' is that it isolates Cairo from the constellation of cities across the globe, all of which underwent similar transformations for different motivations and by various regimes, and transporting urban planning models via differing mechanisms. Vienna, Berlin, Mexico City, Buenos Aires and other cities experimented with urban modernisation models that were later accredited to Haussmann. These cities and others developed in the spirit of the time (zeitgeist) in an increasingly connected world. Cities such as Torino, Barcelona and St Petersburg had already experimented with urban models that later came to be known as Parisian. The dominance of Paris as the capital of modernity is a political one related to the post-colonial continuity of empire's cultural hegemony (Chakrabarty, 2000). Comparative urban studies of 19th- and 20th-century developments across the fault lines of East–West and North–South could reveal that while global knowledge of architecture and planning was already taking place over a century ago with the mobility of architects, planners and their clients, local dynamics and specificities impacted the ways in which such global processes of urbanisation were localised. Understanding the conflicted views and narratives of downtown Cairo's 19th-century origins is an important step towards deciphering the relevance of 'gentrification' as a concept for understanding the district's contemporary transformations.

In the last decade, there has been a growing literature on heritage, memory, cultural landscapes and their relationship to contemporary identities (Staiger, 2009; Orbasli, 2000; Bandarin and Van Oers, 2012). This literature largely focuses on case studies in the European and North American contexts, where there has been a concerted effort over the past several decades by states and business elites to shape contemporary identities through the manipulation of cultural heritage (AlSayyad, 2001). These efforts involve a variety of modes of producing, editing and reconfiguring historical heritage and cultural landscapes in hopes of inculcating certain ideas about the nation (or a smaller community within the nation), and ultimately about the self (the spectator's/observer's self-identity). These highly political processes involve large sums of capital. Post-war culture and heritage production in Western contexts was closely tied to shifting political landscapes. Monuments were created, holidays celebrated, parades planned, cities preserved and rebuilt, museums established, and narratives constructed, and modern tourism was shaped (Lasansky, 2004).

How does Egypt fit into these processes? The early years of the republic, following the 1952 military coup d'état, featured some classic national-level cultural and heritage constructions. The military regime held parades, created monuments, edited history books and established a ministry of culture and guidance. The ministry's mission was to guide Egyptians in a new political landscape towards a newly defined cultural and national identity, one that relied on a certain reading of past heritages and Egypt's cultural landscape. The state invested in cultural programming, restored certain monuments, organised festivals and built 'culture palaces' in the provinces to export Egypt's new cultural landscape as it was conceived in Cairo. Downtown Cairo was affected in several ways during this period. Immediately after the overthrow of monarchy, many streets and squares in the area were renamed and the military held its parades in the newly renamed Tahrir Square at the western edge of downtown and later in Abdeen Square facing the once royal palace in downtown (Lababidi, 2008, p 107). The area also faced its first major wave of depopulation following the nationalisation of the Suez Canal and the subsequent military attack on Egypt by France, England and Israel, when many of the district's residents of European origin emigrated in haste. Abandoned apartments and shops often became properties of the various banks and insurance companies, while others were taken over by military officers and their families wishing to emulate bourgeois life.

Throughout the 1950s and into the 1960s, the district maintained its relevance as the city centre, with many new landmark buildings erected nearby, such as the Nile Hilton Hotel, the Arab League and the Cairo Municipality, which later became the headquarters of the ruling Arab Socialist Union. During this period, downtown cinemas and theatres were abuzz with activity as film production increased and the state supported theatre, opera and ballet, which were performed nearby at the Opera House, National Theatre and several other venues in and around the district. The state also built new facilities for entertainment, such as the Puppet Theatre. Department stores in the district held their place as the city's main shopping destinations. While the social make-up of downtown transformed and was dominated by middle-class Egyptians, the district continued to function as a cultural, entertainment and commercial hub. However, starting in the 1970s, affluent classes began to abandon downtown for the recently built Nasr City to the north-east and Mohandeseen to the west. Some government offices were also relocated to Nasr City, leading the way to a decentralised city. It was only after the exit of affluent classes, and the distance which that exodus created, that downtown's heritage value was assessed in the mid-1990s, sparked by the 1992 earthquake (El Kadi and El Kerdany, 2006, p 351).

Despite the ambivalent place occupied by downtown in Cairo's urban history, the Supreme Council for Antiquities, then an entity affiliated with the Culture Ministry, was charged with the listing, management, conservation, restoration and rehabilitation of a diverse array of patrimony from pre-historic to modern. In 1997, several streets were pedestrianised, such as the streets around the stock exchange. There was an attempt at building public–private partnerships for the restoration and rehabilitation of downtown; however, this optimistic endeavour was short-lived. El Kadi and El Kerdany (2006, p 366) wrote about this gentrification process in a positive light: 'the partnership established between the private sector, municipal officials and public bodies also reflects a new orientation in the domain of protecting and ameliorating the urban environment in general and heritage in particular'. Indeed, there was potential for a public–private partnership to encourage a positive transformation of the urban environment in downtown; however, such a partnership was highly restricted and controlled in ways that did not encourage entrepreneurship on a small scale to flourish.

The emergence of alternative art spaces in downtown

In 1998, the Townhouse Gallery opened as an independent space dedicated to contemporary art (see Figure 7.4).[11] The art space occupies several apartments within an urban townhouse tucked in a backstreet within a part of downtown dominated by car mechanics (see Figure 7.5). In addition to the gallery space, there is a library and nearby gift shops and bookshops. Townhouse became a focal point for the revival of downtown's role as a place for arts and culture, and with time, the gallery acquired a factory space where exhibitions and various events take place, and a nearby garage space was transformed into Rawabet Theater, a space for independent theatre and dance performances. In January 2000, the gallery initiated Nitaq Festival in cooperation with other independent and commercial galleries in downtown (Essa, 2000). The festival consisted of exhibitions, lectures, film screenings and performances and it brought new audiences to downtown, making it a success. The gallery continues to be a cornerstone in downtown's cultural and artistic life, mainly because of its position as a leading art space that functions outside of the controls of the Culture Ministry. Townhouse Gallery opened at the same time as SALT in Istanbul and Askal Alwan in Beirut, which raises questions for a comparative urban study on the impact of these independent art institutions in their respective cities, particularly when it comes to the gentrification of those cities. The presence of the Townhouse Gallery has not resulted in increased rents in the surrounding area or the displacement/eviction of residents.

The second and last Nitaq festival was in 2001. In Egypt's authoritarian political system, arts and culture are tools for political control, often mobilised to create an insular environment uncritical of the governing politics and the pervasive economic inequality. The state's grasp of arts and culture also perpetuated a level of mediocrity that pushed artists to found alternative spaces to practise, display and develop their art. Downtown, with its central location, former position as

Figure 7.4: Cairo exhibition in the winter of 2012 in the Townhouse Gallery

Figure 7.5: An old electronic repair shop that once catered to the district's residents

a place for arts and culture, and relatively affordable real estate due to policies of rent control, became an obvious location for artists to set up alternative arts institutions. While the Townhouse Gallery became a focal point for this alternative arts scene, it did not have the gentrifying effect experienced in Western cities, partly due to its position vis-à-vis the official establishment of culture and due to reluctance by the state to support independent art spaces as catalysts for urban regeneration. As a result, alternative artist spaces that emerged following the lead of the Townhouse Gallery, such as the Contemporary Image Collective (CIC) founded in 2004, had little impact on the urban transformation of the district.[12]

The revolution of 2011 brought an unprecedented mixture of Egyptian society in mass numbers into downtown Cairo. Following major protests in Tahrir Square, restaurants, cafes and bars in the surrounding downtown area were full to capacity with customers. The events reintroduced downtown to the city's bourgeoisie, who participated in protests among activists, artists and others. In the subsequent months, various artist spaces opened in downtown while existing ones experienced resurgence. New art spaces, like the majority of existing ones in downtown, were established in former residential apartments, tucked away from street activity. Apartments are convenient for artists because of the high levels of vacancies in downtown apartments (mostly belonging to absentee landlords) and the prohibitively high prices of commercial street-side spaces.[13] Despite the rise in creative, artistic spaces whose patrons largely consist of the middle class, there has been little visibility to the general public and little impact on the transformation of downtown in the absence of a gentrification policy and with a lack of investment from private capital. In short, while some middle-class audiences have returned to downtown as visitors over the past decade, the lack of municipal policies designed to capitalise on this audience and the lack of investment from private capital have meant that the potential for gentrification (the rent gap) has been unrealised. Despite the existence of creative spaces and their middle-class audiences in downtown, the conditions that encourage the classic appropriation of artists and artist spaces as vehicles for gentrification do not exist in downtown Cairo (see El Shimi, 2013).

Downtown apartment spaces were more readily available, as opposed to street-level commercial space, for non-commercial uses. Artist spaces occupying apartments pay monthly rents and have short-term contracts, causing institutional instability. Furthermore, nearly all artist initiatives outside the realm of the Culture Ministry depend on international funding in the form of grants, making them financially vulnerable. While responding to the clear absence of well-curated and well-managed art/photography/film spaces in Cairo, these spaces remain somewhat hidden from the general public due to their apartment locations. However, they serve an important function in resisting state hegemony over the arts. For example, Cimatheque, a space dedicated to independent filmmakers in Egypt, occupies an apartment in downtown.[14] The space aims to create a hub for Egypt's emergent alternative cinema scene by providing a screening space, a library and a social space in which filmmakers and their audiences can interact.

Open to the public and filmmakers of all levels of experience, Cimatheque is a hub for filmmakers and film lovers alike and works to build a strong platform for alternative cinema in Egypt.[15] Many such spaces are set up in apartments that belong to family or friends. Spaces such as Cimatheque are evidence of the forms of transformation taking place in downtown that do not subscribe to dominant theories of gentrification, most significantly, the presence of such newcomers to the area, in this case, artists, has not led to a systematic increase in rents or resulted in population displacement.

According to a state survey conducted in 2006, Egypt has 5.6 million vacant housing units, more than 3 million of which are in Cairo.[16] In light of the restrictive rent laws, a black market emerged in which deals occur on a personal basis and are outside the realm of government-supervised renter–landlord contracts. The official monthly rent for a downtown apartment may be merely 25 Egyptian Pounds (under USD4, according to exchange rates in 2013, a fair price in the 1960s but not today); however, the owner or old renter may rent it to new residents or a young artist space for a more reasonable but inflated price, as much as 6,000 Egyptian Pounds (under USD900).[17] This kind of transaction is clandestine but widespread. This highly personalised and individualised relationship, which makes these artists spaces possible in downtown Cairo, challenges typical gentrification theories emerging from the Global North that largely draw on case studies where policy controls transactions between renters and landlords in ways that minimise individualised relationships and regulate those relationships under the direct supervision of municipal government.[18]

'10 Mahmoud Bassiouny' is another space established in 2011 in a downtown apartment. The space aims to provide a platform for creativity in various mediums (crafts, dance, film, painting) without subscribing to official institutional guidelines or dominant conceptions of these arts. The apartment occupied by 10 Mahmoud Bassiouny is owned by Al-Ismailia for Real Estate Investments, which aims to refurbish downtown properties and make them available to potential upper-income tenants.[19] Al-Ismailia, established in 2008, owns the building where the artist space of 10 Mahmoud Bassiouny is located and also acquired the building where the CIC is located, as well as the Townhouse Gallery property. The company also owns several other properties in downtown, which it aims to renovate and adapt into new uses or rehabilitate back to their original uses as high-end residential apartments. In the meantime, the company has sponsored several artistic initiatives taking place in company property, such as the Viennoise Hotel, a dilapidated former hotel that has been unused for decades. The ageing, yet charming, space hosted the Cairo Documenta in 2010 and 2012.[20] The event was initiated by six artists who wanted to create a parallel event during the International Cairo Biennial as a form of countering the official event while taking advantage of the audiences that it brings to Cairo. In November 2012, the Viennoise Hotel also hosted a photography exhibition, Studio Viennoise, a tribute to the history of studio photography in Cairo. The company has also been the main sponsor of the Downtown Contemporary Arts Festival, which first ran in

2012 immediately following the revolution, with an expanded second edition in April 2013, bringing international and local performers to downtown Cairo and drawing audiences from around the city.

In other cities, particularly in Europe, independent arts organisations were able to negotiate deals with municipalities in which long-term leases were granted, sometimes with no rent, which has helped such organisations thrive by focusing their funds into their creative activities while catalysing the regeneration of their urban contexts (which municipalities are interested in). Such a process is not possible in Cairo as the state, the governorate (the closest Cairo has to a municipality), does not have a development plan or vision in which independent culture plays a key role in transforming the city. Private capital, such as Al-Ismailia, is not giving away free space either. While the company expresses an interest in the arts as an important component of downtown's cultural life, artists, like other tenants, pay rent. Thus, Cairo's independent artists and the cultural organisations they establish depend on their relationship to private property-owners and their international funders or fundraising abilities when it comes to establishing a space. Egypt's centralised Culture Ministry, with an immense budget and numerous spaces, has not expressed an interest in utilising the arts for urban regeneration. Culture Ministry spaces are often inactive and unwelcoming to not only audiences, but also artists. The ministry's budgets mostly go into paying wages, not into programming.

Downtown gentrification with private capital but without municipal policy?

Al-Ismailia for Real Estate Investments draws its name from the original name of the downtown district, founded during the rule of Khedive Ismail. Al-Ismailia confronts a challenge: what to do with real estate that was built to fit a particular economic strata and architecturally and spatially reflects a level of grandeur associated with that class. The company aims to capitalise on the historical value of this real estate, which it presents as a testament to Egyptian modernity and historical development, returning to imagined past glories (Abaza, 2011; see also Sims, 2010, p 14). However, Al-Ismailia anchors its activities in the present conditions of downtown while speculating on its potential for the future. The company is a new form of private capital formation in Egyptian real estate of mostly Egyptian and Saudi investment and it aims to purchase 10% of downtown's buildings with a total of 1 million square metres (Wood, 2010). News that a private company was purchasing downtown buildings spread rumours and conspiracies about the intentions of the buyers (Abaza, 2006, p 1081). Some warned about the potential for downtown Cairo to be transformed following the model of downtown Beirut, reconstructed by Solidere, a company founded by the former Lebanese prime minister (Sawalha, 2010, p 23). Others who fear that the company is following conventional models of gentrification and appropriating artists for its own long-term benefit have viewed Al-Ismailia's relationship to the arts with scepticism.

Downtown Cairo is not downtown Beirut and the process of privatisation that took place during the rebuilding of Beirut's city centre cannot be replicated in Cairo. There are sharp contrasts and differences that set apart the role of private capital in these two downtowns, summarised in the following points: first, Beirut's downtown was a depopulated city centre heavily damaged by a war that lasted over a decade, leaving much of its architectural fabric in ruins; second, Solidere was a private company created by the country's prime minister for the sole purpose of reconstructing the city centre, thus creating a situation where political power and private capital investment were held in the same hands, a situation that is very different to Egypt; and, third, Solidere acquired nearly all properties in Beirut's much smaller downtown district, which would be impossible in Cairo because the Egyptian state directly or indirectly owns a large percentage of properties in downtown Cairo (through publicly owned banks and insurance companies), in addition to private ownership by various stakeholders, creating a far more complex ownership map in Cairo.

Taking the Lebanese comparison out of the discussion, however, does not respond fully to concerns over the potential gentrification impact from Al-Ismailia in downtown Cairo. Indeed, the company intends to raise the market value of properties that have been either stagnant, underpopulated or utilised by the informal economy, as residential apartments have been unofficially used for storage, for commercial activities or as factories and workshops, contributing little to the official economy and maintenance of the properties and surrounding areas. The company's first public display of its intentions was at the Cinema Radio, built in the 1930s and located on Talaat Harb Street, the most frequently visited street in downtown Cairo. The building is composed of an office building fronting the street and a cinema reached through a passage.[21] The passageway runs under the office building leading to the cinema, with commercial space lined on both sides. During the glory days of downtown, Cinema Radio premiered Egypt's most prominent movies and was frequently visited by Cairo's affluent.[22] The popular television programme *El Bernameg* by Bassef Youssef (Egypt's Jon Stewart) leased the theatre space and refurbished it to host its weekly tapings, which included a pre-screened live audience.

Cinema Radio was part of the golden age of Egyptian cinema and these art deco movie theatres were the spatial manifestation of that new form of public sphere, one rooted in the spirit of the 20th century (Flibbert, 2005, p 448). As the film industry suffered and the former capitalist elite was eradicated after the early 1960s' nationalisation of private wealth, the buildings that stood as testament of a vibrant private sector economy (office buildings) and active film industry (the large screen of Cinema Radio) deteriorated and were later occupied by new tenants who tried to use the space in ways that accommodated their needs. Multiplex cinemas in shopping malls dotted around the city replaced downtown's dying cinemas. Cinema Radio is emblematic of the disappearance of downtown's prestige, which is a story not unique to Cairo, but found in downtowns all across the world, from European capitals such as Lisbon to North American cities such as Detroit. Investors have begun to purchase cinemas in downtown Alexandria, Egypt's second city, with at least one iconic cinema, Cinema Rialto, demolished in 2013 to make room for a shopping mall with a multiplex.

Not only has Alexandria's downtown district begun to lose many of its buildings in the face of market-driven development, but other city centres across the country with buildings dating from the same period have all but disappeared. In this context, some view the efforts by Al-Ismailia in Cairo's downtown as necessary to save a fragment of Egypt's disappearing modern heritage. The state's policies of stagnation, lack of comprehensive planning, bureaucratic hurdles and conflicting interests, in addition to the total absence of any intention to reconsider urban governance structures to allow for communities to partake in urban management, add up to a status quo that can best be described as a neglectful state. The injection of private capital in some downtown properties, such as the reuse of Cinema Radio as the recording studio of a popular television programme, without yet causing the usual effects of gentrification on the current users of the area surrounding the building raises questions about the utility of existing theories and critiques of gentrification based on case studies in the Global North for the case of Cairo.[23]

Conclusion

Is gentrification a stage of capitalist urban modernity with fixed aesthetics, paradigms and processes? Is the question of whether gentrification, a process experienced in Western urban development, has belatedly arrived in the cities of the Global South one that builds on the assumption that gentrification, like modernity, begins and ends in the Global North and is only expanded or exported to the non-West at later stages of development (Mitchell, 2001)? The global mobility of finance, the circulation of urban trends and the production and reproduction of images of urban modernity beg for a global evaluation and a less Eurocentric account of processes of urban transformation, such as gentrification. Cairo, a city that sits at the fault lines of North and South, challenges the linear narrative of urban modernity and tests the limits of the utility of gentrification as a concept for understanding urban transformations in the 21st century.

In the context of downtown Cairo, there are accumulated factors that beg for a reconsideration of how gentrification as a process may take different trajectories in the Global South: high levels of vacancy; deteriorated public amenities and services; the dynamic entrepreneurship of small and medium businesses that benefits from archaic laws such as old rent while manoeuvring around the corrupt municipal system to minimise tax payments; the emergence of artists on the scene for over a decade as a form of resistance to the state's hegemonic grip on art and culture; and the emergence of private capital investment aiming to transform the district following what seems to be conventional gentrification, presenting its efforts as necessary in light of the state's neglectful urban management.

There are multiple processes of urban transformation taking place in Cairo concurrently within different geographies and different economic spheres; some of these transformations carry some of the hallmarks of gentrification. However, conventional gentrification, as understood through European and American experiences, is not present in Cairo as a result of a collapsing municipal management system linked to a failing state that continues to dominate cities while lacking a comprehensive policy and vision, neoliberal or otherwise.

Notes

[1] Gentrification as a concept is not translatable into Egyptian Arabic. Processes described in this chapter that could appear to observers as attempts at gentrification in the context of Cairo are typically described in Arabic as *tatwir* (development), *tansiq* (ordering) or *tagmil* (beautification). All such terms lack the socio-economic component central to the concept of gentrification in the Global North/West.

[2] The term here is used in reference to the classic definition of gentrification – 'the replacement of an existing population by a gentry' – coined in England by Ruth Glass as an attempt to describe processes of urban transformation in post-war London (Lees et al, 2008, p 4).

[3] These transactions are typically freehold sales, sometimes with army officials as partners in the project with a percentage of the profits. These transactions are all very opaque for obvious reasons.

[4] Rent control laws have existed since the 1940s and have been expanded to cover great swathes of the city, including nearly all properties dating from before 1960. Although there has been a new rent control law dating from 1996, which eases transactions involving old rent properties, 'rent controls continued to dampen severely any in-town real-estate investment' (Sims, 2010, p 5).

[5] For more on the urban morphology of Azbakiya Park and surrounding area, see El Kadi (2012, p 37). On the city's metro system, see Sims (2010, p 229).

[6] According to Sims (2010, pp 59–70): 'of the 17 million inhabitants living in Greater Cairo in 2009, a conservative 11 million or 63 percent inhabit areas that have been developed informally or extra legally since 1960'. As Sims notes in his study, informal urbanisation took over large swathes of agricultural land where some infrastructure already existed, beginning in the 1960s and particularly during the wartime period between 1967 and 1974, when formal urbanisation nearly came to a halt yet in-migration and refugees flooded the city seeking affordable housing.

[7] Cairo's municipal system is undemocratic, with the highest official, the governor, appointed directly by the president and not elected. Governors are often retired military generals or police officers who have little or no experience in municipal management. Municipal government lacks effective means for communities to participate in managing urban affairs. Cronies and affiliates of the ruling party dominate local municipal councils. The majority of municipal budgets go to paying salaries rather than urban improvement projects, which are typically the responsibilities of the various ministries, such as housing,

transport and health. These ministries are highly centralised entities responsible for the entire country and their development projects often conflict with one another and are highly uneven: one area may receive favourable attention, such as the newly developed upper-income desert cities, while other densely populated informal urban areas may receive no development attention from these ministries. For more, see Sims's (2010) chapter on governance in *Understanding Cairo*.

[8] For an example of literatures that build on nostalgia in downtown Cairo, see Aswani (2004) and Naaman (2011).

[9] Others have written about how nostalgia for 'better times' and heritage appropriation for gentrification, particularly contested heritage, is seen as colonial (eg Shaw, 2005).

[10] For Ali Mubarak and Khedive Ismail, what had been built in Paris was a response to conditions in cities across the world, including Cairo: unhealthy spaces, crowdedness, sewage problems and a lack of open space (Mubarak, 1887–89, pp 83–7).

[11] For more information, see: http://www.thetownhousegallery.com/

[12] The CIC is an independent non-profit art initiative founded in Egypt in 2004. The CIC's mission spans contemporary art and media educational programming that responds to and develops visual culture and artistic practice, engagement and discourse.

[13] The national minimum wage is 700 Egyptian Pounds a month, though one of the main demands of the 2011 revolution was an increase of the minimum wage to 1,200 Egyptian Pounds a month.

[14] For more information see: https://www.facebook.com/cimathe

[15] Equipped with a screening room, viewing stations and a specialised library of films and books, Cimatheque enables access to films rarely, if ever, shown in Egypt. It provides a year-round educational programme of workshops and courses focusing on key issues like producing, screen-writing, editing and camera work, bringing together local and international filmmakers and industry professionals to exchange skills and experiences. The space also hosts an analogue film laboratory and accordant training programme that allow filmmakers to work with alternative methodologies and film material at affordable rates. However, the space is financially dependent on donations and volunteering and organisers pay rent to the landlord in exchange for maintaining the property.

[16] See: http://www.elwatannews.com/news/details/73611

[17] What is commonly referred to in Egypt as the 'New Rent Law' is law 4 for the year 1996, which was to govern all rent contracts after that date. Old rent contracts were to continue to follow laws 49/1977 and 136/1981. The New Rent Law led to further complications, particularly for landlords, while many tenants preferred obtaining old rent contracts because of their significantly lower rent.

[18] For a summary of Cairo's complex rents, see Sims (2010, pp 148–9).

[19] For more information, see: http://al-ismaelia.com

[20] For more information, see http://cairodocumenta.com

[21] The office building is made up of over 120 rooms and the cinema building (originally one large cinema hall with Cairo's largest screen but later split into two separate levels)

and now hosts a cinema and a theatre, each of 1,500 square metres, which were both vacant for over a decade.

[22] The cinema was among a series of large movie theatres built in Egyptian cities by Egyptian private investors who built up a great deal of wealth in the early 1920s following the 1919 revolution and the establishment of Egyptian financial institutions such as Bank Misr and its companies, including Misr Studio (for film production) (see Davis, 1983).

[23] Bassem Youssef emerged after the revolution as a political satirist who targets politicians, including the president, in his weekly routines. His television programme, among the most watched shows in the region, is filmed at Cinema Radio, which had been unused for nearly a decade. All forms of public and private media had abandoned the city centre and relocated to the walled and policed Media City located on the desert fringes. Additionally, telecommunication and banking have been absorbed into Smart Village, another gated development some 40 kilometres away from downtown. Private capital followed by establishing shopping destinations in far-flung locations such as Designopolis, a shopping destination for urban home decor. The international brands sold at the various shops and galleries in Designopolis are typically found in gentrified urban centres; however, in Cairo, these brands cannot be found in downtown, only in a standalone, and pedestrian, open-air mall on a desert highway outside the city.

References

Abaza, M. (2006) 'Egyptianizing the American Dream: Nasr City's shopping malls, public order, and the privatized military', in D. Singerman and P. Amar (eds) *Cairo cosmopolitan: politics, culture, and urban space in the new globalized Middle East*, Cairo: American University in Cairo Press, pp 193–220.

Abaza, M. (2011) 'Critical commentary. Cairo's downtown imagined: Dubaisation of nostalgia?', *Urban Studies*, vol 48, no 6, pp 1075–87.

Abu Lughod, J. (1965) 'Tale of two cities: the origins of modern Cairo', *Comparative Studies in Society and History*, vol 7, no 4, pp 429–57.

Abu Lughod, J. (1971) *Cairo: 1001 years of the city victorious*, Princeton, NJ: Princeton University Press.

AlSayyad, N. (2001) *Consuming tradition, manufacturing heritage: global norms and urban forms in the age of tourism*, New York, NY: Routledge.

Ashour, R. (2010) 'A piece of Europe', in S. Mehrez (ed) *The literary atlas of Cairo: one hundred years on the streets of the city*, Cairo: American University in Cairo Press.

Aswani, A. (2004) *The Yacoubian building*, Cairo: American University in Cairo Press.

Bandarin, F. and Van Oers, R. (2012) *The historic urban landscape: managing heritage in an urban century*, Chichester: Wiley-Blackwell.

Chakrabarty, D. (2000) *Provincializing Europe: postcolonial thought and historical difference*, Princeton, NJ: Princeton University Press.

Davis, E. (1983) *Challenging colonialism: Bank Misr and Egyptian industrialization, 1920–1941*, Princeton, NJ: Princeton University Press.

Edwards, J. (ed) (2002) *Historians in Cairo: essays in honor of George Scanlon*, Cairo: American University in Cairo Press.

El Kadi, G. (2012) *Le Caire centre en mouvement*, Marseille: Institut de recherché pour le développement.

El Kadi, G. and El Kerdany, D. (2006) 'Belle-epoque Cairo: the politics of refurbishing the downtown business district', in D. Singerman and P. Amar (eds) *Cairo cosmopolitan: politics, culture, and urban space in the new globalized Middle East*, Cairo: American University in Cairo Press, pp 345–74.

El Shimi, R. (2013) 'Downtown Cairo's urban regeneration looks to its artists', *Ahram Online*, April. Available at: http://english.ahram.org.eg/NewsContent/5/35/68446/Arts--Culture/Stage--Street/Downtown-Cairos-urban-regeneration-looks-to-its-ar.aspx

Essa, I. (2000) 'Contemporary voices: Cairo's first arts festival – Al Nitaq', *Medina Magazine*, no 12, pp 84–7.

Fahmy, K. (2002) 'An olfactory tale of two cities: Cairo in the nineteenth century', in J. Edwards (ed) *Historians in Cairo: essays in honor of George Scanlon*, Cairo: American University in Cairo Press, pp 155–87.

Flibbert, A. (2005) 'State and cinema in pre-revolutionary Egypt, 1927–52', in A. Goldschmidt and A. Johnson (eds) *Re-envisioning Egypt 1919–1952*, Cairo: American University in Cairo Press.

Harvey, D. (2006) *Paris, capital of modernity*, New York, NY: Routledge.

Lababidi, L. (2008) *Cairo's street stories: exploring the city's statues, squares, bridges, gardens and sidewalk cafes*, Cairo: American University in Cairo Press.

Lasansky, D. (2004) 'Introduction', in D. Lasansky and B. McLaren (eds) *Architecture and tourism: perception, performance and place*, New York, NY: Berg, pp 1–14.

Lees, L., Slater, T. and Wyly, E. (2008) *Gentrification*, London: Routledge.

Mitchell, T. (1988) *Colonising Egypt*, Cambridge: Cambridge University Press.

Mitchell, T. (2001) 'The stages of modernity', in T. Mitchell (ed) *Questions of modernity*, Minneapolis, MN: University of Minnesota Press, pp 1–34.

Mubarak, A. (1887–89) *Al-khitat al-Tawfiqiyya al-Jadida li-Misr al-Qahirah wa Muduniha wa Biladiha al-Qadima wa al-Shahira, vol. 1*, Cairo: Bulaq Press.

Myntti, C. (1999) *Paris along the Nile: architecture in Cairo from the Belle Epoque*, Cairo: American University in Cairo Press.

Naaman, M. (2011) *Urban space in contemporary Egyptian literature: portraits of Cairo*, New York, NY: Palgrave Macmillan.

Orbasli, A. (2000) *Tourists in historic towns: urban conservation and heritage management*, New York, NY: E & FN Spon.

Reynolds, N. (2012) *A city consumed: urban commerce, the Cairo fire, and the politics of decolonization in Egypt*, Stanford, CA: Stanford University Press.

Sawalha, A. (2010) *Reconstructing Beirut: memory and space in a postwar Arab city*, Austin, TX: University of Texas Press.

Shaw, W. (2005) 'Heritage and gentrification: remembering "the good old days" in postcolonial Sydney', in R. Atkinson and G Bridge (eds) *Gentrification in a global context: the new urban colonialism*, London: Routledge, pp 58–72.

Sims, D. (2010) *Understanding Cairo: the logic of a city out of control*, Cairo: American University in Cairo Press.

Staiger, U. (2009) *Memory culture and the contemporary city building sites*, New York, NY: Palgrave Macmillan.

Wood, J. (2010) 'Remaking Cairo – downtown's faded glamour', *Executive Magazine*. Available at: http://www.executive-magazine.com/special-report/Remaking-Cairo-Downtowns-faded-glamour/736/print

EIGHT

Widespread and diverse forms of gentrification in Israel

Amiram Gonen

Introduction

My ongoing observations over the last three decades on patterns of gentrification in Israeli inner cities, suburban towns and rural communities have led me to view gentrification from a different geographical perspective to the one shared by many Western researchers writing on gentrification. Research on gentrification originated in the heart of some Western cities and, therefore, gentrification was often characterised as primarily an inner-urban phenomenon. It was first observed and defined in an academic fashion in inner London (Glass, 1964) and subsequently studied in the 1980s and early 1990s in the inner city of some North American and British cities (for references to these early studies, see Lees et al, 2008). Indeed, the settling of middle class households in lower-social class neighbourhoods of the inner city has achieved sizeable proportions in Western cities since the 1970s. Much of the debate that developed among social scientists was over whether gentrification posed a substantial challenge to the established socio-spatial structure of Western cities, postulated by the concentric model of the Chicago School (Burgess, 1925). According to this model, based solely on industrialised cities in the US, the lower classes tended to live in the inner city while the middle classes opted for outer-urban and suburban neighbourhoods. The main theoretical question raised in early gentrification debates was whether the renewed interest of the middle classes in the inner city would bring about a reshuffling of the socio-spatial structure of the North American city (eg Smith, 1986).The debate was also centred on identifying the major driving force behind inner-city gentrification: was it economically generated by a rent gap existing in the inner city or was it the result of a growing cultural shift from a suburban to an urban lifestyle? All of this debate was primarily based on the concentric model of socio-spatial structure specific to US cities.

However, the increasing accumulation of urban research on gentrification in a wide variety of cities around the world portrays a much more complex situation that does not lend itself to the sweeping generalisations based on early research on US cities. Motivated by the need for comparative research,Western gentrification researchers first compared cities in their own backyard (eg Carpenter and Lees,

1995), then, propelled by the growing references to 'gentrification' in the 'Global South', researchers leapfrogged to investigate less developed, traditional and decolonised cities (Lees, 2012). However, a focus on the Global South overlooks a whole array of cities in continental Europe and other regions of the Global North, which, though supposedly modern and developed, like North American cities, are characterised at the same time by less developed attributes, such as slums, different socio-spatial urban structures and so on (Lees, 2014). These socio-spatial structures were often shaped by the predominance over a long range of time of the preference among the middle classes for inner-city living, leaving the urban periphery for less advantaged social groups. Such was the case in many of the older Jewish cities and towns in Israel. More so, the socio-spatial structure of European and other non-US cities was occasionally affected by geopolitical and population upheaval due to regional or continental wars. For instance, such upheavals changed the residential geography of inner Istanbul as a result both of Jewish immigration to Israel in the early 1950s as a result of the establishment of the state of Israel, and of Greeks in the late 1950s because of growing tension between Turkey and Greece. Both groups occupied inner-Istanbul's middle-class neighbourhoods. Lower-class Turkish households settled there instead. Since the 1980s, these inner-city neighbourhoods have been gentrified by Turkish middle-class households (Ergun, 2004). Similarly, the 1948/49 political upheaval in Israel, resulting in the forced exit of much of the Arab population followed by the mass entry of lower-class Jewish immigrants, has shaped the residential geography of some Israeli cities in a manner that does not conform necessarily with the orderly concentric pattern postulated by the Chicago model. These three major factors – middle-class preference for inner-urban living, the impact of the 1948/49 political upheaval and the ensuing Jewish mass immigration – combined together to act as the main residential patterns of the Jewish population; patterns that subsequently affected the geography and the forms of gentrification when it rose as a new residential process in the late 1980s.

Israeli urbanists have recognised the existence of gentrification in Israeli cities in their research. They came from among urban geographers and urban sociologists. The sociologists among them, being aware of the great interest in the academic literature in inner-city gentrification, focused their research mainly on the few inner-city neighbourhoods. I and some of my geography students drew attention to gentrification processes taking place in other parts of the urban and metropolitan space, where the 1948/49 political upheaval resulted in Jews taking the place of Arabs and to the mass construction of low-density immigrant housing in outer-urban areas in the 1950s. I had tried to introduce the Hebrew term *hitbargenoot*, which followed the French term *embourgeoisement*, but in vain. Gentrification in Israel is mostly referred to by urbanists and journalists as *gentrificatsia*, following the Italian format, as often applied to many foreign words introduced into the Hebrew language.

Factors affecting the urban socio-spatial structure of urban Israel

Three main factors have affected the urban socio-spatial structure of urban Israel: (i) the preference for inner-city living among the middle classes; (ii) the impact of war and geopolitical upheaval; and (iii) the impact of housing mass immigration on the urban periphery.

In continental European cities, the old emphasis on urban living among the elite and the middle classes endured into the 20th century. Europe's continental elite cherished urban life and were satisfied with a spacious and luxurious apartment in the inner city, while the heart of the English elite was primarily with the country house – a lifestyle transferred to North America by early English settlers. It is therefore not surprising that suburbanisation was eagerly adopted by the newly created British and North American middle classes when industrialisation pushed them out of the city and transport improvements made it conveniently possible. The continental European middle classes did not follow suit and for a long time stayed anchored in the inner city, leaving the suburbs to the lower classes, as is the social role of many Parisian suburbs to this day (Wacquant, 2008, pp 138–45). In many European cities, the inner city has relatively small numbers of lower-class neighbourhoods (Petsimeris, 2005, pp 245–6; Sýkora, 2005, pp 99–100).

In Israel, too, the Jewish middle classes held a preference for the inner city for many decades (Gonen, 1995, ch 3). They cherished access to urban amenities and services, as well as to their place of work, which was more likely to be in the inner city. This long-standing preference for inner-urban living originated in Jewish immigration from Europe, the Middle East and North Africa, where urban living was the ruling norm among the middle classes. Consequently, a spatial pattern of an inner middle-class core encircled by lower-class neighbourhoods soon developed in Israeli cities. Up to the late 1970s, the Jewish middle classes hardly left the inner city for the suburbs, contrary to what happened in North American and British cities and more in line with much of continental Europe, as is the case in many South and East European cities (Kovács, 1998; Petsimeris, 2005; Sýkora, 2005). This steadfastness of the Israeli Jewish middle classes in their preference for the inner city preserved much of that part of the city as their social 'territory' for decades to come. To this day, many Israeli inner-urban neighbourhoods, older or newer, are inhabited by the middle classes. Only a few lower-class neighbourhoods persisted within the inner city of the larger cities.

It was mostly the outer areas of Jewish cities that were left to the lower classes. First in the outer-urban areas were early immigrants from Middle Eastern countries and 'workers' neighbourhoods' (Graicer, 1982). In the 1950s and 1960s, immigrant housing estates were built on the urban periphery (Gonen, 1972, 1975, 1995, ch 6; Hasson, 1977). So strong was the image of the suburbs as obvious 'territory' of the lower classes that when the film *West Side Story*, taking place in the heart of New York City, was brought to Israel in the early 1960s, it was given the Hebrew title of *sippur haparvarim* (*The Story of the Suburbs*), based on the film's content of poor Hispanic immigrants, comparable to the lower-class Jewish

Eastern Sephardic immigrants in Israel, mostly living on the urban periphery at the time (Gonen, 1995, p 27).

Second, as in many cities in continental Europe impacted by geopolitical upheavals caused by war, massive population uprooting and resettlement, some Israeli cities also share such impact. During hostilities between Arabs and Jews in the 1930s and the end of the 1940s, some Jewish neighbourhoods, particularly on the border between Arab Jaffa and Jewish Tel Aviv, were left by their middle-class residents, eventually turning into a strip of low-class neighbourhoods. Years later, these neighbourhoods joined the map of potential gentrification. In 1948, by the duress of war, a large proportion of the Arab population, especially from among its urban middle classes, were forced to leave their homes and neighbourhoods and become refugees in Arab countries. At the same time, a massive wave of Jewish immigrants started to arrive in the country who were desperately in need of housing. One of the main sources of supply of shelter for these impoverished Jewish immigrants and refugees was the vacated Arab neighbourhoods, regardless of the quality of the housing stock. Several Jewish households shared one spacious house or apartment by partitioning it. The former middle-class Arab neighbourhoods, as still evident by their architecture and spacious dimensions, were turned into densely settled lower-class Jewish neighbourhoods (Gonen, 1995, ch 4; Golan, 2009).

Third, massive Jewish immigration in the 1950s also generated state-directed production of new immigrant housing estates on the periphery of almost every existing Jewish city and town, as well as in new immigrant towns established in metropolitan and national peripheries. Most of these housing estates were built on former Arab land, taken over by the Israeli state as a result of the 1948 geopolitical upheaval (Golan, 1995). It so happened that because of a 'ruralist' ideology reigning in the 1950s among housing planners, the common residential mode in these lower-status immigrant housing estates was that of detached or semi-detached houses, sited on relatively large lots. The large lots were intended to enable the new immigrants to grow their own food supply. Several decades later, these detached and semi-detached houses were coveted by suburbanising middle-class households.

Gentrification processes in the inner cities of Jerusalem and Tel Aviv-Yafo

The gentrification of lower-class inner-city neighbourhoods

With the growing interest among part of the Jewish middle classes in inner-urban living in recent decades, some of the lower-class pockets have undergone varying degrees of gentrification. In Jerusalem, there are four such inner-city neighbourhoods: Nahla'ot, Sha'arei Hesed, Mamilla and Yemin Moshe (see Figure 8.1). Nahla'ot (see Figure 8.2) and Sha'arei Hesed are old Jewish neighbourhoods in which gentrification was spontaneous and based on market processes without any intervention of municipal or state authorities. That was not the case in Yemin Moshe and Mamilla – two adjoining neighbourhoods immediately west of the Old City walls, standing close to the armistice line dividing Jordanian-held East Jerusalem and Israeli-held West Jerusalem during 1949–67 (see Figure 8.1). Until 1948, Yemin Moshe was an old Jewish middle-class neighbourhood and Mamilla was a mixed neighbourhood of middle-class Arabs and Jews on both sides of a commercial street coming out of the Old City. The sudden proximity of Yemin Moshe to the hostile 1949 armistice line was the reason for its original Jewish residents leaving their homes and renting them out to newly arrived poor Jewish immigrants. The forced exit of the Arab residents of Mamilla was also followed by the settlement of lower-class Jewish immigrants.

Figure 8.1: Gentrification of Jewish neighbourhoods in Jerusalem

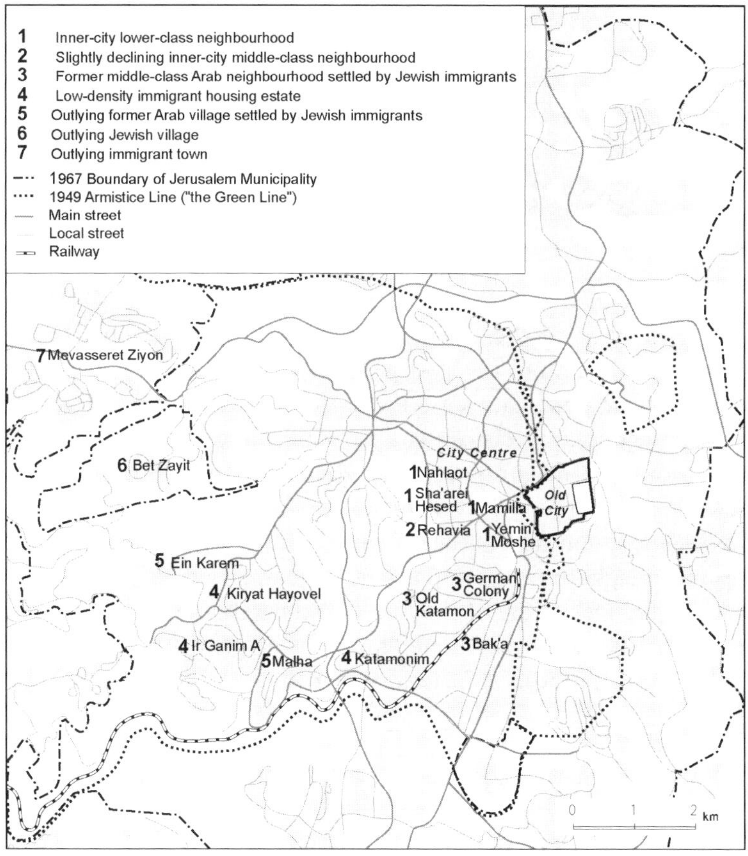

Figure 8.2: Incipient gentrification in the old ethnic neighbourhood of Nahla'ot in Jerusalem's inner city

The 1967 War brought about the annexation of East Jerusalem to West Jerusalem and the disappearance of the occasionally hostile armistice line. The hostile armistice line was lifted and the two neighbourhoods were soon targeted for gentrification by the joint state–city development agency, rushing to make use of the changed geopolitical circumstances by planning the redevelopment and gentrification of these neighbourhoods and employing enforced displacement and relocation of the lower-class tenants.

The displacement and relocation of Yemin Moshe tenants was justified by a plan to turn the neighbourhood into an artists' quarter (Jaffe, 1988). Israeli public policymakers were well aware of the lure of old neighbourhoods for artists and the justification that these artists offered for enforced gentrification projects. This awareness led to the purposeful inclusion of artists as active early participants in their Yemin Moshe gentrification project. However, only a few artists currently reside in the neighbourhood. Most of the partially dilapidated housing stock was sold to upper-middle-class households, having the means to heavily invest in renovation.

In the Mamilla area, there were no special architectural qualities to most of the dilapidated residential buildings and therefore the displacement and relocation of residents was followed by a massive clearance of most of the existing housing stock. An entire new complex of luxury residences, higher-class commercial stores, offices and a hotel was built by a combination of foreign and local capital working in concert with the joint state–municipal development agency. Most of the residential units are presently owned by wealthy households, many of them not permanently residing in Israel.

In the inner city of Tel Aviv-Yafo, two lower-class neighbourhoods have undergone gentrification – Neve Zedek and Florentin – each one characterised by a different urban fabric and a different process. Neve Zedek was established in the 1880s as the first Jewish middle-class neighbourhood in the then northern periphery of the predominantly Arab city of Jaffa. However, with subsequent expansion of the growing Jewish middle classes to new Jewish neighbourhoods to the north, Neve Zedek eventually became a lower-class neighbourhood of Jewish tenants. With the advent of gentrification in the 1980s, the architecture of the neighbourhood attracted artists, architects and other middle-class households who purchased dwellings from their absentee owners and paid 'key money' to lower-class tenants living there for many years, as is often the case in many old neighbourhoods in Israel. The old dwellings were renovated by the new owners according to the municipality's strict preservation rules (Ginsberg, 1993). The role of the municipality focused on proactive urban planning measures. One important supportive measure was the municipal decision to locate the new Susanne Dalal Centre for Dance and Theatre right in the neighbourhood, thus marking it as a desirable place for the culturally active middle classes. This incentive to gentrification is slightly reminiscent of the one provided by the Guggenheim Museum in Bilbao (Vicario and Monje, 2003).

Market-oriented gentrification supported by municipal planning interventions took place from the late 1980s in the Florentin area immediately to the south of Neve Zedek (Erez and Carmon, 1996). Unlike the relatively low density of Neve Zedek, which was attractive to upper-middle-class households, Florentin had been built in the 1930s at high density. Renovation and further intensification as part of the gentrification project attracted mostly young, lower-middle-class households. However, the proximity of Florentin to other lower-class neighbourhoods in Southern Tel Aviv, with a large number of African labour migrants and refugees nearby, most of them entering the country illegally, limited the neighbourhood to the level of lower-middle-class gentrification.

The regentrification of slightly deteriorated middle-class areas in the inner city

The Israeli experience raises the issue of the need to widen the scope of the term 'gentrification' beyond lower-class neighbourhoods. This definitional widening is especially relevant to middle-class neighbourhoods in the inner city that have undergone some social downscaling, later reversed due to the return of middle-class households. I suggest that this return of such neighbourhoods to being again solidly middle-class areas should be included within the definition of gentrification as a special category of 'regentrification', added to the one proposed as 'super-gentrification' for the further gentrification of already-gentrified neighbourhoods by the very rich global elite (Lees, 2003; Butler and Lees, 2006).

In Israel, the most prominent example of regentrification took place in the older southern inner city of Tel Aviv-Yafo, known as Lev Tel Aviv ('Heart of Tel Aviv'). Lev Tel Aviv has emerged in recent decades as a magnet attracting young people, lured by the new occupational opportunities and the intense urban lifestyle offered by the city and particularly by its inner city (Schnell and Graicer, 1993). The inner city of Tel Aviv continuously expanded to the north and, over time, young middle-class households moved to new areas in the city and later even to suburban communities, leaving behind their parent generation in the older neighbourhoods of Lev Tel Aviv in the midst of a growing commercial and financial centre. After the parent generation had to leave for congregated housing facilities or died, the younger generation was already established in its new residential environment and therefore placed the inherited property on the market, for sale or for rent. During the 1960s and 1970s, Lev Tel Aviv turned into a mixture of old residents, young renters and small business firms. As a result, this middle-class area experienced some socio-economic decline. However, in the early 1980s, an increasing preference for inner-city living triggered an influx of young people working in the new financial economy flourishing in the inner city, as well as other young individuals and households, among them inheritors of apartments owned by former residents, all re-enchanted by the image of inner-city living (Schnell and Graicer, 1993, 1996). As a result, Lev Tel Aviv became a fully middle-class area again, but with a much younger population (Schnell and Graicer, 1994).

Encouraged by the new wave of 'back to the inner city' and impressed by what had happened already in other Western cities, the municipality began to encourage upgrading in Lev Tel Aviv. It financially supported and enabled residential improvement guided by architectural preservation, all in order to booster the momentum of young, middle-class households settling in the area (Schnell and Graicer, 1996, p 116). It also intervened by not allowing the continued operation of office firms in residential buildings in order to increase residential supply in the area (Kipnis, 1998, p 78). Municipal intervention was quite effective and young households moved to take advantage of Lev Tel Aviv's growing supply of improved apartments, as well as of new ones added by constructing additional stories on existing buildings. Consequently, the overall socio-economic status of the residential population of Lev Tel Aviv was upgraded. Coffee shops, restaurants and leisure facilities multiplied. Kindergartens were reopened and schools regained the number of pupils they used to serve some decades earlier. The small business and manufacturing establishments had to move to other locations in the inner city slated for commercial use. The displaced residential population consisted of young singles, lower-middle-class households and other short-term transient renters. They were easily able to deal with their displacement by moving a few blocks to streets outside the immediate perimeter of Lev Tel Aviv, including the newly gentrified lower-class Florentin neighbourhood immediately to the south.

A somewhat different course of regentrification is happening in Jerusalem in the Rehavia neighbourhood to the south-west of the city centre (see Figure 8.1).

Between the 1930s and the 1960s, Rehavia was the turf of the city's Jewish upper-middle class. However, with the exodus of its second and third generations for newly built neighbourhoods in the city or in its suburbs, Rehavia's population turned into a blend of older residents, young renting transients and office firms. However, many well-to-do and rich Orthodox Jews from Western countries, mostly from the US, have been purchasing old apartments in the neighbourhood and renovating them. They have also purchased new apartments built in the neighbourhood on top of existing buildings. Many of these new apartment-owners in Rehavia do not live in them permanently; rather, they use them for when they visit the city. Like in the West (on the Hong Kong Chinese in Vancouver, see Ley, 2010), there are growing objections from the Jerusalem public to the growing phenomenon of 'ghost dwellings', which restrict residential supply for the local population and raise housing prices.

Tel Aviv-Yafo and Jerusalem are probably not exceptional in having former middle-class inner-city neighbourhoods experiencing, after partial social downgrading, substantial upgrading of their socio-economic status, as well of the quality of its housing stock, even to a level higher than the one characterising the original stage. In recent decades, a similar process occurred in some post-communist East European cities and particularly in Prague, where it is reported that much of the limited gentrification taking place in the city has concentrated on the traditional middle-class inner-city neighbourhoods that slightly deteriorated during the last decades of the communist period (see Sýkora, 2005, p 95). This kind of renaissance calls for the broadening of the term 'gentrification' to include 'regentrification'.

The gentrification of former Arab middle-class neighbourhoods

Until the 1970s, Jewish middle-class households were not keen to occupy old houses or apartments in former Arab neighbourhoods and take advantage of their architectural qualities, relative low price and closeness to the inner city. For two to three decades, a mismatch existed in these neighbourhoods between the old architectural quality of the houses and the socio-economic status of their Jewish residents. Only later did some sections of these neighbourhoods begin to be coveted by a growing number of Jewish middle-class households, guided by the new vogue of cherishing the old. They purchased the old former Arab houses and apartments from lower-class households, who had been sharing houses and apartments by subdividing them since the 1950s, and returned them into renovated single-family dwellings. As a result of such transactions, the older owners of the existing housing stock moved to new neighbourhoods, some of them even having enough money to help their grown-up children to establish themselves in their own apartments in these new neighbourhoods. This partial gentrification of former Arab neighbourhoods has happened mainly in the large cities of Jerusalem (Cohen, 1985; Gonen, 1995, pp 148–50; Zaban, 2011) and Tel Aviv-Yafo (LeVine, 2001) and to a lesser extent in Haifa.

In Jerusalem, such gentrification took place in the southern former Arab neighbourhoods of Bak'a, the German Colony and Katamon, immediately adjoining the stretch of existing middle-class neighbourhoods to the south-west of the city centre (see Figure 8.1). Gentrification in Bak'a was first started by individual middle-class households moving into the existing housing stock (see Figure 8.3). As gentrification continued with obvious success, other agents joined the scene. Small local construction companies became aware of the new middle-class turnabout in these neighbourhoods and began to make use of the many open lots within them. New houses fitting the demands and tastes of the middle classes were built on these open lots, thus generating a process that came to be termed 'infill gentrification' (Smith, 1996) or 'new build gentrification' (Davidson and Lees, 2005, 2010).

In the city of Tel Aviv-Yafo, the gentrification of former middle-class Arab neighbourhoods, settled in the early 1950s by lower-class Jewish immigrants, took place in the Ajami neighbourhood, not far from the Jaffa port. Jaffa was an Arab town until 1948. In the 1948 upheaval, Arab residents were forced to leave and their town was amalgamated with Jewish Tel Aviv to become the municipality of Tel Aviv-Yafo. Jewish immigrants settled in Jaffa, with only a small Arab minority remaining there. Later, as Jews began to leave for nearby newly built neighbourhoods, Arabs moved in instead. Gradually, much of Jaffa was inhabited by Arabs, a process that Jewish public policymakers were wary of, eventually looking for Jewish gentrification as a solution to their problem. Jewish capital

Figure 8.3: Gentrification in the Bak'a neighbourhood of Jerusalem

from abroad and from Israel joined together with state and municipal agencies to establish a high-class Jewish gated residential complex named Andromeda Hill, marketed exclusively to rich Jewish clients from Israel and abroad (LeVine, 2001; Monterescu and Fabian, 2003; Monterescu, 2009). Arab residents protested against the project as being part of a plot to 'Jewify' Jaffa and in the process make it unaffordable to its Arab residents (Goldhaber and Schnell, 2007, p 610). In spite of Arab protest, the project went ahead as a segregated and gated residential complex (Rosen and Razin, 2009, pp 1702–12).

The gentrification of former Arab villages

There are a few examples in Israel of former Arab villages that after the 1948/49 upheaval were eventually put on the course of gentrification with the settling of artists. One of them is the former Arab village of Ein Karem (see Figure 8.1) on the western outskirts of Jerusalem, where a cluster of artists' homes and galleries located among the predominantly lower-class Jewish immigrant population that had settled there in 1949. The artists moved in to take advantage of the architectural and physical landscape, as well as of the village's role in Christian pilgrimage and tourism. Other artists joined, later being followed by middle-class non-artists who learned to appreciate the qualities of the 'old' and the 'picturesque' (Yakobi, 2008). However, the process of gentrification has not fully taken over. A mixed social composition still characterises the residential population to this day.

The gentrification of peripheral low-density housing estates on the urban periphery

For decades, the low-density outlying immigrant housing estates built in the 1950s maintained their lower-class position in the social map of cities and metropolitan regions. However, since the late 1970s, with the spread among the Jewish middle classes of the newly adopted North American middle-class preference for living in detached ('villa') or semi-detached ('cottage') houses (Lev-Ari, 1977; Gonen, 1995, pp 114–20), the middle classes have started an intensive process of suburban gentrification. Part of this process took place in the outlying low-density immigrant housing estates built in the 1950s, where relatively low-cost detached and semi-detached houses in the low-class outlying housing estates were an affordable supply of potential 'villas' and 'cottages' for lower-middle-class households (Gonen, 1989, 1995, pp 122–4; 2004). As a result, partial gentrification occurred in such housing estates around the country. Some notable examples are Neve Amal in Herzliya (see Figure 8.4), Morasha in Ramat Hasharon and Shikunei Hamizrah in Rishon Leziyon, all three of them being suburban cities in the Tel Aviv metropolis.

Figure 8.4: Gentrification of one part of a semi-detached house in the Neve Amal housing estate in Herzliya

Within Jerusalem, such gentrification of low-density immigrant housing estates is currently going on in a series of housing estates in the south-eastern outer-urban areas of Jerusalem: Katamonim, Kiryat Hayovel and Ir Ganim A (see Figure 8.1).

Place gentrification in immigrant towns on the metropolitan periphery

To date, most definitions of gentrification have been limited to cases in which lower-class residents in an existing housing stock have been replaced by new middle-class residents. Authors had to fight to get new-build developments on ex-industrial, brownfield sites included under the rubric of gentrification (eg Davidson and Lees, 2005, 2010). However, from a wider geographical perspective, examining not only what happened to an existing housing stock, but also to a particular place in its entirety – a neighbourhood, a village or a town – one could argue for the wider concept of 'place gentrification', which includes both gentrification of old housing of lower status and the adjacent construction of new housing for the well-to-do.

In Israel, new immigrant towns on the metropolitan periphery, built in the 1950s, serve as an example of such place gentrification occurring since the 1990s. Among them are Mevasseret Ziyon west of Jerusalem (see Figure 8.1), Rosh Ha'ayin and Yavne, on the eastern and southern periphery of the Tel Aviv metropolitan region, respectfully. Tirat Karmel and Yokne'am Illit, on the southern periphery of the Haifa metropolitan region, are two more examples. For several decades, these towns were harbouring a lower-class population even though they had a share of detached and semi-detached houses built in the 1950s. Since the 1980s, urban and social transformation of these towns happened through the construction of new neighbourhoods adjoining the old ones, catering partly to local upwardly mobile households but mostly to outsiders searching for a suburban lifestyle on the metropolitan periphery (Gonen, 1995, pp 127–30). Despite their physical separation, these newly built middle-class neighbourhoods were able, by their presence, to upgrade the social standing and image of these towns in their entirety, thus changing their overall socio-economic composition, despite the rather limited initial social interaction between the old and new residents, as was the case in Yavne (Ayalon et al, 1993).

It is suggested that this kind of process should be defined as 'place gentrification', even though it is largely based on new construction of new neighbourhoods immediately adjoining old ones and does not necessarily involve the displacement of existing residents. Such place gentrification does enhance the economic value and the social standing of the immediately adjacent older neighbourhoods, as well as of the town in its entirety. This rather close relationship between suburbanisation and gentrification is far removed from the inner-city gentrification formulated by early Western researchers.

Place gentrification of Jewish villages

Rural gentrification is a process witnessed in many countries, including Britain (for a review, see Lees et al, 2008). In Israel, too, the shift to a suburban lifestyle since the late 1970s directed a growing number of middle-class households to set up their homes in Jewish villages. A process of partial gentrification started to evolve in the late 1970s in many villages through the purchase and renovation of old farm houses, a process that can easily be included within the classical definition of gentrification (Applebaum, 1986; Regev-Metuki, 2006). However, a more significant transformation of Jewish villages, starting in the 1990s, was mainly brought about by the construction of new houses on a separate section of land known as 'the extension', assigned for the settling of middle-class suburbanites. Unlike the earlier gentrification, this second stage was triggered by many Jewish villages experiencing severe economic difficulties during the mid-1980s. Allocating tracts of land for residential development was one of the ways to produce a substantial income for these villages, as well as for the Israeli government via its Land Administration Authority, which controlled most of rural land in the country. The result was the raising of the overall socio-economic status of these villages and their place gentrification. Moreover, the settling of middle-class households in an immediately adjacent new neighbourhood avoided the displacement so prevalent in in-situ gentrification, as is the case in some English and Scottish villages undergoing classical gentrification (Phillips, 2005; Stockdale, 2010).

Some general issues concerning gentrification in Israel

The transnational spread of gentrification into Israel

Gentrification in its classical format involves the takeover of old neighbourhoods by the middle classes. However, for many decades, old dwellings and old neighbourhoods were frowned upon by Jewish middle-class households. They had almost an aversion for the 'old' and a deep liking for the 'new', but then a change came about. The news about growing gentrification in Western cities had travelled to Israel, reaching it towards the 1980s, and as a result, aversion for the 'old' started to slowly dissipate among a small but growing part of the Jewish middle classes.

One can point to some 'carriers' of the idea of gentrification in old neighbourhoods coming to Israel from abroad. In Jerusalem, recent Jewish immigrants from North America took an active role in the incipient stage of gentrification of the former Arab middle-class neighbourhood of Bak'a, which turned into a lower-class Jewish neighbourhood in the early 1950s. Being knowledgeable about gentrification in old neighbourhoods in cities of their country of origin, they acted as 'importing agents' for the idea of gentrification by becoming directly involved in it in Israel. Joining them in this role were locally born Israelis, spending time in North American cities for studies or for business, and subsequently becoming aware of ongoing gentrification there. By moving into Bak'a neighbourhood, the North American immigrants not only brought along with them the appreciation of old dwellings in old *urban* neighbourhoods in their home country, but also imported patterns of resident activism, hitherto absent among the incumbent low-class population in Bak'a (Zaban, 2011).

A spontaneous process or driven by a development coalition?

The spread of gentrification in Israel was propelled mainly by the growth in numbers and in wealth of middle-class households as a result of the escalated development of the country's economy. This upward socio-economic mobility was largely expressed in the demand for better and more spacious housing instead of the rather small dwelling standards common in the 1950s and 1960s. This rise in demand was the main driving force in expanding middle-class residential areas, mostly by construction of new middle-class neighbourhoods, but also by gentrification of old ones.

Gentrification in Israel was largely generated by individual middle-class households, some guided by the old preference for urban living while reaping the fruits of a rent gap in lower-class urban neighbourhoods. Others, driven by the newly emerging preference for suburban living, ended up gentrifying low-density sections of low-class immigrant housing estates on the urban periphery, as well as immigrant towns and agricultural villages on the metropolitan periphery. However, there are some instances in which this individually based gentrification acted in concert with public agencies. Municipal agencies in Tel Aviv-Yafo were active in laying the policy and planning foundations for the regentrification of Lev Tel Aviv, as well as the gentrification of Neve Zedek and Florentin, but the rest of the process was carried out mostly by individual gentrifiers, as in Neve Zedek, or by a mix of such individuals and private entrepreneurs, as in Florentin.

This is not to say that there are not some instances of gentrification in Israel in which coalitions of public development agencies and capital have played a decisive role in bringing about an aggressive gentrification process associated with the outright displacement of lower-class residents. The Yemin Moshe and Mamilla areas in the inner city of Jerusalem and the Andromeda Hill area in the former Arab quarter of Jaffa in Tel Aviv-Yafo are examples of such aggressive gentrification.

Place gentrification in peripheral immigrant towns was also generated by a coalition between local and national government. The local government was interested in bringing into town new middle-class residents in order to change the socio-economic composition of the population, raise higher taxes and lift the image of the town. The national government was interested in putting to urban use extensive tracts of land it owned in these towns, thus adding income to the governmental budget. At the same time, the government was interested in opening up a new supply of land in order to serve the growing demand among the expanding middle classes for suburban-style housing. The opening up for residential use of a new supply of land, formerly designated for agricultural use only, was also the way in which the national government, through its National Land Authority, has made possible the construction of a new neighbourhood of detached houses for new middle-class residents next to the original built-up area of villages, thus bringing about their place gentrification.

Displacement or social mixing?

Most instances of gentrification in Israel have been spontaneous in nature, being carried out primarily by individual households or by small entrepreneurs over a long period. In most such neighbourhoods, gentrification is still under way at a relatively low pace. As a result, most of these neighbourhoods still keep a substantial proportion of the lower-class residents. Moreover, in many of the gentrifying neighbourhoods, some of the long-time residents participated in the ongoing gentrification process as incumbent upgraders or by moving to a neighbouring area in the case of place gentrification. This character of gentrification allowed for social mixing in many gentrifying neighbourhoods without it being heralded as a cause of liberal ideology on the part of gentrifiers.

Unlike reports on many gentrification processes in many Western cities (Lees, 2008), in most cases, gentrification in Israel went on without a deep sense of the threat of displacement. This had to do with the fact that much of the housing in Israel is owner-occupied. Moreover, those residents that waited long enough for gentrification to proceed in their neighbourhood saw the value of their property rise enough for them to consider selling. With the receipts, they were able to help themselves and their children to acquire housing outside the gentrifying neighbourhood, where housing prices were much lower.

Only in a few instances, most often where residents were renting or leasing their houses or apartments, was complete gentrification of a neighbourhood the product of aggressive state and municipal intervention in concert with upper-middle-class interests. It is in these instances that conflict with incumbent residents arose, eventually resulting in complete displacement, as in the case of Yemin Moshe in Jerusalem (see Figure 8.1).

Another aspect of social mix and gentrification is its eventual impact on the ethnic mix of a gentrifying neighbourhood (for a neighbourhood of Portuguese immigrants in Toronto, see, eg, Murdie and Teixeira, 2011), since in Israeli cities, as in many others, social class is often correlated with ethnicity. In Israel, middle-class gentrifiers are most often of Ashkenazi or European Jewish ethnicity while the incumbent lower-class residents are most often of Middle Eastern and North African Jewish ethnicity, as was clearly the case in Yemin Moshe, where the displaced lower-class residents were largely immigrants from Turkey (Jaffe, 1988). This was also the case in Neve Zedek and Florentin in Tel Aviv-Yafo, as well as in the low-density sections of outlying housing estates. This ethnic difference between gentrifiers and incumbents also characterised, to some extent, the new and the old neighbourhoods in immigrant towns on the metropolitan periphery. Such was the case of Mevasseret Ziyon near Jerusalem (see Figure 8.1) or Yavne, south of Tel Aviv-Yafo, where the population of the old neighbourhoods was largely of Jewish immigrants from Morocco while the newcomers to the new neighbourhoods were largely of Ashkenazi ethnicity. Therefore, when tension or conflict arose with regard to the impact of gentrification on the incumbent population, the ethnic dimension played an important role. Aware of such potential, public agencies have stipulated that in the planned place gentrification of immigrant towns on the metropolitan periphery, a quota of about a fifth of the new housing in the new neighbourhoods is to be made available to residents of the old neighbourhoods of town, thus trying to bring about some level of ethnic mix in the new neighbourhoods (Ayalon et al, 1993).

Conclusions

Atkinson (2003, p 2343) called for defining gentrification as a middle-class resettlement amenable to a range of new locational and social qualities in which it may be urban, suburban and even rural. His suggestion suits the diversity and widespread nature of gentrification in Israel due to its myriad of historical circumstances and processes. This chapter delineates the various forms of gentrification in Israel and their geographical spread. The inner city does not dominate the scene of gentrification in Israel as it did in much of the early research literature on gentrification in North America and Britain. Gentrification was found to be spread all over the urban and metropolitan space, depending on several historical factors and processes that have shaped the socio-spatial structure of Israeli cities and metropolitan regions, factors often absent in North American and British cities.

One such factor was the preference for many decades among a large part of the middle classes for inner-urban living; Israel's middle classes remained in the inner city like the middle classes in many European and Middle Eastern cities from which many of the Jewish population in Israel originated. As a result, only relatively few small pockets of lower-class populations existed in the inner city, some of them becoming targets of gentrification. The main gentrification process taking place in the inner city in Israel, particularly in Tel Aviv, was the regentrification of middle-class neighbourhoods after a short period of slight decline.

While the middle classes opted predominantly for inner-urban living, outer-urban areas and suburbs were inhabited mostly by lower-class populations, as was the case in many European and Middle Eastern cities. Public agencies enhanced this spatial pattern by constructing large housing estates to house part of the massive inflow of Jewish immigrants. Sections of these estates that were built in the 1950s consisted largely of detached and semi-detached houses. With the onset of suburbanisation among part of the middle classes, these low-density sections were identified as a possible option. The net result was the partial gentrification of such areas.

The 1948/49 upheaval in Israel resulted in the uprooting of the majority of the Arab population and an incoming mass of lower-class Jewish immigrants. Some of the Jewish immigrants were crowded into the vacant, elegant and spacious houses or apartments left behind by former middle-class Arab residents. Since the late 1970s, these neighbourhoods, in inner- or outer-urban areas, have been targeted for gentrification by Jewish middle-class households, recognising the architectural potential of this kind of housing and the rent gap that existed there prior to the onset of gentrification.

The rise in the late 1970s among part of the middle classes of a preference for detached or semi-detached residences resulted in a movement to all kinds of suburban towns and villages, new and old. Among them were two kinds of places in which, it is suggested, a process of 'place gentrification' began to take place in a manner different from the classical gentrification in which middle-class households displace lower-class residents. 'Place gentrification' occurred in immigrant towns built in the 1950s on the metropolitan peripheries of Jerusalem, Tel Aviv-Yafo and Haifa. It was mostly based on middle-class households moving into new neighbourhoods built adjacent to existing lower-class neighbourhoods. The addition of these new neighbourhoods did enhance the economic value and the social standing of the immediately adjacent older neighbourhoods and upgraded the overall social image of the entire area. Another kind of 'place gentrification' was a result of the onset of middle-class suburbanisation in Jewish villages on metropolitan peripheries, where a middle-class neighbourhood of detached houses was built next to an older village.

In recent years, the resistance of Palestinian residents in Jerusalem, in particular, to the neoliberal, ethnocratic planning policies of the mayor – Nir Barakat, who aims to clean up the city, making the Jewish–Arab divide less visible, especially to tourists, and the area even more amenable to gentrification – has been widespread. They have filed lawsuits in Israeli courts challenging house demolition orders and, on other occasions, have refused to allow the police, tax collectors and others into certain areas. Such resistances to more aggressive gentrifications can only be expected.

References

Applebaum, L. (1986) 'Migration of urban families to moshav villages in Israel 1968–1978', unpublished PhD dissertation in geography, The Hebrew University of Jerusalem, Isreal (in Hebrew).

Atkinson, R. (2003) 'Introduction: misunderstood saviour or vengeful wrecker? The many meanings and problems of gentrification', *Urban Studies*, vol 20, no 12, pp 2343–50.

Ayalon, H., Ben-Rafael, E. and Yogev, A. (1993) *Community in transition: mobility, integration and conflict* (Contributions in Sociology, No 14), Westport, CT: Greenwood Press.

Burgess, E. (1925) 'The growth of the city', in R.E. Park, E.W. Burgess and R.D. McKenzie (eds) *The city*, Chicago, IL: University of Chicago Press, pp 47–62.

Butler, T. and Lees, L. (2006) 'Super-gentrification in Barnsbury, London: globalization and gentrifying global elites at the neighbourhood level', *Transactions of the Institute of British Geographers*, vol 31, no 4, pp 467–87.

Carpenter, J. and Lees, L. (1995) 'Gentrification in New York, London and Paris: an international comparison', *International Journal of Urban and Regional Research*, vol 19, no 2, pp 286–303.

Cohen, G. (1985) 'The settling of households of upper socio-economic status in neighbourhoods of lower social status in Jerusalem', unpublished PhD dissertation in geography, The Hebrew University of Jerusalem, Israel (in Hebrew).

Davidson, M. and Lees, L. (2005) 'New-build "gentrification" and London's riverside renaissance', *Environment and Planning A*, vol 37, no 7, pp 1165–90.

Davidson, M. and Lees, L. (2010) 'New-build gentrification: its histories, trajectories, and critical geographies', *Population, Space and Place*, vol 16, no 5, pp 395–411.

Erez, T. and Carmon, N. (1996) *Urban revitalisation: literature review and analysis of the case of the Florentin neighbourhood in Tel Aviv*, Haifa: Center for Urban and Regional Studies, Technion – Israel Institute of Technology.

Ergun, N. (2004) 'Gentrification in Istanbul', *Cities*, vol 21, no 5, pp 391–405.

Ginsberg, Y. (1993) 'Revitalization of two urban neighbourhoods in Tel Aviv: Neve Zedek and Lev Tel Aviv', in D. Nachmias and G. Menahem (eds) *Tel Aviv-Yafo studies of social processes and public policy 1*, Tel Aviv: Ramot Publishing Tel Aviv University, pp 147–66 (in Hebrew).

Glass, R. (1964) 'Introduction: aspects of change', in Centre for Urban Studies (ed) *London: aspects of change*, London: MacGibbon and Kee.

Golan, A. (1995) 'The transfer to Jewish control of abandoned Arab land during the War of Independence', in S.I. Troen and N. Lucas (eds) *The first decade of independence*, Albany, NY: State University of New York University Press.

Golan, A. (2009) 'War and postwar transformation of urban areas: the 1948 War and the incorporation of Jaffa into Tel Aviv', *Journal of Urban History*, vol 35, no 7, pp 1020–36.

Goldhaber, R. and Schnell, I. (2007) 'A model of multidimentional segregation in the Arab ghetto in Tel Aviv-Jaffa', *Tijdschrift voor Economische en Sociale Geografie*, vol 98, no 5, pp 603–20.

Gonen, A. (1972) 'The role of high growth rates and of public housing agencies in shaping the spatial structure of Israeli towns', *Tijdschrift voor Economische en Sociale Geografie*, vol 63, no 6, pp 402–10.

Gonen, A. (1975) 'Locational and ecological aspects of urban public-sector housing: the Israeli case', in G. Gappert and H. Rose (eds) *The social economy of cities* (Urban Affairs Annual Reviews, Vol 9), Beverly Hills, CA: Sage Publications, pp 275–95.

Gonen, A. (1989) 'Obstacles to middle-class suburbanization in Israel', *Contemporary Jewry*, vol 10, no 2, pp 81–9.

Gonen, A. (1995) *Between city and suburb: urban residential patterns and processes in Israel*, Aldershot: Avebury.

Gonen, A. (2002) 'Widespread and diverse neighbourhood gentrification in Jerusalem', *Political Geography*, vol 21, no 5, pp 727–37.

Gonen, A. (2004) 'Non inner-city gentrification in Israel', in M. Pak and D. Rebernik (eds) *Cities in transition*, Ljubljana: Department of Geography, University of Ljubljana, pp 437–44.

Graicer, I. (1982) '"Workers" neighbourhoods: attempts at shaping an urban landscape through social ideologies in Eretz Israel during the Mandate Period', unpublished PhD dissertation, The Hebrew University of Jerusalem, Israel (in Hebrew).

Hasson, S. (1977) 'Immigrant housing projects in the old towns of Israel: a study of social differentiation', unpublished PhD dissertation in geography, The Hebrew University of Jerusalem, Israel.

Jaffe, E. (1988) *Yemin Moshe: the story of a Jerusalem neighbourhood*, New York, NY: Praeger.

Kipnis, B. (1998) 'Location and relocation of class A office users: case study in the metropolitan CBD of Tel-Aviv', *Geographical Research Forum*, vol 18, pp 84–92.

Kovács, Z. (1998) 'Ghettoization or gentrification? Post-socialist scenarios for Budapest', *Netherlands Journal of Housing and the Built Environment*, vol 13, no 1, pp 62–81.

Lees, L. (2003) 'Super-gentrification: the case of Brooklyn Heights, New York City', *Urban Studies*, vol 40, no 12, pp 2487–509.

Lees, L. (2008) 'Gentrification and social mixing: towards an inclusive urban renaissance?', *Urban Studies*, vol 45, no 12, pp 2449–70.

Lees, L. (2012) 'The geography of gentrification: thinking through comparative urbanism', *Progress in Human Geography*, vol 36, pp 155–71.

Lees, L. (2014) 'Gentrification in the Global South?', in S. Parnell and S. Oldfield (eds) *The Routledge handbook on cities of the Global South*, Routledge: New York,, pp 506-21.

Lees, L., Slater, T. and Wyly, E. (2008) *Gentrification*, New York, NY: Routledge.

Lev-Ari, A. (1977) *Centre versus suburb: residential preferences of the upper-middle class in the Tel Aviv metropolis*, Jerusalem: Institute of Urban and Regional Studies, The Hebrew University of Jerusalem (in Hebrew).

LeVine, M. (2001) 'The "new-old Jaffa": tourism, gentrification, and the battle for Tel Aviv's Arab neighbourhood', in N. AlSayyad (ed) *Consuming tradition, manufacturing heritage: global norms and urban forms in the age of tourism*, New York, NY: Routledge, pp 240–72.

Ley, D. (2010) *Millionaire migrants: trans-Pacific life lines*, Chichester: Wiley-Blackwell.

Monterescu, D. (2009) 'To buy or not to buy: trespassing the gated community', *Public Culture*, vol 21, no 2, pp 403–30.

Monterescu, D. and Fabian, R. (2003) 'The golden cage: gentrification and globalization in the Andromeda Hill project, Jaffa', *Theory and Criticism*, vol 23, pp 141–78 (in Hebrew).

Murdie, R. and Teixeira, C. (2011) 'The impact of gentrification on ethnic neighbourhoods in Toronto: a case study of Little Portugal', *Urban Studies*, vol 48, no 1, pp 61–83.

Petsimeris, P. (2005) 'Out of squalor and towards another urban renaissance: gentrification and neighbourhood transformations in Southern Europe', in R. Atkinson and G. Bridge (eds) *Gentrification in a global context: the new urban colonialism*, London and New York, NY: Routledge, pp 209–24.

Phillips, M. (2005) 'Differential productions of rural gentrification: illustrations from North and South Norfolk', *Geoforum*, vol 36, no 4, pp 477–94.

Regev-Metuki, G. (2006) 'Is it rural gentrification? The case of the Moshav Herut', unpublished MA thesis in sociology and urban studies, The Hebrew University of Jerusalem, Israel (in Hebrew).

Rosen, G. and Razin, E. (2009) 'The rise of gated communities in Israel: reflections on changing urban governance in a neo-liberal era', *Urban Studies*, vol 46, pp 1702–22.

Schnell, I. and Graicer, I. (1993) 'The causes of migration to Tel Aviv', *Urban studies*, vol 30, no 7, pp 1187–207.

Schnell, I. and Graicer, I. (1994) 'Rejuvenation of population in Tel-Aviv inner city', *The Geographical Journal*, vol 160, no 2, pp 185–97.

Schnell, I. and Graicer, I. (1996) 'The revitalization of Tel-Aviv's inner city', *Israel Affairs*, vol 3, no 3, pp 104–27.

Smith, N. (1986) 'Gentrification, the frontier and the restructuring of urban space', in N. Smith and P. Williams (eds) *Gentrification of the city*, Boston, MA: Allen and Unwin, pp 15–34.

Smith, N. (1996) *The new urban frontier and the revanchist city*, London: Routledge.

Stockdale, A. (2010) 'The diverse geographies of rural gentrification in Scotland', *Journal of Rural Studies*, vol 26, no 1, pp 31–40.

Sýkora, L. (2005) 'Gentrification in post-communist cities', in R. Atkinson and G. Bridge (eds) *Gentrification in a global context: the new urban colonialism*, London and New York, NY: Routledge, pp 90–105.

Vicario, L. and Monje, P.M. (2003) 'Another "Guggenheim Effect"? The generation of potentially gentrifiable neighbourhoods in Bilbao', *Urban Studies*, vol 40, no 12, pp 2383–2400.

Wacquant, L. (2008) *Urban outcasts: a comparative sociology of advanced marginality*, Cambridge: Polity Press.

Yacobi, H. (2008) 'Architecture, orientalism, and identity: the politics of the Israeli-built environment', *Israel Studies*, vol 13, no 1, pp 94–118.

Zaban, H. (2011) *Neighbourhood citizenship: citizen participation in the Bak'a neighbourhood of Jerusalem*, Jerusalem: Israel Democracy Institute (in Hebrew).

NINE

The endogenous dynamics of urban renewal and gentrification in Seoul

Seong-Kyu Ha

Introduction

Over the past 40 years, urban renewal in South Korea has been characterised by two distinct approaches: a housing provision-led physical approach and a market-oriented (business-driven) approach. These two approaches aim to maximise housing supply and improve the physical environment. They are also expected to have trickle-down effects on the local economy and to create a construction and real estate boom. The resulting wholesale redevelopment programmes have focused on the maximisation of landlord profits rather than on improving low-income residents' housing welfare or revitalising the community. The outcome has been what I term a 'renewal-induced gentrification'.

In South Korea, the term 'gentrification' is not commonly used by the general public. However, the academic world and housing/urban policy authorities are aware of the term and understand it as the restoration of rundown urban areas by the middle class and the displacement of low-income residents through renewal projects. Urban renewal was advocated by the central government in South Korea from the 1980s onwards, being further propelled by the introduction of local autonomy in 1995. However, in comparison with Western cities, gentrification seems to have taken a somewhat different path in South Korea, which has seen real estate development being a central force in urban economic expansion over the last 30 years. In this chapter, I argue that these urban renewal projects are, in fact, a form of urban gentrification because they often involve the displacement of poor residents from their city neighbourhoods, for these tenants are unable to pay the increased rents or afford the pricey new housing.

In the next section, I outline a brief history of urbanisation in South Korea and then turn to the discussion of urban renewal projects as producers of gentrification. I discuss the impacts of urban renewal and gentrification by examining the specific case of Gileum 'new town' in Seoul. The chapter concludes with a discussion of how these urban renewal programmes are a form of gentrification with endogenous dynamics specific to Seoul.

A brief history of urbanisation in South Korea and Seoul

According to the World Bank (2009), urbanisation can progress in three phases: (1) incipient urbanisation; (2) intermediate urbanisation; and (3) advanced urbanisation. In the context of South Korea during the incipient urbanisation phase, most areas were still rural. Urban and housing policies fell short of meeting rapidly rising housing demand and needs during the 1940s and 1950s. Particularly after Korean Independence (1945) and the Korean War (1950–53), the influx of returning emigrants and refugees contributed greatly to the growth of Korea's urban population (Kwon, 1977, p 376). The Korean War (1950–53) resulted in massive population movement, displacing over a million persons (Kim and Ha, 1998). The uprooting effects of the Korean War and the influx of refugees further accelerated the urbanisation process during the 1950s (Ha, 2001, p 387).

In the intermediate urbanisation phase, the World Bank (2009) argues that the benefits of rising economic concentration are widely shared by connective infrastructures, and people are pulled to cities by agglomeration economies. Urbanisation in South Korea began to accelerate in the 1960s. Rapid economic development in South Korea during the 1960s and 1970s was accompanied by an enormous wave of rural to urban migration. An urbanisation rate of 37% in 1960 reached 80% in 1990 (NSO, 2005). Since the 1960s, there has been an average increase in the urbanisation rate of 15.6% every 10 years. Migration had become a serious problem, not only because cities were terribly overcrowded, but also because rural areas were losing the most youthful and productive members of their labour force. The growth of new substandard housing, which took a variety of forms, bridged the gap between low-income housing supply and needs at the time. During the late 1980s, Seoul's average annual population growth rate was more than 3% and the population of Seoul surpassed 10 million people in 1988. In South Korea's intermediate urbanisation phase (1960–90), people generally lived in metropolitan cities with a population of over 1 million. During this period, about 60% of the urban population were concentrated in large cities. The proportion of the urban population living in cities with less than 200,000 people has continued to decrease since 1970.

In the advanced urbanisation phase, people generally decide where to live by considering where they can have easy access to high-quality basic services and by learning where such places are located. Unlike the intermediate phase, South Korea's advanced urbanisation phase saw structural and qualitative transformation. The urban population in the capital region increased its share of the national population from 42.8% in 1990 to 48.1% in 2005. Since the 1990s, the distribution of the urban population experienced some changes: the share of cities with a population of between 500,000 and 1 million has steadily increased, but the share of cities with a population size of less than 50,000 has decreased. It is also interesting to note that even though the population of the capital region as a whole has increased, the population of Seoul has decreased from 10,612,577 in 1990 to 9,820,171 in 2005. This resulted from the relocation of populations to neighbouring satellite cities within the capital region or from suburbanisation processes. In terms of housing policies, the government announced a radical plan to construct 2 million housing units between 1988 and 1992, aimed at increasing the housing supply.

During advanced urbanisation, the population growth rate in South Korea has been decreasing substantially since 2000. Growth accelerated between 1955 and 1966 at an annual average of 2.8%, but slowed down significantly (to 1.7%) during the period between 1966 and 1985. The slow growth of the population has continued: between 2005 and 2010, the total fertility rate for South Korean women was 1.21, which is one of the lowest rates in the world according to the United Nations (2007). The low birth rate has triggered national alarm, with gloomy predictions of an ageing society unable to grow or support its elderly. Recent South Korean governments have prioritised the issue on the national agenda, promising to enact social reforms that will encourage families to have children.

In South Korea, many substandard residential areas that emerged in the intermediate urbanisation phase were removed through urban and housing renewal projects and integrated into cities. In the advanced urbanisation phase, the shortage of housing was alleviated to some extent. However, those communities in substandard residential areas collapsed and became scattered over other urban areas. These redevelopment programmes have focused on the maximisation of housing provision rather than on improving low-income groups' housing welfare. The outcome was a business driven and renewal-induced gentrification.

Urban renewal projects as producers of gentrification in Seoul

During the 1960s and 1970s, urban development was principally geared towards revitalising the urban economy and eliminating the shanties and squatter settlements in what was then the urban centre of Seoul. The central government controlled the clearance process, demolished the shanties and relocated squatters and low-income families to the outskirts of Seoul. In practice, the slum clearance and removal was essentially a police action, and the old units were bulldozed by wrecking crews to prevent their reoccupancy (ACHR, 1990). Relocation programmes destroyed poor people's employment opportunities and provided no alternative. The scheme succeeded in clearing substandard housing from the city centre, but this relocation only served to create other types of low-income settlements in isolated suburbs.

In the Seoul metropolitan region, selective legalisation and self-help programmes were also initiated in 1969, the object being to improve the living conditions in substandard settlements and to help low-income families. In 1972, these programmes were incorporated into the *Saemaul-Undong*, a new community movement sponsored by the central government.[1] This became the primary method of providing support for low-income urban households. The government provided a portion (about 35%) of the rehabilitation costs to improve the areas.

The government contribution came in the form of construction materials and technical assistance. The residents were expected to finance the remainder. Based on the self-help principle, those economically unable to do so were to contribute their labour instead. However, the fact was that the legalisation of substandard settlements and *Saemaul-Undong* achieved little success in improving housing conditions mainly due to unreasonable requirements and the harsh criteria for legalisation (Kim and Ha, 1998).

From the early 1980s, the government began to opt for building high-density and high-rise apartments in preference to relocation or legalisation. A new redevelopment project, the so-called joint redevelopment project (JRP), was supposed to take on a spirit of partnership between homeowners and construction companies. In JRPs, the government designated clearance areas and authorised building removal. Homeowners formed an association that drew up a contract with a construction company (developer) and took on the responsibilities for their project. Large construction companies provided the capital. The government allowed high-density development (high-rise flats) to ensure reasonable profits for all participants. The city government provided no public assistance. It should be noted that these JRP projects were led by property-owners, excluding tenants. The key to the success of JRPs was that they transformed low-rise substandard or unplanned settlements into high-rise commercial housing estates, built to the maximum density permitted by the city government (see Shin, 2009; see also Choi, 2002).

The JRP was accompanied by the booming housing market in the 1980s, when high-rise flats became the most popular type of housing in urban Korea. There is no doubt that the JRP contributed to an increase in the housing stock. The number of redeveloped housing units was more than twice the number of the total units that were there before redevelopment. Also, the average floor area in the newly developed units was almost triple the average of the old units. Considering the quality and size of the units, these new housing units produced by redevelopment were for middle-class households and definitely examples of gentrification (see Lee et al, 2003; Ha, 2004; Shin, 2009).

Urban renewal has been closely linked with the issue of housing reform for the urban poor since the early 1980s. The JRP could have been successful if many of the original residents had remained in the redeveloped area after the completion of the project. However, in reality, the ratio of rehousing in-situ for original residents was very low. Most of them had to move out to other areas where housing costs were lower. Due to the lack of affordability, many original residents sold their right to rehousing to others who could afford it. The result was gentrification, stemming from housing and renewal policies that emphasised housing stock increases rather than housing welfare and community development in the expectation of 'trickle down' or 'filtering' effects. Survey work suggested that nearly 80% of the original residents were displaced in the process of JRP. A considerable share of the development profits from the JRP projects were passed to outside investors (speculators) and real estate brokers instead of going to original residents in the redevelopment sites (Ha, 2004; Housing and Urban Renewal Policy Advisory Committee, 2010). The JRP projects provided on-site rehousing rental flats for eligible tenants, but these were not as popular as one might imagine. This further contributed to the displacement of tenants (see Shin, 2008).

In the 2000s, a new type of urban renewal emerged in Seoul, known as 'new town in town'. The new-town scheme was first introduced in 2002 by a former Seoul mayor, Lee Myung-bak, when the Seoul metropolitan government changed their urban renewal policy and named it the 'new town' project. This was introduced in order to narrow the gap between the rich in South Seoul and the poor in North Seoul, and to improve the deteriorated urban environment, especially in North Seoul. The new-town project set out to improve underprivileged housing areas, turning them into a high-quality residential environment by improving infrastructure and urban functions. In Seoul, the areas of Wangshipri (5,000 housing units), Gileum (14,100 housing units) and Eunpyung (15,200 housing units) were designated as new-town pilot projects in 2002. The Seoul metropolitan government planned to complete the construction of 33 new-town-designated areas by 2015 (Housing and Urban Renewal Policy Advisory Committee, 2010).

The designated areas have seen a sharp increase in their real estate prices. Building upon a policy of building five satellite new towns about 20 kilometres outside the city from the late 1980s to alleviate crowding, Mayor Lee intended to create better living conditions for low-income residents. The financial success of these projects inspired dozens of developers to undertake similar redevelopment efforts throughout the city. The new-town policy seemed like a good idea during the real estate boom, with locals in 'old towns' clamouring for the redevelopment projects because they would greatly increase their property values. However, things began to change in 2008 with the global financial crisis, and some apartment estates in Seoul had many unsold units. The prolonged slump in real estate has made apartments in urban renewal areas less attractive financially, slowing down the drive for new-town projects.

The impacts of urban renewal/gentrification: the case of Gileum new town

Gileum was one of three pilot 'new town in town' projects in Seoul, designated in 2002 and redeveloped by 2006. Gileum was a typical lower-income residential area, accommodating 11,536 households and occupying an area of 950,000 square metres in north Seoul (see Figure 9.1). In order to investigate the impacts of the project and how it led to 'renewal-induced gentrification' in Seoul, I surveyed the newly redeveloped community of Gileum (see Figure 9.2), interviewing 200 randomly selected households between July and August 2012.

Figure 9.1: Gileum before redevelopment

Figure 9.2: Gileum after redevelopment

In the South Korean context, urban renewal as an urban gentrification process involves population migration as poor residents are displaced. It brings about substantial changes to the community in terms of both the physical environment and socio-economic conditions. There has already been a relatively detailed description in the gentrification literature about the positive and negative impacts of gentrification in Western cities (see Lees et al, 2008, ch 6), I move on now to consider the positive and negative impacts in the non-Western city of Seoul.

There are three positive impacts of urban renewal/gentrification projects in Seoul. First, there is no doubt that all the renewal projects have contributed to a housing stock increase. Seoul has been facing a housing shortage for a long time and the most urgent task of urban and housing policy was to meet housing demand and to mitigate the housing shortage. With respect to this goal, the renewal projects have been successful in increasing the housing stock by building new housing and rehabilitating properties without direct state sponsorship in terms of finance. Second, urban renewal projects have upgraded community infrastructures, contributing to the physical improvement of what used to be declining residential areas. Through the renewal projects, old and unplanned settlements have been substantially redeveloped, being equipped with roads, public transportation (bus lines), sewerage systems, community parks and various community facilities (eg nurseries, private institutions, schools, etc) (see Table 9.1). In addition, housing sizes, conditions and facilities have substantially improved.

Table 9.1: Improvements due to the Gileum 'new town in town' project in Seoul

	Before (2002) (A)	After (2006) (B)	Positive impacts
Number of housing units	11,536	13,730	Increase of 2,194 units
Average park space per person(m^2)	0.38	1.17	Increase of 0.79m^2
Public bus lines	22	42	Increase of 20 lines
Number of nurseries	4	33	Increase of 29
Number of private institutions (the number of persons to be admitted)	8 (156)	48 (907)	Increase of 40 (751)
Average number of students per class in elementary school	37.1	29.9	Decrease of 7.2

Sources: Gileum Residents Association for the New Town (2005, p 2), Kim (2009, p 3) and Seoul Metropolitan Government (2004).

The third impact has been an increase in property values. Up until 2012, Seoul experienced a decade of 'new town' policy aimed at demolishing old neighbourhoods in favour of rows of housing towers. Often clustered together, these towers formed giant, echoing, often eerily sterile environments, dubbed 'new towns' by Koreans. Huge banners reading 'Welcome new town and redevelopment!' were often hung in front of old housing units, for Koreans welcomed the demolition of their homes – places filled with priceless memories – in anticipation of higher market values after redevelopment. Such a situation is peculiar to South Korea, for residents in Western cities whose homes were demolished in post-war slum clearance programmes were sad to see their homes destroyed. In Korea, houses have long been seen as objects of investment rather than places to live. During the 1980s and 1990s, as housing prices climbed, more people began to see the real estate market as an investment opportunity. For most ordinary people, housing takes up the largest portion, if not all, of their wealth. Residents hailed the destruction of their old houses for redevelopment projects but loathed any steps that they thought would adversely affect their homes' prices.

Indeed, the direction of housing prices is one of the most important factors determining how votes are cast in elections for civil servants, the president and lawmakers, as well as governors and mayors. Politicians are well aware of this and campaign pledges are made that urban renewal projects or plans will boost property values.

However, there have been many negative impacts caused by these urban renewal projects. Since 2011, the Seoul metropolitan government, headed by the liberal Mayor Park Won-soon, moved to scrap many of the big-scale urban renewal projects due to growing opposition from residents to redevelopment plans. Mayor Park stated that during his term, there would be a moratorium on 'new towns in town' projects, which were initiated by former Mayor Lee Myung-bak and actively promoted by Lee's successor Oh Se-hoon (2006–11) (*Kyunghyang Shinmun*, 2012):

> The New Town has incurred huge sacrifices, with residents being deprived of their rights to reside and rights to live. Today is the day to end the 10 years of New Town in Town history that has made Seoul one huge construction site. (Mayor Park Won-soon, Press conference, 30 January 2012)

The review – and possibly the scrapping of projects in many districts – came from Mayor Park's belief that the large-scale 'new town in town' projects expelled citizens from their long-time places of residence, invited speculators and caused conflicts among interested parties. This is significant and could become an example of the state blocking further gentrification.

In fact, the redevelopment projects have caused many negative impacts. First, the gap in housing conditions between the rich and the poor is deepening as a direct result of the urban renewal projects. Owners could make large capital gains over purchase prices. In fact, the capital gains by owners from the housing redevelopments were so large that the discrepancy of wealth distribution between owners and tenants became wider than before the project. However, as stated, one of the most important factors that property-owners expected from the 'new town in town' development was wealth, that is, capital gains resulting from property value increases. By way of contrast, increases in *Jeonse*[2] deposits did not result in capital gains, but in monetary burdens on tenants. As Table 9.2 illustrates, before the 'new town in town' project, the share of *Jeonse* rental housing units valued at less than USD347,826 (40 million won) was 83% but after the project the figure dropped to 0%. The proportion of small and inexpensive units for low-income families decreased dramatically after the new-town projects in Seoul. Then, things began to change in 2008 with the financial crisis, when the price of apartments fell slightly, and the recovery since then has been flat, with some apartment estates in Seoul having many unsold units. The prolonged slump in the real estate market has made apartments less attractive financially, slowing down the push for redevelopment in many areas.

Table 9.2: The proportion of housing units before and after the Gileum 'new town in town' in Seoul

	Before (2002)	After (2006)
The % of floor space in housing units less than 60m^2	63%	30%
The % of housing units costing less than USD434,782 (500 million won)	86%	30%
The % of *Jeonse* rental housing units less than USD437,826 (40 million won)	83%	0%

Note: 1 USD was approximately 1,150 won in 2012.

Source: Housing and Urban Renewal Policy Advisory Committee (2010).

The second problem caused by the 'new town in town' policy was its social impact. Residents in old communities before renewal had strong unified feelings and relationships and their own community-based culture, even though they encountered economic difficulties. The survey asked whether a sense of community (such as strong unified feelings and relationships/mutual help among them and community-based culture of their own) had changed after the completion of Gileum new town. The number of households who answered negatively (67.3%) in my survey was much higher than those who answered positively (32.7%).[3] It was evident that the characteristics of the old communities changed after the redevelopment.

Third, the housing type after redevelopment shifted totally to apartments. The 'new town in town' projects emerged in the 2000s after a boom in apartment living in the 1990s. Apartments in the 1980s were largely the preserve of the upper-middle class, but they became the norm for the middle class in the 1990s. Apartments were profitable for builders and owners because prices kept going up. They were attractive not only as places to live, but also as investment vehicles. Before the project, households residing in single-detached or multi-family row houses in Gileum occupied the largest share (70–80%) of tenure, rather than apartments. The redevelopment project has massively changed the lives of low-income families who lived in houses before the redevelopment. A number of urban renewal projects over the past three decades have introduced high-rise apartment buildings bearing the names of their *Chaebol*[4] development corporations such as Hyundai and Samsung. Their building configurations have generally obscured visual access to the surrounding terrain. With the disruption to local street patterns, newly redeveloped estates also caused separation from adjacent communities.

Fourth, the majority of displaced tenants had to move to places outside of Seoul or reside in another corner of the city. From the early 1980s, residents in substandard housing settlements were dispersed and relocated to Seoul's suburban areas and satellite cities in the Seoul metropolitan region. According to the municipal government's advisory committee report, only 10–15% of former residents were resettled in redeveloped communities, including Gileum and other renewal areas (Housing and Urban Renewal Policy Advisory Committee, 2010). This is a very low figure and evidence of large-scale displacement.

Table 9.3 illustrates the changes in employment outcomes after the 'new town in town' project in Gileum, based on data from the district government's statistical yearbooks. The number of workplaces and workers decreased substantially after the project. In contrast to the idea of 'trickle down', it is apparent that the Gileum pilot project did not focus on job creation and the expansion of community employment for low-income families. In fact, it is likely that the resettlement of so many former low-income residents has impacted the number of workplaces and employment opportunities within the newly redeveloped community.

Table 9.3: Change of employment in the Gileum 'new town in town' in Seoul

	Before (2002)	After(2006)
Number of workplaces	1,593	1,145
Number of workers	3,224	2,819

Source: Seongbuk-gu (2002–06).

Overall, the ratio of resettled households was very low, and in the case of tenants, it was much lower than that for property-owners. This implies that the 'new town in town' project failed to improve the housing welfare of the original residents. Since the majority of the original residents moved out after the project began, the low-income community was destroyed and their housing security became unstable. The resettlement ratio depended on the marketability of the project and the affordability of housing for residents. The goals of the project, as specified in related urban renewal acts, were to improve the residents' housing welfare and community development. However, the current system of housing renewal does not emphasise welfare policies or the provision of low-cost housing for low-income groups. Emphasis needs to be placed by the government on rental accommodation or low-cost housing in order to bring real benefits to the poor rather than serving the interests of a privileged few, as has occurred with the sale of housing in renewal areas to date.

Fifth, South Korea's basic housing renewal strategy has been based on the filtering or 'trickle down' concept. The government seems to believe that as the housing supply increases, vacated middle-income accommodations will automatically become available for low-income groups, thereby easing housing pressures. In fact, no one has been able to demonstrate that filtering strategies in South Korea promote and encourage a distributional equity in housing renewal areas. Although the original intention of the partnership between homeowners and construction companies was indeed noble, it is estimated that less than 20% of the original owner-residents were able to purchase an apartment unit in the new developments (Ha, 2004, p 126). Due to affordability problems, many original owner-residents sold their right to rehousing to others who could afford it. This was the result of a housing policy that envisaged 'trickle down' effects, emphasising an increase in housing stocks rather than housing welfare for residents. In addition, for the original tenant households, renewal projects led to further deterioration of their housing situation. By way of contrast, the incoming gentrifiers, who accounted for more than 60% of the total population in the redeveloped communities, enjoyed the new, expensive properties (Ha, 2004). Clearly, the major beneficiaries of housing renewal projects have not been the original low-income residents, but the middle- and high-income groups (on similar programmes in the West, see the findings in Bridge et al, 2011).

It is necessary to note here that shelter should not be judged *only* in terms of whether it has a good design and/or decent floor space; although this is undoubtedly important in the West, architectural norms are highly subjective and ethnocentric. Amenities that high-income (Western) groups place high value on are often unnecessary for low-income (non-Western) groups. High housing standards mean that the housing will be more expensive, and this increase in price is often more than what low-income families can bear.[5]

Opposition to redevelopment and new approaches

In contrast to the limited impact of anti-gentrification resistance in Western cities (see Lees et al, 2008), one result of residents' opposition to these redevelopments in Seoul is that the Seoul metropolitan government now plans to cancel the large-scale 'new town in town' and urban renewal projects in some districts, as mentioned earlier. In South Korea, religious organisations and non-governmental organisations (NGOs), along with tenants associations, have taken the lead in anti-urban renewal projects and citizens' housing movements, lobbying for governmental policies favourable to the urban poor. Tenants associations have also tried to implement anti-eviction struggles and anti-business-driven renewal campaigns. One struggle took place on 20 January 2009, when some 40 tenants who had occupied a watchtower on the rooftop of a four-storey building in Yongsan, central Seoul, in protest against insufficient compensation for the redevelopment of their neighbourhood, clashed with riot police. In the pre-dawn raid, a fire broke out and five evictees and one policeman were killed in the blaze (*Korea Times*, 2012b).

The Seoul metropolitan government has designated a total of 247 districts for redevelopment since 2002, but construction has not started in over 80% of these districts. Delays have been largely attributed to the objections from residents and conflicts between resident associations and construction firms. The objections and conflicts were mainly due to a slumping real estate market and collapsing house values after the global financial crisis in 2008. Critics also argued that the simultaneous designation of so many areas as 'new towns in town' caused instability in housing prices in these and surrounding areas, making it difficult for low-income residents to resettle (*Korea Times*, 2012a). The politicians who recklessly promoted these urban renewal projects and the government that neglected them are accountable for the current problems surrounding these renewal projects. Recognising these problems, the Seoul metropolitan government has sensibly taken actions to reduce the number of 'new town in town' project districts, and has also sought a new approach to neighbourhood renewal.

This new approach can be characterised as follows. The metropolitan government is to decide whether or not to proceed with the renewal schemes after inspecting their economic feasibility and other conditions. After collecting residents' opinions, if a majority of the residents want their district to undergo a facelift, the city will help them with fast-tracked and larger administrative support. Poor tenants will also receive government allowances such as housing vouchers (but note that in a similar system in the US – the vouchers associated with the HOPE VI programme – this did not alleviate displacement and, indeed, the ensuing homelessness of poor tenants, see Bridge et al, 2011). Contractors will be banned from forcibly removing tenants at night, especially during the rainy season or in winter, in order to protect their rights. Tenants will be encouraged to participate in drawing up the redevelopment plans (but on the falsehoods of public/community participation in urban regeneration programmes, see Lees, 2014).

Importantly, unlike in the West, if they do not choose the 'new town' type of redevelopment, the plan will be scrapped and the city will help them to find other smaller-scale ways to upgrade their neighbourhoods. If a redevelopment plan is to be cancelled in an area where residents have already formed an association to promote it, the city will pay the association's financial losses. A community-based cooperative approach is to be supported by the government in order to allow for residents' determination and efforts in community development. In this regard, the Seongmisan village could be a model for the future of urban renewal projects, as explained further in the following.

Located in the heart of Seoul, the Seongmisan community is a rare and unique case. There, residents first gathered together for communal child care in 1994: this kind of cooperative child-care system was the very first of its kind in South Korea at the time and it led to the creation of a school, a cafe and even a clothing store. The community brought back the concept of 'neighbourhood' that had/has been long forgotten in a city dominated by apartment buildings due to unrestrained individualism. There are several elements embedded in this bottom-up initiative: co-parenting; an experimental school; and regional recycling ventures. These fostered the resilience of communities and citizens. This fostering of resilience was also done through cultural expressions, as well as direct social and political work: the Seongmisan Town Theatre, for example, was instrumental to this. This community did not accept a 'new town in town' type of urban renewal. Instead, the community chose their own way of community development, mainly based on the concept of cooperative and inclusive methods. In many ways, it is a kind of sustainable development approach that favours bottom-up over top-down approaches, upgrading over demolition, and self-reliance over dependency. It also retains a local rather than a national focus, and is implemented as a small-scale project rather than as a grand-scale or mega-project. The Seongmisan community stands as a good alternative to 'renewal-induced gentrification' in Seoul and could well be copied in other cities around the world who are looking for alternatives to state-led gentrification.

Conclusions

Seoul has been witnessing one of the world's most aggressive residential renewal programmes (Kim, 2001) related to the macroeconomy, national policy, urban management strategies and speculation – what I call 'renewal-induced gentrification'. However, the context and the causes of gentrification in Korea are different when compared to Western cities. First, a housing shortage and housing poverty are the background causes of gentrification. It seems that gentrification in urban Korea has not been based on consumption, for example, the desire for an urban life as opposed to a suburban one (despite the increasing numbers of dual-career couples with no or few children). This is not surprising because in South Korea, suburban development began at the beginning of the 1980s in line with the new-town projects led by central government. During the 1960s and 1970s, very few South Koreans lived in suburbs; indeed, most suburbanites were relocated low-income families due to the slum clearance programme or original farmers who had lived there for a long time – as such anti-suburban sentiments did not develop as they did among gentrifiers in the West.

Second, the first phase of gentrification in South Korea was led by the state via its leading role in shaping the urban renewal policy that generated a gentrification process in South Korea (Lee, 2000). This is quite different to the classic, sweat-equity gentrification undertaken by private individuals in Western cities. There are, however, some parallels between contemporary state-led or state-facilitated gentrification in the West (see Bridge et al, 2011; Lees, 2014) and the wholesale demolition of residential areas and the displacement of poor people in Seoul. Nevertheless, without strong rent control laws or rent subsidies, poor residents have been and will be evicted when they cannot afford the increased rents and housing prices – and these are forced evictees!

Finally, in gentrifying communities in Seoul, the demographic characteristics are different compared to Western cities. In many Western inner cities, gentrifier households have been typically composed of young, more affluent couples without children. In the South Korean context, the demographic characteristics in redeveloped communities are very similar to the city average in terms of age and number of family members (Ha, 2001, 2004). The impact of this on processes of gentrification needs more investigation.

Over the last 40 years, urban regeneration in Seoul has been characterised by two distinct approaches – a housing provision-led physical approach and a market-oriented (business-driven) approach – with both of these approaches having caused gentrification. In addition, not only the central government, but also the local government, was of great significance in managing urban renewal projects in line with neoliberal urbanism.[6] The word 'renewal' is deeply embedded in discussions of real estate and gentrification in South Korea. The socio-political consequences of urban renewal projects have been the redevelopment-induced gentrification of low-income neighbourhoods. External property-based interests in the renewal project areas have enabled the full exploitation of development opportunities at the expense of poor owner-occupiers and tenants. Since the early 1980s under the name 'urban and housing renewal', and since the early 2000s under the name 'new town in town', the city government has designated many old residential areas to be redeveloped into new housing complexes. The designated areas have seen sharp rises in real estate prices. Seoul has spent lavishly on ambitious urban redevelopment projects in recent years to revive fast-decaying city-centre areas starved of investment. However, a slumping real estate market and collapsing house values have made property-owners reluctant to splurge on a facelift of their settlements. As outlined, the 'new town in town' project looks to have hit not just an economic buffer, but a social one too, for the designated renewal areas have become sites of conflict, as seen in the 'low-income class' and NGOs' resistance' to neoliberal projects of renewal-induced gentrification.

In the beginning of 2011, as discussed, the new liberal Mayor Park Won-soon began a major revamping of Seoul's renewal policies, scaling down or scrapping development-oriented projects pursued by his conservative predecessor Oh Se-hoon. This change to an 'enabling approach' to renewal/redevelopment is on the surface proving to be successful. One of the major reasons why it seems so attractive is that it not only conforms to, but also requires, democratic participation and inclusiveness (which is now becoming institutionalised into urban regeneration/renewal programmes like in the West). Since the election of the current Mayor Park, through enabling strategies, the city government aims to give citizens the tools to create and implement solutions to their housing problems. It is important in South Korea that we build on this inclusiveness, especially of vulnerable social groups, particularly low-income tenants. The policy directions for the future of 'urban regeneration' and not 'gentrification' in South Korea must be about the government providing equitable opportunities and outcomes for all community members, particularly the poorest. To this end, both the city and its communities must create democratic processes and open accountable governance structures, and learn from the mistakes made in the institutionalisation of public/community participation in, for example, Europe. It is too early to conclude whether Mayor Park's new ideas will stop 'renewal-induced gentrification' in Seoul; indeed, 'With little undeveloped land left and a burgeoning middle-class population, proponents of redevelopment say Seoul City has no choice but to pursue aggressive gentrification schemes if it hopes to maintain its economic dominance' (*Korea Herald*, 2010).

Notes

[1] *Saemaul-Undong* was started in 1970 under the leadership of the late President Park with the slogan 'Let's improve our livelihood'. The programme was characterised by three basic principles: diligence, self-help and cooperation.

[2] *Jeonse* is a real estate term unique to South Korea that refers to the way apartments are leased. Instead of paying monthly rent, a renter will make a lump-sum deposit on a rental space, at anywhere from 50% to 100% of the market value. At the end of the contract, usually two or three years, the landlord returns the amount in its entirety to the renter.

[3] A similar response was found in the case of the joint redevelopment project in Seoul during the early 2000s. The characteristics of the community on unified feelings and mutual help among residents had changed. The majority of interviewees showed a negative response regarding a sense of community (see Ha, 2004).

[4] *Chaebol* refers to a South Korean form of business conglomerate.

[5] According to the Ministry of Construction and Transportation (MOCT), of the 2,236,800 households in South Korea, more than 16% lived in accommodation that did not meet minimum standards in terms of floor space and basic facilities in 2005.

[6] In this study, neoliberal urbanism broadly refers to a range of punctuated and uneven urban processes taking place in communities. This includes business-driven redevelopment, privatisation, restructuring and the devolution of responsibilities to governments without matching fiscal support (Larner, 2003; Hackworth, 2007; Ong, 2007).

References

ACHR (Asian Coalition for Housing Rights) (1990) *Urban poor housing rights in South Korea and Hong Kong*, Bangkok: ACHR.

Bridge, G., Butler, T. and Lees, L. (eds) (2011) *Mixed communities: gentrification by stealth?*, Bristol: Policy Press. (Republished in 2012 by University of Chicago Press).

Choi, S.-C. (2002) 'The promise and pitfalls of public–private partnerships in Korea', *International Social Science Journal*, vol 54, pp 253–9.

Gileum Residents Association for the New Town (2005) 'Gileum new town', unpublished report.

Ha, S.-K. (2001) 'Substandard settlements and joint redevelopment projects in Seoul', *Habitat International*, vol 24, no 4, pp 385–97.

Ha, S.-K. (2004) 'Housing renewal and neighborhood change as a gentrification process in Seoul', *Cities*, vol 25, no 5, pp 381–9.

Hackworth, J. (2007) *The neoliberal city: governance, ideology and development in American urbanism*, Ithaca, NY: Cornell University Press.

Housing and Urban Renewal Policy Advisory Committee (2010) 'Report for the public hearing', unpublished document, Seoul Metropolitan Government.

Kim, H.K. and Ha, S.K. (eds) (1998) *Urban redevelopment in substandard residential areas in Korea*, Seoul: Nanam.

Kim, H.-R. (2009) 'A study on the characteristics of the new town project in the context of urban regeneration: the case of the Gileum new town project in Seoul', unpublished MA thesis, University of Seoul, South Korea.
Kim, K.J. (2001) 'Residential redevelopment in Seoul: public substandard housing renewal program', in W.Y. Kwon and K.J. Kim (eds) *Urban management in Seoul: policy issues and response*, Seoul: Seoul Development Institute.
Korea Herald (2010) 'Seoul's redevelopment dilemma', *Korea Herald*, 29 March.
Korea Times (2012a) 'Seoul to withdraw redevelopment plans', *Korea Times*, 1 January.
Korea Times (2012b) 'Yongsan disaster revisited', *Korea Times*, 4 July.
Kwon, T.H. (1977) *Demography of Korea: population change and its components, 1926–60*, Seoul: Seoul National University.
Kyunghyang Shinmun (2012) 'Re-examining new town projects in Seoul', *Kyunghyang Shinmun*, 30 January.
Larner, W. (2003) 'Neoliberalism?', *Environment and Planning D: Society and Space*, vol 29, no 3, pp 418–38.
Lee, C.-M., Lee, J.-H. and Yim, C.-H. (2003) 'A revenue-sharing model of residential redevelopment projects: the case of the Hapdong redevelopment scheme in Seoul, Korea', *Urban Studies*, vol 40, no 11, pp 2223–37.
Lee, J.Y. (2000) 'The practice of urban renewal in Seoul, Korea: mode, governance, and sustainability', paper presented at the 2nd International Critical Geography Conference, 9–13 August, Taegu, Korea.
Lees, L. (2014) 'The urban injustices of New Labour's "new urban renewal": the case of the Aylesbury Estate in London', *Antipode*, vol 46, no 4, pp 921–47.
Lees, L., Slater, T. and Wyly, E. (2008) *Gentrification*, London: Routledge.
NSO (National Statistical Office) (2005) *Population and housing census report*, Seoul: NSO South Korea. Available at: http://kosis.kr/statisticsList/statisticsList_01List.jsp?vwcd=MT_ZTITLE&parmTabId=M_01_01 (accessed 7 October 2013).
Ong, A. (2007) 'Neoliberalism as a mobile technology', *Transactions of the Institute of British Geographers*, vol 32, no 1, pp 3–8.
Seongbuk-gu (2002–06) *Seongbuk statistical yearbook, 2002–2006*, Seoul: Seongbuk-gu.
Seoul Metropolitan Government (2004) 'A master plan of Gileum new town development', unpublished report, Seoul Metropolitan Government.
Shin, H.B. (2008) 'Living on the edge: financing post-displacement housing in urban redevelopment projects in Seoul', *Environment and Urbanization*, vol 20, no 2, pp 411–26.
Shin, H.B. (2009) 'Property-based redevelopment and gentrification: the case of Seoul, South Korea', *Geoforum*, vol 40, pp 906–17.
United Nations (2007) *United Nations world population prospects: 2006 revision*, New York, NY: UN Department of Economic and Social Affairs, Population Division.
World Bank (2009) *Reshaping economic geography, World Development Report 2009*, Washington, DC: World Bank.

TEN

Value extraction from land and real estate in Karachi

Arif Hasan

Introduction

This chapter does not theorise, nor does it challenge, any theory of gentrification. It seeks to show how land-use changes and extracting value from real estate takes place in Karachi, a Global South mega-city. This process of extracting value pushes out poor communities from the land and homes of their ancestors and replaces them with richer and/or more politically powerful groups. These processes are very different from those in the Global North; nevertheless, my contention is that these are processes of gentrification. This chapter also shows how the concept of 'gentrification' and its vocabulary and neoliberal planning concepts are shaping academic training and public consciousness regarding heritage and conservation in Pakistan, and how attempts to take over Karachi's beaches (which are extensively used by its working and lower-middle classes) for high-income clubs, condominiums and five-star hotels and marinas have been made in the recent past. It is important to note that this development is taking place in areas located in the Defence Housing Authority (DHA) (a military-controlled housing colony) and those areas that come under the jurisdiction of the Karachi Port Trust (KPT) (a federal government agency, controlled for all practical purposes by the Pakistan Navy).

To understand what this means requires an understanding of land ownership and control patterns in the city. The City District Government Karachi (CDGK) directly controls 30.9% of land in the city. Indirectly, it also controls land allocated to civilian cooperative housing societies. This land amounts to only 1.9% of the total land mass of the Karachi district. Federal agencies – such as Railways, KPT, Port Qasim and the Federal Board of Revenue (BoR) – control 4.7%, the DHA 5% and the military cantonments 2.1%. The rest of the 56% is controlled by various agencies of the provincial government and by the national parks (20.7%). All the federal agencies (which include the military cantonments and the DHA) have their own development programmes, building by-laws and zoning regulations, while the city government has its own plans and regulatory institutions. There is no coordination between these different agencies for planning purposes except for overcoming issues related to utilities. The city government, by virtue of being governed by an elected council, is more influenced by community and citizen concerns than the federal agencies. In addition, federal agencies have the support of the powerful central government and its planning and financial institutions. To understand what projects have been proposed for Karachi and where in the recent past, it is important to understand this difference.

The case of Karachi

Karachi is the fastest-growing mega-city in the world (Cox, 2012). It is Pakistan's only international port and contains 10% of the total population of the country and 25% of its urban population. It generates 15% of the national gross domestic product (GDP) and 42% of value added in large-scale manufacturing. It provides 25% of federal government revenues and 62% of income tax (City District Government, Karachi, 2007). Despite being a major industrial city in Pakistan, three quarters of the working population work in the informal sector, which mostly operates out of low-income settlements mainly in the garment, leather, textile, carpet and light engineering sectors. Since the 1990s, the number of persons working in the informal sector has decreased little in percentage terms but a link between the formal and informal sectors has been established, with the formal sector subcontracting work to informal establishments. The growing importance of the city in the national economy is reflected by the increase of cargo handled by the KPT, which was 2.8 million tons in 1951 and 32.3 million tons in 2005/06 (Government of Pakistan, 2007). All of these factors play an important role in land and real estate conversions and contribute to the continuing migration to Karachi from other regions in Pakistan and from other countries, such as Afghanistan, Bangladesh and Burma.

Karachi's population in 1941, the last census before independence in 1947, was 435,887and its built-up area was less than 100 square kilometres. Today, its population is estimated at 18 million and its metropolitan area is 3,527 square kilometres (City District Government, Karachi, 2007). A major increase in percentage terms took place at the time of independence, when the population increased from about 450,000 to more than 1,435,667 in 1951 (City District Government, Karachi, 2007; Government of Pakistan, 2007). This increase was due to the migration of Muslims from India. It was also accompanied by the out-migration of Hindus to India from Karachi. About 600,000 migrants had to be housed and most of them occupied the houses vacated by the departing Hindus. Most of the departing Hindus came from the merchant and trading communities and lived in lavish homes and beautiful neighbourhoods in what is today Karachi's inner city. However, this beautiful inner city has been devastated because of severe social and physical degradation. The houses in which once-rich Hindu families lived are now inhabited by many poor Muslim families. To house the increase in population, additional floors have been built in concrete over beautiful stone buildings. Many community buildings have also been occupied and converted into homes (Cheema, 2007; Hasan et al, 2013). Cargo terminals, the port and the intercity railway network were also located in the neighbourhood of the old city.

Wholesale markets and small manufacturing units were also within the old city but formed no more than 3% of its area. As Karachi grew, the wholesale markets and small-scale manufacturing and their related warehousing also expanded. In the process, the male-only migrant working-class population increased to serve these facilities. Most of the two- to three-storey homes were pulled down and replaced by warehousing and commercial and industrial activities on the ground floor, with workers' accommodation on the five to six floors above. These developments have also meant a large increase in the movement of the number of heavy vehicles in the narrow lanes of the inner city. This has meant further degradation and traffic congestion. As a result of this degradation, much of the better-off population of the old city relocated to the new housing schemes developed by the Cantonment Boards and the Karachi Development Authority (KDA). Very few old neighbourhoods survive in the old city, and where they do, it is in a very hostile environment (Cheema, 2007). The result of these changes has been a massive increase in the value of land and property in the inner city because the markets and its working class are now located there. Attempts at shifting the markets to the bypasses of the city, which have been proposed many times by the local government, have been resisted by the market operators and the working-class population.

The enormous expansion of Karachi since 1947 has also meant the acquiring of land for development. It is important to understand whose land this was, the manner in which it was acquired and its repercussions on the original inhabitants. Karachi's hinterland consisted of over 3,000 small villages. In almost all cases, these village communities were pastoral and either Sindhi- or Balochi-speaking. The 1947 migrants from India, on the other hand, who today form over 45% of the population, are Urdu-speaking. In addition, the post-independence migrants also consisted of Pushto-speakers from the north-west of Pakistan. Under the Land Settlement Policy of the British colonial administration, the land on which the villages were located was owned collectively by the villages. However, the village pasture lands (mostly desert shrub) were the property of the government's provincial BoR. This pasture land was leased out on an annual basis to the pastoral clans at a very low rate. The purpose was not to collect revenue from this land, but to ensure the loyalty of the clans to the British government by doing them a favour. This land has been (and is still being) acquired for the development of Karachi and is being developed in three very different ways.

First, the Karachi Improvement Trust and later the KDA acquired the pasture land from the BoR for the implementation of their various housing and commercial schemes that were part of their master plans. In many cases, the villages were left intact but those that were in the way of large infrastructure projects were relocated. In the acquiring of village land, promises of providing jobs at some of the infrastructure locations (especially related to industries and port expansion) were also made to the local population. However, since the local population lacked the necessary skills and political power, these promises were never kept. No compensation or alternative was provided to the village communities for the loss of their pasture lands. As a result of the acquisition of pasture lands, the rural economy has been devastated and the village communities have lost their means of livelihood. Studies and surveys show that they have much lower social indicators, social and physical infrastructure, and upward mobility compared with the rest of Karachi (Anwar, 2013).

In addition to the pasture lands, there were also a number of oasis and agricultural belts along the seasonal rivers in the Karachi region. Most of these areas have also been urbanised despite the fact that they were marked as protected green areas under the various master plans (Hasan, 2013). These areas provided a sizeable amount of fruit, milk and vegetables for the city, which now depends entirely on importing these from agricultural zones at considerable distance from the city (Anwar, 2013). These lands have been acquired both by the formal and informal sectors for development purposes. The owners of these lands have made considerable financial gain by selling them to formal and informal developers. What has become of these owners and of the people who worked on these lands has not been adequately studied.

Since the 1960s, there has been an increasing gap in the demand and supply of housing in Karachi. At present, the demand is for 80,000 housing units, as opposed to a supply of 30,000 by the formal sector per year. This supply gap is made up by the supply of 32,000 housing units in the informal settlements known as '*katchiabadis*'. These *katchiabadis* have been developed on BoR lands through an informal agreement between government officials, politicians, informal developers and village elders, who also lay claim to the pasture lands around them. Today, 62% of Karachi's population lives in such settlements. These settlements began as shacks but, over time, proper houses have been built and have acquired physical and social infrastructure through government programmes, lobbying political parties or self-help supported by non-governmental organisations (NGOs) and informal developers. The value of land as a result of this development has increased enormously, and so have rentals. In 1991, land in the *katchiabadis* on the periphery of the city was Rs176 (USD1.76) per square metre, or 1.7 times the daily wage for unskilled labour at that time. By 2008, this had increased to Rs2,500 (USD25) per square metre, or 10 times the daily wage for unskilled labour (Hasan, 2008) (see Figure 10.1).

More recently, the government has initiated what is known as the 'Goth Abad Scheme' (village rehabilitation scheme). According to the scheme, the villages on the periphery of Karachi are given ownership documents if they can prove that they are the original inhabitants of the village. Once regularised, the land of these villages comes into the Karachi land market. This land is either formally or informally developed through a 'joint venture' between the community, an informal developer and relevant government officials. Again, communities have benefitted from the sale of this land while also holding onto land for their homes. However, there is a major difference between the skills that the original inhabitants have compared with the livelihood opportunities that the city offers.

Figure 10.1: The development of Katchi Abadis land

A large number of communities have been displaced to the periphery of the city due to infrastructure projects, especially roads. As a result of this displacement, they have become poorer. However, the value of the properties along the roads has increased considerably. In much of the land that has been vacated and its neighbourhoods, informal and low-income formal housing is being replaced by what is known as commercial 'plazas' and higher-income housing.[1] In addition, parks and amenities are also being occupied illegally for commercial and residential purposes. In this process, government agencies and even the international corporate sector are involved. Communities and concerned citizens have sought relief from the courts against these encroachments.[2]

Two other phenomena are taking place in Karachi. One is the bulldozing of settlements on government land by a powerful nexus of developers, bureaucrats and politicians. This development is for formal sector commercial and residential purposes for lower- and lower-middle-income groups. These bulldozings are taking place on small lots of land marked for development under local government schemes. Their residents are relocating to the city periphery.[3] The second phenomenon is the legal and illegal conversion of residential areas into commercial zones. Legally, the local government declares a certain residential corridor as a commercial one. This means extra floor area ratio, a larger number of storeys and mixed land use compared with residential-only land use. Illegally, people also start opening shops, schools, clinics and offices in their homes. This congests the neighbourhood and taxes the infrastructure but brings considerable economic benefits to the house-owners. However, there are always those individuals and families who go to court against such legal and illegal land-use changes (see Hasan et al, 2013).[4] Over time, the illegal changes are regularised and, as in the legally commercialised areas, high-rise construction catering to the corporate sector and high-end local businesses, often designed by the top architects of the city, begins to replace the old architecture of the area.

Studies have also revealed that the old informal settlements have changed over time. First, they are no longer purely working-class settlements: they have a younger and literate leadership compared with the older-generation leadership; they contain a sizeable number of white-collar workers, teachers and entrepreneurs; they have marriage halls and beauty parlours; and they have a fiercely upwardly mobile population (Hasan, 2003). The other phenomenon is that regularised or soon-to-be-regularised *katchiabadis* are building upwards. Through an understanding between house-owners and developers (formal and informal), individual houses are being replaced by high-rise apartment blocks, which contain very small apartments so as to make them affordable to low-income households for both purchase and rentals. Families who own these houses have become wealthier, since the agreement with the developer means substantial money for the sale of the plot and the retention of two or more flats in the building that is constructed. However, the environment of the *katchiabadi* is environmentally degraded as a result of such unplanned densification and the infrastructure is also overtaxed as a result (Hasan et al, 2010). What the future of these settlements will be has not yet been adequately studied.

The processes described earlier can be divided into two: first, those that degrade; and, second, those that 'gentrify' – meaning improved social and physical conditions and/or a more affluent and politically more powerful class moving in. For instance, in the case of the old city, it is certainly not gentrification. Here, as a result of the expansion of warehousing, wholesaling and manufacturing, its better-off population has abandoned it, leaving behind the lovely institutional buildings that served them. Yet, in economic terms, the old city is booming and its land values have become much higher than those of the elite areas of the city. Again, persons living in better-located formal sector settlements illegally change them into mixed land-use settlements and reap enormous economic benefits. In most such cases, the result is environmental degradation with little hope for future gentrification ('gentrification limited'). But where the nexus of developers, bureaucrats and politicians (including international corporate sector organisations) illegally acquire land marked for utilities and convert it for commercial and residential purposes, and also put pressure on local government to pass laws to change selected residential corridors into commercial ones with higher floor-to-area ratios, the case is different. In such areas where there is a potential for high and commercial usages, gentrification in the form of well-designed office buildings and apartments does take place. Again, where pastoralists are replaced by city dwellers and their economy is ruined, the case is different, for they are replaced by better-skilled communities who, over time, improve their status and extract value from the land and properties on which they live.

Many of the preceding cases can fall under the term of 'development-induced displacement'. However, some of this development does result in developing high-end residential, retailing and commercial neighbourhoods. Can this be classified as 'gentrification' under any of the existing gentrification theories? I feel that this is a subject that needs to be debated in the context of Karachi.

Towards gentrification?

Interest in Karachi's built heritage in the inner city first appeared in the mid-1980s in a series of articles that appeared in *The Herald* monthly magazine and in proposals for pedestrianisation in certain parts of the colonial city (Hasan, 1986). These proposals were more about creating order out of chaos rather than 'gentrification'. In the early 1990s, the Design Bureau of the KDA prepared measured drawings of important Karachi buildings and undertook limited 'repair' work on some of them. In addition, old churches, schools and some 'iconic' public use buildings were also repaired by their owners, though more out of necessity than out of love for their heritage value. This work was not done by trained conservationists or even by persons who had any experience of such work. However, in the decade of the 1990s, two other important things happened. First, the Sindh Cultural Heritage (Preservation) Act 1994 was enacted and a listing of heritage buildings was commenced. An Advisory and a Technical Committee were set up under the Act to assist the Sindh Culture Department. A UK-trained architect, Yasmin Lari, played an important role in pushing for this Act. The second important thing was that another Yasmin, Professor Yasmin Cheema, returned from Turkey after studying and teaching conservation. She became a teacher at the Department of Architecture and Planning at the Dawood College, Karachi, and commenced the first-ever systematic documentation and analysis of Karachi's built heritage. This led to her defining a 'historic district of Karachi' and the publication of her book *The historic quarters of Karachi* (Cheema, 2007). During the 1990s, a number of students at Dawood College undertook 'adaptive reuse' projects related to old buildings in the inner city, and a study of the quarters in which they were located. However, Dawood College had a strong populist tradition built around the concept of 'socially responsive architecture', and, as such, these projects did not aim at displacing people who already lived in these quarters.

Other important developments have taken place in the first decade of the 21st century. Anila Naeem, a graduate of Dawood College, undertook a PhD in Conservation at Oxford Brookes University in the UK. She returned to teach at the Department of Architecture and Planning at NED University in Karachi. NED University's Conservation Cell also became the consultant to the Sindh Culture Department and a member of the Technical Committee. As a result, a larger documentation and categorisation of Karachi's built heritage has been undertaken. The owners of listed buildings have often gone to court against such listings. The Technical Committee has offered them alternatives to demolishing the building. These alternatives aim at providing the owners with the same economic benefits that pulling down and reconstructing the building can offer. A number of such projects have been implemented (along with conservation-related advice to owners of public and corporate sector listed buildings), but they do not aim at changing the land use of the area. However, the buildings that have undergone the adaptive reuse design process have attracted the attention of corporate sector institutions and higher-end users. For example, the Sindh Zamindar Hotel, a 1920s' building in what is now a downmarket area, was redesigned as a downmarket retail shopping centre.[5] Once the facade was rehabilitated, a number of banks contacted the owner, who was unhappy that he had not foreseen this, for if he had, he would have had the building redesigned differently. There are indications that if these heritage buildings are beautifully conserved, even for downmarket activities, they will eventually help in changing the land use to a higher-end market.

Students' projects and proposals from the Conservation Cell at NED University have not really proposed 'gentrification' in the conventional sense of the term. They have only made proposals for protecting and conserving existing neighbourhoods where heritage is still intact and communities still exist (on social preservation versus gentrification, see Brown-Saracino, 2010). A debate on shifting wholesaling and warehousing from the inner city to the city bypasses is ongoing; however, given Karachi's political violence and the role of real estate development and battles for turf between conflicting interest groups in the inner city, this is not likely to happen in the near future.

Karachi has an active and rapidly expanding theatre, film, fashion, media and art scene. Most of this is located in the elite and middle-income areas or near the administrative centre of the city. Abandoned warehouses in the industrial areas on the periphery of the city are increasingly used for this purpose. Talk of shifting this to the inner city now often takes place in academic and art circles, though, for reasons given earlier, this is unlikely to materialise. However, the desire to preserve and use old buildings for cultural purposes is strong and has been promoted by the small but increasingly vocal conservation lobby, and a number of organisations have emerged to promote concepts related to heritage.[6] As a result, a number of old listed colonial buildings in the cantonment and elite areas have been conserved and are being reused as museums, schools and expensive restaurants.

A major boost to promoting development at the cost of relocating and evicting communities (gentrification) took place in 1999 when General Musharraf dismissed the democratically elected government in Pakistan and became the country's chief executive. He appointed an important World Bank person as the minister for finance, planning and development in Sindh province, in which Karachi is located, who was subsequently made federal minister for privatisation and investment. He appointed a chief vice executive of Citibank as finance minister, who was subsequently appointed prime minister. He also appointed a very senior economist of the World Bank as the governor of the State Bank of Pakistan, whose additional job was that of chairperson of the National Commission for Government Reforms. As a result of the neoliberal agenda followed by the new government, decentralisation was carried out and indirectly elected mayors replaced the old colonial bureaucracy. 'Devolution' led to the implementation of the provincial Local Body Ordinances. In Sindh, the Sindh Local Government Ordinance (SLGO) was enforced, and in 2001, Karachi became an autonomous city district/government. Its first mayor initiated a major signal-free road-building programme, complete with flyovers and underpasses, displacing over 300,000 people. Civil society organisations and also the city planners had serious concerns regarding these initiatives. However, unlike earlier, the city planners were not the decision-makers. The programme, though, remained modest due to the conservatism of the mayor. With the election of the second mayor, things changed. He was 'dynamic', had international links and represented Karachi's main political party. The road-building programme was expanded and projects for 'beautifying' Karachi were aggressively developed. A new vocabulary entered the development and planning process, terms such as 'World-Class City', investment-friendly infrastructure, foreign direct investment, cities as engines of growth, golden handshake, public–private partnership and build, operate and transfer began to be used more extensively in planning circles and in the media. This vocabulary and the culture that it promoted also found its way into academia and was/is being promoted by many teachers, especially those who have studied in the West. In addition, foreign companies started visiting Karachi and missions from international financial institutions also increased substantially. International companies and international financial institutions flooded the city seeking to invest in it. Due to all these new developments, projects replaced planning, and during the period 1991–2006, Dubai-based companies with multi-billion-dollar portfolios (including Dubai World, Emaar, Limitless and Nakheel) entered into negotiations with the government of Pakistan and other prospective private sector partners.

The Karachi Strategic Development Plan 2020 (KSDP-2020) (City District Government, Karachi, 2007), approved by the City District Council Karachi in 2007, specifically states in its vision that Karachi is to be a 'World-Class City'. Under this vision, initiated in 2002, not only were signal-free roads, flyovers and underpasses built, but the gentrification of Karachi's coastline was also attempted by federal land-owning agencies. This coastline is 27 kilometres long and has numerous creeks and mangrove forests. It is dotted with ancient fishing villages and more than half of it is visited by hundreds of thousands of Karachiites every week for recreation and entertainment. A large service sector serves the visitors. In 2006, the prime minister signed a Memorandum of Understanding (MoU) with Dubai-based developers and ordered federal land-owning agencies to provide land to the developers by transferring state land to them and by cancelling the existing leases of non-state entities. An MoU for handing over two islands off the coast was also enacted.[7] The development projects proposed consisted of condominiums, five-star hotels, marinas, elite clubs and housing and commercial facilities. All these projects were located in the jurisdiction of the KPT. One of these projects, Sugarland City, consisted of 26,000 hectares of land (the size of Washington), with a total investment of USD68 billion. This land was to be handed over to Limitless, a Dubai-based company launched by Dubai World.

These development projects were not surprising (even if their scale was) given that Karachi's coastline had long been threatened by coastal gentrification. Even before 2006, the DHA, which began as the Pakistan Defence Officers' Housing Society in 1960, had initiated development projects along its coastline. The DHA consists of 3,530 hectares of land and is the most elite area of the city. It contains luxury apartments and homes, schools, colleges, clubs, posh shopping centres with designer boutiques, and five- and six-star hotels. The functioning of the DHA is vested in two bodies: the Governing Body, headed by the secretary of the ministry of defence; and the Executive Board, headed by the Karachi corps commander of the Pakistan Army. The housing society also holds about 18 kilometres of coastline and creeks that are the nearest coastal areas to the city. In 2002/03, the DHA built a promenade along a stretch of beach, it came to be known as Sea View and was a major addition to recreation for the city of Karachi. As a result, people shifted from other beachfronts to it. Hawkers, jugglers, animal performers, camels and horses for riding invaded it (see Figure 10.2). The DHA was horrified, for it wanted its beach to be used by 'decent people', so it banned all hawkers, performers and other persons serving the poorer sections of the population from the beachfront. It set up expensive food outlets along this stretch of beach. As a result, poor people stopped going there. This stretch came to be known as 'the rich man's beach' and a beach adjacent to it in the jurisdiction of the city government, where all activity was permitted, came to be known as 'the poor man's beach'. The Urban Resource Centre (URC) took up this issue in articles and letters in the press, and the media also made it an important issue. Finally, the DHA residents' society intervened and made the DHA management relax the conditions that they had imposed. Meanwhile, the city government developed the poor man's beach as a park (see Figure 10.3) and turned away all

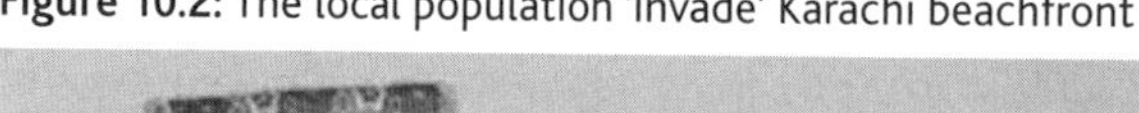

Figure 10.2: The local population 'invade' Karachi beachfront

the hawkers and performers from there as well. However, they have come back at the entrances to the park and in the lanes next to it by informally paying city government staff and officials.

Figure 10.3: The beach redeveloped by the city government as a park

In 2004, the DHA initiated another project – the Waterfront Development Project – with the involvement of Emaar, a well-known Dubai-based company. Its promotional literature described the project as follows:

> In Karachi, DHA has a virgin, unspoiled waterfront of nearly 14 kilometres ready with full potential for development.... The residents of Karachi will soon see a qualitative change in their lives and their concept of relaxation, style and fun. The fire of creativity and imagination is promising to make Karachi beachfront a much sought-after tourist destination in the foreseeable future. Entirely practical and wholly realizable projects will have a deep impact on the lifestyle of the people of Karachi whose perception of enjoying the sea at present consists of riding a camel or a horse or just taking a walk on the wet sand and watching the waves crash on the shore. They will soon have access to multiple recreational activities within their reach. (Emaar promotional literature, no date)

This proposed 'coastal gentrification' project (see Figure 10.4) also involved the development (privatisation) of the city's public beaches and the 'reclamation of 74.5 acres of land for a high-end hotel complex', '5-star hotels owning private segments of the beach' and a 'private beach with lagoon for hotel and residential blocks'. It also included Emaar's 'Crescent Bay Project', with a seven-star hotel and 4,000 super-luxury apartments with private beaches and lagoons. Civil society organisations argued that as a result of these developments, 20% of the DHA beach will not be available to the public and that even the remaining 80% that is meant to be available is beyond the disadvantaged and the poor's economic power to access.

Figure 10.4: The Defence Housing Authority proposal for the Karachi beachfront

This project, along with the other projects located in the KPT areas and the sale of the islands, were opposed by civil society organisations backed by prominent Karachi citizens: the Wildlife Fund Pakistan; national, provincial and Karachi-based fishermen's organisations; trade unions; low-income schools and community based organisations from all over Sindh through a signature campaign by the URC; academia; and concerns voiced by some corporate sector heads, planners from within the city government and senior provincial bureaucrats. These organisations and individuals argued that, as a result of these developments: Karachiites would lose an important part of their entertainment and recreation assets; the services sector that served these facilities would lose its livelihood; fishing villages would lose access to their fishing grounds and livelihoods and a large number of them would be evicted; immense environmental damage would be caused to wildlife and the natural environment, especially to the mangrove marshes; and also that these projects were strictly speaking 'illegal' as they violated the Public Trust Doctrine and the government's own environment-related laws.

The most important role in opposing the projects was played by the Pakistan Mahigeer Tahreek – the Pakistan Fisherfolk Forum – which is a network of indigenous coastal fishing communities from all over Sindh province. They were able to mobilise their network and carry out large-scale demonstrations in various Sindh cities. They produced a position letter referring to the project as a 'Development to destroy nature and displace people' (September 2007). The letter was an outcome of consultations between various stakeholders, especially fishing and low-income communities. Among other things, the letter pointed out that the projects posed a threat to the coastal ecosystems as they were destroying major breeding areas of the green turtle, the resting place of migratory birds and the nurseries for shrimps and several fish species. The letter also pointed out that fishing communities have been living on the coast for centuries and that the proposed developments would destroy not only their economy, but also their cultural heritage, and make access to the tombs of their saints, where their yearly festivities are held (see Figure 10.5), difficult, if not impossible. The letter also mentioned that lower- and lower-middle-income Karachiites would no longer be able to go to the beaches in search of recreation and entertainment and that this would increase the divide between the rich and poor in the city.

Figure 10.5: The festivities of the shrine

Civil society opposition consisted of court cases, forums, demonstrations, walks, writings in the press and the making of films. Finally, Limitless backed out of the project in 2009 and the projects were shelved because of opposition from all segments of Karachi society. The president presented the DHA beach as a 'gift' to the people of Karachi, except for a small portion of Emaar's 2.4-billion-dollar Crescent Bay Project, which was well on its way before the other projects and opposition to them was launched. In the areas where the projects were supposed to take place, the DHA has now planned residential and commercial schemes consisting of small plots. In these schemes, the beaches are accessible and no further reclamation from the sea is being carried out. The reasons for the shelving of the projects are not clear. Maybe it was because of the recession of 2010, because of the deteriorating law-and-order situation in Karachi, because of civil society opposition (an example of the success of this anti-gentrification campaign?), or a combination of all three. However, as a result of this opposition, certain criteria for the preservation of the coastline were incorporated into the KSDP-2020 (City District Government, Karachi, 2007), which was being formulated while opposition to the projects was taking place. These criteria designate that no reclamation from the sea, mangrove marshes and mudflats (which are fish and turtle nurseries) is permitted. Also, all the beaches are to be accessible to the fishing communities and to the public. No development between the high-water mark and 150 metres beyond it, or on the seaward side of the coastal roads, is permissible. The KSDP-2020 was approved by the city council in December 2007. Under the provisions of the KSDP-2020, none of the proposed projects can possibly be built. However, two of these projects do not fall in the jurisdiction of the city government but of military cantonments and the DHA, who are under no obligation to follow the KSDP-2020 provisions. Meanwhile, another form of gentrification has taken place in the shape of the Port Grand Project in Karachi, and gentrification through small-scale improvement projects are being discussed for various locations in the city centre.

The Port Grand Project in Karachi is a clear example of gentrification. The Native Jetty Bridge was built by the British in the 1850s, linking the island of Keamari, where the port is, to the Karachi mainland. In the decade of the 1990s, a new bridge – Jinnah Bridge – which was linked to a number of flyovers, was built parallel to the Native Jetty Bridge, which was abandoned as a result. From the time the Native Jetty Bridge was built, it also served as a place for gatherings and various cultural activities: 'common' people sat at the edge and watched the water; boys jumped off it to swim; and older men fished while sitting at its edge. Furthermore, the water catered to a number of religious superstitions: fish were fed; birds were released from cages; trysts were consolidated; and many religious processions terminated at the water's edge. Old religious manuscripts were also ceremoniously given to the water. After the construction of the Jinnah Bridge, these activities continued at the Native Jetty Bridge. However, in 2003, the bridge was taken over by the Grand Leisure Corporation. As a result, all the popular activities shifted to the Jinnah Bridge (see Figure 10.6). Meanwhile, the Grand

Figure 10.6: Jinnah Bridge activities before being blocked to the public

Leisure Corporation has constructed the Port Grand Project on the Native Jetty Bridge. Its promotional literature[8] says:

> The project is a food, shopping and entertainment complex which has been built with over Rs 1 billion investment by Grand Leisure Corporation. Port Grand project is a 13-acre world-class facility that has been designed and built in collaboration with top international architects/designers who employed the latest technology and building techniques to deliver a state of the art facility. About 40 outlets are being made operational at this stage while more outlets will be opened soon. The native jetty bridge has been entirely rebuilt to ensure a world-class tourist destination and a source of pride for Karachites that will ultimately attract millions of people from all over the country and beyond. Visitors will come to Port Grand not only for food and entertainment but for over a hundred different concepts, including free wifi, a port bazaar, a bookstore, a florist, Art Lane, gifts and antiques etc. Parking for over eight hundred cars with complimentary valet service, and pristine public restrooms and plenty of pedestrian friendly walkways are additional attractions at the project. Port Grand is also one of the first projects in the City that has been dedicated to building an open eco-friendly/green environment, with a special focus on urban regeneration. Port Grand is going to be a model for a lot of good to be followed in the city.

Politicians, the middle classes, the Karachiite elite and the media are all full of praise for Port Grand. Various Karachi websites are very appreciative of it. However, Jinnah Bridge looks down onto Port Grand, and as a result, poor people on the bridge, while carrying on their various 'cultural activities', can look down into

Port Grand, which also hosts fashion shows. As a result, it was felt that Port Grand should be protected from such voyeurs and so barriers were built on either side of Jinnah Bridge, making the populist activities that took place there impossible. So far, no protests against this discontinuation of popular activities have been registered.

Conclusion

This chapter shows that extracting value through land-use changes has caused degradation (both in social and physical terms) as opposed to gentrification in Karachi, even in heritage areas. However, it also shows that gentrification has taken place in Karachi as a result of development that has displaced people from their traditional lands and homes in peri-urban areas and replaced them with better-off and better-educated populations ('peri-urban gentrification'). Gentrification has also taken place in inner-city areas (not necessarily heritage zones) where there is a potential for high-end commercialisation. How all this fits into the existing theories of gentrification from the Global North is up for debate (see Lees, 2012). However, any debate will have to accommodate the views of the pro-poor development activists in Karachi and members of Pakistan's academic and professional institutions if that theorisation is to have a relationship with reality.

At the moment (but then, things can change), the neoliberal-related trends described in this chapter, along with the increasing number of Western-trained Karachi professionals who, in turn, are educating future generations in Pakistan, are having an impact on both practice and policy. The question that one is forced to ask is whether the Dawood College concept of 'socially responsive architecture' and the powerful hangover of populism that still lives in the media will survive the neoliberal onslaught? If it does not, will it be possible to mount a civil society movement against the gentrification of the inner city if at some stage it is proposed and seems possible? It is difficult to answer this question. However, it is important to note that almost all those professionals and academics who actively opposed the gentrification of Karachi's coastline were either trained at Dawood College as architects, belonged to the environmentalist lobby in the city or belonged to a strong left-wing tradition – and they are to be congratulated for their efforts and successes to date.

Architects and planners have played an important role in developing a very large number of anti-poor projects. I have advocated (without success) an oath for architects and planners, something similar to the Hippocratic Oath for the medical profession. The theory is that the Council of Architects should deregister anyone that violates this oath. In 1983, I took such an oath:

> I will not do projects that will irreparably damage the ecology and environment of the area in which they are located; I will not do projects that increase poverty, dislocate people and destroy the tangible and intangible cultural heritage of communities that live in the city;

> I will not do projects that destroy multi-class public space and violate building byelaws and zoning regulations; and I will always object to insensitive projects that do all this, provided I can offer viable alternatives.

I have kept to my words. I feel that if other prominent architects had taken a similar oath in 1983 and stuck to it, Karachi would have been, and would be, a different city.

Notes

[1] See Urban Resource Centre. Available at: www.urckarachi.org

[2] See: www.shehri.org

[3] See Urban Resource Centre. Available at: www.urckarachi.org

[4] See also: www.shehri.org

[5] See: www.arifhasan.org

[6] See: www.seeds.org

[7] The islands measure about 4,800 hectares and were to be sold for USD42 billion. Access to the islands is only by boat and so a USD50 million bridge was proposed by the federal government connecting the islands to the DHA.

[8] Available at: http://forum.xcitefun.net/port-grand-karachi-food-street-t63136.html

References

Anwar, F. (2013) 'People and the land: rural Karachi: a case study', Affiliated Network for Social Accountability, South Asia Region.

Brown-Saracino, J. (2010) *A neighbourhood that never changes: gentrification, social preservation and the search for authenticity*, Chicago, IL: University of Chicago Press.

Cheema, Y. (2007) *The historic quarters of Karachi*, Karachi: Oxford University Press, Pakistan.

City District Government, Karachi (2007) *Karachi strategic development plan 2020*, Karachi: Master Plan Group of Offices.

Cox, W. (2012) 'Pakistan: where the population bomb is exploding', *New Geography*. Available at: http://www.newgeography.com/content/002940-pakistan-where-population-bomb-exploding

Government of Pakistan (2007) *Pakistan economic survey 2006–07*, Islamabad: Finance Division.

Hasan, A. (1986) 'A pedestrian Saddar', *The Herald*, 29 July.

Hasan, A. (2003) 'The changing nature of the informal sector in Karachi due to global restructuring and liberalisation and its repercussions', in A. Roy and N. Al-Sayyad (eds) *Urban informality*, Oxford: Lexington Books.

Hasan, A. (2008) 'Housing security and related issues: the case of Karachi' unpublished paper prepared for UN-Habitat.

Hasan, A. (2013) *Karachi rising: the densification of low income settlements in Karachi* (film), London: International Institute for Environment and Development (IIED).

Hasan, A., Sadiq, A. and Ahmed, S. (2010) *Planning for high density in low income settlements: four case studies from Karachi*, London: International Institute for Environment and Development (IIED).

Hasan, A., Noman, A., Raza, M., Sadiq, A., Saeedud Din, A. and Sarwar, M.B. (2013) *Land ownership, control and contestation in Karachi and its implications for low income housing*, London: International Institute for Environment and Development (IIED).

Lees, L. (2012) 'The geography of gentrification: thinking through comparative urbanism', *Progress in Human Geography*, vol 36, no 2, pp 155–71.

ELEVEN

Gentrification in Buenos Aires: global trends and local features

Hilda Herzer, María Mercedes Di Virgilio and María Carla Rodríguez

Introduction

Despite the fact that gentrification processes are far from a new phenomenon in the field of urban studies (see Lees et al, 2008), their importance nowadays lies in the *scale* of changes that cities are undergoing, as well as in the links that such transformations seem to have within the globalised economy. As Sassen (1997) pointed out, the transformation of the global economy restored the importance of large cities as sites of certain types of production, services, commercialisation and innovation. In a globalised economy, cities became centres for the growth and consolidation of capital investment and for the development of an international real estate market. Latin American cities do not appear to have bucked this trend. Indeed, a new phase of territorial capital accumulation has had a strong impact on urban processes in Latin American cities, promoting what some authors have identified as a redefinition of *the sense of urbanity* from 'the notion of demographic concentration and urbanisation towards the idea of dispersal and fragmented socio-spatial structures' (Carrión, 2010, p 7). In fact, evidence shows that Latin American cities are facing a new phase of increasingly deeper redevelopment in new centralities, which is creating new displacement-related conflicts (see Coulomb, 2010).

Within this framework, gentrification is a phenomenon that has become widespread and integrated into wider processes, both urban and global, and is differentiated from what happened during previous decades when these processes were circumscribed within specific sites (Smith, 2002). It is important to question, as Marcuse and Van Kempen (2000) did with respect to North American cities, the extent to which gentrification processes in Latin American cities are part of the establishment of a new urban order or if, on the contrary, they are historic processes of urban change in city centres that have only recently become more noticeable. It is important to note that the rehabilitation of old quarters in the privileged locations of large Latin American cities has made more visible existing divisions among different social sectors: barriers are no longer virtual, as in past decades, but are constructed in such a way as to create highly unequal conditions regarding access to urban facilities, urban aesthetics, green spaces, and so on. Although these new processes are similar to those apparent during the 1990s, they have changed in terms of their degree and intensity, making economic and social differences more profound.

This chapter looks at the development of gentrification processes in the city of Buenos Aires in Argentina. These processes started at the beginning of the 1990s, but during the last decade, and particularly as a way out of the 2000–02 political and financial crises, they have gained an unusual strength and have extended to different quarters and locations in the city. In this chapter, we deal more specifically with the process as it has taken place in the city's southern area. We begin by summarising the main findings of a longitudinal study (as yet unusual in the gentrification literature, but see Butler and Lees, 2006), which began in 1998 in the La Boca, San Telmo and Barracas quarters in Buenos Aires, Argentina (see Figure 11.1).[1] It examines gentrification through an analysis of household characteristics – socio-economic levels, living standards and employment statistics – in order to determine which aspects of their lives make residents vulnerable to displacement. We scrutinised the residents' perceptions of change, as well as the local and national governments' interventions that encouraged the developments. The purpose of our research was to increase the empirical 'evidence' about 'gentrification' in Latin American cities, given the wide range of processes under way, and to contribute to the existing theoretical body in this field.

Clues to gentrification processes in Buenos Aires

For some time, the gentrification literature revealed an entrenched divide between production (the role of supply) and consumption (the role of demand) theses on the causes of gentrification; then, in the 1990s, researchers urged a synthesis of these two sides (for an account, see Lees et al, 2008). In this vein, we consider how market conditions and consumer preferences interact in the southern neighbourhoods of the city of Buenos Aires, where it is possible to notice different forms of articulation and cleavages in the role of supply and demand. Uitermark et al (2007, p 510; see also Lees and Ley, 2008) discuss the role of urban policies in the promotion of gentrification 'by encouraging middle-class households to move into working-class neighbourhoods'. This seems to be particularly important in Latin American cities in general (Steel and Klaufus, 2010; Salinas Arreortua, 2013), and particularly in some neighbourhoods in the southern area of the City of Buenos Aires. In this chapter, we pay special attention to public regulations and to urban policies as key factors through which to understand the course taken by gentrification in Buenos Aires, focusing on those factors producing market opportunities and the necessary conditions for the arrival of new populations (Smith, 1999; Janoschka et al, 2014). In so doing, we add to debates over new forms of gentrification (Lees, 2003; Butler, 2007).

Figure 11.1: Buenos Aires City and its quarters

Public policies promoted in central and peri-central areas of different Latin American cities have varied in their extent and objectives. On the one hand, some were geared towards direct intervention in the gentrification process by promoting investment and real estate reactivation through the creation of public–private consortiums and a stimulus to supply and demand – for example, through the Programa de Repoblamiento Habitacional in Santiago de Chile (Salinas Arreortua, 2013), which encouraged: population re-densification; the implementation of specific neoliberal planning instruments and building liberalisation (López-Morales, 2011); tax exemptions, such as building rights, a reduction in advertising prices and building permits (Rodríguez et al, 2008, 2011); and changes in land use and new forms of land occupation, such as the Project Puerto Maravilla in Rio de Janeiro and the building on the river bank in the southern area of the city of Buenos Aires. On the other hand, public policies that accompany and complement direct interventions (socio-territorial closing down or closure; see Di Virgilio, 2013) have been developed. They are policies geared to reinforce public safety, to improve public street-lighting systems, to qualify public open spaces such as parks and public squares, and to displace informal traders (eg street vendors) and homeless individuals and families. Such policies are seen in the cases of Quito and Guayaquil, in Ecuador (Swanson, 2007), in Mexico City (Crossa, 2009), in Sao Paulo, Brazil (Mieg and Töpfer, 2013), and in Buenos Aires, Argentina, itself (Carman, 2005, 2006; Guevara, 2012). In many cases, these initiatives articulate with other policies linked to the upgrading of city heritage, gentrification and displacement (Salinas Arreortua, 2013, p 286). The purpose of the initiatives seems to be the generation of attractive spaces for tourism and for private investment. In the southern area of Buenos Aires, these kinds of processes were particularly evident in San Telmo after the enaction of policies[2] geared towards 'heritagisation' processes:

> Facing this urban management scenario, growing private investment is noticed in business premises, hotels, museums, and fashion stores, thereby conforming ... to an 'elitization' of public spaces as well as commercial activity; two dimensions of the gentrification process that characterizes several Latin American cities. (Salinas Arreortua, 2013, p 287)

Thus, public and private investment seems to integrate with cultural innovation processes (Zukin, 1995), often promoted by the very same public cultural policies. Following Zukin (2010, p 13), we understand:

> the emergence of culture as both a strategy and a theme of urban redevelopment and the rise of the symbolic economy of art, finance, food, and fashion that has done so much both to nourish and to destroy the city's distinctive cultures.... We cannot consider power to control urban spaces, usually seen as the economic power of capital investors and the legal power of the state, without considering the cultural power of ... consumers' tastes. All of these factors now shape the struggle to control the city's future.

As Casgrain and Janoschka (2013, p 23) suggest, in Latin American cities, 'gentrification is more than the exploitation of a monopoly rent by investors and speculators, since it also involves a series of cultural, relational and symbolic capitals that condition the efficiency of this type of process'.

Berry (2010 [1985]) showed nearly 30 years ago that the rhythm of gentrification processes was linked to the dynamics of the regional real estate market. Thus, the opportunities and limitations that buyers and sellers find when involved in real estate businesses in a city's central areas will depend on the interplay of supply and demand at the metropolitan scale (see Lees et al, 2010). A relationship between the processes of gentrification and suburbanisation also seems to be present in the case of Buenos Aires. Since the 1990s, the city of Buenos Aires has undergone both forms of urban growth: an intense residential movement towards the periphery (centrifugal mobility); and a densification of central spaces (centripetal mobility). In recent years, there have been many studies of gated communities (Svampa, 2001; Arizaga, 2005; Janoschka, 2006; Ciccolella and Mignaqui, 2008), their real estate dynamics and the role played by municipal governments (Vio, 2011 ; Pintos and Narodowski, 2012), as well as the transformation dynamics of those centres in general (Torres, 2001; Guevara, 2012). Nevertheless, except for some studies on squatting (Rodríguez, 2005, 2009; Carman, 2006), researchers have rarely envisaged these processes from the perspective of the social groups involved. Furthermore, Berry (2010 [1985]) showed that gentrification processes may achieve different intensification levels. In this sense, he stated that:

> certain cities with strong cores (New York, Washington and Boston) showed extensive areas of housing improvement; in others, improvement was restricted to one or two neighbourhoods near the core if the core was healthy. When the core was stagnant or deteriorating, there was little rehabilitation. (Berry, 2010 [1985], p 42)

Despite the fact that it is widely known that Buenos Aires has a strong centre, it is possible to identify different intensities of this process in its southern neighbourhoods. Even in the neighbourhood of La Boca, gentrification seems to have created 'an island of renewal' based on the development of businesses and services geared to tourism. As a result, its marked contrast with the surrounding areas increases the feelings of deterioration and even danger in neighbouring areas. This mixture of images seems to discourage and even slow down gentrification in the neighbourhood.

Finally, it is impossible to overlook the growth of middle- and upper-middle-class sectors in gentrified areas and, concurrently, the displacement of poorer families. This change in the social composition of the urban landscape underlines the fact that gentrification is an aspect of social inequality (Smith and LeFaivre, 1984). In most of the analysed cases, low- and moderate-income sectors accept their displacement because they lack the financial or political resources needed to oppose gentrification. In other cases, despite a lack of resources, they struggle against the displacement and they encourage the development of neighbourhood organisations, even if some of them do not last long, as has happened in some of the neighbourhoods in the southern area of the city of Buenos Aires. The direct or indirect displacement of lower-income groups constitutes a core element of gentrification processes. Buenos Aires is no exception. Such displacements occur under different forms: through the rehabilitation of dwellings occupied by low-income groups, but requalified as high-level housing; the involuntary abandonment of the neighbourhood by poor sectors (large families, old people, etc) who cannot pay the increasing property taxes; the lack of resources that young emancipated youths who were born in the neighbourhood face in order to pay for their living quarters; the emigration of residents due to the closure of social, economic and religious institutions, and even the loss of friends in the neighbourhood; and so on. Nonetheless, as López-Morales (2010, p 148) points out in the Chilean case, for Buenos Aires:

> inequalities related with market-driven inner city redevelopment seem to emerge less as a matter of direct displacement (as the global northern literature claims for those realities; see Atkinson, 2000b; 2000a; Freeman, 2005; Newman and Wyly, 2006; García-Herrera et al, 2007) but more as an indirect, invisible form of 'exclusionary displacement' and 'displacement pressure' (Slater, 2009) in addition to other forms of physical rupture of vibrant working-class neighborhoods.

Some of the impacts caused by gentrification are: the creation of new opportunities for speculative investment in the housing market in the city centre; the displacement caused by increases in rents and property prices; the psychological costs of displacement suffered by those who have to leave the site; social tension and conflict; permanent emergency solutions for the homeless; the displacement of households that are always forced to look for dwellings in cheaper areas – Marcuse (2000) calls this phenomenon exclusionary displacement; commercial and industrial displacement; increases in the cost of services; the loss of social diversity; and the introduction of new discriminatory forms of surveillance and social control.

Gentrification in Buenos Aires

The trigger for the gentrification process on the south side of Buenos Aires City was the implementation of an urban renewal plan for the Río de La Plata and Riachuelo riverside, which establishes the east and south-east city limits. Launched in 1993, the conversion of the Puerto Madero waterfront stimulated the urban recovery of the riverside as a whole, as well as the city's south-side quarters, La Bocca and Baraccus, which sit next to the old harbour in Buenos Aires. At the same time, the area where the city was founded – the San Telmo quarter – was declared as historic; a process that had begun during the previous decade (Lourés Seonae, 1997). The riverside recovery plan set about enlarging the central area by incorporating urban land through the development and functional change of underused areas and urban infrastructures in a city in which land was very limited. The new quarter of Puerto Madero was annexed to the old quarters located in the city's original area – San Telmo, among them – and the process of the urban 'integration' of La Boca and Barracas began with the renewal of the riverside promenade and investment in a coastal defence structure against flooding with Inter-American Development Bank funding. These changes enabled the development of new commercial services and housing uses for activities that involved high-income populations. Also, roads were built, making travel in and out of the central area easier through motorways and so on. In 1995, a renowned architect explained that:

> the South-side quarters are areas that can be revalued and recycled in the same way as Eastern Paris or Soho in New York. What can be done? Money is needed, but also awareness is lacking. Ventures such as the Intercontinental hotel produce movement. Parks may be recovered, and employment, leisure and housing imagined. Otherwise, these large quarters are underused, and may become impenetrable, as the Bronx in New York where not even the police can go. (*Clarín*, 3 December 1995)

The implementation of the State Reform and Economic Emergency Law 1989 and the launching of the 'Convertibility' Plan in 1991 set the bases for change. The reduction of interest rates in the local financial market and the launching of housing loans and the incorporation of state land and buildings that were not used for their original purpose into the real estate market promoted a building boom. The process benefitted from new flexibility applied to urban regulations and urban planning that enabled an increase in the size of buildings in residential districts and also eased the procedures for modifying and making exceptions to the building code (Mignaqui, 1998). This meant the opening up of new opportunity areas for real estate firms in the central and southern side of the city, and its correlation was: an increase in the number of building permits granted and the surface upon which improvements could be built (see Figure 11.2);[3] a readjustment of the selling prices of buildings and plots; and the proliferation of a new residential supply geared towards high- and upper-middle-income sectors in high-standard, high-rise buildings and in gated communities.[4]

It is evident that within this framework, the governments – national and local – played a role as managers of the necessary, though not sufficient, conditions for the emergence of the economic, social and environmental changes in the city's degraded areas in general, and in the southern quarters in particular. The mechanisms that enabled these processes were the changes in their regulatory functions and the adaptation of rules and regulations, particularly: the flexibilisation of the Urban Planning Code (CPU) in 1990 and its numerous exceptions; the privatisation of water, electricity and telephone services; and, finally, the subsidised transfer of resources, such as urban land or public debt. Within this context, the continuity in the direction taken by successive local governments between 1988 and 2005 regarding the city's public expenditures was to assign a large amount of resources to infrastructure works in the southern area. In 1999, 'for each US $100 of public funds invested in the North, $130 were allocated to the South', following the government slogan to 'incorporate the South to the North' (Rodríguez and Redondo, 2001, p 3). The foreign direct investment that the city

Figure 11.2: Total square metres of construction authorised in the city of Buenos Aires, 1935–2010

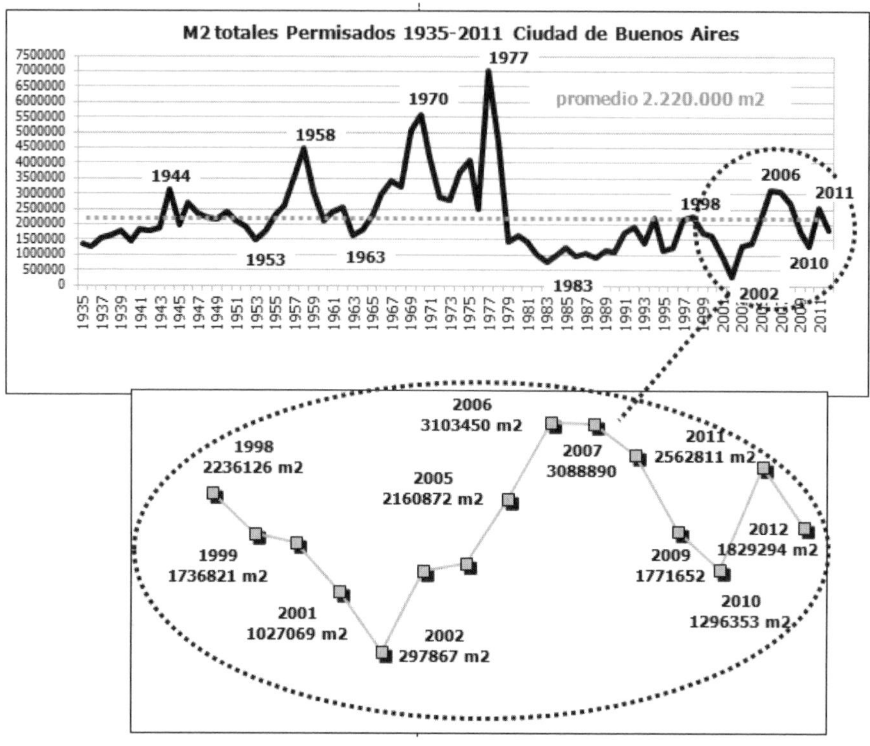

Source: Reporte Inmobiliario. Available at: http://www.reporteinmobiliario.com/nuke/index.php

received from the 1990s would have been unthinkable without this framework of public action. In fact, it:

> enabled the arrival and settlement of a group of agents and actors linked to the real estate global market [among them, Richard Ellis, Bovis and Lend properties, Ernst and Young, Cushman and Wakefield], who found in Buenos Aires attractive niches for capital investment. The intervention scales and strategies were developed by these actors through the construction of sites for hotels and international enterprises, shopping centres, hypermarkets, private urbanisations on the metropolitan periphery, high standard residential ventures (El Porteño Building, El Faro Tower, among others), or investments in the renewal of the old Puerto Madero area in Buenos Aires, that promoted a selective valuation process of the metropolitan territory and an increase in the demand for real estate products geared to [high-income] social segments. (Ciccolella and Mignaqui, 2008, p 56)

The dynamics of reactivating the building and real estate industries became evident in the sustained increase in the average purchase and sale price per square metre (see Figure 11.2). This prosperity was interrupted between 1998 and 2001, when one of the 20th-century's deepest social, economic and institutional crises befell Argentina. Within this context, the average purchase and sale price per square metre reached rock bottom; nevertheless, from 2002, the appreciation process began to grow slowly (see Figure 11.3). After the 2001 national crisis, public investment was revived in the city's southern area: in 2004, the foreseen building investment plan for those quarters involved 38% of the city's budget versus 12% forecasted for the northern side of the city. This trend changed in 2005 when the southern area's budget was increased to 52% of the forecasted city's budget, as against 8% assigned to the northern area (Herzer, 2009).

Figure 11.3: Apartment price per total square metre (average value per two to three rooms in USD)

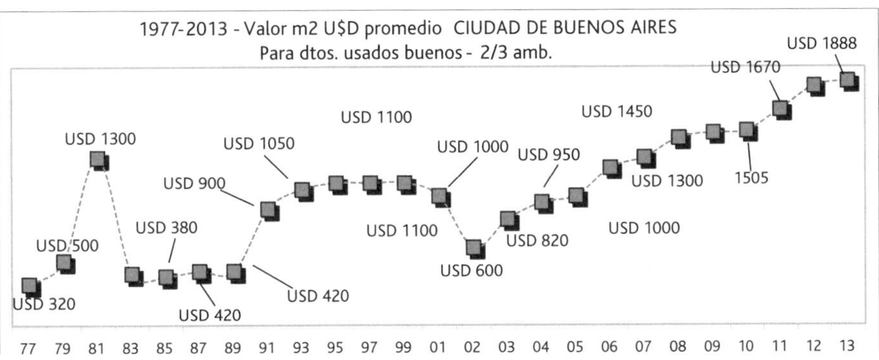

Source: Reporte Inmobiliario. Available at: http://www.reporteinmobiliario.com/miembros/informes

Moreover, a new reform to the CPU of the city of Buenos Aires within the context of the crisis worked as a trigger for a new vertical densification stage. This process is clearly expressed in the 2010 census: while population growth was 10% between 2001 and 2010, housing stock growth showed a striking 41% increase. In the neighbourhoods of the southern area of Buenos Aires, the housing stock also increased, though at a smaller proportion than the city average. Barracas was the neighbourhood that most benefitted from the increase (see Table 11.1).

Table 11.1: Population and dwelling units in three neighbourhoods of Buenos Aires, 2001 and 2010

Area/neighbourhood	Year	Population	% of total population	Dwelling units	% housing units	Inhabitants/ housing unit
Ciudad Autónoma de Buenos Aires	2001	2,776,138	100.00	1,008,867	100.00	2.75
	2010	3,058,309	100.00	1,423,973	100.00	1.50
La Boca	2001	43,413	1.56	14,227	1.41	3.05
	2010	47,117	1.54	15,441	–	–
San Telmo	2001	23,198	0.84	9,420	0.93	2.46
	2010	25,557	0.84	10,378	–	–
Barracas	2001	73,377	2.64	22,762	2.26	3.22
	2010	83,410	2.73	25,874	–	–

Source: Population data and number of dwelling units for 2001 from National Census 2001, INDEC. Population data for 2010 from Dirección General de Estadística y Censos (2008), *Informe de resultados*, no 368, Buenos Aires: GCBA.

Note: Dwelling unit data for 2010 were estimated by the author.

Gentrification in the southern neighbourhoods of Buenos Aires

La Boca

La Boca developed as a working-class neighbourhood of European immigrants who, after merging with the local society, moved to the city's middle-class quarters. Initially, La Boca was strongly linked to the port activities of the Riachuelo, the centre of the local economy. However, between 1947 and 1991, La Boca lost 40% of its population and suffered severe degradation, which intensified in the 1970s when the port was dismantled and many factories in the neighbourhood were closed.

In the 1990s, the city government launched a neighbourhood revival project, including the building of river embankments to take advantage of the quarter's prime location close to the city centre. This intervention was developed together with the launching of initiatives geared towards the consolidation of residents' presence in the area: the first one, called RECUP Boca, was developed at the beginning of the 1980s and was associated with the context of democratic recovery; the second one, called Procedure 525, took place during the mid-1990s and was linked to the resistance displayed by neighbourhood social organisations that risked eviction when the coastal defence works were concluded; and the third one, occurring during the 2000s, was linked to the development of another scheme proposed by social organisations and destined to promote cooperative habitat-building, which gained some traction within the context of the 2001 crisis.

However, these programmes to alleviate the problems of lower-income residents were discontinuous and had limited scope (see Guevara, 2010). Nonetheless:

> [it is] difficult to evaluate the effects of the purchase of premises by the Government of Buenos Aires City during the 1990s (21 within the programme RECUP La Boca and 36 during Procedure 525), because their general deterioration may have 'discouraged' investment in their area of influence. (Guevara, 2011, p 16)

Within this context, higher-income groups began to buy low-cost warehouses, shipyards and dwellings to be recovered and later used mainly for commercial and cultural activities in the neighbourhood. According to Herzer et al (2000), the market for commercial buildings was most directly affected by the appreciation process triggered by urban renewal in the quarter, and a new commercial area emerged inside the tourist sector that showed the highest activity, Caminito-Vuelta de Rocha, which is an area where the coastal defence system also has a touristic function and rents are nearly eight times more expensive that in other sectors of the quarter. While in the first sector, premises were rented very quickly despite their price, in deteriorated sectors like Necochea Street, they were on the market for months, even years, without reaching a tenancy agreement. In Caminito-Vuelta de Rocha, the warehouse market has been directly affected by the new coastal defence system, the disappearance of flooding conditions increased the price per square metre of the warehouses located in the areas affected by recurrent flooding, multiplying two- or threefold the price per square metre.

It is important to note that the neighbourhood's appreciation process, in general terms, was strongly affected by the crisis that exploded at the end of 2001 and the beginning of 2002. According to a 2005 report by the Buenos Aires City's GIS General Offices, in December 2002, there was an important dip in the prices established in dollars – a dip originated by the end of the convertibility of pesos. In December 2003, the price of property began to rise, being, at present, slightly over the figures registered by Herzer et al (2000) at the end of the 1990s (USD620 versus USD600, respectively). Nevertheless, the price of dwellings has increased in general terms, despite the fact that the quarter is near the city centre, and the price is low in relation to the Buenos Aires housing market, where the average is USD1,515 per square metre. Some environmental factors, such as high truck traffic and the deterioration of buildings, as well as the social conditions of a large part of the inhabitants, tend to keep the prices lower than those of the rest of the city (cr Ley and Dobson, 2008).

Since the beginning of the gentrification process, working-class households in La Boca have seen their existence threatened by the increasing value of real estate. Since 1998, the neighbourhood has gone through a systematic process of population change. According to a follow-up survey carried out on a group of approximately 430 dwellings in 2000, 1.2% had changed in use, 3.7% had been demolished and 5.6% were unoccupied. Also, approximately 54.5% of the surveyed households no longer lived in those premises. Given the nature of the survey, it is impossible to know with any certainty why, and to where, those families moved. Nevertheless, if we bear in mind the characteristics of those who replaced them, it is gentrification-induced displacement. When we examined the population characteristics that replaced the oldest residents in 2000, we were able to conclude that the first stage of the renewal process was driven by higher rentals. At that time, however, a closer look did not reveal significant differences in the characteristics of the buildings or their occupancy. In 2008, it was evident that the new households that occupied the dwellings visited in 2000 had integrated themselves into the neighbourhood under better conditions than the old residents. In the new homes, the heads carried out white-collar activities and were less vulnerable than the old residents in terms of the labour market. The changes in the characteristics of the resident households were also evident in the feminisation of family heads, particularly among the new surveyed families. In spite of this, we noted that the proportion of heads of household with a highly vulnerable occupational position was larger in the group of new households than in those that were revisited. This phenomenon shows that La Boca was still attracting disadvantaged populations who did not manage to stay in their dwellings for long periods and were slowly displaced by others that were better positioned in the labour market or, at least, had better incomes. When we look at the characteristics of the process, monitored since 1998, it adds up to a process of population change in which the old households are being progressively replaced by new ones that, although better positioned socially and economically, are close to them in the social structure. Inzulza-Contardo (2012) shows something similar in Bellavista, a neighbourhood in Santiago de Chile.

San Telmo

San Telmo is the south-side quarter that is closest to national and city governmental centres. This is a small historical quarter with many landmarks that remain from the time when the city was founded and began developing. Changes began in the quarter at the beginning of the 1980s. One of the first actions that opened the way to renewal was the declaration, in 1979, of a number of blocks as an area of historic preservation. Since then, activities linked to services – particularly hotels, gastronomy and cultural services – have progressively expanded in the neighbourhood. This process took off especially after the 2001/02 crisis and was linked to the international touristic boom in the city that promoted new commercial and real estate businesses. During the last few years, activities related to tourism have diversified and become more complex, ranging from traditional antiques to a wide range of gastronomic services, boutique hotels, hostels, shops selling designer clothing and so on. The quarter has also become an educational magnet and has consolidated as a cultural area since the enlargement of the Museum of Modern Art and the remodelling and opening of the Spanish Cultural Centre. In this framework, historic protection policies have moved backwards to favour market initiatives. Gentrification seems to have rapidly moved forward and the characteristics of the population who live there expresses that development: its social structure is more polarised and heads of household hold higher and better-paid occupational positions than their equals in the neighbouring quarters. These characteristics make them less vulnerable to the conditions of gentrification. The surveyed San Telmo residents were, in fact, those who managed to stay despite the process and/or those who have recently arrived, attracted by the 'virtues' of the surroundings. The important presence of self-employed people and the characteristics of their labour position mark a particular gentrification process: artists, craftsmen and professionals replacing manual workers and unskilled employees.

Barracas

Historically, the characteristic feature of Barracas has been its important industrial dynamics; at first linked to port activities carried out at the mouth of the Riachuelo River, in the 1930s it consolidated its industrial profile, producing a large range of products. Successive crises and the gradual push to drive industry away from the city led to the neighbourhood's decline and downgrading, leaving a large number of vacant industrial buildings. Barracas is marked by the presence of urban barriers: the Buenos Aires–La Plata motorway, the General Roca railway line, the 'Buenos Aires' railway station and a building complex made up of the Borda, Moyano and Tobar García neuropsychiatric hospitals. As a result, three clearly differentiated macro-areas have emerged. One is predominantly residential, and, here, renewal started earlier. The second is the industrial and services area, which is the most deteriorated of the three. The third macro-area includes the Villa 21-24 shantytowns and the Zavaleta quarter. Over the last two decades, this area has experienced the largest population growth of the entire neighbourhood. Public intervention is evident in Barracas: for example, works carried out on sites located under the 9 de Julio Sur motorway include new street lighting, new concrete pavements, the moving of fences and border railings, bicycle paths, ramps for disabled people, skate ramps, wastepaper baskets and planting of trees and bushes, and so on. More recently, the Fish Market has been proposed as a Historic Protection Area. Concomitantly, private investment has grown and is evident in the construction of residential units for the upper-middle classes. At the end of 2000, the price of a square metre of land in Barracas was under USD1,000, compared with USD3,000 in more expensive neighbourhoods; this incentivised investment in the area. Incentives for private investment were also provided: in 2007, building permits were granted for 20,000 square metres; a year later, the permitted building area was triple that amount. This increase relates to the development of a technology pole, a civic centre and amenities buildings for middle- and upper-middle-income families.

In the 2009 follow-up survey carried out on approximately 173 dwellings in San Telmo and 204 in Barracas, there were improvements in both areas, but changes in building use were much more apparent in San Telmo and there was a greater mobility among its residential households. Population change was also evident, for improved buildings housed different people from those who lived there in 2005. For example, in San Telmo, the gap between old and new households was very marked: among old residents, the proportion of dwellings in bad condition was 12.9%, and for new households, it was only 3.3%. The different urban structures found in the neighbourhoods under investigation enable us to understand why the process of change did not follow the same course in both. In Barracas, a set of factors hindered the uniform development of gentrification, while in San Telmo, the process itself was two decades old and encountered few urban barriers.

Differential gentrifications and displacements

As initially pointed out in this chapter, cultural and symbolic aspects are key clues in the development of gentrification. In this frame, the construction of touristic and/or residential enclaves allows different agents to engage with the re-signification of uses and spaces. It is important to note that their participation in such processes is heterogeneous, and even though they do not necessarily agree with the development and/or the outcomes they produce, directly or indirectly, they contribute by placing it on the public agenda and/or by giving it visibility. Zukin (1989), in her characterisation of the renewal process in Manhattan, observes that touristic and cultural development constitutes the axis of a successful strategy for real estate appraisal.

Buses full of groups that come and go, passengers that roam about the streets with curiosity, and tourists that like to have their photographs taken against the backdrop of historic buildings in the neighbourhoods are scenes an observer finds in La Boca, San Telmo and, in fewer numbers, in Barracas. Tourists calmly stroll around and look with curiosity at what the artists are doing. With gentrification, neighbourhood iconography has gone global. Urban icons have become legitimate elements that structure the mental images of a place. There is a multiplication of expressions destined for mass consumption that are subject to different perceptions and ephemeral appropriations. The history that gives them meaning becomes trivial and ends up in a simple anecdote with which an external image, strongly related to the media, is built. Diversity is the distinctive sign of others and is clearly linked to tourists. Tourists mix (at least for a short while) with peddlers and the old residents of boarding houses and tenements. These situations of co-presence reinforce the difference. The space prepared for tourism delimits a sphere for the others in which the *use* of the neighbourhood's residents is, in itself, a form of displacement.

On weekends, craft fairs, like the artisan fair in La Boca and the antiques fair in San Telmo, become protagonists. Fairs are not a novelty in these quarters; on the contrary, they constitute long-standing initiatives that have been articulated and redefined along with the gentrification process (see Figure 11.4). Tourists and residents are linked in different ways to the process of gentrification and

Figure 11.4: Bar La Perla and artisan fair

the activities that take place in the fairs. For stallholders and shopkeepers, work constitutes the element that draws them together in a territory that goes beyond the limits of residence. Although they do not live in the neighbourhood, their belonging to the neighbourhood is defined by the bond established in their daily activities. The neighbours maintain an ambiguous relationship with the fair and its protagonists (stallholders and tourists): for them, the fair implies an *invasion* of people who disrupt the neighbourhood's everyday life and who describe *exotic* and *picturesque* situations that crystallise deep social inequalities, such as the living conditions in tenements in La Boca.

The La Boca urban renewal process used the tenement as a referent that interwove the neighbourhood's history. Within the context of gentrification, those who do not live in tenements or who only have indirect contact with the tenements in their daily lives evoke the tenement as dissociated from the precarious conditions that the inhabitants experience. The senses that are built incorporate the tenement as a curiosity, as a matter of interest for visitors and for foreigners. It thus appears as a product that may be culturally consumed; a promotional ad (see Figure 11.5) features it as a tour by which the tourist may go back to the neighbourhood's 'picturesque' past, ignoring the fact that the tenement is still a very real present. Thus, the tenement shows in a paradigmatic way the ideological operation of symbolic substitution through the introduction of new ritualised practices. Its presentation as a cultural product and the tourists' pilgrimage to that space – now having a commercial use cloaked with a 'mythical' past – omits its present-day validity as a housing facility linked to poverty and precariousness. In this case, contrary to what happens with the artisans' spaces, there is no space for insertion in the urban landscape. One use has been displaced by another one, and one of history's narratives has been omitted.

Figure 11.5: Advertisement for tenement tour La Boca

Conventillo anterior a 1885

Conozca por dentro un auténtico conventillo de madera y chapa, ubicado en el patio de la casa. Vea la escritura original que dice "Se vende lote de terreno con casilla de madera" con fecha 11 de julio de 1885. arqueólogos e historiadores afirman que la construcción es anterior a 1870, ya que es la típica vivienda que hace el genovés para su familia. Visite la "Galería del Recuerdo" con testimonios de Benito Quinquela Martín y Juan de Dios Filiberto, junto a fotos y objetos antiguos que recuerdan la inmigración en el barrio de La Boca.

Pinturas sobre Buenos Aires en los años cincuenta

Vea la Costanera Sur, el Balneario, la antigua Vuelta de Rocha, el Viejo Puente con transbordador de La Boca y otras imágenes que evocan lugares y costumbres de aquellos tiempos con un relevamiento arquitectónico fiel y pintadas en estilo naif.

Visita Guiada

Boutique de Arte - Souvenirs - Salón de Conferencias
Sábados, Domingos y feriados de 14 a 19 hs. Entrada $ 2.-

Atención de grupos en la semana: Turismo, Colegios e Instituciones
Informes: Tel.: 4302-2337, E-mail: celia_chevalier@yahoo.com.ar

IRALA 1162 a dos cuadras de Caminito y Av. Patricios al 900

Un paseo histórico, divertido e *Inolvidable!...*

Declarado de Interés Cultural por la Legislatura de la Ciudad Autónoma de Buenos Aires

Actions carried out by the private sector in the recovery of neighbourhoods through architectural and historical interventions are strongly linked to cultural activities – one of the most renowned cases in San Telmo is that of a well-known architect who, at the end of the 1960s, established his studio and an auditorium in an old recycled tenement and later on added a real estate business that has become one of the most important in the area. These actions shape revitalisation processes:

> the result of which (seen from the standpoint of renewal promoters) is a landscape that does not betray San Telmo: it does not have, for example, the neat finish of the restauro alla italiana but the graphic presence of coarseness that is the evidence of a neighbourhood history. (Quoted in *Revista Dos Puntos*, no 4, March–April 1982, p 45)

The actions of the private sector were articulated with preservation policies through isolated urban interventions and government campaigns called 'awareness and sensitivity'. Preservation policies are thus cultural policies, as shown in the transfer of the San Telmo–Montserrat programme to the Culture Secretariat. They also articulate with urban interventions, binding together the meanings of urban history and cultural values with improvements to physical spaces. These interventions have ranged from façade recovery and the improvement of public spaces, to urban transport regulations. Greenlining was also evident in a number of loans: the Historical Quarter Offices opened a mortgage credit line in 1999, granted by the City's Bank, for the purchase of dwellings in the quarter. Another credit line was opened as the Secretariats for Culture and Production, Tourism and Sustainable Development provided loans of up to USD50,000 for building firms engaged in renovation and 1 million pesos for condominiums that wanted to renew their façades.

The promotion of intangible heritage took place through cultural policies, such as: the events of 'Open Space' and the establishment of a cultural hub, with art, a cinema and museums; the preservation of the fair and of tango; and the preservation of those crafts that are considered in danger of extinction – in 2003, a puppeteer, an architect, a clockmaker and the person who runs a roundabout were declared so by Buenos Aires City Heritage (*La Nación*, 2003). In San Telmo, Barracas and La Boca, a large number of artists have established studios, creating a bohemian environment and offering their work in the colourful courtyards of tenements, thus articulating with the other museums in the quarter.

In recent years, the media have also echoed the changes in the city's south side by pointing to the commercial boom in leisure, entertainment and tourism; including commercial development in hotels and gastronomy. There has also been an unexpected residential trend in the case of San Telmo – the purchasing of real estate by foreigners. Newspaper commentaries express and reinforce the mythicising discourse about the south zone by tying economic success to the testimonial site of cultural identity and diversity. Here, La Boca is still the testimonial site of our history as porteños (a person born in Buenos Aires city), as well as a tourist attraction. One of the most important real estate developers in the San Telmo quarter has targeted 90% of its supply to foreigners, explaining that:

> the patrimonial architecture, the bohemian spirit and the low cost of San Telmo properties are irresistible for foreign investors. In the last two years the number of real estate operations grew by 20 percent and the area became one of the main temporary rental zones for foreigners. (*El Clarín*, 2005)

Foreign investment in the area is mostly through the purchase of apartments that are rented to tourists; the larger investments are linked to the purchase of boutique hotels, restaurants and even antique dealers who are able to sell in international circuits. Thus, those who appreciated the San Telmo quarter when they came as tourists, later came back as investors. Little by little, identity and diversity coalesced with local attractions and successful commercial renovation. In April 2005, there was a Latin American meeting of antique dealers in San Telmo – it is the quarter that gathers the largest number of antique dealers in all of Latin America. As the antique dealers' chairman said: 'San Telmo is a brand!'

Conclusions

What are the features that globalisation imprints on gentrification processes in Latin American cities, in particular in Buenos Aires? It is evident that the processes we have observed in the city's south-side quarters have been strongly promoted by the development of public policies that generated the conditions for, and eased the process of, price increases in an important but empty real estate stock, as well as by the expansion of real estate investments. A feature that seems to have become consolidated is that gentrification in Buenos Aires is not exclusively geared to provide housing for higher-income groups; such a supply is subsidiary to the processes that provide, for example, cultural, touristic, educational and commercial services for those same groups. In San Telmo and La Boca, in particular, commercial and service uses have expanded at the expense of residential uses. The changes in use of the existing housing stock produced direct and indirect displacements. The direct ones were due to the decrease in the supply of available housing in both neighbourhoods, and the indirect ones were due to the fact that the new amenities were geared to population sectors that had little to do with those who lived in the neighbourhood 30 years ago. In Buenos Aires, particularly in Barracas and San Telmo, some magnificent mansions have become integrated into the supply of restaurants, hotels, universities, museums and so on, aimed at middle- and upper-middle-class consumers. When the conditions are not yet ripe for success, as happened in La Boca, the process is organised under the logic of an enclave that re-signifies realities that are far away from the situation of the sectors that consume the services provided by that enclave.

The gentrification process in the south side of Buenos Aires City has been strongly promoted by local government and pushed forward by the development of public policies implemented in the area since the end of the 1980s. The local government's actions have been more or less explicit, sometimes through direct intervention in infrastructure works and at other times by creating the conditions that made private investment possible. Investment in public works has been significant; the most important works were developed in La Boca – such as the building of the coastal defence. Nevertheless, they were accompanied by cosmetic public investments. The ornamental nature of these initiatives has been even more evident in San Telmo and Barracas; within that context, investments have accompanied the development of different urban businesses (real estate and services), which are linked to different opportunities for finding a way out in moments of crisis.

Within this framework, what has been the role played by local real estate firms? Large real estate developer firms have opened subsidiaries in San Telmo. In Barracas, it seems that these agents became involved in building the new properties and it is still necessary to inquire whether they became involved or not in the purchase. In La Boca, they were the recent protagonists of the building of a new museum. They also seem to have played a leading role as middlemen with small- and middle-sized buyers.

The gentrification process in these quarters has also triggered the emergence of rivalry and conflict related to the appropriation and use of urban space. This competition has taken place through the development of different practices linked to the quarters and their heritage. These practices have developed through a set of re-significations that include the ways in which urban space is used, discussed and thought about. The tourist circuit and cultural supply have shaped this paradigmatic space for the redefinition of centrality.

Within this framework, the space prepared for tourism delimits an environment where the neighbourhood's residents are the object of displacement and the community is built partly from cultural activities devised for other publics. In La Boca, tenements are presented as 'culture' and tourists pilgrimage to them, spaces now having a commercial use cloaked with a 'mythical' past that omits their present-day reality as housing linked to poverty and precariousness. One use has been displaced by another one, and one of history's narratives, together with the inhabitants, has been omitted, though not completely substituted.

Notes

[1] This research was funded by the University of Buenos Aires Grants Programme for Urban Studies, Gino Germani Research Institute (UBA).

[2] As can be seen in the cases of: Cuenca, Ecuador, and Cusco, Perú (Steel and Klaufus, 2010); Buenos Aires, Argentina (Lourés Seonae, 1997; Gómez Schettini and Zunino Singh, 2008; Herzer, 2012); Santamarta, Colombia (Ospina, 2012); and Porto Alegre and Salvador, Brazil (Nobre, 2003; Sanfelici, 2007).

[3] The surface to be built is registered in the building permits issued for private works. The sharp decline observed in the permitted areas in 1995 shows the consequences of the so-called Tequila Effect: the economic consequences of the 1994 Mexican financial crisis.

[4] The growth of the city seems to be consolidating at a higher socio-economic level and the gentrification process in the central city is contemporaneous with high-income suburbanisation.

References

Arizaga, C. (2005) *El mito de la comunidad en la ciudad mundializada. Estilos de vida y nuevas clases medias en urbanizaciones cerradas*, Buenos Aires: Ediciones El cielo por asalto.

Atkinson, R. (2000a) 'The hidden costs of gentrification: displacement in Central London', *Journal of Housing and the Built Environment*, vol 15, no 4, pp 307–26.

Atkinson, R. (2000b) 'Measuring gentrification and displacement in Greater London', *Urban Studies*, vol 37, no 1, pp 149–65.

Berry, B. (2010 [1985]) 'Islands of renewal in seas of decay', in L. Lees, T. Slater and E.K. Wyly (eds) *The gentrification reader*, London: Routledge.

Butler, T. (2007) 'For gentrification?', *Environment and Planning A*, vol 39, no 1, pp 162–81.

Butler, T. and Lees, L. (2006) 'Super-gentrification in Barnsbury, London: globalisation and gentrifying global elites at the neighbourhood level', *Transactions of the Institute of British Geographers*, vol 31, pp 467–87.

Carman, M. (2005) 'La máxima de intrusión socialmente aceptable, o los diversos grados de legitimidad de las ocupaciones urbanas', paper presented at Primer Congreso Latinoamericano de Antropología, Universidad Nacional de Rosario, Rosario.

Carman, M. (2006) *Las trampas de la cultura: los' intrusos' y los nuevos usos del barrio de Gardel*, Buenos Aires: Paidos.

Carrión, F. (2010) 'Prólogo', in R. Coulomb, *México: centralidades históricas y proyectos de ciudad*, Quito: OLACCHI.

Casgrain, A. and Janoschka, M. (2013) 'Gentrificación y resistencia en las ciudades latinoamericanas. El ejemplo de Santiago de Chile', *Andamios. Revista de investigación social*, vol 10, no 22, pp 19–44.

Ciccolella, P. and Mignaqui, I. (2008) 'Metrópolis latinoamericanas: fragilidad del estado, proyecto hegemónico y demandas ciudadanas. Algunas reflexiones a partir del caso de Buenos Aires', *Revista CENDES*, vol 69, pp 47–68.

Coulomb, R. (2010) *México: centralidades históricas y proyectos de ciudad*, Quito: OLACCHI.

Crossa, V. (2009) 'Resisting the entrepreneurial city: street vendors' struggle in Mexico City's historic center', *International Journal of Urban and Regional Research*, vol 33, no 1, pp 43–63.

Di Virgilio, M.M. (2013) 'Buenos Aires: gentrificacion, neoliberalismo y políticas públicas', paper presented at Contested Cities Seminar, 20–23 May, Buenos Aires, Centro Cultural Haroldo Conti.

El Clarin (2005) 'San Telmo, up', 15 March. Available at: http://edant.clarin.com/suplementos/arquitectura/2005/03/15/a-938657.htm

Freeman, L. (2005) 'Displacement or succession? Residential mobility in gentrifying neighborhoods', *Urban Affairs Review* vol 40, pp 463-91.

García-Herrera, L. M., Smith, N. and Vera, M. (2007) 'Gentrification, displacement, and tourism in Santa Cruz de Tenerife', *Urban Geography* vol 28, no 3, pp 276-98.

Gómez Schettini, M. and Zunino Singh, D. (2008) 'La [re]valorización de la zona sur y su patrimonio histórico-cultural como recurso turístico', in H. Herzer (ed) *Con el corazón mirando al sur. Transformaciones en el sur de la ciudad de Buenos Aires*, Buenos Aires: Espacio Editorial.

Guevara, T. (2010) 'Políticas habitacionales y procesos de producción de hábitat en la Ciudad de Buenos Aires. El caso de LA Boca', Master's in Public Policy dissertation, Buenos Aires, Facultad de Ciencias Sociales, Universidad de Buenos Aires.

Guevara, T. (2011) *El proceso de valorización inmobiliaria selectiva como política pública en la Ciudad Autónoma de Buenos Aires*, Buenos Aires: Mimeo.

Guevara, T. (2012) '¿La ciudad para quién? Políticas públicas urbanas, procesos de producción del hábitat y transformaciones territoriales en la Ciudad de Buenos Aires (2001–2011)', Doctor in Social Sciences dissertation, Buenos Aires, Facultad de Ciencias Sociales, Universidad de Buenos Aires.

Herzer, H. (2009) 'Globalización y cambio en el sur de la ciudad de Buenos Aires', paper presented at Seminario Ciudadanía y Problemas Sociales Urbanos, Buenos Aires, Universidad 3 de febrero.

Herzer, H. (2012) *Barrios al sur. Renovación y pobreza en la Ciudad de Buenos Aires*, Buenos Aires: Café de las Ciudades.

Herzer, H., Di Virgilio, M.M. and Rodriguez, M.C. (2000) *¿Revalorización de* áreas *centrales en la ciudad de Buenos Aires? El caso de La Boca*, Buenos Aires: Mimeo.

Inzulza-Contardo, J. (2012) '"Latino gentrification"? Focusing on physical and socioeconomic patterns of change in Latin American inner cities', *Urban Studies*, vol 49, no 10, pp 2085–107.

Janoschka, M. (2006) 'El modelo de ciudad latinoamericana. Privatización y fragmentación del espacio urbano en Buenos Aires: el caso Nordelta', in M.W. Guerra (ed) *Buenos Aires a la deriva: transformaciones urbanas recientes*, Buenos Aires: Editorial Biblos.

Janoschka, M., Sequera, J. and Salinas, L. (2014) 'Gentrification in Spain and Latin America – a critical dialogue', *International Journal of Urban and Regional Research*, vol 38, no 4, pp 1234–65.

La Nación (2003) 'For the first time, four people are declared Buenos Aires heritage. It is a puppeteer, an architect, a watchmaker and calesitero', 10 November. Available at: www.lanacion.com.ar/543928-por-primera-vez-cuatro-personas-son-declaradas-patrimonio-porteno

Lees, L. (2003) 'Super-gentrification: the case of Brooklyn Heights, New York City', *Urban Studies*, vol 40, pp 2487–510.

Lees, L. and Ley, D. (2008) 'Introduction to special issue on gentrification and public policy', *Urban Studies*, vol 45, no 12, pp 2379–84.
Lees, L., Slater, T. and Wyly, E. (2008) *Gentrification*, New York, NY: Routledge.
Lees, L., Slater, T. and Wyly, E. (eds) (2010) *The gentrification reader*, London: Routledge.
Ley, D. and Dobson, C. (2008) 'Are there limits to gentrification? The contexts of impeded gentrification in Vancouver', *Urban Studies*, vol 45, no 12, pp 2471–98.
López-Morales, E. (2010) 'Real estate market, state-entrepreneurialism and urban policy in the "gentrification by ground rent dispossession" of Santiago de Chile', *Journal of Latin American Geography* vol 9, no 1, pp 145–73.
López-Morales, E. (2011) 'Gentrification by ground rent dispossession: the shadows cast by large-scale urban renewal in Santiago de Chile', *International Journal of Urban and Regional Research*, vol 35, no 2, pp 330–57.
Lourés Seonae, M.L. (1997) *Buenos Aires, centro histórico y crisis social*, Alicante: ECU.
Marcuse, P. (2000) *Globalizing cities. Studies in urban and social change*, Oxford: Backwell.
Marcuse, P. and Van Kempen, R. (2000) *Globalizing cities*, London: Blackwell.
Mieg, H.A. and Töpfer, K. (2013) *Institutional and social innovation for sustainable urban development*, Abingdon, Oxon: Routledge.
Mignaqui, I. (1998) 'Dinámica inmobiliaria y transformaciones metropolitanas. La producción del espacio residencial en la Región Metropolitana de Buenos Aires en los '90: una aproximación a la geografía de la riqueza', in R. Bustos Cara and S. Gorestein (eds) *Ciudades y regiones frente al avance de la globalización*, Bahía Blanca: Universidad Nacional del Sur.
Newman, K. and Wyly, E. (2006) 'The right to stay put, revisited: gentrification and resistance to displacement in New York City', *Urban Studies*, vol 43, pp 23–57.
Nobre, E. (2003) 'Intervençães urbanas em Salvador: turismo e 'gentrificação no processo de renovação urbana do Pelourinho'. Available at: http://www.usp.br/fau/docentes/depprojeto/e_nobre/intervencoes_urbanas_Salvador.pdf
Ospina, N. (2012) '¿A quién pertenece el Centro Histórico de santa Marta? Análisis sobre la recuperación del Centro Histórico. Entre los discursos hegemónicos y las desigualdades sociales', Master's in Urban and Regional Planning dissertation, Buenos Aires, Facultad de Arquitectura y Urbanismo, Universidad de Buenos Aires.
Pintos, P. and Narodowski, P. (2012) *La privatopía sacrílega. Efectos del urbanismo privado en humedales de la cueca baja del río Luján*, La Plata: UNLP/Imago Mundi.
Rodríguez, M.C. (2005) *Autogestión, políticas del hábitat y transformación social*, Buenos Aires: Espacio Editorial.
Rodríguez, M.C. (2009) *Como en la estrategia del caracol... Ocupaciones de edificios y políticas municipales del hábitat en la ciudad de Buenos Aires*, Buenos Aires: Editorial El Cielo por Asalto.
Rodríguez, M.C. and Redondo, A. (2001) 'Procesos de renovación urbana en la zona sur de la ciudad de Buenos Aires. San Telmo y La Boca', paper presented at XXIII International Congress LASA, Washington, DC, LASA.

Rodríguez, M.C., Bañuelos, C. and Mera, G. (2008) 'Intervención – no intervención: ciudad y políticas públicas en el proceso de renovación del área sur de la ciudad de Buenos Aires', in H. Herzer (ed) *Con el corazón mirando al sur: transformaciones en el sur de la ciudad de Buenos Aires*, Buenos Aires: Espacio Editorial.

Rodríguez, M.C., Mejica, S.A., Rodríguez, M.F., Schettini, M.G. and Zapata, M.C. (2011) 'La política urbana PRO: Continuidades y cambios en contextos de renovación en la Ciudad de Buenos Aires', paper presented at Permanent Research Workshop, Buenos Aires, Area de Estudios Urbanos, Instituto de Investigaciones Gino Germani, Universidad de Buenos Aires.

Salinas Arreortua, L. (2013) 'Gentrificación en la ciudad latinoamericana. El Caso de buenos aires y ciudad de méxico', *Geographos*, vol 4, no 44, pp 281–305.

Sanfelici, D. (2007) 'Urbanismo neoliberal e gentrificação: as políticas de revitalização do centro de Porto Alegre/RS', *Ciênc. let.*, no 41, pp 188–203.

Sassen, S. (1997) *Losing control? Sovereignty in an age of globalization*, New York, NY: Columbia University Press.

Slater, T. (2009) 'Missing Marcuse: on gentrification and displacement', *CITY: analysis of urban trends, culture, theory, policy, action* vol 13, no 2, pp 292–311.

Smith, N. (1999) 'Which new urbanism? New York City and the revanchist 1990s', in R.A. Beauregard and S. Body-Gendrot (eds) *The urban moment: cosmopolitan essays on late 20th century city*, London: Sage.

Smith, N. (2002) 'New globalism, new urbanism: gentrification as global urban strategy', *Antipode*, vol 34, no 3, pp 427–50.

Smith, N. and LeFaivre, M. (1984) 'A class analysis of gentrificaton', in J.J. Palen and B. London (eds) *Gentrification, displacement, and neighborhood revitalization*, Albany, NY: State University of New York Press.

Steel, G. and Klaufus, C. (2010) 'Displacement by/for development in two Andean cities', paper presented at 2010 Congress of the Latin American Studies Association, Toronto.

Svampa, M. (2001) *Los que ganaron. La vida en los countries*, Buenos Aires: Biblos.

Swanson, K. (2007) 'Revanchist urbanism heads south: the regulation of indigenous beggars and street vendors in Ecuador', *Antipode*, vol 39, no 4, pp 708–28.

Torres, H. (2001) 'Cambios socioterritoriales en Buenos Aires durante la década de 1990', *Revista EURE*, vol 27, p 80.

Uitermark, J., Duyvendak, J.W. and Kleinhans, R. (2007) 'Gentrification as a governmental strategy: social control and social cohesion in Hoogvliet, Rotterdam', *Environment and Planning A*, vol 39, no 1, pp 125–41.

Vio, M. (2011) 'Política habitacional y producción de la Ciudad Metropolitana. Análisis de las contribuciones del Programa Federal de Construcción de Vivienda al desarrollo urbano de los partidos de la región metropolitana de Buenos Aires', in M.M. Di Virgilio and M.C. Rodríguez (eds) *Caleidoscopio de las políticas territoriales: Un rompecabezas para armar*, Buenos Aires: Prometeo.

Zukin, S. (1989) *Loft living. Cultural and capital in urban change*, New Jersey, NJ: Rutgers University Press.

Zukin, S. (1995) *The cultures of cities*, Cambridge, MA, and Oxford: Blackwell.

Zukin, S. (2010) *Naked city: the death and life of authentic urban places*, Oxford: Oxford University Press.

TWELVE

Promoting private interest by public hands? The gentrification of public lands by housing policies in Taipei City

Liling Huang

Introduction

In the West, the discussion about gentrification to date has mainly referred to how certain social classes were replaced by others due to changes in the spatial economy and public policies (see Lees et al, 2008). Increasingly, it has focused on how private developers partner with government bodies, especially in the provision of urban infrastructures, to mobilise the process of gentrification. The mechanisms that Western governments employ in redevelopment mostly rely on financial, planning and legal tools. By way of comparison, to date, the role of public lands and their influence on gentrification has been much less significant.[1] In Taipei, however, processes of gentrification seem to be different. Due to the legacy of Japanese colonial rule and the authoritarian regime after the Second World War, central and local governments own more than 40% of the urban land in Taipei. Because a high percentage of the public lands are located in the city center and in strategic areas, in recent decades, the development of public lands has played an important role in the gentrification of Taipei.

This chapter reviews the development of public lands in Taipei and its impact on the urban gentrification of the city center. I focus on two issues. The first is the commodification of public housing in the 1980s. From the mid-1970s to the 1980s, central government built a block of public housing in the city center that was not for permanent rental and could be sold after a certain number of years, normally five years. Due to the colonial legacy and the later role of public lands in the city, these public housing developments in central Taipei were mostly for military dependants and the rising new middle class. The national and local governments collaborated in the provision of military lands with good planning and design, sound infrastructures, and good locations; as such, many public housing units became an upscale commodity in the real estate market and pushed up housing prices in the surrounding areas. Second, over the past decade, the relationship between public housing and gentrification in Taipei has ascended to another stage. The deregulation of public lands and housing under the Urban Renewal Act (URA) inaugurated in 1998, in conjunction with the power of private capital, has turned public land and housing in good central city locations into enclaves for the super-rich and elite professionals, and created a phenomenon similar to the 'super-gentrification' in first-tier global cities such as New York or London that Lees (2003; see also Butler and Lees, 2006) has conceptualised. However, in Taipei, it is not super-gentrifiers that are gentrifying, but rather the government itself, in that it is privatising public lands, making them ripe for urban redevelopment. Taipei, then, presents a somewhat unique case of gentrification.

Public lands, housing policies and urban development

Public lands should serve the public by providing social services, providing public investment and mitigating social inequality. However, in primary cities in East Asia, which have experienced rapid economic development since the Second World War under the leadership of developmental states, public lands have often played a leading role in generating economic growth rather than redistributing wealth in urban transition. In recent years, in many East Asian cities, public lands are witnessing a neoliberal trend towards further privatisation and deregulation. Even in Hong Kong and Singapore, where governments used to build public housing units on a massive scale to reduce the cost of labour reproduction and to allow them to compete globally (Castells et al, 1990), the privatisation of public housing following the neoliberal model has been adopted. By way of contrast, public housing policy in Taiwan, through the mechanism of almost absolute ownership from the mid-1970s to the 1980s, has led to the privatisation of public lands and gentrification. Moreover, public lands often occupied the most central and strategic locations in the city; as such, with the later (re)development of public housing estates and the surrounding urban facilities, they became a major source for the recent wave of super-gentrification. In what follows, I analyse the specific features of these public lands with a focus on the unbalanced land resource power between national and municipal governments. Then, I outline their intertwining relationship with urban development and their impact on gentrification, seen through the privatisation of public housing, the development of urban infrastructures and redevelopment based on urban renewal policies. The political history of Taipei is of special relevance with respect to subsequent gentrification processes.

The Japanese occupation and early post-Second World War era

During the Japanese occupation (1895–1945), institutions for modern urban planning were established, allowing the colonial government to obtain centralised power in commanding urban development. The urban renewal and urban planning ordinances endowed the government with the right of land acquisition, and by establishing state enterprises, the colonial government further monopolised the national lands and economy (Zhang, 1991). The centralisation of these lands reflected the political function and weight of the institutions in the colonial system.

In Taipei, the central government agencies and the residential areas for their staff formed a number of clusters in the urban centre, fulfilling the regulation of living within walking distance of their workplaces. This was a result of the practices of segregating the living quarters of the Japanese from local people, as well as the need to immediately respond to any urban uprisings (Zhang, 1991). After the Second World War, the large swathes of national lands incorporated by the Japanese government were returned to the Kuomintang (KMT [Chinese Nationalist Party]) government, and because Japanese colonial power was an urban military regime, in a later period, with this locational advantage, the military lands continued to have strong leverage in urban development. The outbreak of the Chinese civil war between the Communist Party and KMT in 1949 brought a huge population into Taipei. Meanwhile, in 1949, Martial Law was enforced island-wide, which helped to shape the authoritarian state until the democratisation of Taiwan after 1987.

In the first two decades after the Second World War, the rule of the KMT in Taiwan was consolidated by its military, semi-feudal and autocratic power. Under the new authoritarian state, military finance was often separated from the government finance system and escaped scrutiny by the Legislative Yuan (Congress). Through national enterprises, national properties and US aid, the central government took two thirds of the national revenue from the 1950s to the mid-1960s. While the military sector took about 80% of central government expenditure at that time, keeping about 60% to 70% in the mid-1960s, and more than 45% by the late 1980s, in this sense, the KMT government, before the lifting of Martial Law in 1987, could be termed a Regime of Military Finance, with centralised and commanding power over the military sector (Gold, 1981; Liu, 1992). With the consolidation of the authoritarian state thereafter, between 1949 and 1954, the KMT government successfully conducted land reform in rural areas. By redistributing the lands to peasants, it enhanced agricultural productivity and paved the way for industrial development from the early 1960s. In the 1960s and 1970s, economic development was rapid and public lands were provided for the provision of infrastructures for national development plans, such as ports, airports and new towns. Exportation-oriented Industrial Zones were set up to develop the manufacturing industry as the backbone of the national economy. By the 1980s, an economic miracle had been created, and Taiwan was considered to be one of the four Asian tigers (Wang, 1989).

Urban land use in the period of rapid economic development

Before the early 1960s, the shadow of war still remained and in hopes of returning to mainland China, the KMT government utilised the existing buildings, including the Japanese residences left by the colonial government, without making many changes on their new investment. However, with nearly 2 million people relocating from mainland China with the KMT government to Taiwan, and a significant share of the population concentrated in Taipei, the city faced serious housing shortages. Military people and public servants were allocated housing in the original living quarters of the Japanese, with some extra residences built to cope with their immediate needs. On the other hand, low-ranking soldiers or military dependants were allowed to build their own units on public lands, and the government was relatively tolerant of this before the lands were used for development. At that time, in Taipei, a long-term plan for developing public lands was not in place, and only spontaneous measures existed. However, since the mid-1960s, with the economic take-off of Taiwan, military finance and public lands became key resources for the KMT government with respect to fast urbanisation. As Taipei served as the model city for the provisional capital of the Republic of China (ROC), it functioned as the show window for modernisation, as well as an engine for economic growth. For the following three decades, Taiwan enjoyed nearly double-digit gross domestic product (GDP) growth and witnessed continuous waves of migration from rural to urban areas seeking better life opportunities. In this context, the population of Taipei grew fast: from a population of nearly 500,000 people in 1959, it reached 1.5 million in 1965, and continuously grew to 2.7 million by 1990, the historical peak to this day (Chen, 1997).

Public housing and public lands before the mid-1970s

During this period of fast urbanisation, unlike in Hong Kong or Singapore, the Taiwanese government mostly left housing demands to be met by the market. The goal of housing policy was promoting ownership, so much so that even public housing stocks were provided for sale. This particular commodification led to the current odd situation of the coexistence of 'three highs' in housing – high ownership, high housing prices and high vacancy rates – indicating the nature of speculation regarding real estate in Taipei. For example, housing ownership in Taipei city is over 80%, while there is a 13% vacancy rate in market housing. At the same time, public rental housing only occupies 0.6% of the total housing stock in Taipei City (Chen, 2013). However, governmental interventions in public housing and its relationship to the market changed over time. In the early post-Second World War era, US aid played an important role in supporting the Taiwanese government in constructing public housing in order to maintain social security. As early as 1955, the national government set up the Committee for National Housing to build housing or provide loans for members of the Legislative Yuan or high officers in central government. Later, in 1959, the Committee for National Housing was moved to be affiliated with the provincial government of Taiwan. By combining US aid and funding for national public housing, the first group of resettlement housing was built in Taipei for the relocation of squatters. Nationally, between 1957 and 1975, there were in total 125,534 units of public housing completed. The resettlement housing was for disaster refugees, low-income groups, relocated squatters and also teachers and government staff (Hsia, 1988). In Taipei, between 1963 and 1975, a total of 10,806 units of resettlement housing were built, in contrast to the demolition of 23,488 units of squatted structures (Huang, 2002). At this time, public housing construction was not based on a comprehensive or long-term plan. No level of government secured long-term finance for public housing and most relied on US aid, which consolidated the alliance between the US and Taiwan during the Cold War. Governmental intervention in public housing only appeared in the provision of housing for the staff of government agencies, especially for state enterprises, the military sector and representatives of the KMT party-state. However, despite being built by the government, they could hardly be viewed as public goods. After completion, most of the housing stock was sold to individuals.

Public housing and public lands from the mid-1970s to the late 1980s

In the 1970s, this somewhat passive approach to public housing policy was forced to change. The oil shock led to general inflation, and housing prices skyrocketed. In 1971, under the influence of the People's Republic of China, the KMT government became a non-UN member and thus faced a series of political crises. A way to strengthen the legitimacy of the government was necessary (Wang, 1996). In this context, in 1975, the national government announced the Six Years of Economic Development Plan to lead economic development. A six-year programme for building national housing and developing new towns was incorporated. The Ordinance for National Housing was also passed in the same year to provide a legal backbone. Between 1974 and 1981, 180,000 units of public housing were built in total (Chang, 1981). In 1979, national housing policy was then expanded into a six-year plan and also incorporated into the Twelve Projects for National Development Plan. This seemed to announce the determination of the government to intervene in the housing market. However, during implementation, it encountered a few problems. The mechanisms for organisation, personnel and funding were not in place, and obtaining land for construction was very difficult. This may sound odd for a country that owns a large portion of national land, but as Lin and Dong (1991) point out, 'sectionalism' over the management of national lands was a problem. Similarly, housing provision was used as a welfare subsidy for the party-state sectors. Although built by the government, the housing stock built under the national housing programme is only 'public' housing in a limited sense (Hu, 2013).

As progress dragged on, by 1981, only 72,532 units, about 67.83% of the planned number of public housing units, were built. Meanwhile, the management of public housing estates was a big concern for government agencies; therefore, a policy to build ownership-oriented public housing rather than public rental housing was developed. However, the ownership-oriented public housing encountered market fluctuations, and therefore criticism and increased financial burdens. From the 1980s, the government gradually changed the policy on public housing from building by the government to building by developers (Hsia, 1988). This approach to public housing reflected a particular mode of collaboration between national and local government in providing public housing and taking care of their target groups during social transformation. The area of Taipei City is about

27,180 hectares, and public lands covered about 45.7% of the city area (Taipei City Government, 1996a); therefore, public lands were significant in urban (re)development. The ownership shares in the public lands in Taipei City were 50.29% national government, 9.06% provincial government and 40.1% Taipei City government. The weight of the national government in the urban development of the city was/is evident (Taipei City Government, 1996b).

Table 12.1 shows the land sources used for the building of public housing in Taipei between 1976 and 1985. More than half of the total produced units came from land provided by the national government, while, by contrast, the city government played an even smaller role than the private sector in land supply. Table 12.2 shows that the six-year housing construction programme included the sale of housing units to ordinary families (43.48%), military dependants' families (23.33%), families affected by public works (22.54%) and government employees (7.78%). The criterion for 'ordinary family' was one with below-average income who could qualify for a mortgage to be a first-time house-buyer. This type of public housing provision excluded low-income groups that could not afford to buy. Military dependants' families were those who originally resided on the national lands and were entitled to purchase the developed public housing units on these sites. According to Lee (1988), the Ministry of Defense, the main land supplier of the central government, tended to choose high-price areas for developing public housing because it could receive 70% of the land sale revenue from the city government, which it redistributed to military dependants for the purchase of the newly built units. Meanwhile, the Ministry of Defense could obtain the rest of the 30% of the land price. Therefore, the military dependants originally residing in better locations could get one unit by paying less or even nothing due to public housing development. This model formed a skewed approach that subsidised the military sector through public housing development (Luo, 1991). Nevertheless, public housing policy played an indispensable role not only for

Table 12.1: The accomplishments of the six-year housing construction programme

LAND SOURCE	UNIT		SITE AREA		FLOOR AREA	
	unit	(%)	(m^2)	(%)	(m^2)	(%)
Central government	14,388	60.36%	373,831	54.32%	1,246,226	61.53%
City government	3,018	12.66%	112,184	16.30%	254,720	12.58%
Province government	922	3.87%	26,214	3.81%	79,936	3.95%
Central government, province, city and private	338	1.42%	11,517	1.67%	34,897	1.72%
Private	5,172	21.70%	164,469	23.90%	409,615	20.22%
TOTAL	23,838	100.00%	688,215	100.00%	2,025,394	100.00%

Source: Housing Department of Taipei City Government (1987, pp 34–35).

Table 12.2: Categories of housing sold and for sale in the six-year housing construction programme

	HOUSING ALLOCATED											HOUSING FOR SALE					TOTAL
	SOLD									RENTED	TOTAL	Ordinary family	Shops	Military dependants	Employee of Railroad Bureau	Subtotal	
	Overseas Chinese refugees	Military dependants	Police	Government employee	Family affected by public works	Ordinary family	Original property-owner	Shops	Subtotal								
1977	126				307				433		433					0	433
1978	38			9	149			4	200		200					0	200
1979		94			1,374			84	1,552		1,552		2			2	1,554
1980									0		0					0	0
1981		509	121	167	448	1,372		45	2,662		2,662		5			5	2,667
1982		330		416	460	1,058		7	2,271	72	2,343	50	5			55	2,398
1983		1,305		309	352	2,614		21	4,601	673	5,274	274	32	40	47	393	5,667
1984		790		295	217	593		5	1,900	490	2,390	27	19	47	27	120	2,510
1985		704		49	298	1,318	1	7	2,376		2,378	685	22	799		1,506	3,882
TOTAL	164	3,732	121	1,245	3,605	6,955	1	173	15,995	1,235	17,232	1,036	85	886	74	2,081	19,311
	(1.03%)	(23.33%)	(0.76%)	(7.78%)	(22.54%)	(43.48%)	(0.00%)	(1.08%)	(100%)			(49.78%)	(4.08%)	(42.58%)	(3.56%)	(100%)	

Source: Housing Department of Taipei City Government (1987, p 86).

housing itself, but also for urban development. Without providing the hope or nominal qualification for purchasing public housing estates, it was difficult for local government to acquire private land by using eminent domain or relocating squatters on public lands and completing the necessary urban development. The assistance with land and finance from the national government for public housing also helped Taipei City government to develop necessary urban infrastructures, including public roads, parks, schools and institutional facilities, and turned Taipei into the showcase modern capital city for the state.

This formula explains that to overcome the political crisis happening at the domestic and international level, the authoritarian party-state chose to win the support of government-related agencies, as well as the rising middle class, to stabilise political legitimacy (Wang, 1996). The ownership-oriented public housing policy helped to serve that goal. Due to the important role of the Ministry of Defense in providing the land, the military sector was the main group entitled to public housing. Besides this, a certain portion of the public housing stock was reserved for the rising urban middle class through a lucky draw. Low-interest mortgages were also offered to the first-time buyers of these public and market housing units. However, this ownership (market) approach undoubtedly excluded low-income groups from public housing because, during that time, rental housing occupied only 3.3% of total supply. In the end, according to Chang (1981), 82.36% of the residents of national housing estates belonged to the middle-income level, the middle classes.

From the late 1980s to the early 1990s, Taipei was at the peak of urban growth and encountered a crisis of collective consumption in the shortage of housing, urban parks, open spaces and urban services, similar to capital cities in other developmental states. However, at the same time, with the economic miracle, a new middle class who wanted a better urban environment emerged. For example, 17 urban parks were planned in the Japanese colonial period but most of them were kept undeveloped until the late 1980s when the issue of quality of life was raised by the urban middle classes, sometimes by citizen mobilisation or protests. The emerging middle class in Taipei had some features akin to those in the Western context (see Lees et al, 2008). It was composed of various social classes, including owners of small/medium businesses, skilled workers, professionals and managers in the service sector, and it replaced the previous middle-income group in the public sectors, such as the military, civil servants and teachers (軍公教; JunGongJiao), the conventional supporters of the KMT party-state. This urban middle class was a generation 'ascending from hardship to abundance', and 'legitimated the export-led, market-oriented mode of production' (Chu, 1996, p 207). By the late 1980s, it was estimated to occupy around 20% to 30% of the total population in Taiwan (Hsiao, 1989a).

Scholars have also pointed out the ambiguous identity of this new class. For example, according to Hsiao (1989b), the rising middle class in the 1980s, especially in urban areas, were actively engaged in political democratisation through participating in a wide range of social movements, such as consumer rights, environmental conservation and feminist movements. Their participation in community planning and historical preservation also pushed for a shift from the top-down planning model of the developmental state to a more participatory one (Huang, 2005). However, the rising middle class is also sometimes described as self-interested, tending to identify themselves with consumption cultures and distinguishing themselves from others by cultural taste and new lifestyles (Yeh, 1989). Indeed, the East District of Taipei, with its concentration of department stores, boutique shops and fashionable restaurants, has served as the power station for producing an urban consumption lifestyle, especially for highly educated working women.

The transformation of public housing units in the urban renewal era

In the 1990s, a trend towards deregulating public lands and expanding the role of the market emerged. After the lifting of martial law in 1987, the centralised power of the authoritarian state faced strong challenges. The Legislative Yuan was gradually entrenched through the influence of developers. Local factions allied with political elites, and together they controlled urban planning and the land use of public lands. By identifying the real estate sector as the leading industry for economic development, they mobilised related legal mechanisms such as tax breaks and land priority to continuously bolster the booming housing market and construction industry (Wang, 1996). Meanwhile, there was pressure from the public and the opposition party to push the KMT party-state to release its monopoly over state enterprises and relinquish national lands. However, instead of a genuine process of further democratising public lands, a policy of privatisation was pushed by the opposition party and a neoliberal model was employed for new urban governance. The deregulation of public lands mainly proceeded from the weakening of the authoritarian and centralised state in the face of local capitalists (Chen, 1995).

This privatisation of public lands by developers did not go uncriticised. In 1992, a movement called 'the Second Land Reform' was launched, mostly by scholars of urban planning and land economy. They proposed measures such as land tax increases to curb land speculation and defend public interests regarding public lands. However, their urge did not get much response from the government. Eventually, a new power bloc of the new landlord class and political elites was formed and became dominant (Lee, 2012). At the same time, the privatisation of public housing was deepened. The government introduced subsidies on a massive scale for people to purchase market housing and retreated from building public housing estates. From 1993 to 1998, the Ministry of Interior and Ministry of Labor Affairs together provided loans for more than 200,000 units for housing purchase, outnumbering the units of public housing constructed by the government at the same time. Meanwhile, agencies in charge of public housing were gradually abolished. In March 2004, the Public Housing Division of the Taipei City government was incorporated into the Division of Urban Renewal under the

Bureau of Urban Development, and its main task has shifted to facilitating urban renewal projects led by the private market. All these phenomena have been identified by some as evidence of the neoliberalisation of housing policy in Taiwan (Chen and Li, 2011). Amid the general withdrawal of government from public housing, the Ministry of Defense was exceptional. It continues to expand the scale of building housing for military dependants by inputting its rich land resources and independent finance.

The privatisation of public housing went hand in hand with the privatisation of public lands. After the mid-1990s, new mechanisms, including Build, Operation and Transfer (BOT) and land sale to developers, were generally incorporated in the development of public land. The inauguration of the URA in 1998 epitomised a new phase for government in participating in the speculation of urban lands. By providing bonus Floor Area Ratio and tax breaks as incentives, the URA encourages developers to conduct urban renewal projects in urban areas. Furthermore, Article 27 of URA states that the public lands and properties within the boundary of the Urban Renewal Project should all participate in the urban renewal schemes submitted by the private sector. To attract private capital into redevelopments, the national government, under the name of 'revitalising public lands', sped up the auction of public lands. In addition, it assigned large parcels along waterfront, railway or light industrial sites in Taipei City as 'strategic development sites' to collaborate with developers for urban renewal. This new approach has turned public lands into real estates and bolstered another wave of gentrification (cr Lees, 2014, on the gentrification of public housing in London).

In parallel, the National Housing Act (NHA) was revised in 2005. The main purpose was to equalise the status of public housing with market housing in terms of regulation and management, landownership, the rights to rebuild, and the qualifications for first-time buyers. The revision of the ordinances abolished these related regulations and turned public housing into a free market for speculation awaiting urban renewal. This wave of urban renewal undertaken by both the public and private sectors has changed Taipei City. From 2003 to 2008, the housing price boom bolstered by urban renewal policy has pushed 50,000 people, mostly middle-class, away from Taipei City to the suburban areas in Taipei County (now called New Taipei City), which is an hour's commute away. This wave was made possible with the completion of the Taipei Metro network and/or the upgrade of railways. This group included double-income families like university professors and civil servants, who used to be the main dwellers in Taipei City (Chen and Huang, 2008). Taipei has become more and more difficult for middle-class or young people to live in, and they have been replaced by the super-rich. In 2008, the Price and Income Ratio (PRI) (the ratio of median housing prices to median family annual income) in Taipei rose to 10, and in 2012, further rose to 14, one of the highest in Asia. The fast-rising curve of the PRI indicates Smith's (2002) 'generalization of gentrification' as a global urban strategy, which is happening not only in first-tier global cities like New York, London and Tokyo, but also in other upscaling cities in Asia. The term 'phenomenon of luxury housing' (Hao-zai-hua豪宅化) has been used by local people to describe the effect of urban renewal in Taipei.

This massive recasting of the city has caused serious disputes. For example, the Taiwan Alliance for Victims of Urban Renewal (TAVUR) was established in May 2010 to fight the forced demolition of the urban renewal policy. TAVUR is mainly organised by property-owners who encountered unfair compensation from developers or who suffered from forceful displacement under the URA. A great number of university students also joined and they seriously questioned the public interests of the URA and its violation of private property rights. However, the anti-renewal movement, though it challenged the renewal regime formed by the governments and developers, has left the issue of gentrification more or less untouched. Meanwhile, the Social Housing Advocacy Consortium was formed in August 2010 to protest against the deepening market approach to housing. It declared 'the right to the city' and has promoted a policy of public rental housing to protect the housing rights of the low-income and disadvantaged social groups who suffer most from the gentrification of the city.

Two cases help illustrate how government intervention in public housing has resulted in the gentrification of central urban areas in Taipei. The first case, Da-an (Great Peace) Public Housing Estate, exemplifies how ownership-oriented public housing in an advantageous location with sound amenities favoured the rising middle class and led to the earlier stage of gentrification in the central city. The second case, Zhen-Yi (Justice) Public Housing Estate, illustrates how ownership-oriented public housing, with the assistance of the URA, has further enlarged the ground rent, enriched speculators and led to a new wave of gentrification.

A comparison of two examples of government intervention in public housing causing gentrification

Example 1: Da-an Public Housing Estate

In Taipei, land costs are about 70% of the building costs; therefore, the age, conditions or management of housing units are less dominant than location as a factor for determining the land and housing price. The Da-an Public Housing Estate is located in the Da-an district, which has the highest average housing and land prices among the 12 districts in Taipei. The site has good urban facilities in adjacent areas (see Figure 12.1), including the city library, three national universities, two private universities, the former American Institute at Taipei and renowned primary and high schools nearby. This site was chosen due to its good location, the potential high price of land after development and relatively few original dwellers living on the site (Luo, 1991).

Before the development of public housing, there were 319 military households living on the site belonging to the Ministry of Defense. According to the development plan, the public housing estate would accommodate 1,397 households with the construction of 12 buildings, ranging from seven to 18 storeys

Figure 12.1: Land use and services surrounding the Da-an Public Housing Estate

Source: Author

high. On the site, public facilities were provided, including gardens, a playground and roller-skating court, and a community centre. In terms of style, it was the first public housing estate of the city featuring design by renowned architects. Y.C. Lee, the architect, who later became the designer of the 101 Building, was famous for his postmodern approach. He decorated the Da-an Public Housing Estate with elements of traditional Chinese gardens, such as curved corridors and rooflines (see Figure 12.2). This distinguished the Da-an Public Housing Estate from those completed in earlier times with largely standardised designs.

The Da-an Public Housing Estate was completed in 1985, more than 1,000 units were sold to the public at NT$2.16 million each at that time. By 2013, the market price had already increased more than 10 times. In comparison with other public housing, the rent gap created by the development of the Da-an Public Housing Estate was much higher. It also generated increased land values in surrounding areas on a massive scale. According to its management board: 'except for those units sold to military staff and policemen, most of the units were open for the public to purchase. Most residents have a degree of advanced higher education, including public servants, teachers, self-employed and business people'.[2] In addition to its accessibility to a wide array of urban services nearby, there were city infrastructures that helped to enhance the cultural and educational attractiveness of the area, and brought up land prices. These included the Da-an Forest Park (also known as No. 4 Park) developed in 1994 and Xin-sheng Primary school, the first public bilingual primary school in Taipei. Da-an Forest Park covered about 26 hectares, including 14.9 hectares of private land, 6.4 hectares of city government land and the rest of the lands belonging to national (mostly Ministry of Defense) and provincial governments. During the land acquisition, nearly 2,000 households, including squatters who had arrived at different times to the site, strongly protested against their relocation and demanded to be resettled

Figure 12.2: Da-an Public Housing Estate

Source: Author. In the background is the 101 Building designed by the same architect, Y.C. Lee.

on the existing site with the provision of public housing, or to receive enough compensation to purchase a new unit nearby. However, their demands were refused by the city government. Instead, it offered public housing for them to purchase in the Nang Kang District, a relatively remote area in the north-eastern part of Taipei (Huang, 2001). Their displacement to peripheral areas due to gentrification echoes that found in many cities, from Istanbul to Shanghai.

Da-an Forest Park was designed to be like Central Park in Manhattan – the lungs of the city – at the behest of citizens and non-profit organisations. However, this new concept in urban facilities, in a unique location, soon pushed up the land prices in neighbouring areas. Furthermore, it was evident that the completion of the Da-an Public Housing Estate and Da-an Forest Park together led to the gentrification of its surrounding areas. Table 12.3 shows the comparative land prices between the Da-an Public Housing Estate and its neighbouring areas. In the first three years after its completion in the late 1980s, the ratio of increase in the land prices of Da-an Public Housing Estate was about 66% of its adjacent land, but in the past three years, it has jumped to 134%. More recently, the land prices of Da-an Public Housing Estate itself has been catching up fast. The rent gap between the privatised public housing and market housing has narrowed.

Table 12.3: Land price increases in the Da-an Public Housing Estate and the neighbouring area

	Land prices Da-an Public Housing Estate (298)	Ratio of increase	Neighbouring land (342)	Ratio of increase
June 1987	124,165		138,843	
June 1988	160,198	29.02%	198,347	42.86%
June 1989	193,488	20.78%	304,132	53.33%
June 1990	382, 347	97.61%	687,603	126.09%
Average increase of land price		49.14%		74.09%
January 2010	721,855		1,123,967	
January 2011	838,638	16.18%	1,223,140	8.82%
January 2012	936,020	11.61%	1,358,678	11.08%
January 2013	1,041,835	11.30%	1,490,909	9.73%
Average increase from 2010 to 2013		13.03%		9.88%
Average increase from 1980 to 2013		12.47%		13.77%

Example 2: Zhen-Yi Public Housing Estate

The completion of the Zhen-Yi Public Housing Estate in 1987 attracted a large number of applicants. It was unique because many of the other public housing estates at that time encountered difficulties with their sales, and location was the main reason for its popularity (Housing Department of Taipei City Government, 1987). However, as the East District continued to grow as the most vibrant commercial and cultural area in Taipei, the government and developers targeted the site for redevelopment to turn its five-storey-high apartment blocks into high-rise commercial and residential buildings. In 2003, the urban renewal plan for the Zhen-Yi Public Housing Estate passed the review of the urban planning commission of the city. The original low-rise public housing units, including residential and commercial uses on the first floor (see Figure 12.3), were to be replaced by a cluster of 31-storey-high buildings with seven floors of underground space, super-expensive apartments and a fancy shopping mall. The price could reach as high as USD20,000 per square metre. Some units are as big as 330 square metres, about three times larger than other regular housing units in this location, creating a niche market targeting the super-rich.

Most of the original land belonged to Taipei's City government and the Ministry of Defense; private land only occupied a small share. The excellent location is the main reason for the extremely high housing and land prices; it has also been a prestigious housing area since the 1970s. It is also only two subway stops from the Hsing-Yi Planning District, which houses the city government, the headquarters

Figure 12.3: The Zhen-Yi Public Housing Estate before redevelopment

Source: Author

of major enterprises, bustling business and commercial activities, and a major urban mega-project developed in the mid-1990s – 'Taipei Manhattan' – to aid Taipei's ascent to a global city (Jou, 2005). It is also located next to the Zhongxiao Fuxing Metro Station, but Taipei Metro means more than transportation convenience: through its employment of high technology, its clean and aesthetic style shaped by coordinated interior design, its public arts, and its foreigner-friendly environment, it brought a new cultural landscape and imaginative geography of globalisation to Taipei City (Wang, 2005).

The rising milieu of a cultural economy cluster is further shaping a new identity for this area. The Bureau of Cultural Affairs of the city government has been promoting the chic stores in the alleys run by local designers and has named this area the Creative Cluster of Taipei East. In addition, on a bigger scale, one stop from Zhongxiao Fuxing Station is the Huashan 1914 Creative,[3] and two stops away is the Songshan Cultural and Creative Park[4] opened in 2012 (see Figure 12.4). The result of collaboration between government and private developers, these two mega-projects target the differentiated tastes of the new upper-middle class, composed of new professionals, global elites and the super-rich.

For the renewal of Zhen-Yi Public Housing Estate, the developer invited Paul Tange, the son of the renowned Japanese architect Kenzo Tange, to conduct the landscape and architectural design. The new project is to be named 'Diamond Tower' and the selling price of the residential units has been estimated to be as high as NT$2 million per square metre, increasing about 100 times in comparison with its original price in 1987 of about NT$20,000. The development of the

Figure 12.4: Zhen-Yi Public Housing Estate and surrounding areas

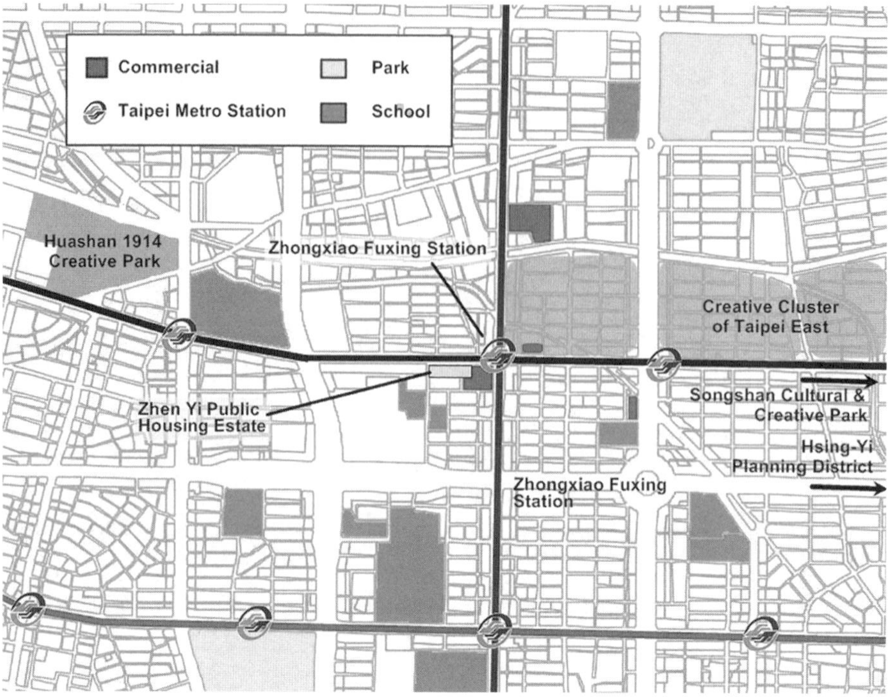

project, following the URA, created huge ground rent for landowners and developers. Among the 175 landowners, 78 people who are original military dependants could purchase their share of national lands at one sixth of the market price, but the other land investors are still estimated by real estate analysts to gain after development. Despite the Urban Planning Review Committee of Taipei City requesting the developers offer public spaces, pedestrian spaces and parking lots as the feedback for increasing the Floor Area Ratio according to the Urban Renewal Ordinance, the profit from the development is huge.

Smith (1979) theorised his gentrification-producing rent gap as the difference between present capitalised ground rent and future potential ground rent: when devalorisation occurs and enlarges the rent gap, enough capital will flow into disinvested areas to make profit. However, in Taipei, the formulation of gentrification seems to be different. Landownership in the old areas of Taipei was/is often complicated and overly subdivided, and from the 1970s, governments and developers had more room/power to incorporate strong planning mechanisms that increased land values and rents. The economy and the convention of mixed land use in Taipei City also differentiate it from the contexts of gentrification in Western cities. Since colonial times, Taipei has functioned as a city combining political, administrative, cultural and service functions; light industrial sites have mostly spread into the urban fringe and heavy industry was developed in Kaohsiung, a major city in the south of the island. Thus, the population of the city of Taipei has long been majority white-collar or service sector, though the composition of service sector workers has transformed from the party-state sectors to a diversified urban middle class and a new upper-middle class belonging to the global elite.

In the Da-an case, a rent gap was created through the provision of ownership-oriented public housing and the improvement of surrounding areas. This echoes what Tekeli (1994) points to in the fast-growing cities of developing countries: that by providing urban infrastructures and services, governments create huge land rents and redistribute them among favoured social groups under patronage-clientelist regimes. In Taipei, through public housing, military dependants have continuously benefited the most from this process, while the then rising urban middle class have gotten their share by purchasing one-unit public housing. In the process, huge numbers of squatters have been marginalised. This indicates the footprints of an authoritarian and military state in terms of land and financial resources that can be traced back to the colonial time and post-war era, and, more recently, the influence of private developers in public housing redevelopment and its indirect impacts on gentrification. The sectionalism of public land in early periods and the privatisation of public land in the late 1980s are two critical threads that have led to the situation of unchecked land speculation and social inequality that we see in Taipei today.

Harvey (2006) points out that under the neoliberal model, the process of spatial fix based on government planning incentives and deregulation has helped developers to create particular locations to produce or maintain monopoly rents. Neil Smith (2002) also observed that the 'generalization of gentrification' as a 'global urban strategy' was happening in Asia as an urban strategy to compete for capital accumulation in the new globalism. In Taipei, the new wave of gentrification was triggered by the URA and its coupling policies, including expanding and speeding up the auction of public land and compulsory collaboration with private developers in urban renewal. This approach has further deepened the commodification of former public housing stocks. Although the urban renewal policy in Taiwan claimed to improve the condition of poor housing, the majority of renewal projects in Taipei did not occur in run-down areas but in existing areas of expensive land that continuously generated a potential ground rent due to planning (de)regulations and government investment in the new economy or mega-projects.

It is clear that in the Zhen-Yi Public Housing Estate, government investment in infrastructures like Taipei Metro, mega-projects, a creative economy cluster and the planning deregulation under the URA created the monopoly rent for the site. The renewal of the Zhen-Yi Public Housing Estate also demonstrates a case of gaining 'spatial capital' (see Rerat and Lees, 2011) from new-build gentrification in the city. The location provides gentrifiers with very convenient access to urban services through transportation, and the locational advantages also attract the 'new' middle classes who differentiate themselves through symbolic aspects, such as conspicuous consumption and aesthetic values. In some ways, this case echoes the phenomenon of 'new urban renewal' as state-led gentrification discussed by Lees (2014); however, public housing in Taipei was not disinvested in, as in inner

London, nor did it house the lower-income sectors of society. This was/is not a simple case of reinvestment following disinvestment.

Conclusion

The Western gentrification literature shows that a rent gap can be created through government intervention, including changing (rezoning) land use and providing incentives for developers (Lees et al, 2008). In comparison, Taipei's experience shows a more direct government-led gentrification through a privatisation process, including building ownership-oriented public housing, selling public lands, participating in urban renewal initiated by private developers and making public investments that favour strategic locations. Da-an and Zhen-Yi both show the interplay of the supply and consumption sides of gentrification and different legal and political circumstances at different temporal stages. By way of contrast, focusing on the Joint Redevelopment Programme, Shin (2009) points out that development potential arose from rent-gap expansion through dilapidated areas that featured 'informal characteristics', while the two cases discussed in this chapter show that even neighbourhoods of public housing with 'formal characteristics' could be 'recycled' and begin a new cycle of use, adding to Lees' (2003) critique of stage models of gentrification.

The case of the Da-an Public Housing Estate illustrates how ownership-oriented public housing policy favoured first-time house-buyers from the emerging urban middle class and the social groups close to the KMT party-state, especially the military sector. This shows the features of 'sectionalism' over the management of national lands since the colonial time and the transformation of Taipei into a middle-class urban society in the late 1980s. In the period of fast urban growth, public housing sites with strategic locations offered huge potential ground rents.

While the urban renewal of the Zhen-Yi Public Housing Estate indicates another stage of government-led gentrification, akin to the phenomenon of 'super-gentrification' (Lees, 2003), it was brought on by the advent of the URA and its continuous privatisation of public lands. As the middle class was further divided by skyrocketing housing prices, a new form of social inequality was formed. Only the upper-middle class and super-rich could afford to live in the city centre while a new wave of suburbanisation is emerging as a way to respond to the generalised gentrification in Taipei.

Gentrification is a neighbourhood expression of class inequality (Lees et al, 2008). As urban redevelopment is more and more driven by the politics of property, and property-owners are eager to get financial gains from their assets, Taipei has become an emerging society dominated by a 'property regime' that is eroding the strong sense of civil society influenced by the middle class who pushed for a liveable city with better urban infrastructures. As the concepts of home-ownership and individual property rights have been deeply shaped by the government through housing policy, Taipei is only beginning to develop anti-renewal and anti-privatisation movements in the face of this generalised gentrification.

Notes

[1] Although see Lees (2014) on the gentrification of public land and state rent gaps in inner London.

[2] Introduction by the management board of Da-an Public Housing Community. Available at: http://www.udd.taipei.gov.tw/webhouse/area1.aspx?commnbr=E10

[3] See the official website of Huashan 1914 Creative Park. Available at: http://www.huashan1914.com/en/index.html

[4] Relevant information can be found on the official website of Songshan Cultural and Creative Park. Available at: http://www.songshanculturalpark.org/en/index.html

References

Butler, T. and Lees, L. (2006) 'Super-gentrification in Barnsbury, London: globalisation and gentrifying global elites at the neighbourhood level', *Transactions of the Institute of British Geographers*, vol 31, pp 467–87.

Castells, M., Goh, L. and Kwok, R.Y.-W. (1990) *The Shek Kip Mei syndrome: economic development and public housing in Hong Kong and Singapore*, London: Pion.

Chang, S.-D. (1981) Research on the planning and design of the National Housing projects in Taiwan area. Taipei: Research, Development and Evaluation Commission, Executive Yuan. (In Chinese) 張世典(1981)「台灣地區國民住宅規劃設計之研究」。臺北:行政院研考會。

Chen, C.S. (1997) *The history of Taipei City*, Taipei: SMC Publisher. (In Chinese) 陳正祥 (1997)《臺北市誌》。臺北市:南天。

Chen, D.-S. (1995) *Cities of money power: business groups and Taipei urban development*, Taipei: Chu-liu Publisher. (In Chinese) 陳東升 (1995) 金權城市。臺北市:巨流。

Chen, Y.-L. (2013) 'Taiwan's housing system: the crisis under free and market and commodification', *Urban Planning International*, vol 28, no 4, pp 10-17. Available at: http://www.upi-planning.org/. (In Chinese) 陳怡伶 (2013)〈台灣的住宅體系:自由市場和住宅商品化下的居住危機〉, 收錄於《國際城市規劃》, 第28期, 第4卷。

Chen, Y.-L. and Li, W.D. (2011) 'Neoliberalism, the developmental state, and housing policy in Taiwan', in B.-G. Park, R.C. Hill and A. Saito (eds) *Locating neoliberalism in East Asia: neoliberalizing spaces in developmental states*, Oxford: Wiley-Blackwell, pp 196–224.

Chen, Y.-S. and Huang, Y.-Y. (2008) 'Spring beyond the city: the middle class is moving out and the second wave of sub-urbanization', *Common Wealth*, vol 403, pp 38–47. (In Chinese) 陳一姍、黃亦筠 (2008)〈城外有春天:中產階級向外走與第二波郊區化〉收錄於《天下雜誌》, 第403期:頁38–47。

Chu, J.-J. (1996) 'Taiwan: a fragmented "middle" class in the making', in R. Robison and D.S.G. Goodman (eds) *The new rich in Asia: mobile phones, McDonalds and middle-class revolution*, London: Routledge, pp 207–24.

Gold, T.B. (1981) *Dependent development in Taiwan*, Harvard University.

Harvey, D. (2006) 'Neo-liberalism as creative destruction', *Geografiska Annaler: Series B, Human Geography*, vol 88, no 2, pp 145–58.

Housing Department of Taipei City Government (1987) *Housing Taipei: 1976–1985*, Taipei: Taipei City Government. (In Chinese) 台北市政府國民住宅處 (1987)《國宅十年：台北市(1976–1985)》。台北市：台北市政府國民住宅處。

Hsia, C.J. (1988) 'Housing policy in Taiwan: sociological analysis of "public housing plan"', Graduate Institute of Civil Engineering, National Taiwan University, Taipei. (In Chinese)夏鑄九 (1988)《台灣的住宅政策：國民住宅計劃之社會學分析》。台北市：台灣大學土木工程學研究所都市計劃室。

Hsiao, M.H.-H. (1989a) 'The analytical framework of the new social movements in Taiwan', in C.-K. Hsu and w.-L. Soong (eds) *The new social movements*, Taipei: Ju Liu Publisher, pp 21–46. (In Chinese) 蕭新煌 (1989)〈台灣新興社會運動的分析架構〉, 收錄於徐正光, 宋文里編《台灣新興社會運動》, 頁21–46。台北市：巨流圖書公司。

Hsiao, M.H.-H. (1989b) *The middle class in the transforming society of Taiwan*, Taipei: Ju Liu Publisher. (In Chinese) 蕭新煌 (1989)《變遷中臺灣社會的中產階級》。台北：巨流圖書公司。

Hu, H.-W. (2013) 'Social exclusion/inclusion and housing : research on the Nan Chi Chang Resettlement Estate in Taipei', Graduate Institute of Building and Planning, National Taiwan University, Taipei. (In Chinese) 胡皓瑋 (2013)《都市居住的社會排除與包容：以臺北市南機場整建住宅社區為例》。國立台灣大學建築與城鄉研究所碩士論文。

Huang, D.-J. (2001) *Transformation: the birth of Da-an Forest Park*, Taipei: Chen Chung Publisher. (In Chinese) 黃大洲 (2001)《蛻變：大安森林公園的誕生》。臺北市：正中。

Huang, L.-l. (2002) 'Urban redevelopment and urban governance: a comparative study between Taipei and Hong Kong', Graduate Institute of Building and Planning, National Taiwan University, Taipei. (In Chinese) 黃麗玲 (2002)《都市更新與都市統理：台北與香港的比較研究》。國立台灣大學建築與城鄉研究所博士論文。

Huang, L.-l. (2005) 'Urban politics and spatial development: the emergence of participatory planning in Taipei', in R.Y.-W. Kwok (ed) *Globalizing Taipei: the political economy of spatial development*, New York, NY: Routledge, pp 78–98.

Jou, S.-C. (2005) 'Domestic politics in urban image creation: Xinyi as the "Manhattan of Taipei"', in R.Y.-W. Kwok (ed) *Globalizing Taipei: the political economy of spatial development*, New York, NY: Routledge, pp 120–40.

Lee, C.-J. (2012) *The analysis of land policies in Taiwan: Formosa from revolution to speculation*, Taipei: Wu-nan Press. (In Chinese) 李承嘉 (2012)《臺灣土地政策析論：從改革到投機的福爾摩沙》。臺北市：五南。

Lee, R.-N. (1988) *A research on the redevelopment of military dependents villages*, Taipei: Agency of Construction, the Ministry of Interior Affairs. (In Chinese) 李如南 (1988)《臺灣地區軍眷村更新配合都市發展之研究》。臺北市：中華民國內政部營建署。

Lees, L. (2003) 'Super-gentrification: the case of Brooklyn heights, New York City', *Urban Studies*, vol 40, no 12, pp 2487–509.

Lees, L. (2014) 'The urban injustices of New Labour's "new urban renewal": the case of the Aylesbury Estate in London', *Antipode*, vol 46, no 4, pp 921–47.

Lees, L., Slater, T. and Wyly, E. (2008) *Gentrification*, New York, NY, and London: Routledge.

Liu, G.-C. (1992) *Economical analysis of post-war Taiwan*, Taipei: Ren Jen Publisher. (In Chinese) 劉進慶 (1992)《台灣戰後經濟分析》。臺北市：人間出版。

Luo, Y.L. (1991) 'Military dependent villages: definition and redefinition of the spatial meaning', Graduate Institute of Building and Planning, Taipei, National Taiwan University. (In Chinese) 羅於陵 (1991)《眷村：空間意義的賦與和再界定》。國立台灣大學建築與城鄉研究所碩士論文。

Rerat, P. and Lees, L. (2011) 'Spatial capital, gentrification and mobility: evidence from Swiss core cities', *Transactions of the Institute of British Geographers*, vol 36, pp 126–42.

Shin, H.B. (2009) 'Property-based redevelopment and gentrification: the case of Seoul, South Korea', *Geoforum*, vol 40, no 5,pp 906–17.

Smith, N. (1979) 'Toward a theory of gentrification: a back to the city movement by capital, not people', *Journal of the American Planning Association*, vol 45, no 4,pp 538–48.

Smith, N. (2002) 'New globalism, new urbanism: gentrification as global urban strategy', *Antipode*, vol 34, no 3, pp 427–50.

Taipei City Government (1996a) *The statistics of Taipei City*, Taipei: Taipei City Government. (In Chinese) 台北市政府 (1996a)《台北市統計要覽》。台北市：台北市政府。

Taipei City Government (1996b) *The statistics of the land administration of Taipei*, Taipei: Taipei City Government. (In Chinese) 台北市政府 (1996b)《台北市地政統計》。台北市：台北市政府。

Tekeli, I. (1994) 'The patron–client relationship: land-rent economy and the experience of "urbanization without citizens"', in S.J. Neary, M.S. Symes and F.E. Brown (eds) *The urban experience: a people environment perspective*, London: E & FN Spon, pp 9–18.

Wang, C.H (2005) 'Modernization ideoscape: imaginative geography and aesthetic landscape in Taipei rapid transit system', in R.Y.-W. Kwok (ed) *Globalizing Taipei: the political economy of spatial development*, New York, NY: Routledge, pp 195–218.

Wang, J.-H. (1996) *Who rules Taiwan?*, Taipei: Ju Liu Publisher. (In Chinese) 王振寰 (1996)《誰統治臺灣？轉型中的國家機器與權力結構》。臺北市：巨流。

Wang, T.-Y. (1989) *How we created the economic miracle*, Taipei: China Times Publishing Company. (In Chinese) 王作榮 (1989)《我們如何創造了經濟奇蹟》。台北市：時報文化。

Yeh, C.-J. (1989) 'The cultural myth of the middle class in Taiwan', in M.H.-H. Hsiao (ed) *The middle class in the transforming society of Taiwan*, Taipei: Ju Liu Publisher, pp 103–26. (In Chinese) 葉啟正 (1989)「臺灣中產階級的迷思」收於蕭新煌編《變遷中臺灣社會的中產階級,頁103–26。台北:巨流圖書公司。

Zhang, J.-S. (1991) 'The contemporary cities planning in Taiwan: an investigation of political economy history (1895–1988)', Graduate Institute of Civil Engineering, National Taiwan University, Taipei. (In Chinese) 張景森 (1991)《台灣現代城市規劃:一個政治經濟史的考察(1895-1988)》。國立台灣大學建築與城鄉研究所博士論文。

THIRTEEN

The making of, and resistance to, state-led gentrification in Istanbul, Turkey

Tolga İslam and Bahar Sakızlıoğlu

Introduction

The gentrification literature has long been dominated by studies of gentrification in Western European and North American cities (Lees, 2012). In addition, investigations and conceptualisations of gentrification in the Global South have tended to make use of a conceptual toolbox developed for explaining gentrification in Anglo-American cities. This ignores the various important issues that scholars have highlighted and discussed in the literature regarding the peculiarities of processes of gentrification in cities in the Global South. These include: the formalisation of hitherto informal housing and labour markets (Shin, 2009a; Winkler, 2009; Kuyucu and Unsal, 2010); the state and market making land ready for gentrification by international developers through red-lining and ground rent dispossession (López-Morales, 2011); the state's higher capacity and propensity for repression (Cabannes et al, 2010); the peripheralisation of low-income residents (Wu, 2004; He and Wu; 2007; Shin 2007; Islam, 2010); and the infiltration of clientelism into pro-gentrification policies while eliminating populist-clientelist policies for neoliberal ones (Bartu and Kolluoglu, 2008). These 'Southern' peculiarities deserve our scholarly attention.

Moreover, the comparative imagination in the gentrification literature has, until more recently, been restricted to the cities of the Global North (eg Lees, 1994; Slater, 2004; Carpenter and Lees, 1995), leaving cities outside of these 'cores' off the research agenda. Harris's (2008) comparative work on London and Mumbai was perhaps the first to counter this trend in the gentrification literature in any significant way. Likewise, Lees (2012) has underlined the need for a fresh comparative urbanism of gentrification, one that will 'begin the task of decentring the dominant narratives of gentrification from the Global North' (p 6), thus potentially refining gentrification theories. Indeed, a comprehensive focus on the different dynamics, actors and processes involved in gentrification in different cities, and even in the same city, is needed to shed light on the different geographies of gentrification within the Global South. To face this challenge, there is a need for a much more grounded approach in researching different geographies of gentrification. Understanding the local political contexts – the actually existing neoliberalisms in different cities/regions/countries, the role and power of the state, elite coalitions and so on – that give rise to urban policies promoting gentrification, together with research into the strategies of actors facing gentrification, is a crucial part of this grounded approach. Such an attempt requires a historical perspective to analyse the evolution of gentrification in a specific context in discussion with its peculiarities. It should also be sensitive to, and enable the researcher to explore, the different geographies of gentrification within the same city, as well as across cities.

In an attempt to follow through on this, this chapter draws on two case studies of the making of, and resistance to, state-led gentrification in Istanbul. It aims to shed light on the diversity of state-led gentrification processes within the same city. The case studies chosen are from two disadvantaged neighbourhoods in the historical inner city – Sulukule and Tarlabasi – which have been transformed based on the same renewal law enacted by the district municipalities. We discuss the differences between these cases, for even in two seemingly similar cases within the same city, the making of, and resistance to, gentrification has taken quite different forms.

We begin with a review of the gentrification literature in Turkey, not only to discuss the applicability of gentrification theories to the Turkish case, but also to provide an overview of the discussions regarding the concept of gentrification in academia in Turkey. Next, a short review of the evolution of gentrification in Turkey is made and then, using a comparative perspective, we analyse the way state-led gentrification has proceeded in the Turkish context with a focus on two case studies in Istanbul.

Gentrification studies in Turkey

Until the late 1990s, gentrification was not used as a conceptual tool by urban researchers in Turkey to describe the upgrading processes in run-down neighbourhoods. However, hitherto, gentrification became a very popular research topic from the mid-2000s following new changes in urban policy that embraced urban transformation as its central element. This has accelerated more recently as worldwide media attention was focused on the anti-gentrification riots in Istanbul in the summer of 2013. The early works on gentrification focused on the classical gentrification cases in the city in an attempt to explore the process within the frameworks developed from/for the Anglo-Saxon world (eg Keyder, 1999; Uzun, 2001; Islam, 2005; Şen, 2006). Gentrification is seen and reflected in these works as a local manifestation of a global phenomenon that started in core cities elsewhere and reached more peripheral ones down the line.

However, recent writings on gentrification in Turkey have focused more on the changing role of the state in the large-scale urban transformation of neglected yet central areas. Urban transformation was put forward by politicians in the early 2000s as a remedy for the existing problems of rapid urbanisation. While it was used in the past as a tool to formalise informal settlements (*gecekondu*), the recent transformation agenda targets formal inner-city neighbourhoods as well as the *gecekondu* areas.[1] For the first time, urban transformation was declared as the main urban policy by the state with a high level of determination.

Contrary to the classical gentrification processes, this recent wave of urban transformation has attracted significant academic attention, both from Turkish and international scholars. Although terms with more neutral tones such as 'urban transformation', 'urban regeneration' or 'urban renewal' have a wider usage, 'gentrification' has also been used as an analytical tool to understand these recent transformations (see Güzey, 2006; Sakızlıoğlu, 2007; Islam, 2009), focusing on the direct or indirect displacement effects of these projects and referring to the similarities of these projects with state-led/post-recession/third-wave gentrification processes in North America and Europe (see Hackworth and Smith, 2001; Smith, 2002; Davidson and Lees, 2005; Uitermark et al, 2007).

The translation of the term 'gentrification' into Turkish has been rather problematic. It took around 20 years for urban researchers to conceptualise the gentrification processes that had begun in the early 1980s in Istanbul. Several words are now used that are equivalents to the concept of gentrification; among them, two have a wider usage – *soylulaşma* and *mutenalaşma*. '*Soylulaşma*' is formed by the conjugation of the adjective '*soylu*' (noble) and means *becoming noble*. '*Mutenalaşma*' is conjugated by the adjective '*mutena*' (an old word of Arabic origin) and has meanings such as becoming *select, distinguished, carefully done* or *exclusive*. Some scholars prefer the use of '*seçkinleştirme*', the Turkish equivalent of '*mutenalaştırma*'. All the terms have been coined as a response to the need to find a Turkish translation for the concept of 'gentrification'. In the Turkish context, it is true to say that the process followed the term, and not the other way round. As a result, scholars have not produced original conceptual tools based on pure observation; rather, they have tried to analyse the transformation of inner-city neighbourhoods using already-existing concepts and theories from the Western gentrification literature.

There is, of course, a question about the applicability of gentrification theories created in/for the Anglo-Saxon world, and this has been the subject of discussion in Turkish academia. In the introduction to the first-ever edited book on gentrification in Istanbul (Behar and Islam, 2006), for example, Behar and Perouise (2006) raised their concerns about the applicability of the gentrification concept to the urban transformation processes taking place in Istanbul. The authors highlighted the importance of treating 'imported' concepts with a certain level of caution: 'as it is the case for every imported material', they say, 'concepts might get damaged during the "transportation" process: their expiration date might have passed, they might be overloaded by "additional tax", or they can be sent back from the customs' (Behar and Perouise, 2006, p 6). Reflecting on these sentences, Güvenç (2006) claimed that unlike other urban concepts (such as segregation, exclusion or urban renewal) whose meanings have been rather smoothly translated into the Turkish context, there is a problem in the adaptation of the term 'gentrification' for Turkish cases because of the 'context-specific' character of gentrification and its being loaded with too many side-meanings (cultural, economic, etc).

We believe that 'gentrification' is a useful term and conceptual tool for urban researchers to analyse most of the typical cases of middle-class invasion in run-down neighbourhoods in Istanbul since the early 1980s, and for more recent urban transformations too. Yet, we want to reiterate Behar and Perouise's (2006) concerns that one should be careful regarding the importation of a concept as loaded as gentrification. Overall, there is an urgent need for a grounded approach to describing and analysing the processes of neighbourhood change in Istanbul, with a solid grip on the contextual peculiarities, not only to do justice to the context, but also to potentially amend the existing theories of global gentrification. In fact, in the policy context of urban transformation, where public authorities are using their extended powers to take urban space and resources from the poor and put them into the use of the rich, we assert that it is politically very important to embrace the concept of gentrification regardless of its translation into Turkish.

Gentrification in Turkey

In contrast to most cities in the Anglo-Saxon world, Istanbul (see Figure 13.1) did not experience a depopulation and abandonment of its central areas; the

Figure 13.1: Map of Istanbul and its neighbourhoods

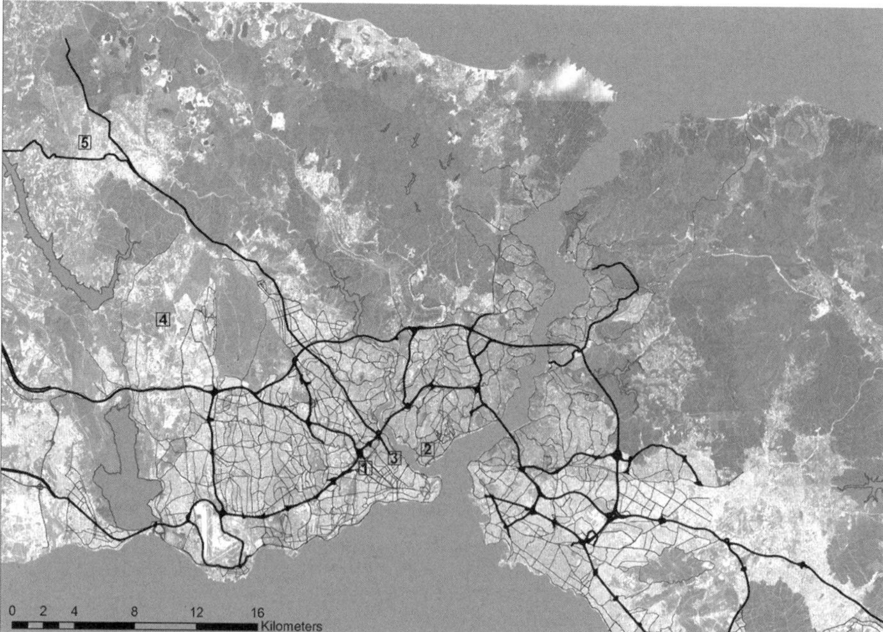

Notes: 1. Sulukule; 2. Beyoglu Region, which includes Taksim Square, Tarlabasi, Istiklal Street, Cihangir, Galata and Asmalimescit; 3. Fener-Balat; 4. Kayabasi; and 5. Tasoluk.

central city has always hosted people, even in times of devalorisation. The centre has been subject to a disinvestment cycle but the dynamics of this cycle were not related to industrial decentralisation. The neighbourhoods that were subjected to gentrification in the 1980s had a predominantly non-Muslim minority population until the 1950s and 1960s. An important segment of this population were tradesmen, and they had middle- and upper-middle-class backgrounds. A sort of filtering process happened in the minority neighbourhoods but the rationale behind this social change was political rather than economic. The imposition of an enormous wealth levy on non-Muslim businessmen in 1942, the riot against the Greek population that destroyed their properties in 1955 and the legislation requiring the departure of the population of Greek origin in 1964 all led to the abandonment of these neighbourhoods by their original residents, most of whom also left the country as well. This process of middle- and upper-income flight coincided with the rapid industrialisation and urbanisation era of the 1950s, as a result of which the masses started to migrate to Istanbul from rural parts of the country. The abandoned housing stock in the centre absorbed some of this immigrant population, and within a few years, the social status of these neighbourhoods had undergone dramatic changes.

During the 1980s and 1990s, gentrification was confined to minority neighbourhoods. According to the literature on gentrification in Turkey, the first signs of gentrification were seen in the early 1980s in two urban villages along the Bosphorus, Kuzguncuk and Arnavutköy (Uzun, 2001; Islam, 2003, 2005; Ergun, 2004). Other instances of gentrification were observed in Beyoglu, the historic centre of the city, in the early 1990s, and in Cihangir, Galata and Asmalimescit. The impetus behind this gentrification wave was the new status that İstiklal Street had acquired as the main hub of cultural and leisure activities after it was pedestrianised in the 1990s. This pedestrianisation was only possible by the transfer of the car traffic to its parallel axis, the Tarlabasi Boulevard, which was constructed in the 1980s after the demolition of hundreds of historic buildings. In a highly ironic way, while the existence of this boulevard opened the way for gentrification on one side (the İstiklal Street), by cutting its relationship and acting as a barrier, it triggered the dilapidation processes on the other side (Tarlabasi), which would be subject to another round of (state-led) gentrification two decades later. In the late 1990s, gentrification spread to the poorer areas in the city, to neighbourhoods like Fener and Balat around the Golden Horn. All these pre-2000 examples of gentrification fit into the definitions of classical gentrification to a great extent: the social profile of the neighbourhoods changed gradually over time with the incoming of higher-status groups, followed by accompanying changes in the physical fabric and real estate prices.

Until the 2000s, the pace of this gentrification was slow: there were institutional, legal and economic barriers that brought to a halt the recapitalisation of historical neighbourhoods. One of these barriers to gentrification was the heavy bureaucracy involved in any renovation action in the highly regulated historical conservation areas (eg getting permits from conservation committees). In addition, the history of ad hoc policy measures and the flight of non-Muslim minorities had created a complicated ownership structure, with many unknown owners and multiple ownerships. Furthermore, the concentration of marginalised groups such as sex workers, recycling workers and groups involved in drug-dealing, burglary and pickpocketing constituted a barrier for individual gentrifiers to invest in these areas.

Following the 2004 municipal elections, the Justice and Development Party (AKP) started to rule most of the district municipalities. With the metropolitan municipality and the central government under its rule, the AKP gained enormous political power, sufficient to overcome these hurdles. With the intention to make Istanbul a global city, the AKP pushed an urban transformation agenda[2] that resulted in gentrification in several neighbourhoods. Alterations were made in legislative and institutional frameworks to form the legal and organisational basis of the future urban transformation projects. The Mass Housing Administration (MHA) emerged as a powerful actor with strong public powers to make use of public land stocks in its operations and to intervene in *gecekondu* areas for transformation activities. The administration has been a key actor in urban transformation in Istanbul. District and metropolitan municipalities were given extended authorities regarding the designation and implementation of the transformation projects. This was done by the introduction of a series of laws and draft laws to reconfigure the legal infrastructure of urban transformation, among which Law No. 5366, the law for 'Preservation by Renovation and Utilisation by Revitalising of Deteriorated Immovable Historical and Cultural Properties' (from now on the Renewal Law), played the most critical role in terms of overcoming the barriers to, and forming the basis of, (state-led) gentrification.

The Renewal Law regulates the transformation of historical sites that are dilapidated, and arms local administrations to designate renewal areas within their jurisdictions. After getting the approvals from the special area conservation committees and the cabinet, they prepare and implement the projects and plans to renew these areas. The law enables the local administrations to aggregate the property rights in the project areas, to transfer the property rights to another area, to allocate property rights for only one part within a multi-unit building (eg for a storey in a single building) and to expropriate the properties of the owners who do not agree with the terms and conditions of the projects. Moreover, all the transactions and costs within the project area are exempt from all taxes and duties, which means a 35% reduction in the construction costs.

While arming local governments with strong powers and rights, the law does not clearly frame their public duties and responsibilities to protect residents' rights to housing and access to decision-making. As the only mechanism for participation, it mentions informative meetings to be held by the local administration with property-owners and/or local residents. That is to say, property-owners – but not necessarily other tenure groups – are to be informed about the process. However, it does not specify any defined mechanisms and measures to ensure the participation of the property-owners and local residents in the decision-making and implementation of the project. The law also does not consider tenants as 'rightful' parties in the process of urban renewal and their rights are not guaranteed in the law. Furthermore, it does not guarantee any social policy measures, such as relocation compensation or a relocation property, to be offered to affected residents. The law also encourages corporate agents through the insertion of public–private partnerships in the urban renewal field. This means that local municipalities have gained a new role[3] as powerful mediators between private investors and property-owners with respect to the project. This opens the way for developers, investors, builders and financial institutions to be involved in the process as early as the planning stage. Not only are the corporate agents able to enjoy the powers of the local administration to intervene into the urban space through the use of, for example, planning rights, expropriations, land-use decisions and so on, but they also have easy access to the subsidies, tax concessions, other public funds and incentives available.

Based on these institutional and legal frameworks, new forms of gentrification have emerged, in a way proving Smith's (2002, p 446) prophecy that '"urban regeneration" represent[s] the next wave of gentrification'. In the 2000s, Istanbul witnessed the expansion of these urban transformation projects, which spurred state-led gentrification in disadvantaged inner-city neighbourhoods with favourable locations with respect to the city centre and/or main transportation axes of the city. Top-down policies for urban transformation have been implemented through public–private and public–public partnerships. On the opposing side of this strong coalition between Istanbul's political and economic elite is resistance from residents and activists contesting these projects. In what follows, we present two case studies that are emblematic of the recent state-led gentrification processes in Istanbul. The data are based on the PhD projects of the authors and were gathered mainly through in-depth interviewing with the municipal authorities, project developers and local residents of these two neighbourhoods.

State-led gentrification in Tarlabasi and Sulukule

Two disadvantaged neighbourhoods

Tarlabasi (see Figure 13.1) is a deprived neighbourhood in Beyoğlu, the commercial, entertainment and cultural centre of Istanbul. Hitherto a neighbourhood for lower-middle-class non-Muslim minorities, it suffered from the flight of non-Muslim minorities, who were replaced by incoming rural migrants and disinvestment by the state. The construction of the Tarlabasi Boulevard in the late 1980s cut the connection and increased the disparity between Tarlabasi and its immediate surroundings, especially with İstiklal Street, the main cultural axis of the city. While adjacent neighbourhoods were gentrifying in the 1990s, Tarlabasi dilapidated more and more and became home to displaced people – including stigmatised groups like sex workers and workers in the informal economy like recyclers – and to forced Kurdish migration as the result of the war in the south-east and east of Turkey from the 1980s onwards.

Sulukule (see Figure 13.1) was once a residential inner-city neighbourhood located within the Historic Peninsula along the city walls. Officially, the area known as Sulukule by the general public is located within the boundaries of two neighbourhoods, Neslişah and Hatice Sultan. Although not as much as Tarlabasi, the neighbourhood had a central location, and was close to main transportation axes and to the central tourist and hotel zones. The area was characterised by low-rise housing and an organic street pattern (see Figure 13.2). The housing stock had a lower quality and lesser historical significance than that of Tarlabasi. However, one of the discerning characteristics of the neighbourhood was the unique settlement pattern, the 'courtyard houses', where individual units open to and have access from courtyards, and courtyards open to the streets. Another discerning characteristic of the neighbourhood was the high concentration of Roma living in the area for decades. In the past, Sulukule had a vibrant economy in famous 'entertainment houses', where food and drinks were served to the customers, accompanied by live Roma music and dancers. Entertainment houses were closed in the late 1980s as the state accused them of engaging in prostitution. The closure of the entertainment houses that had acted as the main income source for the local residents for decades had a deep impact on the economy of the neighbourhood. Economic decline was followed by physical decay since the residents could not afford the maintenance of their houses (Karaman and Islam, 2012). Like Tarlabasi, Sulukule was also a highly stigmatised neighbourhood, perceived as a no-go zone by the great majority. Unlike Tarlabasi, probably because

Figure 13.2: Sulukule before the demolitions

Note: Photograph taken 2007.

it was a little less central, the gentrification of Sulukule was never on the agenda until the declaration of the urban transformation project.

The renewal processes

In early 2005, Beyoglu's mayor announced the initial plans for the renewal of Tarlabasi. He declared in an interview (see Erdem, 2006) that Prime Minister Erdogan supported the transformation of Tarlabasi and had said 'May you solve the issue of Tarlabasi' to the mayor. This top-down decision forced the municipality to take an active role in the preparation of a new urban renewal law to ease the bureaucratic barriers to the recapitalisation of the area. With cooperation between the local and central governments, the law-making process was quick and the new Renewal Law for historical areas that is known as the 'Tarlabasi Law' was enacted the same year. The preparations for the renewal process in Tarlabasi had actually started before the introduction of the Renewal Law. The municipality started with surveys in the neighbourhood in order to understand the tenure structure in the area. No information was provided to the residents about the forthcoming transformation project during this survey; they learned about the project from the media.[4]

Tarlabasi was designated as one of six renewal areas in Beyoglu in 2006. In 2006, it received the approval of the cabinet for its urgent expropriation, and in 2007, a tender was made for the design and implementation of the renewal project. A big developer firm, the GAP Construction Company, part of Çalık Holding, won the tender to realise the renewal project, covering an area of around 20,000 square metres, with 278 buildings in nine building blocks. Around 2,200 people were living in the renewal area, 75% were tenants, 5% were non-paying residents and the remaining 20% were owners (Kentsel, 2008). The Tarlabasi renewal project was based on a model of public–private partnership, where the partners were/are the GAP Construction Company and the district municipality of Beyoglu. The project aimed at preventing decay and creation of a new safer, healthier, livable area that is integrated to the city, with an emphasis on the historical and cultural heritage in Tarlabasi (see Figure 13.3). Hotels, luxurious residences and offices were to be built in the renewal area, designed by nine renowned architects. The municipality drew on already-existing stigmas portraying Tarlabasi as a 'criminal', 'terrorist' and 'decaying' neighbourhood to legitimise the renewal project.

The Sulukule renewal project formally started in September 2005, with a joint protocol signed between Fatih Municipality, the MHA and the Greater City Municipality. This protocol was renewed in 2006 following the enactment of the implementation procedures of the Renewal Law. The official declaration of Sulukule as a renewal area took place in April 2006 with the decision of the cabinet. In December 2006, the local municipality was given the right of urgent expropriation. However, the transformation model in Sulukule is different from that in Tarlabasi since the model does not involve any private actors. Two public institutions, Fatih Municipality (local municipality) and the MHA, were responsible

Figure 13.3: The Tarlabasi renewal project

for the design and implementation of the project.[5] An area of around 90,000 square metres, encompassing 12 blocks and 382 plots, was declared a transformation area on the basis of the Renewal Law. The project area was home to around 3,500 people. Around half of the population were owners (48.5%), whereas renters and non-paying households constituted 42.5% and 9%, respectively (Sulukule Platform, 2007). The project envisaged the construction of new residential units, a school, a cultural unit and a hotel following the demolition of all the existing buildings. Just like in Tarlabasi, the Fatih Municipality mobilised already-existing stigmas about the Roma population, and claimed that they would create a better Sulukule after renewal.

Not everybody has the right to stay put

In both neighbourhoods, similar rules applied to the owners. They were given two options: (i) to be a partner of the project and get new units from the area by fulfilling certain conditions; or (ii) to give the rights of their property to the authorities in exchange for money or another property elsewhere in the city that was equivalent to the current value of the asset. The owners were not given a third option of keeping their units as they were. Those who did not agree with these terms were threatened by the new expropriation tool that the municipalities gained with the Renewal Law. To be a partner of the project, the owners had to pay the difference between the value of their current houses and the unit they would get at the end of the project in long-term payments, which many could not afford. The tenants were not given the right to live in the project area, but were provided with some options. The ones with formal tenancy contracts were offered the right to buy a house on a newly built mass housing estate in Kayabasi on the periphery, around 35–40 km outside the city centre. In Tarlabasi, the percentage of formal tenants was very low, so very few tenants could use this right. The occupants who did not pay rent constituted approximately 5% of the households, whereas tenants with no formal contract constituted almost 75% of tenants and 55% of all households. Unlike Tarlabasi, in Sulukule, almost all the renters who were able to prove that they were residents in the project area before the declaration of the renewal plan got the right to buy a property in Kayabasi and Tasoluk mass housing estate on the periphery of the city. Here, apart from the official rental agreements, the municipality's survey, undertaken before the declaration of the renewal plan, and any bills (telephone, water, etc) showing an address within the project area were accepted as proof of tenancy.[6] However, most of the residents who bought housing in the Toki mass housing estate could not pay their instalments and moved back around their old neighbourhoods.[7]

In the end, the majority of the residents were displaced from both areas as a result of the renewal projects. In the case of tenants, all of them were displaced at the very beginning since they were not given the right to stay in the project area in both neighbourhoods. In the case of the owners, an important segment of them have sold their properties and left the area. Very few in both renewal sites would be able to afford to live in the new Tarlabasi or Sulukule.[8]

Contesting the renewal projects: anti-gentrification strategies in Tarlabasi and Sulukule

Tarlabasi Solidarity Organisation for Property Owners and Tenants (the Tarlabasi Organisation from here on) was founded by a group of commercial property-owners in early 2008, and mainly struggled for the rights of the property-owners. The founders of the Tarlabasi Organisation mobilised people through one-to-one talks, drawing on their own social networks in the neighbourhood and gaining members to the organisation. Thereafter, the organisation collected letters of attorney from every member who was a property-owner. Through this, it aimed to hold the collective rights to bargain with the municipality as the representative of the property-owners. This would not only ensure that the individual properties would not be sold without the organisation knowing it, but also weaken the impact of the municipality's one-to-one talks with property-owners when the municipality was pressing property-owners to sell.

The organisation's starting point was that the property-owners were not content with the terms of the project – to be precise, rent redistribution in the project – even though they were not opposed to the idea of renewal in Tarlabasi. It aimed to change the terms of the project, trying to open up space for participation, and when this was not possible any more, it aimed to annul the project entirely. Even though it tried to get members among the tenants as well, tenants' right to housing was not a priority agenda and the tenants were only strategic allies for the organisation so as to gain more members and support. These facts hallmarked the organisation's strategies and action repertoire as they tilted the balance between participation in, and contestation to, the process.

The tactical line started with negotiations with the municipality to increase the share that property-owners would get from the project and to get some compensation for the tenants. Soon after, the negotiations with the municipality and the GAP Construction Company were ended by the organisation as their demands were not acknowledged. The only improvement achieved as a result of the negotiations was that commercial property-owners were offered commercial space in the new Tarlabasi, whereas this was not hitherto the case. Then, the organisation started a national juridical battle for the annulment of the project with the Chambers of Architects and City Planners. After the negative decision of the court, the organisation scaled up its resistance to an international juridical battle started at the European Court of Human Rights on behalf of its members and through an application to UNESCO to stop the project. Furthermore, several demonstrations and media campaigns were actualised and the organisation also recruited the support of other organisations, such as Amnesty International.

In Sulukule, an association against the renewal project, the Association to Develop Roma Culture and Solidarity (the Roma Association from now on), was established in May 2006. The Sulukule Platform was also established in order to bring together activists in the city to support resistance to the urban renewal project. The resistance in Sulukule was mainly organised by the Sulukule Platform (Uysal, 2012). The active resistance to the project started in 2007. Between March and May, the Sulukule Platform organised a festival that lasted '40 days and 40 nights' in order to focus public attention on the neighbourhood and the renewal process. The organisation continued its efforts to increase the visibility of the neighbourhood and to a great extent reached its aims: Sulukule, a small neighbourhood in Istanbul, gained such visibility that its popularity reached beyond the borders of Turkey via national and international media coverage. The resistance of the activists did not stop the project, but did act as a support mechanism to the residents.[9] As a result of this resistance, some informal residents who did not initially have any rights got compensation and the right to buy a house on a mass housing estate.

The Sulukule Platform emphasised the livelihood of the Roma population in Sulukule and the entertainment houses. This tactical choice, however, was not welcomed by a segment of the population, who believed that the use of the word 'Sulukule' created further stigmatisation. As a reaction to this, a second neighbourhood association, the Association for Cooperation, Solidarity and Development of Neslişah and Hatice Sultan (the Neighbourhood Association from now on), was established in October 2007. The aim of this association was similar to that of the Tarlabasi Organisation; as stated by Kaya, the head of the association, they were "seeking ways to get the maximum from the project". Another aim of the association was "to build a bridge between the residents and the municipality".[10] However, this internal conflict among the local residents made it much easier for the municipality to proceed with the project. In 2008, the municipality started to demolish the units. Parallel to these demolitions, activists' efforts continued: prominent national and international figures made visits to the neighbourhood (Tony Gatlif, Gogol Bordello, Sezen Aksu, etc) and concerns about the development were mentioned in a number of international reports on human rights (eg reports of human rights of the Council of Europe, OECD, the Advisory Group on Forced Evictions).

The end ...

In both neighbourhoods, many were displaced despite the strong contestations against the projects. Even though some would benefit from the renewal process, many suffered from the effects of displacement. Besides the material effects of the process (such as loss of house, job, income, solidarity networks, etc), living under the constant threat of displacement was heavy for most of the residents (see Sakızlıoğlu, 2014a). Even before the actual displacement of the residents, the neighbourhoods went into a spiral of decline as vacancies increased and safety and the sense of community decreased as the neighbours moved out (cr Lees, 2014a, 2014b). Besides these changes, the municipalities put pressure on the remaining residents to sell and/or to move out (by using expropriation as a tool, etc). Even though the resistance was relatively strong in both cases, in the end, the municipalities managed to divide and rule the residents using different tactics, such as: using differential treatment of different tenure groups (Sakizlioglu and Uitermark, 2014); pressuring remaining residents with the threat of expropriation; leaving the debris of the demolitions in the neighbourhood; and leaving the residents in a state of uncertainty and anxious waiting. As a result, resistance weakened in both neighbourhoods over time and fell short of stopping the processes. Many were dispossessed and displaced as a result.[11]

Conclusion

Sulukule and Tarlabasi are cases of state-led gentrification as their renewal, initiated by the local municipalities, has displaced the poor from these neighbourhoods and transformed them for the use of the upper classes. Even though these two renewal projects are based on the same renewal law, there are important differences. The Tarlabasi renewal project is a public–private partnership, whereas the Sulukule project is a public–public partnership. What is common in these two different models is that they are based on a coalition of elites: a coalition of political and economic elites in the Tarlabasi case and that of political elites (at different scales of government) in the Sulukule case. Both coalitions are possible because the AKP is in power at three different government scales.

In both neighbourhoods, the process of renewal proceeded similarly: it pushed the neighbourhoods into a spiral of decline that impeded everyday life in the neighbourhoods. Community feeling and solidarity networks collapsed as some neighbours moved out. As the vacancies increased, people did not feel safe in their neighbourhoods anymore. Local shops closed down as there was less and less business. The residents were not informed about the process in advance (most learned about the renewal from the media). This uncertainty first brought about hopes for an in-situ upgrading in the neighbourhoods, but resulted in anxious waiting as residents understood in time that they would be displaced from their neighbourhoods. The presence of the threat of expropriation from the very beginning of the process (thanks to the new powers given to the authorities by the Renewal Law) acted as 'a sword of Damacles' to create pressure on the residents to move out. Thus, the extension of the implementation process, over time, proved to be a good recipe for the authorities to break active resistance in both neighbourhoods.

There are certain peculiarities in the way the renewal process in the two neighbourhoods proceeded. Renters were, for instance, treated differently in the two neighbourhoods. In Sulukule, most of the renters got compensation at some level by being given the right to own a house in the mass housing on the periphery; in Tarlabasi, only a few renters were given such rights. There were differences in the dynamics, tactics and impacts of the resistance as well. There are at least two reasons for this. First, the composition of the resisters was different in both neighbourhoods. A group of property-owners in Tarlabasi started the resistance to protect their own property rights. They had similar backgrounds: early migrants, mostly Turkish, the only commercial presence in Tarlabasi, and relatively higher-, lower-middle- and middle-class. Sulukule lacked such a group to lead the resistance and this gap was filled with the activists who fought against the displacement of Sulukule residents. This affected the characteristics, tactics and impacts of the resistance. Second, and related, the rent gap was higher in Tarlabasi compared to Sulukule, which attracted investors to the area, thus pressurising the local residents and making their displacement inevitable.

Starting as a property-owners' alliance, the Tarlabasi Organisation strategically chose to enlarge itself by including renters. Even though the cross-class or tenure alliance did not last long – as is the case in other contexts such as China (Shin, 2013) – this alliance made the organisation bigger and stronger for a while. The urban activists' contribution was limited to giving support: they never became the main actors. The organisation managed to get support from the majority of the property-owners on the one hand, but could not manage to use media tools to publicise their case as effectively as those in Sulukule. In Sulukule, however, the resistance was organised by an umbrella platform formed by urban activists. The platform was able to get the support of some of the residents but they could never be as representative as the Tarlabasi Organisation. The Sulukule Platform made strategic moves in order to get public attention through the media. They used symbols to highlight the Roma character of the neighbourhood and managed to get the attention of the national and international press; however, on the other hand, they were not welcomed by some residents, who wanted to distance themselves from the name of Sulukule in order not to be stigmatised. The result, however, was almost the same in the two neighbourhoods: the resistance helped to delay the projects, which in the end went on. However, some provisions were gained for some groups thanks to the contestations in both neighbourhoods.

Building on this overview, we can now focus on what these case studies tell us about gentrification in Istanbul and the Global South at large and how to study them.

1. The centrality of the state and the need for inserting theories of the state into theories of gentrification

In Istanbul, the state has had a very central role in gentrification in the post-2000 era. The state, on the one hand, shapes the demand for, and produces, the gentrifiable stock that will serve the demands of the gentrifiers. On the other hand, the capacity of the state to implement the new gentrification-centred urban policies occurred only after a single party (the AKP) had been in power for many years and had control over different levels of government and bureaucratic institutions that had critical positions. It is this coherence among different levels of government and bureaucracy that made the shift to the new urban policy possible. If any part of this mechanism was missing, or incomplete, the policy was doomed to fail. There are similar examples from cities in China, India, Korea and Chile, among others, where the state's fine-tuned interventions make massive-scale urban redevelopment-led gentrification possible (He and Wu, 2007; Shin, 2009b, 2013; López-Morales, 2011). Third-wave gentrification, in general, is characterised by the central role of the state. Yet, we think, in countries like Turkey, where the authoritarian state's practices are embedded in the tradition of making politics, the state's involvement in contemporary urban processes may be more violent and harsh. Thus, in order to comprehend how gentrification proceeded in Istanbul – and perhaps many other cities in the Global South – it is important to understand how power relations worked/work at different levels of government and why they pushed the agenda of gentrification.[12]

2. Tilting the balance between the formal and the informal

While the state is formalising informal housing markets, it also creates an informal space in which to manoeuvre. The urban policy change in the 2000s in Istanbul was based on the formalisation of the informal housing market as a way to control disadvantaged neighbourhoods and to reregulate the housing market (Kuyucu and Unsal, 2010). This formalisation, on the one hand, incorporates informal elements into market mechanisms through the proactive agency of the state. Hitherto widely tolerated, informal housing markets together with other informalities, such as informal work, drugs and prostitution, embedded in disadvantaged neighbourhoods are now seen as unwanted elements that need to be cleared away. On the other hand, the way this formalisation is actualised still leaves a space for public authorities to exercise discretionary power regarding the management of the process and the allocation of the urban rent created through the projects. This stems from the ambiguity of the new Urban Renewal Law in framing the obligations of public authorities and the rights of renters. For instance, there is no uniform relocation policy and the rights of renters are not guaranteed by law, which leaves considerable space for discretionary power and informality. Such ambiguities regarding the regulation of urban renewal are probably not issues overlooked by policymakers, but are 'precisely the basis of state authority and serve(s) as the modes of sovereignty and discipline' (Roy, 2009, p 83). Public authorities use their discretionary power to manage the process of urban renewal in different neighbourhoods; in both Sulukule and Tarlabasi, this discretionary power enabled the public authorities to manoeuvre and act according to the cases. Henceforth, it was possible to both meet contingencies and also divide resistance by using the tactic of divide and rule – by providing informal provisions to some but not all.[13]

To conclude, gentrification researchers in Turkey have mostly used existing conceptual toolboxes developed outside of the Turkish context to analyse gentrification processes. We believe that this is mostly because the cases labelled as 'gentrification' in Istanbul comprise all the 'core elements'[14] of gentrification in the West. In other words, the use of gentrification as the main analytical tool to grasp neighbourhood transformations involving socio-economic and physical upgrading that brings about displacement is an appropriate choice. Yet, until quite recently, the gentrification literature in Turkey has tended to focus on cases of classical gentrification taking place in historic city centres, and has been quite disconnected from other urban literatures such as on *gecekondu* transformations or on informal urbanisation. As our case studies show, there is a need for integrating theories of power and state into gentrification theories to grasp the crucial role of the state and the interchangeable use of formality and informality in cities outside the Global North.[15] This signals an urgent need for theory building with a grounded approach.

Notes

[1] In addition, the gentrification literature has not been connected to the *gecekondu* literature until very recently (Dündar, 2003; Islam, 2005), when the state targeted these areas to transform them into upper-class neighbourhoods. While *gecekondu* transformation was often in situ in the past and enabled upwards mobility for the poor, the recent projects of the local and central state for the *gecekondu* areas have displaced people from their neighbourhoods, which are being transformed into middle- and upper-class areas. Connecting the gentrification and *gecekondu* literatures has the potential to bring fresh insights to both literatures.

[2] A devastating economic crisis, the accumulated problems of ad hoc and speculative urbanisation, and the political victory of the liberal-conservative AKP created the impetus for the urban transformation agenda.

[3] This law exemplifies what Hackworth (2007) refers to as municipalisation under neoliberalism in the Turkish context.

[4] The fact that the survey was conducted prior to the enactment of the Renewal Law on 16 June 2005 is important for two reasons. First, it shows the relationship between the

local and central state. The local municipality had information about the forthcoming law that was going to be enacted by the central government, which is not a surprise since both are run by the same political party. Second, and more importantly, it shows the level of confidence that the mayor had in the power of the existing government (the confidence that the Urban Renewal Law would pass without any problems).

[5] The MHA does not have its own construction firms to develop renewal areas; it tenders the projects to construction and developer companies.

[6] Compared to 474 households in Sulukule, only 150 households were given rights in Tarlabasi to have units in the mass housing estates in the periphery. See: http://www.gazetea24.com/sondakikahaber/magduru-olmayan-donusum---tarlabasi_69436.html and http://www.sabah.com.tr/Yasam/2010/06/23/sulukuleli_127_aileye_daha_kayabasinda_yeni_konut

[7] According to Funda Oral, an activist who had been working in Sulukule since 2007, except for 10 families, all the families that were given units in the mass housing estates have left these units and settled around Sulukule, bearing the burden of increasing rents (see: www.insanhaber.com/guncel/sulukule-artik-cok-uzaklarda-h11751.html).

[8] In Sulukule, for example, it has recently been stated by the head of the MHA that among the 600 households, around half of them consist of those who have been living in the area before the declaration of the project (see: www.hurriyet.com.tr/ekonomi/23330363.asp). Apart from the monthly instalments for 10 years, the new units in the now-luxurious settlement require additional costs as well (ie for security, heating or maintenance). According to a survey in 2007, around half of the population earned less than TL500 (around €300 according to the currency at that time), whereas only 7.5% had an income of TL1000 (€588) or more.

[9] Other than trying to draw public attention to the case, the activists in Sulukule also provided legal support to help bring cases to the national and international courts, undertook surveys, and sought to minimise the traumatising effects of the renewal process on children. Some of the activists are still supporting the children even though the renewal process is completely over.

[10] Interview with the head of Neighbourhood Association on 16 March 2008.

[11] The resistance was local, attracted limited people and did not become a massive movement until the Gezi Park riots in May–June 2013. For the first time in Turkish history, urban resistance of a massive scale took place with the Gezi riots, which started in order to protest the cutting down of some trees in Gezi Park, regarded as the first step in the construction of a massive building in the park, one of the rare remaining open spaces in the city centre. The protests transformed into anti-government (and anti-gentrification) protests due to the excessive use of power by the riot police to suppress the riots in Taksim and the protest spread to other cities.

[12] Many other comparative questions also await answers, for example: 'Why does gentrification result in contestation in some contexts but not in others?'; 'Who are the parties pushing the agenda of gentrification?'; and 'How does gentrification get into the policy agenda in the cities of the Global South?'.

[13] While these ambiguities and discretionary powers are found mostly in the urban political contexts of cities of the Global South, such as Latin American cities, they are also common in Western cities, which are characterised by a, relatively, more formal political structure. In the latter, however, process works in a reverse manner, creating informalities within a formal structure, through deregulations, to open up political space to manoeuvre (Sakizlioglu, 2014b).

[14] According to Davidson and Lees (2005), the core elements of gentrification are: '(1) the reinvestment of capital; (2) the social upgrading of locale by incoming high-income groups; (3) landscape change; and (4) direct or indirect displacement of low-income groups'.

[15] Despite many differences, state-led gentrification processes in Istanbul and also in other cities in the Global South, pushed forward by the state through the agenda of 'urban renewal', converge with processes in the Global North that Hyra (2008) and Lees (2014a) call 'the new urban renewal' and Merrifield (2013) calls 'neo-Haussmannization'.

References

Bartu, A. and Kolluoglu, B. (2008) 'Emerging spaces of neoliberalism: a gated town and a public housing project in Istanbul', *New Perspectives on Turkey*, no 39, pp 5–46.

Behar, D. and Islam, T. (eds) (2006) İstanbul*'da soylulaştırma: Eski kentin yeni sahipleri*, İstanbul: İstanbul Bilgi Üniversitesi Yayınları.

Behar, D. and Perouise, J.F. (2006) 'Giriş', in D. Behar and T. Islam (eds) İstanbul*'da soylulaştırma: Eski kentin yeni sahipleri* [*Gentrification in Istanbul: the new owners of the old city*], İstanbul: İstanbul Bilgi Üniversitesi Yayınları.

Cabannes, Y., Yafai, S.G. and Johnson, C. (2010) *How people face evictions*, London: Development Planning Unit, University College London.

Carpenter, J. and Lees, L. (1995) 'Gentrification in New York, London and Paris: an international comparison', *International Journal of Urban and Regional Research*, vol 19, no 2, pp 286–303.

Davidson, M. and Lees, L. (2005) 'New-build "gentrification" and London's riverside renaissance', *Environment and Planning A*, vol 37, no 7, pp 1165–90.

Dündar, Ö. (2003) *Kentsel dönüşüm politikaları* üzerine *kavramsal bir tartışma*, TMMOB Şehir Plancıları Odasi Kentsel Dönüşüm Sempozyumu, 11–13 June, Istanbul: YTU Press, pp 159–72.

Erdem, S.E. (2006) 'The history is revitalizing', *Radikal*, 20 April.

Ergun, N. (2004) 'Gentrification in Istanbul', *Cities*, vol 21, no 5, pp 391–405.

Güvenç, M. (2006) '"Gentrification" Kavramı Nasıl Türkçeleştirilmeli?' ['How should the concept of gentrification be translated into Turkish?'], *Mimarist*, vol 6, no 21, pp 39–45.

Güzey, O. (2006) 'Understanding the logic of gentrification in different geographies: a comparison of five regeneration projects in Ankara, Turkey', 42nd ISoCaRP Congress.

Hackworth, J. (2007) *The neoliberal city: governance, ideology, and development in American urbanism*, Ithaca, NY: Cornell University Press.

Hackworth, J. and Smith, N. (2001) 'The changing state of gentrification', *Tijdschrift Voor Economische En Sociale Geografie*, vol 92, no 4, pp 464–77.

Harris, A. (2008) 'From London to Mumbai and back again: gentrification and public policy in comparative perspective', *Urban Studies*, vol 45, no 12, pp 2407–28.

He, S. and Wu, F. (2007) 'Socio-spatial impacts of property-led redevelopment on China's urban neighbourhoods', *Cities*, vol 24, no 3, pp 194–208.

Hyra, D.S. (2008) *New urban renewal: the economic transformation of Harlem and Bronzeville*, Chicago, IL: University of Chicago Press.

Islam, T. (2003) 'Istanbul'da Soylulaştırma: Galata Örnegi' ['Gentrification in Istanbul: the case of Galata'], unpublished Msc thesis, Yıldız Technical University, Istanbul.

Islam, T. (2005) 'Outside the core: gentrification in Istanbul', in R. Atkinson and G. Bridge (eds) *Gentrification in a global perspective: the new urban colonialism*, London: Routledge, pp 121–36.

Islam, T. (2009) 'Devlet Eksenli Soylulaşma ve Yerel Halk: Neslişah ve Hatice Sultan Mahalleleri (Sulukule) Örneği' ['State-led gentrification and local people: the case of Sulukule'], unpublished PhD thesis, Yıldız Technical University, Istanbul.

Islam, T. (2010) 'Current urban discourse, urban transformation and gentrification in Istanbul', *Architectural Design*, vol 80, no 1, pp 58–63.

Karaman, O. and Islam, T. (2012) 'On the dual nature of intra-urban borders: the case of a Romani neighborhood in Istanbul', *Cities*, vol 29, no 4, pp 234–43.

Kentsel, A. (2008) 'Tarlabaşı Stratejik Sosyal Plan 2008–2010', unpublished research report.

Keyder, Ç. (1999) 'A tale of two neighborhoods', in C. Keyder (ed) *Istanbul: between the global and the local*, Maryland, MD: Rowman & Littlefield, pp 179–86.

Kuyucu, T. and Unsal, O. (2010) '"Urban transformation" as state-led property transfer: an analysis of two cases of urban renewal in Istanbul', *Urban Studies*, vol 47, no 7, pp 1479–99.

Lees, L. (1994) 'Gentrification in London and New York: an Atlantic gap?', *Housing Studies*, vol 9, no 2, pp 199–217.

Lees, L. (2012) 'The geography of gentrification: thinking through comparative urbanism', *Progress in Human Geography*, vol 36, no 2, pp 155–71.

Lees, L. (2014a) 'The urban injustices of New Labour's "new urban renewal": the case of the Aylesbury Estate in London', *Antipode*, vol 46, no 4, pp 921–47.

Lees, L. (2014b) 'The death of sustainable communities in London?', in R. Imrie and L. Lees (eds) *Sustainable London? The future of a global city*, Bristol: Policy Press, pp 149–72.

López-Morales, E. (2011) 'Gentrification by ground rent dispossession: the shadows cast by large-scale urban renewal in Santiago De Chile', *International Journal of Urban and Regional Research*, vol 35, no 2, pp 330–57.

Merrifield, A. (2013) 'The urban question under planetary urbanization', *International Journal of Urban and Regional Research*, vol 37, no 3, pp 909–22.

Roy, A. (2009) 'Why India cannot plan its cities: informality, insurgence and the idiom of urbanization', *Planning Theory*, vol 8, no 1, pp 76–87.

Sakızlıoğlu, B. (2007) 'The impacts of urban renewal projects: the case of Tarlabasi, Istanbul', unpublished Msc thesis, Middle East Technical University, Ankara.

Sakızlıoğlu, B. (2014a) 'Inserting temporality into the analysis of displacement: living under the threat of displacement', *Tijdschrift voor Economische en Sociale Geografie*, vol 105, no 2, pp 206–20.

Sakızlıoğlu, B. (2014b) 'A comparative look at the experiences of displacement: the cases of Amsterdam and Istanbul', unpublished PhD thesis, Utrecht University, The Netherlands.

Sakızlıoğlu, B. and Uitermark, J. (2014) 'The symbolic politics of gentrification: the restructuring of stigmatized neighborhoods in Amsterdam and Istanbul', *Environment and Planning A*, vol 46, no 6, pp 1369–85.

Şen, B. (2006) 'Kentsel Gerilemeyi Aşmada Çelişkili Bir Süreç Olarak Soylulaştırma: Galata Örneği', unpublished PhD thesis, MSGSÜ, Istanbul.

Shin, H.B. (2007) 'Residential redevelopment and social impacts in Beijing', in F. Wu (ed) *China's emerging cities: the making of new urbanism*, London: Routledge, pp 163–84.

Shin, H.B. (2009a) 'Property-based redevelopment and gentrification: the case of Seoul, South Korea', *Geoforum*, vol 40, no 5, pp 906–17.

Shin, H.B. (2009b) 'Residential redevelopment and entrepreneurial local state: the implications of Beijing's shifting emphasis on urban redevelopment policies', *Urban Studies*, vol 46, no 13, pp 2815–39.

Shin, H.B. (2013) 'The right to the city and critical reflections on China's property rights activism', *Antipode*, vol 45, no 5, pp 1167–89.

Slater, T. (2004) 'North American gentrification? Revanchist and emancipatory perspectives explored', *Environment and Planning A*, vol 36, no 7, pp 1191–213.

Smith, N. (2002) 'New globalism, new urbanism: gentrification as global urban strategy', *Antipode*, vol 34, no 3, pp 428–50.

Sulukule Platform (2007) 'Neighbourhood survey', unpublished work by the Sulukule Platform, Istanbul.

Uitermark, J., Duyvendak, J.W. and Kleinhans, R. (2007) 'Gentrification as a governmental strategy: social control and social cohesion in Hoogvliet, Rotterdam', *Environment and Planning A*, vol 39, no 1, pp 125–41.

Uysal, Ü.E. (2012) 'An urban social movement challenging urban regeneration: the case of Sulukule, Istanbul', *Cities*, vol 29, no 1, pp 12–22.

Uzun, N. (2001) *Gentrification in Istanbul: a diagnostic study*, Utrecht: KNAG.

Winkler, T. (2009) 'Prolonging the global age of gentrification: Johannesburg's regeneration policies', *Planning Theory*, vol 8, no 4, pp 362–81.

Wu, F. (2004) 'Residential relocation under market-oriented redevelopment: the process and outcomes in urban China', *Geoforum*, vol 35, no 4, pp 453–70.

FOURTEEN

Gentrification, neoliberalism and loss in Puebla, Mexico

Gareth Jones

Introduction

In 2002, Neil Smith published a characteristically provocative article in which he claimed that gentrification, which had 'initially emerged as a sporadic, quaint, and local anomaly in the housing markets' of cities in the advanced capitalist world, had become a 'thoroughly generalized' 'urban strategy' (Smith, 2002, p 427). The incidence of this strategy was, he argued, now 'global' and a 'consummate expression of neoliberal urbanism' (Smith, 2002, p 446). Smith acknowledged the rescaling of urban relations in a more global economy, but he took aim at writers who regarded the process as driven by finance and consumption, arguing that globalisation was based on production, albeit now in broader and more tightly connected circuits of capital and culture. Smith, however, paid little explicit attention to the relation between culture and gentrification, and he illustrated his claims of a global urban political economy from the experience of New York City.

In this chapter, I want to consider Smith's broad arguments in and from the perspective of Mexico. Specifically, the chapter revisits the city of Puebla, the site of a set of articles that had their point of departure in whether the debates surrounding the 'ideal type' of gentrification as conceptualised in the North could 'travel' and offer analytical traction in the South (Jones and Varley, 1994, 1999). I outline the arguments of this research later in the chapter. However, for now, it is useful to note that we perceived gentrification in Puebla at that time to be very different from what we understood to have happened in New York City, London or Vancouver. What was unclear to us then, however, and what I want to explore in this chapter as I take the experience of Puebla forward, is whether the particular form of gentrification in the 1990s represented a 'variation' on a norm or a different process. In particular, this chapter considers how gentrification is affected by the changing processes of urban change in neoliberal times.

Following Smith, the link between gentrification and neoliberalism requires some specificity. I am cautious about making a claim that gentrification is intrinsically linked with neoliberalism or that the latest 'phase' of one is coterminus with the most recent iteration of the other. I prefer to think of neoliberalism as a messy project that, in practice, is often removed from the theoretical principles of its promoters (Peck, 2013). There does seem some relevance, however, in considering how capitalism in neoliberal times relies on a series of enigmatic representations of the world: consumption disconnected from production; the promise of surplus without labour; vibrant markets with less state; enterprise without social reproduction; and recurrent crises depicted as forms of rejuvenation (Smith, 2002). As Comaroff and Comaroff (2000) indicate, what they call 'millennial capitalism' presents these relations in especially abstract terms, provoking the call to explore their interconnections. For cities, this call has special resonance. Gentrification springs up as a magical solution to a host of social and economic ills, a claim to re-imagine an urban landscape synonymous with economic crisis, discrimination and anger as one of potential 'value added' through the reinvention of place (Harvey, 2000, p 11). However, although the aim of capital is often blatant, what is kept hidden or disconnected is the association of gentrification with the representational work and commodification of identity. It is this point that was ignored by Smith and that I want to keep in mind when analysing the experience of Puebla.

I deploy gentrification as a concept-metaphor to expose two points. First, how urban change has taken place based on constructs of culture and cultural difference. At work is a tension over what one might term 'Mexicaneity' as an aesthetic commodity that can serve as a cipher for space through particular notions of history (Garcia Canclini, 1995; Alonso, 2004). Critically, from the perspective of capital, this fashioning of culture in order to invigorate space needs to reconcile a tension: commodification can work to 'soften' certain identities, threatening their potential to refashion space, while resistant identities are deemed menacing and need to be controlled. The compromise is achieved through affording ethnicity a weak position on the one hand, and packaging a 'history' of poverty and exploitation as a set of nostalgic representations on the other (Comaroff and Comaroff, 2009; Overmyer-Velasquez, 2010). Thus, cultural identities are recognised up to the point that they threaten economic imperatives: markets trump cultural and social rights while giving the impression that cultural identities remain vital to the undertaking of everyday life. Cultural identities at the service of neoliberalism provide a 'field' on which gentrification has been imagined but also resisted.

The second point is to understand gentrification as an idea of 'loss' and emptiness. The reliance of gentrification on the representation of others and 'other spaces' entails a simplification of culture and cultural difference. Such a device legitimates the removal of particular users and uses regarded as threatening to the new urban imagination. For the removed, gentrification is a loss in terms of physical displacement, as well as a range of emotional attachments to place. Resistance to gentrification, therefore, is shown to stress the richness of place, its multivalent qualities and enigmatic representations. While gentrification often promises a streetscape marked by a 'cafe culture' and museum queues, this filling of urban space is predicated on its prior emptying. What appears to be happening in Puebla is that the nostalgia that drove early gentrification processes has given way to a 'thinner' vision of space 'without history', apparently emptied of cultural significance but that, of course, simply reminds many residents on a daily basis of what has been lost.

Gentrificación a la Poblana: rescue and representation of the 'historic centre'

A walk through 'el centro' of Puebla in the late 1980s was an exciting experience. The pavements – often broken – were crowded with street traders, many of them indigenous women, often with children, selling fruit and vegetables or preparing food, with steam rising from pots over charcoal stoves. Small children would sell chewing gum and lottery tickets, sing at tables, or beg. Fixed-point stands would sell newspapers, books, soft drinks, clothes, toys, household utensils and electrical items, many of which were contraband (*fayuca*), or provide services such as knife sharpening or haircuts. These activities would often spill into the street, which trader organisations would attempt to close off from traffic, motivating periodic removal campaigns led by the municipal police. The streets would be clogged, car horns would blare out almost constantly and collective *combi* vans would pick up and set down at any corner, making a mockery of traffic light or transit police attempts at regulation. Larger buses would belch diesel that would leave the centre dark long before the sun had gone down. Trading and traffic would continue late in to the night, helped by low-wattage street lights that would make walking among the detritus of the day's activity all the more hazardous. By early evening, the prostitutes who had mostly plied their trade in the brothels and cheap hotels would now be walking the street. The cantinas would add pungency to the atmosphere – a combination of cane alcohol and vomit – but also contribute the noise of music, laugher and shouting. The centre had buzz.

Back from the street, numerous derelict buildings, many dating from the 18th and 19th centuries were close to collapse: roofs would often have fallen in, outer walls would be propped and inside there would be piles of garbage, vermin and the occasional occupant. Tenements (*vecindad*) would provide accommodation, usually consisting of no more than one room per family, around a communal courtyard, with shared facilities (Gilbert and Varley, 1991). Certain streets had a reputation for 'hard living', controlled by heavies (*matones*) that gave barrios such as San Antonio a notoriety as hotbeds of criminal organisation involved in contraband, small-scale drug-dealing and trafficking. Activities would be 'tolerated' through a tacit agreement between politicians, the police and barrio leaders in which the latter could be called upon to threaten opponents, especially student groups and street trader organisations, and control competitors among taxi and *combi* owners. Almost every day, the centre would experience a march or sit-in (*plantón*), which would often be met with police in riot gear.

From the late 1980s and through the 1990s, the centre underwent a form of 'gentrification'. The spatial focus was the UNESCO-accredited 'historic centre'[1] and involved the removal of signs associated with poverty, disorder and indigeneity, from street traders, workshops, 'popular' cinemas and cantinas (Jones and Varley, 1994, 1999; Patiño Tovar, 2002; Mendiola García, 2008). Formerly broken pavements were fixed, some tarmac streets were replaced with cobbles or block, fountains were restored, and advertising hoardings, TV aerials and external electricity cables were removed. There was evidence of tenements being replaced with apartments and offices, and the appearance of higher-end restaurants and cafes, galleries and museums (see Figures 14.1 and 14.2; see also Bélanger, 2008). However, as Ann Varley and I argued, rather than constituting a material process of middle-class residential replacement, gentrification was a symbolic redefinition of the centre constructed around discourses of a past 'golden age', associated with Spanishness, whiteness and elite 'good taste', and in opposition to notions of Indianness and popular culture. Gentrification involved very few gentrifiers.

In line with Smith's argument, Mexico had been a key site for the shift of economic production to the South, but this process had largely ignored Puebla at this point. Gentrification, therefore, was a *response* from a threatened class and state. It was justified locally as 'rescue' (*rescate*) and reconquest (*reconquista*), an attempt to regain the city's heritage (*patrimonio*) and especially its 'dignity', drawing from a deep historical imagination. It was nostalgia for a city that Graham Greene described following his visit in 1938 as:

> the only Mexican town in which it seemed to me possible to live with some happiness. It had more than the usual wounded beauty: it had grace. Something French seemed to linger from Maximillian's

Figure 14.1: A boutique hotel opens a few blocks from the Puebla main square

Figure 14.2: A high-end restaurant in a former colonial mansion

> time. You could buy old French glass and portraits of Carlotta on paperweights; even the arts and crafts of Puebla was civilized in a Victorian, European way.... A kind of social Catholicism lingered here. (Greene, 1982 [1939], p 201).

Greene's 'Puebla' captures a widely held sentiment for a 'lost' past. For a middle class suffering from a crisis of confidence and a belief that it had lost moral and political authority over the city, gentrification was an existential project: reclaiming the centre was synonymous with shoring-up a class identity. There was little desire to live in the centre; the older suburbs, country clubs and gated estates would do just fine.

There is an important distinction to be made here between the nexus of gentrification and 'heritage' (*patrimonio*). As Ferry (2006) has pointed out, the original meaning of the Spanish term *patrimonio* referred to the state tutelage of natural resources and territory. Close to its Latin root, *patrimonium*, meaning a paternal estate, patrimony was charged with notions of property, nationalism and masculinist power. In contemporary guise, however, *patrimonio* has become a 'mnemonic', a device to teach people about a past and a time of national cultural integrity. In order to secure a particular representation of an 'inherited' past, 'history' is displayed across the city as plaques, renamed streets, retro street furniture, museums and cultural festivals. Who defines contemporary patrimony gives greater voice to media, religious organisations, tourist agencies and corporations

(Garcia Canclini, 1995).[2] This version of *patrimonio* is complementary to both an emergent post-nationalism in the late 20th century and one variety of neoliberal urbanism, namely, an opportunism to commodify a landscape now associated with a 'narrative' of cultural identity made material through the emptying out of competing users and complicating representations of place.

The mega-project and reconstructing the historic centre

By the mid-1990s, gentrification as a 'return to the centre' was a key component of both urban policy and private capital investment across a range of Mexican cities (Melé, 2002; Herzog, 2006; Crossa, 2009).[3] The underlying political economy, however, was fragile and gentrification could barely mask a decadence that, in the case of Puebla, had witnessed the city losing its position economically through the crisis of the 1980s and subsequent restructuring. Puebla's industrial base of Volkswagen, Ciba-Geigy, Chicle-Adams and textiles was in contrast to the 'new economy' of cities across the North. Politically, too, formerly dominant groups in the state had less influence nationally, and the city's characteristic Catholic conservatism seemed culturally out of step with the liberalisation of moral norms. By the mid-1990s, Puebla was regularly referred to as a 'Southern' state, in the same breath as Oaxaca, Guerrero and Chiapas, and ranked in the bottom five states for poverty and social deprivation (World Bank, 2003).[4]

On 6 July 1993, a candidate for state governor and political heavyweight, Manuel Bartlett, announced his intention to modernise Puebla by launching what he claimed to be a USD1 billion 'mega-project' called Angelópolis. The key component of the 'mega' was a range of 'sub-projects' that included major highway upgrades, a recycling plant and a complex of malls, private universities and gated communities (Patiño Tovar, 2002; Jones and Moreno-Carranco, 2007). In the round, Angelópolis was unambiguously about neoliberalism. The programme aimed, in the words of the now-elected governor, to 'detonate' private investment via an entrepreneurial mode of 'metropolitan' governance. A dedicated government office, also known as Angelópolis, was charged with negotiating investment contracts and marketing the city brand (Patiño Tovar, 2002). The Angelópolis programme logo, another innovation, used a capital 'A' crossed with angel wings, a direct reference to the colonial name of Puebla de los Angeles. Promotional materials deployed a set of representational devices that aimed to simultaneously ground the project in a local identity and project a future urban vision to national and international capital. Explicitly, Angelópolis aimed to 're-found' and to 'recover the grandeur' of Puebla, a message communicated in slick programme documents that interspersed punchy non-technical text and high-colour diagrams detailing investments with full-page images of the city's iconic *talavera* pottery.

The goal was to open up the introverted political economy that had brought the city large-scale manufacturing during the 'miracle decades' of import-substitution industrialisation but had left it lagging behind in the NAFTA era.[5] Puebla's idiosyncratic gentrification was no longer compatible with this agenda. Instead, guided initially by McKinsey and Company, and later refined by HKS-Sasaki of Dallas, a sub-project of Angelópolis called the Paseo del Río San Francisco was set out. The intention of the Paseo was to establish a cultural, tourist and business district across 27 city blocks in an area of the historic centre largely ignored by the earlier phase of 'rescue'-cum-gentrification. Crucially, the Paseo covered the 'barrios' of El Alto, La Luz, Xanenetla and Analco, which had been designated for indigenous groups in the colonial period and served as an area of workshops, factories and working-class residences from the 19th century. Angelópolis proposed to expropriate and then transfer the 18.9 hectares to a Fideicomiso (Trust), which would manage the installation of infrastructure, including cable networks, and then reassemble land parcels for sale to private developers. The centrepiece of the project would be an international conference centre, a range of international hotels, a mall and, in an obvious imitation of the San Antonio (Texas) Riverwalk, a reopening of the San Francisco river, which had been paved over in 1963 to install the 5 de Mayo highway, and on which it was intended that small launches would take people between two artificial lakes. From a base near the church of San Francisco at one end of the Riverwalk, a cable-car system would link the Paseo with two forts on a hill overlooking the centre. The fort site would be renovated to include new museums, hotels and a library.

The Paseo offered a state guarantee to real estate speculation. Moreover, it fundamentally changed the representation of the 'historic centre', which had previously focused on the Spanish 'traza' around the main square (*zócalo*), cathedral and the city's principal institutions. The barrios were largely ignored, in the sense that they were represented as 'traditional' and '*popular*', and therefore inappropriate for rescue to retrieve an imagined golden age (Jones and Varley, 1999). Angelópolis now claimed the barrios as beyond rescue, as incapable of becoming 'modern' and 'global'. The infrastructure was crumbling, textile factories were either abandoned or on the verge of bankruptcy (as production shifted to *maquila*), and they were full of low-rent tenements. From the perspective of the Paseo, only the barrios' colonial and early 19th-century churches, convents and seminaries merited saving. Everything else was slated for demolition or major remodelling.

A neoliberal space and recapturing the barrio

The 'rescue' of the centre during the 1980s and early 1990s involved considerable violence: street traders were confronted with water cannons, sit-ins were removed by force and leaders were beaten. However, although the population of the centre and barrios fell enormously from 340,000 people in 1978 to around 108,000 in 2011, property-owners and tenants were rarely the target of state power. In this regard, the Paseo project marked a muscular form of gentrification similar to the revanchism described by Smith (1998) in New York City. Between 1994 and 1997, I met with activists opposing the Paseo project, many of whom talked about verbal and physical threats. At one meeting in the barrio of Analco, a spokesperson for an association of residents demonstrated the degree of state surveillance and intimidation. He indicated how his phone was tapped and introduced me to two state security agents in a car across the street.[6] In 1997, the state showed how far it was willing to go to remove barrio residents. The move came after three years of resistance that had coincided with a financial crisis that undermined investor confidence in large real estate projects. With Bartlett's term as governor entering its final year, patience had worn thin. In mid-May, police and judicial officers beat up leading anti-Paseo activists and initiated a stand-off with around 500 officers, mostly in riot gear and some wearing balaclavas, occupying the streets of the barrios. With the power cut in the early hours, a bulldozer was brought in to demolish buildings, with some of the barricaded occupants leaving just before the walls and roofs collapsed (Churchill, 1999).

Despite a state being willing to use violence and to operate in a grey area of the law, resistance had mobilised tenants, property-owners, labour organisations, street trader and artisan groups, academics, and cultural organisations. Two of the most vocal groups were the Unión de Barrios (UB) and the well-named Asociación Civil por los Ideales de la Puebla Tradicional, which united to form the Unión de Ciudadanos Libres (UCL). From interviews with members of the Unión and Asociación, as well as revision of newspaper and magazine articles and internal memoranda, and observation of rallies, resistance offered a counter-representation to the Angelópolis vision of a 'world-class' barrio in the service of neoliberalism. Specifically, campaigns presented the barrios as 'deep-rooted' cultural spaces, appreciative of social norms (if not always compliant) and spaces of conviviality (if not unequivocally harmonious relations), hard work and the embracing of modernity. Many of these claims were exaggerations and relied on celebratory re-imaginations of the barrio that bordered on caricature. However, to some extent, this was the point. Rather than accept a set of imposed common-sense and tangible identities, legitimated through an association of the barrio with inferiority, the activist discourse blurred the Indian–white, popular–elite and historic–modern distinctions. As Churchill indicates, the 'intangibility' of culture is precisely what was at stake; the Unión and others argued that working out their culture was their 'inalienable right' (Churchill, 1999, p 164).

A key dimension of activist discourse was to challenge the neoliberal conceptualisation of the Paseo as a dynamic symbol of enterprise and globalisation, in step with NAFTA. The Unión suggested that nothing less than national identity – or *patrimonio* – was at stake. The Asociación condemned Angelópolis as 'Made in the USA' and pointed to the 'foreign' consultants that made the programme 'undemocratic and unMexican', and the French companies lined up to run hotels around the proposed convention centre. Activist texts and conversations were punctuated with references to the barrios being converted in to 'Disneylandia', a 'Moll' (mall), Las Vegas or 'McDonald's and other things norteamericano'. The Riverwalk (anglicised in official documentation and press accounts) was derided as a NAFTA import, and somewhat melodramatic allusions got drawn with the 'pain' of adopting a concept devised in San Antonio (or 'Texas City' as it was often referred) to bring tourists to the Alamo. The state government was accused of being 'sell-outs' (*vendepatrias*) or 'prostitutes' looking for a fast buck; Bartlett was drawn as General Santa Ana, whose defeat at San Jacinto, following the Alamo, started a process that would lead to the loss of over one-half of the national territory in the Treaty of Guadalupe in 1848.[7] The barrio presented itself as a heroic safeguard against the repeated connivance of the city's political elite and its ambivalence to both the resonance of history and local identities.

Asserting cultural difference as resistance

The atmosphere for revanchism was not without opportunity for activists to ridicule state claims to history and space. In discussions, speeches and press releases, the UCL and Unión de Barrios deliberately referred to the city by its republican name, Puebla de Zaragoza. For a time, the UCL also undertook weekly 'occupations' of the Analco bridge, a five-arch stone bridge that once connected the barrios to the 'centre' and which, since 1964, had been left stranded by the 5 de Mayo boulevard. The Paseo project referred to the bridge as the Puente de Ovando (Ovando Bridge), drawing attention to the bridge's construction by the Ovando family, the city's richest family during the colonial period, but referred to as Analco Bridge by most people.[8] Drawing on a repertoire of satirical strategies, graffiti and cartoons, a magazine published by the UCL showed people striking out the word Ovando from the bridge and overwriting it with Analco. Representations of resistance often invoked images of Chiapas and the symbol of the UCL became a masked dove wearing a helmet with the symbol 'C', often modifying public statements from Sub-comandante Marcos to refer to the barrios instead. Figure 14.3 shows a renovated Puente de Ovando with the yellow sculpture by the Mexican artist Sebastián in the background, which was referred to at the time as The Terminator.

Critics also took aim at a neoliberal gaze that regarded urban lived spaces as assets. The discovery that consultants to the Paseo project had described the Church of San Francisco as the city's 'cathedral' on some documents was discussed at length as an example of how the mega-project was predicated on a mobile knowledge divorced from local significance. Even the sub-director of the Concejo del Centro Histórico, a rather hastily created office of the municipality charged with overseeing the renovation of the centre and who admitted to me that she had not seen the original plans for the Paseo, described the logic as: "Angelópolis did not look, they just imposed. They must have studied the area by helicopter". The comment highlights a contradiction of the Paseo project. On the one hand, the Angelópolis office deployed various devices to present an image of government as transparent and willing to engage with criticism. Symbolically, its office on the main avenue in the centre had a large window in which a series of project maquettes was displayed. The office also had a communications officer and did a good job of distributing leaflets, some of which provided detail on project budgets, time frames and predicted benefits. On the other hand, Angelópolis and the state were constantly being 'found out' for using inaccurate or no information

Figure 14.3: The renovated Puente de Ovando and The Terminator

on key aspects of project design and expected impact, and a repeated liability to contradiction in the media. Despite references to studies, surveys and assessments, basic data appeared beyond the grasp of Angelópolis officials or leading politicians. Thus, the original conceptual project for the Paseo claimed that the affected area of the barrios possessed only 46 designated monuments, a figure that INAH would later reveal to be false. The catalogue of historical monuments showed 175 properties in the barrios, including 80 that were classed as 'Grade A' and therefore untouchable.[9]

As well as exposing the disjuncture between the claimed technocracy of the state and the shortcomings in its knowledge, these disagreements spoke to the haste that many felt characterised Angelópolis as a whole. It also had significance for how the 'impacts' of the Paseo project were to be presented and understood. The original claim for the 27-block version of the project was that it would displace around 700 people – a figure that critics regarded as a convenient underestimate given rampant landlordism and inaccurate cadastral records. Eventually, officials would admit to 4,590 people being displaced. These figures were a long way from the almost 10,000 claimed by the UCL, which gave quantitative weight to their association of displacement with 'cultural genocide' and the barrios as 'AIDS victims'.

Perhaps the most subtle shift in conceptualisation and contest for history and spatial identities in the aftermath of the Paseo was in relation to claims regarding the barrios as an indigenous space. Prior to the launch of Angelopolis, and through the initial phase of gentrification in the centre, the barrios were represented as indigenous space. Now, the state was arguing that the barrios were not indigenous enough. Press statements pointed to the lack of indigenous languages spoken in the barrio and residents not wearing traditional dress. A private research consultancy was contracted by the state to compare the 'intangible culture' of the barrios with cultural markers in the town of Zacapoaxtla in the Sierra Norte (Churchill, 2006). Unsurprisingly, the barrios came out of the analysis rather badly. Furthermore, the state government published a book accompanied by a series of talks and exhibitions that went in to great detail about archaeological discoveries (pre-Columbian and colonial) and the 16th- and 17th-century history of the city, but the only imagery related to the 20th century was of abandoned buildings and factories in decline (Gobierno del Estado de Puebla, 1994). The Paseo project, it was claimed, would 'liberate' buildings and recover 'customs and traditions' that had been lost by misuse.

In response, the UCL and others attempted to promote a barrio identity, raising the profile of festivals and markets, and drawing a connection between the barrios and the identity of the city and nation generally. Conversations with UCL leaders stressed the importance of the barrios as symbols of Puebla's uniqueness, notably, in the location of important potteries for the firing of talavera and of kitchens for the preparation of 'traditional' foods, such as *camotes*, *chalupas* and breads. There was also significant attention to music concerts and religious festivals, notably, the 'Procession of the Cross' from Calvario to San Francisco, the Epiphany, La Candelaria procession of saints and the week-long Procession de Nuestra Senora de la Luz, with mariachi, choirs and a mass dedicated to potters. The events became opportunities for the UCL and politicians to denounce Angelópolis in the press and to 'verify' cultural importance through the presence of large crowds and attempts to measure attendance: one survey showed upwards of 80% of barrio residents participated regularly in religious festivals.

Resistance, however, had to avoid what I would call a 'barriology': the tendency to perceive barrios as natural repositories of popular culture, superstition and indigeneity. Activists were mostly not indigenous, most were mestizo and identified as such, and went to considerable lengths to present the barrios as sites of modernity. One UCL pamphlet discussed Le Corbusier's Letter of Athens as a template for modern urban life and stressed how the barrios were sites of modernity-denied. Demonstrations focused on a state school that would be forced to close through the Paseo project, noting the prevalence of illiteracy in the barrios (and that Governor Bartlett had been national secretary for education). Some argued that if the state believed in markets, then the residents should be supported to improve – even gentrify – the area themselves (Churchill, 1999). In what the UCL called a 'discourse of greater vision', there were requests to extend micro-credit programmes, community housing and special zones for the promotion of food and artisanal goods to the barrios. The UCL repeatedly attempted to pitch their development proposals to international organisations, including the World Bank and Inter-American Development Bank, neither of which responded to their requests.

Cultural difference was an unstable discursive and performative weapon of resistance. The state condoned cultural practices that presented the barrios as a 'repository' of authenticity and that did not threaten the project of regeneration and gentrification. Nancy Churchill has conducted a rare ethnography of the carnival in the barrios as a focal point for debates over claims to representative 'authentic' culture, as well as a loaded political message of subversion to authority, including in ethnic terms. As she has noted:

> Here is a carnival with a long, rich history, annually uniting the people of the barrios in community. It is not an exaggeration to claim that carnival defines El Alto, Xonaca, and the colonias populares of Lomas Cinco de Mayo and Lomas Diez de Mayo; nor is it too much to claim that it defends the people who live in these working class neighborhoods as good, family people, rather than the dangerous classes that many Pueblans believe them to be. (Churchill, 2006, pp 19–20)

The public dancing of the *huehues* and *maringuilla* projected a 'popular' re-appropriation of the barrio space.[10] However, she notes, the attention to carnival prompted state efforts to regulate routes and establish patron–client relations with some troops (*cuadrilla*) through efforts to formalise carnival 'shows' in the *zócalo* and later at the new convention centre. Although to the UCL and many *carnivaleros*, the carnival represented a 'deep Mexico' respectful of long-standing beliefs and practices in contrast to the 'sharp practices' of neoliberal times, the carnival itself was under constant pressure to be exoticised and eventually excised, just like the space it represented.

Touring a space of emptiness

The actions and accounts of activists communicated a fear of impending loss, an emotion that seemed only to be confirmed by the emptiness of the space that the Paseo redevelopment eventually produced. In 1998, the first phase of building work on the downscaled Paseo was well under way, and through repeated visits in the 2000s, it was possible to witness the changing landscape of the site, the surrounding barrios and the rest of the historic centre. At the Paseo, a large convention centre, a modern art museum, the office of the Free Trade for the Americas (Área de Libre Comercio de las Américas; ALCA) and an 'archaeological zone' outside, mostly laid to gardens, were taking on shape (see Figure 14.4). The site was moving upmarket. A mall, opened in 2006, had designer brand stores, mobile phone booths and a handmade ice-cream shop; the convention centre boasted a high-class restaurant, a bar and a cigar shop humidor. Surrounding the site, houses and factories were converted to studio apartments and boutique hotels. Although most properties were fairly 'low key', a close observer could pick out

Figure 14.4: Site of former textile factories, workshops and homes from the convention centre

CCTV, electrified security fencing on adjoining rooftops and reinforced steel doors made to resemble wood (see Figures 14.5 and 14.6).

Yet, in contrast to the crowded streets, tenements, workshops and markets before the Paseo, this was an empty or, more accurately, an emptied space. Interspersed across the site were the facades of the evicted and demolished properties, which provided pathos. The 'archaeological' gardens to the back of the convention centre seemed to be rarely visited. The trees provided some shade for workers during their break and for groups of school children to have a crafty cigarette. However, people mostly walked through on their way to work. At night, the area was a favoured spot for kids to smoke marijuana and drink, despite conspicuous security. Adding to the sense of emptiness was the contemporary art museum. The space itself, a former textile factory, had been remodelled to the highest specification to include performance and video space. In-keeping with neoliberal times, the museum was intended to have no permanent collection. Rather, its 'business plan' relied on the acquisition of donated pieces or new artists' work, which could then be sold to reinvest in a portfolio and cover running costs. The practice seems to have been more modest and the space has been used for occasional corporate-sponsored or -owned exhibitions. On countless visits, the museum was mostly closed or open but empty. As such, the museum remains pristine and an elite space – especially since it is now named after Angeles Espinosa Yglesias, daughter of Espinosa Yglesias, former chief executive officer of Mexico's largest

Figure 14.5: Gentrification of the barrio, note the electric fence on roof

Figure 14.6: Gentrification in progress in the barrio

bank, Puebla's richest man, patrician of the arts and a major property-holder in the centre of the city.

The sense of emptiness seems to have been intentional. In a glossy publication put out by the state government, it was argued that the Paseo project would provide the 'recuperation of the physical and symbolic elements that formed the colonial and historical settlement in the area' (Gobierno del Estado de Puebla, 2004, p 4). The text is broken up by drawings of tiles found during rather rushed excavations, numerous aerial photos showing archaeological works and images from the early 20th century and more recent disused factories. People are only mentioned obliquely under 'improved quality of life' and the text only makes reference to two residents, both ex-textile workers who were interviewed for an 'oral history'. Their views are summarised on the report's penultimate page. For a former resident who can still see her former home protruding from between the convention centre and the mall, the sense of loss was akin to violence. During my interview, she compared it with being witness to authoritarian regimes in the past and lamented that then the violence seemed "a long way from us, it was something painful, something unjust... but always distant". Now, the violation was personal, gentrification took her home, a property that had been in her family for generations, and converted it to an ill-painted facade devoid of purpose (Churchill, 1999).

Cartesian gentrification: refilling the centre

By the late 1990s, the activist organisations disintegrated as members accepted the inevitable, their legal injunctions were lost or ignored, their properties were demolished and the ground was broken on the Paseo buildings. In the centre, gentrification seemed to have gathered pace. Restaurants and cafes were more prominent, small squares where street traders had once pitched their spots were made over to art shows, music festivals and corporate events. Civil society groups funded by philanthropic organisations and volunteers initiated wall-painting and graffiti projects to 'reclaim' barrios near the centre. A number of municipal governments extended pedestrian areas and improved street lighting, and the administration of Blanca Alcalá (2008–11) re-initiated a programme of cultural 'pathways' (*sendas*) linking together key historic sites, and attempted to install cycle lanes. Business groups continued to urge 'dignification', though the concerns were expressed now in terms of bars playing over-loud music and demands to remove newspaper stands from the route of the cultural pathway.[11] The elites and middle classes, however, still displayed a reluctance to live permanently in the centre or barrios.

There has been, however, a growing sense that the state is interested in repopulating the centre, along the lines already undertaken in Mexico City and elsewhere in Latin America. In 2009, the municipality floated the idea to 'repopulate' abandoned or underused houses.[12] In 2011, a major federal investment programme intended for high-growth and suburban projects announced that it would launch its first intervention in a city centre in Puebla. The aim was to transform underused spaces into parks and improve the image of the barrios through painting walls and improving infrastructure and connectivity, via a sub-project called Mi Barrio Vive (My Barrio Lives). A crucial component of the programme was financial support for housing to more than double the population of the centre to 238,000 by 2020, taking advantage of a relaxation of building codes to allow densities to increase from 50 units per hectare to 400 (DUIS, 2011). Desarrollo Urbano Integral Sustentable (DUIS) was pitched by the new governor, Rafael Moreno Valle, as the 'rebirth' of the centre and an explicit attempt to bring the 'new' middle class to live in the centre.

Governors and controversy, however, go hand in hand, especially where the sensitivities of the city centre are concerned. A proposal to install what was announced as the tallest Ferris wheel in Latin America, La Estrella de Puebla, in a central park was abandoned after opposition from environmental groups. The governor had greater success with his 'plan' to build a 1.2-kilometre elevated highway, the Viaducto de Zaragoza, despite not having either requisite licences, a municipality-approved impact study or, as the route clipped the 'historic centre', the approval of INAH. Nevertheless, with support from the national president, the project went ahead and was completed in just over one year. However, in late 2012, the governor outdid even the highway project when it was revealed that his government intended to build a 2-kilometre cable-car system (*teleférico*), situating a number of 80-metre-high pylons at points through the centre starting from the art market in the downtown. The cable car would link the centre to another controversial project, the already-constructed 'interactive museum' that had remodelled spaces and installed a glass canopy over the historic forts on the hill overlooking the city designed by TEN, Mexico's premier architectural consultancy. Ground was broken on the first pylon within weeks, again without approvals from relevant authorities and with the unauthorised demolition of a 17th-century listed building. Conservation groups were outraged and lobbied the International Council on Monuments and Sites-Mexico (ICOMOS) as the 25th anniversary of the UNESCO accreditation loomed.[13] In December 2012, ICOMOS demanded the suspension of the *teleférico* and rumours circulated that Puebla might be placed on a 'watch list' of 'heritage at risk' by UNESCO. An embarrassed government halted work on 8 January 2013 but then announced that the project would be completed before Puebla hosted the International Tourist Fair (*Tianguis Turístico*) in March 2013. The deadline was missed, and in June 2013, INAH gained an injunction to suspend the works but officials sent to apply the suspension notices were met by state police and work continued on the towers regardless.

The audacity of these projects, the quantity of public finance going to the needs of the middle classes and capital, and the lack of restraint on state power by legal process speaks to the high stakes to fashion the urban space economy that Smith would recognise all too well. It remains unclear if a new middle class will 'repopulate' the centre or if the arts, media and information technology will provide a new economic dynamic to the increasingly embedded tourism and leisure functions. Future visitors will still need to negotiate crowded streets, locate parking and find places to eat but they will also have the option to 'look over' the centre from a variety of vantage points. Twenty-first-century gentrification will engage with *patrimonio* from above.

Conclusion

Gentrification in neoliberal times is entangled with representations of culture. If we accept that culture is a matter not only of self-definition and practice, but also of representation, then it matters how people's culture is displayed, performed and received by others, especially those with greater power. This is especially vital where ethnicity is concerned as, to paraphrase Bonfil Batalla (1989), it is the white who defines the Indian. In Mexican cities, culture has long marked out the value of spaces socially and whether they are therefore 'valuable' economically. In Puebla, early gentrification was understood as an elite and middle-class response to the perception of the centre as 'popular' and Indian. The space had lost its 'dignity': it was dirty, noisy, contentious and in need of being 'recaptured'. As this process unfolded, there was little attention given to the barrios, which were, after all, the 'natural' space for the popular class and represented as indigenous even though this was inaccurate of their ethno-demography.

However, as Mexico embraced neoliberalism, the economic potential of this space became obvious to successive governors concerned with the state's relative decline. Public intervention became more overtly linked with the interests of capital rather than the existential insecurities of a particular class. The efforts to bring corporate capital to the centre became bolder and the spatial compass wider. In order to extend gentrification to the barrios, the state represented its plans as 'objective' and 'strategic' but subsumed within its discourse the idea of barrio degradation and claims to the absence of 'living' and tangible culture and an overtone of class and ethnic blame. Activists challenged these representations, highlighting the hard work of occupants – as street traders had done unsuccessfully in the 1980s – the architectural value of the area and the importance of embedded cultural practices, and satirised the pastiche 'Spanish colonial' Americana of the emergent gentrified landscape. Puebla was different from Smith's note that gentrification's role in 'retaking the city' was *initially* a housing strategy predicated on the middle class, but with the Paseo, it *became* closer to his observation that gentrification would serve as means to engineer 'whole areas into new landscape complexes that pioneer a comprehensive class-inflected urban remake' (Smith, 2002, p 443). If, as the Comaroffs suggest, neoliberalism deploys culture as a 'copyrighted possession' within an 'identity economy' (Comaroff and Comaroff, 2009, p 139), then gentrification marks the emotional violence of losing place-bound memories derived from a deeper 'lived experience'.

Notes

[1] An area of 6.99 square kilometres with 2,619 'historic' buildings and 27 public squares was granted Patrimonio de la Humanidad in 1987, the same year as Oaxaca City and Mexico City.

[2] Control of the legal framework shifted accordingly. The 1972 legislation on 'historic monuments and archaeological sites' empowered a preservationist ethos and a federal agency, the Instituto Nacional de Antropología e Historia (INAH). With decentralisation of governance from the 1980s, the INAH's power has given way to state and business groups.

[3] The obvious example is the involvement of Carlos Slim, the world's richest man, in the acquisition of large areas of downtown Mexico City and the deliberate intent to 'repopulate' the area with students, artists and young professionals (Leal Martínez, 2007).

[4] Although ignoring the city, the notion would crystallise as the Plan Puebla–Panama programme, launched in 2001 to construct an infrastructure corridor linking Puebla with, eventually, Colombia, through which a series of mega-projects would be located (see Martin, 2005).

[5] Angelópolis can be understood as part of a wider set of state responses to globalisation and pressures within the political apparatus to reconfigure state–nation arrangements (Martin, 2005).

[6] Bartlett continued actions against the main street trader organisation, the Unión Popular de Vendedores y Ambulantes (UPVA) 28 de Octubre. In March 1995, 200 UPVA members were arrested and pitched battles took place between traders and police over one week, with tear gas and reports of live shots.

[7] Activists and the press pointed to the precedent from the 1980s when traders were removed from the city's major market – La Victoria – on the pretext that it was to be renovated, only for the site to be leased free of charge to a private foundation that promptly converted it to a shopping mall and leased the space to Walmart (Mendiola García, 2008).

[8] Analco means 'other side of the river' in nahuatl. As one person put it, '"the other side of the river", or the imprisoned side, the side that the Indians that built the city, the oldest side, most often flooded, poorest, most combative when it is necessary to show it regionally or nationally'.

[9] No prior survey, it was later revealed, had measured building conditions and eventually data would show 45% of buildings to be in a good condition, 20% poor and 9% in ruin (Patiño Tovar, 2002).

[10] Carnival is a hybrid of folk Catholicism, indigenous, working-class and mestizo symbolisms. The principal dancers, the *huehues* ('old one' in nahuatl), represent 'whites' as folk devils with painted masks, who dance in a troop that usually passes from bar to bar, led by a *maringuilla*, a male member of the troop dressed as a woman. In some troops, the *maringuilla* is explicitly sexualised, though this is often not the case and is frowned upon.

[11] *Proceso*, 23 September 2012.

[12] *La Jornada de Oriente*, 19 November 2009.

[13] Specifically, the Comité de Defensa del Patrimonio Histórico, Cultural y Ambiental, the Comité Mexicano de Conservación del Patrimonio Industrial and Concejo Ciudadano del Centro Histórico.

References

Alonso, A.M. (2004) 'Conforming disconformity: "Mestizaje", hybridity, and the aesthetics of Mexican nationalism', *Cultural Anthropology*, vol 19, no 4, pp 459–90.

Bélanger, H. (2008) 'Vivir en un centro histórico en Latinoamérica: Percepciones de los hogares de profesionales en la ciudad de Puebla, México', *Estudios Demográficos y Urbanos*, vol 23, no 2, pp 415–40.

Bonfil Batalla, G. (1989) *México Profundo: una civilización negada*, México DF: Grijalbo.

Churchill, N. (1999) 'El Paseo de San Francisco: urban development and social justice in Puebla', *Social Justice*, vol 26, no 3, pp 156–73.

Churchill, N. (2006) 'Dignifying carnival: the politics of heritage recognition in Puebla, Mexico', *International Journal of Cultural Property*, vol 13, no 1, pp 1–24.

Comaroff, J. and Comaroff, J.L. (2000) 'Millennial capitalism: first thoughts on a second coming', *Public Culture*, vol 12, no 2, pp 291–343.

Comaroff, J. and Comaroff, J.L. (2009) *Ethnicity, inc.*, Chicago, IL: University of Chicago Press.

Crossa, V. (2009) 'Resisting the entrepreneurial city: street vendors' struggle in Mexico City's historic center', *International Journal of Urban and Regional Research*, vol 33, no 1, pp 43–63.

DUIS (2011) *Desarrollo Urbano Integral Sustentable: centro histórico*, México DF: DUIS.

Ferry, E.E. (2006) 'Memory as wealth, history as commerce: a changing economic landscape in Mexico', *Ethos*, vol 34, no 2, pp 297–324.

García Canclini, N. (1995) *Hybrid cultures: strategies for entering and leaving modernity*, Minneapolis, MN: University of Minnesota.

Gilbert, A. and Varley, A. (1991) *Landlord and tenant: housing the poor in urban Mexico*, London: Routledge.

Gobierno del Estado de Puebla (1994) *La Fundación y Desarrollo de la Ciudad de Puebla de los Angeles*, Puebla: INAH.

Gobierno del Estado de Puebla (2004) *Rescate y Remodellacion del Paseo de San Francisco en la Ciudad de Puebla*, Puebla: Gobierno del Estado.

Greene, G. (1982 [1939]) *The lawless roads*, Harmondsworth: Penguin.

Harvey, D. (2000) *Spaces of hope*, Edinburgh: University of Edinburgh Press.

Herzog, L.A. (2006) *Return to the center: culture, public space and city-building in a global era*, Austin: University of Texas Press.

Jones, G.A. and Moreno-Carranco, M. (2007) 'Megaprojects: beneath the pavement, excess', *City*, vol 11, no 2, pp 143–63.

Jones, G.A. and Varley, A. (1994) 'The contest for the city centre: street traders versus buildings', *Bulletin of Latin American Research*, vol 13, no 1, pp 27–44.

Jones, G.A. and Varley, A. (1999) 'The reconquest of the historic centre: urban conservation and gentrification in Puebla, Mexico', *Environment and Planning A*, vol 31, no 9, pp 1547–66.

Leal Martínez, A. (2007) 'Peligro, proximidad y diferencia: negociar fronteras en el Centro Histórico de la Ciudad de México', *Alteridades*, vol 17, no 34, pp 27–38.

Martin, P. (2005) 'Comparative topographies of neoliberalism in Mexico', *Environment and Planning A*, vol 37, pp 203–20.

Melé, P. (2002) '(Ré)investir les espaces centraux des villes mexicaines', in C. Bidou-Zachariasen, D. Hiernaux-Nicolas and H. Riviere d'Arc (eds) *Retours en Ville: des processus de 'gentrification' urbaine aux politiques de 'revitalisation' des centres*, Paris: Descartes & Cie, pp 175–204.

Mendiola García, S.C. (2008) 'Street vendors, marketers, and politics in twentieth-century Puebla, Mexico', PhD dissertation, Rutgers University, New Brunswick.

Overmyer-Velasquez, R. (2010) *Folkloric poverty: neoliberal multiculturalism in Mexico*, Philadelphia: University of Pennsylvania Press.

Patiño Tovar, E. (2002) *El Pasado en el Presente: pobreza, centro histórico y ciudad*, Puebla: UAP.

Peck, J. (2013) *Constructions of neoliberal reason*, Oxford: OUP.

Smith, N. (1998) 'Giuliani time: the revanchist 1990s', *Social Text*, vol 57, no 16, pp 1–20.

Smith, N. (2002) 'New globalism, new urbanism: gentrification as global urban strategy', *Antipode*, vol 34, no 3, pp 434–57.

World Bank (2003) *Mexico: Southern states development strategy*, Washington, DC: World Bank.

FIFTEEN

Capital, state and conflict: the various drivers of diverse gentrification processes in Beirut, Lebanon

Marieke Krijnen and Christiaan De Beukelaer

Introduction

This chapter responds to several recent calls to extend the geographical scope of gentrification studies and to consider the potential contribution of theory-making from the Global South (Robinson, 2006; Roy, 2009a; McFarlane, 2010; Lees, 2012). We present two cases of gentrification in Beirut, Lebanon, and demonstrate the ways in which they differ from the existing literature on gentrification. Employing a post-colonial perspective, we argue that an account of these differences is essential if gentrification studies are to make a meaningful contribution to our understanding of uneven geographical development and social exclusion in a Southern context. Evidence from Beirut shows how and why historical and politico-economic specificities matter: the point of theory formation should not be to articulate a one-size-fits-all model that can be applied to apparent cases of gentrification anywhere in the world at any time. Indeed, the case of Beirut shows just how much gentrification processes can diverge within a single city, with different networks of capital formation and visions of the urban future reflecting Lebanon's history of confessional conflict and the various ways in which neighbourhoods and social groups are linked to regional and global circuits of capital. However – notwithstanding these differences – our case studies demonstrate that the driving forces and results of urban transformation in Beirut are much the same as elsewhere: gentrification has been instigated by a privileging of the logic of the market in housing provision and it has resulted in the displacement and exclusion of lower- and middle-income groups from central city locations. Gentrification in Beirut has been driven by transnational capital and facilitated by state interventions, including – inter alia – tax breaks for investors and the liberalisation of rental contracts.

It is hardly surprising that Beirut is sensitive to gentrification. Real estate is one of the most important sectors of the Lebanese economy. Post-civil war real estate booms have been numerous, and the sector has grown continuously during the past decade despite political turmoil and the financial crisis (which Beirut largely escaped due to considerable bank liquidity and the resources of its diaspora population; see Habib, 2011). For the past two years, the real estate sector has slowed down and stagnated, but land and apartment prices are still high (*Daily Star*, 2013; Makarem, 2013; Sakr, 2013). On average, apartments in downtown Beirut sell from USD3,500/m^2 to USD5,000/m^2, while outside the centre, prices start at around USD3,000/m^2.[1] Investors and buyers come from the Middle East or the Lebanese diaspora (Lloyd-Jones, 2005; Halawi, 2010; Karam, 2010). Inevitably, this frenetic real estate activity has led to the rapid gentrification of many sectors of the city and consequent population displacement. Neighbourhoods that were previously characterised by low-rise 1950s' apartment buildings with shops on the ground floors are now dominated by glitzy high-rises that remain uninhabited during most of the year. A growing body of scholarship has documented the social, economic and political impact of these urban redevelopments. There is ample literature on the transformation of downtown Beirut into a luxury quarter by a private company (Makdisi, 1997; Leenders, 2003, 2004; Becherer, 2005; Summer, 2005) and other work on the effects of private urban planning agencies or the role of political parties in planning (Harb, 2001; Khayat, 2007; Fawaz, 2009a; Roy, 2009b), gated communities in Lebanon and other forms of spatial segregation (Glasze, 2003; Alaily-Mattar, 2008). Until now, however, only Ross and Jamil (2011) and Achkar (2011) have specifically researched gentrification processes in Beirut.

Besides contributing to extending the geographical scope of gentrification studies towards the Global South, our chapter points towards the influence of processes that are not typically mentioned in the literature on gentrification, such as the role of civil conflict and sectarianism (a system that ties civil status and political representation to a person's religious affiliation), the overlap between public and private spheres in Lebanon's political system (where many politicians are involved in real estate activities), and the role of diaspora capital, which is the main driver of gentrification processes in Beirut. These factors influence gentrifiers' and developers' preferences, as some prefer to invest in areas with a distinct sectarian identity while, to the contrary, others look for a more diverse space. They also influence the way in which residents resist gentrification, as political parties are usually the only viable means of negotiating compensation and strengthening sectarian allegiances. Also, religious organisations are the only actors providing affordable housing.

The complex dimensions shaping gentrification processes in Beirut lead to very different outcomes locally. While gentrification is mostly new-build, there are cases of renovation with a role for creative entrepreneurs, commercial gentrification, classic loft-living construction or large-scale urban renewal projects involving the displacement of slum dwellers and highway construction (Harb, 2001; Deboulet and Fawaz, 2011). This chapter will employ two case studies highlighting new-build and creative/commercial gentrification. We ask: what forms of gentrification can be seen in Beirut? What is the role of the state? Who is being displaced and what forms of resistance to displacement or impediments to gentrification exist? Who are the gentrifiers? What are the key points to keep in mind when developing a post-colonial perspective on gentrification processes in Beirut? What questions can be formulated and directed 'back' to other contexts? In order to achieve these goals, we will proceed as follows: after providing a background of the Lebanese context, we discuss gentrification processes in Beirut by looking at new-build gentrification, including the role of rent controls and the displacement of residents, building laws, and the role of the state. We then look at creative and commercial gentrification, using the case study of the Mar Mikhael area. Then, we describe the gentrifiers and explain their presence, and move on to various forms of resistance and impediments to gentrification. We conclude by listing the various findings that can help us formulate a post-colonial perspective on gentrification processes in Beirut. We argue that a post-colonial perspective has to partially 'unlearn' (Spivak, 1993, cited in Lees, 2012) Western intuitions about the role of the state in gentrification, and pay attention to the dimensions mentioned earlier.

Figure 15.1: Beirut in Lebanon

Lebanon: a background

Beirut, Lebanon's capital and largest city (see Figure 15.1), with some 2 million inhabitants,[2] hosts most of the country's administrative bodies, companies and universities. The Lebanese civil war (1975–90) divided the city into two parts: a predominantly Christian eastern section and a largely Muslim western section. Each area was exclusively controlled by militias representing the dominant groups. This demographic rearrangement prevails to date, though at a lesser extent in certain areas (Genberg, 2002).

After Lebanon gained its independence from France in 1943, a political system based on confessional power sharing and a minimalist state was tacitly accepted as the country's political model. This facilitated and promoted foreign direct investment, focusing on services and finance (Gates, 1998; Dibeh, 2005; Traboulsi, 2007; Shwayri, 2008). Hence, contrary to most Western contexts that have a history of Keynesian state interventionism and welfare provision, the state role in Lebanon has never been that of a social provider;[3] this was left to private initiatives, mostly religious authorities and political sectarian groups (Gates, 1998; Chaaban and Gebara, 2007; Hoeckel, 2007; Hilal, 2008; Fawaz, 2009b). The laissez-faire policies of post-independence Lebanon protected the interests of the dominant mercantile-bourgeoisie, who had traditionally used politics to achieve this protection (Chaaban and Gebara, 2007; Gates, 1998; Boudisseau, 2001; Traboulsi, 2007; Hourani, 2010; Krijnen and Fawaz, 2010). After the outbreak of the civil war in 1975, these fundamental characteristics of the Lebanese economy remained unaltered (Leenders, 2004; Shwayri, 2008; Hourani, 2010). Hence, historically, the interests of market actors have always taken precedence in the Lebanese political economy. This is evident in laws passed during the post-independence period that increased maximum building heights (El-Achkar, 1998) and exploitation factors, with never fulfilled promises of public housing provision (Bekdache, forthcoming). As of the 1950s, a zoning plan allocated the highest exploitation ratios to areas closest to the urban centre (Achkar, 2011; MAJAL, 2012). Developers can exceed height limits by applying for a building permit at the Higher Council for Urban Planning, a politically connected body that makes decisions on a seemingly ad hoc basis. In one case, the developer obtained a building permit by agreeing to fund roadworks (Ghodbane, 2012). Urban planning is thus characterised by a public–private overlap that is also seen in the country's political economy (Makdisi, 1997; Glasze, 2003; Leenders, 2003, 2004; Summer, 2005; Krijnen and Fawaz, 2010; Ross and Jamil, 2011).[4] As we will argue in our conclusion, this overlap provides us with some interesting questions to ask 'back' to other (Western) contexts.

Post-civil war government policies continued to protect the dominant elite's interests by facilitating trade, finance and services sectors, but this time, the reconstruction[5] was influenced by the neoliberal turn (Leenders, 2004; Makdisi, 1997). Prime Minister Hariri was keen on facilitating national and foreign investors and regaining Beirut's position as a financial centre and primary tourist destination in the Arab world, signing several free-trade agreements and launching an ambitious privatisation plan. Downtown Beirut, a devastated no-man's-land during the civil war, became a symbol of Hariri's ambitions when it was reconstructed into a centre of business for the global neoliberal elite.

Gentrification in Beirut

The classical definition of gentrification, as coined by Ruth Glass (1964), describes an influx of middle-class residents into working-class neighbourhoods. The new inhabitants renovate low-income and downgraded properties into expensive residences, displacing the original residents and changing the entire social character of the district. This definition has been expanded in recent decades to include, among others, new-build developments (Davidson and Lees, 2005, 2010), gated communities, super-gentrification and commercial and rural gentrification (see Lees et al, 2008). However, Lees et al (2008) argue that these different types of gentrification have in common a socio-economic and cultural transformation due to middle-class colonisation or recolonisation of working-class spaces: people with less power and means are displaced involuntarily from their homes by people with more power and means (see also Davidson and Lees, 2005, 2010; Slater, 2006, 2011). Following this argument, we use the definition of Lees et al (2008, p xv): gentrification is 'the transformation of a working-class or vacant area of the central city into middle-class residential and/or commercial use'. Whether this happens through new construction or renovation, and whether this process is state-led or not, is related to the geography of gentrification (Lees, 2000), that is, how similar processes play out differently in different geographical contexts.

Keeping this in mind, we now look at gentrification processes in Beirut. Who is driving these processes? Why do they take their particular shape? How do they relate to processes of gentrification in other contexts? Who are the gentrifiers? Who is being displaced and what is the role of the state?

New-build gentrification in Beirut

Gentrification in Beirut is usually new-build and involves direct displacement. Historical preservation as a means of preventing devalorisation and, hence, a cause of gentrification (Lees et al, 2008) is rare: money is made by demolition. This can be explained by huge rent gaps (Smith, 1987). Stringent rent controls for contracts signed before July 1992 and increasingly high maintenance/renovation costs of older buildings mean that landlords get little to no return from buildings with these tenants, while they are usually located in coveted central city locations. Moreover, high exploitation ratios via zoning and building laws, coupled with a sufficient demand, mean that enormous profits can be made by demolishing older, three-to-six-floor buildings and replacing them with 20- to 40-storey high-rises, especially given the relatively low costs of construction and abundance of cheap labour power provided by Syrian migrant workers. The role of conflict in widening rent gaps has been pointed out by Ross and Jamil (2011): developers buy cheaply in times of political turmoil and cash in once peace 'breaks' out (provided enough demand exists), leaving Beirutis with the bitter false choice of either living through conflict in affordable housing while facing possible displacement through war, or facing displacement through real estate development when their buildings are bought by developers in times of peace. Developers are willing to pay large sums of money for these buildings, vacant or not. The role of rent controls, the process of eviction and production of supply, the different forms of displacement, and the role of building regulations will be explained and illustrated in the following.

Rent controls

In theory, rent controls can limit processes of gentrification (Ley and Dobson, 2008). In Beirut, in a context of escalating apartment prices, making them unaffordable to even middle-class Beirutis (see later), rent control is one of the few reasons that low- and middle-income dwellers have managed to retain homes in central city locations. All in all, 40,000 families in Beirut alone are estimated to benefit from rent controls, despite lack of census data on who and where they are.[6] Tenants pay rents based on pre-war rates, only slightly corrected for inflation. This means that a building can yield as little as USD120 a year for a landlord (Cochrane, 2012; Fisk, 2012) at a time when in real market value, the rent of that building can rise above USD100,000. Landlords have formed a committee that has been lobbying for a new rental law to replace the temporary law introduced for pre-July 1992 rental contracts that has, until now, been extended every four years, with new rent law drafts rejected by landlords and tenants alike. When a building collapsed in January 2012, killing 27 people, the landlord committee was quick to blame the old rent law. Other causes for the collapse, such as a nearby construction site and the addition of floors, were dismissed. Another law proposal was drafted, involving a gradual transition to higher rent, compensation and eviction to state-provided housing with a rent-to-own scheme (Cochrane, 2012). If and how this law will be implemented is unclear but, clearly, any proposal regards displacement as inevitable.

Displacement

A landlord wanting to evict for new construction risks a lengthy battle in court. To avoid this, many landlords sell their buildings to developers who negotiate with tenants and pay them a higher compensation than they would receive in court (Bekdache, forthcoming). Sometimes, residents themselves track down multiple heirs of small plots and sell them together to a developer (Ghodbane, 2012). Landlords also resort to the tagging of buildings, warning of a possible collapse and obtaining a notice from the municipality for eviction and cutting off services (Bekdache, forthcoming).

These winkling practices (bribery and harassment practices to evict tenants; see Lees et al, 2008) have resulted in successful evictions in most cases. In the 1970s, leftist parties protected the interests of the tenants, but they are a lot smaller today and are suppressed by the neoliberal consensus that was formed under Hariri (Makdisi, 1997). A committee to protect tenant rights exists, but it has yet to succeed in preventing evictions or securing alternative housing. Instead, one by one, buildings with old-rent tenants are vacated and demolished. Besides direct displacement, displacement pressure (Marcuse, 1985) is an issue as well (as we will see later): neighbourhoods change beyond recognition, shops close, social networks fall apart and living in a half-empty building in disrepair would pressure most people into looking for alternative housing.

Most tenants who were not protected by old rent contracts have faced direct displacement through enormous rent increases (Lee, 2009). As low-cost housing disappears, and other apartments face rent increases, exclusionary displacement (Marcuse, 1985; Davidson and Lees, 2010) follows because the Lebanese who might otherwise have wished to live in these areas can no longer afford to do so. Displacees usually have no other choice than to move to the periphery of the city, into politically segregated neighbourhoods that first emerged during mass displacement during the civil war. Most rent-controlled clusters, however, were among some of the last remaining diverse sections in the city (Bekdache, forthcoming). This points to another dimension of gentrification processes in Beirut, namely, the role of sectarianism and civil conflict. The next section elaborates upon these dimensions with a case study of Zokak el-Blat.

New-build gentrification: the case of Zokak el-Blat

The case of Zokak el-Blat illustrates processes of new-build gentrification. Located south-west of downtown Beirut, this area was one of the first to develop outside Beirut's city walls, urbanised by a merchant elite that owned businesses in the city centre (Mollenhauer, 2005). They later moved out to suburbs while workers from the nearby port moved in. The 1975–90 civil war led to the relocation of most Christian and Sunni elite families of the neighbourhood to other areas. They were replaced by a large, mainly Shi'ite, refugee population from the South, often squatting in the abandoned mansions or renting apartments in newly built 10–12-storey apartment buildings. With them came militias that ensured their protection and provided social services (Hanssen, 2005; MAJAL, 2012). Post-civil war reconstruction and road extensions involved the destruction of many buildings in the area's northern part and the eviction of squatters through a post-civil war state programme[7] involving compensations used to buy apartments in the area. New construction activities have built buildings up to 12 stories high in the area, more than five per year on average between 1991 and 2003. The proximity of the high-end downtown area has increased the attractiveness of the neighbouring Patriarchate sector and hence driven up prices. Most owners on the eastern side of Zokak el-Blat are Shi'ites who have invested capital in the area (Bodenstein, 2005; Hanssen, 2005).

Two political actors prevail in the area: (1) Hezbollah, a major party in Parliament, with a primarily Shi'ite constituency and famous for leading the resistance against the Israeli occupation of South Lebanon (1978–2000); and (2) Haraket Amal, a predominantly Shi'ite party sprung from Imam Moussa Sadr's 'Movement of the dispossessed' in the 1970s. The presence of these actors might influence choices of investors; indeed, our informants have told us that especially in the inner areas, developers are mostly local Shi'ites and buyers mostly Muslim. On the highways surrounding the area, however, not all developers are local Shi'ites.

Zokak el-Blat is facing intensive real estate development. Cadastral data show an increase in sales transactions[8] and empty lots have disappeared rapidly (MAJAL, 2012). Most projects cluster around the area bordering the Fuad Chehab and airport roads, offering a view of the sea and downtown: 'It is as if they built it for us to look at', one developer stated.[9] A developer usually acquires several lots, merges them, demolishes existing structures and constructs a high-rise. From 2000 to 2011, 30 buildings were demolished, and buildings from that time period now occupy 9% of the area. A survey of several projects under construction revealed that they average 12 floors, with apartments generally larger than 200m^2 (MAJAL, 2012). Real estate brochures for the area do not promote the neighbourhood itself, but its proximity to major thoroughfares and shopping districts. This matches the tendency of developers to construct buildings on the fringes of the quarter. Apartments are built for sale, and around half of them are bought for personal, permanent use. Prices ranged from USD1,300/m^2 to USD4,000/m^2 in 2011 (MAJAL, 2012).

One large-scale development is the Jamil Agha/Binadar project, consisting of three 14-floor towers (see Figure 15.2). According to a Binadar representative, the 210–250m^2 apartments sell for an average of USD3,200/m^2 and target middle-class buyers, with 80% being foreigners or Lebanese expatriates, mostly well-off families living and working in Qatar or Dubai, proving that most buyers are non-residents. Most apartments sold rapidly, attesting to high demand, while some were retained to make a higher profit later. Initially, one tower was planned, but due to high demand, three were built.[10] According to cadastral records, three lots (610, 611 and 1014) were bought in 1994[11] and merged to create the large parcel.

We will now explicate the role of the state and building laws in the processes of new-build gentrification mentioned earlier, showing how changes in institutional and legal frameworks have assisted developers and can be explained through looking at the Lebanese political economy.

Building laws and the role of the state

Today, the previously mentioned real estate booms have led to a construction frenzy, as the Lebanese government seeks to facilitate real estate developers in line with neoliberal governance, prioritising capital over social reproduction (Smith,

Figure 15.2: Binadar Highland, La Citadelle and Solitaire towers

Note: Photograph taken by Marieke Krijnen in 2010.

2002). Measures include the lifting of restrictions on (foreign) investments and foreign property-ownership, delegating planning tasks to private actors, exempting investors from certain taxes or registration fees, and providing exceptions and exemptions applicable to large-scale projects and hotels (for an overview, see Krijnen, 2010; Krijnen and Fawaz, 2010). The Building Law was revised in 2004 to include extra built-up areas and increase the maximum building height, in some cases allowing for the doubling of the exploitation ratio (Achkar, 2011). Most empirical studies emphasise a strong role for the state in creating conditions conducive to gentrification processes (see Lees and Ley, 2008). However, as explained earlier, the distinction between state and market interests is not very easy to make. In fact, many politicians are involved in real estate and banking (Hourani, 2010; Achkar, 2011). Another example is the fact that developers have personally helped draft the new 2004 Building Law that increased exploitation ratios (Krijnen and Fawaz, 2010). When looking at the role of the state in gentrification processes in Lebanon, this is something any researcher should keep in mind.

The role of the state: the example of heritage buildings

The state ordered several studies on heritage buildings in the peri-central areas of Beirut, but the vast majority have been demolished (sometimes in fear of being listed) or remain unprotected. Landlords lobbied to get their buildings off the list, stating in one letter: 'we also ask you to preserve the wealth of a large portion of the middle class by releasing all the buildings on the list' (quoted in Bekdache, forthcoming). From over 1,000 buildings classified in 1995, only about 270 remain protected (MAJAL, 2012; Bekdache, forthcoming). There are no subsidies for renovation, and illegal demolitions are frequent. A draft law to better protect buildings has been under study since 2007 (including the right for owners to sell their land development rights) but has so far not been voted on because of political conflict (Byrns, 2011; MAJAL, 2012). Any attempts at curbing Beirut's real estate development or preserving what remains of the city's architectural heritage are met with fierce resistance on the part of developers (Fielding-Smith, 2010). Developers interviewed have complained about the difficulties of getting a demolition permit, but also made clear that with the right connections, anything is possible.[12] In Zokak el-Blat, from 94 heritage buildings identified in 1995, only 26 are officially protected, and from those, only 14% are in a good state (MAJAL, 2012). With a state unable and unwilling to curb exploitation ratios, old buildings and their tenants become an obstacle to profit accumulation. The overlap between public and private interests becomes visible in the state's failed attempts at heritage preservation. Unlike other cases (see, eg, Lees, 2003), obtaining landmark status represents an obstacle to, not incentive for, gentrification.

Creative and commercial gentrification in Beirut

The past decade has seen a considerable interest in creative cities as a way forward to revitalise (often European) urban centres that struggled to find ways to cope with changing post-industrial realities. This idea also gained some attention in Beirut, particularly through a British Council-sponsored report:

> This is a call, an invitation to work together for a better future for Lebanon, a call to put in place a structure that will plan and prepare for the release of Lebanon's economic and creative potential. The importance of creativity and content in any present-day economy presents to Lebanon unique opportunities for growth, development and stability. Grasping these opportunities can transform all our futures. (Hill, 2008, p 15)

This call is far from exceptional, as many places have been trying to *do a Florida thing* (McGuigan, 2009), referring to the optimistic advocacy for creative city strategies by Richard Florida (2002, 2005).

There are a variety of ways in which creative industries discourse is used around the world, as Cunningham (2009, p 376) describes: it can be 'thought of as a Rorschach blot, being invested in for varying reasons and with varying emphases and outcomes'. In the case of Beirut, for example, state and non-state actors supporting the emerging creative industries in Lebanon argue that it would facilitate a transition to, or at least a more significant role for, the so-called knowledge economy, and transfer resources and investments from real estate development and financial services to this sector, so that young, highly educated people that are currently leaving the country would be inclined to stay and the Lebanese diaspora would be inclined to return (Hill, 2008). It seems unlikely, however, that this bottom-up strategy will help combat social stratification and sectarian segregation in the city. In Beirut, the creative city discourse also exists alongside the ongoing structural problems of uneven development and ignores potential gentrification and, hence, displacement effects. The 'Creativity Fix' (Peck, 2007) is as equally unlikely to provide a structural solution to the social issues in Beirut as it is elsewhere. The main difference, however, is how this 'fix' made its way into urban practice.

Contrary to the literature on creative gentrification, the Lebanese state has not formulated any policies at the local level to assist creative entrepreneurs or facilitate gentrification. This recently changed with the introduction of the Beirut Digital District in the quarter of Bachoura, a poor area south of downtown. Backed by the Ministry of Telecommunications, it intends to turn Lebanon into a digital hub by facilitating the clustering of companies and shops, sparking justified fears of displacement among local residents (Whiting, 2012).

Most instances of creative gentrification, however, have not benefited directly from any state support (although the state has intervened generally to facilitate real estate development). The initiative to transform Beirut into a creative city was proposed, developed and supported by local and international non-governmental organisations (NGOs). The two primary actors are the local branch of GAIA Heritage, an international NGO founded by a Lebanese-French economist that seeks to promote the preservation of cultural heritage and the arts while activating their economic potentials, and the local branch of the British Council, who has a programme of advancing and supporting creative economies worldwide (Hill, 2008; Zouain et al, 2011). Their plan is to create an interactive database and map of creative activity in Lebanon to allow 'creatives' to cooperate. This tool will support the nascent industry and fill the gap that local authorities left. So far, these tools have not materialised, but the clustering of creative industries is present, helped by family members and, in some cases, the British Council by facilitating access to finance. As Peck (2005) points out, Richard Florida's most celebrated creative cities are actually not a product of government intervention. Moreover, the case of the Mar Mikhael neighbourhood in the following illustrates how the very diversity that made the area attractive is threatened by gentrification. It also provides us with a different form of gentrification from what we have seen in Zokak el-Blat, where the construction of new high-rises has remained unaccompanied by commercial changes.

Gentrification in Mar Mikhael and the 'creatives' dimension

Mar Mikhael is a mixed residential/commercial area where many villas from the 1930s survive, alongside more recent structures. Until 2008, it was generally described as a sleepy quarter, not fully recovered from the closure of the railroad in 1976 and the civil war. After the Armenian genocide in 1915, many refugees settled in the district. The character of the area remains distinctly Armenian today (Ashkarian, 2012; Zouain et al, 2011). Most inhabitants are tenants on old rental contracts.

Mar Mikhael started transforming around 2008, as nightlife from the bordering Gemmayzeh district spilled over (Lee, 2009). Restaurants, pubs, boutiques and art galleries opened one after another. The lower prices of land attracted many property investors and developers, who viewed the area as the next place to be and sold it as such on their projects' websites and in brochures. Property and rental prices have risen rapidly, tripling in some cases (Lee, 2009; Sherwood, 2010; Chardon, 2011; Zouain et al, 2011; Ashkarian, 2012). A few 'pioneers' bought empty lots or old houses, followed by larger real estate developers, who bought several lots at the same time, merged them and demolished existing structures in order to build as high as possible. Because many tenants live on old rental contracts, owners are willing to sell their properties to developers, who convince tenants to leave upon compensation (Salem, 2010).

The 'revival' of Mar Mikhael was accelerated by the settlement of young creative entrepreneurs in the neighbourhood. A survey of creatives carried out by Zouain et al (2011)[13] shows that there were two waves of creative entrepreneurs entering the neighbourhood: the first attracted by the area's low prices and village-like characteristics around 2008; and the second attracted by the area's developing cultural and creative industries around 2010/11. They consist of designers, architects and art and information technology (IT) professionals. Their clients hail mostly from outside Mar Mikhael, are 25 to 40 years old and are well-off.

The transformation of Mar Mikhael has had far-reaching effects for the area's existing commercial establishments. A recent survey by Ashkarian (2012) revealed that 12 original shops have closed over the past three to four years and inhabitants are worried about the changing character of the district and their precarious social situation. They face a form of sociocultural displacement (Davidson and Lees, 2005). Other Lebanese-Armenians take this seriously as well, as the following quote illustrates:

> 'How do we know that gentrification is "destroying" Mar Mikhael? Well, today, when our march for the 98th commemoration of the Armenian genocide passed through Mar Mikhael, shops owned by Lebanese-Armenians were closed, shops that have been owned by Lebanese who have been living with the Lebanese-Armenians for a long time in Mar Mikhael were also closed. However, many of the new trendy places do not seem to care: Chez Sophie and 3enab for example: shame on you! As a journalist from Al-akhbar once put it: "Mar Mikhael fi intizar el Barabera"[14] ... well ... they are already here!' (Kevork Baboyan, 24 April 2013)

The influx of creative entrepreneurs, bars and restaurants has been visualised in the map shown in Figure 15.3, comparing two surveys undertaken by Marieke Krijnen (MK) in 2011 and 2013. It also shows real estate projects.

Figure 15.3: Influx of real estate projects and venues between 2011 and 2013

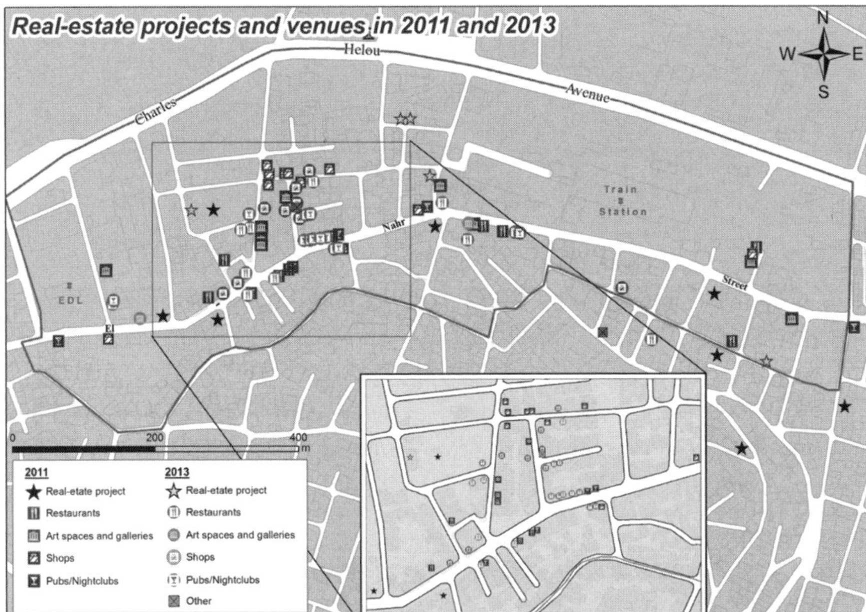

The first large-scale real estate project in Mar Mikhael was the AYA tower (see Figure 15.4), by HAR Properties, one of whose founders and major shareholders is the son of the former Prime Minister Rafik el-Hariri, Fahed el-Hariri. Forbes estimated his inherited fortune at USD1.4 billion in 2010.[15] Activists of the local Save Beirut Heritage (SBH) group have accused Hariri of using political pressure to obtain demolition permits, something that HAR Properties vehemently denies (Sikimic, 2011).

HAR Properties bought several lots in September 2009 and merged them in the same month.[16] Construction started in spring 2010 and involved the demolition of an old cinema plus a few old houses. According to one of the partners in HAR Properties, the intention was to preserve the existing structures. Finally, they decided against it because the cost was too high and the structure would not allow the required 25 parking spaces. Instead, they created 'a thin tall building that cannot be seen from anywhere.... The idea was to not have a big impact.'[17] The demolition was not without controversy, and SBH protested.[18] Although the developer proposed a solution to preserve heritage, the project itself has merely preserved a building facade because the minister of culture ordered them to do so.[19]

Salem (2010) reports that eight tenants remained in the old buildings and were paid a total of USD900,000 to leave. HAR Properties stated: 'the building belonged to eight brothers and sisters, they don't get the rent, it's the old system'.[20] This illustrates yet another case of the rent gaps created by rent controls.

The project is marketed on HAR Properties' website (available at: www.har-properties.com) as low-cost housing in a once-forgotten neighbourhood full of architectural charm. About 70% of the planned apartments have been sold at the time of writing. According to HAR Properties, prices start at USD3,000/m^2 and rise to USD4,200/m^2 for higher floors, allowing people to buy a property from USD500,000 to around USD1.2 million.[21] Facilities include a gym and a swimming pool. The developer is adamant that he does not sell to speculators (Salem, 2010, p 2): clients are '100% Lebanese, but about half of them are living abroad, in Europe, Dubai, Qatar'. The smaller apartments go to people actually living in Lebanon.

Another project is 'Bobo', by the Zardman company, a residential-commercial building with luxury apartments starting at USD3,300/m^2, ranging from 200m^2 to 350m^2, with a 425m^2 penthouse and 108m^2 roof garden. The project incorporates the facade of an older building and has been completely sold. Initially, the company wanted to demolish the entire structure, but was only given a permit after preserving the building as a whole, according to SBH. The then-minister

Figure 15.4: AYA

Note: Copyright HAR Properties.

of culture pressured them into the preservation.[22] While these cases may point to a change in state policy regarding heritage preservation, we have to point out that this minister has since been replaced, and his successor does not display an interest in heritage preservation.

The name 'Bobo' clearly plays with the area's 'hip' and creative image, as '*Bobo*' stands for 'bohemian-bourgeois', the francophone equivalent of '*hipster*'. The project was launched in February 2011 and sold out in 27 minutes: 'Bobo project is the new luxurious, residential estate; located in the new hotspot of Beirut, Mar Mikhael, combining a luxurious lifestyle with a non-stop lifestyle.'[23] This shows how the creative city discourse subliminally permeates the urban imaginary and that it fuels further gentrification of the neighbourhood. The next section will explore the demand for these and other new buildings.

Who are the gentrifiers?

Real estate developers refer to their buyers mostly as 'Lebanese middle class'. It is safe to say, however, that the vast majority of what is usually considered the middle class by politicians and residents (self-employed persons, teachers, doctors) cannot afford housing in Beirut unless assisted in some ways. If we try to define the middle class in Lebanon by relying on income data, we see that 50% of households in Lebanon live on less than USD6,500 a year. When real estate developers refer to their buyers as 'middle class', then, they usually refer to expatriate Lebanese that are employed abroad and can hence afford to buy. Most of these people buy for their children or are assisted by family, according to a real estate consultant,[24] who said that he had just sold a USD800,000 apartment to a Lebanese dentist living in France. Developers in Zokak el-Blat have also stated that most demand comes from Lebanese expatriates, while hardly any developer claims to have sold to foreigners. They claim their clients work mostly in white-collar professions and are university-educated. They buy the apartment for themselves and their family (MAJAL, 2012).

Keeping in mind the role of family support and expatriate Lebanese, we can distinguish two groups of gentrifiers. On the one hand, we see creative entrepreneurs who set up shop in Mar Mikhael, as described earlier. They include (fashion) designers, art professionals, owners of 'concept' stores and restaurants. There are likely some emancipatory effects of the gentrification (Lees, 2000). Many shop-owners are women, and there is a feminist cafe. Developers have noted that some clients prefer Mar Mikhael because of its allegedly non-sectarian character (even though it is distinctly Armenian, but perhaps that is viewed as more neutral). Indeed, political flagging, omnipresent in Zokak el-Blat, is mostly absent, except for Armenian banners calling for the recognition of the genocide by Turkey.

Lees et al (2008) describe how many initial gentrifiers are interested in preserving the social diversity of the area they live in. In Mar Mikhael, this mostly takes the form of preserving old buildings. The self-proclaimed non-profit Karaj-media lab (founded by two expatriate Lebanese designers/artists in 2010) states:

> Karaj is located in a historic Lebanese house in Mar Mikhayel, a neighborhood that is home to young arts and non-profit organizations, galleries and emerging designers. Amidst rapid gentrification and rampant real estate crimes, Karaj takes a pro-active stance in support of architectural and cultural preservation.[25]

Indeed, most new bars and restaurants are located on the ground floors of Mandate-era buildings (1920–43).

According to developers and brokers, most buyers are Lebanese working abroad who only reside in their apartments in summer, buy it for their children or as an investment, or rent it out. Hence, the majority of buyers do not actually move into their apartments right away. That the vast majority of gentrifiers do not actually live in Lebanon most of the year means that they do not have the same influence on changing landscapes of consumption as elsewhere (Slater, 2011). These establishments exist in other, commercial areas of the city, such as Hamra, Verdun, Achrafieh and, of course, Mar Mikhael, but in Zokak el-Blat, they have remained absent. It is probable that gentrifiers use facilities in other areas, but if they lived in Beirut permanently, it is likely that consumer spaces would flourish in the neighbourhood itself.

Apart from the distinction between creative entrepreneurs and residents, the main difference between gentrifiers is sectarian, according to experts: Muslims will buy in predominantly Muslim areas in West Beirut; Christians in the East. Mar Mikhael is an exception, attracting a diverse, hip clientele consisting of singles or young couples, and with less families because of the large amount of restaurants and bars. The apartments are generally smaller as well, making them attractive to rent out to foreigners, with whom Mar Mikhael is very popular. Within Zokak el-Blat, the towers overlooking downtown attract more upmarket buyers, while the inner neighbourhoods cater to lower market segments (a difference of USD1,000/m^2), and most buyers are families. This is another proof of the immense diversity that exists within gentrification processes in Beirut. However, focusing solely on gentrifiers' preferences provides neither a complete picture nor explanation of gentrification. It is important to also talk about the people who are the victims of gentrification processes, the displaced (Slater, 2006), and discuss their resistance tactics and other factors that may impede gentrification processes.

Resistance to displacement, impediments to gentrification

Some 'spaces of hope' (Harvey, 2000) are created when social movements mobilise against gentrification. This has become more of a challenge recently as many community activists are displaced (Lees et al, 2008, p 248), but it is exceedingly difficult in Lebanon, where civil society activists concerned with social justice hardly escape sectarian politics, and where few people can afford to miss a day at work. At a meeting concerned with resisting gentrification processes in Beirut, one girl exclaimed: "The only way to occupy a building and resist displacement is if you have your own militia!"[26]

Deboulet and Fawaz (2011) mention a successful effort at resisting displacement by highway projects in the southern suburbs of Beirut that involved political parties negotiating on behalf of the residents, coupled with protests. The fact that these mobilisations take place through political parties, which are usually closely linked to people's sectarian affiliation, serves to strengthen sectarian religious identities, even though not all residents support those parties. They are, however, dependent on them for information and a share in negotiated compensations because the Lebanese political system does not provide any other means of participation (Fawaz, 2009b; Deboulet and Fawaz, 2011). In Zokak el-Blat, some squatters probably enjoy political protection and are, hence, difficult to evict. Bodenstein (2005) mentions that during the war, militias protected buildings squatted by Kurds and Palestinians from demolition. Their role is ambiguous: in the case of informal settlements in Beirut, political parties such as Amal and Hezbollah have played a role in either facilitating or resisting processes of displacement (Harb, 2001; Fawaz and Peillen, 2003). In Mar Mikhael, there is no overlapping structure to organise collectively on the local level, a fact that encourages clientelism when people try to resist displacement (Ashkarian, 2012). Hence, resistance opportunities are limited in Lebanon.

The provision of affordable housing can impede gentrification (Ley and Dobson, 2008). In Lebanon, this is mostly done by religious organisations, which own large tracts of land to use in the interests of their constituencies. Hezbollah, the Maronite Church (Lebanon's biggest landowner) and the Syriac Patriarchate have all provided affordable housing (Brundiers and Odermatt, 2002; Ghodbane, 2012), even their role is ambiguous though here as well: in one case, ostensibly affordable housing turned out to be a luxury project with large profits (Bekdache, forthcoming). Rent controls do not necessarily prevent displacement either, as we have seen earlier.

Organisations that intend to preserve heritage such as SBH, and the state's heritage protection efforts themselves, solely look at the built environment and disregard the social fabric of neighbourhoods (Bekdache, forthcoming). They generally side with the landlords. If they get their way, buildings might be preserved, but tenants will be displaced since they advocate for the abolition of rent controls. As potential for resistance is limited, and actors that can prevent displacement have ambiguous roles – spaces of hope are hard to find in Lebanon.

Conclusion: a post-colonial perspective on researching gentrification in Beirut

Most processes of gentrification described earlier follow the same logic as gentrification processes elsewhere: they can be explained via the rent-gap thesis, coupled with sufficient demand. Yet, in the Lebanese case specifically, and probably many other countries in the Global South, it is important to think about the role of the diaspora. As Smith (2002) has pointed out, global capital is reaching down into local neighbourhoods. While keeping in mind that the global is always locally embedded, and hence the local–global dichotomy should be treated with suspicion (Tsing, 2005), we do see a crucial role for transnational capital investment and (expatriate) demand. The place-making projects associated with gentrification deploy the global–local dichotomy in ways that make them legible to capital: Mar Mikhael's 'local authenticity'; Beirut's place as a global hub on the crossroads between East and West; and so forth (see also Parker, 2008).

Anyone researching gentrification should keep in mind that there are big differences within one and the same urban region. As we have shown, Mar Mikhael experienced rampant changes in its commercial establishments; Zokak el-Blat did not (MAJAL, 2012). We have also seen, as Butler and Robson (2001) noted, that different areas attract different types of gentrifiers. Moreover, Mar Mikhael has seen the rehabilitation of some older structures and the preservation of facades. In Zokak el-Blat, this is entirely absent, apart from some renovated mansions that house schools (MAJAL, 2012). Furthermore, we should not forget gentrifiers' sectarian preferences. All these complex dynamics come together and influence the shape of gentrification processes in specific areas.

The role of war and conflict in processes of displacement and creating rent gaps is important. Permanent displacement of different sectarian groups into more homogeneously populated neighbourhoods and regions, as explained earlier, has reinforced sectarian divisions in the country, while the role of political parties in negotiating compensation has done the same for some groups. These displacements 'free up' space for profitable reinvestment, which is another spatial fix after a crisis (Lees et al, 2008). We argue that it is not only the financial crises of capitalism, but also the crises of conflict and war, that should be taken into account in providing the opportunity for spatial fixes. As we have shown, conflict can become part of a speculator's game and widen rent gaps (Ross and Jamil, 2011).

This leads towards our final point, namely, that a post-colonial perspective should look beyond the 'usual suspects'. Anyone who wants to perform a discourse analysis using policy documents will have a hard time in Lebanon, since these are hardly produced. Instead, state involvement is merged with non-state actors' practices. Scholars should keep this in mind when researching gentrification processes in any context. This goes for resistance to gentrification as well: political parties in Lebanon are an important factor in processes of displacement, and we need to look beyond social movements based on location or class alone and pay attention to the dynamics of sectarianism, political connections and clientelism to investigate how these complex interactions shape the contemporary city in the Global South.

The research presented here has sought to clarify the different ways in which processes of gentrification in Beirut unfold, and how they are influenced by context-specific factors. We hope that our work will raise questions on similar dimensions of gentrification taking place in their context of research, hence bringing more 'Southern' experiences into scholarship and using these findings to question how we view the process in the dominant literature about the West (drawing on Roy [2009a] and Robinson [2006]; Lees [2014] makes a similar observation).

Notes

[1] To compare: prices in the most important city centers in Europe include USD24,900/m^2 (United Kingdom), USD19,150/m^2 (France), USD6,000/m^2 (Netherlands) and USD4,000/m^2 (Germany). For the US, it is USD13,377/m^2; for the Middle East, Beirut is only preceded by Israel (USD8,258/m^2) and Abu Dhabi (USD4,010/m^2). See: http://www.globalpropertyguide.com (accessed 26 June 2013).

[2] There is a distinction between the area of Beirut City proper and the Greater Beirut or Beirut Metropolitan Area. The latter counts the suburbs as part of the city, and is the scale from which the estimate of 2 million has been derived.

[3] Except for a short period of state interventionism in the 1960s following a severe civil conflict. This period saw the introduction of some forms of social security and large investments in infrastructure.

[4] One extreme example is the case of a minister passing a temporary decree allowing the building of his project in the mountains near Beirut and cancelling it after the building permit was passed. Another is the project of a major developer (MENA Capital) to destroy an old garden whose architect (Ziad Akl) is on the Higher Council for Urban Planning, and hence on the committee deciding to approve it. He is also the head of the Urban Planning Department at ALBA University training a new generation of city builders.

[5] Reconstruction was initiated in 1992 with the National Emergency Reconstruction Plan (NERP), developed by the Council for Reconstruction and Development (CDR) into the long-term Horizon 2000 plan (Dibeh, 2005). The reconstruction of downtown Beirut was a private enterprise, executed by a private company called Solidere, which was created in 1994 by the Hariri government.

[6] The last census in Lebanon took place in 1932 and has not been repeated for political reasons related to the distribution of government posts and parliament seats based on sectarian affiliation.

[7] Which was confined to war displacees and has not been used for other operations involving the displacement of dwellers, such as highway construction. The Ministry of Displaced People is in charge of a 'return programme' for people displaced by war (Fawaz and Peillen, 2003) and negotiating on their behalf.

[8] In 2005, 1,339 sales were registered, of which 64 were to foreigners, 25 were lot mergers and 15 demolitions took place. In 2011, 1,870 sales were concluded, of which 65 were to foreigners, 32 were mergers and 14 demolitions took place.

[9] Interview by Marieke Krijnen for MAJAL, 30 September 2010.

[10] Interview with Binadar representative, conducted by MK for MAJAL, 28 September 2010.

[11] Three cadastral records were analysed by MAJAL in autumn 2010.

[12] Interview with developer 2, carried out by MK for MAJAL, 27 September 2010.

[13] In Mar Mikhael, 35 creative entrepreneurs were identified, of which 26 completed a questionnaire. Of these, 22 were actual 'creators', while four were exhibitors of creative work and six provided services to the creators and exhibitors, including restaurants.

[14] 'Mar Mikhael: waiting for the barbarians.'

[15] See: www.forbes.com/lists/2010/10/billionaires-2010_Fahd-Hariri_F5B7.html (accessed 2 January 2013).

[16] As evidenced by a cadastral record requested by MK on 15 December 2011.

[17] Interview conducted by MK, 13 December 2011.

[18] See: http://www.dailystar.com.lb/News/Local-News/Sep/27/Hundreds-march-in-support-of-Beiruts-historic-architecture.ashx

[19] According to an interview by MK with one of the partners of HAR Properties, the developer of AYA, 13 December 2011. In the original renders of the project, no such preservation can be seen.

[20] Interview conducted by MK, 13 December 2011.

[21] Interview conducted by MK, 13 December 2011.

[22] See the debate on the Skyscraper City forums. Available at: http://www.skyscrapercity.com/showthread.php?p=83830747andhighlight=save+beirut+heritage+bobo#post83830747 (accessed 21 December 2012).

[23] From Zardman's Facebook page. Available at: www.facebook.com/zardman

[24] Personal communication, June 2013. This space has been forced to close due to rent increases.

[25] Quote from: www.karajbeirut.org

[26] Meeting organised by MK and a friend, April 2010, t-marbouta cafe, Beirut.

References

Achkar, H. (2011) *The role of the state in initiating gentrification: the case of the neighborhood of Achrafieh in Beirut*, Beirut: Lebanese University.

Alaily-Mattar, N. (2008) 'Beyond gated communities? Detachment and concentration in networked nodes of affluence in the city of Beirut', *Urban Design International*, vol 13, no 4, pp 263–71.

Ashkarian, V. (2012) 'Le développement local du quartier Mar Mikhaël', research paper, Master 2 Recherche, Department of Urban Planning, Lebanese University, Beirut.

Becherer, R. (2005) 'A matter of life and debt: the untold costs of Rafiq Hariri's New Beirut', *The Journal of Architecture*, vol 10, no 1, pp 1–42.

Bekdache, N. (forthcoming) 'Evicting sovereignty: old housing tenants from citizens to obstacles', ACSS working paper to be published in Arab Studies.

Bodenstein, R. (2005) 'The making and remaking of Zokak el-Blat: a history of the urban fabric', in H. Gebhardt, D. Sack and R. Bodenstein (eds) *History, space and social conflict in Beirut: the quarter of Zokak el-Blat*, Beirut/Wuerzburg: Orient-Institut/Ergon Verlag in Kommission (Beiruter Texte und Studien no 97), pp 35–108.

Boudisseau, G. (2001) *Espaces commerciaux, centralités et logiques d'acteurs a Beyrouth: le cas de Hamra et de Verdun*, Tours: Université François-Rabelais de Tours.

Brundiers, K. and Odermatt, A. (2002) 'Analyzing socio-spatial processes of integration and disintegration by examining the local housing market: a case study of Beirut, Lebanon', *The Arab World Geographer*, vol 5, no 4, pp 209–31.

Butler, T. and Robson, G. (2001) 'Social capital, gentrification and neighbourhood change in London: a comparison of three South London neighbourhoods', *Urban Studies*, vol 38, no 12, pp 2145–62.

Byrns, K. (2011) 'Beirut: under destruction', *The Executive*, 3 April, pp 1–18.

Chaaban, J. and Gebara, K. (2007) 'Development in a polarized society: looking at economic and social development in Lebanon through a different lens', *Abaad*, no 11, Lebanese Center for Policy Studies (in Arabic).

Chardon, L. (2011) 'Mar Mikhaël, le nouveau quartier bobo', *Le Commerce du Levant*, February.

Cochrane, P. (2012) 'Turning tragedy into transformation. New legislation is set to remake rental markets in the wake of building collapse', *The Executive*, 3 May.

Cunningham, S. (2009) 'Trojan horse or Rorschach blot? Creative industries discourse around the world', *International Journal of Cultural Policy*, vol 15, no 4, pp 375–86.

Daily Star (2013) 'Most Beirut properties completed in 2012 unsold', *The Daily Star*, 6 June.

Davidson, M. and Lees, L. (2005) 'New-build "gentrification" and London's riverside renaissance', *Environment and Planning A*, vol 37, no 7, pp 1165–90.

Davidson, M. and Lees, L. (2010) 'New-build gentrification: its histories, trajectories, and critical geographies', *Population, Space and Place*, vol 16, no 5, pp 335–43.

Deboulet, A. and Fawaz, M. (2011) 'Contesting the legitimacy of urban restructuring and highways in Beirut's irregular settlements', in D.E. Davis and N. Libertun de Duren (eds) *Cities and sovereignty. Identity politics in urban spaces*, Bloomington and Indianapolis, IN: Indiana University Press, pp 117–51.

Dibeh, G. (2005) 'The political economy of postwar reconstruction in Lebanon', research paper 44, United Nations University, World Institute for Development Economics Research.

El-Achkar, E. (1998) 'Réglementation et formes urbaines: le cas de Beyrouth', *Cahiers du Cermoc*, No 20, Beirut, CERMOC.

Fawaz, M. (2009a) 'Hezbollah as urban planner? Questions to and from planning theory', *Planning Theory*, vol 8, no 4, pp 323–34.

Fawaz, M. (2009b) 'Neoliberal urbanity and the right to the city: a view from Beirut's periphery', *Development and Change*, vol 40, no 5, pp 827–52.

Fawaz, M. and Peillen, I. (2003) *Urban slums reports: the case of Beirut, Lebanon. Understanding slums: case studies for the global report on human settlements 2003*, London: Earthscan.

Fielding-Smith, A. (2010) 'Property boom raises fears for Beirut heritage', *The Financial Times*, 16 September.

Fisk, R. (2012) 'Poverty is main culprit as 19 die in slum tragedy', *The Independent*, 17 January, pp 18–19.

Florida, R. (2002) 'Bohemia and economic geography', *Journal of Economic Geography*, vol 2, no 1, pp 55–71.

Florida, R. (2005) *The rise of the creative class and how it's transforming work, leisure, community and everyday life*, New York, NY: Basic Books.

Gates, C. (1998) *Merchant Republic of Lebanon: rise of an open economy*, London: Centre for Lebanese Studies/I. B. Tauris.

Genberg, D. (2002) 'Borders and boundaries in post-war Beirut', in A. Erdentug and F. Colombijn (eds) *Urban ethnic encounters: the spatial consequences*, London: Routledge, pp 81–96.

Ghodbane, D. (2012) 'Les acteurs du renouvellement urbain. Le cas du quartier Syriaque de Beyrouth', MA thesis, Ecole Nationale Supérieure d'Architecture de Paris-La-Villette.

Glass, R. (1964) *London: aspects of change*, London: MacGibbon and Kee.

Glasze, G. (2003) 'Segmented governance patterns – fragmented urbanism: the development of guarded housing estates in Lebanon', *The Arab World Geographer*, vol 6, no 2, pp 79–100.

Habib, O. (2011) 'Lebanon safe from debt crisis fallout', *The Daily Star*, Lebanon, 10 August, pp 6–8.

Halawi, D. (2010) 'Non-residents buying bulk of Lebanese real estate', *The Daily Star*, Lebanon, 17 April.

Hanssen, J. (2005) 'The birth of an education quarter: Zokak el-Blat as a cradle of culture in the Arab World', in H. Gebhardt, D. Sack and R. Bodenstein (eds) *History, space and social conflict in Beirut: the quarter of Zokak el-Blat*, Beirut/Wuerzburg: Orient-Institut/Ergon Verlag in Kommission (Beiruter Texte und Studien no 97), pp 143–74.

Harb, M. (2001) 'Urban governance in post-war Beirut: resources, negotiations and contestations in the Elyssar Project', in S. Shami (ed) *Capital cities: ethnographies of urban governance in the Middle East*, Toronto: Toronto University Press, pp 111–33.

Harvey, D. (2000) *Spaces of hope*, Berkeley and Los Angeles, CA: University of California Press.

Hilal, N. (2008) *Governance and public participation in post-war reconstruction projects: Haret Hreik, Beirut as a case study*, Beirut: American University of Beirut.

Hill, S. (2008) *Creative Lebanon. A framework for future prosperity*, Beirut: British Council. Available at: http://www.britishcouncil.org/lebanon-creative-lebanon-full-report.pdf

Hoeckel, K. (2007) *Beyond Beirut: why reconstruction in Lebanon did not contribute to state-making and stability*, Occasional Paper 4, Crisis States Research Centre, London: LSE.

Hourani, N. (2010) 'Transnational pathways and politico-economic power: globalisation and the Lebanese Civil War', *Geopolitics*, vol 15, no 2, pp 290–311.

Karam, Z. (2010) 'Luxury building boom transforms Beirut as Lebanon becomes a financial draw', *AP*, 22 January, pp 7–9.

Khayat, N. (2007) 'Case studies: the Elyssar Reconstruction Project; The Ministry of the Displaced; The Economic and Social Fund for Development'. Available at: www.integrityaction.org/sites/www.integrityaction.org/files/documents/files/Lebanon%20Case%20Studies.doc

Krijnen, M. (2010) *Facilitating real estate development in Beirut: a peculiar case of neoliberal public policy*, Beirut: American University of Beirut.

Krijnen, M. and Fawaz, M. (2010) 'Exception as the rule: high-end developments in neoliberal Beirut', *Built Environment*, vol 36, no 2, pp 245–59.

Lee, H. (2009) 'Mar Mikhael, the new Gemmayzeh?', *NOW Lebanon*, 16 August.

Leenders, R. (2003) 'Public means to private ends: state building and power in post-war Lebanon', in E. Kienle (ed) *Politics from above, politics from below. The Middle East in the age of reform*, London: Saqi Books, pp 304–35.

Leenders, R. (2004) 'Nobody having too much to answer for: laissez-faire, networks, and post-war reconstruction in Lebanon', in S. Heydemann (ed) *Networks of privilege in the Middle East: the politics of economic reform revisited*, Basingstoke: Palgrave Macmillan, pp 169–200.

Lees, L. (2000) 'A reappraisal of gentrification: towards a "geography of gentrification"', *Progress in Human Geography*, vol 24, no 3, pp 389–408.

Lees, L. (2003) 'Super-gentrification: the case of Brooklyn Heights, New York City', *Urban Studies*, vol 40, no 12, pp 2487–509.

Lees, L. (2012) 'The geography of gentrification: thinking through comparative urbanism', *Progress in Human Geography*, vol 36, no 2, pp 155–71.

Lees, L. (2014) 'Gentrification in the global south?', in S. Parnell and S. Oldfield (eds) *The Routledge handbook on cities of the global south*, Routledge: New York, pp 506–21.

Lees, L. and Ley, D. (eds) (2008) 'Special issue on gentrification and public policy', *Urban Studies*, vol 45, no 12.

Lees, L., Slater, T. and Wyly, E. (2008) *Gentrification*, New York and London: Routledge.

Ley, D. and Dobson, C. (2008) 'Are there limits to gentrification? The contexts of impeded gentrification in Vancouver', *Urban Studies*, vol 45, no 12, pp 2471–98.

Lloyd-Jones, T. (2005) 'Beirut property takes the fast lane again', *Business Intelligence Middle East*, 24 June.

MAJAL (2012) *Urban observation, Zokak el-Blat*, Beirut, http://www.scribd.com/doc/192861400/Urban-Obervation-Zokak-El-Blat-Beirut-Lebanon

Makarem, K. (2013) 'A buyer's market. Three trends keeping housing afloat', *The Executive*, 5 April, pp 11–16.

Makdisi, S. (1997) 'Laying claim to Beirut: urban narrative and spatial identity in the age of Solidere', *Critical inquiry*, vol 23, no 3, pp 661–705.

Marcuse, P. (1985) 'Gentrification, abandonment and displacement: connections, causes, and policy responses in New York City', *Urban Law Annual, Journal of Urban and Contemporary Law*, vol 28, pp 195–240.

McFarlane, C. (2010) 'The comparative city: knowledge, learning, urbanism', *International Journal of Urban and Regional Research*, vol 34, no 4, pp 725–42.

McGuigan, J. (2009) 'Doing a Florida thing: the creative class thesis and cultural policy', *International Journal of Cultural Policy*, vol 15, no 3, pp 291–300.

Mollenhauer, A. (2005) 'Continuity and change in the architectural development of Zokak el-Blat', in H. Gebhardt, D. Sack and R. Bodenstein (eds) *History, space and social conflict in Beirut: the quarter of Zokak el-Blat*, Beirut/Wuerzburg: Orient-Institut/Ergon Verlag in Kommission (Beiruter Texte und Studien no 97), pp 109–42.

Parker, C. (2008) 'Re-orienting Amman: neoliberalism and the iconography of the local', *Traditional dwellings and settlements review*, vol 20, no 1, pp 28–30.

Peck, J. (2005) 'Struggling with the creative class', *International Journal of Urban and Regional Research*, vol 29, no 4, pp 740–70.

Peck, J. (2007) 'The creativity fix', *Eurozine*, 28 June.

Robinson, J. (2006) *Ordinary cities. Between modernity and development*, London: Routledge.

Ross, R. and Jamil, L. (2011) 'Waiting for war (and other strategies to stop gentrification): the case of Ras Beirut', *Human Geography*, vol 4, no 3, pp 14–32.

Roy, A. (2009a) 'The 21st-century metropolis: new geographies of theory', *Regional Studies*, vol 43, no 6, pp 819–30.

Roy, A. (2009b) 'Civic governmentality: the politics of inclusion in Beirut and Mumbai', *Antipode*, vol 41, no 1, pp 159–79.

Sakr, E. (2013) 'Central Bank package to revitalize real estate', *The Daily Star*, Lebanon, 5 February, pp 6–7.

Salem, R. (2010) 'Tradition in trouble', *The Executive*, 2 September, pp 1–4.

Sherwood, S. (2010) 'The creative set heads east in Beirut', *The New York Times*, 12 September.

Shwayri, S.T. (2008) 'From regional node to backwater and back to uncertainty: Beirut 1923–2006', in Y. Elsheshtawy (ed) *The evolving Arab city*, London: Routledge, pp 69–98.

Sikimic, S. (2011) 'Activists protest against demolition of Beirut buildings', *The Daily Star*, Lebanon, 3 May.

Slater, T. (2006) 'The eviction of critical perspectives from gentrification research', *International Journal of Urban and Regional Research*, vol 30, no 4, pp 737–57.

Slater, T. (2011) 'Gentrification of the city', in G. Bridge and S. Watson (eds) *The new Blackwell companion to the city*, Oxford: Blackwell, pp 571–85.

Smith, N. (1987) 'Gentrification and the rent gap', *Annals of the Association of American Geographers*, vol 77, no 3, pp 462–5.

Smith, N. (2002) 'New globalism, new urbanism: gentrification as global urban strategy', *Antipode*, vol 34, no 3, pp 427–50.

Spivak, G. (1993) *Outside in the teaching machine*, Routledge: London.

Summer, D. (2005) *Neoliberalizalizing the city: the circulation of city builders and urban images in Beirut and Amman*, Beirut: American University of Beirut.

Traboulsi, F. (2007) *A history of modern Lebanon*, London: Pluto Press.

Tsing, A. (2005) *Friction. An ethnography of global connection*, Princeton, NJ: Princeton University Press.

Whiting, R. (2012) 'Beirut digital district: high-tech development or gentrification?', *Al Akhbar (English)*, 28 December.

Zouain, G.S., Liatard, F. and Fournier, Z. (2011) 'Les industries créatives dans la ville: le cas du quartier de Mar-Mikhayel à Beyrouth', *Travaux et Jours*, no 85, pp 139–85.

SIXTEEN

Gentrification in Nigeria: the case of two housing estates in Lagos

Chinwe Nwanna

Introduction

Nigeria has experienced an unprecedented rate of urbanisation, from 10% in 1951 to 48.2% in 2010, a gain of nearly 40% over a period of 60 years. The current rate of urbanisation is 50%, with an urban population growth of 5.8%. This is higher than the average population growth of 2.8% (Ibrahim, 2012). The rate of in-migration into major cities in Nigeria has been so high that the pace of settlement development and housing provision could not, and cannot, accommodate it. Since the in-migrants must have shelter, all forms of informal procedures are being adopted to provide housing. This has resulted in non-compliance with physical planning regulations and development control standards. This, in turn, has culminated in slum development in most Nigerian cities. Currently, the slum population in Nigeria's urban areas is estimated at 66%, resulting in unplanned towns and cities, inadequate housing infrastructure, and so on.

Slums and squatter settlements in Nigeria are both the products of, and vehicles for, modernising activities. Lagos Mega City is no exception when it comes to this problematic impact of urbanisation. Agbola and Jinadu (1997) reported that a 1981 World Bank-assisted urban renewal project identified 42 'blighted areas' in the Lagos metropolis alone and the State Urban Renewal Board has identified more in recent years. The majority of urban residents are crowded into these areas and other enclaves of low-income groups. Atere (2001) has shown that these areas are in dire need of upgrading or regeneration. Most often, the Nigerian government's response is demolition or slum clearance after the eviction of the residents. Such efforts are largely undertaken to improve the city's international public image, or justified for health reasons, or as maintaining standards. However, it could also be argued that this is about profit maximisation when a settlement is located on prime development land, which a number of slums are. After evictions and demolitions, such areas are often redeveloped into condominiums such that the former residents cannot afford the new properties. This transformation, I would argue, is a form of 'gentrification' in Lagos.

'Gentrification' is relatively a contemporary term that refers to an ongoing, cyclical process that is widespread in the developed Western world. The term 'gentrification' has received significant attention in a number of academic disciplines, most notably, urban geography and urban sociology. The US Centre for Disease Control and Prevention defines gentrification quite simply as a transformation of neighbourhoods from low value to high value (see Nwanna, 2012). However, it is more than that, Lees et al (2008) argue that gentrification is a physical, social, economic and cultural phenomenon whereby working-class and/or inner-city neighbourhoods are converted into more affluent middle-class communities through the remodelling of buildings, resulting in increased property values and the displacement of the poor. They describe it as a powerful and now more likely state-led process that plays an important role in fashioning the physical and social form of Anglo-American cities. Gentrification is not spatially or temporally limited and thus even though the term is relatively new, any process that fits the basic description of the displacement of one group by another would constitute gentrification (see Smith, 1996). Gentrification fits well as a term for, and explanation of, similar processes that have occurred in Lagos but have yet to be studied in any detail.

Gentrification in Lagos can be seen in the state government's infrastructural developments and its restoration of law and order, which have resulted in the revanchist treatment of marginal people. Governor Ahmed Tinubu's administration (1999–2007) inherited a near-failed state from the military regime and adopted visionary and exemplary leadership approaches to promote development, resuscitate the state's value systems and bring back Lagos' lost glory. His major objectives were to create wealth, provide jobs, provide affordable mass housing schemes through the creation of the New/Satellite Town Development Scheme, reduce poverty, reorient value systems, and so on. Governor Fashola succeeded him in 2007 with the same vigour and commitment. His goal is to turn Lagos into one of the most modern mega-cities of the 21st century. His initiatives include the establishment of the Lagos Metropolitan Development and Governance Project and the Lagos Island Revitalization project, which aims to 'upgrade derelict residential areas' in Lagos (Abosede, 2006), and the formulation of the Medium Term Sector Strategy of the Housing Sector for Lagos for 2011–13, which has an ambitious vision to achieve 'a Lagos State where every citizen has access to quality housing that meets their needs' (ibid). Unfortunately, most of the houses commissioned so far by Governor Fashola and his predecessor favoured the rich. For instance, in the Ifako/Ijaye 'low-cost' housing estate, a flat sells for about N4.5 million (£18,750). No indigent person or salary earner can afford that. Their promises are, therefore, mere propaganda and remain mere rhetoric. As if that is not enough, the state is currently converting the Atlantic Ocean into a bourgeois enclave, Eko Atlantic City.

During Fashola's second inauguration into office in May 2011, he claimed that his policies and programmes were not intended to discriminate against any person(s). However, shortly after this, his administration has been meting out revanchist treatments to the poor, the marginalised and the downtrodden. For instance, beggars and the destitute have been forcibly removed from Lagos streets and taken to the rehabilitation centre in Ikorodu, an outstretch of Lagos, or deported to their various home states or countries as part of the government's strategy to gentrify the mega-city. In February 2013, the government took this revanchism against the beggars to another level by charging a number of them with 'constituting a nuisance in public by begging for alms' and for conducting themselves as disorderly persons without any visible means of livelihood. They were sent to Kirikiri Prison, one of the worst prisons in the world, and Badagry Prison for one month pending the final judgement by the court. Furthermore, a new immigration department was opened in Lagos. 'Illegal aliens' are being expelled and are shipped back to their homelands in the middle of the night.

As well as removing the destitute and mentally ill off the streets of Lagos, the government has also set out to gentrify slums. On 23 February 2013, the government forcibly razed houses in Badia East, a large slum neighbourhood in Lagos with a population of about 40,000 people. Workers had settled there 50 years ago upon taking jobs in the city centre. The government said that it could evict the community because the land was federal property. Early that fateful Saturday, a black police vehicle pulled up, armed and uniformed policemen sprang out to quell any restiveness while the houses were destroyed before the dismayed residents. Badia is one of the nine beneficiaries of the USD200 million World Bank-funded slum upgrading under the Lagos Metropolitan Development and Governance Project and so could have been upgraded rather than demolished. The government no longer tolerates the existence of slums in the centre of a state with a mega-city plan for a 'world-class', middle- and upper-class Lagos. Lagos State has also resisted any attempts to make the state financially responsible for the costs of resettling the slum dwellers; indeed, they rely on a weak legal system and the rights and powers they have under the Land Use Act to carry out this visceral gentrification. To buttress this point, slums in Mushin, Oluwole and Makoko have been demolished. The residents were evicted from their homes, with no talk of rehabilitation. They were given only 72 hours' notice to leave, just like in Badia East. In Makoko/Iwaya, the government's quit notice described them as 'environmental nuisances' that 'undermined the mega-city status' of Lagos. It stated that their menial existence was detrimental to the government's determination to beautify the Lagos waterfront. This is to justify Fashola's resounding slogan '*Eko o ni baje*', which means 'Lagos will not spoil or degenerate'.

Recently, an edict was passed banning motorcycles popularly known as '*okada*' in most parts of Lagos. The government refused to provide alternative means of transportation for those riders who do not have cars or even jobs before banning the *okadas*. Many people in Lagos are now compelled to walk for kilometres or stand for hours at bus stops, waiting in readiness to struggle for the few spaces available in the few buses when they finally arrive. Some riders are now jobless, increasing the level of unemployment in the state. Markets in Tejuoso, Yaba and Oshodi were demolished and rebuilt beyond the pockets of the earlier poor occupants. To crown it all, petty and street trading was banned, leaving the poor traders with no means of livelihood. The 'Kick Against Indiscipline' (KAI) brigade will seize anyone's goods if apprehended. Everywhere in Lagos, the poor are becoming persona non grata. All these measures translate into revanchism against the poor.

Hamnett (1984) insisted that all geographers and sociologists should be examining the phenomenon of gentrification by asking the questions: 'Why has gentrification occurred?'; 'When?'; and 'Where?' I do this in the context of Nigeria, specifically Lagos, by focusing on two different cases: the gentrification of Maroko, a densely populated slum area in Lagos, and 1004 Estate, a deteriorated and dilapidated federal government quarter located in the highbrow Victoria Island area of Lagos City.

Context: urbanisation and housing in Nigeria and Lagos

Nigeria is the most populous country in Africa, with a population of 140 million and a growth rate of 3.2% (FGP, 2007). The country is a federation, operating a three-tier governance system at the national, state and local government levels. Nigeria is made up of 36 states including a Federal Capital Territory and 774 Local Government Areas (LGAs). For ease of administration and accelerated development, the states were divided broadly into six geopolitical zones, namely, North East (NE), North Central (NC), North West (NW), South East (SE), South South (SS) and South West (SW). Nigeria is currently under a democratic government after about 30 years of military rule.

In Nigeria, land allocation and title distribution were, and are still, based on the kinship system. However, with the advent of colonialism, urban land allocation and title distribution became the affair of government at various levels. Public intervention in housing in Nigeria began in the colonial period following the outbreak of bubonic plague in Lagos in the 1920s. During the period between 1900 and 1960, government involvement was centred essentially on the provision of quarters for expatriate staff and for selected indigenous staff. There was no effort made to construct houses for the general public. Thereafter, successive governments in Nigeria sought to confront the nagging problem of accommodating an increasing number of Nigerians through the Low-Cost Housing Project (1972–79 and 1975–83), and Site-and-Services Programme (1984 –88) (Aribigbola, 2008).

The first explicitly formulated national policy on housing was launched in 1991, with the aim of providing housing for all Nigerians by the year 2000. As the set goal failed, the policy was reinvigorated in 2002, aiming to provide necessary solutions to the hitherto intractable housing crisis in Nigeria (Okewole and Aribigbola, 2006). The 2002 National Housing Policy sought to ensure that all Nigerians own or have access to decent, safe and sanitary housing accommodation at an affordable cost with secure tenure through private sector initiatives with government encouragement and involvement.

Ibrahim (2012) has identified the numerous challenges facing the housing sector: the lack of political will to unleash a housing revolution; policy inconsistencies; institutional inabilities; undue politicisation; and piecemeal strategies of housing delivery at the expense of mass housing being developed. Others are the lack of ownership/title rights partly attributable to the challenges associated with the implementation of the Land Use Act 1978, other land issues, the non-availability and high cost of construction materials, and so on. In view of the aforementioned challenges, a new National Housing Policy was recently approved by the federal government. This new policy is expected to boost infrastructural development in the sector. Highlights of the policy include the introduction of a mass housing policy, which would enable Nigerians, irrespective of their financial and social status, to have their own houses (Ikuomola, 2012). The government will make funds available for people in the informal sector. Over and above this, the policy hopes to drive employment and income generation in the country.

Lagos state is located in South-Western Nigeria on a narrow coastal flood plain. Administratively, Lagos State is divided into 20 LGAs; the metropolis comprises both the islands (Lagos Island, Victoria Island and Ikoyi Island) and the mainland. Lagos is the economic hub of Nigeria and is well connected by all known modes of transportation. Lagos port is Nigeria's leading port and one of the largest and busiest in Africa. Until 1991, Lagos served as the federal capital of the country. Abuja is now the country's administrative and political capital but Lagos is still Nigeria's industrial, commercial and financial centre and therefore attracts a good number of in-migrant and immigrant settlers. The ethnic configuration is diverse, with Yorubas constituting 65%, Hausa 15%, Igbo 15% and others 5% (Lagos State Government, 2004; Nwanna, 2011).

Lagos epitomises the phenomenal growth that many African cities have experienced. In 1950, its population was 230,256, while in the 2006 census, it stood at over 9.0 million inhabitants (FGP, 2007). Moreover, a parallel census conducted by the state produced a higher figure of 17.6 million people (Obia, 2007; Nwanna, 2011). Lagos is the only African city, other than Cairo, said to be one of the world's mega-cities. This massive population growth in metropolitan Lagos has raised the demand for housing. However, the provision of urban infrastructure and housing to meet this demand has remained low, resulting in an acute shortage of housing for the teeming population of the state (Oshodi, 2012). Abosede (2006) stated that the Master Plan for Metropolitan Lagos (1980–2000), which was sponsored by the United Nations Development Programme (UNDP), accurately analysed the housing needs of Lagos and recommended that between 1980 and 2000, 1.4 million additional housing units should be constructed, out of which 1 million should be deliberately earmarked for low-income households. However, by the year 2000 when the plan expired, no more than 10% of this housing was built. Abosede (2006) also reported that it was not only in Lagos, but also in many other Nigerian towns and cities, that the housing problem was quite acute, due simply to government inertia and anomalies in the National Housing Policy and finance.

According to more recent reports, the stock of habitable housing in Lagos is 1.25 million units. With a population conservatively put at 15 million people, Lagos alone needs 926,562 units, and the city, in effect, suffers a 10% housing deficit (Alitheia Capital REInsight, 2012). Oshodi (2012) maintains that the absence of sustainable access to quality and affordable housing has compelled the urban poor, who constitute about 91% of the state's population, to take the initiative in providing their own housing. These self-help efforts contravene zoning and subdivision regulations. The major outcome of the contravention is slum proliferation, which has increased from 45 in 1985 to more than 100 in 2010, and control has remained a demanding challenge to urban planners and policymakers. Indeed, Nigeria has one of the highest slum proliferation rates among African nations: Lagos has a slum growth rate of more than 2.5% of the Nigerian average population growth rate. Alitheia Capital REInsight (2012) reported in a study of the housing conditions in Nigeria that over 70% of houses in urban areas were developed by informal/individual efforts.

Abosede (2006) noted that the high incidence of slum growth in Metropolitan Lagos culminated in the creation of the Urban Renewal Division in the then Ministry of Economic Planning and Land Matters in 1985, which later metamorphosed into the Lagos State Urban Renewal Board in 1991. The Board was restructured and renamed the Lagos State Urban Renewal Authority (LASURA) in 2005. Various strategies aimed at providing housing were adopted by the government, but these only yielded less than 1,000 units per annum, when 500,000 units were required annually over a 10-year period to bridge the deficit. Kadiri (2012) has reported that Lagos's state government has recently adopted a hybrid strategy as part of its pragmatic approach to developing housing in the state.

The real estate sector in Nigeria has become the ultimate destination for most investors (Sanyaolu and Sanyaolu, 2010). With the untamed increase in population, the heightened economic activity in the country and the concomitant demand for space for both residential and official use, the sector has taken a prime position for those with resources and seeking worthwhile avenues in which to invest. In late 2007, alongside the surge in equity markets, property prices in Lagos escalated by between 50% and 60% (Kantai, 2009). Bullish from the incredible returns on share prices, Lagos' nouveau riche invested in real estate. In addition, banks flush with cash following a wave of consolidations also began investing in property, further pushing up prices. The nexus between the banking sector, real estate and the capital markets was further reinforced with the securitisation of real estate, which enabled big stock exchange operators to buy property without having their dividends taxed. This has made housing virtually unaffordable for most of Lagos' 9 million residents. Still, many are bullish about the future. Savvy developers are already casting an eye on some of the new growth areas – the last of the undeveloped spots in the Lekki peninsula along the coast from Victoria Island, or the expressway from Lagos to Ibadan.

The emergence of private estate developers, building initially more for the elite, in the early parts of the new millennium expanded the frontiers of the real estate industry and paved the way for huge funding and multinational interest in the real estate development market. This was encouraged by the instant success of primary developments like Lekki Phase One and the Victoria Garden City (VGC) development, also in Lekki, Lagos. Today, this emergence of private real estate developers and their huge resources, which they have put into shopping malls, residential apartments, multipurpose office spaces and even multi-storey car parks, underscores its current assessment by analysts as the most profitable investment vehicle and a goldmine of a sort. House prices, driven up by expatriate demand, the oil boom and Nigerians returning from the diaspora have soared and made Lagos one of the most expensive cities in Africa. For example, a three-bedroom house in Lagos with three to four bathrooms would sell for £163,396.69 compared to £142,194.19 in Johannesburg, South Africa, £77,149.58 in Casablanca, Morocco, or £61,076.75 in Accra, Ghana. The real estate business is very viable despite an economic depression. This fact makes any dilapidated house attractive to real estate developers and affluent members of society, who will want to purchase and renovate the house into a condominium. The activities of property speculators have increased, as have criminalities regarding land transactions – particularly the nefarious activities of landowners popularly known as '*omo onile*', who sell and resell already-sold properties to unsuspecting buyers.

Analysts believe that the key constraints in the industry are more centred on unfavourable government policies (Sanyaolu and Sanyaolu, 2010). However, for the ordinary individual, nothing could be worse than an encounter with an '*omo onile*'. From analysis, it can easily be inferred that the well-known inscription 'Not for sale – beware of 419' that appears on buildings and landed properties (see Figure 16.1) is a result of the activities of these miscreants. The number 419 originally represented a section of the Nigerian criminal code that prescribed punishment for any person obtaining property by false pretence. It was made popular by the

Figure 16.1: Beware of 419

Nigerian police who were saddled with the responsibility of investigating this class of crime (Sanyaolu and Sanyaolu, 2010). The investigating officers usually recited this section when taking statements from plaintiffs and the accused. Lagos being a place where people are used to lining their words with slang, the policemen would probably have used 419 to describe the offence for which suspects were being held. It is not hard to imagine a police officer asking his colleague, 'Why is this man here?' and the other responding, '*na 419*' (meaning that he was there for a section 419 offence). The number, now tagged the 419 scam, soon became an alternative for advance-fee fraud and the tricksters. Every country has a similar section in their criminal codes but the massive proliferation of such confidence tricks in Nigeria since the 1980s has internationalised this particular section of the Nigerian criminal code (Sanyaolu and Sanyaolu, 2010). The real estate sector in Nigeria remains a realm to tread in with serious caution, with minimal policy protection and weaker than weak institutions in the judiciary and the police.

Slum clearance in Nigeria

Slums in Nigeria are areas of authorised housing that are 'underserviced, overcrowded and dilapidated', for example, Ilaje and Ijora Badia. Slums are run-down or dilapidated houses that were once in excellent condition but, due to old age or lack of maintenance, have deteriorated. According to Marris (1981), the definition of a slum is contextual and depends on the individual defining it. Similarly, the response to slums is situational. Housing is usually condemned as a slum when in the eyes of those who make policy, its appearance and use contradict the requirements of society. UN-Habitat (2010) defines a slum household as that which consists of one or a group of individuals living under the same roof in an urban area lacking one or more of the following five amenities: durable housing, sufficient living space, access to improved water, sanitation facilities and secure tenure. Slums exist and can be legally built in established areas. Inhabitants can have tenural rights over the land. When dealing with these slum dwellers, governments are forced to recognise their rights and usually compensate the owners in case of acquisition. By way of contrast, squatter settlements are informal, unauthorised, residential settlements consisting of makeshift dwellings that are generally (but not always) located on the periphery of cities.

UN-Habitat (1981) defines squatter settlements as aggregates of houses built on land not belonging to house builders, but invaded by them, sometimes in individual household groups, sometimes in collective action. Such possession with respect to land held without title indicates the use of the term 'squatter'. They can be found on swampy areas, areas prone to flooding and other wastelands, marginal land parcels like railway setbacks or 'undesirable' marshy land. These can be the result of an organised invasion or a gradual occupation. A good example of a squatter settlement in Lagos State was Makoko in the Lagos Mainland LGA. Houses were made from available cheap materials, such as bamboo, packing cases, metal cans, plywood and cardboard. There were no minimum sanitation practices, to say nothing of controlled construction or essential service provision.

'Slum clearance', 'urban renewal', 'urban redevelopment' and 'urban regeneration' are common terms used in Nigeria. Slum clearance refers to the clearing of old decrepit buildings to allow the land to be put to a better and more productive use. It is also frequently referred to as 'urban renewal'. Urban renewal is the rehabilitation of city areas by renovating or replacing dilapidated buildings with new housing, public buildings, parks, roadways, industrial areas and so on, often in accordance with comprehensive plans. It is also a programme of land redevelopment in areas of moderate- to high-density urban land use. Its modern incarnation began in the late 19th century in developed nations and experienced an intense phase in the late 1940s – under the rubric of reconstruction. The earliest emphasis was placed on slum clearance or 'redevelopment', which was followed by a focused effort to conserve threatened but not-yet-deteriorated neighbourhoods. In many cases, this strategy leads to gentrification and a revival in the fortunes of a decaying area. Osuide (2004) describes urban regeneration in Nigeria as a deliberate effort to change the urban environment through planned large-scale adjustment of existing city areas to create future requirements for urban living and working. Kayes (1973, discussed by Dimuna and Omatsone, 2010) argues that: 'unlike the slum clearance formula that replaces each demolished structure with nine new low-cost units, there is no necessary link in the redevelopment programme between the torn down units and the units that go up in their place' (Dimuna and Omatsone, 2010, p 143).

Slum clearance is not of recent origin in Nigeria; it dates back to 1920 when there was a demolition by the Lagos Executive Development Board (LEDB) in response to the outbreak of bubonic plague. This was followed by the pre-independence demolition that resulted in the celebrated Isale-Eko clearance to give the visiting Queen of England a pleasing view of the area. The pre-independence and immediate post-independence clearances in Nigeria were marked by a series of evictions between 1973 and 1995. Urban renewal was launched in 1949 (Dimuna and Omatsone, 2010). It emerged out of the public housing slum clearance movement and became known as urban redevelopment, as expressed in the 1949 Act. The Act was aimed at providing better housing through the spot removal of residential slums. The initial programme was bitterly criticised. Dimuna and Omatsone (2010) revealed that the deficiencies of the initial programmes led to the revision of the 1949 Act in 1954. The amended 1954 Act transformed the programme from one aimed at bulldozing residential slums to one concerned with conserving and rehabilitating the existing stock within the broad framework of the workable programme. An innovation in the Housing Act 1954 placed responsibility upon local agencies to develop an action plan for renewal – an overall community programme for the removal of slums and blight. In many cases in Nigeria, slum clearance, urban regeneration, urban renewal and/or urban redevelopment has led to gentrification.

Slum gentrification: the case of Maroko

In 1990, a large-scale eviction took place in Maroko, which was demolished and handed over to the rich as a new condominium development (the Oniru Private Housing Estate) well beyond the reach of the urban poor (Agbola and Jinadu, 1997). Before its demolition, Maroko was a sprawling settlement on the outskirts of Lagos (see Figure 16.2). It was a densely populated slum of about 11,425 hectares (Nwanna, 2012), located adjacent to Victoria Island, the main business and financial area of Lagos, and Ikoyi, an upscale residential area and the former governmental centre of Nigeria (Morka and Goldsmith, 2008; Nwanna, 2012). It was controlled by a traditional leader, Chief Murtallab Folami, the Baale of Oroke. The Oniru and the Elegushi families were said to be the landowners, from whom people bought land. The majority of Maroko's residents were low-income earners working in unskilled, low-wage and often informal sector jobs and trades. It had an estimated population of about 300,000 socially heterogeneous inhabitants (Amnesty International, 2006). Though largely poor, it was a fully functioning slum with a middle-class sector, businesses, schools, churches, mosques, a police station and an active and organised civil society.

Figure 16.2: Maroko slum

The majority of the residents were young and middle-aged, mostly in the age group 30–49, and polygynous with large families. The housing stock was of spontaneous nature (makeshift plank buildings) and was easily flooded during the rainy seasons. There were some brick buildings as well, mostly owned by wealthy landlords, many of whom did not necessarily reside in Maroko (Kehinde, 2003). The residents of Maroko had no access to piped water, electricity or a proper drainage system and sewage disposal. Bucket toilets were used.

Maroko's location within the heart of Victoria Island, a wealthy residential and commercial area of Lagos, made it attractive for property development. It was demolished in phases: first, during Governor Jakande's (1979–85) era to transform the slums into civilised cities and towns while dual development was to be stopped so that the ugly juxtaposition of 'heaven' in Victoria Island and 'hell' in Maroko would be erased. The second demolition was in 1985 by the Buhari–Idiagbon government. The third demolition took place on Saturday, 14 July 1990 by Governor Rasaki (Kehinde, 2003). The major reason offered for this demolition was that Maroko was occupying an area below sea level and was dangerous for human habitation, and that the people had to be removed so that the government could sand-fill the land and improve its infrastructure. Morka and Goldsmith (2008) reported that the demolition continued for 12 days, by the end of which the entire area of Maroko, extending five miles east of Victoria Island, was completely destroyed. About 15,000 houses, shops, schools, churches and other buildings, including approximately 10,000 residential structures, were destroyed. The only building that remained standing was the Maroko police station. Some 300,000 Maroko residents were rendered homeless. The demolition was said to be characterised by violence, chaos, theft, rape and death.

The issue over which family was the genuine owner of Maroko had been a tussle between the Oniru and the Elegushi Chieftancy Families of Lagos since 1965. The Oniru Chieftancy Family was able to prove that the Maroko land belonged to them. A portion of the land was conceded to them, duly derequisitioned and published in the Official State Gazette in 1977. The state government paid a total of N6.8 million (£28,333) as compensation to the Oniru Chieftaincy Family for both the land and the structures thereon. What was left to the Oniru family was 732 hectares out of about 11,425 hectares. Some of the land was sold while 200 plots were given to Oniru family members. Condominiums were then built on this area, now known as the Oniru Private Housing Estate. The entire estate is under the administration of His Royal Majesty, Oba (Dr) Idowu Abiodun Oniru (Aki Ogun the 2nd). The Oba manages the affairs of the people in the estate, ensuring social order.

Gentrification is a highly visible expression of wider social and economic change. There are obvious differences in the socio-economic profiles of the old Maroko 'slum' and the new Oniru Private Housing Estate (see Figure 16.3). The new estate is low-density and, as yet, 'there is no estimate of the population of the people living here because there has been no effort yet to conduct a census of people living in the estate yet as development is still going on' (interview with official in the Oba's palace, quoted in Nwanna, 2012, p 170).

The majority of the residents were observed to be young and middle-aged and the predominant type of family in the estate was the nuclear family with between two and four children (Nwanna, 2012). This was contrary to the polygynous and large families of old Maroko. There was also hardly any class distinction among them in terms of property and family settings. The majority of the residents are highly educated with a postgraduate education (mostly masters and PhDs); they

Figure 16.3: Oniru Private Housing Estate 2013

are professionals with a high disposable income. Unlike the semi-skilled, unskilled and petty traders of Maroko, the Oniru Private Housing Estate occupants are mostly business executives, senior bureaucrats and a range of well-paid workers in financial and oil services, advertising and the media. Their workplaces are situated in neighbouring areas on the island and its environs. They have long or irregular hours of work and therefore desire to live close to work and the cultural and entertainment facilities offered by these areas. Access to the city and key facilities is vital for these groups to maintain their positions in a dynamic and insecure economic environment. A central location and apartment living reduces the time lost in the traditional suburban pursuits of commuting and house maintenance.

Like in other gentrified cities of the world, the feminisation of the professional workforce and the formation of dual-career families were also observed. There was a high proportion of women in professional and technical occupations and many women chose to continue their careers once they became mothers. Location in the area to avoid travelling long distances and consequently saving time was important.

In contrast to Maroko, the estate was totally residential and well-planned. The land and buildings in the Oniru Private Housing Estate are very expensive. A plot of land of about 1,500 square metres costs about N180 million (£75,000 as of 2013). There are three categories of houses: terraced houses, fully detached houses and semi-detached houses. House prices in the area range from a three-bedroom flat at £33,333–37,500 (excluding the service charges of N1.5million or £6,250 per annum), this is far beyond the reach of the original occupants. Within the estate, there is another mini-estate where a room alone costs about N800,000 or £3,333 per annum. The Oba built this for members of his extended family. There have been significant local reductions in the neighbourhood's property crime rate, as one resident said: 'there are no miscreants' (Nwanna, 2012, p 171).

At the entrance to the estate, the famous Shoprite Shopping Mall was built to serve the population of the estate and others in its environs. Unlike in Maroko, the area is now served with electricity, good roads, drainage, waste and sewage disposal systems, and other social amenities within the home. However, despite the regeneration of the Maroko area, one problem remains for the residents of the Oniru Private Hosing Estate – the issue of water. There is no water because the estate is built on a freak topographical feature. According to one of the residents: 'we have spent close to N10 million *(£41,667)* trying to find a lasting solution to the issue of water but all have failed instead' (quoted in Nwanna, 2012, p 171). They have resorted to buying in water at a cost of N7,000 (£29.17) per tanker every week.

The gentrification of the 1004 Estate

There have been other examples of gentrification in Lagos too, ones that are not related to slum clearance. The 1004 Estate is the single largest luxury high-rise estate in sub-Saharan Africa and comprises over 1004 flats, maisonettes and studio apartments in the Victoria Island district of Lagos (see Figure 16.4). The estate was a government-owned housing scheme that was originally opened in 1979 as a high-amenity and upscale estate for the accommodation of senators and members of the House of Representatives. It was subsequently occupied by senior federal civil servants. The residents were made up of members of the armed forces (40%) and civil servants working for various federal ministries, agencies and parastatals in Lagos. The estate was in good condition before but, due to neglect and lack of maintenance, became deteriorated and dilapidated; in addition, the federal government claimed that most of the residents were illegal occupants (Aborisade, 2011). Furthermore, the 2004 monetisation policy privatised government-owned housing stock. The booming real estate industry in Nigeria, particularly in Lagos, was a factor contributing to the desire to sell off the estate to investors other than the occupants. The chairman of the 1004 Estate Association reported that the government never gave the residents the first option in the sale of the property: 'The Government had reneged on its promise that the sitting tenants would be given the first option in the sale of the property' (quoted in Aborisade, 2011).

The residents resisted the attempt by the government to sell the estate and went to court to challenge their proposed eviction (Aborisade, 2011). They also sent separate petitions to the House of Representatives Committee on Petitions and the Senate Committee on Housing and Urban Development. The estate was acquired from the federal government by a consortium led by UACN Property Development Company Plc and Union Homes Saving and Loans Plc. The former residents were directed by the government to vacate the estate before 15 May 2005 and then, at 4.30am on 9 December 2005, armed policemen violently evicted all the tenants despite a court injunction. In 2007, it was bought by 1004 Estates Limited (a private limited liability company established by a group of investors in 2004) for N7 billion (£29,167), representing the single largest property transaction

Figure 16.4: The 1004 Estate

in 2007. Actual renovation, however, started in 2006 due to the sales completion period taking nearly 24 months, though work on the redevelopment was stalled following the closure of the site by government agents due to the numerous litigations against the acquisition. The company commenced refurbishment of the estate in 2008, which involved extensively remodelling the exterior facade to a modern finish, increasing the apartment sizes and replacing all the internal mechanical/electrical fittings and internal partitions. All the external services equipment for power, water and sewage was also extensively redesigned and constructed to meet the changing needs of the housing market.

The newly gentrified 1004 Estate comprises over 1,000 flats arranged in four clusters. It has six high-rise buildings and 33 low-rise buildings. Each flat is fully serviced with a fitted kitchen, pre-paid meter (electromechanical smart meters in which consumers pay prior to actual consumption), air-conditioning, washer/dryer machines, water heaters and microwave ovens. Each of the high-rise buildings has had two brand new elevators installed. The estate also has a dedicated sewage treatment plant and a power plant. 1004 Estates Limited opened sales in mid-2009 with the pre-sale of 600 apartments, with Zenith Bank and United Bank of Africa (UBA)-funded mortgages. The estate has now attained 95% occupancy due to its excellent location in the heart of Victoria Island's business and recreational district, coupled with its power/recreational facilities and its secure environment. Its large landscaped garden provides a safe backdrop for jogging and walking. Four swimming pools and tennis courts provide a vibrant sporting lifestyle for residents. To facilitate communication, one of the communication outfits is partnering with the 1004 Estate to provide information and communications infrastructure within the complex.

Kantai (2009) reported that the newly improved 1004 Estate units were advertised as one of the hottest properties on Victoria Island and ideal for visiting Nigerians from the diaspora on short-term stays or Lagosian yuppies with young families. Individual units are selling at between N25 million (£104,167) and N45 million (£187,500). This indicates that no civil servant can afford to rent a flat in this estate. People who can afford to live in the estate are those who talk, purchase and pay in US dollars even though they are living in Lagos. Besides these, the other people who can afford the flats are those working in the oil industry.

Conclusion

In summary, in Lagos, both slum gentrification (Maroko) and neighbourhood renewal/upgrading (1004 Estate) have seen the forcible eviction of residents and redevelopment into properties well beyond the reach of the former residents. The redevelopment of Maroko into the Oniru Private Housing Estate, I argue, can be described as contemporary gentrification. It is characterised by reinvestment of capital, social upgrading of locale by incoming high-income groups, landscape change and direct displacement of low-income groups, as argued by Davidson and Lees (2005). I would argue that the process in the 1004 Estate is a more classical form of gentrification: the disinvested and derelict old government quarter was renovated; wealthier residents displaced less wealthy ones (Glass, 1964; Kilmartin, 2003; Lees et al, 2008); the neighbourhood character changed; and property values increased. However, in both cases, the gentrification processes were state-led and attained profit maximisation as the areas were located on prime development land.

I have argued elsewhere (Nwanna, 2012) that gentrification has brought benefits to these communities: it has increased their status and wealth and improved social problems, reducing crime and so on. It has beautified the environment and slowed suburban sprawl and environmental degradation. However, the negatives associated with gentrification in Lagos have massively outweighed the positives. The negatives have been especially visceral. They include physical and psychological trauma, the dislocation of families, the loss of sources of livelihood and the disruption of children's education (Morka and Goldsmith, 2008). The displaced residents should be adequately relocated, compensated and have their human rights protected.

References

Aborisade, S. (2011) '1004 Estate: residents vow to resist forceful ejection', *The Punch News*.

Abosede, F. (2006) 'Housing in Lagos mega city – improving liveability, inclusion and governance', paper presented at the International Conference on Building Nigeria's Capacity to Implement Economic, Social and Cultural Rights: Lessons Learned, Challenges and the Way Forward held at Abuja, 27–28 September.

Agbola, T. and Jinadu, A.M. (1997) 'Forced eviction and forced relocation in Nigeria: the experience of those evicted from Maroko in 1990', *Environment and Urbanization*, vol 9, no 2, pp 271–88.

Alitheia Capital REInsight (2012) 'Housing – creating the right environment: lessons from other economies in tackling the housing crisis', *Alitheia Capital*, vol 24.

Amnesty International (2006) 'Nigeria: making the destitute homeless – forced eviction in Makoko, Lagos State', AI Index AFR 44/001/2006, 24 January. Available at: http://www.amnesty.org/library/Index/ENGAFR440012006?open&of=ENG-NGA

Aribigbola, A. (2008) 'Housing policy formulation in developing countries: evidence of programme implementation from Akure, Ondo State, Nigeria', *Journal of Human Ecology*, vol 23, no 2, pp 125–34.

Atere, T.S. (2001) 'Urban slums increase in Lagos', *Daily Independent*, 8 October, p 40.

Davidson, M. and Lees, L. (2005) 'New-build "gentrification" and London's riverside renaissance', *Environment and Planning A*, vol 37, pp 1165–90.

Dimuna, K.O. and Omatsone, M.E.O. (2010) 'Regeneration in the Nigerian urban built environment', *Journal of Human Ecology*, vol 29, no 2, pp 141–9.

FGP (Federal Government Printer) (2007) 'Legal notice on publication of the details of the breakdown of the national and state provisional totals 2006 census', *Federal Republic of Nigeria Official Gazette*, vol 94, no 24 (15 May), pp B175–98.

Glass, R. (1964) *London: aspects of change*, London: MacGibbon and Kee.

Hamnett, C. (1984) 'Gentrification and residential location theory: a review and assessment', in D. Herbert and R.J. Johnston (eds) *Geography and the urban environment: progress in research and applications* (vol 6), London: Wiley, pp 283–319.

Ibrahim, L. (2012) 'Nigeria short of 17m housing units, faces crisis in 2020', *Compass*, 13 November.

Ikuomola, V. (2012) 'Fed govt approves new housing policy', *The Nation*, 21 June.

Kadiri, F.A. (2012) 'Lagos state adopts hybrid strategy for housing development', *Blueprint*, 27 March.

Kantai, P. (2009) 'Real estate: Lagos becomes one of the most expensive cities in Africa', *Financial Times*, 20 July. Available at: http://www.ft.com/cms/s/0/363287f4-7502-11de-9ed5-00144feabdc0.html#ixzz23SGff8Gy

Kayes, L.C. (1973) *The rehabilitation planning game: a study in the diversity of neighbourhood*, Cambridge, MA: M.I.T. Press.

Kehinde, S.O. (2003) *Maroko: the agonies of displacement*, Lagos: Rebonik Publications Limited.

Kilmartin, C. (2003) *Port Phillip: change and gentrification*, Victoria: Urban and Regional Research DSE.

Lagos State Government (2004) *History of Lagos*, Lagos: Lagos State Government.

Lees, L., Slater, T. and Wyly, E.K. (2008) *Gentrification*, New York, NY: Routledge/Taylor & Francis Group.

Marris, P. (1981) 'The meaning of slums and patterns of change', in UN-Habitat (ed) *The residential circumstances of the urban poor in developing countries*, New York, NY: Praeger.

Morka, F.C. and Goldsmith, P.H. (2008) 'Communication: Social and Economic Rights Action Center v. Nigeria', a report submitted by the Social and Economic Rights Action Center (SERAC) on behalf of the former residents of the Maroko district, 3 December.

Nwanna, C.R. (2011) *Socio-economic status and HIV-related discrimination in Lagos, Nigeria*, Germany: LAP Lambert Academic Publishing GmbH & Co. KG.

Nwanna, C.R. (2012) 'Gentrification in Lagos State: challenges and prospects', *British Journal of Arts and Social Sciences*, vol 5, no 2, pp 163–76.

Obia, V. (2007) 'Census: an unusual survey', *Sunday Independent*, 11 February, p B8.

Okewole, I.A. and Aribigbola, A. (2006) 'Innovations and sustainability in housing policy conception and implementation in Nigeria', in I.A. Okewole, A. Ajayi, A. Daramola, K. Odusanmi and O. Ogunba (eds) *The built environment: innovation policy and sustainable development*, Ota, Ogun State, Nigeria: Covenant University, pp 414–20.

Oshodi, L. (2012) 'Formulating a social housing policy in Lagos state – the participatory approach', *International Development and Urban Governance*, 27 April.

Osuide, S.O. (2004) *Strategies for affordable housing stock delivery in Nigeria*, 18th Inaugural Lecture of Ambrose Alli University, Ekpoma, Benin City: Floreat Systems, p 15.

Sanyaolu, T. and Sanyaolu, K. (2010) 'Not for sale – anatomy of a real estate cliché', *Minority report, International Corporate Research*, no 1, March.

Smith, N. (1996) *The new urban frontier: gentrification and the revanchist city*, London: Routledge.

UN-Habitat (1981) *The residential circumstances of the urban poor in developing countries*, New York, NY: Praeger.

UN-Habitat (2010) *State of the world's cities: 2010/2011 – bridging the urban divide*, New York, NY: Routledge.

SEVENTEEN

Gentrification in China?

Julie Ren

Introduction

Urban China is experiencing tremendous change, inspiring an intensification of academic attention. While there is an emerging body of literature on gentrification in China (eg He, 2007, 2009; Song and Zhu, 2010), there is concurrently a wave of urban researchers critiquing the nature of 'parochially derived' urban concepts (Robinson, 2011, p 19). Similar to other researchers interested in theorising urban China (eg Fainstein and Logan, 2008), I have also struggled with the selection of urban concepts and theoretical framings to help interpret its various urban transformations. Like with 'gentrification', many urban concepts that might ease this task originate from empirical works done mostly in North America and Western Europe. In light of this reflection, this chapter questions the tendency to 'stretch' existing concepts such as gentrification in order to interpret urban change processes across a variety of cases and sites.

This chapter is framed by a twofold doubt. First, given the growing body of research on urban China, I examine whether gentrification is an accurate or relevant means to describe the changes it is undergoing. Reviewing some existing research provides certain insights into reasons for this interpretive choice. Studying gentrification in China produces an understanding of China as part of a global neoliberal system of urban development, but focusing on gentrification is also limited in its ability to account for major structural transformations in class structures and housing, as well as basic problems of urban governance, tax structures, land use, citizenship/property rights and housing shortages, which all play a part in displacement. While there is not enough space to go through these in detail, a brief overview will help to show the descriptive limits of the gentrification lens;[1] the example of *hutongs* in Beijing will serve to illustrate the complexity that such interpretive determinism might efface.

Second, I am concerned about the embedded normative question: '*Should* urban change in Beijing be interpreted in terms of gentrification?' There are perhaps some imperatives that help to answer this question. Of increasing urgency, there is a normative obligation to deal with the rapidly growing urban inequality in urban China. Many have argued that the strength of gentrification lies in its critical analysis of class inequality (eg Lees, 2007; He, 2009). Yet, this argument also brings with it assumed notions of urban inequality and social justice that allude to a context in which mobility and privilege function in tandem. While there is a need to critically engage with issues of inequality in China, a brief discussion of some of the factors of marginalisation and polarisation will highlight the limits of relying on prevalent urban concepts like gentrification. In addition, there is an academic imperative to address the sites of theory (eg Parnell, 2012; Robinson, 2011). Where is the space for theory-building when urban researchers in under-researched sites are compelled to limit their work to validating, expanding, reinforcing or otherwise responding to prevailing canons of urban thought?

The final thoughts will weigh the potential for a strategic instrumentalisation of gentrification in the context of urban China against the potential for developing 'urban theory on a world scale' (Robinson, 2011, p 19). While the former may help to directly address decisions about spatial developments and reap concrete results, the latter has far-reaching implications for getting urban China research out of the 'urban shadow' (McFarlane, 2008, p 341). Perhaps it is a false binary construction, but this pointed deliberation nevertheless underscores what is at stake when asking about gentrification in China.

Interpreting gentrification in China

> Perhaps unsurprisingly, if you go looking for gentrification you tend to find it, but if your concerns are different you may find less evidence of it. (Butler, 2007, p 164)

So, why are researchers 'looking for gentrification' in China? One rationale for studying gentrification in China might stem from the academic pressure to situate Chinese cities as part of a global neoliberal system of urban development.[2] Atkinson and Bridge (2005, p 1, emphasis added), in their developmentalist view, assert that 'gentrification is *now* global. It is no longer confined to Western cities', implying along the way that Shanghai has now caught up to London. Given the transformation of the Chinese economy, and following Harvey (1985) and Fraser (2003, 2011) on the mobility of capital in shaping urban spaces, such reasoning is not surprising. It can be sketched out as a transitive relationship: since gentrification is understood as a neoliberal urban process and neoliberalism is understood to be a global system, gentrification must also be occurring globally. Gentrification experts argue that the strength and interest in gentrification stems from the fact that gentrification remains at the leading edge of neoliberal urbanism and is intertwined with processes of globalisation (Lees et al, 2008, p xvii). Moreover, 'just as capital and culture have become quintessentially global, class and politics are also global. Gentrification, as a class conquest of the city, is one of the touchstones of that recognition today and its globalisation requires a global response' (Smith, 2008, p 25).

Indeed, interest in gentrification research maintains its strength through its explicit focus on displacement, and has also influenced academic research on urban China. While gentrification research in China remains relatively sparse, many scholars have insisted on its application and relevance to the interpretation of displacement in urban China. State-led gentrification, for instance, has been systematically analysed in its various phases, by adapting a New York City-based stage model of gentrification (He, 2007; He and Liu, 2010; cf Clay, 1979; Berry, 1985). He and Liu (2010) describe it in three phases: first, the state stimulates and accommodates the consumption demands of the middle class through land and housing reform; second, the state makes policy interventions and invests in environment and infrastructure to optimise conditions for capital circulation; and, third, the state mobilises land and resettlement housing resources to address fragmented property rights and facilitate gentrification. Ultimately, they argue that this leads to growth and urban development, resulting in large-scale residential displacement. Further differentiating the role of the Chinese state in gentrification, Iossifova (2009) has analysed the macro-level of state-sponsored gentrification and the micro-level involving low levels of government in compliance with higher levels of state action.

Focusing on the role of the state as a driver of gentrification is one method that researchers have used to account for the contextual drivers and sources of influence. Others have looked at China in its historical context, 'cautiously examining' the underlying explanations for gentrification, and arguing that the 'post-reform restructuring of urban space in China has to take into account the legacy of socialist construction and, as a consequence, should not necessarily view the marketization of housing consumption as the sole determinant in the process' (Tang and Wong, 2007, p 211). Therefore, even if spatial differentiation outcomes seem to fit well with socio-spatial restructuring patterns in post-socialist contexts such as China, there may be different mechanisms at play.

Still others focus on the social and moral aspects of gentrification arising from issues of inequality in urban China. Some call for an increased attention to the social impacts of gentrification, and not just to physical renewal (Song and Zhu, 2010). Gentrification is further stretched in its meanings, as Pan (2011, p 156) newly defines it for a study in Shanghai: 'in this chapter, gentrification refers to a cultural and moral process of urban change brought forth by socialist engineering and community development during the reform era (1978–present)'. Gentrification is not only found when looked for, as Butler (2007) claimed, but can be constructed, encompassing various forms and symbolic meanings.

This broad range of work stretching the concept of gentrification into China also references a diversity of structural changes, which perhaps warrant alternative theorisations of urban change. For instance, these gentrification researchers recognise that there is displacement tied to property development in China. Yet, they also point to structural shifts that are simultaneously transforming the urban sphere in ways unlike those experienced in the cities studied by the pre-eminent scholars of gentrification. These shifts include the emergence of a massive middle class tied to urbanisation and resulting in tremendous population density in urban centres. Indeed, demographic changes have already been used to question gentrification: 'Are neighbourhoods being gentrified or is it simply that there are more of those people that we now view as gentrifiers? Are people displaced or are there simply fewer people working in blue-collar and manual positions?' (Atkinson, 2003, p 3243). Since the 1978 market reforms, China has lifted 600 million people out of poverty (World Bank, 2013a), creating a mass consumer market that is also transforming its urban space. Using one Organisation for Economic Co-operation and Development (OECD) measure for 'middle class', China's middle class ranks second (to the US) in absolute terms, with 157 million people (Kharas, 2010, p 30); average income has almost tripled in recent years, from USD3,180 in 2003 to USD8,390 in 2011 (World Bank, 2013b).[3] Moreover, the major cities, frequently the focus of academic research, show disproportionately higher income levels (Sicular et al, 2006). Businesses speculating over the new consumer market in the early 2000s were driven by mantras, as postulated by McKinsey and Co, that 'tomorrow's middle-class consumers are today's urban workers', anticipating the growth of an enormous Chinese middle class (Farrell et al, 2006).

Another major shift referenced by urban researchers in China is the transformation of housing. Due to its gradual introduction, housing reform resulted in both gated luxury villa communities and migrant enclaves: 'the housing context in Chinese cities and the dynamics of housing inequality and residential segregation are more complex than those in both market and socialist economies' (Huang, 2004, p 193). Until the end of the 1990s, housing was mostly provided by employers (through work-units called the *danwei*) and local governments (through municipal housing bureaus); their allocation was based on non-monetary factors like job rank, seniority and marital status (Huang, 2004). While the *danwei* system underwent various stages of demolition, redevelopment or commercialisation, government institutions provided housing exclusively for employees in central areas and in former *danwei* compound locations, privileging access to housing for public sector employees (Shin, 2010a). Thus, housing inequality is driven not simply by the displacement of lower-income by higher-income residents, but also from policies privileging access to government workers.

There are also a number of structural barriers exacerbating unequal access to housing. One important determinant of housing inequality is related to the rights afforded by *hukou* status. For instance, migrant enclaves are not solely determined by the prohibitive challenges of finding affordable, alternative housing. Rather, the antiquated *hukou* registration system remains a major barrier for potential renters, since *hukou* status is granted by place of birth, and attaining an urban *hukou* is a prerequisite for public housing and other social services (Huang, 2004, p 194; Wu, 2010). Even the *hukou* reforms under way fail to grant full rights to the 'non-local' resident of the city (Smart and Lin, 2007): 'The spatial manifestation of housing inequality resulting from the *hukou* system is islands of rural villages' (Huang, 2004, p 195). Beyond the *hukou* system, however, Zhou and Logan (2002, p 137) have also argued that post-reform trends (from 1978) in inequality can be traced to existing inequalities in pre-reform periods: 'Since housing was a very scarce resource, its access was highly unequal'. Therefore, structural legal barriers and entrenched systems of gatekeeping serve as cornerstones driving housing issues in urban China. While market-oriented reforms are under way, these processes hardly bring the experience of Shanghai closer to that of London. Rural migrants to Shanghai experience fundamentally different barriers to housing, for instance, than newcomers in London. Unlike the accommodations for government workers in China, public sector workers in London do not receive exclusive access to gated housing communities in the city centre. Indeed, decades-long inequalities driven by government nepotism are not equivalent to inequalities resulting from the inflation of property prices from speculation-driven real estate markets.

So, how is it possible to reconcile class transformation and the transformation of housing with even a general definition of gentrification as 'the transformation of a working-class or vacant area of the central city into middle-class residential or commercial use' (Lees et al, 2008, p xv)? The focus on commodification, commercialisation and the general neoliberalisation of urban China offers some guidance (Wu et al, 2007). The class and demographic shifts that have resulted in an urban housing crunch have put immense pressure on both the state and a newly growing private property development industry to construct higher-density buildings. An additional force pushing land commodification and facilitating private property is the fractured tax system. Lin (2012) has called attention to the simultaneous decentralisation of responsibilities in terms of government expenditures in infrastructure and social services, and the recentralisation of tax revenue. This has created a gap for municipalities faced with budgetary pressures, which is resolved through their land-use policies. Thus, land commodification is a major source of financing for the municipal budget, funding nearly 40% of all urban maintenance and construction costs (Lin, 2012). While the construction engine, land commodification and 1990s' rebuilding policy of the Old and Dilapidated Housing Redevelopment Programme (ODHP) resemble a form of new-build gentrification (see He, 2009; Davidson and Lees, 2010), this confluence of forces in fact reveals that urban China is shaped by a complex state–market relationship that is itself in transition. A better understanding of these forces may provide a theoretical basis for enriching knowledge about the 'spatiality of neoliberal urbanism' (Lin, 2012), perhaps also suggesting alternatives to the gentrification lens.

Whether it is new-build gentrification (He, 2009; Davidson and Lees, 2010) or state-led gentrification (Hackworth and Smith, 2001; He, 2007), the elasticity of gentrification (Clark, 2005) has certainly long been a topic of discussion. Beauregard (1985) argued that gentrification had become an ideology with universalistic tendencies; Lees (1994) has emphasised the context-specific nature of gentrification, pointing to an Atlantic gap in the differences in land and housing markets in London and New York; and Harris (2008) has similarly focused on London and Mumbai, emphasising the need for a more regional theorising with regards to gentrification. Following decades of discussion, however, the term continues to be submitted to conceptual stretching. Perhaps these efforts are a consequence of the descriptive limits of gentrification across different contexts;

an empirical example can help to more clearly define what these limits in urban China might be.

The gentrification of hutongs

To illustrate some of the previous points, I take the example of *hutongs* and apply the 'gentrification lens' to them, looking at the changes that they have been undergoing. A *hutong* is an alleyway connecting single-storey courtyard residencies (*siheyuan*), though the term can refer to both the neighbourhood and the alleyway.[4] Most commonly identified in Beijing, many of these neighbourhoods date back to the Qing Dynasty (1644–1911).

Figure 17.1: Heizhima Hutong, Beijing

Note: Copyright Julie Ren, 2012.

According to the Beijing Urban Planning Society, there were 3,250 *hutongs* in 1949, shrinking to 1,204 by 2004 (Stone, 2008). This was the result of the 1990 ODHP policy, which demolished *hutongs* to make way for the construction of higher-density residential buildings (Zhang, 2008; Shin, 2009a, 2010b). Starting in the early 2000s, cultural preservation policies served to counter these demolitions, designating 25 historic areas that account for 17% of the total area of Beijing's Old City (Shin, 2010b, p 43).

Figure 17.2: Beijing conservation areas within the second ring; compare with the Beijing map on the right

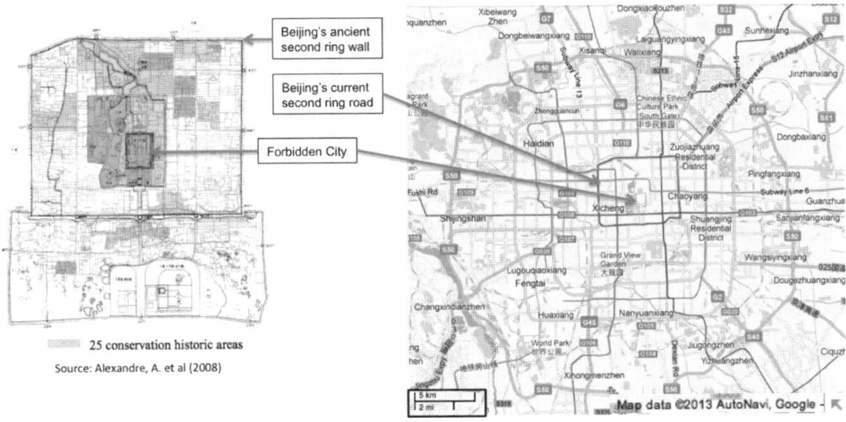

Sources: Alexandre et al (2008) and Google Maps (2013).

The cultural preservation policy affected about 285,000 people, covering 1,038 hectares of land (Alexandre et al, 2008). In advance of the Beijing Olympics in 2008, an uneven urban transformation was undertaken (Shin, 2009b; Shin and Li, 2013), which included a number of renovations to improve basic infrastructure, such as moving electricity underground, improving sewage piping and paving roads, as well as more superficial improvements, such as painting building facades and walls (Alexandre et al, 2008, pp 49–54), leading Shin (2010b) to argue that residents faced inevitable displacement.

A superficial reading of this history has already resulted in novel interpretations of *hutong* gentrification. An aesthetic interpretation might adapt Jager's (1986) analysis of Victorian style (Victoriana) to that of the Qing Dynasty, or seek out recognisable, familiar amenities that have recently been seen in some *hutongs*. In several Beijing *hutongs*, including Nanlougouxiang and Wudaoying, main alleyways have been converted into commercial shopping streets, with cafes, bars, restaurants, street vendors and small stores that signify an aesthetic familiarity, especially for foreigners. As destination areas for entertainment, foreigners residing in these areas are quick to associate the amenities with gentrification. Compare, for instance, these two editorials drafted by different Beijing-based journalists from *The New Yorker* and the *Financial Times*, respectively:

> Within that layout, however, gentrification was inevitable – the *hutong* had become so rare that they now had cachet in the new economy. The change had already begun in my neighborhood. In 2004, bars, cafés, and boutiques started moving into a quiet street that intersects Ju'er, where locals were happy to give up their homes for good prices. (Hessler, 2006)

> Boutique hotels, gentlemen's clubs, cocktail bars and cafés, microbrew pubs, countless restaurants and an alternative music scene have all taken root. This gentrification is not cultural preservation in the purest sense of leaving things untouched but nor is it wholesale demolition and reconstruction. It is building on the framework of the *hutongs* that has existed for centuries, adding one more layer of sediment to their history. (Rabinovitch, 2013)

These descriptions resonate with writings about gentrifiers that overwhelm working-class neighbourhoods with their 'cafes and boutiques' (Zukin, 2010, p 1), or discussions about 'how taste is explicitly or implicitly part of the discourse of gentrification' (Krase, 2005, p 192; see also Zukin, 1998), as well as more extensive writings on commercial gentrification (eg Beauregard, 1986; Kloosterman and Van Der Leun, 1999; Zukin and Kosta, 2004). While commercial gentrification has been tied to residential gentrification (Beauregard, 1986, p 44), it is prudent to remember Tang and Wong's (2007) caution that familiar-looking outcomes may be concealing different underlying mechanisms of change.

Beyond looking at these superficial signifiers, there is a diversity of drivers instigating *hutong* change. First, the main housing problem in the *hutongs* is not a rent-gap issue, but a basic supply–demand problem of providing sufficient housing for all the people. Overcrowding is the major concern for residents living in the *hutongs*, as one resident of Nanlougouxiang explains:

> improving the physical condition of houses is of no use. If the housing space cannot be increased, it's not really improvement.... The best solution would be for the state to take out money, compensate residents for their displacement and reduce the population density. (Quoted in Shin, 2010b, p 51)

Thus, public infrastructural investments undertaken in electricity, sewage, street pavements and general dilapidation failed to address the primary problem. This is further confirmed by the continued preference of residents to move to alternative housing over the option of financial compensation, because it indicates an older and broader problem of insufficient housing in urban China (Huang, 2003). More money will not help them to rent homes that do not exist. This housing insufficiency is what triggered the ODHP and the resulting construction imperatives that pushed 'many inner-city urban areas to construct at higher and higher densities' (Wu, 1999, p vii).

A related driver of change in the *hutongs* is a result of the forms of privatisation whereby the state is leasing to private property developers, allowing for individual ownership and creating opportunities for profit. Residents, who were also private owners, had a number of financial opportunities opened to them. For instance, 'there were residents who made gains by exercising landlordism (seeking rent income) or entrepreneurialism (running businesses themselves)' (Shin, 2010b, p

50). Depending on the location of their homes, they found opportunities for subletting while moving out of the area themselves, or opening new businesses. The area renovation that helped to increase the value of the *hutongs* thus played an important role in the way that some residents benefited (Shin, 2010b, p 51). While this increasing property value was not directly relevant for residents in government-owned *hutongs*, they were interested in renovations that would potentially improve their buildings and neighbourhood infrastructures, as the valuation plays a direct role in the potential future compensation they may receive from the state. Displacement resulting from state development plans in China is compensated according to the land appraisal value (Shin, 2007). While the state may be interested in the potential future gains that they may reap from privatising their properties, this is somewhat mediated by the increasing value of compensation they would owe residents.

The cultural preservation policies previously mentioned were also a driver in the *hutong* renovations. A result of the destruction that the ODHP caused in the 1990s, cultural preservation had multiple functions. In addition to protecting the remaining *hutongs* from demolition, Zhang (2008, pp 195–6, 206) has argued that these policies served to simultaneously placate the growing public outrage about *hutong* demolition while conceding to the construction imperatives by defining and legitimising the remaining demolition areas. The cultural preservation label also turned *hutongs* into entertainment districts, fuelling both domestic and international tourism to *hutong* areas (Zhang, 2008, p 203). The branding of these areas was additionally aided by various state-sponsored awards and designations that promoted *hutongs* as 'commercial districts with characteristics' (Shin, 2010b, p 49). With regards to the cultural preservation driver, there are two important aspects worth mentioning. First, cultural preservation in China has historically often implied the wholesale destruction and reconstruction of a similar form. Thus, 'conservation' implied a commitment to a particular style, but not necessarily to the preservation of existing material structures. In these reconstructions, residents have complained that 'old Beijing' features often disappear (Shin, 2010b, p 52). Second, the state lacks the resources to do these reconstructions, even falling short on the renovations already promised (Zhang, 2008, p 192). Cultural preservation is therefore intrinsically tied to private property developers, as the state depends on these lease agreements to finance the reconstructions and renovations that they are committed to but are themselves unable to afford (Shin, 2010b, p 50).

Even though the *hutong* example is different from the new-build models that imply 'large-scale demolition and displacement' (Shin, 2010b, p 53), it is still a useful illustration of the complex relationships between drivers and consequences that a gentrification lens fails to incorporate. It points to familiar drivers of urban change, such as housing shortages, real estate privatisation/valorisation and the cultural preservation of neighbourhoods. The consequences of these various drivers, however, are intertwined in pivotal relationships with the state and its mixed bag of facilities and limits. While it is possible to focus on the exceptional characteristics of the Chinese state, this serves only to reduce the experience of urban China to a case study. Yet, there are questions being raised by the empirical work in urban China that breach the national and regional frames. What does it mean when privatisation is never total, but on a temporal lease basis? What is the impact of this co-dependent relationship between the state and private developers on land value, urban growth and social inequality? How does middle-class consumerism shape the urban space? Like Lin (2012), I wonder how this empirical work can help to build more inclusive theories on the 'spatiality of neoliberal urbanism'.

Should we interpret urban change in China in terms of gentrification?

Like Butler (2007) has posited, if we look for gentrification, we will probably find it; but *should* we look for it? This is the kind of question that this edited collection set out to ask, and the growing body of research on urban China makes this a question worth reflecting on. Even if there are limits to the applicability of gentrification in its current forms, there are many reasons to conceptually stretch gentrification and to explore if, and how, gentrification has travelled from the Global North to the Global South (Lees, 2012). Unlike Atkinson and Bridge (2005), Lees does not assume a trajectory for the concept of gentrification from the 'Global North' to the 'Global South' (see also Lees, 2006, 2014); she sees such a trajectory to be as yet unproven. Nevertheless, Lees (2007, p 232) argues:

> it is crucial that we do not stick to outdated historical representations of gentrification and gentrifiers, but it is also crucial that we stick to the term 'gentrification' and use its political purchase to contest and resist the most onerous aspects of this often unjust and morphing process.

Similarly, He (2009, p 359) contends that 'the critical aspects of gentrification are indispensible and valuable', especially in its analysis of class inequality and the impacts on 'indigenous', 'local communities'. These voices thus insist on the importance not to discredit the strategic value attached to the term 'gentrification'.

Given the pressing concerns around economic inequality in China, gentrification may certainly offer a powerful instrument to critically assess the spatial impacts of this on the city. Wu (2010, p 72) estimates that between 15 million and 37 million urban residents have fallen into absolute poverty. Given a Gini coefficient of .474 in 2012,[5] the head of the National Bureau of Statistics spokesperson extrapolated that it 'demonstrates the urgency for our country to speed up reform of the income distribution system to narrow the poor–rich gap' (Yao and Wang, 2013). The official recognition of growing inequality is also evident in China's 12th Five-Year Plan (2011–15), which explicitly addresses social imbalances (World Bank, 2013a). Indeed, Ren (2013, p 146) argues that capitalism in China has created new class strata that 'differentiates the entire population along multiple lines of power, wealth and risk'.

In view of this normative concern about addressing inequality, there may be strategic reasons to remain committed to gentrification; however, there are also potential shortcomings. Substantively, the prevailing conceptualisation of 'gentrification' privileges particular forms of economy over others – macroeconomic shifts and neoliberal forces over the informal sector, for example (McFarlane, 2008, p 344). The political economy of globalisation has been charged with a Marxist pedigree and overdetermination in its 'privileging of capitalism as the only mechanism and class struggle as the only resolution to urban problems' (Ong, 2011, p 2). Class inequality is not the same everywhere and the critical engagement with new class structures in China requires particular caution, as 'the meanings of the Chinese middle class are diverse and highly contested' (Ren, 2013, p 11; see also Lees, 2014). Scholars are investigating 'the emergent moment of class-making in a formerly socialist society that had passionately denied the existence of social class in its recent history', and are focusing on 'the amorphous, disjointed, and unstable nature of the new Chinese middle classes shaped by this specific historical juncture' (Zhang, 2010, p 3). If gentrification is understood as a 'class conquest of the city' (Smith, 2008, p 25), how does the disjointed nature of China's contested class stratification manage such a coup?

Moreover, the complexity of the changing class structures in China reinforces the need to re-examine inequality itself. For instance, Wu and Webster's (2010) edited volume on *Marginalization in urban China* discusses a diversity of factors that drive urban inequality, poverty and deprivation. Rather than using fixed understandings of class or inequality, they look at the simultaneous processes generating a 'massive accumulation of wealth and the formation of a marginalized population' (Wu and Webster, 2010, p xii). Instead of assuming the categories of 'urban poor' and 'middle class', these studies look at the mechanisms of inequality in urban China, such as the intertwining issues that property rights and *hukou* play in generating these groups (Wu, 2010), the union of rural–urban migration with the formation of urban villages (Liu and He, 2010), and the complexity of property rights resulting from multiple household, policy and historical changes (Shin, 2010a). These studies signal a need to deal critically with inequality in China. Yet, their focus remains on the 'formalisation and differentiation of rights', which are fundamental to the spatialisation of inequality and drive processes of displacement in China (Wu and Webster, 2010, p 12; Zhang, 2010, p 161). In other words, various strategies for addressing inequality in urban China are being laid out; by dealing with the drivers of inequality more directly, perhaps these approaches offer a sharper toolkit than gentrification to tackle unjust spatial processes.

A second consideration is an academic concern regarding the sites of theory. Critiques of the parochialism of urban theory (Robinson, 2011) highlight the disciplinary failure that:

> urban theory has been slow in contributing to important advances in political, economic, social and cultural theories that have had a longer tradition of moving beyond theoretical agendas dominated by North

> American and European traditions. In these terms, urban theorists have tended to remain entrenched in conceptual and empirical approaches that have barely moved beyond the study of a small number of 'Western' cities which act as the template against which all other cities are judged. (Edensor and Jayne, 2012, p 1)

This is particularly a danger for researchers of urban China, who risk consigning their work to the realm of case study. Asking 'What is gentrification with Chinese characteristics?' limits the nature of research in China to a variation-finding model, excising or at least limiting its theory-building potential (McFarlane, 2010; Ward, 2010; Robinson, 2011). As a 'variation' of a dominant model, research of urban China becomes a case study, a derivative of the original, and does not enjoy an equal footing in the field of urban knowledge. It becomes one of:

> those spaces at the edges of urban theory, so often 'added-on' as case study, or measured against Euro-American theoretical constructs and claims. The shadows cast are those cast by the particular reoccupations of Euro-American urban theory; these are spaces that often do not register as agents on the map of urban theory. (McFarlane, 2008, p 341)

These variation-finding tactics construct core and second-tier cities, situating the 'Western city' as model and 'Southern city' around the trope of copy/unique (McFarlane, 2008, p 344). Therefore, in studying gentrification in China, researchers may want to reflect on the ways in which they are measuring Shanghai against a model of change that is contextual to London. Even though London may also gain from the theoretical insights learned in Shanghai,[6] the directionality of travelling knowledge (gentrification travelling to and finally arriving in Shanghai!) that results from this case study-ism precludes alternative grounded theoretical insights. Less researched sites become case studies of a dominant model or understanding of urban change, not a site of theorisation. Indeed, if researchers are perpetually validating, expanding, reinforcing and responding to dominant canons of thought derived from a limited set of empirical cases, where is the space for 'theorising back' and building from new empirical results (Ward, 2010)?

The reliance on concepts like gentrification as the starting point for designing research about under-studied sites limits the possibility for developing new theoretical insights from empirical work in these places and also, more fundamentally, holds implications for how urban researchers might conceptualise the 'urban'. Designing research frameworks based on concepts developed about places like London for other places privileges the experience of London in the realm of urban theory. Parnell (2012) has argued to address this issue by parochialising urban theory, and McFarlane (2010, p 726) echoes this view when he contends that researchers should examine their 'implicit objects of reference'. When making claims about the 'urban' as a category, careful consideration is required as to what extent these claims are based on a limited set of experiences.

The task of reconceptualising the city, especially for scholars seeking to think beyond deterministic, hegemonic frames, has given rise to a need for experimentation:

> Instead of seeing the city as a fixed space or node, we approach the metropolis as a milieu of experimentation where diverse actors and institutions invent and aspire to new ways of being global, and in doing so, recuperate the global not as the endpoint to an already given urban developmental process, but as a terrain of problematization. Instead of abstract hierarchies and typologies of cities and citizenship, we are open to the variety of ideas, idioms, methods, and solutions that political leaders, developers, citizens, workers, and slum-dwellers deploy in a global game of claiming the world's attention through the staging of showy architecture, cutting-edge industry, and homegrown urban aesthetics. (Ong, 2011, p 23)

Unfortunately, the call to experimentation offers few concrete recommendations for methodologies and alternative concepts. Grouped as a call for 'comparative urbanism', the critical works of McFarlane (2010), Ong (2011), Robinson (2011), Ward (2010) and others currently offer more guidance for critiques of existing modes of urban research and theory-building than alternatives (see Lees, 2012; Luger and Ren, forthcoming). It begs the question: if urban China researchers do not select 'gentrification' as a strategic weapon in the battle over spatial justice, what are the alternatives? Still, the fact that there is not a fully concretised research agenda is hardly a sufficient reason to dismiss the call – especially for researchers asking 'What can the Chinese experience offer to an understanding of enlarging social inequalities in the twenty-first century?' (Wu and Webster, 2010). In fact, it may be an enticing invitation for those keen on pushing epistemological and methodological boundaries. Furthermore, it recognises the limits of the current canon of urban theory and that:

> the experience of Western capitalist cities is *not* adequate to understand the transitional cities and that the understanding of the Chinese cities as well as other cities outside the extensively researched Western economies will inform the debate of the nature of contemporary urban restructuring in general. (Wu and Ma, 2005, p 234, emphasis in original)

Conclusion

Weighing the strategic, instrumental value of gentrification for critically addressing inequality against the need to develop urban theory on a world scale is impossible to measure. Yet, this constructed binary invites researchers to reflect on the theoretical and conceptual choices they make. To summarise, there may be a value in studying gentrification in China, but perhaps at the cost of producing research that more directly investigates the drivers and consequences of urban inequality in China. Despite its critical perspective, gentrification research in China may thus obscure a more contextually relevant understanding of urban inequality.

Moreover, if urban research is concerned with inequality, it should also take seriously the critique of inequity in urban theory (this is something that Lees [2012] and this edited collection try to do). There is an inequality of interpretive instruments, wherein the power to describe, to name, and to represent things in a certain way remains within the terms of a few constantly reified and stretched urban concepts. These 'regimes of truth' (Hall, 1997, p 49) effectively shape not only how we understand the urban, but also the urban itself. In critiquing knowledge-production processes, authority and disciplinary accounts, post-structuralists may have inspired the move towards 'embracing the richness of the local and the particular' (Hubbard, 2006, pp 44–5) but this has yet to be reconciled with the need to address the parochial nature of urban theory.

Of course, there is a need to balance context and 'the particular' given the danger of isolating research in China into its own parochial frame (Luger and Ren, forthcoming). Pow (2012, p 47) has warned that underlying a significant amount of research on urban China is an assumption of 'Chinese exceptionalism', rendering it unique and different from all other urban experiences. Yet, suggesting the need to include existing research on urban China in building theoretical concepts does not necessitate the canonisation of Beijing. Rather, it is a renewed call for grounded theory, especially given the volume of research being generated on urban China. A clear alternative to 'Chinese exceptionalism' would mean asking: how can research on urban China inform an understanding of not only 'Chinese urbanism', but 'Urbanism', with a capital 'U'?

Notes

[1] Indeed, the descriptive limits of gentrification are not a new topic of discussion. See, for example, Lambert and Boddy's (2002) discussion on new-build gentrification, as discussed in Davidson and Lees (2010) and Slater (2006).

[2] There is little questioning about the applicability of the neoliberalisation framework for understanding China's urbanisation (compare He and Wu [2009] with Brenner et al [2010] and Ong [2006]).

[3] These figures are measured in 'PPP GNI': gross national income (GNI) converted to international dollars using purchasing power parity (PPP) rates (World Bank, 2013b).

[4] For example, Fuqian *Hutong* is the name of a specific alley, whereas 'life in the *hutongs*' would refer to the neighbourhood comprised of these alleys.

[5] 'China has not provided an official Gini coefficient since 2005, claiming that it was too difficult to calculate given rampant under-reporting of incomes, particularly by the wealthy. The index ranges from 0 to 1, with the 0.4 mark viewed by analysts as the point at which social dissatisfaction may come to a head' (Yao and Wang, 2013).

[6] Harris's (2008) comparative study of London and Mumbai points to this circulation when he posits that Mumbai might offer 'significant sources of learning in terms of new forms of community resistance to predatory processes of gentrification' (Harris, 2008, p 2424). Lees (2012, 2014) also makes the same argument.

References

Alexandre, A., Hirako, Y., Dorje, L., and de Azevedo, P. (2008) 'Beijing Hutong conservation plan', Tibet Heritage Fund International. Available at: http://www.tibetheritagefund.org/media/download/hutong_study.pdf

Atkinson, R. (2003) 'Introduction: misunderstood saviour or vengeful wrecker? The many meanings and problems of gentrification', *Urban Studies*, vol 40, no 12, pp 2343–55.

Atkinson, R. and Bridge, G. (2005) 'Introduction', in R. Atkinson and G. Bridge (eds) *Gentrification in a global context: the new urban colonialism*, London and New York, NY: Routledge, pp 1–17.

Beauregard, R. (1985) 'Politics, ideology and theories of gentrification', *Journal of Urban Affairs*, vol 7, no 4, pp 51–62.

Beauregard, R. (1986) 'The chaos and complexity of gentrification', in N. Smith and P. Williams (eds) *Gentrification of the city*, Boston, MA: Allen & Unwin, pp 35–55.

Berry, B. (1985) 'Islands of renewal in seas of decay', in P. Peterson (ed) *The new urban reality*, Washington, DC: The Brookings Institution.

Brenner, N., Peck, J. and Theodore, N. (2010) 'Variegated neoliberalization: geographies, modalities, pathways', *Global Networks*, vol 10, no 2, pp 182–222.

Butler, T. (2007) 'For gentrification?', *Environment and Planning A*, vol 39, no 1, pp 162–81.

Clark, E. (2005) 'The order and simplicity of gentrification – a political challenge', in R. Atkinson and G. Bridge (eds) *Gentrification in a global context: the new urban colonialism*, London and New York, NY: Routledge.

Clay, P.L. (1979) *Neighbourhood renewal*, Lexington, MA: D.C. Heath.

Davidson, M. and Lees, L. (2010) 'New-build gentrification: its histories, trajectories and critical geographies', *Population, Space and Place*, vol 16, pp 295–411.

Edensor, T. and Jayne, M. (2012) 'Introduction', in T. Edensor and M. Jayne (eds) *Urban theory beyond the West: a world of cities*, New York, NY: Routledge.

Fainstein, S. and Logan, J. (2008) 'Introduction: Urban China in comparative perspective', in J. Logan (ed) *Urban China in transition*, Malden, MA: Blackwell.

Farrell, D., Gersch, U. and Stephenson, E. (2006) 'The value of China's emerging middle class', *The McKinsey Quarterly*, June special edition.

Fraser, N. (2003) 'From discipline to flexibilization? Rereading Foucault in the shadow of globalization', *Constellations*, vol 10, no 2, pp 160–71.

Fraser, N. (2011) 'Marketization, social protection, emancipation: toward a neo-Polanyian conception of capitalist crisis', in C. Calhoun (ed) *Business as usual: the roots of the global financial meltdown*, New York, NY: New York University Press.

Hackworth, J. and Smith, N. (2001) 'The changing state of gentrification', *Tijdschrift voor Economische en Sociale Geografie*, vol 92, no 4, pp 464–77.

Hall, S. (1997) 'The work of representation', in S. Hall (ed) *Representation: cultural representation and signifying practices*, London: Sage Publications.

Harris, A. (2008) 'From London to Mumbai and back again: gentrification and public policy in comparative perspective', *Urban Studies*, vol 45, no 12, pp 2407–28.

Harvey, D. (1985) *The urbanization of capital*, Oxford: Blackwell.

He, S. (2007) 'State-sponsored gentrification under market transition: the case of Shanghai', *Urban Affairs Review*, vol 43, no 2, pp 171–98.

He, S. (2009) 'New-build gentrification in central Shanghai: demographic changes and socioeconomic implications', *Population Space and Place*, vol 16, pp 345–61.

He, S. and Liu, Y. (2010) 'Mechanism and consequences of China's gentrification under market transition', *Scientia Geographica Sinica*, vol 30, no 4, pp 496–502.

He, S. and Wu, F. (2009) 'China's emerging neoliberal urbanism: perspectives from urban redevelopment', *Antipode*, vol 41, no 2, pp 282–304.

Hessler, P. (2006) 'Hutong Karma', *The New Yorker*. Available at: http://www.newyorker.com/archive/2006/02/13/060213fa_fact_hessler

Huang, Y. (2003) 'A room of one's own: housing consumption and residential crowding in transitional urban China', *Environment and Planning A*, vol 35, pp 591–614.

Huang, Y. (2004) 'From work-unit compounds to gated communities: housing inequality and residential segregation in transitional Beijing', in L. Ma and F. Wu (eds) *Restructuring the Chinese city: changing society, economy and space*, London and New York, NY: Routledge.

Hubbard, P. (2006) *City*, London: Routledge.

Iossifova, D. (2009) 'Negotiating livelihoods in a city of difference: narratives of gentrification in Shanghai', *Critical Planning*, vol 16, pp 98–116.

Jager, M. (1986) 'Class definition and the esthetics of gentrification: Victoriana in Melbourne', in N. Smith and P. Williams (eds) *Gentrification of the city*, Boston, MA: Allen and Unwin.

Kharas, H. (2010) 'The emerging middle class in developing countries', Working Paper No. 285, OECD Development Centre.

Kloosterman, R. and Van der Leun, J. (1999) 'Just for starters: commercial gentrification by immigrant entrepreneurs in Amsterdam and Rotterdam neighbourhoods', *Housing Studies*, vol 14, no 5, pp 659–77.

Krase, J. (2005) 'Poland and Polonia: migration and the re-incorporation of ethnic aesthetic practice in the taste of luxury', in R. Atkinson and G. Bridge (eds) *Gentrification in a global context: the new urban colonialism*, London and New York, NY: Routledge, pp 189–213.

Lambert, C. and Boddy, M. (2002) 'Transforming the city: post-recession gentrification and re-urbanisation', Paper presented at 'Upward neighbourhood trajectories: gentrification in the new century', 26-27 September, University of Glasgow.

Lees, L. (1994) 'Gentrification in London and New York: an Atlantic gap?', *Housing Studies*, vol 9, no 2, pp 199–217.

Lees, L. (2006) 'Gentrifying down the urban hierarchy: "the cascade effect" in Portland, Maine, USA', in D. Bell and M. Jayne (eds) *Small cities: urban experience beyond the metropolis*, London: Routledge, pp 91–104.

Lees, L. (2007) 'Afterword', *Environment and Planning A*, vol 39, no 1, pp 228–84.

Lees, L. (2012) 'The geography of gentrification: thinking through comparative urbanism', *Progress in Human Geography*, vol 36, no 2, pp 155–71.

Lees, L. (2014) 'Gentrification in the Global South?', in S. Parnell and S. Oldfield (eds) *The Routledge Handbook on Cities of the Global South*, Routledge: new York, pp 506–21.

Lees, L., Slater, T. and Wyly, E.K. (2008) *Gentrification*, New York, NY, and London: Routledge.

Lin, G.C.S. (2012) 'Chinese metropolises in transformation: state power reshuffling, land commodification and uneven urban development', International Conference on Spatial and Social Transformation in Urban China, Hong Kong Baptist University.

Liu, Y. and He, S. (2010) 'Chinese urban villages as marginalized neighbourhoods under rapid urbanization', in F. Wu and C. Webster (eds) *Marginalization in urban China: comparative perspectives*, Basingstoke: Palgrave Macmillan.

Luger, J. and Ren, J. (forthcoming) 'Comparative urbanism and the "Asian city": implications for research and theory', *International Journal of Urban and Regional Research*. Available at: http://onlinelibrary.wiley.com/doi/10.1111/1468-2427.12140/abstract

McFarlane, C. (2008) 'Urban shadows: materiality, the "Southern city" and urban theory', *Geography Compass*, vol 2, no 2, pp 340–58.

McFarlane, C. (2010) 'The comparative city: knowledge, learning, urbanism', *International Journal of Urban and Regional Research*, vol 34, no 4, pp 725–42.

Ong, A. (2006) 'Neoliberalism as a mobile technology', *Transactions of the Institute of British Geographers*, vol 32, no 1, pp 3–8.

Ong, A. (2011) 'Introduction: worlding cities, or the art of being global', in A. Roy and A. Ong (eds) *Worlding cities: Asian experiments and the art of being global*, Malden, MA: Wiley-Blackwell, pp 1–25.

Pan, T. (2011) *Deep China: the moral life of the person, what anthropology and psychiatry tell us about China today*, Berkeley and Los Angeles, CA: University of California Press.

Parnell, S. (2012) 'The Global South and building theory', conference paper presented at University of Manchester Cities' Group Annual Lecture, March.

Pow, C.P. (2012) 'China exceptionalism? Unbounding narratives on urban China', in T. Edensor and M. Jayne (eds) *Urban theory beyond the West: a world of cities*, New York, NY: Routledge.

Rabinovitch, S. (2013) 'Structural revolution', *Financial Times*. Available at: http://www.ft.com/intl/cms/s/2/eb0384c0-a812-11e2-b031-00144feabdc0.html#slide0

Ren, H. (2013) *The middle class in neoliberal China: governing risk, life building, and themed space*, London and New York, NY: Routledge.

Robinson, J. (2011) 'Cities in a world of cities: the comparative gesture', *International Journal of Urban and Regional Research*, vol 35, pp 1–23.

Shin, H.B. (2007) 'Residential redevelopment and social impacts in Beijing', in F. Wu (ed) *China's emerging cities: the making of a new urbanism*, London: Routledge, pp 163–84.

Shin, H.B. (2009a) 'Residential redevelopment and entrepreneurial local state: the implications of Beijing's shifting emphasis on urban redevelopment policies', *Urban Studies*, vol 46, no 13, pp 2815–39.

Shin, H.B. (2009b) 'Life in the shadow of mega-events: Beijing summer Olympiad and its impact on housing', *Journal of Asian Public Policy*, vol 2, no 2, pp 122–41.

Shin, H.B. (2010a) 'Empowerment or marginalization: land, housing and property rights in poor neighbourhoods', in F. Wu and C. Webster (eds) *Marginalization in urban China: comparative perspectives*, Basingstoke: Palgrave Macmillan.

Shin, H.B. (2010b) 'Urban conservation and revalorisation of dilapidated historic quarters: the case of Nanluoguxiang in Beijing', *Cities*, vol 27, pp 43–54.

Shin, H.B. and Li, B. (2013) 'Whose Games? The costs of being "Olympic citizens" in Beijing', *Environment and Urbanization*, vol 25, no 2, pp 559–76.

Sicular, T., Yue, X., Gustafsson, B. and Li, S. (2006) 'The urban–rural income gap and inequality in China', *Review of Income and Wealth*, vol 53, no 1, pp 93–126.

Slater, T. (2006) 'The eviction of critical perspectives from gentrification research', *International Journal of Urban and Regional Research*, vol 30, no 4, pp 737–57.

Smart, A. and Lin, G.C.S. (2007) 'Local capitalism, local citizenship and translocality: rescaling from below in the Pearl River Delta Region, China', *International Journal of Urban and Regional Research*, vol 31, pp 280–302.

Smith, N. (2008) 'The evolution of gentrification', in J.J. Berg, T. Kaminer, M. Schoonderbeek and J. Zonneveld (eds) *Houses in transformation: interventions in European gentrification*, Rotterdam: NAi Publishers, pp 14–27.

Song, W. and Zhu, X. (2010) 'Gentrification in urban China under market transformation', *International Journal of Urban Sciences*, vol 14, no 2, pp 152–63.

Stone, A. (2008) 'Farewell to the Hutongs: urban development in Beijing', *Dissent*, vol 55, no 2, pp 43–8.

Tang, Y. and Wong, C. (2007) 'Large urban redevelopment projects and socio-spatial stratification in Shanghai', in F. Wu (ed) *China's emerging cities: the making of new urbanism*, London: Routledge.

Ward, K. (2010) 'Towards a relational comparative approach to the study of cities', *Progress in Human Geography*, vol 34, no 4, pp 471–87.

World Bank (2013a) 'Country overview: China'. Available at: http://www.worldbank.org/en/country/china/overview

World Bank (2013b) 'China', World DataBank – World Development Indicators. Available at: http://databank.worldbank.org/data/views/reports/tableview.aspx

Wu, F. (2010) 'Property rights, citizenship and the making of the new poor in urban China', in F. Wu and C. Webster (eds) *Marginalization in urban China: comparative perspectives*, Basingstoke: Palgrave Macmillan.

Wu, F. and Ma, L. (2005) 'The Chinese city in transition: towards theorizing China's urban restructuring', in L. Ma and F. Wu (eds) *Restructuring the Chinese city: changing society, economy and space*, London and New York, NY: Routledge.

Wu, F. and Webster, C. (eds) (2010) *Marginalization in urban China: comparative perspectives*, Basingstoke: Palgrave Macmillan.

Wu, F., Xu, J. and Yeh, A. (2007) *Urban development in post-reform China: state, market and space*, London: Routledge.

Wu, L. (1999) 'Rehabilitating the old city of Beijing: a project in the Ju'er *Hutong*', *Neighbourhood*, Vancouver: UBC Press.

Yao, K. and Wang, A. (2013) 'China lets Gini out of the bottle; wide wealth gap', *Reuters*. Available at: http://www.reuters.com/article/2013/01/18/us-china-economy-income-gap-idUSBRE90H06L20130118

Zhang, L. (2010) *In search of paradise: middle-class living in a Chinese metropolis*, Ithaca, NY, and London: Cornell University Press.

Zhang, Y. (2008) 'Steering towards growth: symbolic urban preservation in Beijing, 1990–2005', *Town Planning Review*, vol 79, nos 2/3, pp 187–208.

Zhou, M. and Logan, J. (2002) 'Market transition and the commodification of housing in urban China', in J. Logan (ed) *The new Chinese city: globalization and market reform*, Oxford: Blackwell.

Zukin, S. (1998) 'Urban Lifestyles: Diversity and Standardisation in Spaces of Consumption', *Urban Studies*, vol 35, pp 825–39.

Zukin, S. (2010) *Naked city*, Oxford and New York, NY: Oxford University Press.

Zukin, S. and Kosta, E. (2004) 'Bourdieu off-Broadway: managing distinction on a shopping block in the East Village', *City and Community*, vol 3, no 2, pp 101–14.

EIGHTEEN

Emerging retail gentrification in Santiago de Chile: the case of Italia-Caupolicán

Elke Schlack and Neil Turnbull

Introduction

Chile is enjoying sustained economic growth accompanied by a boisterous real estate market, transforming its capital, Santiago. De Mattos (1999) states that this is the product of a strategy of economic liberalisation that has been in operation since the 1970s. This transformation is identified in the many manifestations of investment across the city, including inner-city renewal. These operations are taking place within an existing urban social context characterised by inequality and spatial segregation (Sabatini et al, 2001; Rodriguez, 2008). In this context, the concept of 'gentrification', while having been discussed for some time within academic and government circles in Chile, is now emerging in recently published academic work that, for the most part, is focused on metropolitan Santiago (see López-Morales, 2008, 2010, 2013; Contreras, 2009, 2011; Sabatini et al, 2009; Borsdorf and Hidalgo, 2012; Inzulza, 2012; Janoschka and Casgrain, 2012; López-Morales et al, 2012).

The main body of this work concentrates on new-build gentrification, by way of contrast, there is comparatively little evidence concerning urban renewal in inner-city Santiago through the rehabilitation of existing structures. The focus on new-build gentrification is understandable given its residential impact; however, it leaves an important field of urban development under-examined: the commercial-oriented transformations that are putting pressure on residential neighbourhoods in inner Santiago. If viewed under the lens of gentrification, this process could broaden the debate in Chile to include fields of urbanisation where profit is made through the exploitation of distinctive neighbourhood cultural attributes.

Our case study is the neighbourhood of Italia-Caupolicán in central Santiago, where there is strong evidence of conflict between the long-established land users, the residential inhabitants and tradespeople (who satisfy local everyday needs), and the new entrepreneurs who are focused on innovating consumerism (and who aim to captivate a floating elite population). The circumstances of a change in landscape brought about by reinvestment in both the tangible and intangible cultural attributes of the neighbourhood is important to gentrification debates in

Chile and serves as a warning of a powerful business model that could potentially be rolled out in other similar neighbourhoods in Santiago.

In this chapter, we apply the concept of 'gentrification' developed in the Global North to similar processes of change observed in Italia-Caupolicán. We explore why certain aspects of neighbourhood change in Italia-Caupolicán might be catalogued as gentrification and analyse our case using part of the broad definition of gentrification outlined by Davidson and Lees (2005, 2010), focusing on the reinvestment of capital, landscape change and displacement. Reinvestment of capital is explored by analysing the motors of commercial profit. Landscape change is documented through field observations, by registering cultural and commercial infrastructure in the area, and includes interviews with key informants. Finally, we outline possible theoretical approaches to commercial gentrification in order to analyse displacement in this context. However, we first begin by outlining the local context and manifestations of gentrification in Santiago de Chile.

The gentrification debate in Chile

In the words of De Mattos (1999), Santiago is a 'globalised archipelago' where there are many forms of urban transformation operating at different scales. This fragmented development includes: new office and commercial developments, gated communities, high-rise towers, '*tugurización*' ('decline' – from the Spanish '*tugurio*', meaning 'hovel'), social housing on the periphery, and new road networks and infrastructure (Hidalgo and Arenas, 2011; Borsdorf and Hidalgo, 2012). These developments are taking place throughout the metropolitan region in both the inner city and on the periphery of the city.

If the physical and geographical expressions of change in Santiago are complex, the economic drivers and social problems are more evident. The imperative in the development of the city is profit, where transnational investors and real estate companies are the protagonists in search of profit through land exploitation (Hidalgo and Arenas, 2011). However, the outcomes of this development are not shared by all the inhabitants of Santiago and there is concern about the (re) production of severe social segregation and urban inequality, as highlighted in a recent report on Chilean urban policy that identifies Santiago as having the highest economic urban inequality of all metropolitan regions in the Organisation for Economic Co-operation and Development for which there are data (OECD, 2013). In this context, adopting the term 'gentrification' and drawing on theories from the Global North permits a critical reflection on the predominant patterns of urban development in the metropolitan areas of Chile. The strong dialogue of Chilean scholars with theories from the North is understandable given a shared interest in a critical take on gentrification (see Lees et al, 2008) in the face of the predominant local practice of urban development and renewal.

Most of the gentrification literature in Chile to date has analysed residential gentrification; however, there is divergence on which aspects of the concept are essential to understanding the process and its impacts. While some Chilean authors use the term 'gentrification' in their analysis of urban transformations, considering the economic causes of the phenomenon and outlining social upgrading as an important aspect (see Sabatini et al, 2009; Contreras, 2011; Borsdorf and Hidalgo, 2012), others study the relationship between gentrification processes and the planned decline of neighbourhoods as a pattern of class appropriation of land to the detriment of those on lower incomes in the city (see López-Morales, 2008, 2010, 2013; Inzulza, 2012; Janoschka and Casgrain, 2012; López-Morales et al, 2012). These different foci on gentrification are formed and influenced by the different fields in which gentrification has been identified in Chile to date, depending on its peripheral or inner-city location in Santiago.

The manifestation of gentrification on the periphery involves new-build condominiums, following the typology of the gated or non-gated community. Sabatini et al (2009), for example, describe as gentrification situations where real estate developers profit by turning land on the poor periphery into condominiums for the middle and upper-middle classes. While Sabatini et al (2009) praise the opportunity to establish physical proximity between social groups and discard the idea that displacement is inevitable, stating that most existing residents are owner-occupiers and that there is sufficient vacant land to build on without tearing down existing social housing, Janoshka and Casgrain (2012) contest this, claiming that the arrival of gentrifiers reduces the opportunity for land for the poor.

By contrast, inner-city gentrification in Santiago involves a relationship with the existing built environment. One type of inner-city gentrification involves the demolition of traditional housing with continuous facades and historic '*cités*' ('workers' housing') and their replacement by towering residential blocks (Janoschka and Casgrain, 2012). This gentrification of the inner city occurs where working-class areas are bought at low cost by large-scale private developers who profit from government urban renewal subsidies and the opportunities offered by permissive planning legislation (López-Morales, 2010). The existing owner-occupiers had suffered a form of 'red-lining' by the state, whose building regulations frustrated efforts to add small-scale value to the land, and combined with the failure of local authorities to implement existing social housing subsidies, this caused decay (López-Morales, 2010, 2013). The result was and is indirect displacement, where the ground rent capitalised by proprietors is not enough to find replacement accommodation of a similar quality and central location (López-Morales, 2010). By drawing on Neil Smith's (1979) rent-gap thesis, López-Morales (2010) has called this 'gentrification by ground rent dispossession', stating that the renovation of Santiago's city centre is a class monopolisation of land whereby the capitalisation of property achievable by current residents is considerably less than the higher-capitalised ground rent achievable by large-scale real estate developers.

Gentrification in the inner city has also been associated with the cultural and physical upgrading of some areas of heritage value and their subsequent exploitation by real estate developments. In contrast to the demolition of the built environment, the renewal of heritage areas involves the rehabilitation of existing historic structures and a limited construction of new-build units. This has been undertaken by the recycling of deteriorated mansions or the construction of new-build 'lofts' to attract people with greater incomes than the existing population (Rodriguez, 2007; De Mattos, 2008; Contreras, 2009). Here, there is evidence of a moderate scale of reinvestment, which is the result of planning legislation that restricts the building height to match the existing buildings and therefore removes the opportunity for profit through high-rise blocks.

Gentrification in historic central areas in Chile is understood to relate to residential use; however, some authors have begun to suggest that the characteristics of gentrification may also be present in other forms. Borsdorf and Hidalgo (2012) cite the presence of a floating population of students and patrons of restaurants and bars as an indicator of gentrification. However, they refrain from a conclusive diagnosis of gentrification, stating that in some historic neighbourhoods, it is mainly the lower-income bracket of the population who have moved in, enticed by the 'alternative' atmosphere, whereas bohemians only visit in the evenings and at weekends, shying away from living in the centre permanently.

In Chile, then, the phenomenon of residential gentrification is becoming well-established and debated. However, in academic circles, much less attention has been directed at commercial gentrification in heritage areas and those neighbourhoods with a bohemian connotation. The transformation of residential neighbourhoods into consumer clusters is a phenomenon that is under way in the Italia-Caupolicán neighbourhood, as well as in other central neighbourhoods like 'Bellavista', 'Lastarria' and 'Brasil-Yungay'. However, while all these neighbourhoods demonstrate similar characteristics of retail gentrification, they also show differences in its cause-and-effect relationship to residential gentrification and in the kind of retail that is present there. While the characteristic of 'Bellavista', 'Lastarria' and 'Brasil-Yungay' is a gentrification predominantly pushed by restaurants and bars, in 'Italia-Caupolicán', design shops and boutiques prevail.

The neighbourhoods of 'Lastarria' and 'Brasil-Yungay' correspond to districts where renewal and cultural policies have been developed. A key factor in the development of 'Lastarria' was the construction of a new metro line and underground parking, while in 'Brasil-Yungay', it was the construction of new cultural infrastructure that promoted retail gentrification. By way of contrast, 'Bellavista' as well as 'Italia-Caupolicán' have developed in a more spontaneous way; like in classic/first-wave cases of gentrification from the Global North, the process here has been directed by private investment and marked by an absence of promotion through public policies.

The transformations in all four of these neighbourhoods have been heavily influenced by private initiatives that, in some cases, have counted on public support. Both the private and public actors behind these initiatives have been strongly influenced by renewal practices realised in Barcelona, Lisbon, London and Paris. The private entrepreneurs involved in the renewal of 'Bellavista' and 'Italia-Caupolicán' mention how they have been inspired by renewal projects like 'Covent Garden' in London and tourist neighbourhoods in Paris, and the municipality of Santiago has likewise been influenced by European cities in developing policy for urban renewal. This is evident in the important technical support given in the plan for the repopulation of the inner city by the Atelier Parisene D'Urbanisme (APU, 2000), and renewal based on the experience of Spanish cities like Barcelona and Bilbao is obvious in the development of an ensemble of cultural infrastructures, such as the Matucana 100 Cultural Centre, as well as the Museum of Memory and the Library of Santiago. A strong European influence on urban renewal approaches is common across all these cases of inner-city commercial gentrification in Santiago de Chile.

The case of Italia-Caupolicán

The neighbourhood of Italia-Caupolicán, located in the Providencia district of Santiago, is a patchwork quilt of smaller areas located along the streets of Santa Isabel, Italia and Caupolicán, all of which have lent their name to the neighbourhood at different times and for different people. Providencia is a well-established district that attracts significant revenue due to its central location and status as an important commercial sub-centre. From 1900 onwards, Italia-Caupolicán was established as an affluent neighbourhood where homes and local shops coexisted with some medium-sized factories that occupied part of, but never the whole of, the area. During a stage of decline and abandonment (1970–90), several houses were replaced by garages and warehouses. However, in the 1990s, especially from 2005 onwards, this working-class neighbourhood saw a marked turnaround in its fortunes. Retail selling high-end design emerged and capitalised on the existence of artists, furniture restorers and the built environment. This process, in turn, attracted other initiatives that joined in this narrative and sought to benefit from this transformation, exerting pressure on the existing population.

Reinvestment of capital

The role of the economic exploitation of land has been vital to understanding gentrification in Chile in the literature to date; in Italia-Caupolicán, profit is also an important issue with regards to gentrification. There is evidence that gentrification in Italia-Caupolicán was a market response to a lucrative opportunity to exploit deteriorated neighbourhoods, as set out by Smith's (1979) rent-gap theory. However, in Italia-Caupolicán, the financial gain from the 'highest and best' use is not found in larger, newer structures, but in a change of land use, as described by Ingram (2006). Here, the maximum economic return is augmented by other neighbourhood characteristics that are in the process of being commodified, such as the mark of a 'distinctive place', as described by Bourdieu (1983), and the 'spatial embeddedness' and 'real cultural capital', as discussed by Zukin (1990). These geographical and sociological theories inform the basis of the following analysis and characterisation of gentrification in Italia-Caupolicán.

Smith (1979) described the decline of the inner city as led by interrelated processes, including the deterioration of property, decline through a change of tenancy, unscrupulous actions by real estate agents, disinvestment by financial institutions and abandonment. In Italia-Caupolicán, decline has been associated with the degradation of original properties and small-scale developer agency, which has installed marginal uses that sit cheek by jowl with existing residential uses, undermining the quality of life and economic value of the individual properties. Signs of reinvestment in the built environment began to appear in Italia-Caupolicán from the 1990s onwards. Reinvestment took the form of the rehabilitation of existing buildings. In a sample of planning permissions issued between the years 1994 and 2011, only 6% relate to 'new buildings', whereas the remaining 94% related to 'extensions and alterations'. Calculations of the physical size and volume of these developments indicate floor area ratios of between 0.7 and 1.5, reaching a maximum height of two storeys, which indicates that the building works maintain the existing structures, while analysis of the local planning legislation shows that a potential maximum land use is permitted for buildings with floor area ratios of 2.7, reaching a maximum height of five storeys (see Figure 18.1, image 2). The actual developments in terms of their physical size and height therefore fall short of what is available, exploiting only part of the building rights permitted by the local planning legislation. In the Chilean context, this model of land reinvestment stands in stark contrast to the developments that exploit opportunities for larger new building volumes from which profit is made. These developments are taking place in neighbouring inner-city municipalities whose planning codes theoretically permit floor area ratios of 28 distributed over 48 floors (see Figure 18.1, image 3). It should be noted that, in practice, the actual floor area ratios being created by developers in inner-city Santiago are around 14 (López-Morales, 2010). In Italia-Caupolicán, by contrast, value is being found in the rehabilitation of existing structures and not in new-build, high-rise redevelopment.

Reinvestment in Italia-Caupolicán is still associated with exploitation of the land market but the opportunity for profit is sought through a change to commercial land use. This change of land use is evident in the rise in the number of new commercial licences issued by the municipality, a total of 100 during the period

Figure 18.1: Scales of reinvestment on building plots of 5,000m^2

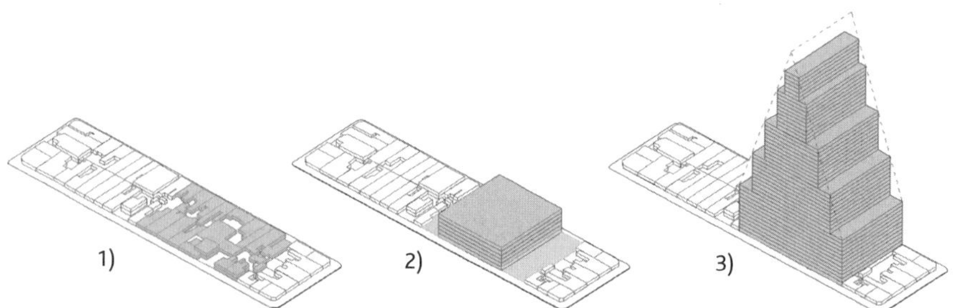

Note: 1) Existing reinvestment undertaken in the neighbourhood; 2) Potential offered by legislation; 3) Potential offered in neighbouring municipalities.

2009–12, compared with eight issued during 1990–95 (Ilustre Municipalidad de Providencia, 2009, 2012). Ingram (2006) offers an economic explanation for this switch to commercial use in the neighbourhood, stating that in central areas with high land values, residential uses are only financially justified if they are high-density, whereas commercial use is capable of capturing the necessary profit to justify the investment. Since there are many central and cheaper areas in Santiago that offer a variety of land uses under conditions where profits through larger building volumes are restricted, Italia-Caupolicán offers an additional attraction. Italia-Caupolicán is also different from other areas in Santiago as the appreciation of renovated properties by artists and furniture restorers signals the existence of a cultural capital that gives the neighbourhood the mark of a 'distinctive place' (see Zukin, 1990; Holm, 2010). It is this distinction that is operational in supplying an additional economic return from the ground rent. Based on Bourdieu (1983), Zukin (1990) and Holm (2010) outline a process where the individual cultural capital of artists is transferred to the physical environment, which then becomes systematically exploited as a distinctive place, with this mark of distinction then being transformed into a commodity. Zukin (1990) highlights how the built environment obtains a special value by embodying cultural capital in a 'spatial embeddedness' of culture, calling this 'real cultural capital'. She explains this relationship between culture and commerce in her concept of the 'Artistic Mode of Production' (Zukin, 1989), where artists in New York City created a commercial stimulant for the commercial redevelopment of Lower Manhattan (see Lees et al, 2008). Through such processes, a culturally loaded neighbourhood can be transformed into a successful prototype of consumerism, which permits real estate developers to capture economic profit in an environment that has presented challenges to their habitual practices of urban renewal in a seemingly modest redevelopment strategy based on the arts and historic preservation (Zukin, 1989).

In Italia-Caupolicán, it is not residential loft living that has capitalised on cultural capital, but rather the proliferation of high-end design retail in a process of commercial gentrification (see Zukin, 2009). The way in which reinvestment attempts to capture this 'highest and best' use has a defined pattern in the neighbourhood. New businesses have land-occupancy patterns of single commercial uses and subdivided uses, where the new commercial licences in individual properties number 40, while in subdivided properties, they number 60 (Ilustre Municipalidad de Providencia, 2012). It is notable that landlords have exploited the individual cultural capital created by the design outlets for their own profit; this is a technique of 'milking' property cited by Smith (1979) as evidence of residential neighbourhood decline. In Italia-Caupolicán, the rent gap is not yet 'closed' by the direct sale of the property; rather, developers have become landlords and maintain ownership in order to capitalise on their investment by renting out the units for commercial use.

The new profit that is being extracted from those properties subdivided for rent is also demonstrated by the rise in rental values of properties in the neighbourhood. The information in Table 18.1 records the change in the value of commercial property in the district. Despite the significant variations in rental values in the years selected, the average variation in rental value calculated over the 23-year period of the survey shows an increase of 0.7% per annum in the district of Providencia overall and an increase of 5.8% per annum in the neighbourhood of Italia-Caupolicán, over eight times that of the district as a whole. This increase is all the more significant considering that Providencia is already an important commercial sector in Santiago. Rental accommodation in Italia-Caupolicán is becoming more exclusive and a more attractive financial investment.

The process of gentrification in Italia-Caupolicán is emerging from a neighbourhood differentiated by cultural capital to one where this capital is being financially exploited. Here, it is useful to characterise these new forms of exploitation of urban space as spaces for consumption. Following Zukin's (2009) classification, it is possible to document stages in the transformation of retail capital, from 'local' to 'new entrepreneurial' and towards 'corporate' investment. Here, we classify shops considering the type of owner, who the customers are and what the business consists of, through, for example, the sale of goods or the letting of space. The 'local' shops are individually owned (SII, 2013). They are oriented towards the local population, catering to their everyday needs, including groceries, hairdressing, bicycle repair and restaurants serving simple lunches. Shopkeepers are often noted

Table 18.1: Variation in rental values in the district of Providencia and the Italia-Caupolicán neighbourhood

	Providencia			Italia-Caupolicán		
	Cases	Value UF/m²	Variation (%)	Cases	Value UF/m²	Variation (%)
1990	20	0.45	–	5	0.14	–
1993	97	0.57	27.2	1	0.24	73
1995	102	0.42	–25.6	6	0.20	–15.3
1998	79	0.43	2.2	4	0.21	5.5
2000	68	0.31	–27.3	6	0.14	–33.8
2003	63	0.31	–0.5	3	0.14	1.1
2005	17	0.33	4.6	1	0.08	–43.3
2008	27	0.39	20.5	3	0.17	107.2
2010	31	0.37	7.6	4	0.15	–7.8
2013	20	0.45	23.1	3	0.23	47.4
	Average of variation (per annum) (%)		0.7	Average of variation (per annum) (%)		5.8

Notes: Variation in the rental price in metres squared of commercial properties in the Municipality of Providencia, compared with the rental price in metres squared in Italia-Caupolicán between the years 1990 and 2013 (values are in the Chilean UF or '*Unidad de fomento*', which express values adjusted for inflation).

Source: Classified adverts from the national newspaper, El Mercurio, each Saturday fortnight during the months of April and September for the years shown. This was expanded for Italia-Caupolicán to include the months of January and March in order to increase the sample but does not include Internet advertisements, which would significantly raise the number of statistics available but are only available for 2013.

actors in the community and have a close relationship with their customers. 'New entrepreneurial' boutiques fall under two patterns of operation: the first is where individual properties are put to commercial use by their owners; the second is where shopkeepers rent space in subdivided properties from landlords. They make their business from selling 'classic' and 'modern' design products, handicrafts and antiques of national origin supplemented by international goods from Argentina and Europe (CNCA, 2012). These high-end expensive products are oriented towards a floating tourist population, which is enticed into the neighbourhood by a promotional website set up by the new shopkeepers, who have also invited many 'local' shops to participate (available at: www.barrioitalia.cl). The landlords of the rented shops make profit by the lease of land rather than the sale of products, capitalising on the promotional efforts of the individual shopkeepers.

The international retail chain stores that characterise the 'corporate' stores referred to by Zukin (2009) have not yet arrived in the neighbourhood but there is evidence of an economic interest beyond that of individual units. Some landlords who are renting space to the 'new entrepreneurs' are involved in an incipient process of real estate capital accumulation and now own four, seven and up to 14 properties (SII, 2013). A new project to renovate a former factory space is emblematic of this shift in the neighbourhood economy. This project will recreate the small boutiques, design stores and restaurants typical of the neighbourhood while, at the same time, including office space, a 'gastro' food market and boutique hotel. This project is the product of a carefully developed programme to capitalise on the 'trendy' mark of the neighbourhood (see: www.plataformaarquitectura.cl), in part created by the activities that have been held in the former factory, which include commercial events promoting national design, international clothing and footwear.

These three categories where capital is exploited at each stage of the transformation underlines the importance of each actor in the accumulation of capital. So far, 'local' capital still serves as an important element in the financial success of the new entrepreneurs. The 'added value' that local shops bring is evident as they have been invited to participate in a promotional website set up by the 'new entrepreneurs'. The individual capital of the traditional shops adds authenticity and serves as Bourdieu's (1983) mark of 'distinction' for the neighbourhood. In turn, the capital captured by the 'new entrepreneurs' is being capitalised on by the landlords who sell space. The temporary corporate events are a sign of progression in the capitalisation of the cultural capital of the neighbourhood, which is still yet to be consolidated by a business model that renovates buildings for retail use and sells them on to third parties for profit or a 'closing' of the rent gap.

Landscape change

While the international gentrification literature has documented neighbourhoods where new designer shops, cafes and restaurants are a sign of gentrification (eg Bridge and Dowling, 2001; Atkinson and Bridge 2005; Gotham, 2005; Zukin,

2009), in the Chilean literature, only a few case studies have described the landscape change that has occurred through retail gentrification in the central districts of the Chilean metropolis (eg Matus, 2010; Contreras, 2011). In fact, only a few areas in the centre of the city have managed to preserve their built heritage and are in this sense a fertile ground for retail gentrification, and contrast notably with the high-rise developments and new-build gentrification discussed by López-Morales (2008, 2010, 2013; López-Morales et al, 2012).

Italia-Caupolicán was established as a place for an affluent population at the end of the 19th century; it subsequently suffered decline and changed from a residential to a mixed-use semi-industrial area in the 1960s, and was occupied by artists from the early 1980s. This process seems to fit comfortably with the classic descriptions of inner-city neighbourhood gentrification in the Global North. The physical characteristics of this neighbourhood also correspond to the historical urban spatial evolution of the classic residential gentrification that Glass (1964) described in London. In Italia-Caupolicán, there is extensive evidence that retail gentrification is under way, demonstrating actual consumption practices and reflecting Zukin's (1990, 2009) early work on 'socio-spatial prototypes of consumption' and her more recent work on 'boutiquing'. The process of gentrification in Italia-Caupolicán is also akin to the patterns of cultural-mediated renewal described by Holm (2010), which parallels Ley's (2003) discussion on the commodification of cultural capital in the process of gentrification. These threads constitute the theoretical framework for our step-by-step analysis of landscape change in Italia-Caupolicán.

The first step in describing landscape change is to identify the existing, individual cultural capital of certain groups that is transformed into 'real cultural capital' (Zukin, 1990). The next step is to show how this capital is transformed into 'real cultural capital' and what role the buildings and urban space play in embedding this cultural capital (Zukin, 1990). The specific sites of transformation, the kind of shops, the type of products and atmosphere, and finally the type of promotion they undertake characterise the specific way in which the idea of a 'special' or 'distinctive' place is created and is capable of 'closing the gap' for profit (Holm, 2010). At which point, the neighbourhood becomes a competitive 'consumer landscape' in comparison to other sites of consumerism in Santiago de Chile. Finally, this leads to a 'culture of upgrading' (Holm, 2010) as the modus operandi of capitalist urban development.

The characteristics of individual 'incorporated' cultural capital

Through interviews with artists, identified in the register of artists, we sought to identify the presence of actors who were endowed with a high level of individual cultural capital, as described by Bourdieu (1983), Lloyd (2010) and Holm (2010). Data from interviews with artists, neighbours, shopkeepers and workers demonstrated that the cultural capital that characterises the neighbourhood has been provided by two groups. Since the beginning of the 1980s in the south-western area of the Providencia district, the proportion of artists living and working there has grown in relevance. This is shown by a register of artists made by the Unión de Artistas del Barrio Santa Isabel, a group of well-known and influential Chilean artists who moved their ateliers and individual showrooms to this area, bringing with them a lot of art students and colleagues (Unión de Artistas del Barrio Santa Isabel, 2009). By 2009, more than 70 artists lived or worked in the area they call 'Barrio Santa Isabel', an area that includes Italia-Caupolicán (see Figure 18.2). This neighbourhood – traditionally known as a bedraggled residential area – is, for them, a place where they find plenty of appropriate space for their work and a 'neighbourhood ambience' in exchange for a cheap rent. From the 1990s, some smaller bars and neighbourhood restaurants became known as meeting points for visual artists, writers and poets, and where artwork such as writing, paintings and photographs were put on display. The neighbourhood began to be a subject in paintings and installations by some artists and some of the street facades began to express the presence of this artistic production.

Data from interviews with key informants show that there is another group with cultural capital that was also relevant for the future development of the neighbourhood. From the end of the 1970s, a group of furniture restorers who lived in the disadvantaged periphery of Santiago settled with their stalls, workshops and warehouses along Caupolicán Street in the neighbourhood. This location

Figure 18.2: Plan of the Italia-Caupolicán neighbourhood.

Note: Actors and enterprises in the transformation of capital

ensured them an accessible venue, where buyers from all over Santiago and also from abroad would come to buy restored furniture. From 2009, they occupied almost the whole northern front of the street along two blocks and 20 shops (Lamour, leader of furniture restorers, interview, 2013). Through the permission to use the pavement for their restoring work, they created a very characteristic landscape along Caupolicán Street (see Figure 18.3).

Figure 18.3: Furniture restorers along Caupolicán Street

The cultural 'charging' of the space and its transformation into 'real cultural capital'

Artists' and furniture restorers' activities contributed to the symbolic transformation of the image of this bedraggled residential and light-industrial neighbourhood into a 'special place' with a 'bohemian' atmosphere, where it 'still is possible to see original craftsmanship'.[1] Interviews with artists revealed that this was a time when artists began to establish an explicit relationship with the neighbourhood in their direct marketing and where 'pioneer' art galleries began to flourish in the neighbourhood. Between 2006 and 2010, four 'pioneer' art galleries were opened in the Santa Isabel neighbourhood, especially in the area of Infante Street (Galeria Florencia Löwenthal, Galería Die Ecke, Galeria Bloc- YONO). Several newspaper articles appeared between 2003 and 2009 reporting on, and highlighting, projects, activities and architectural renewal in this 'new bohemian' neighbourhood (Schlack and Turnbull, 2009). Since 2010, this 'special' location has become explicit in the promotion of local, new renewal projects: 'Immersed in the traditional scene known as Barrio Italia where antique shops, design, furniture, clothing, cafes, restaurants and art galleries coexist daily'.[2]

The transformation of this neighbourhood has been accompanied by some initiatives undertaken by the state at the local and national level. At the local level, the municipality contributed to the modernisation of the neighbourhood through the construction of a new sports centre, social and cultural infrastructures, and new bicycle routes, and the renovation of the pavement in front of the stalls of the furniture restorers (Bannen and Chateau, 2007). At the national level, in 2012, the Chilean government's National Council for Culture and Arts (CNCA) declared the area of Avenue Italia as the 'Neighbourhood of Design'. This designation was given by the new 'Design' area of the council, which was set up to create programmes and public policy to develop the 'spatial impact of the market of the creative industries' (CNCA, 2012). In practice, this backing does little more than support private initiatives, which, in this case, was an association of design shops, restaurants and boutique-owners who promote the 'design & deco'-, 'accessories & style'-, 'heritage'-, 'culture'- and 'gastronomic'-themed tourist routes through the neighbourhood, as well as cultural and promotional activities.

The transformation of cultural capital into real cultural capital is evident in the urban space (demonstrating the spatial embeddedness of this cultural capital). In Avenue Italia renewal has taken the form of a 'distinctive place' for consumerism, where the ambience is constructed mostly by the traditional building typologies of 'patios' and 'houses with continuous facades' that are home to boutiques, restaurants, cafes and design shops where the expression of heritage features, old timber finishes and old adobe walls are all part of setting the scene. The changes in the Italia-Caupolicán neighbourhood, unlike the intense physical changes that occur in the cases of new-build gentrification in inner-city Santiago, do not structurally alter the buildings, the building height or the form of the facades. The big changes are in the rehabilitation of space, the change in use and at a symbolic level. It is the remodelling of the interior space through the application of new colours, materials and textures through which an aesthetic is created where the patina of the 'old' is capitalised on to give new value (see Figure 18.4). Neighbourhood change comes in the form of a change of use, where homes, car mechanic garages and local services such as the grocer or dry cleaners are transformed into design stores, shops for decoration and clothing, and fine dining.

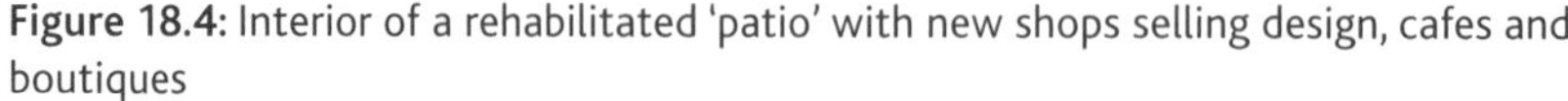

Figure 18.4: Interior of a rehabilitated 'patio' with new shops selling design, cafes and boutiques

The transformation of the profile of these shops is expressed symbolically in the local shop signs. Some of the existing premises do not have signs with names as they are already known to local customers. Other premises have cardboard signs in their windows that simply state 'bicycle workshop'; still others bear the nickname of their owner, such as 'Almacen Zulita' (Schlack and Turnbull, 2009, 2011) (see Figure 18.5). By contrast, the facades of newly installed commerce are adorned with banners and signs with sophisticated typography. Each shop sign is exposed to competition from the other evoking landscapes of foreign sophistication, 'Little Italy', 'Espacio Italia' and 'Italia Mía', or gamble on something more fashionable or contemporary, calling themselves 'Bazar de la Fortuna', 'Composit', 'Oops', 'The Popular Design', 'Amoble' and so on. This new retail not only symbolises an aspiration to cater for a more sophisticated clientele, but neither their product offer nor prices correspond to the usual lifestyle of the neighbourhood. The original landscape for inhabitants is replaced by a landscape for other consumers, most of them from other neighbourhoods in Santiago.

Figure 18.5: Cardboard signs of a local shop: the 'locksmith for cars, homes, safes' and a local restaurant that offers home-cooked dishes

The retail landscape and relationship to other spatial prototypes of consumption in Santiago

The renewal of the Italia-Caupolicán neighbourhood means more than merely a change of use, it has embedded a specific prototype of consumption, an alternative to Shopping Malls and 'Strip centres' (shopping parades), and is similar to other typologies in Santiago, like Patio Bellavista (see Figure 18.6), Patio Lastarria and

Patio Mulato Gil in central Santiago. What these cases have in common is that they all developed as bohemian neighbourhoods that were subsequently converted into a new retail typology, such as a 'patio', new-build or restored, administrated by one owner, which have also been sold on to mall entrepreneurs.

Displacement

Although the reinvestment of capital and landscape change in Italia-Caupolicán and the data from interviews with long-term residents suggest a socio-economic restructuring of the neighbourhood, census data from 1982–2002 (the latest

Figure 18.6: The retail prototype of the patio: 'Patio Bellavista'

Source: Photograph taken by the authors.

census available) demonstrate most revealingly a shrinking residential population. In the supposedly most-gentrified area around Italia Avenue, the total population consisted of 705 inhabitants in 1982, falling to 544 in 1992 and then to 366 in 2002, a decrease of 56% (INE, 1982, 1992, 2002). This differs from general population changes in the wider district of Providencia, where the population has increased by 4.6% between 1992 and 2002, and also from the population changes in the entire metropolitan region of Santiago, which has seen a growth of 15.6% between 1992 and 2002 (INE, 1992, 2002). This decrease of population in the neighbourhood could be explained by the change of use, as shown by data on commercial licences: of the 48 properties newly brought into commercial use during 2009–12, only 8% have changed their commercial use, whereas 92% are in properties that previously were not of commercial use. What these properties were used for before is difficult to ascertain. However, field observations confirm that 90% of the properties identified as coming into recent commercial use are surviving examples of domestic architecture that date from 1900–30, that is to say, they were originally constructed for residential use. This may serve as a key indicator, as many structures have been altered in the neighbourhood over the years in order to accommodate new uses and it is often only the domestic uses that have maintained the domestic architecture.

As these data from the census show that low-income and lower-middle-income groups decreased in Italia-Caupolicán by 53% between 1982 and 2002, and as the decrease of these occupational groups nationally amounts to only 1.8%, we interpret this as evidence of gentrification. However, more recent evidence on displacement is not available as the information from the 2012 census has not been released and other sources of population data do not allow for investigation of specific neighbourhoods. Research in the Global North has found that displacement is often difficult to prove. However, we concur that displacement is crucial to the gentrification debate (Slater, 2009) and is a key factor of gentrification, which, to paraphrase Marcuse (1985), takes place with the arrival of new residents with a higher educational profile and income who replace older, poorer, working-class residents to a degree that is disproportionate to changes in general society. In its widest sense, displacement touches on the fundamental concept of the 'right to the city' (Lefebvre, 1969). Further analysis of displacement in Italia-Caupolicán must be based on these concepts. The comparative study of commercial gentrification in Harlem and Williamsburg in New York City undertaken by Zukin (2009) offers a useful framework for the study of retail gentrification; it shows 'retail landscapes in transition' but concludes that there is no evidence of replacement. Another approach to researching retail gentrification can be found in the work of Moreno (2010), who investigates gentrification in Barcelona using a classification developed by Sergi Martínez Rigol (2010). Moreno (2010) directs attention to the commercial typologies characterised according to social groups that share similar lifestyle values. The main categories are 'traditional establishments' that meet the daily needs of long-term residents (greengrocers, grocers, etc), those that are for recreation (bars, local restaurants) and 'fashionable' establishments that are oriented towards a more 'modern' and 'sophisticated' lifestyle. He concludes that these categories stand for the sociocultural changes that happen in the renewal processes in the central city. Although both Zukin's (2009) and Moreno's (2010) studies have very different theoretical frameworks and aims, they share in common an emphasis on the importance of qualitative indicators behind the numbers. Zukin refers to the change of 'sense of place' due to the diminution of local shops and the increase in the visibility of new entrepreneurial and corporate stores that risk 'disrupting local social life and may alienate and displace long-term residents' (Zukin, 2009, p 62). She opens up discussion about the 'right to shop' as part of the 'right to the city' principle. By way of contrast, Moreno (2010) reflects on the kind of population that the traditional and the fashionable establishments attract and what this means for a change of lifestyles in the neighbourhood. His reflections are interested in indirect displacement, in the terms of Marcuse's 'pressure of displacement', which is brought about by neighbourhood factors, such as loss of social networks and facilities, that conspire to undermine quality of life (see Marcuse, 1985).

Holm (2010) also reflects on displacement in central areas where gentrification has been driven by the cultural capital of creative groups. His analysis comes from the perspective of 'cultural capital as an instrument of displacement' and he argues that cultural and creative activities have sociocultural effects over the existing population because of a displacement by 'distinction'. From this point of view, research on displacement needs to focus on the perceptions of cultural change by the existing population, for example, Butler (2003) has described existing inhabitants feeling that they were 'being left behind'.

These slightly different approaches seem to be appropriate for further studies in neighbourhoods like Italia-Caupolicán where the economic interests of retail entrepreneurs who are transforming the landscape are perceived by long-term local residents as provoking a loss of social networks and the alienation of their sociocultural environment (Schlack and Turnbull, 2013). A long-term female resident told us: "normally we know almost nothing about the others [referring to the new shopkeepers and owners]; there is a lot of distrust between us".

Disaffection of existing residents with respect to this new landscape is a central theme, particularly for groups of older people, those of lower income and those who have lived there all their lives. There are two main reasons for this. The first, argued by residents who are also local shop-owners, is that they feel challenged to adapt their local small-scale businesses to a more competitive context. A woman that owns a local greengrocers shop said: "I feel happy with my display of fruit and vegetables. And I feel happy with my neighbours that come along to buy something and gossip. So, I don't want to change either my clients or my products."

The second reason, argued by long-term residents – mostly older people – is the feeling of being abandoned because their old neighbours – their social network – has been replaced by boutiques, restaurants or designer shops (Schlack and Turnbull, 2013), and the whole neighbourhood lifestyle has become full of noise, traffic pollution and criminality. 'A neighbourhood without neighbours doesn't work!', said one long-term inhabitant. He added:

> 'the encounter between the old and new inhabitants of the neighbourhood is not amicable. As families, we are left alone. The renewed architecture could be very nice, but the big problem is the loss of inhabitants. We prefer to live together with the furniture restorers, than with the new restaurants and cafes. In spite of the rubbish the furniture restorers leave behind, they take part in the life of the neighbourhood.'

The data from interviews with long-term residents shown earlier suggests a socio-economic restructuring of the neighbourhood, even if we have no definitive evidence on displacement in Italia-Caupolicán since the 2002 census. As data from interviews with diverse participants of renewal and long-term residents from our study show,s the diverse actors in the neighbourhood are threatened or benefit by the rise of commercial activity differently. To assess the differentiated way in which diverse actors are affected, research needs to be based on data on housing tenure distribution and take account of the differences between residential and commercial land use, as discussed in similar international gentrification processes (see Shin, 2010).

Through the analysis of census data, rental prices and the register of commercial licences, we identified the specific housing tenure distribution in the neighbourhood. On the one hand, data on the residential population demonstrates that between 23% and 31% of the population in the Italia-Caupolicán neighbourhood lived in rented properties in 2011 and that 67.6–74.9% were residential owner-occupiers (Biblioteca del Congreso Nacional, 2011). On the other hand, an estimate of the tenure pattern of the commercial activity shows that 63% of the commercial activities were in rented accommodation and only 17% of the business premises owned the same property in which they operated (Ilustre Municipalidad de Providencia, 2012). Through this tenancy pattern, we interpret that differentiated consequences from the rising commercial activity in the Italia-Caupolicán neighbourhood could emerge. Further studies would have to survey if tenant-residents are indeed vulnerable to a rise in rents and direct displacement and to what extent homeowners are also threatened by indirect displacement. Existing data from interviews show that most homeowners sold their property and left the neighbourhood. Yet, our survey does not identify if they left because the sale of a housing unit did not generate the necessary financial return to buy a new house in the same location.

With regards to commercial premises, it is possible to assert that since rental prices for new premises have almost doubled in the last 13 years (see Table 18.1), and where there may be a similar rise in the rent for existing premises, the issue of how commercial use can adapt to meet these new financial demands becomes important. For example existing shops would need to adapt their offer in order to service a higher rental cost. Local shops such as the grocers, locksmiths and bicycle workshops might find it difficult to raise their incomes through their current offer. The ability for renting shopkeepers to adapt to a more expensive environment will depend on the specific type of commerce, the relationship shopkeepers have with the existing community and their ability to capture a new market.

The neighbourhood's new image has led some of the old shop-owners to take part as new entrepreneurs. This is the case mostly with local restaurants and bars, where shop-owners are flexible to the new clientele. Instead, other long-term shop-owners insist on their traditional services for the neighbourhood. This is the case of grocery and greengrocery shops, as well as car repair workshops. For them, even if the changes in the neighbourhood are not as direct as for tenant shopkeepers, the rise in commercial activity means a pressure for them to leave their specific type of commerce.

Understanding the decisive role that planning legislation plays in shaping commercial activities in the neighbourhood provides insight into the failures of pro-entrepreneurial, neoliberal urbanism where these regulations are absent. Here, owners might also be vulnerable (as tenants are) depending on their respective role as residents or shopkeepers in the neighbourhood. Due to the specific characteristics of commercial activity in the neighbourhood, we presume that the rising rents influence, first, the tenant seller but, through him or her, also indirectly the consumer. As Zukin (2009) stated, displacement in the context of commercial gentrification should also consider the displacement of potential consumers that are forced to buy more expensive and more sophisticated products.

Conclusion

Gentrification in Italia-Caupolicán is a different variant from other processes of private developer-led gentrification in Santiago. Here, gentrification is not the product of a coherent and planned strategy of urban renewal, as witnessed in inner-city Santiago, but an opportunistic exploitation by private developers of a number of key neighbourhood factors that are transformed into capital gain, which in the absence of state intervention, has left local communities vulnerable to private initiatives. This is an emerging process that has not yet reached 'completion' in the sense that 'corporate' interests have not yet arrived en masse to capitalise on this process. The findings in this chapter are complementary to the discussions about gentrification in the form of high-rise towers and gated communities in the Chilean gentrification literature, for they show the class appropriation of land, in this case, being sold as a consumer enclave. Ultimately, the emerging retail gentrification in Italia-Caupolicán is evidence that gentrification is adapting itself to different spatial contexts and conditions in Santiago and is yet another expression of an unwelcome process of unequal land access in the urban landscape.

The specifics of gentrification here pose several questions, including how to defend heritage areas from the pressure of competitive retail clusters that are embedded in attractive and authentic urban spaces, and how to avoid culturally 'distinctive' places capitalised on as new spatial prototypes of consumption that have similar characteristics to those in the Global North. Ultimately, is all urban transformation generated by private capital investment in the form of retail clusters in the inner city of Santiago inevitably a form of gentrification? Could this 'gentrification' be a limited phenomenon (see Ley and Dobson, 2008) and can we find some examples of 'gentrification-free' territories in the inner city of Santiago?

Notes

[1] Quote from: www.barrioitalia.cl

[2] Quote from: www.iarmas.cl

References

APU (Atelier Parisien D'Urbanisme) (2000) *Santiago poniente desarrollo urbano y patrimonio* [*West Santiago, urban development and heritage*], Paris and Santiago de Chile: Dirección de Obras Municipales de Santiago and Atelier Parisien D'Urbanisme.

Atkinson, R. and Bridge, G. (2005) *Gentrification in a global context: the new urban colonialism*, London: Routledge.

Bannen, P. and Chateau, F. (eds) (2007) *La Ciudad de Providenica en la obra de Germán Bannen* [*The city of Providencia in the work of Germán Bannen*], Santiago de Chile: Ediciones ARQ.

Biblioteca del Congreso Nacional (2011) 'Reportes estadísticos sobre la encuesta CASEN de Caracterización Socioeconómica Nacional' ['Statistical reports on the national poll of socio-economic categories']. Available at: http://reportescomunales.bcn.cl/2013/index.php/Providencia#Tipo_de_tenencia_de_la_vivienda_CASEN_2003-2011

Borsdorf, A. and Hidalgo, R. (2012) 'Revitalization and tugurization in the historical centre of Santiago de Chile', *Cities*, no 31, pp 96–104.

Bourdieu, P. (1983) 'Ökonomisches Kapital, kulturelles Kapital und soziales Kapital', ['Economic capital, cultural capital, social capital'], in R. Krekel (ed) *Soziale Ungleichheiten, Soziale Welt Sonderband 2*, Göttingen: Göttingen University Press, pp 183–9.

Bridge, G. and Dowling, R. (2001) 'Microgeographies of retailing and gentrification', *Australian Geographer*, vol 32, no 1, pp 93–107.

Butler, T. (2003) 'Living in the bubble: gentrification and its others in London', *Urban Studies*, vol 40, no 12, pp 2469–86.

CNCA (2012) *Guía, 'Barrio Italia', Barrio del Diseño* [*Guide to the 'Barrio Italia' Design neighbourhood*], Santiago de Chile: Consejo Nacional de la Cultura y las Artes.

Contreras, Y. (2009) 'Movilidad Residencial Centrípeta: El rol del mercado inmobiliario y del nuevo habitante urbano en la recuperación del centro de Santiago de Chile' ['Centripetal residential mobility: the role of the housing market and the urban inhabitant in the recovery of the centre of Santiago de Chile'], XII ENCUENTRO DE GEÓGRAFOS DE AMÉRICA LATINA, Uruguay, 3–7 April. Available at: http://egal2009.easyplanners.info/area08/8223_Contreras_Gatica_Yasna_del_Carmen.pdf

Contreras, Y. (2011) 'La recuperación urbana y residencial del centro de Santiago: Nuevos habitantes, cambios socioespaciales significativos' ['The urban and residential renovation of central Santiago: newcomers and significant sociospatial changes'], *Revista EURE*, vol 37, no 112, pp 89–113.

Davidson, M. and Lees, L. (2005) 'New-build "gentrification" and London's riverside renaissance', *Environment and Planning A*, vol 37, pp 1165–90.

Davidson, M. and Lees, L. (2010) 'New-build gentrification: its histories, trajectories, and critical geographies', *Population, Space and Place*, vol 16, pp 395–411.

De Mattos, C. (1999) 'Santiago de Chile, globalización y expansión metropolitana: lo que existía sigue existiendo' ['The globalisation and metropolitan expansion of Santiago de Chile: what existed still exists'], *Revista EURE*, no 76, pp 29–56.

De Mattos, C. (2008) 'Cambios socio-ocupacionales y transformación metropolitana del Gran Santiago, 1992–2002' ['Social-occupational changes and metropolitan changes in Greater Santiago 1992–2002'], in P. Allard (ed) *Mercado y ciudad: desafíos de un país urbano. Observatorio de Ciudades UC/BBVA*, Santiago: Editorial Valente.

Glass, R. (1964) 'Introduction: aspects of change', in Centre for Urban Studies (ed) *London: aspects of change*, London: MacGibbon and Kee.

Gotham, K. (2005) 'Tourism gentrification: the case of New Orleans' Vieux Carre (French Quarter)', *Urban Studies*, vol 42, no 7, pp 1099–121.

Hidalgo, R. and Arenas, F. (2011) 'Negocios inmobiliarios y la transformación metropolitana de Santiago de Chile: Desde la renovación del espacio central hasta la periferia expandida' ['Real estate markets and the metropolitan transformation of Santiago de Chile'], *Revista Geográfica de América Central*, Número Especial EGAL, II semestre, pp 1–16.

Holm, A. (2010) 'Gentrifizierung und Kultur: Zur Logik kulturell vermittelter Aufwertungsprozesse' ['Gentrification and culture: on the logic of culturally mediated enhancement processes'], in C. Hannemann (ed) *Jahrbuch StadtRegion 2009. Stadtkultur und Kreativität*, Opladen: Budrich, pp 64–80.

Ilustre Municipalidad de Providencia (2009) *Listado de Patentes Comerciales* [*Register of commercial licenses*], Santiago de Chile: Ilustre Municipalidad de Providencia.

Ilustre Municipalidad de Providencia (2012) *Listado de Patentes Comerciales* [*Register of commercial licenses*], Santiago de Chile: Ilustre Municipalidad de Providencia.

INE (Chilean National Institute of Statistics) (1982) *Census 1982*.

INE (1992) *Census 1992*.

INE (2002) *Census 2002*.

Ingram, G. (2006) 'Patrones del desarrollo metropolitano ¿qué hemos aprendido?' ['Patterns of metropolitan development, what have we learnt?'], in A. Galetovic (ed) *Santiago dónde estamos hacia dónde vamos*, Santiago de Chile: Ediciones Centro de Estudios Públicos.

Inzulza, J. (2012) '"Latino gentrification?" Focusing on physical and socioeconomic patterns of change in Latin American inner cities', *Urban Studies*, vol 49, no 10, pp 2085–107.

Janoschka, M. and Casgrain, A. (2012) 'Urbanismo Neoliberal y gentrificación en Santiago de Chile' ['Neoliberal urbanism and gentrification in Santiago de Chile'], unpublished paper for *Revista OTRA*, pp 1–10.

Lees, L., Slater, T. and Wyly, E. (2008) *Gentrification*, London and New York, NY: Routledge.

Lefevbre, H. (1969) *El derecho a la ciudad* [*The right to the city*], Barcelona: Edición 62.

Ley, D. (2003) 'Artists, aestheticisation and the field of gentrification', *Urban Studies*, vol 40, no 12, pp 2527–44.

Ley, D. and Dobson, C. (2008) 'Are there limits to gentrification? The contexts of impeded gentrification in Vancouver', *Urban Studies*, vol 45, no 12, pp 2471–98.

Lloyd, R. (2010) *Neo-Bohemia: art and commerce in the post industrial city* (2nd edn), London and New York, BY: Routledge.

López-Morales, E. (2008) 'Destrucción creativa y explotación de brecha de renta: discutiendo la renovación urbana del peri-centro sur poniente de Santiago de Chile entre 1990 y 2005', ['Creative destruction and rent-gap exploitation: discussion of the urban regeneration of the south-west centre of Santiago de Chile between 1990 and 2005'], *Scripta Nova*, p 12.

López-Morales, E. (2010) 'Real estate market, state-entrepreneurialism and urban policy in the "gentrification by ground rent dispossession" of Santiago de Chile', *Journal of Latin American Geography*, vol 9, no 1, pp 145–73.

López-Morales, E. (2013) 'Measuring the invisible: the dispossession of the rent gap as a form of displacement', paper presented at the RC21 Conference, Berlin, Germany.

López-Morales, E., Gasic, K. and Meza, D. (2012) 'Urban state-entrepreneurialism in Chile: policies and planning within high-rise residential production in the pericenter area of greater Santiago', *Revista INVI*, no 76, vol 27, pp 75–114.

Marcuse, P. (1985) 'Gentrification, abandonment and displacement: connections, causes and policy responses in New York City', *Urban Law Annual; Journal of Urban and Contemporary Law*, vol 28, pp 195–240.

Martínez Rigol, S. (ed) (2010) *La cuestión del centro. El centro en cuestión* [*The question of the centre. The centre in question*], Lleida: Editorial Milenio.

Matus, C. (2010) 'La cultura urbana y los estilos de vida en la revitalización de un barrio patrimonial del centro histórico de Santiago. El caso de Lastarría-Bellas Artes' ['Urban culture and lifestyles in the renewal of a historic neighbourhood in the historic centre of Santiago'], PhD thesis, Santiago de Chile, Faculty of Architecture, Design and Urban Studies, Catholic University of Chile.

Moreno, S. (2010) 'Actividades comerciales, centralidad y gentrificación' ['Commercial activity, centrality and gentrification'], in S. Martínez Rigol (ed) *La cuestión del Centro, el Centro en cuestión* [*The question of the centre, the centre in question*], Lleida: Editorial Milenio.

OECD (Organisation for Economic Co-operation and Development) (2013) *Working party on territorial policy in urban areas. National urban policy reviews, the case of Chile*, Paris: Organisation for Economic Co-operation and Development.

Rodríguez, J. (2007) 'Paradojas y contrapuntos de dinámica demográfica metropolitana: algunas respuestas basadas en la explotación intensiva de microdatos censales' ['Paradoxes and counterpoints in metropolitan population dynamics: some answers based on the intensive exploitation of census microdata'], in C. De Mattos and R. Hidalgo (eds) *Santiago de Chile: Movilidad espacial y reconfiguración metropolitan*, Colección EURE Libros, Serie GEOlibros No 8, pp 19–52.

Rodríguez, J. (2008) 'Dinámica sociodemográfica metropolitana y segregación residencial: ¿qué aporta la CASEN 2006?' ['Metropolitan sociodemographic dynamics and residential segregation: what does the CASEN 2006 show?'], *Revista de Geografía Norte Grande*, no 41, pp 81–102.

Sabatini, F., Cáceres, G. and Cerda, J. (2001) 'Segregación residencial en las principales ciudades chilenas: Tendencia de las tres últimas décadas y posibles cursos de acción' ['Residential segregation in the major Chilean cities: trends of the last three decades and possible courses of action'], *Revista Eure*, vol XXVIII, no 82, pp 21–42.

Sabatini, F., Robles, M. and Vásquez, H. (2009) 'Gentrificación sin expulsión, o la ciudad latinoamericana en una encrucijada histórica' ['Gentrification without expulsion, or the Latin American city at a historic crossroad'], *Revista 180*, no 24, pp 18–25.

Schlack, E. and Turnbull, N. (2009) 'La Colonización de barrios céntricos por artistas' ['The colonisation of central neighbourhoods by artists'], *Revista 180*, no 24, pp 02–05.

Schlack, E. and Turnbull, N. (2011) 'Capitalizando lugares autenticos' ['Capitalising upon authenticity'], *Revista ARQ*, no 79, pp 28–42.

Schlack, E. and Turnbull, N. (2013) Unpublished meeting notes from public consultations in Italia-Caupolicán.

Shin, H.B. (2010) 'Urban conservation and revalorisation of dilapidated historic quarters: the case of Nanluoguxiang in Beijing', *Cities*, vol 27 (Supplement 1), S43–S54.

SII (Servicio de Impuestos Internos [National Tax Office]) (2013) *Local property tax register 2013*, Santiago de Chile: Servicio de Impuestos Internos.

Slater, T. (2009) 'Missing Marcuse on gentrification and displacement', *City: Analysis of Urban Trends, Culture, Theory, Policy, Action*, vol 13, nos 2/3, pp 292–311.

Smith, N. (1979) 'Toward a theory of gentrification, a back to the city movement by capital, not people', *Journal of American Planning Association*, vol 45, no 4, pp 538–48.

Unión de Artistas de Barrio Santa Isabel (2009) Unpublished record of artists who live and work in the Santa Isabel neighbourhood.

Zukin, S. (1989) *Loft living culture and capital in urban change* (2nd edn), New Brunswick, NJ: Rutgers University Press.

Zukin, S. (1990) 'Socio-spatial prototypes of a new organization of consumption: the role of real cultural capital', *Sociology*, vol 24, no 1, pp 37–56.

Zukin, S. (2009) 'New retail capital and neighborhood change: boutiques and gentrification in New York City', *City & Community*, vol 8, no 1, pp 47–64.

NINETEEN

Gentrification dispositifs in the historic centre of Madrid: a reconsideration of urban governmentality and state-led urban reconfiguration

Jorge Sequera and Michael Janoschka

Introduction

Fuelled by major social, political and economic transformations occurring since the early 1990s, the historic centre of Madrid, home to roughly 145,000 inhabitants, has undergone a series of fundamental re-articulations that have boosted its functional role and symbolic imaginary. Among others, the implementation of different urban renewal programmes[1] has strategically targeted its economic revalorisation. Additionally, specific master plans[2] for the area have structured the investment policies around joint and coordinated actions between public administrations and private initiatives, chiefly aiming to bolster capital investment in commercial, cultural and real estate activities. Beyond this, an extensive 'touristification' of the area has been taking place. As a consequence, many parts of the historic centre of Madrid (such as the neighbourhoods of Malasaña, Chueca and the Las Letras quarter) can now be considered as gentrified or at least as spaces that have been experiencing intensive processes of gentrification. During the long boom decade between 1995 and 2007, the price increases in real estate transactions in the central district outperformed all other neighbourhoods of the city, and since then, the historic centre's housing prices have consolidated at above-average prices – both for purchase and rental agreements.

Public administrations have played a crucial role in this reconfiguration of the historic city centre (Blanco et al, 2011), configuring contemporary geographies of gentrification and creating a symbolically and strategically unique space within the metropolitan area (Díaz Orueta, 2007). In this chapter, by exploring the powerful logics of the private and public interventions that are causing gentrification in Madrid, we develop an understanding of the locally specific adaptation of neoliberal urban policies in a Spanish city so far little discussed in the gentrification literatures. It is our contention that debates about gentrification in Spain must move beyond the two iconic examples of Barcelona and Bilbao that have been dominating the literature (eg Vicario and Martínez Monje, 2005; Ribera-Fumaz,

2008; González, 2011). In this chapter, we move beyond these 'usual Spanish suspects' and consider two contemporary gentrification frontiers in the historic city centre of Madrid: the neighbourhoods of Lavapiés and Triball. Both areas have recently experienced significant public and private reinvestment, but they are related to quite different policies and the strategic targeting of gentrification in Madrid. Lavapiés is an example of how cultural production can be considered as a principal driving force behind gentrification. By way of contrast, our second case study, Triball, is a gentrification frontier that has been established primarily by private investors targeting the area for revalorisation via commercial branding (Justo, 2011). In addition, they are of a different size,[3] and the social composition of their populations varies substantially. The latter has made researching these neighbourhoods extraordinarily interesting, but also a very challenging endeavour, both analytically and intellectually.

In analytical terms, the discussions presented here are based on empirical work that included participant observation, the analysis of official planning documents and media reports, 26 semi-structured interviews with key actors in both neighbourhoods, and 12 group discussions with neighbours.[4] The interpretation draws on the concept of governmentality – a perspective that helps us to explain how *gentrification dispositifs* can be considered simultaneously as a biopower and disciplinary power that disguise the arts of governing the self and the population (Uitermark, 2005; Foucault, 2006; Huxley, 2007; Ettlinger, 2011). We will focus on three specific gentrification dispositifs in Madrid that are comprehensively developed through the empirical examples, related to (i) creativity and cultural production, (ii) retail and design, and (iii) the governance of public space to both enforce and promote gentrification. However, before moving on to this, we provide a characterisation of contemporary gentrification discourses in Spain to point out some of the key differences from those in anglophone gentrification studies.

Gentrification discourses in Spain and Madrid

Although certain evidence suggests that gentrification processes have shaped Spanish cities such as Madrid and Barcelona since the early 1990s (Vázquez, 1992; Sargatal, 2001), it was not until the mid-2000s that gentrification emerged as a powerful discourse across the Spanish-speaking scientific community. Many scientists initially failed to recognise and adapt the concept to the social, political and urban contexts in which gentrification was occurring, especially as its symbolic and material expressions differ notably from the iconic cases in London and New York that have dominated the perception of gentrification for decades. However, to a certain extent, this delay also responds to scientific trends. For instance, the 1992 Olympic Games provided a significant impetus for the tracking and 'selling' of the 'success story' of Barcelona's regeneration processes (Monclús, 2003; Marshall, 2004). On the other hand, discussions from Bilbao concentrated on the 'Guggenheim effect' (Gómez, 1998; Plaza, 1999; Gómez and González, 2001), and since the mid-2000s, major attention was paid to the consequences of transnational migration processes (Arbaci, 2007; Pareja-Eastaway, 2009; Portes et al, 2010) and the real estate bubble (López and Rodríguez, 2010). Such prominent debates relegated gentrification research in Spain to a secondary place.

The situation, though, has changed, and gentrification is now being regularly applied to the study of urban transformation in all major Spanish cities. Among others, gentrification discourses shape a broader criticism of the social and spatial consequences of contemporary urban policies such as segregation, classism, inequalities and displacement – especially as the term has not been depoliticised or naturalised as a non-critical concept thus far. As such, in this chapter, we critically engage with contemporary gentrification as a crucial expression and key outcome of urban neoliberalisation – a process that has been widely recognised in Spanish cities as a very specific form of urban capital accumulation (Swyngedouw et al, 2002; López and Rodríguez, 2011; Naredo and Montiel, 2011). This necessitates reconsidering gentrification through the territorial and sociolinguistic lens of Spanish researchers, enabling critical dialogues with the mainstream anglophone discourse. Additionally, this performs an emancipatory approach that emphasises the distinctiveness of gentrification outside of the anglophone core (see Lees, 2012; Maloutas, 2012), so as to provide 'nuanced, complex and contextual accounts' of urban realities and processes (Robinson, 2011, p 18). Spanish researchers have brought in new and, at the same time, challenging perspectives that have contributed to decentring theoretical approaches for a better understanding of contemporary gentrification through a 'Spanish' lens (Janoschka et al, 2013). Following this lineage, we develop four key points of argumentation here, which help us to better frame our empirical case studies in Madrid.

First, it should be acknowledged that gentrification in Spain has been taking place within the context of a massive influx of more than 5 million migrants to the country. Many of them settled in inner-city areas that were at the same time subject to renewal schemes, as described earlier. Lavapiés and Triball illustrate this perfectly; in both neighbourhoods (mostly non-European) foreigners made up nearly 40% of the total population. In Lavapiés, the arrival of immigrants and gentrification took place simultaneously, which introduces the interesting question of how both mechanisms can coexist in Spanish city centres. Based on empirical work, Arbaci (2008, p 595f) displays the discontinuity of gentrification, a process that apparently has not transgressed to entire neighbourhoods. This means that at least two sharply differentiated and separated housing markets coexist in the same place (Sargatal, 2001), perpetuating segregation and spatial exclusion. In other words, Triball and Lavapiés stand for other Spanish cities that represent non-homogeneous areas of revalorisation and fragmented territories in a continuous struggle about the re-appropriation of space (Janoschka et al, 2013).

Second, gentrification in Spanish cities cannot be fully understood without attention to the key role that the different levels of public administration play within the promotion of policies that target tourism-related and other symbolic gentrification processes, especially those linked to an institutionalised cultural production. In this regard, it is important to consider how urban tourism has increasingly appreciated cultural assets, establishing different logics of spatial appropriation that have paired themselves with gentrification induced by tourism (Janoschka et al, 2013). We suggest that this 'state-led tourism gentrification' can be noticed in the daily activity of the neighbourhood of Lavapiés, due to its multiculturalism, museums and cultural facilities, as well as its nightlife and multi-ethnic gastronomy. Furthermore, the rhetoric of the creative city as a *leitmotiv* for urban renewal is also a key issue for recent discussions. Not only in Bilbao and Barcelona, but also in Madrid and specifically in Lavapiés, public policies have applied Richard Florida's creative paradigm, attempting to establish a discursive environment that attracts cultural entrepreneurs. In a meaningful critique of this logic, Rodríguez and Vicario (2005) state that urban marketing only covers evident gentrification strategies, while it displaces urban problems instead of resolving them. In Madrid, the long-term consequences of urban renewal have been interpreted as an introduction of new lifestyles based on distinctive practices of consumerism and models of citizenship (Sequera, 2010). Delgado (2008) names this effect 'artistification' (*artistización* in Spanish): a process that is enacted by urban policies that embrace the entrepreneurial and consumerist re-appropriation of a city transformed into a cluster of thematic parks and a place for cultural performances. Such strategies are a key factor in the renewal schemes applied in Lavapiés, converting a working-class neighbourhood into a place for new knowledge economies. The relationship has been labelled by Dot et al (2010) as 'productive gentrification' – creativity and knowledge appear as new resources that express the paradigmatic shift towards post-Fordism.

Third, in this chapter, we propose placing a major emphasis on the policies related to the reconversion of working-class neighbourhoods through commercial restructuration. To a certain degree, this is related to the previous aspect, but it responds primarily to suggestions that retail can be considered a key issue for explaining contemporary gentrification processes (see Kloostermann and Van der Leun, 1999; Zukin et al, 2009; Wang, 2011; González and Waley, 2013). In Madrid, commercial gentrification is taking place in several neighbourhoods, and similar aspects have been reported from Barcelona (Ribera-Fumaz, 2008). In some cases, such as the Las Letras neighbourhood, these transformations are primarily related to urban tourism and/or nightlife. However, Triball is the most important and, at the same time, aggressive attempt to reconstruct a neighbourhood as a specific commercial product (*barrio marca* in Spanish). Such policies aim at the general gentrification of the area: first symbolically, by producing a favourable environment for the middle- and upper-middle classes; then through the renovation of buildings and the construction of new housing units to attract new residents with higher incomes – with both aspects then necessarily inducing the displacement of lower-income residents. Triball can be considered an exemplary case of this. While the issue is different in Lavapiés – where although new shops have also begun to mushroom, the process is more associated with the incoming cosmopolitan middle classes with high cultural levels than with a specific entrepreneurial strategy – nevertheless, there is an impact on the neighbourhood.

Finally, the Spanish gentrification debate should also take into consideration how resistance against gentrification is theoretically framed by a close collaboration between academics and social movements. Following the legacy of Manuel Castells (1983), the literature on urban social movements has an important presence in Spanish urban studies. This has motivated many gentrification researchers to focus their arguments towards neighbourhood struggles and demands (Gómez, 2006; Delgado, 2007; Díaz Orueta, 2007). The case of Lavapiés is no exception: since the very beginning of the implementation of the renewal programmes, the residents' demands have attracted the attention of academics. In line with our own observations, different studies have recognised that activism in Lavapiés is symbolically loaded with a pronounced left-wing atmosphere. It allows maintaining the fight against speculation, evictions and indiscriminate immigrant detentions, as well as the police state that has besieged the neighbourhood. The situation is similar in Triball, for important struggles against gentrification, as well as the increasing policing strategies, emerged as soon as the commercial association was founded. Since then, the area has been subject to different squatting initiatives. Additionally, several militant researchers have studied the transformations that are taking place by visualising and contextualising the gentrification strategies applied, while the city has been suffering a profound economic and social crisis. As further discussed by Janoschka et al (2013), the close relation between activists and academics is something that is a key feature in gentrification debates in Madrid and, in more general terms, also in other Spanish cities.

'Gentrification dispositifs' as a conceptual perspective

The conceptual underpinnings to this chapter stem from the work of the French philosopher Michel Foucault, in which he reflects upon how discipline is exercised through bodies, and how security is performed upon the collective population as a whole. Ettlinger (2011, p 538) states that this governmentality approach 'offers an analytical framework that is especially useful towards connecting abstract societal discourses with everyday material practices'. In relation to the city, governmentality provides us with an understanding of how social relations have been incorporated into productive relationships (Negri, 2006), especially as the city can be considered to be an encoded objective of the strategies of political extraction (Agamben, 2006). In this regard, Dominguez (2008) affirms that a sharp diminution of social spaces that escape the logics of capitalist exploitation and domination has been taking place in Spanish cities. Resulting from these dynamics, a series of dispositifs transform the processes of urban restructuration into a mechanism to discipline citizens (Delgado, 2007). Within neoliberal governmentality, the governed apparently possess the autonomy to decide their doom, but 'technologies of the self' make them suffer procedures of individualisation and self-coercion (Vázquez, 2005). Zukin (2010) has approached this empirically, investigating how individuals look for a supposedly authentic lifestyle. However, such a quest transforms the subject itself into an enterprise, and it stimulates the creation of new markets and ways to commercialise additional parts of everyday life. Hence, the governance that is established within neoliberalisation processes is a specific form of governmentality – built upon the illusion that allegedly free subjects establish non-hierarchical relations (Lorey, 2008). However, in the terms of Elias (1990), such apparently free individual governance is at the same time a disciplinary act that strengthens internal fears. As a consequence, figuratively, sovereign individuals can be considered as governed through the practice of invisible power relations.

This makes us wonder how public administrations actually understand the governance of a population: in the handling and naturalisation of specific scripts and procedures for a population that self-regulates in relation to the resources that it has previously been provided with (Foucault, 2006). Such a government can be considered as reflexive – it does not directly manage the living conditions or the productive relations of its population, but produces subjectivities that are closely related to biopolitical technologies and disciplinary practices (Coleman and Agnew, 2007). Taking into consideration the relationship between subjectivities and space, this can mean the application of disciplinary dispositifs (spatial policing practices, CCTV surveillance and control over or the appropriation of public space). Governance also makes use of the proper biopolitics of the neoliberal era – liquid relations, creative production and consumerism. Such a perspective helps us to understand how distinctive practices unfold in relation to public space and how discipline, security and biopower model the 'exemplary neighbour'. In addition, we may discover how these practices are able to co-opt ongoing hybridisation processes and how they create a new gentrification dispositif that includes discourses, institutions, architecture, rules and laws, administrative measures, scientific production, philosophy, and much more – a grid that brings together all these elements (Foucault, 1980 [1977]). Following Agamben (2011), a dispositif is considered to be: (i) a heterogeneous set that includes both the linguistic and the non-linguistic aspects of our life: (ii) a specific function that is inscribed in a power relation: and (iii) a network, understood as an episteme that includes everything considered as legitimate or not in a society. Together, these three aspects create a position that allows us to investigate more subtle power relations than those considered by Foucault (eg asylums, prisons and schools), and the ways in which they are implemented in contemporary urban societies. This perspective will be further developed during the subsequent empirical discussion about the application of governmental technologies in Lavapiés and Triball, especially with regard to those dispositifs applied to the control of public space.

Gentrification dispositifs in Lavapiés and Triball: creativity–cultural production–retail

> The city needs the drive of the creative class, and the centre must receive the talents that will trigger economic competition. The new creative classes, university students and small-scale R+D entrepreneurs

will be extremely well received in the centre. (Municipality of Madrid, 2011, p 55)

In recent years, the knowledge economy has become a key battlefield for urban competition between cities, especially if the social, economic and spatial reconfiguration of symbolically important city centres is considered (Peck, 2010). This situation is similar in Madrid: one of the key elements is the strategic importance that has been given to 'creativity' as a signifier for a whole array of symbolic transformations taking place. This narrates broader trends on the global scale, through which discourses about creativity, culture and other knowledge-related activities have been strategically reinforced (Pratt, 2008). In the case of Madrid, there are policies that explicitly track and demand qualified human capital to relocate to the city in general, with a specific emphasis on the historical city centre (Méndez et al, 2012, p 6). One of the priorities is to strengthen creative industries, and in comparison to other cities, Madrid is especially successful in this task. Roughly a third of all jobs in Spain's creative businesses are concentrated in Madrid, which is double the national gross domestic product (GDP) share of the metropolitan region (Méndez and Sánchez, 2010). The promotion of creative industries and its human capital has been increasingly boosting processes of gentrification. Furthermore, the place, in itself and in its socio-historical context, promotes a type of cultural inertia that defines the character of some of the creative work – an essential aspect that directly relates to planning policies. Since the transition from an industrial to a post-industrial city, public administrations have been decisively supporting a type of employment that cannot be easily relocated: it requires the city and its physical and cultural environment, heritage and traditional cultural activities (eg museums, libraries, festivals, crafts, etc), arts, media, science, and design (eg software, digital content, advertising, architecture, etc) to be addressed by this strategy. As culture and creativity are a main source of economic growth, this sector should also be understood as a way of producing the contemporary capitalist city: innovation, entertainment, performances and tourism play very similar roles in attracting capital and investment and enhancing international competition between cities. Moreover, instead of competing for the largest or the cheapest factory, the metropolis itself competes now as a product and as a factory of multiple 'creative' necessities and of symbolically charged cultural products. In this context, innovative cultural practices have become the new 'production line' that is enhanced by public administrations – for example, to 'transform the centre of Madrid into an international reference of culture, projecting its creative potential beyond our borders' (Municipality of Madrid, 2011, p 69). Such a statement underlines the key focus of public policies to foster gentrification dispositifs in the two areas discussed in this chapter, Lavapiés and Triball.

By means of a series of interventions by public administrations, Lavapiés has been symbolically reconstructed, with a new, if artificial and somewhat pretentious, identity, as a fancy neighbourhood and a place for new culture and art trends (Pérez-Agote et al, 2010). Lavapiés, which has the highest percentage of immigrants in the city, has a rich social and cultural mixture, and was targeted as an 'exotic' environment in which alternative and artistic realms could reaffirm themselves as globalised and attract the 'creative classes'. Díaz Orueta (2007) asserts that Lavapiés can be evaluated as a laboratory for new lifestyles that can draw, simultaneously, on representations of bohemian and left-wing identities. Accordingly, the discourses of many of the incoming younger professionals include, simultaneously, an instrumental relationship to the neighbourhood, based on its centrality, cultural production and the leisure activities developed there. Furthermore, strong identifications with, and reifications of, counter-hegemonic struggles, anti-capitalistic ideologies and political activism, as part of an active and, at the same time, activist cultural production, have been taking place (Barañano et al, 2006). In fact, public policies have overtly taken advantage of a set of allegedly important (subcultural and countercultural) characteristics that emerged at least two decades ago in the neighbourhood. These identities have been in a constant struggle with traditional practices, as well as with the practices of many of the immigrants settling in the area. Regarding the inherent struggle about the appropriation of space that lies behind the commodification of culture and creativity, these references can also be evaluated as a tool that might permit at least a superficial consensus between initially antagonistic social groups – especially if this refers to identity constructions in the neighbourhood. However, many of the myths ascribed to Lavapiés are now being utilised by public and private capital, producing an important reconfiguration of the neighbourhood. In this case, it is additionally important to state that local, regional and national administrations have increasingly developed an unequivocal cultural profile of the area, favouring a suitable environment for private investment that aims at creating new subjectivities. Different investment plans have not only reinforced the revitalisation of this historic enclave in the city centre, but also created, amplified and improved a series of infrastructures that value its cultural character, imaginaries and lifestyles. In this regard, Lavapiés is a perfect example of the development of innovative cultural processes that are then converted into commoditised arts and elements of distinction.

As a result of this investment, Lavapiés can today be considered the neighbourhood with the highest density of cultural institutions in Spain – more than a dozen public museums, universities, film and arts centres, theatres, and so on have opened their doors over the last two decades, and this has had an important impact on the configuration of identities, the symbolic dimensions of cultural segregation and, of course, the potential of the neighbourhood to be gentrified. Additionally, an almost-innumerable array of countercultural spaces, as well as private theatres, art galleries, spaces for different kinds of performances and so on, settled in the area. Such a unique concentration of different cultural institutions generates specific urban experiences and laboratories. The applied aesthetics began mixing with ethics, moving towards a notion of civility that is increasingly defined by supposed 'good taste' – which now means the taste of the creative urban middle class. The construction of such culture-places can be evaluated as paradigmatic and symptomatic of post-Fordism. Creative industries and culture are key assets of contemporary capitalism (Yúdice, 2002), simultaneously promoting urban development, tourism and other dynamics that promise economic growth. As such, public investment was focused upon interventions that would create a positive environment for, and attract, new social and economic activities closely related to the general globalisation that the city was experiencing.

Although many of the aspects mentioned in Lavapiés have been reproduced in similar ways in Triball, the preparation of this neighbourhood for gentrification has been somewhat different, and discussion of this can provide us with a better understanding about how gentrification dispositifs are applied across Madrid, especially with regard to retail. Here, gentrification was born as an entrepreneurial strategy developed by a company specialised in purchasing historic housing estates and rehabilitating them into luxury apartments. The corporation bought several dozens of buildings and shops, of which of specific importance was the purchase of several brothels and sex shops that were then transformed into aparthotels and restaurants. However, at the same time, private investment was flanked by a public renewal scheme implemented by the local administration in 2008, among other things, comprising a series of housing renovation subsidies and the significant redesign of the central square of the neighbourhood. Additionally, and as part of a plan to attract designers of individual clothing, shoes and different fashion products, as well as other retailing activities for upper-middle and upper-class clients, the private investor granted major subsidies for new entrepreneurs settling in the area. The neighbourhood was subsequently renamed and promoted as Triball (*Tri*angle *Ball*esta, after a street at the core of the neighbourhood formerly renowned for drug-dealing and street prostitution), evoking a semantic relationship with the gentrification of 'TriBeCa' in Manhattan. Additionally, the investors cemented their influence over the regeneration schemes through the foundation of a commercial association that has now attracted more than 170 members, which evolved as a key actor for translating the changing neighbourhood demands into policy propositions. Similar to Lavapiés, Triball reinforced an imaginary of 'a unique concept'.[5] However, this was not anchored in its alleged historical and cultural assets, but represented a newly created and labelled place for a specific type of urban entertainment related to fashion, design and gastronomy. In the words of the commercial association, its model is related to 'a proper personality that will be the focus and the style to be imitated in the rest of the country', while the neighbourhood 'does not compete with other commercial areas of Madrid'.[6] This is somewhat true, as the specific location and the characteristics of the new trendy fashion designer shops aspire to attract a public that is entirely different to the traditional public of the area.

Although the dispositif that was applied here puts a clear-cut emphasis on the genuine character of the neighbourhood, Triball is much more a commercial project and projection than Lavapiés. It closes a gap in the corridor between the already-gentrified neighbourhoods of Malasaña (eastbound, with a very international population of mainly 'European' origin), Chueca (southbound, the traditional neighbourhood of gays and lesbians in Madrid, and, at the same time, the first gentrified area of the city) and the central commercial arterials of Madrid's city centre (westbound). It had suffered a somewhat calculated abandonment during the late 1990s and early 2000s, while the surrounding areas were experiencing gentrification. By that time, its population changed dramatically, attracting first Moroccan and later Philippino, Chinese and Latin American immigrants, who remain an important part of the population. Especially after the closure of a traditional cinema located in the central square of the area, media discourses began to focus negatively on decay, abandonment, drug trafficking and prostitution, creating a script in which different actors allegedly demanded social cleansing of the area. Nevertheless, this discourse diverges widely from the perception of the inhabitants. As the area was home to several brothels and street prostitution for decades, most local residents had naturalised the scenery that surrounded these activities. However, by that time, the rent gap had become so obvious that the area was being targeted by investors who then created the commercial association. The pursued strategy was a logical extension of the gentrified areas that were nearby and that were functionally geared towards globalised creative middle-class residents.

While retail gentrification has been rapidly advancing, the economic crisis that Spain has been suffering since 2007/08 has lowered the capital return for investors. This means that 'the neighbourhood has only changed with regard to the commercial activities, it is now facing the people who come from outside. Before Triball, the junkies came to deal, and now the posh girls come to shop here' (interview with the president of the pro-gentrification initiative 'Foro Cívico'). This statement raises a specific question that brings together the two case studies. In our empirical work, we can clearly identify a disaffection of the local population with the transformations in Lavapiés and Triball. In both neighbourhoods, the target population for commercial activities has been transformed from local residents to (mainly wealthy) clients from the whole city and also short-term visitors and tourists. While space has been prepared for these groups, most of the local demands for neighbourhood need have been ignored. In other words, the politics of gentrification applied have strategically pursued the *mise en scène* of symbolic, historical and cultural aspects. The consequence is an increasing segregation with regard to the potential use of the public and private spaces that have been reformed and assigned with new uses. The museums, theatres and art galleries in Lavapiés are as useful for the local population as are the designer fashion shops that sell shoes and clothing from €300 upwards in Triball. Even incoming medium- and higher-income residents have complained about the ongoing eviction of commercial activities that a lively Southern European neighbourhood requires for the daily reproduction of its inhabitants (ie traditional bakeries, butchers, grocers, places to eat at reasonable prices). Although both Lavapiés and Triball still possess a certain social mixture, the transformation of the population has been significant, and the new controls over urban public space are pushing the gentrification process further.

A common dispositif – the gentrification of public space

We have analysed how different gentrification dispositifs around culture and creativity (Lavapiés) and retail (Triball) have been playing a key role in the transformation of both neighbourhoods. However, as we will now discuss, the references to cultural economy, the creative classes and the commercial appropriation of space have worked out successfully only because they have been simultaneously addressed and targeted through a common dispositif applied in both neighbourhoods, one that relates to security governance and the control of public space.

Public space has played a crucial role within the governance of gentrification processes in Madrid. A variety of control mechanisms have been applied in the management of public space, bringing about the 'domestication of public space by cappuccino' (Zukin, 1995, p xiv) and a deeper form of the revanchism outlined by Smith (2002) and Atkinson (2003). The contemporary management of public space privileges the displacement of social problems instead of providing solutions for them, and this means that regulation and control increasingly threatens the inclusion of users that are not considered as 'legitimate clients' (Sequera and Janoschka, 2012). Given the deprived living conditions of broader parts of the immigrant population, but also of many of the 'traditional' residents, this is especially virulent in our two case studies of Lavapiés and Triball. However, beyond this, it is important to state that the transformation of public space as a target of gentrification policies seems to be a common feature appearing in many Southern European cities. The use of open spaces has transformed them into a key dimension for social reproduction, especially as the intensity of use and the needs to appropriate public space differ noticeably from those observed in different parts of (the climatically more unpleasant parts of) Europe. In Southern Europe, the traditional meaning and function of public space is much closer to common spaces, and its popular usage is prior (and obviously different) to the interest that public administrations and market actors have been developing in recent years for assuring their hegemony over them. In this regard, the control over the use and appropriation of open spaces in Southern European cities can be considered a key threshold that decides the future of a neighbourhood (Stavrides, 2010).

However, there are different ways to analyse the control policies that are currently applied in public space: returning to Foucault, we can state that disciplinary society was successively replaced by a post-disciplinary order that has applied new types of biopolitics. In this regard, control and rescue strategies can now be considered as key elements of the repertoire of securitisation, for which the case of Madrid provides an interesting case. By studying the politics of surveillance in Madrid's central Retiro Park, Fraser (2007, p 677) has shown how the symbolic gentrification of supposed public spaces is part of a broader dominance of the public realm by private actors' interests that aim at a general gentrification of the urban sphere. Additionally, this reminds us about the mutual relations that gentrification and the management of public space may have, interpreting the dialectics between the public and the private as one of the multiple expressions of the speculative nature of capital in the contemporary city. This gives a meaningful critique of the rising exclusion of undesired persons from public spaces as preparation for an increasingly 'aseptic' public sphere. It goes hand in hand with Mitchell (1997), who discusses the diffusion of public regulations that have 'destroyed' public space as such in the US, and that affect precisely the population that typically uses and frequents open spaces – the prohibition of begging or the criminalisation of traditional cultural practices in public space, for example. For instance, in Madrid, public administrations have not only forbidden the consumption of alcohol in public spaces, but also singing and playing music, for which an official permission is required. At the same time, public space in Lavapiés has been repeatedly used to organise concerts to stage the multi-ethnic character of the neighbourhood. In other words, it depends on the specific arrangement if playing music in a square is considered as legal or not. This leads us to two aspects that bring together the case studies of Lavapiés and Triball with regard to the application of gentrification dispositifs in and through the strategic management of public space: (i) control by architectonic design and neoliberal civility; and (ii) control by implementing security dispositifs.

The control of public space is undertaken through a wide variety of policies that range from physically closing public space at night to the architectonic modification of squares using the best defensive and preventive design. The key idea is to foster circulation and commercial appropriation and prevent people from appropriating open spaces by implementing municipal ordinances that hamper everyday use. Such physical transformations have been accompanied by discursive strategies that create sensations of insecurity. The objectives of different security plans that have been applied in Madrid in recent years, as well as the installation of control facilities (eg mobile but permanently present police forces in the different squares of Lavapiés and a police station in the central square of Triball), have resulted in social, political and ethnic cleansing, and the preparation of these neighbourhoods for gentrification, rather than to fight crime. In other words, many of the crime-prevention strategies encourage the success of other gentrification dispositifs such as those related to tourism, retail and culture; in general terms, they cater to the new middle classes that inhabit both neighbourhoods.

CCTV cameras in both Lavapiés and Triball have been very efficient cleansing strategies for complex areas in which only a 'controlled' dose of multiculturalism and exotic flair should exist to provide a reminder of the supposed authenticity of the place. The video surveillance in both neighbourhoods is of importance, especially as beyond Lavapiés and Triball, only three additional areas exist in Madrid that count on CCTV control (the squares Plaza Mayor and Puerta del Sol, both tourism destinations par excellence, and the Montera street, another habitual place for female sex workers). In this regard, it is important to remember that CCTV cameras are not intrinsically related to crime control (prior to the surveillance, Lavapiés had a crime rate significantly below average), but rather to scare and calm simultaneously, to create different models of knowledge and power in supposedly conflictive neighbourhoods. Additionally, the video surveillance promotes explicit models of civic conduct, which have to be maintained in front of the cameras. In other words, the panoptic view and the internalisation of civic behaviour are fundamental centrepieces of this logic of control. The individual should not be punished, but civilised, by being submerged in a field of complete visibility. The opinion, the views and the discourses of the surrounding sociability establish a control in which one cannot even imagine acting incorrectly (Foucault, 1980 [1977]). As a consequence, the limits between architecture and order have been increasingly dispelled, and the police can now be considered a key actor in urban planning in Madrid (Sequera and Janoschka, 2012). By attempting a naturalisation of the 'public' as a 'civic' place, certain practices are governed through prevention. Hence, the disciplinary power, under the trilogy of body–discipline–institutions, develops technologies of civilisation that effectively distribute and segregate individuals and their activities across space. For this, specific models of civic conduct in which appearances also interiorise in the orbit of the social panoptic are promoted (Goffman, 2009).

Conclusions

Many of the debates presented in this chapter are related to the different dimensions of symbolic gentrification. In this regard, we have discussed how creativity, culture and retail operate as gentrification dispositifs that classify neighbourhoods into different 'products' that are targeted by differential governmental strategies. Beyond these spatially selective politics of gentrification, the historic city centre of Madrid as a whole is experiencing new civilities that exclude unwanted populations. This strategy is related to the 'management' of public space in general, and especially to the policing strategies that are widely applied to control and punish. Based on a strategy of ongoing commodification of public space, such policies limit the possibilities, especially of the weakest social groups, to appropriate centrally located spaces and places for a meaningful social reproduction. Otherness is evicted from the public sphere. As Rose (1996) has said, different subjectivities and ways of producing knowledge are serving this 'art of governing'. Furthermore, they have the power to articulate themselves with the purpose of excluding other behaviours, understanding society as 'a set of energies and initiatives for facilitating and enhancing' (Vázquez, 2009, p 14). In other words, dispositifs such as architecture, urbanism in general, public facilities or institutions interact and weave a net of power relations that shape the sense of a place in which the subject is traversed (Amendola, 2000, p 162).

While in Lavapiés, dispositifs relate strongly to culture, creativity and the control of the public sphere, Triball is about the fashion and retail gentrification that goes hand in hand with a commercialisation, festivalisation and banalisation of public space. Nevertheless, Triball also expels the unwanted: primarily junkies, prostitutes and irregular migrants, who suffer the policing strategies – but similar rejections apply to children, parents and the elderly, who are strategically evicted from appropriating a public space that is increasingly used as a stage to promote the activities of the commercial association. More than this, some items such as migration, counterculture and the 'authentic' taste of the neighbourhoods are additionally staged as potential sources of 'prosperity' – an important vocabulary in times of economic crisis. Such features imply a logic that articulates the increasing value of capital and investment through the creation of new values of use – a consumerism of multicultural, alternative, creative or bohemian symbols. Space is not exempt from these powerful logics; rather, it is a material expression that is reproduced in place, and urban planners often make efforts to fit sociability into architecture, trying to manage and supervise the unpredictable aspects of life. Such policies not only harass the most vulnerable subjects in an increasingly unequal society, but also give priority to the diffusion of hegemonic social practices. Moreover, they limit access to public space and simultaneously promote social cleansing.

Nevertheless, the social complexity of Lavapiés and Triball affirms that despite its notorious transformation of public space, public sphere and commercial uses, the gentrification process is paradoxically hampered by: (i) an underprivileged non-European immigrant population that has not declined substantially, giving place to rising inter-ethnic solidarity networks; (ii) a counterculture that has increased its roots in the neighbourhoods; (iii) increasing struggles for the right to housing as a response to the dramatic social and economic crisis that the city is experiencing; and (iv) new residents that are not part of the expected profile of the neighbourhood as desired in the intervention plans. The Spanish housing crisis has not helped to generalise the process of price increases for many of the recently renovated buildings. In other words, the gentrification processes in Lavapiés and Triball are unfinished. In this regard, the examples from Madrid provide us with a comprehensive understanding about the manifold differences that exist between gentrification in the 'Anglo-Saxon world' and the variegated processes of urban capital accumulation in Spain.

Notes

[1] The renovation schemes in Madrid have been, first, the Priority Rehabilitation Areas (Áreas *de Rehabiliación Preferente* [ARP], since 1994) and, later, the Integral Rehabilitation Areas (Áreas *de Rehabiliación Integral* [ARI], since 1997).

[2] The general plan for the municipality of Madrid (*Plan General de Ordenación Urbana*) of 1997 established the historic centre as a Special Planning Area (Área *de Planeamiento Espacial*). Based on this, the local government developed a strategic renewal scheme (*Plan Estratégico para la Revitalización del Centro Urbano*) in 1997, which was recently replaced by the *Proyecto Madrid Centro* (Municipality of Madrid, 2011).

[3] Lavapiés has about 50,000 inhabitants, and the immigrant population predominantly comes from Bangladesh, Ecuador, Morocco, China, sub-Saharan Africa and Pakistan. On the other hand, the area of Triball consists of less than 5,000 inhabitants, with a predominance of Latin American, Chinese and Philippine immigrants.

[4] This research has been supported by the research grant CIUDAD Y CRISIS (Plan Nacional I+D+i: CSO-2012-34729), provided by the Spanish Ministry of Economy and Competition.

[5] Triball Commercial Association (2011).

[6] Triball Commercial Association (2011).

References

Agamben, G. (2006) 'Metropolis', lecture given in Venice on 11 November. Available at: http://www.egs.edu/faculty/giorgio-agamben/articles/metropolis-spanish/ (accessed 22 April 2013).

Agamben, G. (2011) 'Qué es un dispositivo?', *Sociológica*, vol 26, no 73, pp 240–64.

Amendola, G. (2000) *La ciudad postmoderna*, Madrid: Celeste.

Arbaci, S. (2007) 'Ethnic segregation, housing systems and welfare regimes in Europe', *International Journal of Housing Policy*, vol 7, no 4, pp 401–33.

Arbaci, S. (2008) '(Re)Viewing ethnic residential segregation in Southern European cities: housing and urban regimes as mechanisms of marginalization', *Housing Studies*, vol 23, no 4, pp 589–613.

Atkinson, R. (2003) 'Introduction: misunderstood saviour or vengeful wrecker? The many meanings and problems of gentrification', *Urban Studies*, vol 40, no 12, pp 2343–50.

Barañano Cid, M., Riesco Sanz, A., Romero Bachiller, C. and García López, J. (2006) *Globalización, inmigración transnacional y reestructuración de la región metropolitana de Madrid, Estudio del Barrio de Embajadores*, Madrid: Edición GPS.

Blanco, I., Bonet, J. and Walliser, A. (2011) 'Urban governance and regeneration policies in historic city centres: Madrid and Barcelona', *Urban Research & Practice*, vol 4, no 3, pp 326–43.

Castells, M. (1983) *The city and the grassroots: a cross-cultural theory of urban social movements*, Berkeley, CA: University of California Press.

Coleman, M. and Agnew, J. (2007) 'The problem with Empire', in J. Crampton and S. Elden (eds) *Space, knowledge and power: Foucault and Geography*, Aldershot: Ashgate, pp 317–39.

Delgado, M. (2007) *La ciudad mentirosa. Fraude y miseria del 'Modelo Barcelona'*, Madrid: La Catarata.

Delgado, M. (2008) 'La artistización de las políticas urbanas: El lugar de la cultura en las dinámicas de reapropiación capitalista de la ciudad', *Scripta Nova, Special Issue: X Coloquio Internacional de Geocrítica*. Available at: http://www.ub.edu/geocrit/-xcol/393.htm

Díaz Orueta, F. (2007) 'Madrid: urban regeneration projects and social mobilization', *Cities*, vol 24, no 3, pp 183–93.

Dominguez, M. (2008) 'Trabajo material e inmaterial. Polémicas y conceptos inestables, marco teórico y estado de la cuestión', *Youkali, Revista Crítica de las Artes y el Pensamiento*. Available at: http://www.youkali.net/5a1-YOUKALI-Dominguez-Sanchez-Pinilla.pdf

Dot, E., Casellas, A. and Pallares-Barbera, M. (2010) 'Gentrificación productiva en Barcelona: efectos del nuevo espacio económico' ['Productive gentrification in Barcelona: effects of the new economic space'], acts of the 4th *Jornadas de Geografía Económica*. Available at: http://age.ieg.csic.es/geconomica/IVJornadasGGELeon/Comunicaciones%20Jornadas%20de%20Leon/I%20Ponencia/Dot-Casellas-Pallar.pdf (accessed 8 August 2011).

Elias, N. (1990) *La sociedad de los individuos*, Madrid: Ediciones Península.

Ettlinger, N. (2011) 'Governmentality as epistemology', *Annals of the Association of American Geographers*, vol 101, no 3, pp 537–60.

Foucault, M. (1980 [1977]) 'The confession of the flesh', in M. Foucault and C. Gordon (eds) *Power/knowledge selected interviews and other writings, 1972–1977*, New York, NY: Pantheon Books, pp 194–228.

Foucault, M. (2006) *'Seguridad, territorio, población', Curso en el Collège de France: 1977–1978*, Buenos Aires: Fondo de Cultura Económica.

Fraser, B. (2007) 'Madrid's Retiro Park as publicly-private space and the spatial problems of spatial theory', *Social and Cultural Geography*, vol 8, no 5, pp 673–700.

Goffman, E. (2009) *La presentación de la persona en la vida cotidiana*, Buenos Aires: Amorrortu.

Gómez, M. (1998) 'Reflective images: the case of urban regeneration in Glasgow and Bilbao', *International Journal of Urban and Regional Research*, vol 22, no 1, pp 106–21.

Gómez, M. (2006) 'El barrio de Lavapiés, laboratorio de interculturalidad' ['The district of Lavapiés, laboratory of interculturality'], *Dissidences, Hispanic Journal of Theory and Criticism*, 2.1. Available at: http://digitalcommons.bowdoin.edu/dissidences/vol1/iss2/12/ (accessed 5 February 2013).

Gómez, M. and González, S. (2001) 'A reply to Beatriz Plaza's "The Guggenheim-Bilbao museum effect"', *International Journal of Urban and Regional Research*, vol 25, no 4, pp 898–900.

González, S. (2011) 'Bilbao and Barcelona "in motion". How urban regeneration "models" travel and mutate in the global flows of policy tourism', *Urban Studies*, vol 48, no 7, pp 1397–418.

González, S. and Waley, P. (2013) 'Traditional retail markets: the new gentrification frontier', *Antipode*, vol 45, no 4, pp 965–83.

Huxley, M. (2007) 'Geographies of governmentality', in J. Crampton and S. Elden (eds) *Space, knowledge and power: Foucault and geography*, Aldershot: Ashgate.

Janoschka, M., Sequera, J. and Salinas, L. (2014) 'Gentrification in Spain and Latin America – a critical dialogue', *International Journal of Urban and Regional Research*, vol 38, no 4, pp 1234–65.

Justo, A. (2011) 'Transformaciones en el barrio de Malasaña. Hacia la gentrificación', *Viento Sur*, vol 116, pp 73–9.

Kloostermann, R. and Van der Leun, J. (1999) 'Just for starters: commercial gentrification by immigrant entrepreneurs in Amsterdam and Rotterdam neighbourhoods', *Housing Studies*, vol 15, no 4, pp 659–77.

Lees, L. (2012) 'The geography of gentrification. Thinking through comparative urbanism', *Progress in Human Geography*, vol 38, no 2, pp 155–71.

López, I. and Rodríguez, E. (2010) *Fin de ciclo. Financiarización, territorio y sociedad de propietarios en la onda larga del capitalismo hispano (1959–2010)* [*End of a cycle. Financialization, territory and ownership society in the large wave of Spanish capitalism (1959–2010)*], Madrid: Traficantes de Sueños.

López, I. and Rodríguez, E. (2011) 'The Spanish model', *New Left Review*, vol 69, no 3. Available at: http://newleftreview.org/II/69/isidro-lopez-emmanuel-rodriguez-the-spanish-model (accessed 5 February 2013).

Lorey, I. (2008) 'Gubernamentalidad y precarización de sí. Sobre la normalización de los productores y las productoras culturales', in Proyecto Transform (ed) *Producción cultural y prácticas instituyentes, Líneas de ruptura en la crítica institucional*, Madrid: Traficantes de sueños, pp 72–4.

Maloutas, T. (2012) 'Contextual diversity in gentrification research', *Critical Sociology*, vol 38, no 1, pp 33–48.

Marshall, T. (2004) *Transforming Barcelona*, London: Routledge.

Méndez, R. and Sánchez, S. (2010) 'Spanish cities in the knowledge economy: theoretical debates and empirical evidence', *European Urban and Regional Studies*, vol 18, no 2, pp 136–55.

Méndez, R., Michelini, J.J., Prada, J. and Tébar, J. (2012) 'Economía creativa y desarrollo urbano en España: una aproximación a sus lógicas espaciales', *EURE (Santiago)*, vol 38, no 113, pp 5–32.

Mitchell, D. (1997) *The lie of the land: migrant workers and the California landscape*, Minneapolis, MN: University of Minnesota Press.

Monclús, F.-J. (2003) 'The Barcelona model: and an original formula? From "reconstruction" to strategic urban projects (1979–2004)', *Planning Perspectives*, vol 18, no 4, pp 399–421.

Municipality of Madrid (2011) 'Proyecto Madrid Centro. Madrid'. Available at: http://www.madrid.es/portales/munimadrid/es/Inicio/Ayuntamiento/Urbanismo-e-Infraestructuras/Proyecto-completo?vgnextfmt=default&vgnextoid=2ed4488f7c742310VgnVCM1000000b205a0aRCRD&vgnextchannel=8dba171c30036010VgnVCM100000dc0ca8c0RCRD&idioma=es&idiomaPrevio=es&rmColeccion=0b65488f7c742310VgnVCM1000000b205a0aRCRD (accessed 22 March 2013).

Naredo, J.M. and Montiel, A. (2011) *El modelo inmobiliario español y su culminación en el caso valenciano* [*The Spanish real estate model and its culmination in the case of Valencia*], Barcelona: Icaria.

Negri, A. (2006) *Movimientos en el Imperio. Pasajes y paisajes*, Barcelona: Paidós Ibérica.

Pareja-Eastaway, M. (2009) 'The effects of the Spanish housing system on the settlement patterns of immigrants', *Tijdschrift voor economische en sociale geografie*, vol 100, no 4, pp 519–34.

Peck, J. (2010) *Constructions of neoliberal reason*, Oxford: Oxford University Press.

Pérez-Agote, A., Tejerina, B. and Barañano, M. (eds) (2010) *Barrios multiculturales. Relaciones interétnicas en los barrios de San Francisco (Bilbao) y Embajadores/Lavapiés (Madrid)*, Madrid: Trotta.

Plaza, B. (1999) 'The Guggenheim–Bilbao museum effect: a reply to María V. Gomez "Reflective images: the case of urban regeneration in Glasgow and Bilbao"', *International Journal of Urban and Regional Research*, vol 23, no 3, pp 589–92.

Portes, A., Aparicio, R., Haller, W. and Vickstrom, E. (2010) 'Moving ahead in Madrid: aspirations and expectations in the Spanish second generation', *International Migration Review*, vol 44, no 4, pp 767–801.

Pratt, A. (2008) 'Creative cities: the cultural industries and the creative class', *Geografiska Annaler: Series B, Human Geography*, vol 90, no 2, pp 107–17.

Ribera-Fumaz, R. (2008) 'Gentrification and retail in Ciutat Vella, Barcelona', in L. Porter and K. Shaw (eds) *Whose urban renaissance? An international comparison of urban regeneration policies*, London: Routledge.

Robinson, J. (2011) 'Cities in a world of cities: the comparative gesture', *International Journal of Urban and Regional Research*, vol 35, no 1, pp 1–23.

Rodríguez, A. and Vicario, L. (2005) 'Innovación, competitividad y regeneración urbana: los espacios retóricos de la "ciudad creativa" en el nuevo Bilbao' ['Innovation, competitiveness and urban regeneration: the rhetorical spaces of the "creative city" in the new Bilbao'], *Ekonomiaz*, vol 58, no 1, pp 262–95.

Rose, N. (1996) 'Governing "advanced" liberal democracies', in A. Barry, T. Osborne and N. Rose (eds) *Foucault and political reason: liberalism, neo-liberalism and rationalities of government*, London: UCL Press, pp 37–64.

Sargatal, M.A. (2001) 'Gentrificación e inmigración en los centros históricos: el caso del barrio del Raval en Barcelona' ['Gentrification and immigration in the historic centres; the case of el Raval in Barcelona'], *Scripta Nova. Revista Electrónica de Geografía y Ciencias Sociale*, 6.94(66). Available at: http://www.ub.es/geocrit/sn-94-66.htm (accessed 12 February 2008).

Sequera, J. (2010) 'Prácticas distintivas y control urbano como mecanismos de gestión de las conductas. El caso de Lavapiés (Madrid)' ['Distinctive practices and urban control as behaviour management mechanisms'], in C. Cornejo, J. Sáez and J. Prada (eds) *Ciudad, territorio y paisaje: reflexiones para un debate multidisciplinario* [*City, territory and landscape; reflections on a multidisciplinary debate*], Madrid: CSIC.

Sequera, J. and Janoschka, M. (2012) 'Ciudadanía y espacio público en la era de la globalización neoliberal', *ARBOR Ciencia, Pensamiento y Cultura*, vol 188, no 755, pp 515–27.

Smith, N. (2002) 'New globalism, new urbanism: gentrification as global urban strategy', *Antipode*, vol 34, no 3, pp 427–50.

Stavrides, S. (2010) *Towards the city of thresholds*, Trento: Professionaldreamers.

Swyngedouw, E., Moulaert, F. and Rodríguez, A. (2002) 'Neoliberal urbanization in Europe: large-scale urban development and the new urban policy', *Antipode*, vol 34, no 3, pp 543–76.

Uitermark, J. (2005) 'The genesis and evolution of urban policy: a confrontation of regulationist and governmentality approaches', *Political Geography*, vol 24, no 1, pp 137–63.

Vázquez, C. (1992) 'Urban policies and gentrification trends in Madrid's inner city', *Netherlands' Journal of Housing & Built Environment*, vol 7, no 4, pp 357–76.

Vázquez, F. (2005) 'Empresarios de nosotros mismos. Biopolítica, mercado y soberanía en la gubernamentalidad neoliberal', in J. Ugarte (ed) *La administración de la vida. Estudios biopolíticos*, Barcelona: Anthropos.

Vázquez, F. (2009) *La invención del racismo. Nacimiento de la biopolítica en España*, Madrid: Akal.

Vicario, L. and Martínez Monje, M. (2005) 'Another "Guggenheim effect"? Central city projects and gentrification in Bilbao', in R. Atkinson and G. Bridge (eds) *Gentrification in a global context: the new urban colonialism*, London: Routledge.

Wang, S. (2011) 'Commercial gentrification and entrepreneurial governance in Shanghai: a case study of Taikang Road creative cluster', *Urban Policy and Research*, vol 29, no 4, pp 363–80.

Yúdice, G. (2002) *El recurso de la cultura: usos de la cultura en la era global*, Barcelona: Gedisa.

Zukin, S. (1995) *The cultures of cities*, Oxford: Blackwell.

Zukin, S. (2010) *Naked city: the death and life of authentic urban places*, Oxford: Oxford University Press.

Zukin, S., Trujillo, V., Frase, P., Jackson, D., Recuber, T. and Walker, A. (2009) 'New retail capital and neighborhood change: boutiques and gentrification in New York City', *City & Community*, vol 8, no 1, pp 47–64.

TWENTY

When authoritarianism embraces gentrification – the case of Old Damascus, Syria

Yannick Sudermann

Introduction

When the *New York Times* published an article titled 'Next stop Damascus' in June 2005, it did not refer to US fighter jets, but to Western jetsetters celebrating Old Damascus, the oldest continuously inhabited capital of the world, with its restaurants and boutique hotels, as a destination for luxury city breaks. There, they came across and benefited from an already-gentrifying urban landscape that, up to then, was primarily aimed at Syrian middle-class professionals, regime cronies and their changing consumer preferences. Gentrification– 'the production of urban space for progressively more affluent users' (Hackworth, 2002, p 815) – can best be seen in approximately 100 themed restaurants that, since the mid-1990s, have mushroomed throughout Old Damascus. After 2005, these restaurants were joined by a fast-growing number of *boutique hotels*, small luxury hotels situated in opulently renovated courtyard houses targeting international business travellers and moneyed tourists.

In this chapter,[1] I scrutinise to what extent gentrification can be considered a successful upgrading strategy for Syria's authoritarian regime, whose legitimacy has been permanently contested, especially so since the outbreak of the Syrian Civil War in March 2011. I argue that the production of gentrification in the Syrian capital not only followed the logics of the market, but also depended on an authoritarian state that had been trying to exploit gentrification in order to secure its power at the local level. The chapter thus sheds light on the interrelations between gentrification and authoritarian rule in the historic old town.

The chapter is organised in the following way. As literature on gentrification in Damascus is almost non-existent, the first section of this chapter aims at connecting the Damascene case to research in other Arab cities. The second section investigates to what extent the principles of the Islamic City – namely, segregation along sectarian instead of class lines – shaped the preconditions for gentrification. In so doing, it provides an overview of the social and political-economic history of Damascus, a task that continues in the second section, which focuses on the rise of gentrifiers in terms of their class constitution. Furthermore, the third section looks into ways in which Damascenes involved in gentrification differ from their counterparts in the West. In the fourth section, by offering an empirical account of gentrification and its impacts on the old city and its residents, the chapter presents a history of gentrification in the old city of Damascus. Finally, I analyse links between the bourgeoisie and the authoritarian state in the field of gentrification.

Gentrification and the Arab city

In the early 2000s – as this chapter will show in terms of gentrification in Old Damascus – the process of gentrification was no longer limited to cities in the Global North and it had become a 'crucial urban strategy' (Smith, 2002, p 440) embedded in the context of globally advancing neoliberalism. However, many cities, as well as much local knowledge on gentrification – in the Global South in particular – remained 'off the map' (Robinson, 2002) and under the radar of urban research. Damascus is one such city and the capital of a state with a state-directed economy and authoritarian political system. Hence, it is neither a democracy nor fully integrated into the global economy – two contexts under which gentrification theory has been developed.

So far, gentrification in the Syrian capital has hardly been researched. Therefore, accounts from other Middle Eastern cities are helpful in contextualising regional particularities and thus facilitating a better understanding of the Damascene case. In one of the first articles on gentrification in the Arab World, Escher et al (2001) investigated the arrival of foreign home-buyers in the *medina* (old town) of the Moroccan desert city Marrakech, a process that has seen a genuine boom since the late 1990s. Only recently, in an article on state involvement in the Bouregreg project (a large-scale urban development project close to the Moroccan capital, Rabat), did Bogaert (2012) address the risk of displacement caused by gentrification. In the Egyptian capital, Cairo, gentrification simultaneously emerged in distinct forms: first, like in Damascus, the historic old town has been affected by heritage and tourism gentrification (Sutton and Fahmi, 2002); second, the formerly colonial city and Cairo's belle époque downtown experienced 'classic' residential gentrification (Sutton and Fahmi, 2002; Abaza, 2011); and, finally, like in Damascus, new-build gentrification can be detected in the form of large-scale residential and commercial upmarket development projects on the city's fringes (Abaza, 2001; Kuppinger, 2005). Since the mid-1990s, research on urban development in Beirut has been shaped by a focus on the city's post-civil-war reconstruction process (eg Schmidt, 2009; Nagel, 2000, 2002). Informal policymaking is a general characteristic of authoritarian rule in Syria, which has been rarely linked to the urban sphere. In this context, Krijnen and Fawas's (2010) research on informal practices and ad hoc decision-making, which had become the rule in high-end development projects in neoliberal Beirut, is most useful in this analysis of the Damascene case.

Comparing the impact of globalisation on the historic cities of Marrakech and Damascus, Escher (2001) mentioned the 1980s as the starting point for globalisation-induced urban change, when a small number of Old Damascene houses were renovated. After that, restoring historic property became the topic of several studies on the Syrian capital. Salamandra (2004) investigated how parts of the bourgeoisie used the renovation and commercialisation of Old Damascene real estate as a means of identity creation and for social distinction, without directly referring to 'gentrification' however. In the context of 'revitalising' traditional courtyard houses, discourses dealing with the issue of tradition versus modernity were seen to play a crucial role (Totah, 2009). Like elsewhere in the Global South, the state, both local and central, also played a dominant role in facilitating large-scale luxury redevelopment projects, which were located in central as well as suburban settings (Goulden, 2011). Whereas many redevelopment projects in Damascus's periphery were still in the planning stage, gentrification – as will be shown in this chapter – became an everyday reality in the capital's historic neighbourhoods prior to the current civil war.

Social segregation and the production of gentrifiable housing in Old Damascus

Compared to cities in the Global North, where unrestricted access to public space was taken for granted until the emergence of privatisation under neoliberal municipal regimes, in cities throughout the Islamic Orient, privacy and segregation are structural *leitmotifs* of residential quarters. Furthermore, segregation is observed between different ethnic and religious groups, as well as between the sexes (Wirth, 2000). This resulted in the development of quarters for different religious groups, that is, besides quarters for different fractions of the Muslim majority, there were quarters for the Christian and Jewish minorities. Internally, these quarters were subdivided based on regional origin. However, unlike in Western cities, social class did not represent a criterion for such urban quartering: rich and poor families were living side by side (Wirth, 2000).

Since the late 19th century, first under the late Ottomans and thereafter under French colonial rule, Damascus experienced the construction of Western-style administrative buildings and upscale residential quarters outside its walled old town (Dettmann, 1969). Seger (1975) highlighted the existence of two cores within the city centre: first, the *suq* (traditional market) in the old city; and, second, the central business district (CBD). After independence in 1946, affluent Damascenes continued leaving the old town in order to live in the newly constructed neighbourhoods. These colonial or post-independence upscale quarters were considered to be a symbol of a modern, Western lifestyle – the narrow streets and the traditional courtyard houses of the old town (see Figure 20.1) being the antithesis (Dettmann, 1969, pp 100ff; Abu Lughod, 1980; Escher et al, 2001). In Old Damascus, despite these suburbanisation-like processes, the traditional patterns of segregation along sectarian divisions did not change significantly.[2] Houses abandoned by the bourgeoisie were rented to lower-class families, often migrants of rural origin. The outcome was the decline of social status within the old city and the successive transformation of Old Damascus into a heavily populated, disinvested lower-class area. Newcomers to Old Damascus normally moved into quarters according to their religion. By contrast, within the prestigious new neighbourhoods, religion as a criterion for segregation became irrelevant; in the meantime, social status became crucial. In these quarters, even occasional intermarriages among elite families – until then unthinkable – could be observed (Salamandra, 2004).

Figure 20.1: An Old Damascene courtyard house

At the same time, members of the Damascene bourgeoisie started to develop a culture of leisure and consumption resembling their Western counterparts. As the old town was considered to represent the country's backwardness, New Damascus became the focal point of this development (Dettmann, 1969; Salamandra, 2004). Nevertheless, during the 1970s, in an attempt to return to 'the old', a small number of intellectuals moved to the old city (Pfaffenbach, 2004; for Istanbul, see Dokmeci et al, 2007; for Cairo, see Fahmi and Sutton, 2010). In contrast to their Western counterparts 'who, not for reasons of exogenous style but of *desire*, find suburbs and modernist spaces unlivable' (Caulfield, 1989, p 140, emphasis in original), and therefore increasingly resettled in old-city neighbourhoods since the 1970s, calling these individuals 'urban pioneers' would overstate their part in the Old Damascene gentrification process, which only started at the end of the 1990s. These changed consumer preferences contributed to suburbanisation followed by disinvestment, which, as will be demonstrated later, added significantly to the production of inexpensive centrally located real estate and set the (pre)conditions for subsequent gentrification.

Producing the potential gentry

Gentrification in the West is often considered to be a middle-class activity. In Damascus, by contrast, gentrifiers are usually from a 'higher' social stratum – often, they are part of the country's new bourgeoisie. However, what potential gentrifiers on both sides of the Mediterranean share is being part of a privileged class, seeking to establish themselves through social distinction vis-a-vis other actors: in the West, from the working class and the upper class; in the Damascene context, from the middle class and the old bourgeoisie. This section intends, first, to trace the impact of class constitution on gentrification in Damascus and, second, to shed light on the constitution of Syria's new bourgeoisie.

David Ley's (1980) 'post-industrial thesis' on gentrification considered changes in the mode of production and related shifts within the labour force, namely, the increase of white-collar jobs, as causative for gentrification. Consumption-side explanations of gentrification subsequently emphasised the emergence of a new professional and managerial middle class (Hamnett, 1991; Williams, 1986) and their aesthetic tastes (Jager, 1986; Zukin, 1988), desires (Caulfield, 1989) or occupations, often within new 'creative' industries (Florida, 2005). They were buttressed by the capitalist state investors exuberantly seeking profit in centrally located, gentrifiable real estate, thereby causing marginalisation and displacement of working-class residents (Marcuse, 1986; Slater, 2006). For that reason, gentrification has also been described as 'new urban colonialism' (Atkinson and Bridge, 2005) and, accordingly, gentrifiers as profit-driven urban colonialists (Smith, 1996). The influence of neoliberalism has reduced the role of the state to providing/granting a functioning free-market economy in which the state is becoming 'a junior if highly active partner to global capital' (Smith, 2002, p 428). In Syria, too, it is the market driving the production of potential gentrifiers but the role of allocation is in favour of the authoritarian state: authoritarianism puts the state in the powerful position of being able to control 'classical' agents of gentrification (eg investors, landlords, tenants and potential gentrifiers) through measures like the country's planned economic opening (Law No 10 of 1991). The interrelations between the Syrian state and potential gentrifiers, in that they are majority members of the bourgeoisie, will be addressed in the following section, especially regarding the specific dynamics that unfold in an authoritarian context. Prior to that, however, it is vital to shed light on the constitution of Syria's bourgeoisie embedded in the country's newer history.

At the time Ruth Glass (1964) coined the term 'gentrification', Syria was in the midst of a populist socialist restructuring following the Ba'th Party's revolution of 1963. Until then, the country was ruled by members of landed urban elites, which accumulated fortunes under Ottoman and French rule and retained their political and economic privileges in the post-colonial era. The Ba'th Party's takeover involved radical efforts to redistribute political and economic power, the latter through the nationalisation of key industries during the 1960s (Rabinovich, 1972, pp 141–3). It further induced the recruitment of formerly marginalised parts of the population (workers and peasants, often from a rural minority background) into the civil services, which resulted in the displacement of the traditional urban ruling class from power (Perthes, 1991, p 32; Hinnebusch, 2001, p 48).

Since the Ba'th Party came to power, Damascus and Aleppo, the country's largest cities and, respectively, the political and economic centres, became key destinations for the steady rural–urban migration that was further fuelled by heightened upward social mobility. Some of the rural newcomers were recruited into Syria's growing public sector or into the ranks of the extensive security forces. Those who acquired affluence and political influence frequently underwent a process of embourgoisement, challenging the traditional urban ruling class. The political marginalisation of the old elites changed Damascus's demographic stability, which 'aimed at making it possible for the (Ba'th) party to entrench itself in Syria's hostile urban environments' (Hinnebusch, 2001, p 53, referring to Devlin, 1983, pp 23, 121). When the new bourgeoisie consolidated its power and managed to enter the urban stage, '[t]hey tried to emulate the lifestyles of the old bourgeoisie, but more ostentatiously' (Perthes, 1991, p 34).

The rule of radical Ba'thi factions ended in inner-party struggles, which led to the coup of Hafiz al-Asad and his 'Corrective Movement' in 1970. Whereas the radicals had based their power on trade unions and intellectuals, al-Asad – whose leadership was described as 'less ideologically inclined, more pragmatic politically, far more careerist and, most important, fundamentally outward looking' (Haddad, 2009, p 36) – got his support from the military and parts of the bourgeoisie. Hafiz al-Asad and his government were facing several political challenges, the rivalry with neighbouring Israel and the regime's tense relation with urban (business) society being of prime importance. Syrian–Israeli relations escalated in the Arab–Israeli War of 1973 and further direct and indirect confrontations between Israel and Syria or their Lebanese proxies. The demands of the urban bourgeoisie were addressed by limited economic liberalisation and reducing state control over foreign trade, which, combined with attracting Arab investment and remittances of Syrians working abroad, contributed to the economic recovery of the 1970s, as well as – at least partially – relaxing state–business relations (Hinnebusch, 2001, p 64f; Haddad, 2009, p 36).

In order to secure its power: first, the al-Asad regime gained 'control over key levers of power', such as for instance the Ba'th Party, which functioned as a means of 'popular incorporation' and became one foundation of what Rabinovich (1972, p 212) termed 'army–party-symbiosis'; second, Hafiz al-Asad crafted a personalised presidential system in Syria; third, the power became guaranteed by various security services, as well as a state of emergency that – already put in place in 1963 (Leverett, 2005, pp 22–7; for the Syrian state under Hafiz al-Asad, see Seale 1988, pp 169–84) – was suspended only in 2011; and, finally, forging a broad social base to safeguard his power. In contrast to the Ba'thi radicals, who between

1963 and 1970 incorporated a populist agenda aiming at mobilising additional constituencies and thereby widely bypassing traditional urban elites, al-Asad's approach aimed at putting an end to the marginalisation of the bourgeoisie and the private economy. Therefore, since the Corrective Movement, Syria experienced striking changes regarding the composition of its elites. Within the stratum of Syrian society, which nowadays can be referred to as the country's bourgeoisie, one can distinguish four subcategories based on their background. First, there is the traditional bourgeoisie with origins dating to the Ottoman period. However, within this group, it is only the merchant class who managed to rehabilitate its pre-1963 role due to al-Asad's *infitah* (open door) policy (Perthes, 1991, p 32). Second, new industrialists emerged as a group that 'caught up with and surpassed the old bourgeoisie in wealth and influence' (Perthes, 1991, p 33) by producing mostly consumer goods, for example, under licence of Western brands. Third, what can be called the State Bourgeoisie evolved as a group of actors that owed 'its position to its loyalty to the regime and often its personal connections to President al-Asad' (Perthes, 1991, p 34). The success of this group – whose members usually shared a petty-bourgeois or middle-class background – had its origin in privileges and not always legal practices: 'To put it less politely, this group became rich from theft, bribes and commissions' (Perthes, 1991, p 34). Finally, linked to the regime by kinship or personal relations, the new bourgeoisie only appeared after 1973 and can best be described as an oligarchy 'composed of high-ranking officials and their offspring' (Ismail, 2009, p 18). Causative for its advent was:

> a state in which the bureaucracy directly controls essential parts of the national economy, including state planning, yet with no democratic control over those who run the state and little ability to prevent private business from organizing the external relations of the state economy. (Perthes, 1991, p 36)

The rise of an increasingly influential (new) bourgeoisie, as well as the accelerated social polarisation since the 1990s, was framed by the production and consumption of a 'return to the old' (*awda lil-qadim*) accompanied by a growing awareness of cultural heritage. Both the 'return to the old' and the 'rehabilitation' of the bourgeoisie, including the ascent of *awlad al-sultah*, found their expression in a place-specific gentrification process alongside an expanding leisure sector and the spread of lavish consumptions patterns.

Producing gentrification in Old Damascus

Asked for the starting point of gentrification, most interviewees were not specific, but mentioned a point in time around 2000.[3] This raises the question of why gentrification started at that time and not earlier. Salamandra's (2004) research, which gives valuable insight into how Old Damascus 'has become a commodity for the consumption of the Damascene bourgeoisie', is based on numerous interviews with members of Damascene elite families and illustrates a shift in these elites' consumption habits and leisure practices during the early 1990s, a decade before gentrification actually started. She considers the consumer preference for an 'authentic' Old Damascene urban fabric as a factor contributing to increasing interest in the old city. However, she emphasises the temporary and leisure-driven character of this return of the bourgeoisie: 'Restaurants and cafés remain the Damascenes' only mode of physical return; the Damascene elite has not resettled Old Damascus' (Salamandra, 2004, p 77). Nevertheless, as early as 1979, Neil Smith warned: 'To explain gentrification according to the gentrifier's actions alone, while ignoring the role of builders, developers, landlords, mortgage lenders, government agencies, real estate agents, and tenants, is excessively narrow' (Smith, 1979, p 540). Smith also questioned the demand-side prototype of the 'back to the city' movement by assuming that gentrification is 'a back to the city movement all right, but of capital rather than people' (Smith, 1979, p 547), a position shared and corroborated by several interviewees in the spring of 2011.

Gotham (2005) introduced the concept of 'tourism gentrification', which conceptually links both demand-side and production-side explanations of gentrification. Concerning the production side, 'tourism is about shifting patterns of capital investment in the sphere of production, new forms of financing real estate development and the creation of spaces of consumption' (Gotham, 2005, p 1103). With regards to the demand side, Gotham emphasised that spaces related to gentrification can be seen as what Carpenter and Lees (1995, p 288) described as a 'highly visual expression of changing patterns of consumption in cities'. As will be elaborated later, in Old Damascus, gentrification first occurred in the form of traditional courtyard houses being transformed into Middle Eastern-themed restaurants and cafes. During the peak season, these businesses definitely attracted numerous foreigners (Escher and Schepers, 2008, p 130). Their main target group, however, seemed to be, from interviews in 2011 and my own observations, members of the Damascene upper-middle and upper classes. In an article on gentrification in Brazil, Rubino (2005) described affluent users of gentrified old-city locations who 'had constructed new and temporary bonds with the place' as 'night or weekend gentrifiers' (Rubino, 2005, p 233), a term that accurately depicts well-off Damascenes living in modern neighbourhoods who – prior to the current crisis – occasionally went to Old Damascus for their individually consumed *return to the old*.

In the early 1970s, it looked as if several preconditions for gentrification were fulfilled: first, the availability of inexpensive, centrally located real estate; second, the accessibility of potential investment capital in the form of petrodollars and foreign aid (political rent); and, third, a period of relative economic prosperity following the Arab–Israeli War of 1973. However, reasons for the postponement of gentrification during the 1980s were manifold: among other things, the regime had not yet entirely consolidated its power (as can be seen in the Muslim Brotherhood Revolt and the failed coup of Rif'at al-Asad during the early 1980s); consumer preferences for the 'new' were predominant; and, furthermore,

Syria's hesitant opening of the *infitah* era had been accompanied by a socialist agenda and found its expression through, for example, tenant-friendly tenancy laws. By contrast, during the 1990s, in particular, after the end of the Cold War and the country's participation in the US-led war against Iraq in 1990, Syria saw the creation of a capital-friendly investment climate following state-controlled economic liberalisation (Law No 10 of 1991 and the landlord-friendly tenancy law of 2004; see Totah, 2009). Until the 1990s, Old Damascus was not appreciated as a weekend or evening destination among leisure-seeking members of the Damascene bourgeoisie and upper-middle class. At that time, the choice of restaurants within the old city was limited to 'small restaurants which just sold hommus and foul [chickpeas and beans]' (author's interview, April 2011), a small number of restaurants located in former commercial buildings in the Christian Quarter, Bab Tuma, being the sole exceptions. Since the early 1990s, however, in connection with *awda lil-qadim*, affluent Damascenes started giving up their hostile stance vis-à-vis the old city that they – up to then – considered to be the epitome of the country's undesired past and that subsequently transformed into an arena of consumption and class distinction (Salamandra, 2004). 'Pioneers', best understood as trendsetters giving a blueprint for successful business models,[4] had a major stake in initiating the renovation of suitable traditional Damascene courtyard houses (see Figure 20.2) and their transformation into cafes and restaurants. Many followed the example of Beit Jabri, which opened in 1999 as the first themed restaurant in a renovated Old Damascene courtyard house.

In 2005, there were 65 restaurants within the walled old town, and three years later, their number reached 99 (data from Maktab al Anbar[5]). The rising demand for restaurants was, first, a chance for investors to buy into the world's oldest, continuously inhabited capital and, second, an expression of the earlier-mentioned considerably changed leisure practices and consumption patterns of affluent Damascenes. When asked where and how they used to spend their spare time in terms of going out, many respondents answered like this business consultant:

> 'Usually, if we want to have dinner in Damascus itself, we prefer to go to the old city, not outside the city, always in the old city because the atmosphere is different. You love to see that kind of atmosphere.' (Author's interview, April 2011)

Also referring to the unique atmosphere of Old Damascene restaurants, this tour guide recalled:

> '[P]eople – whether we are talking about Syrians or non-Syrians, Europeans or other non-Syrians – were interested in having exotic dinners in an old house which has history, a background and a fountain in the middle. So people who live in the modern part of Damascus let's say, in the evening they were interested to come to an exciting place for dinner or to smoke arghile.' (Author's interview, April 2011)

Figure 20.2: An Old Damascene courtyard house under renovation

Both accounts testify to the changing leisure practices of affluent Damascenes. However, these new habits had a significant impact on old-city residents' everyday lives. Evening gentrifiers competed for the limited parking space available in the old city's narrow alleys, making conflict a daily occurrence. The high demands for fresh water, electricity and waste-water capacity brought the obsolete public networks close to collapse. Additionally, noise caused by restaurants and the leisure-seeking nouveaux riche affected residents, as did the traffic caused by suppliers. Another field of conflict was the social behaviour of the mostly young guests, which did not meet residents' traditional values:

> 'Usually, if you kiss in a traditional neighbourhood they [the residents] will come and beat you. Yes. But now they are seeing more than that. They are seeing ladies in mini-jupes, drinking alcohol in the street; the young people are having relations etc.' (Author's interview, April 2011)

Like this Damascene, many residents felt upset by publicly displayed affection between unmarried individuals or the consumption of alcohol.

In 2007, as a reaction to widespread resentment among old-city residents, the local authorities implemented an integrated master plan for the old city, aiming at appeasing the residents and, meanwhile, protecting the status quo for business interests. The master plan set out different zones and allotted specific functions to them. Its main achievement, however, was formally banning the construction of new restaurants from residential areas and all locations off the main tourist thoroughfares.

Figure 20.3: Inside a Damascene boutique hotel

At the same time, the existence of investment capital (often, remittances from Syrian expatriates living abroad or petrodollars) forced investors to find alternatives to investing in restaurants. Beit Mamlouka, the first boutique hotel in Old Damascus, opened in 2004. Its owner set the standard for a new business model that the international travel press celebrated as the new insider destination for authentic upmarket city breaks (author's interview, April 2011). This attracted the attention of further investors, Syrian as well as foreign, and the prospect of high profits accelerated the demand for houses suitable for being transformed into boutique hotels. Whereas restaurants within the walled old city were the subject of far-reaching regulations, the master plan did not lay down comparable rules for boutique hotels. Obviously, some investors took advantage of the situation and boutique hotels have since mushroomed throughout the old city. Between 2005 and 2008, their number rose from 10 to 65, and by the spring of 2012, Maktab al-Anbar estimated there to be more than 100 boutique hotels (author's interview, April 2011). The successive development of boutique hotels throughout the old city emblematised the transformation of traditional residential neighbourhoods into a gentrified landscape for the consumption purposes of affluent Damascenes and tourists (see Figure 20.3). This yielded rising property prices,[6] a shortage of inexpensive housing and changes that, as a resident from the old city stated:

> 'resulted in the fact that gradually people started either to be tempted to sell their properties or to be bothered by the commercial places and its disadvantages. Then they wanted to get rid of living in the old city as soon as possible.' (Author's interview, April 2011)

This vivid account documents a phenomenon that occurs in the context of gentrification even in cases where no direct displacement can be observed, which Peter Marcuse (1986) terms 'pressure of displacement':

> When a family sees its neighbourhood changing dramatically, when all their friends are leaving, when stores are going out of business and new stores for other clientele are taking their place (or none at all replacing them), when changes in public transportation patterns, support services, are all clearly making the area less and less liveable, then the pressure of displacement is already severe, and its actuality only a matter of time. Families under such circumstances may even move as soon as they can. (Marcuse, 1986, p 157)

Meanwhile, though on a very low flame, 'new' business ideas including the residential use of historic buildings for upmarket housing or as luxury holiday homes became part of investors' portfolios. Reflecting on these changes in the old city, an artist working in the Jewish Quarter contemplated the growing demand for gentrifiable property with fear:

> 'Every place, every area becomes like this. At the beginning, there was poverty, poor artists.... With little money, you could have a house here, small place or big place. But after.... Now I think artists can't have places here anymore.' (Author's interview, April 2011)

Marcuse (1986) defined circumstances in which changing external conditions excluded a family from moving into a property as 'exclusionary displacement'. Thereby, he focused on those changes of conditions that:

(a) [are] beyond the household's reasonable ability to control or prevent;
(b) occur despite the household's being able to meet all previously imposed conditions of occupancy;
(c) differ significantly and in a spatially concentrated fashion from changes in the housing market as a whole; and
(d) makes occupancy by that household impossible, hazardous, or unaffordable. (Marcuse, 1986, p 156)

For Ross and Jamil (2011, p 27), evidence from the Lebanese capital, Beirut,[7] revealed the internal contradictions of advanced capitalist urbanisation in general and gentrification in particular: 'given adequate effective demand, that which makes neighborhoods, if not entire cities, attractive and livable, also makes them unaffordable. That which sullies the beauty, safety, or desirability of urban spaces, in turn, makes housing more affordable'. The authors concluded that '[t]he only market factor that has merely dampened rising housing prices in Beirut is the debilitating fear of renewed political violence' (Ross and Jamil, 2011, p 27). The pressures on Old Damascus, its residents and infrastructure were forecast to accelerate in the coming years. However, in the context of the Syrian civil war, it is not yet foreseeable if gentrification will continue as predicted or rather come to a halt.

Authoritarian resilience, gentrification and the new bourgeoisie

Having elaborated on the preconditions for gentrification – the production of both gentrifiable real estate and potential gentrifiers – and how gentrification gained momentum in Old Damascus, it becomes necessary to articulate the links between the authoritarian state and the bourgeoisie within the process of gentrification. Encouraged by the transition of formerly socialist states into democracies, the assumption of a predetermined changeover towards full democracy was appreciated by many Western politicians and scholars. According to this 'transition paradigm', all states have to be seen as situated on a continuum somewhere between authoritarianism and democracy (for a critique, see Carothers, 2002; Snyder, 2006, p 219). However, authoritarian regimes across the globe remained resistant to democratisation, and, until recently, especially so in the Arab world (Bellin, 2004). Exposure to external pressures made these states develop strategies for coping with the demands and, meanwhile, build up new forms of power solidification. These days, authoritarian upgrading is a main focus of authoritarianism research (eg Posusney, 2004; Pratt, 2007; King, 2009). In this context, authoritarian regimes developed forms of control that, from the perspective of an authoritarian regime, could be termed an approved aim at responding 'aggressively to the triple threat of globalization, markets, and democratization' (Heydemann, 2007, p 3). One such response is co-opting new clients.

The al-Asad regime expanded its base of support by co-opting the (new) bourgeoisie, whose interests were not that incongruent with those of the formerly radical constituency (Hinnebusch, 1995). On the subject of differentiating between the 'old' and 'new' bourgeoisie, Perthes (1991, p 33) identified the year 1963 as a turning point. However, this distinction increasingly became less important, as a certain amalgamation of formerly inimical elites took place due to economic liberalisation. Damascene elites sharing a common lifestyle and level of wealth helped to overcome formerly dividing categories such as religion or regional origin. Involving the new class means creating an investor-friendly environment, offering new business opportunities and allowing consumption of a cosmopolitan lifestyle. As illustrated earlier, members of new social classes seek to establish themselves either through emulating established elites (Perthes, 1991) or through distinction in a Bourdieuian sense. Regarding the production of a gentrified Old Damascus,[8] this applied to factions of the state bourgeoisie and the new bourgeoisie, as well as to those members of the old business elite who were co-opted in the regime's attempt to broaden its power base during the economic crises of the 1980s. State contracts and other privileges brought regime cronies into the position of representatives of international enterprises; others gained influence as middlemen or were granted privileged access to new business sectors, for instance, the fast-growing tourism industry and real estate, which both had a direct impact on gentrification in Old Damascus.

As will be shown in the following paragraphs, the context of gentrification provided the regime with a plenitude of occasions for employing informal policies. Measures comprised petty favours as well as distinct corruption. Oligarchic networks based on kinship or family ties granted strong cohesion within what Syrians call *the clique*. Rami Makhlouf, a cousin of Bashar al-Asad, most prominently embodied this practice. His widely ramified business empire included the mobile phone company Syriatel, construction, real estate and the touristic services provider Talisman Group. The latter operated two boutique hotels of the same name, both located in Old Damascus. Other members of the Makhlouf family also invested in the tourism industry: Khaldoun Makhlouf's Julia Dumna Group owned the centrally located Shahbandar Palace Hotel and had the monopoly for taxi travel from Damascus International Airport to the city centre. Others gained privileges through friendship and comradeship dating back to the wars against Israel, and privileges seemed to translate into an inheritable asset. Awlad al-sultah, for example, as the son of long-standing Minister of Defence Mustafa Tlas, had real-estate interests and invested in boutique hotels and restaurants too (Ismail, 2009, p 19; Schmidt, 2009, pp 29–32). To sum up, and using the words of Aita (2007), one can argue that 'opening a restaurant in a lucrative location is reserved to the *happy few*, often the offspring of regime figures' (Aita, 2007, p 565, emphasis in original, author's translation from French).

Also, outside the inner circle, patronage and clientelism seemed to be 'successful' strategies to tighten state–business relations. Under Bashar al-Asad, 'no significant business venture was possible without regime insiders taking a percentage'

(Hinnebusch, 2012, p 101). Consequently, every business depended on protection from within the security apparatus. For instance, according to a Damascene political consultant, this was facilitated by letting officers have their share in joint business activities:

> 'Usually, you have somebody working behind the owner, behind the *direct* owner.... If you are an officer and you would like to embark on a project like that, you would be quite keen to involve a businessman ... so that you would be responsible and you would have an interest in making it [the business] a success.' (Author's interview, April 2011)

For example, running boutique hotels or restaurants as joint businesses generated benefits for all partners involved and thus became an opportunity to reinforce the 'military–commercial coalition', 'which unites high-ranking officers and private-sector entrepreneurs' (Donati, 2013, p 40).

Likewise, opening hotels and restaurants before the necessary licences were granted became a widespread practice that enabled owners of gentrified property to quickly raise profits. In this regard – and with a focus on the guests of many newly opened restaurants – the owner of a small guesthouse who grew up in an Old Damascene courtyard house recalled:

> 'Many of their guests are famous people, sometimes even powerful people ... decision-makers let's say in the governorate of Damascus who usually give the licence. Even before the licences were granted, these restaurants became well-known, mentioned in guidebooks and so on. So, the government found itself eventually forced ... to license those places.... Their existence became a reality.' (Author's interview, April 2011)

The respondent gave a vivid account on how building up a client base, often among well-connected decision-makers, helped to create a fait accompli that the local administration had to accept. For investors with good contacts in the regime, it was possible to obtain ex post permissions despite violations of construction or licence regulations and thus privileged access to promising business activities. Informal practices like including members of the security services in joint business activities or opening a restaurant before obtaining the necessary licences and thereby creating a fait accompli demonstrated a shared interest by most stakeholders in preserving the status quo instead of threatening their privileges by introducing the rule of law or more transparency. As a result, it can be argued that selective access to the production of a gentrified Old Damascus functioned as one tool to bind new constituencies, namely, producers of gentrification, to the regime.

After 2005, foreign investors, mostly from the Gulf Cooperation Council (GCC) states, but also from Turkey and Europe, discovered the high profitability of investment in Old Damascus. However, the lack of legal certainty and transparency was a major constraint for doing business in Syria. Nevertheless, inconveniencies could be bypassed by using the service of well-connected middlemen, often members of the new bourgeoisie.

The remaining paragraphs in this chapter investigate mainly tourism-based authoritarian gentrification in Old Damascus in the context of open domestic and external opposition to the authoritarian rule that has rocked the county since the outbreak of the Syrian uprising in March 2011.

As a business sector, the tourism industry is particularly vulnerable to political tension. In April 2011, only one month into the uprising – up to then, security in Damascus was only marginally affected by the events – interviewees already observed a substantial decline in international tourist arrivals and explained how they postponed or even cancelled intended investment and considered dismissing some of their employees. Other private stakeholders had already done so and left the county. By the autumn of 2011, tourism, which accounted for 11.2% of the country's gross domestic product (GDP) in 2009 (Oxford Business Group, 2010), had come to a standstill.

Attempting to put pressure on the Syrian government, Turkey and Arab and Western states imposed several rounds of sanctions. These measures restricted trade and included an arms embargo, as well as an import ban on Syrian crude oil products. Furthermore, the Syrian regime faced an asset freeze, as well as a travel ban targeting some of its most influential supporters. Investigating the European Union's (EU, 2012) *Official Journal* illustrates striking links to gentrification in Damascus, both in the old city and in the capital's modern neighbourhoods: while the document lists individuals, entities and bodies targeted by sanctions, it meanwhile exposes the involvement of a number of key institutional and private stakeholders in the Damascene real estate market and thus producers of gentrification in the current crackdown. Among the individuals targeted by the EU for financing the regime were: the tycoons Rami Makhlouf and Mustafa Tlas (see earlier); Mohammad Hamsho, the founder of the development group Hamsho International and brother-in-law of the president's younger brother, Maher al-Asad; Riyad Chaliche, a cousin of al-Asad and director of military housing; and Bassam Sabbagh, a lawyer and partner of al-Asad in a real estate project in the port city Lattakia. The list of entities and bodies targeted by EU sanctions included, among others, the real estate and tourist developers Cham Holding, Beno Property, Hamcho International, Cham Investment, Military Housing and the Real Estate Bank Syria.

Meanwhile, and despite the fact that the bloodshed increased, international sanctions began to make an impact. In a recent interview, Syrian economist Samir Seifan mentioned that:

> governmental projects are stopped, private investment is stopped, capital has fled abroad, the tourism sector ... is close to zero, industrial production has shrunk and demobilised part of its workforce,

> agriculture is affected heavily due to the vast army operations, the market is shrinking, exports are reduced by half, unemployment has increased to around 25% and prices have risen due to a lack of many goods. (Quoted in *The Guardian*, 14 November 2011[9])

Under these circumstances, it is questionable whether authoritarian upgrading remains a successful strategy for regime maintenance. Regarding the co-optation of producers of gentrification, this means monitoring these stakeholders' behaviour when their expected revenues from tourism fail to materialise. Will these individuals continue to remain indifferent towards the regime's atrocities when faced with personal disadvantages or economic loss? Whom will they blame for the deteriorating situation: the regime, the opposition or a foreign conspiracy? It could be argued that those co-opted only by economic incentives such as ad hoc permissions for starting a business or preferential access are likely to change sides as soon as there is an alternative to the status quo. By way of contrast, for those linked to the regime not only by business, but also by religion or kinship, all or nothing is the stake.

Conclusion

This chapter has examined the interrelations between gentrification and authoritarian rule in Old Damascus with the objective of broadening scholarly research on gentrification beyond the Global North. The chapter has investigated how the particular principles of the Islamic city, namely, segregation along sectarian instead of class boundaries, shaped the preconditions for gentrification in Old Damascus, such as the production of gentrifiable, meaning inexpensive and centrally located, real estate. Further, it was argued that suburbanisation, a process preceding gentrification, accelerated the decline of Old Damascus's status as a place to live. In addition, by comparing Damascene gentrifiers to their Western counterparts, common grounds and differences between both groups have been pointed out. Besides individual gentrifiers and the market, an additional dimension for analysing gentrification in Damascus was introduced: the authoritarian state. The focus on the history of class formation in Syria underlines the importance of identifying potential gentrifiers; in contrast to the case in the West, where gentrifiers often have a professional middle-class background, it was shown that it was the new bourgeoisie that spurred gentrification in Old Damascus.

In the Damascene context, gentrification can best be understood as the production of urban space for temporary consumption by affluent users, mostly local 'evening or weekend gentrifiers', as well as tourists. Gentrification only gained momentum when the state's attempts to economically open up the country met changes in consumer preferences, most importantly, a 'return to the old'. Moreover, although this chapter is based on the accounts of producers of gentrification who are often members of the Damascene bourgeoisie, social issues, most prominently, displacement, which was identified in the form of exclusionary displacement and displacement pressure, cannot be ignored in the analysis of gentrification in Old Damascus.

In considering the extent to which gentrification contributed to the solidification of authoritarian power in Syria, this chapter argues that the context of gentrification in Old Damascus provided the regime with various tools to co-opt the new bourgeoisie, for example, by granting ex post permissions for previously illicitly commercialised residential property, or granting licences (or by declining to do so) for transforming residential into commercial property. Allowing investment in, and the commercialisation of, Old Damascene real estate meant creating profitable business opportunities for members of the new class. Moreover, the creation of private sector jobs in both the production of a gentrified Old Damascus and in the new leisure industry attached many Syrians to the businesses of regime cronies and consequently to the regime.

By scrutinising informal urban policies in the context of clientelism and patronage, the findings from Old Damascus presented in this chapter contribute to a broader understanding of gentrification in authoritarian states. The chapter casts light on informal forms of state involvement in the gentrification process beyond the state-led gentrification discussed elsewhere. Meanwhile, the Damascene case adds to the literature on authoritarian upgrading by linking the concept and the actors involved to the urban scale. With regards to the years prior to the Syrian Civil War, gentrification can be considered to have been a successful tool for sustaining authoritarian rule.

Since March 2011, citizens across Syria have been peacefully demonstrating for freedom and an end to Bashar al-Asad's authoritarian rule. From the beginning, the regime reacted with brute force (eg arrests, torture and a shoot-to-kill policy, which escalated to the current Syrian Civil War). More recently, the brutality of the regime has been marked by evidence of their use of chemical weapons on their own people. Observing the events in Syria from afar reveals that the centre of Damascus – despite the increasing level of violence in some of the capital's suburbs and elsewhere in the country – has remained relatively calm. On the one hand, this can be explained by the high concentration of regime security forces in central Damascus; an additional explanation, however, could be that the regime's attempts to broaden its constituency by embedding huge factions of the urban bourgeoisie through privileges such as access to a gentrified Old Damascus was regrettably 'successful' – at least for the time being.

Notes

[1] This chapter is based on qualitative interviews with producers of gentrification and ethnographic observations conducted in Damascus in 2010 and 2011 as part of my PhD research. Fieldwork in March/April 2011 would not have been possible without a travel grant from the Council for British Research in the Levant (CBRL). Furthermore, I want to thank Leila Vignal and Christa Salamandra for their valuable comments on earlier versions of this chapter.

[2] However, the influx of Palestinian refugees into the Jewish Quarter is a noteworthy exception.

[3] This coincides with Bashar al-Asad's rise to power in the summer of 2000, an event that is perceived as a turning point by many Syrians.

[4] For a critical assessment of the term 'urban pioneer', see Smith (1986, pp 16–17).

[5] Division of the Ministry of Local Administration responsible for the old city.

[6] An informant mentioned that prices for some properties went up thirtyfold within 10 years (author's interview, April 2011).

[7] Between 1975 and 1990, Lebanon was the stage of a bloody civil war; since then, the political situation has remained unstable.

[8] Based on the case of Victoriana in Melbourne, Jager (1986) investigates the specific ambiance of gentrified neighbourhoods, which he terms 'aesthetics of gentrification' (p 78). This phenomenon, which includes '[t]he return to historical purity and authenticity' (p 83), is the expression of gentrifiers' increasing interest in the cultural heritage of 'their' neighbourhoods, as was also described by my Damascene informants in the spring of 2011.

[9] Available at: http://www.theguardian.com/commentisfree/2011/nov/14/economic-sanctions-syria-bashar-al-assad-regime (accessed 20 September 2012).

References

Abaza, M. (2001) 'Shopping malls, consumer culture and the reshaping of public space in Egypt', *Theory, Culture and Society*, vol 18, no 5, pp 97–122.

Abaza, M. (2011) 'Critical commentary. Cairo's downtown imagined: Dubaisation or nostalgia?', *Urban Studies*, vol 48, no 6, pp 1075–87.

Abu-Lughod, J. (1980) *Rabat: urban apartheid in Morocco*, Guildford: Princeton University Press.

Aita, S. (2007) 'L'économie de la Syrie peut-elle devenir sociale?' ['Syria's economy – can it become social?'], in B. Dupret, Z. Ghazzal, Y. Courbage, M. al-Dbiyat (eds) *La Syrie au présent – Reflets d'une société* [*Syria at present – reflections about a society*], Paris: Sindbad Actes Sud, pp 541–79.

Atkinson, R. and Bridge, G. (2005) *Gentrification in a global context: the new urban Colonialism*, London: Routledge.

Bellin, E. (2004) 'The robustness of authoritarianism in the Middle East – exceptionalism in comparative perspective', *Comparative Politics*, vol 36, no 2, pp 139–57.

Bogaert, K. (2012) 'New state space formation in Morocco: the example of the Bouregreg Valley', *Urban Studies*, vol 49, no 2, pp 255–70.

Carothers, T. (2002) 'The end of the transition paradigm', *Journal of Democracy*, vol 13, no 1, pp 5–21.

Carpenter, J. and Lees, L. (1995) 'Gentrification in New York, London and Paris – an international comparison', *International Journal of Urban and Regional Research*, vol 19, no 2, pp 286–303.

Caulfield, J. (1989) 'Gentrification and desire', *Canadian Review of Sociology and Anthropology-Revue Canadienne de Sociologie et d' Anthropologie*, vol 26, no 4, pp 617–32.

Dettmann, K. (1969) 'Damaskus. Eine orientalische Stadt zwischen Tradition und Moderne' ['Damascus. An Eastern city between tradition and modernity'], *Mitteilungen der Fränkischen Geographischen Gesellschaft*, vols 15/16, pp 183–312.

Dokmeci, V., Altunbas, U. and Yazgi, B. (2007) 'Revitalisation of the main street of a distinguished old neighbourhood in Istanbul', *European Planning Studies*, vol 15, no 1, pp 153–66.

Donati, C. (2013) 'The economics of authoritarian upgrading in Syria: liberalization and the reconfiguration of economic networks', in S. Heydemann and R. Leenders (eds) *Middle East authoritarianisms – governance, contestation, and regime resilience in Syria and Iran*, Stanford, CA: Stanford University Press, pp 35–60.

Escher, A. (2001) 'Globalisierung in den Altstädten von Damaskus und Marrakesch?' ['Globalization in the old cities of Damascus and Marrakech?'], in H. Roggenthin (ed) *Stadt – der Lebensraum der Zukunft?*[*City – lebensraum for the future*], Mainz: Geographisches Institut, Johannes Gutenberg-Universität, pp 23–38.

Escher, A. and Schepers, M. (2008) 'Revitalizing the medina of Tunis as a national symbol', *Erdkunde*, vol 62, no 2, pp 129–41.

Escher, A., Petermann, S. and Clos, B. (2001) 'Gentrification in der Medina von Marrakech', *Geographische Rundschau*, vol 53, no 6, pp 24–31.

EU (European Union) (2012) *Official Journal of the European Union*, L16, 19 January.

Fahmi, W. and Sutton, K. (2010) 'Reclaiming Cairo's downtown district: contesting the nineteenth- and early twentieth-century European Quarter', *International Development Planning Review*, vol 32, no 2, pp 93–118.

Florida, R. (2005) *Cities and the creative class*, New York, NY: Routledge.

Glass, R. (1964) 'Introduction: aspects of change', in Centre for Urban Studies (ed) *London aspects of change*, London: MacGibbon and Kee.

Gotham, K.F. (2005) 'Tourism gentrification: the case of New Orleans' Vieux Carre (French Quarter)', *Urban Studies*, vol 42, no 7, pp 1099–121.

Goulden, R. (2011) 'Housing, inequality, and economic change in Syria', *British Journal of Middle Eastern Studies*, vol 38, no 2, pp 187–202.

Hackworth, J. (2002) 'Post recession gentrification in New York City', *Urban Affairs Review*, vol 37, no 6, pp 815–43.

Haddad, B. (2009) 'Enduring legacies: the politics of private sector development in Syria', in F. Lawson (ed) *Demystifying Syria*, London: The London Middle East Institute, pp 29–55.

Hamnett, C. (1991) 'The blind men and the elephant – the explanation of gentrification', *Transactions of the Institute of British Geographers*, vol 16, no 2, pp 173–89.

Heydemann, S. (2007) 'Upgrading authoritarianism in the Arab world', Analysis Paper, no 13, The Saban Center for Middle East Policy at the Brookings Institution.

Hinnebusch, R.A. (1995) 'The political-economy of economic liberalization in Syria', *International Journal of Middle East Studies*, vol 27, no 3, pp 305–20.

Hinnebusch, R.A. (2001) *Syria: revolution from above*, London: Routledge.

Hinnebusch, R.A. (2012) 'Syria: from "authoritarian upgrading" to revolution?', *International Affairs*, vol 88, no 1, pp 95–113.

Ismail, S. (2009) 'Changing social structures, shifting alliances and authoritarianism in Syria', in F. Lawson (ed) *Demystifying Syria*, London: The London Middle East Institute, pp 13–28.

Jager, M. (1986) 'Class definition and the aesthetics of gentrification: Victoriana in Melbourne', in N. Smith and P. Williams (eds) *Gentrification of the city*, London: Allen and Unwin, pp 78–91.

King, S.J. (2009) *The new authoritarianism in the Middle East and North Africa*, Bloomington, IN: Indiana University Press.

Krijnen, M. and Fawas, M. (2010) 'Exception as the rule: high-end developments in neoliberal Beirut', *Built Environment*, vol 36, no 2, pp 245–59.

Kuppinger, P. (2005) 'Globalization and exterritoriality in metropolitan Cairo', *Geographical Review*, vol 95, no 3, pp 348–72.

Leverett, F.L. (2005) *Inheriting Syria: Bashar's trial by fire*, Washington, DC: Brookings Institution Press.

Ley, D. (1980) 'Liberal ideology and the postindustrial city', *Annals of the Association of American Geographers*, vol 70, no 2, pp 238–58.

Marcuse, P. (1986) 'Abandonment, gentrification and displacement: the linkages in New York City', in N. Smith and P. Williams (eds) *Gentrification of the city*, London: Allen and Unwin, pp 153–77.

Nagel, C. (2000) 'Ethnic conflict and urban redevelopment in downtown Beirut', *Growth and Change*, vol 31, no 2, pp 211–34.

Nagel, C. (2002) 'Reconstructing space, re-creating memory: sectarian politics and urban development in post-war Beirut', *Political Geography*, vol 21, no 5, pp 717–25.

Oxford Business Group (2010) *The report – Syria 2009*, London: Oxford Business Group.

Perthes, V. (1991) 'A look at Syria's upper class: the bourgeoisie and the Ba'th', *Middle East Report*, vol 21, no 170, pp 31–7.

Pfaffenbach, C. (2004) 'Damaskus. Von der traditionellen orientalischen Stadt zur kulturell globalisierten Metropole des Südens' ['Damascus. From the traditional Eastern city towards a culturally globalized metropolis of the South'], in G. Meyer (ed) *Die Arabische Welt im Spiegel der Kulturgeographie* [*The Arab world through the lens of cultural geography*], Mainz: ZEFAW, pp 62–9.

Posusney, M.P. (2004) 'Enduring authoritarianism – Middle East lessons for comparative theory', *Comparative Politics*, vol 36, no 2, pp 127–38.

Pratt, N.C. (2007) *Democracy and authoritarianism in the Arab world*, Boulder, CO: Lynne Rienner Publishers.

Rabinovich, I. (1972) *Syria under the Ba'th 1963–66. The army–party symbiosis*, Jerusalem: Israel Universities Press.

Robinson, J. (2002) 'Global and world cities: a view from off the map', *International Journal of Urban and Regional Research*, vol 26, pp 531–54.

Ross, R. and Jamil, L. (2011) 'Waiting for war (and other strategies to stop gentrification): the case of Ras Beirut', *Urban Geography*, vol 4, no 3, pp 15–32.

Rubino, S. (2005) 'A curious blend? City revitalization, gentrification and commodification in Brazil', in R. Atkinson and G. Bridge (eds) *Gentrification in a global context: the new urban colonialism*, London: Routledge, pp 225–39.

Salamandra, C. (2004) *A new Old Damascus: authenticity and distinction in urban Syria*, Bloomington, IN: Indiana University Press.

Schmidt, S. (2009) 'The developmental role of the state in the Middle East: lessons from Syria', in R. Hinnebusch and S. Schmidt (eds) *The state and the political economy of reform in Syria*, St Andrews: University of St Andrews Centre for Syrian Studies, distributed by Lynne Rienner Publishers, pp 25–44.

Seale, P. (1988) *Assad of Syria: the struggle for the Middle East*, London: Tauris.

Seger, M. (1975) 'Strukturelemente der Stadt Teheran und das Modell der modernen orientalischen Stadt' ['Structural elements of the city of Teheran and the model of the modern Eastern city'], *Erdkunde*, vol 29, no 1, pp 21–38.

Slater, T. (2006) 'The eviction of critical perspectives from gentrification research', *International Journal of Urban and Regional Research*, vol 30, no 4, pp 737–57.

Smith, N. (1979) 'Toward a theory of gentrification – back to the city movements by capital, not people', *Journal of the American Planning Association*, vol 45, no 4, pp 538–48.

Smith, N. (1986) 'Gentrification, the frontier, and the restructuring of urban space' in N. Smith, and P. Williams (eds) *Gentrification of the City*, London: Allen & Unwin, pp 15–34.

Smith, N. (1996) *The new urban frontier: gentrification and the revanchist city*, London: Routledge.

Smith, N. (2002) 'New globalism, new urbanism: gentrification as global urban strategy', *Antipode*, vol 34, no 3, pp 427–50.

Snyder, R. (2006) 'Beyond authoritarianism: the spectrum of nondemocratic regimes', in A. Schedler (ed) *Electoral authoritarianism: the dynamics of unfree competition*, Boulder, CO: Lynne Rienner Publishers, pp 292–310.

Sudermann, Y. (2012) 'Contested heritage? Gentrification and authoritarian resilience in Damascus', in B. Ahmad and Y. Sudermann (eds) *Syria's contrasting neighborhoods: gentrification and informal settlements juxtaposed*, St Andrews: University of St Andrews Centre for Syrian Studies, distributed by Lynne Rienner Publishers, pp 29–54.

Sutton, K. and Fahmi, W. (2002) 'The rehabilitation of Old Cairo', *Habitat International*, vol 26, no 1, pp 73–93.

Totah, F. (2009) 'Return to the origin: negotiating the modern and the unmodern in the old city of Damascus', *City & Society*, vol 21, no 1, pp 58–81.

Williams, P. (1986) 'Class constitution through spatial reconstruction? A re-evaluation of gentrification in Australia, Britain and the United States', in N. Smith and P. Williams (eds) *Gentrification of the city*, London: Allen and Unwin, pp 56–77.

Wirth, E. (2000) *Die orientalische Stadt im islamischen Vorderasien und Nordafrika* [*The Eastern city in the Islamic Middle East and North Africa*], Mainz: Verlag Philipp von Zabern.

Zukin, S. (1988) *Loft living: culture and capital in urban change*, London: Radius.

TWENTY-ONE

The place of gentrification in Cape Town

Annika Teppo and Marianne Millstein

Introduction

Consider these events in Cape Town in 2009:

- *Gugulethu*: A gleaming new mall is built in the township approximately 20 kilometres from the city centre: the developers are interested in attracting black middle-class clientele to the area. However, this means that the local merchants, many of whom had traded in the area for more than a decade, are displaced far from Gugulethu's best trading sites.
- *Central Business District (CBD)*: Right before the 2010 FIFA World Cup, the central city is rejuvenated. However, the facelift involves moving the poorest people away from the area and transferring them to distant temporary relocation areas (TRAs) in which they face exceedingly difficult circumstances.
- *Woodstock*: This charming old area in central Cape Town is looking better by the day. The services in the area cater for an increasingly exclusive class, and the housing prices are soaring. Many families who have been residing in the area for decades can no longer afford to stay there. Some of these destitute residents try to take action against landlords, who want to evict them in order to develop their homes into upmarket flats.

These events can be labelled gentrification, as they involve the movement of middle-income people into low-income neighbourhoods, thus causing the displacement of all, or many, of the pre-existing low-income residents (Lees et al, 2010, p xvi). According to gentrification literature from the Global North, the process involves some level of reinvestment, social upgrading, landscape change and displacement. While all these signs are present in Cape Town and other South African cities, the public justifications of, and discussions and disputes about, these processes differ greatly from those employed in the Global North. Furthermore, the material and social conditions often differ completely.

The developers building the Gugulethu mall lean on revolutionary imagery and proclaim the racial upliftment of the people. Despite the ensuing evictions, the FIFA World Cup is supposed to bring glory to all (South) Africans and thus unite the nation(s). In 2003, President Thabo Mbeki stated:

> [t]he basis of [South Africa's] bid was a resolve to ensure that the 21st century unfolds as a century of growth and development in Africa.... We want, on behalf of our continent, to stage an event that will send ripples of confidence from the Cape to Cairo.... We want to ensure that one day, historians will reflect upon the 2010 World Cup as a moment when Africa stood tall and resolutely turned the tide on centuries of poverty and conflict. We want to show that Africa's time has come. (Quoted in Desai and Vahed, 2009, p 154).

Those defending these urban changes appeal to a moral, post-colonial, racial discourse. The language and terminology used are more often than not that of a moral project. The Afrikaans term '*opheffing*', for example, originally referred to the social upliftment of 'poor white people', and later expanded to signify a number of other social and spatial improvement processes. In order to achieve these aims, any and all change begins to sound justifiable – the eviction of some of the urban poor seems almost a minor detail.

However, these projects were not accepted unanimously and without resistance. Citizens, politicians and civil societies hotly debated and contested the urban transformations in and around the malls, stadiums and suburbs.

Many urban changes in South African cities seemingly fit the notion of gentrification and especially its ensuing displacement. However, the issues at hand are vast and complicated. They include the colonial and post-colonial inheritance, the social hierarchies of a settler society, and ideas of 'race', all of which have numerous sociocultural implications. Moreover, the material circumstances are challenging: according to the GINI coefficient, South Africa continues to have one of the most unequal divisions of income in the world (UNDP, 2012). Middle-class South Africans, who have access to employment, proper education and medical services, are members of a relatively small elite. The middle class differs from the less affluent middle-income group, earning ZAR3,500–7,000 per month (about USD350–700). As one delves into these processes in South Africa, the concept of gentrification seems an inadequate lens through which to study these intricate material and discursive processes. In this country, they involve academic debates, vast social engineering projects, civil society, malls and housing, extreme wealth and poverty, and urban planning, as well as a complex, historically shaped, local system of moral values.

In this chapter, we aim to discuss the place that the notion of gentrification occupies in the South African context, and the terms according to which it is applicable. We contribute to the gentrification debate by exploring different histories and socio-spatial processes related to urban changes and displacements in Cape Town. We study gentrification using certain 'keywords' – a term that Emile Boonzaier and John Sharp's (1988) seminal work *South African keywords: the uses and abuses of political concepts* inspired. These keywords – such as 'upliftment', 'regeneration' and 'development' – have historically been used in relevant discussions, or they have taken different forms over the years. They reflect the discursive formations of urban change, while the authors argue that these keywords also reflect and reproduce the moral ordering of urban spaces in South Africa.

Theoretical underpinnings

As previously outlined, there are a number of South African examples that could easily fit one or several of the broader theoretical perspectives on gentrification. Urban transformation involves changing neighbourhoods and communities, and leads to direct and indirect displacements. These processes sometimes fit the earlier-mentioned definition of gentrification and sometimes do not. Nevertheless, when researchers touch on gentrification processes, their framework is mainly based on theories from gentrification research in the Global North.

The gentrification research on Cape Town seems to reflect exactly what classic studies of gentrification expect to find: neat cases of the gentrification and urban renewal of inner-city neighbourhoods. Visser and Kotze (2008), for instance, discuss the recent transformations of the central district as examples of new-build gentrification that directly echo the characteristics of recent 'third-wave' gentrification debates in the Global North. This way of applying a framework developed from the research carried out in Northern cities constitutes a problem, as gentrification is usually associated with a number of local elements. What seems like a straightforward case of gentrification may turn out to be much more complicated upon further investigation.

A number of writers have questioned the extent to which gentrification is actually a recent phenomenon that is integral to the hegemonic neoliberal urban policies currently expanding across the globe (Butler, 2007; McCann and Ward, 2011; Lees, 2012). Moreover, the recent literature on gentrification in South Africa tends to treat it exclusively as a new urban process, linking it to broader economic globalisation processes. Tania Winkler (2009) approaches inner-city regeneration in Johannesburg as 'nothing more than a euphemism for gentrification' (p 363) driven by a blind belief in new global policies or, as her study's title suggests, the prolongation of the global age of gentrification as it moves towards Southern cities. Her analysis presents the market-driven regeneration of Johannesburg's CBD as a fitting example of how gentrification has become a focal point for global urban policymakers and underlines the current state-led gentrification processes (Winkler, 2009, p 364). Similarly, Visser and Kotze (2008, p 2569) argue that, in South Africa, urban policies for regeneration and renewal also show 'the imprint of global economic forces and urban redevelopment thinking'.

These perspectives thus fall within a strong tradition of critical research on South African cities. They emphasise that the hegemonic power of neoliberal urban governance, which originates in the North, or in Western societies, shapes urban transformations (Didier et al, 2012; Bénit Gbaffou et al, 2012). Since their main emphasis is on the political economy of capital and consumption, Smith (2002, pp 437–46), as summarised by Clark (2005, p 260), generalises gentrification processes as 'a global urban strategy' based on 'the mobilization of urban real-estate markets as vehicles of capital accumulation'. Furthermore:

> [t]he language of this strategy is sugar coated with images of revitalization, regeneration, renewal, reinvestment and redevelopment, while its legitimacy is anchored in the 'necessity to become a 'global city', a 'creative city', an attractive city, in competition with other cities. The social costs of the strategy are, if at all recognized, deemed necessary and unavoidable. (Clark, 2005, p 260)

Similar language can be perceived in the South African urban policy discourse. Referring to Slater (2006), Winkler (2009, p 366) argues that:

> [c]oncepts such as economic competitiveness, responsive governance, social cohesion, and social mix, embroiled in New Urban Policy and New Conventional Wisdom, serve as excellent examples of how the reality of gentrification is being replaced by a discursive policy language to deflect criticism.

The discourses on South African urban changes should not only be interpreted by means of a hegemonic, neoliberal urban governance lingo, or as policy discourses aimed at avoiding criticism. They reflect a deeper and much older moral ordering of urban spaces. In this ordering, global hegemonic discourses are tied to and renegotiated through national and local discursive frameworks. On a more pragmatic note, Sue Parnell (2008) has also noted that the lack of a national urban policy framework in South Africa is a challenge as it is open to very localised interpretations of critical rights, such as water, electricity and housing.

Not even the most powerful ideas and 'best practices' are simply copied or replicated; they are renegotiated and often challenged. Recent discussions on the mobility and transferability of policies have paid attention to this in a debate on the hegemony of neoliberal ideas and on opportunities to create and propose alternative imaginaries and strategies (McCann and Ward, 2011). Some debates in the gentrification literature recognise opportunities for positive or 'third way' gentrification, with the state playing a more central role through its public policies for urban renewal. Lees and Ley (2008) provide a critical discussion of such state-led and managed gentrification. In this type of gentrification, public policies – such as social mixing – are integral to broader neoliberal urban policies. Gentrification, therefore, should be an empirical question in terms of its effect on displacements and redistribution. If not, 'uncritical optimism about the benign results of gentrification can readily be incorporated into a [hegemonic discourse], ranging across policy, politics and popular opinion' (Lees and Ley, 2008, p 2382). We do not contest that such hegemonic, external forces have massively shaped the urban transformations in South Africa. In line with many others, we do, however, argue that analyses of urban change and gentrification can easily miss an engagement with history and geography, or an understanding of the social processes and domains that underpin these ideas (see Lees, 2012, 2014). As Beauregard (1986, p 40) points out, 'gentrification must be theorized as a part of the organic totality of social formation'.

Other researchers have also called for this theorisation, emphasising the need for contextual and concrete analyses of neoliberal policies' manifestations. Butler (2007, p 165) argues that analyses of gentrification as a travelling policy require 'an understanding of the local social relations in which the gentrification process is taking place'. In her research on Cape Town, Miraftab (2007), for instance, rejects the idea that the implementation of the Central City Improvement District was merely a roll-out of neoliberal gentrification. While keeping the neoliberal discursive and spatial practices in mind, Miraftab's analysis reveals that this process was also challenged and contested from within the state and by citizens on the ground.

While there are clear linkages to global hegemonic ideas and best practices, we suggest that certain *discursive formations* also emerge from the particular histories and geographies of South African urban transformations. These discursive formations can be found behind certain keywords in South African gentrification. The term 'gentrification' might be relatively new to the country, but the concepts and policies of renewal, upliftment, urban regeneration and community development are not, and are often used synonymously with gentrification. Consequently, in order to assess gentrification's position in South African urban discourses, we investigate its historical continuity in the language – from apartheid's 'social engineering' to the lingo used in contemporary urban policies. This language frames ongoing gentrification processes. We further argue that this language is tainted with previous racial hierarchies and the ensuing ideas regarding the moral order between races.

By unpacking the rationalisation of the moral ordering of urban spaces, we present discursive formations in the form of keywords that have legitimised policies involving multiple forms of displacement, but that have also been appropriated and reinterpreted through local social relations. Because the use of these words has changed over time, we explore their formations and their function as a moral framework that politically legitimises urban change processes and the ensuing spatial practices. We also explore this beyond the bounds of the inner city, which many eminent writers have suggested (eg Phillips, 2004). We are concerned with the multiple ways in which these urban discourses, strategies and practices are mediated, contested and negotiated in South African cities.

The keywords of fragmented urbanity in South Africa

As discursive formation consists of different, often contradictory, opinions, all the stakeholders in urban issues – from civil society to planners and people on the street – might have differing stances regarding urban changes. They have different ways of expressing different viewpoints, which are subsequently interpreted differently. However, all residents of Cape Town are familiar with a number of ideas about being a proper person in the city, which constitute a framework of moral thinking about urban life and its changes. This means that those involved draw from particular local discourses and systems of culturally and historically defined values, which they employ when they make, justify and implement their points of view regarding urban changes. While these moral perspectives have formed a historical continuity of thinking since the days of apartheid, they continue to shape the stakeholders' reasoning and legitimacy. These local moral perspectives can also be seen as complementary ways of addressing the questions raised by gentrification processes. In practice, this is noticeable in disputes over spaces, which often escalate into battles for the highest moral standing in the community. This is a particularly valuable point in a country that has experienced its negotiated revolution against ethically untenable governance. It is important to be seen as the beholder of the 'right' values.

In apartheid South Africa and even before, the hegemonic framework of white minority power defined the urban discussions. A quick look at some of the earlier examples shows that complex developments were at play. Cape Town's history of, and geography due to, colonialism and apartheid inform these processes in ways that are not easily understood through the existing perspectives on gentrification or urban theories. Also known as the 'Mother City', Cape Town was a segregated society since its humble beginnings in 1652. At that time, the East Indian Trading Company established it as a provisioning station at the Cape of the Good Hope. Slaves lived in crowded lodges, while the free burghers inhabited spacious Cape Dutch-style houses. In the colonial era, this social hierarchy was occasionally breached: a number of African and 'coloured'[1] people became prominent members of society, mainly in Cape Town. Nevertheless, the basic pattern was always the same: white people were higher up and the darker the skin tone, the lower a person's rung on the social ladder.

While the city grew and experienced numerous phases and developments, segregation remained. Official segregation began in 1901, at which time most Africans were forcibly removed to the Ndabeni area outside the city limits – allegedly to prevent bubonic plague from spreading. In his classic essay 'The sanitation syndrome', Maynard Swanson shows how 'urban race relations came to be widely conceived and dealt with in the imagery of infection and epidemic disease' (Swanson, 1977, p 387). This was consequently used to justify apartheid. However, it did much more. Many social discourses of the time suggested that there was a connection between illness and a lack of morals. Thus, classifying Africans as 'contagious' also reflected their low social ranking and assigned them to a morally low rank. Public administration and ideas of race, urban space, health and morality were already firmly intertwined by the late 19th and early 20th centuries.

Upliftment part 1: apartheid city – bringing up proper white people

Segregation in urban spaces was reinforced by the apartheid era's (1948–84) spatial policies. The effect on urban areas was to exaggerate the already-existing segregation in South African cities. Apartheid-era social engineering was an extension of colonial spatial and racial policies, while it also took on unique malign features. Petty and grand apartheid rules divided the cities. All spaces – schools, parks, public benches, post offices and private homes – were racially divided. In 1950, the implementation of the Group Areas Act forced people to reside in their designated racial areas, while the Population Registration Act of 1950 divided all citizens into 'white', 'African' or 'black', and 'coloured' (and, later, 'Asian') categories. The categorisation took place according to outward appearance, habitus and general acceptance as a member of a certain racial group. The already-established moral values were the unspoken content of these categories. It is important to note that the racial categories underlying spatial divisions were, as in many other African colonies, hierarchical: white people were presumed to be superior to any other 'race' in every respect. White people were therefore granted the best opportunities and privileges in every area of life. The 'coloured' people shared some of these advantages, while the Africans, who were pushed to the least-developed and most distant urban spaces, received no privileges. Not only were material resources considered as belonging to white people, but they were also believed to embody the highest values and morality. They were presented as the pinnacle of human goodness and decency. These values were reflected in policymaking and urban spaces (Teppo, 2004, 2009).

Apartheid was not only for segregating people, it was also used to rehabilitate them, and make them apt representatives of their designated racial groups. An excellent example of this endeavour was the 'upliftment' of 'poor white people' – impoverished white people. In the 1930s, half of the white Afrikaners were poor, and social engineering was deployed to help them. The Carnegie Commission carried out a large research project on poor white people, uniting white South African intellectuals and policymakers in their goal to uplift them to a level considered suitable for white people. Their rehabilitation would take place in suburbs especially built for this racial upliftment. To 'uplift' (the word can be used as either a noun or verb) was a much-used term in the five volumes on the 'poor white problem' that the Carnegie Commission published in 1932, and originates from the Afrikaans word '*opheffing*' (to lift up). Upliftment of the poor white people meant that they had to look and behave like 'good white people'. They needed to acquire good jobs, have happy family lives and enjoy a stable economy. Being unemployed, alcoholic or poor marginalised a white person, who, according to the apartheid ideology, was inherently better at everything. As white people were considered superior, their behaviour was closely monitored. The mere virtue of being white meant that poor white people had a number of advantages, but industrious social workers also watched and controlled them in their areas. Being a good white person was the ideal, and becoming one was presented as a moral duty linked to simultaneous ascension in the racial and social hierarchies. This process was concluded when rehabilitated white people moved to middle-class areas to live a fulfilling, white life (Teppo, 2004, 2009).

While some poor white people succeeded in taking their new place in the social hierarchy, some never left the poor white areas. They stayed there, living on the apartheid state's seemingly endless support, while people of colour in the neighbouring areas lived under much harder conditions with much less, if any, support. There is evidence that, after the 1960s, the remaining poor white people fought endless deadlocked battles over the highest moral standing in their suburbs. They accused one another of being immoral, thus directing the social worker's intruding gaze elsewhere. Over the decades, they became the most stigmatised people in South Africa, and were generally regarded as morally inferior.

The poor white project was one of apartheid's many social engineering exercises, which meant that only 1% of white South Africans were poor at the end of apartheid. The preferential treatment of white people throughout the apartheid era ensured that those classified as 'black' or 'African' began to regard themselves in a very different light than those classified as 'coloured' or 'white', which made the racial categories 'subjectively real' (Erasmus, 2008, p 172).

This is just one of the many ways in which apartheid social engineering linked moral, social, spatial and racial aspects. However, these ideas persist in South African thinking. Wherever urban upgrading ideas, which also include gentrification, are presented – whether in an everyday discussion or in a policy paper – they are immediately merged with the ideas of moral upliftment. The apartheid legislation was dismantled in 1990, when the Group Areas Act was declared null and void. While South Africa boasts a radically advanced constitution, the racially and morally justified categories of space are still central in many people's everyday thinking about the city (Salo, 2003; Teppo, 2004, 2009; Ross, 2005; Jensen, 2008); and the status of an area is often still defined accordingly. In addition, these salient urban divisions remain at the very core of many social issues in South Africa and public spaces remain unequal – with some notable exceptions.

Upliftment part 2: from a township to a suburb

Language and moral and spatial upliftment did not only influence former white areas, their influences are also noticeable in traditionally African areas. An example is Gugulethu, a quintessential apartheid township, which was established in the late 1950s on the sandy, windy Cape Flats – far from the then central Cape Town – to accommodate people classified as 'black' or 'African'. As the Christian-nationalist ideology of apartheid emphasised the principle of 'separate development', which meant that each race would have its space to become whatever God had destined it to become, African townships had to survive on their own.

According to earlier, colonial thinking and apartheid ideology, the 'natives' did not belong in cities. In apartheid South Africa, they were considered citizens of their distant homelands, and they could only live and work in cities if they had a permit in a passport, which was hard to acquire. The cities only offered Africans temporary accommodation, and the townships were equipped accordingly. Few or no services were offered in Gugulethu, which remained a dusty, poverty-ridden place dotted with what were referred to as matchbox houses (apartheid standard dwellings) and shacks. The degradation of the people forced to live in dire circumstances reflected their perceived moral degradation.

During the apartheid era, the township remained poor. After apartheid ended, state property was developed in keeping with neoliberal principles and the state's economic policy changed the ownership relations in the township. Soon, a central piece of state-owned land was sold to a new parastatal organisation, which then sold it for a very nominal price to private companies. Some of these were state-owned, while development companies run by South African politicians and businesspersons owned others. A new mall was built on the land in 2009 (see Figure 21.1). The developers marketed the mall as changing the face of the township. They branded the change as empowering and uplifting for the entire area. The architecture was carefully designed to reflect the political mood in the township: the external walls were decorated with huge concrete reliefs depicting the people, and were adorned with revolutionary poetry (see Figure 21.2). The inside of the mall is also decorated with revolutionary slogans (Teppo and Houssay-Holzschuch, 2013).

The figurehead of the mall project in Gugulethu is Mzoli Ngcawuzele, one of the politically connected businesspersons who owns a chunk of the mall. He is also known as a former local sports hero and the owner of a very successful sports bar/restaurant/venue called Mzoli's. As a successful businessman, Ngcawuzele represents a link between the capital and the township. Everyone in Gugulethu can identify with the experiences and hardships that characterise his life. As a young boy, Ngcawuzele was forcibly removed from the Bo-Kaap central area in 1960 to live on the Cape Flats. While he, his friends and his family were struggling in the townships, they witnessed the apartheid machinery increasing white South Africans' standard of living. They saw the white people of Cape Town becoming wealthier and their houses growing bigger and better, while they eked out an existence in the townships:

> 'You know ... we better [improve] the bush to become a suburb, wherever you are, in order to make a difference to your neighbour, to mankind, to human beings. I followed this philosophy and began to put it into practice, began to say that my main focus is to change the lives of needy communities.' (Ngcawuzele, Interview, 2010)

Ngcawuzele's ideas involved creating better services in the townships to replace the substandard ones. He presented the mall as part of a solution to remove the anomie in the townships. Yet, the new mall was met with fierce resistance from the local civil society. There used to be a number of local shops and a small Eyona mall on the land on which it was built. These shopkeepers were evicted and had

Figure 21.1: Gugulethu Square mall: entrance to the main building

Note: Photograph courtesy of Myriam Houssay-Holzchurch.

Figure 21.2: Gugulethu Square mall: poetry and sculpture celebrating African pride

Note: Photograph courtesy of Myriam Houssay-Holzchurch.

to settle in far less profitable spaces. The civil society strongly disapproved of these evictions, making moral arguments against the new developments. The civil society representatives condemned Ngcawuzele's actions as shameful (Teppo and Houssay-Holzschuch, 2013).

While many in the community appreciated the new mall and the services it offered (though many found the shops too expensive), the chairman of the Lagunya Business Association, which represents about 150 small shops in Gugulethu and the surrounding areas, expressed his distrust in the developers' morality in racial and moral terms:

> Lagunya Chairman: 'This guy, they call him Mzoli, he uses window dressing [to impress] people.'
>
> Annika Teppo: 'Who is behind the window?'
>
> Lagunya Chairman: 'It's the whites.... This mall belongs to whites. Not only the whites, it belongs to ... the cruel whites who make everything happen.' (Interview with local business-owners, 2010)

Ngcawuzele, unfazed by these accusations, described his vision of the township during an interview in 2010. He explained that offering high-quality services would uplift the community. He stated that building the mall was part of a moral exercise to erase the poverty and damage that the apartheid era had caused in Gugulethu. He describes his mission as philanthropic, helping the township and changing its people's lives forever: "If you look at Gugulethu ... in the past it was a bush ... gravel roads leading to homes with no foundations ... no ceilings. And then I began to say: 'let me change that mentality'" (Ngcawuzele, interview, 2010).

Ngcawuzele describes the changes in Gugulethu as an upliftment of the township and its dwellers – he uses very similar arguments and language as those employed when the poor white people were rehabilitated. These ideas are also parallel to the ideas of gentrification, which involves displacing earlier residents or businesses by introducing middle-class residents or businesses into the area, by reinvesting in the area, and by changing the landscape. The mall was not built for Gugulethu's poorest, but for the new, hoped-for middle-class residents: "It's a philosophy of saying, beginning to say: 'black man, black woman, you are on your own ... you have to create your own middle class'" (Ngcawuzele, interview, 2010). Ngcawuzele's new plans further clarify his agenda. He aims to build 'high-rise and luxury condos' in the centre of the area instead of matchbox houses. His stated mission is to "make a suburb out of a township". In South African lingo, 'suburb' is a term previously, and even now, mainly used for white areas, while 'township' was and is almost exclusively reserved for African areas. His philanthropic success remains unknown, but, in 2012, the mall was sold to multinational investors in accordance with the principles of neoliberalism. Ngcawuzele earned millions, as he owned 9% of the mall, which was sold for ZAR250 million (around USD25 million) (see Teppo and Houssay-Holzschuch, 2013).

In the case of post-apartheid urban change in Gugulethu, a discursive formation is at play. This formation consists of displacement processes and racial discourses combined with the ideas of moral and spatial upliftment, the ideals of community development, and neoliberal trends and developments that can be labelled gentrification. In Gugulethu and in Delft (to be discussed later), upliftment or regeneration reflects the intermingling of historical formations with more recent public policies through the construction of mixed communities to regenerate supposedly degenerated and broken communities (see Lees and Ley, 2008; see also Bridge et al, 2011).

South Africa's housing policies' aim is to create sustainable human settlements. In order to do this, they promote upgrading and development through the construction of mixed-income neighbourhoods. The urban battles are fought and the tensions become visible in the moral arguments used to justify the actions taken. These arguments are partly inherited from the previous eras, partly mixed with new trends and ideas, and heatedly served by and to all those involved.

Urban development: better houses for better people?

Like the mall in Gugulethu, development projects in Delft inform and are informed by local moral discourses and contestations. Delft was one of the first areas built in Cape Town after apartheid to cater for the urban poor from the black and coloured areas of the city. People appreciate this diversity in their daily lives, but the legacy of racial identities informs residents' perceptions of themselves and others (Millstein, 2008). Delft receives many of those being displaced from other areas of the city. At the same time, Delft is a site of massive state-led interventions. Ongoing housing developments build subsidised housing for the urban poor. A second objective is to construct units for the 'not so poor', who can afford a mortgage, in order to create sustainable human settlements consisting of various housing opportunities. Some local residents call these settlements, which are fortified with barbed-wire fences and their own security gate, their own 'gated communities' (personal conversations, March 2013). This situation has meant that Delft has houses for 'better people' and for those who were displaced from elsewhere in the city, which triggers local contestations over inclusion and exclusion. For those already living in Delft, the influx of new residents threatens their access to scarce resources, and is framed in racial terms, as well as by feelings of belonging and residency. This addresses both the moral ordering from above and ideas of moral righteousness from below.

Cultural diversity, sprinkled with a notion of moral righteousness (perceived unfairness), is mobilised to challenge the government's allocation of houses:

> 'We went as far as to say … [there is] institutionalised racial prejudice in terms of housing allocation on the part of the state … we say we

> are living in a diverse community, Xhosa and Afrikaans-speaking, but only the Xhosa are allocated houses.' (Interview with a community activist, 27 March 2013)

Such local contestations have also led to local 'Not In My Back Yard' (NIMBY) community activism, which means that citizens in poor communities object to poor(er) people moving into their area (Garmany, 2012). Some community groups have objected to the establishment of TRAs, and to outsiders' perceived preferential treatment regarding housing. The activists deliberately referred to themselves as 'Xhosa-speaking' or 'Afrikaans-speaking', instead of the previously prevalent 'African' or 'coloured'. This was a way of seeking distance from any racial tensions that could impede the working of the groups. These objections are thus not only about racial identity (or language, as in the quotation mentioned earlier), but also about belonging, regardless of racial identity (Delft against the rest/newcomers). Delft backyarders have lived in the community for many years. For them, a right to housing has been a critical grievance in response to the influx of 'newcomers':

> 'I think you have heard those echoes from the meeting ... we know the backyarders and the backyarders have been marginalised in the process, which is the Delft backyarders [implicitly those who have lived in Delft for many years]. And then we say [that when] housing allocation occurs, it only occurs from the TRAs [for the newcomers].' (Interview with a community activist, 27 March 2013)

Local community politics thus revolves around who should be included and excluded from local moral communities, who regard themselves as more eligible for the housing resources built in their community (Millstein and Jordus-Lier, 2012).

Gentrification as displacement

While Gugulethu and Delft may seem like unlikely gentrification areas, Woodstock could be seen as an ideal showcase for classic urban renewal and gentrification in an inner-city working-class neighbourhood (see Figure 21.3). The food market, which was established in the Old Biscuit Mill in 2006, has become a Saturday outing for many middle-income and wealthier citizens. While the renewal of the area has escalated over the last 10 years, Woodstock's gentrification process has a much longer history. Throughout apartheid, parts of Woodstock were known as 'grey' areas, where white and coloured people lived together. At the end of apartheid, the Group Areas Act was somewhat relaxed, allowing wealthier coloured residents to move in. Today, Woodstock is a vibrant, desegregated neighbourhood, and a popular spot for creative industries.

Figure 21.3: Woodstock foundry

Note: Photograph courtesy of Robyn Rorke.

The transformation of Woodstock has had mixed effects. The people moving into Woodstock reflect the diversity of the emerging middle class in the city in terms of race and income. In the last survey, Woodstock had 14% white and 50% coloured residents (City of Cape Town, 2012a). New creative industries and private-led real estate developments have not yet completely replaced the older commercial activities (see Figure 21.4), but there are concerns that increasing indirect displacement will do so (Booyens, 2012). While some streets and areas are becoming more middle-class, pockets of working-class areas and residencies for the urban poor are still visible. However, in some parts of Lower Woodstock, private-led developments have led to intense evictions and direct displacement struggles.

So, to some extent, urban change processes in Cape Town, such as those in Woodstock, mirror examples of gentrification across the globe. Shifting the class composition towards the middle class, creating incentives for private investments, the use of public–private partnership in urban governance and the adaptation of global policies, such as City Improvement Districts, have shaped transformations in inner-city areas, such as the CBD, Bo-Kaap, Greenpoint and Woodstock (Visser, 2002; Miraftab, 2007; Visser and Kotze, 2008; Booyens, 2012; Donaldson et al, 2013). In contrast to some of the recent research that celebrates the vibrancy and creativity of gentrified inner-city neighbourhoods in Western cities (for a critical

Figure 21.4: Woodstock shops

Note: Photograph courtesy of Robyn Rorke.

account, see Slater, 2006), it is vital that we continue to critically assess these policies in relation to negative effects, such as displacements. Yet, the complexity of the spatial changes in Woodstock also highlights the need to understand and unpack the specific context in which these transformations and their effects occur.

These and other urban interventions in Cape Town draw on a mix of discourses on nation-building, non-racialism and democracy, but also visions of a world-class city well-positioned as a hub for international investments and Africa's number one tourist destination. Locally, the City of Cape Town has framed a master plan, the Integrated Development Plan (IDP), using notions such as 'the secure city', 'the inclusive city' and 'the caring city' (City of Cape Town, 2012b). While these phrases might appear neutral and apolitical, they reflect how '[c]ity builders promote and market urban revitalization through the judicious use of moralizing narratives of past harmony, present decline, and future regeneration' (Murray, 2008, p 209). Global, national and local discourses are mobilised simultaneously to legitimise renewal policies that are difficult to challenge. They also conceal important continuities from previous justifications of the moral ordering of urban spaces. The simultaneous workings of various discourses legitimise policies that privilege the interests of the urban middle class and the elite at the expense of the urban poor. Post-apartheid policies thus continue to reproduce racial and class segregation that excludes citizens conceived as morally wrong and undesirable from desirable spaces. Increased surveillance and policing to improve the city's security become technological tools for continued racial exclusion (Visser and Kotze, 2008; Samara,

2010). Such moral orderings of urban spaces in this post-apartheid context are not far removed from the discursive framings and legitimisation of policies for urban upliftment and renewal during the colonial and apartheid eras.

The workings of such discursive practices (Miraftab, 2007) provide good reasons for research to explore gentrification in terms of its effect on displacement and socio-spatial inequality. As a politicised concept, gentrification may counteract discourses that appear benign or apolitical, such as renewal, development and upliftment dialogues, which are pursued in the name of nation-building and democracy. Again, Woodstock is a case in point. The negative effects of contemporary urban renewal and gentrification in Woodstock boil down to questions of class, though they mostly affect poor black and coloured residents. One of the most visible displacement struggles was the eviction of residents in Gympie Street – labelled Cape Town's most dangerous street – in Lower Woodstock. The street is portrayed as a criminal hotspot, but it has also been home to many. For years, the residents of Gympie Street fought against their arbitrary eviction by property-owners. In one of the buildings, the owner sought to evict tenants due to non-payment. According to the residents, the owner had bought the property cheaply at an auction and then raised the rent immediately. They challenged the new rent, stating that they would withhold it and put it into a trust until the owner fixed the house (interview with Gympie Street resident, 25 March 2013). After the owner lost the court case to evict them, the residents claimed that he started using other tactics:

> 'We won the court case, but at the end of the day, we were getting tired of the owner, because he then started making the houses inhuman [uninhabitable] for us. He switched off the electricity and he switched off the water, so it was as if we were staying in shacks. But we were staying in shacks in the suburbs. Because you can't live without water and you can't live without power.' (Interview with Gympie Street resident of Blikkiesdorp TRA, 25 March 2013)

Many of the residents in this building, tired of the uncertainties and arbitrary harassments, eventually gave up and decided to accept temporary accommodation in Blikkiesdorp (Delft). In another building in Gympie Street, the tenants did not move voluntarily, but were eventually forcefully evicted by law enforcement officers and relocated to the TRA.

In the case described here, the aim was to gain more profitable tenants. The original tenants were not given the opportunity to find other solutions that would allow them to stay:

> 'Before we moved here [to Blikkiesdorp TRA], we found that the house, the whole blocks of flats of 11 houses, was 5,000 rand each when he bought it. Somehow, something was wrong, because we didn't even get first privilege [choice]. Nobody asked us: 'Are you interested

> in buying the house or what?' Nobody asked us, so we didn't get the opportunity to even make a plan. If they had asked us 5,000 rand for a house, we could have gone in, taken our salaries, bought the houses, and fixed [them] ... but we didn't get that opportunity.' (Interview with Gympie Street resident of Blikkiesdorp TRA, 25 March 2013)

At the height of the struggle, the activists linked the owner's strategies to the developments that were ongoing before the World Cup was presented in 2010:

> 'And what is the owner going to do with the property once he evicts the tenants? Sell it to the highest bidder and make a nice profit on the building. This is part of a continued process of World Cup gentrification in Woodstock which is forcing more and more poor people away from the city centre and away from jobs.' (Woodstock Anti-Eviction Campaign Press Release, 26 May 2009)

For the Gympie Street residents, gentrification means displacement and exclusion, and thus a violation of their right to the city, which led to their struggle against it. There is no permanent place for the urban poor in the renewed urban spaces. The city government's policy option is to offer them temporary accommodation far from their community and their sources of livelihood. Two of the residents in the building mentioned earlier said that they had lived in the area for 30 and 50 years, respectively.

In contrast to Northern cities, where the neoliberal hegemony of renewal policies seems to have taken a common-sense position and is often unchallenged (Hackworth and Smith, 2001), Cape Town's social movements have actively contested these policies of renewal and privatisation. The struggle in Gympie Street was part of the Western Cape Anti-Eviction Campaign that mobilised many poor communities in the city. Fighting an uphill battle, these actors challenged the exclusionary effects of urban regeneration and strategically mobilised a discourse of gentrification as displacement against the seemingly apolitical and benign urban renewal terminology. These struggles have had a limited effect on changing dominant ideas and strategies, but they have been instrumental in creating some space for critical debates about urban changes in the city.

Conclusion

The persistent inequality in South African society ensures that the poor will be displaced regardless of whether an urban change project is referred to as 'gentrification', 'upliftment', 'development' or something else. These keywords are influenced by historical continuities of inherited economic inequality and racial classifications, as well as morally loaded ideas for improvement or the upliftment of the population by means of urban social engineering. The poor white people example shows the long-lasting links between the moral ordering of urban spaces, policy and politics, which may have global or local origins. These historical continuities surface in the discursive formations of urban change that reflect the moral ordering of urban spaces. This ordering pervades all layers of South African society. In the post-apartheid era, people's inclusion and exclusion from urban spaces has allowed class hierarchies to replace some of the past racial hierarchies. This does not render the racial hierarchies meaningless. The hierarchies of race and class are continuously re-evaluated through nation-building and democracy discourses, as well as neoliberal visions for a global and creative city.

Neo-liberal urban policies, through which the state acts as a facilitator of urban regeneration projects (Winkler, 2009), through public policies (Lees and Ley, 2008), are also evident in Cape Town. If we look at the various discourses and policies, there is a certain spatiality regarding discursive practices. This spatiality allows ideas of social mixing to be employed to construct sustainable communities from supposedly dysfunctional and degenerated poor neighbourhoods – the townships and informal settlements around the city. While it is imperative for the state to challenge the legacy of apartheid urban segregation, the current policies reproduce patterns of socio-spatial exclusion. Discourses and public policies on social mixing are also similar to those underlying a developmentalist approach, which aims to create sustainable settlements on the outskirts of the city in order to fix degenerated and broken poor communities. As we argued in the cases of Gugulethu and Delft, these discourses and policies are negotiated in and through national and local discourses and moral frameworks.

The resulting discursive formations involve ideas of upliftment, renewal and development, as well as the ordering of the good citizen. They provide moral frameworks and justifications for a range of interventions – processes of state-led social engineering – in all areas of the city. These frameworks conjoin with new global ideas and policies that, in effect, thereafter reproduce the existing socio-spatial patterns of exclusion and segregation, instead of creating integrated and just cities. The Gugulethu mall example shows how promoting the neoliberal processes of urban change as upliftment/renewal/development creates concrete framings for the local appropriations of neoliberal policies, which take on particular forms and rationalities that create desirable and undesirable spaces and citizens.

Eventually, the discursive formations of urban change define the place of gentrification as both a discourse and a practice shaping the complex geographies of gentrification in Cape Town. Gentrification processes lead to the displacement of the most vulnerable people, thus manifesting the continued moral ordering of urban spaces. In Woodstock, gentrification, which is followed by displacements of the urban poor, also impacts the receiving community of Delft. The eviction of people to Delft and the ensuing contestations of identity and belonging exemplify the complex ways in which gentrification affects these communities. Delft is simultaneously a site of massive interventions to create 'better communities' through mixed-income housing developments and a site where displaced citizens are being dumped. This ambiguity also informs the local moral politics of place.

In Woodstock, activists use gentrification strategically as a synonym for the displacement of the poor and a symbol of social injustice. To some extent, it has become a more politicised concept, which emphasises evictions and displacements, and contradicts syrupy official concepts, such as 'urban renaissance' and 'community development'. This – and other examples of the multiple experiences of displacement – constitutes an argument for the continuous need to explore gentrification's *effects* as a critical research agenda (Slater, 2006) in the cities of the South (see Lees, 2014).

In the case of Cape Town, the effects of gentrification, which is combined with the local discursive formations of urban space, morality, race and class, point to a number of directions. Although being white is no longer the only determining factor for elite membership, the ideals and norms of whiteness are still strongly represented and reproduced. Similarly to the gentrification of the former Aboriginal areas of Sydney (Shaw, 2005, p 60), the colonial past is celebrated and reproduced in the renovated old buildings of Woodstock, now inhabited by those with money and means. In some parts of Cape Town, gentrification thus clearly marks the era of 'new urban colonialism' (Atkinson and Bridge, 2005, p 3). However, the colonial ideals of whiteness are not the only ones used in these new colonisation processes: in Gugulethu, nostalgia for the South African revolution is used as a tool to sell the mall, which global investors own, to the locals.

Still, the end results are the same in both these cases: in the aftermath of the South African negotiated revolution, the elite colonise the urban areas from those who are less privileged, claiming the city for themselves. The question remains, will the new black and coloured elites participate equally in the political life of their new communities in their search for identity, belonging and a moral community, as happened in Harlem in the 1970s and 1980s (Taylor, 1992)? Or, will the boundaries of class drawn in the urban spaces be more difficult to circumvent than the previous racial boundaries?

Note

[1] For a thorough explanation of racial categories, see Christopher (1994, pp 103–5). In this chapter, while aware of the political implications of each term, we follow the usual conventions and use the categories mentioned earlier as they are understood in the South African context.

References

Atkinson, R. and Bridge, G. (2005) 'Introduction', in R. Atkinson and G. Bridge (eds) *Gentrification in a global context: the new urban colonialism*, London: Routledge.

Beauregard, R. (1986) 'The chaos and complexity of gentrification', in N.S. Smith and P. Williams (eds) *Gentrification of the city*, Boston, MA: Allen and Unwin, pp 35–55.

Bénit Gbaffou, C., Didier, S. and Peyroux, E. (2012) 'Circulation of security models in Southern African cities: between neoliberal encroachment and local power dynamics', *International Journal of Urban and Regional Research*, vol 36, no 5, pp 877–89.

Boonzaier, E. and Sharp, J. (1988) *South African keywords: the uses and abuses of political concepts*, Cape Town: David Phillips.

Booyens, I. (2012) 'Creative industries, inequality and social development: developments, impacts and challenges in Cape Town', *Urban Forum*, vol 23, no 1, pp 43–60.

Bridge, G., Butler, T. and Lees, L. (eds) (2011) *Mixed communities: gentrification by stealth?*, Bristol: The Policy Press.

Butler, T. (2007) 'For gentrification?', *Environment and Planning A*, vol 39, pp 162–81.

Christopher, A.J. (1994) *Atlas of apartheid*, Johannesburg: Witwatersrand University Press.

City of Cape Town (2012a) '2011 census suburb Woodstock', December. Available at: http://www.capetown.gov.za/en/stats/2011CensusSuburbs/2011_Census_CT_Suburb_Woodstock_Profile.pdf (accessed 25 October 2013).

City of Cape Town (2012b) *Integrated Development Plan (IDP) 2012–2017*, Cape Town: City of Cape Town.

Clark, E. (2005) 'The order and simplicity of gentrification – a political challenge', in R. Atkinson and G. Bridge (eds) *Gentrification in a global context: the new urban colonialism*, London: Routledge.

Desai, A. and Vahed, G. (2009) 'World Cup 2010: Africa's turn or the turn on Africa?', *Soccer & Society*, vol 11, nos 1/2, pp 154–67.

Didier, S., Morange, M. and Peyroux, E. (2012) 'The adaptive nature of neoliberalism at the local scale: fifteen years of city improvement districts in Cape Town and Johannesburg', *Antipode*, vol 45, pp 121–39.

Donaldson, R., Kotze, N., Visser, G., Park, J., Wally, N., Zen, J. and Vieyra, O. (2013) 'An uneasy match: neoliberalism, gentrification and heritage conservation in Bo-Kaap, Cape Town, South Africa', *Urban Forum*, vol 24, pp 173–88.

Erasmus, Z. (2008) 'Race', in N. Shepherd and S. Robins (eds) *New South African keywords*, Ohio: Ohio University Press, pp 169–81.

Garmany, J. (2012) 'Spaces of displacement and the potentialities of (post) citizenship', *Political Geography*, vol 31, no 1, pp 17–19.

Hackworth, J. and Smith, N. (2001) 'The changing state of gentrification', *Tijdschrift voor economische en sociale geografie*, vol 92, pp 464–77.

Houssay-Holzschuch, M. and Teppo, A. (2009) 'A mall for all: race and public space in post-apartheid Cape Town', *Cultural Geographies*, vol 16, no 3, pp 351–79.

Jensen, S. (2008) *Gangs, politics and dignity in Cape Town*, Oxford/Chicago/Johannesburg: James Currey/The University of Chicago Press/Wits University Press.

Lees, L. (2012) 'The geography of gentrification: thinking through comparative urbanism', *Progress in Human Geography*, vol 36, no 2, pp 155–71.

Lees, L. (2014) 'Gentrification in the Global South?', in S. Parnell and S. Oldfield (eds) *The Routledge Handbook on Cities of the Global South*, Routledge: new York, pp 506–21.

Lees, L. and Ley, D. (2008) 'Introduction to special issue on gentrification and public policy', *Urban Studies*, vol 45, no 12, pp 2379–84.

Lees, L., Slater, T. and Wyly, E. (eds) (2010) *The gentrification reader*, London: Routledge.

McCann, E. and Ward, K. (eds) (2011) *Mobile urbanism: cities and policymaking in the global age*, Minneapolis, MN: University of Minnesota Press.

Millstein, M. (2008) 'Challenges to community organising in a context of spatial fragmentations: some experiences from Delft, Cape Town', *Critical Dialogue. Public Participation in Review*, vol 4, no 8, pp 34–40.

Millstein, M. and Jordhus-Lier, D. (2012) 'Making communities work? Casual labour practices and local civil society dynamics in Delft, Cape Town', *Journal of Southern African Studies*, vol 38, no 1, pp 183–201.

Miraftab, F. (2007) 'Governing post-apartheid spatiality: implementing City Improvement Districts in Cape Town', *Antipode*, vol 3, no 4, pp 603–26.

Murray, M.J. (2008) *Taming the disorderly city: the spatial landscape of Johannesburg after apartheid*, Ithaca, NY, and London: Cornell University Press.

Parnell, S. (2008) 'Urban governance in the South: the politics of rights and development', in K. Cox, M. Low and J. Robinson (eds) *The SAGE handbook of political geography*, London: SAGE Publications Ltd, pp 595–609.

Phillips, M. (2004) 'Other geographies of gentrification', *Progress in Human Geography*, vol 28, no 1, pp 5–30.

Ross, F. (2005) 'Model communities and respectable residents? Home and housing in a low-income residential estate in the Western Cape, South Africa', *Journal of Southern African Studies*, vol 31, no 3, pp 631–48.

Salo, E. (2003) 'Negotiating gender and personhood in the new South Africa', *European Journal of Cultural Studies*, vol 6, no 3, pp 345–65.

Samara, T.R. (2010) 'Order and security in the city: producing race and policing neoliberal spaces in South Africa', *Ethnic and Racial Studies*, vol 33, no 4, pp 637–55.

Shaw K. (2005) 'Heritage and gentrification: implications for a new urban policy', in L. Lees, T. Slater and E. Wyly (eds) *The Gentrification reader*, London: Routledge, pp 285–98.

Shepherd, N. and Robins, S. (eds) (2008) *New South African keywords*, Ohio: Ohio University Press.

Slater, T. (2006) 'The eviction of critical perspectives from gentrification research', *International Journal of Urban and Regional Research*, vol 30, no 4, pp 737–57.

Smith, N. (2002) 'New globalism, new urbanism: gentrification as global urban strategy', *Antipode*, vol 34, no 3, pp 427–50.

Swanson, M.W. (1977) 'The sanitation syndrome: bubonic plague and urban native policy in the Cape colony, 1900–09', *The Journal of African History*, vol 18, no 3, pp 387–410.

Taylor, M.M. (1992) 'Can you go home again? Black gentrification and the dilemma of difference', in L. Lees, T. Slater and E. Wyly (eds) *The gentrification reader*, London: Routledge, pp 285–98.

Teppo, A. (2004) 'The making of a good white: a historical ethnography of the rehabilitation of poor whites in a suburb of Cape Town', PhD thesis, University of Helsinki. Available at: http://ethesis.helsinki.fi/julkaisut/val/sosio/vk/teppo/themakin.pdf (accessed 11 October 2013).

Teppo, A. (2009) 'A decent place? Space and morality in a former "poor white" suburb', in M. Steyn and M. van Zyl (ed) *The price and the prize: shaping sexualities in South Africa*, Cape Town: HSRC Press, pp 220–33.

Teppo, A. and Houssay-Holzschuch, M. (2013) 'Gugulethu™: revolution for neoliberalism in a South African township', *Canadian Journal of African Studies/La Revue canadienne des études africaines*, vol 47, no 1, pp 51–74.

UNDP (United Nations Development Programme) (2012) 'United Nations development data', October.

Visser, G. (2002) 'Gentrification and South African cities', *Cities*, vol 19, no 6, pp 419–23.

Visser, G. and Kotze, N. (2008) 'The state and new-build gentrification in Central Cape Town, South Africa', *Urban Studies*, vol 45, no 12, pp 2565–93.

Winkler, T. (2009) 'Prolonging the global age of gentrification: Johannesburg's regeneration policies', *Planning Theory*, vol 8, no 4, pp 362–81.

TWENTY-TWO

Conclusion: global gentrifications

Loretta Lees, Hyun Bang Shin and Ernesto López-Morales

This edited collection has been like a leap onto a moving train, not quite knowing where it might lead, and having only a vague sense of where it has been. It has been exciting and we have learnt a lot. What the different chapters offer is a wider and deeper view of 'gentrification' from around the globe than has been managed to date. However, here, the editors and contributors have done more than merely offer a large number of empirical accounts of the diverse forms of gentrification (and its interaction with other urban processes) around the world. In this conclusion, drawing on Ward (2010), we conceptualise and theorise back from the different empirical cases in this book to reveal what we have learned from looking at gentrification globally, and from comparing beyond the usual suspects.

The chapters in this edited collection show that a vast number of cities around the world, from Mumbai to Rio de Janeiro, from Santiago to Cape Town, from Buenos Aires to Taipei, are simultaneously experiencing intensive and uneven processes of capital-led restructuring with significant influxes of upper- and middle-income people and large doses of class-led displacement from deprived urban areas. The chapters show the uneven development of global gentrification connected to planetary urbanisations, and a significant number of these are in the vein of neo-Haussmannization (Merrifield, 2013a, 2013b) through processes of 'accumulation by dispossession' (Harvey, 2003). This exploitative process of value extraction from the built environment is a phenomenon that has been in place in the Global South for some time now but has often been overlooked by urban researchers, though work is emerging (see Shin, 2009, 2014; López-Morales, 2010, 2011; Goldman, 2011; Desai and Loftus, 2013). Globally, the process of value extraction has been accelerated, unevenly, by the faster pace of financial capital mobility invested in real estate circuits of capital, by rampantly entrepreneurial urban policies, by the lack of available land for the urban expansion that many cities are experiencing and by the increasing cost of peripheral (suburban) expansion and long-distance transportation (re-emphasising the importance of the notion of 'spatial capital' vis-a-vis gentrification; see Rerat and Lees, 2011). This intense intervention in the built environment and especially in residential and commercial landscapes is something that previous urban and political theories in Latin America and Asia have little explained, but it is our conclusion that a properly understood and hermeneutically adapted gentrification studies, in conjunction with a well-founded critique of political economy (eg Henri Lefebvre, David Harvey and Neil Smith), can effectively explain and predict it. The phenomenon of gentrification is global to an extent that urban spaces around the world are increasingly subject to global and domestic capital (re)investment to be transformed into new uses that cater to the needs of wealthier inhabitants. Indeed, it has become an important process in the growing inequality of cities and societies worldwide.

The chapters in this book however show that statements about gentrification arriving in the Global South and East need to be rethought, and that there is no simple trajectory. We find that there are multiple gentrifications in a pluralistic sense rather than 'Gentrification' with a capital 'G'. The trajectories are affected by the ascendancy of neoliberal policy ideas, especially revanchist behaviours on public space aimed at propping up or instigating gentrification (as seen in the chapters on Athens, Madrid, Puebla, Taipei and Karachi). Such multiplicities require gentrification researchers to undertake fresh debate on the control and privatisation of public space in relation to gentrification and in the context of: a) places that do not follow the Western democratic conception of a democratic public space (in some places, there is no direct translation for the Western notion of 'public space') based on the Greek agora and the democratic public sphere; b) places where a welfare state has been absent or poorly developed; and c) places where dwellings and land are subject to commodification (eg in post-socialist economies) and intense speculation.

The transnational mobility of gentrification or its endogenous emergence is complex: first, the process is not always North to South (as shown in the capital and design ideas moving from Dubai to Karachi); second, the process sometimes emerges in an endogenous way as part of city-making in times of condensed urbanisation and late industrialisation (as seen in the chapters on Seoul and Taipei; see also Shin, 2009); and, third, sometimes policymakers are not involved in the expansion of gentrification, for other drivers or agents creating gentrification are the learnings and desires due to the global mobility of people – eg Israelis living in gentrified areas of cities like London and New York City taking ideas about gentrification with them to Israel. Here, the gentrifiers' desires are not politically anti-suburban (eg as seen in Caulfield, 1989), but rather desires for sameness, the sameness of the now internationally recognisable, Western gentrified inner-city neighbourhood. Furthermore, fourth, the global circulation of corporate capital seeking out profit has become increasingly important, for example, money from the Middle East (Dubai) funding gentrification in Karachi, Pakistan. Last, but not least, we have learnt that the contradictions in the indigenous logics of accumulation and urban politics play a pivotal role in producing, slowing down and resisting gentrification (as the chapter on Cairo demonstrates).

As Eric Clark (2005) once suggested, gentrification is not confined to the inner city, but can be suburban and rural too, as the chapters on Egypt and Israel show. As Martin Phillips (2004) urged some time ago now, 'other geographies of gentrification' need to be brought into the mainstream literature on gentrification. Phillips's plea now has new urgency not just in light of the expansion of gentrification spatially, but also due to recent proclamations about the expansion (or the 'explosion and implosion') of urbanisation processes that go beyond city boundaries (see, eg, Keil, 2013; Brenner, 2014). The gentrification process itself has become much more suburban and multi-centric (rather than focused on the inner city as a singular centrality). The conventional Western distinctions between inner city and suburb make less sense globally, and, indeed, are more complex in the Global South (but also the Global North) these days. In many ways, scholars from the South have come to pay more attention to the close relation between gentrification and peripheral suburbanisation, though the question about where the poor go after being displaced from central areas is still relatively under-researched. Governments and businesses are increasingly mobilising their power and resources to intervene in the real estate sector for extracting exchange value, and there seem to be no geographical restrictions (at least in principle, though there is an emergent urban social mobilisation to fight speculation) on the target areas of such intervention. Gated communities on city peripheries can be examples of gentrification in the same vein as those in city centres. Indeed, the dialectical play between these two in cities like Buenos Aires, Cairo and Abu Dhabi need further investigation. The chapters in this book have underlined for us that we are at a point in time when the extension of urbanism has meant that (Anglo-American and beyond) processes and categories like suburbanisation, gentrification, urban regeneration and informal urbanism are increasingly blurred.

Maloutas (2012) has argued that the idea of urban regeneration as gentrification may not be adequate to travel around the world. He is concerned that gentrification scholars are projecting onto different forms of urban regeneration the features of gentrification's dominant conceptualisation. However, the chapters in this book show that although the 'actually existing' gentrifications in the Global South do not necessarily resemble those previously found in the Global North, it is obvious that they are embedded in contexts that are largely characterised by the state-led class restructuring of urban space intertwined with speculative land/housing markets and a growing lack of affordable housing and spaces for social reproduction. In fact, it is evident from the chapters that urban regeneration and urban renewal globally have become major facilitators of gentrification. Merrifield (2013a, p 52) has recently used the (Global North) term 'neo-Haussmannization' to describe this, arguing that neo-Haussmannization is now a global urban strategy that has peripheralised millions of people everywhere. In many places, especially in East Asia, as the chapters on Taipei and Seoul in this book testify to, this has some real resonance. Of course, this does not mean that we should automatically assume that any form of urban regeneration or urban renewal everywhere is a case of gentrification, only a poor scholar would do that, but it does seem more often to be the case. It is as if governments and policymakers around the world are hoodwinked by policies that ultimately produce gentrification and can see no alternative, a hoodwinking that is even more problematic when situated in the current context of social and economic crisis for many nations around the world. Different forms of urban renewal also result in different types of policy interventions, as well as the mobilisation of factions of capital. While urban renewal projects involving the large-scale, wholesale clearance and reconstruction of neighbourhoods require large businesses (eg the construction firms affiliated with large conglomerates in Seoul or Abu Dhabi), the urban conservation of historic neighbourhoods often involves smaller capital that aims to exploit the niche market left unturned by large businesses (see, eg, Shin, 2010). A deeper comparison of these two different types of gentrification in, for example, Chile – large-scale new-build (see López-Morales, 2010, 2011) and small-scale commercial and niched (see the chapter on Santiago in this book) – is much needed. There has not been enough research into the impact of scale on capital mobilisation and displacement.

So, what makes a case of urban regeneration a process of gentrification? We claim that it is 'social cleansing' – the class-related conflicts often channelled as processes of class-led displacement (Roderos [2013] makes a similar case for Manila in the Phillipines). Maloutas (2012) has argued that the label 'gentrification' is ideological and political, and that its use projects onto other forms and processes 'the features of gentrification's dominant conceptualization as a process fuelled by neoliberal policies' (Maloutas, 2012, p 42). We do not have a problem with this, and would underline the political significance of the term itself for not just the Global North (see Davidson and Lees, 2005; Lees et al, 2008), but also the Global South. As Shin (2009) argues, gentrification policies show the strong arm of the developmental state, with its national goals of increased housing production and rising homeownership, albeit at the cost of social redistribution. Indeed, accumulation through property development has been a significant goal of many developmental states. As attested to by Lees's (2014a, 2014b) work on council tenants being socially cleansed from inner London by gentrification, what Hyra (2008) has called the 'new urban renewal' in the US, tenants need to know when urban regeneration *is* gentrification and that it is not a good thing! Then they can fight it for what it is, not what it is pretending to be. However, even urban renewal must be understood in ways different from how it has been conceived in the Global North, and scale is again important, for in the neoliberalised South, urban renewal can be entrepreneurial and piecemeal speculative redevelopment or it can be more large-scale, entwined with land-grabbing and large capital.

There are also epistemological (even generational) hurdles that need to be overcome to critically understand class-led urban change in an increasingly urbanised world. Early in 2013, one of the editors of this book was confronted by an infamous development geographer towards the end of his long career who vehemently rejected that 'slum gentrification' existed. This is an example of how part of the already-established academia reacts when new evidence contradicts established urban categorisations that nonetheless prove to be of little use in explaining current processes of displacement-led urban change. The fact is that there has only been occasional and limited discussion about displacement and redevelopment-led exclusion in Asia, Latin America and the Middle East. Moreover, depoliticised urban research has tended to characterise contemporary academic practices in these regions due to various political constraints and market logics that place academics in increasingly precarious and vulnerable positions. Critical researchers in the South often have to ameliorate their perspectives so that they can apply for research funding, as states at various scales adopt 'gentrification as a housing policy' and therefore have 'little self-interest in collecting the kind of data that documents the level of displacement and the fate of displacees, data that would be tantamount to exposing the failure of these policies' (García-Herrera et al, 2007, p 280).

The use of 'slum' terminology helps researchers understand the relationship between class-led displacement and informality, but it is necessary to refrain from overgeneralisation as we do not want the term 'slum' to become the label for everything related to high levels of urban informality outside of the Global North. In fact, a much deeper understanding of the causes, effects and characteristics of urban change in 'slums' is urgently needed. Significantly, low-income settlements known as 'slums' or 'favelas' in some parts of the globe are often more resilient to gentrification due to their fragmented land and tenures, as well as social stigma and segregation (as the chapter on Rio de Janeiro discusses). However, many others are demolished as part of infrastructure provision (eg motorways) or urban beautification (eg public parks and amenities). In addition, significantly, slum/barrio/favela gentrification has become a significant feature of gentrification in the Global South since the 1990s, as 'slums' have become increasingly subject to urban policies that aim to demolish them to make way for real estate projects for higher-income groups (see the chapters on Lisbon and Lagos, where slum gentrification is seen as modernisation). Of course, gentrification in the Global North has a long history of locating in inner-city slums –let us not forget that the Lower East Side in New York City was a slum, as was Islington in London – but many of the slums now gentrifying in the Global South are much larger in size and population and the racial- and class-based politics are quite different (as the chapter on India discusses).

In this book, there are discussions of slum gentrification in Brazil, Portugal, Nigeria, South Africa, India and so on (the gentrification of low-income quarters in Southern Buenos Aires can, in many ways, be seen as slum gentrification too). A key tactic in 'slum gentrification' is that despite their potential to be upgraded and remain as stable neighbourhoods, low-income dilapidated settlements are often socially constructed and stigmatised as slums by the local state to justify their demolition (as the chapter on Lisbon shows well). Low-income, informal settlements often occupy strategic locations in cities, and, as such, they become potentially profitable sites for capital investment, thus attracting selective intervention by the state and capital. As the chapter on Brazil shows, the new culture of favela chic in Rio de Janeiro, which, to some degree, protects slums from demolition, still nevertheless leads to gentrification, in similar vein to the pioneer gentrifications in the inner-city slum areas of Western cities in the 1960s and 1970s. The use of geographical knowledge by the state and businesses, as discussed by Christophers (2010), has some useful implications in this regard. The stigmatisation and social construction of low-income settlements as slums takes place not only in the Global South, but also in the Global North (as Lees [2014a] shows in the case of the Aylesbury Estate, the largest public housing estate in Europe) and Chicago (on Cabrini Green, see Lees et al, 2008; see also Hyra, 2008). What all this demands is not only that the gentrification literature needs to engage properly with the slum literature, as Lemanski (2014) has tried to do in the context of 'downward raiding' on slums in South Africa, but that there also needs to be better engagement between the slum literatures in the Global North and the Global South – an endeavour that partly responds to Ananya Roy's (2009) call for 'new geographies of imagination and epistemology'. In addition, slum gentrification is taking place not only within inner cities, but also on city fringes and on the slum peripheries of cities in the Global South, and even the Global North. Slum gentrification and rapid peripheral urbanisation are common development features not just in the economically 'emerging' societies of Asia and some parts of Africa, but in cities in the Global North too, and this is creating new kinds of effects and different results.

One feature of gentrification in the Global South that quickly became apparent in the production of this book is the expropriation of public land and housing for gentrification. Like in the Global North (as seen in mixed communities policies, see Bridge et al, 2011), this includes public housing being offered up by the state for gentrification (as seen in Taipei), and also military land (as seen in Karachi) and military housing (as seen in Lagos) being offered up for gentrification. The forceful acquisition of non-market properties and their release for capital (re)investment indicates that dispossession acts as an important precondition for subsequent gentrification. This tallies with the argument made by Macleod and Johnstone (2012, p 1) that accumulation by dispossession 'licenses state-orchestrated gentrification' in post-industrial cities in the UK. López-Morales (2010, 2011) has also called this 'gentrification by ground rent dispossession', in relation to the class-monopoly accumulation of land value in Santiago's inner area. These discussions suggest that we need to pay attention to other urban processes and theories at work, which can complement gentrification theories. Indeed, this is one of the questions that this book raises, and it is also the point strongly emphasised by some of the contributors in this volume (see Doshi on India and Ren on China). Building on this perspective further, gentrification often works in tandem with other urban processes and state projects in the Global South in particular, involving the production of particular state spaces and the establishment of state legitimacy. This is another area of research that requires further attention from urban researchers in both the Global North and the Global South, and we expect further theorisation to emerge from both areas in the near future.

There are evidently different types of state-led gentrification worldwide that warrant further investigation and some new typologies, for example, 'modernising gentrification', 'authoritarian gentrification' and so on. To date, the extant gentrification literature has been largely dominated by discussions of residential gentrification, but 'other' gentrifications, for example, commercial, retail and tourist gentrifications, which have had less presence in the gentrification literature to date, have become increasingly important processes in many cities worldwide operating under various types of political regimes. Indeed, in some Latin American cities like Rio de Janeiro, Buenos Aires and Santiago de Chile, and European cities like Madrid, these gentrification processes are sometimes more important than residential gentrification in certain neighbourhoods. A discussion of tourist gentrification must engage with the recent discussions of 'slum tourism' (see the special issue of *Tourism Geographies*, 2012), as the chapter on Rio de Janeiro testifies to. Very little has been written on 'tourist gentrification' (Gotham, 2005) in either the Global North or Global South, and it is time for gentrification studies to talk to tourism studies and heritage studies, and vice versa. Finally, the as-yet-under-studied relationship between residential and employment issues with respect to gentrification deserves our attention (see the cases of Cairo or Santiago de Chile). Indeed, the chapter on Seoul shows not only that businesses were displaced in the process of gentrification, but also that the economic 'trickle-down' promised from gentrification did not happen, echoing findings emerging about economic trickle-down theory in the West.

The gentrification stories collated in this book urge us to underline Slater's (2006, 2009) plea for more research on displacement. The displacements are different in type (residential, commercial, retail, public space, community, racist, classist), scale (some are small-scale, some are mega-displacements), operation (the ins and outs of how people are actually displaced legally and physically) and impact (on home/residence, employment [past job and any future job], small businesses and intergenerational cohabitation [extended families living near to each other]). As Ley and Teo (2014) point out, in the Global South, eviction and demolition is perhaps more naturalised as an inevitable part of life, and eviction for publicly initiated urban renewal opens up opportunities for negotiations that can lead to improved public housing accommodation in cities like Hong Kong (even if, in reality, this is for a few, not the many). As such, when conflict arises, it is usually about the scale of the (monetary and/or in-kind) compensation package rather than the eviction itself. However, it needs to be noted that the politics of displacement accompany both consensus (as seen in the rise of a particular 'culture of property' in Ley and Teo's discussion of Hong Kong) *and* the use of force and coercion, especially in the context of urbanisation by authoritarian non-democratic states. These complexities are important and can have an impact on attempts to resist gentrification.

Resistance to gentrification seems to have been both significant (eg Istanbul, Karachi, Seoul) and possibly even more successful in the Global South (eg Karachi, Seoul). The 'Right to the City' idea that emerged in the West and has travelled to Asia, South Africa and Latin America may not, however, serve post-colonial cities (eg like Mumbai) well, where the promise of development/modernisation holds sway and identity politics are significant. Some may even argue that the 'Right to the City' is a white, middle-class, Western European idea (see the chapter on India). Even housing activists working on the social cleansing of London's council estates have issues with it, seeing it as a trendy, bourgeois project (see Lees, 2014a, 2014b), though some social movements in Latin America use it along with the term 'gentrification' for their claims (López-Morales, 2013).

Nevertheless, if we conceptualise gentrification as defined by capital reinvestment in the built environment accompanying the displacement of existing users, be they inhabitants or workers (see also Clark, 2005), the main tenets of the 'Right to the City', which emphasise the taking back of the power to produce space from the state and capital, may still hold. How these tenets are going to be realised and the 'Right to the City' put into practice in urban strategies remains subject to various interpretations and disputes. Resistance needs to be contextualised in each locality, critically understanding the temporal and spatial dimensions of urban problematics and historicising the ways in which rights claims have been exercised (for discussions on China's experience, see Shin, 2013, 2014).

This book shows a number of different examples of impeded gentrification – as caused by war and civil unrest (Damascus and Cairo) or public protest (Seoul and Karachi). The economic crisis may have stalled gentrification in some cities around the world, but it has also triggered gentrification in, for example, Athens or Madrid, where the arrival of so-called *buitre* (vulture) speculative foreign funds is helping to accumulate devalued properties and causing the transformation of once lower-income residential neighbourhoods into commercial areas, like the post-crisis scenario did in areas of New York City in the 1970s and 1980s. In fact, we think that the scope of Ley and Dobson's (2008) discussion of 'gentrification limited', that is, of the contexts of impeded gentrification, needs to be expanded with further research. The experiences of economic crisis in many Asian cities in the 1990s and 2000s also indicate that speculative real estate markets quickly followed economic crisis, prompting a further round of commercial real estate projects that resulted in gentrification (see, eg, the chapters on Seoul and Taipei; see also Lützeler, 2008; Shin, 2009; Ley and Teo, 2014). Finding out much more about what limits, stalls and even stops gentrification, but also how crises push it forward, is important in the global fight against it.

One of our goals, and a very difficult one at that, was the post-colonial challenge of 'decentering the reference points for international scholarship' (Robinson, 2006, p 169); to that end, some genuinely alternative starting points can be excavated from these chapters. We could, for example, compare processes between cities through unlikely comparisons, for example, focusing on war zones or military lands. An important thematic across the chapters is that in the context of different forms of political order or state (authoritarian, informalised, corrupt, centralised, etc) and different dynamics of land use or property development, the processes of urban change require different kinds of rubrics of interpretation than found in current analyses of gentrification, but also, in some cases, the same rubrics of interpretation already found in the gentrification literature. There is some indication that an exploration of the early 20th-century experiences of displacement and urban social change across many former colonies and other 'developing' contexts might reveal much longer and more situated histories to urban processes there, in contrast to the idea of the globalisation of gentrification from its Western origins. Unfortunately, researchers like Maloutas (2012), in their search for context-dependent attachment, disempower global debate and weaken the comparative and explanatory possibilities that gentrification theory offers, especially in times where fast-expanding neoliberal policy prescriptions and financial capital are reproducing similar trends of displacement and exclusion in a wide array of different cities across the world.

At the end of the day, gentrification around the globe is an essentially simple concept and few would disagree with Clark's (2005, p 258) definition:

> Gentrification is a process involving a change in the population of land-users such that the new users are of a higher socio-economic status than the previous users, together with an associated change in the built environment through a reinvestment in fixed capital. The greater the difference in socio-economic status, the more noticeable the process, not least because the more powerful the new users are, the more marked will be the concomitant change in the built environment. It does not matter where, it does not matter when. Any process of change fitting this description is, to my understanding, Gentrification.

Furthermore, as Henri Lefebvre (2003) and David Harvey (1978) argued at different times, post-industrial cities in the West saw the retreat of industrial production and the switching of capital into the secondary circuit of the built environment (especially the real estate sector), with the resulting speculation breeding gentrification. Such a rise of the real estate sector has also become the main feature of urbanisation in the Global South and the Global East, and it fits our understanding of gentrification. Given that the rise of the secondary circuit of the built environment and the real estate sector is geographically uneven, it is important to understand the geographically and historically uneven ways in which various agents of capital investment, as well as the functions of a range of state apparatuses and hegemonic ideologies, have contributed to both the safeguarding and reproduction of (often speculative) investment in the built environment.

By way of conclusion, we agree with Atkinson (2003, p 2347) that 'the problem of gentrification is less its conceptualization and more about the need for a project which will begin to address the systematic inequalities of urban society upon which gentrification thrives'. This should be the research agenda now, and gentrification scholars should be at the forefront of pushing for more just urban policies and programmes worldwide. They should also help inform anti-gentrification movements with global evidence while reflecting on their own local realities. At the same time as we distance ourselves from specificities and particularities in the descending process of abstraction to come to a consensus on a core definition of gentrification, we need to ascend to the reality of the cases in this book to contextualise the rise of gentrification (almost always in tandem with other urban processes) in particular places and make our anti-gentrification strategies attuned to local specificities. In fact, we have used what we have learned by editing this book to inform a new book on *Global gentrifications and comparative urbanisms* (Lees et al, forthcoming), where we have the space to expand on the lessons outlined here. While we do not claim that gentrification is the only process that requires our attention, the intensifying struggles over who is in control of our everyday space certainly highlight that gentrification is one of the key battlegrounds in the contemporary world. As the late Neil Smith (1996, pp 185–6) argued:

> I do not think it makes sense to dissolve all these experiences into radically different empirical phenomena. It seems to me that it is of primary importance to retain a certain scalar tension between, on the one hand, the individuality of gentrification in specific cities, neighbourhoods, even blocks, and on the other hand a general set of conditions and causes (not every one of which may always and necessarily be present) which have led to the appearance of gentrification across several continents, at approximately the same time. The power of a more general theoretical stance is augmented by the suppleness that comes from a sensitivity to the details of local experience – and vice versa.

References

Atkinson, R. (2003) 'Introduction: misunderstood saviour or vengeful wrecker? The many meanings and problems of gentrification', *Urban Studies*, vol 20, no 12, pp 2343–50.

Brenner, N. (ed) (2014) *Implosions/explosions: towards a study of planetary urbanization*, Berlin: Jovis Verlag.

Bridge, G., Butler, T. and Lees, L. (eds) (2011) *Mixed communities: gentrification by stealth?*, Bristol: The Policy Press. (Republished in 2012 by the University of Chicago Press).

Caulfield, J. (1989) 'Gentrification and desire', *Canadian Review of Sociology and Anthropology*, vol 26, pp 617–32.

Christophers, B. (2010) 'Geographical knowledges and neoliberal tensions: compulsory land purchase in the context of contemporary urban redevelopment', *Environment and Planning A*, vol 42, no 4, pp 856–73.

Clark, E. (2005) 'The order and simplicity of gentrification – a political challenge', in R. Atkinson and G. Bridge (eds) *Gentrification in a global context: the new urban colonialism*, London: Routledge, pp 256–64.

Davidson, M. and Lees, L. (2005) 'New build "gentrification" and London's riverside renaissance', *Environment and Planning A*, vol 37, no 7, pp 1165–90.

Desai, V. and Loftus, A. (2013) 'Speculating on slums: infrastructural fixes in informal housing in the Global South', *Antipode*, vol 45, no 4, pp 789–808.

García-Herrera, L.M., Smith, N. and Vera, M. (2007) 'Gentrification, displacement, and tourism in Santa Cruz De Tenerife', *Urban Geography*, vol 28, no 3, pp 276–98.

Goldman, M. (2011) 'Speculative urbanism and the making of the next world city', *International Journal of Urban and Regional Research*, vol 35, no 3, pp 555–81.

Gotham, K.F. (2005) 'Tourism gentrification: the case of New Orleans' Vieux Carre (French Quarter)', *Urban Studies*, vol 42, no 7, pp 1099–121.

Harvey, D. (1978) 'The urban processes under capitalism: a framework for analysis', *International Journal of Urban and Regional Research*, vol 2, nos 1–4, pp 101–31.

Harvey, D. (2003) *The new imperialism*, Oxford: Oxford University Press.

Hyra, D. (2008) *The new urban renewal: the economic transformation of Harlem and Bronzeville*, Chicago, IL: University of Chicago Press.

Keil, R. (ed) (2013) *Suburban constellations: governance, land and infrastructure in the 21st century*, Berlin: Jovis Verlag.

Lees, L. (2014a) 'The urban injustices of New Labour's "new urban renewal": the case of the Aylesbury Estate in London', *Antipode*, vol 46, no 4, pp 921–47.

Lees, L. (2014b) 'The death of sustainable communities in London?', in R. Imrie and L. Lees (eds) *Sustainable London? The future of a global city*, Bristol: The Policy Press, pp 149–72.

Lees, L., Slater, T. and Wyly, E. (2008) *Gentrification*, New York, NY: Routledge.

Lees, L., Shin, H.B. and López-Morales, E. (forthcoming) *Global gentrifications and comparative urbanisms*, Cambridge: Polity Press.

Lefebvre, H. (2003) *The urban revolution*, Minneapolis, MN: University of Minnesota Press.

Lemanski, C. (2014) 'Hybrid gentrification in South Africa: theorising across Southern and Northern cities, *Urban Studies,* DOI:10.1177/0042098013515030

Ley, D. and Dobson, C. (2008) 'Are there limits to gentrification? The contexts of impeded gentrification in Vancouver', *Urban Studies*, vol 45, no 12, pp 2471–98.

Ley, D. and Teo, S.-Y. (2014) 'Gentrification in Hong Kong? Epistemology vs. ontology', *International Journal of Urban and Regional Research*, vol 38, no 4, pp 1286–303.

López-Morales, E. (2010) 'Real estate market, urban policy and entrepreneurial ideology in the "gentrification by ground rent dispossession" of Santiago de Chile', *Journal of Latin American Geography*, vol 9, no 1, pp 145–73.

López-Morales, E. (2011) 'Gentrification by ground rent dispossession: the shadows cast by large scale urban renewal in Santiago de Chile', *International Journal of Urban and Regional Research*, vol 35, no 2, pp 1–28.

López-Morales, E. (2013) 'Insurgency and institutionalized social participation in local-level urban planning: the case of PAC comuna, Santiago de Chile, 2003–2005', in T. Samara, S. He and G. Chen (eds) *Locating right to the city in the Global South: transnational urban governance and socio-spatial transformations*, New York, NY: Routledge, pp 221–46.

Lützeler, R. (2008) 'Population increase and "new-build gentrification" in central Tokyo', *Erdkunde*, vol 62, no 4, pp 287–99.

Macleod, G. and Johnstone, C. (2012) 'Stretching urban renaissance: privatizing space, civilizing place, summoning "community"', *International Journal of Urban and Regional Research*, vol 36, no 1, pp 1–28.

Maloutas, T. (2012) 'Contextual diversity in gentrification research', *Critical Sociology*, vol 38, no 1, pp 33–48.

Merrifield, A. (2013a) *The politics of the encounter: urban theory and protest under planetary urbanization*, Athens and London: The University of Georgia University.

Merrifield, A. (2013b) 'The urban question under planetary urbanization', *International Journal of Urban and Regional Research*, vol 37, no 3, pp 909–22.

Phillips, M. (2004) 'Other geographies of gentrification', *Progress in Human Geography*, vol 28, no 1, pp 5–30.

Rerat, P. and Lees, L. (2011) 'Spatial capital, gentrification and mobility: lessons from Swiss core cities', *Transactions of the Institute of British Geographers*, vol 36, no 1, pp 126–42.

Robinson, J. (2006) *Ordinary cities: between modernity and development*, London: Routledge.

Roderos, R.S. (2013) 'Reshaping metro Manila: gentrification, displacement and the challenge facing the urban capital', *Social Transformations*, vol 1, no 2, pp 79–103.

Roy, A. (2009) 'The 21st century metropolis: new geographies of theory', *Regional Studies*, vol 43, no 6, pp 819–30.

Shin, H.B. (2009) 'Property-based redevelopment and gentrification: the case of Seoul, South Korea', *Geoforum*, vol 40, no 5, pp 906–17.

Shin, H.B. (2010) 'Urban conservation and revalorisation of dilapidated historic quarters: the case of Nanluoguxiang in Beijing', *Cities*, vol 27 (Supplement 1), S43–S54.

Shin, H.B. (2013) 'The right to the city and critical reflections on China's property rights activism', *Antipode*, vol 45, no 5, pp 1167–89.

Shin, H.B. (2014) 'Contesting speculative urbanisation and strategising discontents", *City: analysis of urban trends, culture, theory, policy, action,* vol 18, no 4-5, pp 509-16.

Slater, T. (2006) 'The eviction of critical perspectives from gentrification research', *International Journal of Urban and Regional Research*, vol 30, no 4, pp 737–57.

Slater, T. (2009) 'Missing Marcuse: on gentrification and displacement', *City – Analysis of Urban Trends, Culture, Theory, Policy and Action*, vol 13, no 2, pp 292–312.

Smith, N. (1996) *The new urban frontier: gentrification and the revanchist city*, London and New York, NY: Routledge.

Tourism Geographies (2012) 'Special issue: global perspectives on slum tourism', vol 14, no 2.

Ward, K. (2010) 'Towards a relational comparative approach to the study of cities', *Progress in Human Geography*, vol 34, pp 471–87.

Afterword
The adventure of generic gentrification

Eric Clark

"Oh, no, we don't have any gentrification here", said this eminent researcher of the rise of the Taiwanese middle class. On only my third visit to Taipei, I was not inclined to challenge his reply, though the ongoing and newly completed large redevelopments I saw as he drove me around Taipei some 10 years ago did stir doubt. Gentrification cannot be simply read off the urban landscape as if visible in a momentary view. So, who was I to jump to conclusions? Nevertheless, I imagined that these redevelopments – state- or market-led (or both), commercial or residential, inner-city or suburban – involved the massive accumulation of rent-seeking capital, the displacement of homes and livelihoods, and the suffering of many people who pay those costs of 'improvement' that fail to appear on financial balance sheets or glossy plans for 'revitalisation'. In addition, I wondered what the victims of the process in Taipei called it, if not 'gentrification'. What particularities might a vernacular term for the process highlight?

A decade and a dozen visits later, research into urban development in Taipei in collaboration with Taiwanese colleagues tells me that this was not sheer imagination, a travelling theory about a travelling problem. Gentrification is part of Taipei's contemporary geography and history (Jou et al, 2014). However, as could be said of gentrification in Swedish cities in the early post-war period, when massive urban renewal projects were carried out with strong social-democratic legitimacy, and as Ley and Teo (2014) have observed more recently in Hong Kong, public debate and media discourse on urban transformation did not engage with the concept of gentrification. My knowledgeable Taipei guide spoke prior to 'an ontological awakening' spurred by growing inequality (Ley and Teo, 2014).

Ruth Glass introduced her now-classic analysis of London with: 'London can never be taken for granted. The city is too vast, too complex, too contrary and too moody to become entirely familiar' (Glass, 1989, p 133). The same can be said of Abu Dhabi, Athens, Beijing, Beirut, Buenos Aires, Cairo, Cape Town, Damascus and the other cities included in this volume. The rich empirical analyses presented here reflect how gentrification is characterised by particular social, economic, cultural, political and legal contexts. We see diverse forms and processes in Beirut and Jerusalem, authoritarianism in Damascus, favela chic in Rio de Janeiro, multiple processes under a failing state in Cairo, the spectre of development in Indian cities, value extraction in Karachi, endogenous dynamics in Seoul, and a tendency to assume exceptionalism in Chinese cities.

How can we talk of gentrification in such different contexts? Can we conceptualise gentrification as a generic notion while avoiding the two opposing traps of travelling theory: overextending categorical generalisations or 'reification of contextual epiphenomena'. (Whitehead called this the fallacy of misplaced concreteness). With Swedish colleagues, I used the concept of generic gentrification to make sense of widely varying particularities in Swedish cities (Hedin et al, 2012). The much greater scope of variation presented in this volume gives reason to reconsider what generic gentrification might mean.

Generic notions, says Whitehead (1978 [1929], p 17), 'should make it easier to conceive the infinite variety of specific instances'. Stengers (2011, p 19) elaborates:

> When Whitehead uses the word 'generic', and also when he speaks of 'generality', he is not thinking like a logician and is not giving the term the power to define a class of particular cases.... The generic notion does not authorize any definition. It suggests a way of addressing a situation whose eventual success will be the relevance of the questions to which it gives rise. Generalities in the logical sense authorize classifications, with each particular case exemplifying the general characteristic that defines a set of notions. Whiteheadian philosophical generalities, and the notions he calls 'generic', make the wager that the questions to which they will give rise will shed light on features that are important for each situation.

This is very different from Weberian ideal-types or the empiricist idea of an unambiguously defined concept coupled with observations allowing categorisation of events included in or excluded from the concept. This is gentrification: true or false? The point, continues Stengers (2011, p 40), is to construct a concept:

> that requires the highest power of invention: not to privilege any particular mode of knowledge. This is why, in Whitehead's vocabulary, the terms 'general' and 'generality' will never have the meaning given to them in logic. They will never provide the power to forget particularities, but, on the contrary, will point to the ambition to affirm all of them together.

In close engagement with Whitehead's relational process philosophy, Harvey (1996, p 261) argued that 'some sort of theoretical basis can be forged for all that diverse information', clarifying that, 'On the one hand, the radically different cartographies have to be respected since they have a real foundation in highly differentiated socio-ecological processes, but on the other it is erroneous to regard them as totally disconnected' (Harvey, 1996, p 285).

The endurance of a generic notion of gentrification as an 'adventure of ideas' (Whitehead, 1933) is due not to successes in logical-empirical 'testing', but to the relevance of questions it has given rise to in ever-wider contexts. These questions consistently echo Karl Polanyi's (2001 [1944], p 35) problem formulation – 'Habitation versus Improvement' – whereby 'investments' profitable for investors involve 'catastrophic dislocation of the lives of the common people' (for analysis of two profoundly different forms of investment, see Sayer, 2012). The social polarisation and expanding commodification of land and labour pervading recent decades underlies the tenacity of questions surrounding conflict-laden processes in which 'investments' in 'improvement' bring 'growth', wealth and 'gentrified happiness' (Schulman, 2012, p 166) to some, and displacement (Davidson, 2009; Lees, 2014), domicide (Porteous and Smith, 2001; Shao, 2013) and root shock (Fullilove, 2004) to others.

Were it not for Ruth Glass, we may be using another name for the generic notion. Furthermore, thinking through comparative urbanism (Lees, 2012) may lead us to use different concepts that raise questions better suited to shed light on important features. Maybe gentrification was less apposite to 1960s' Stockholm or 1990s' Hong Kong and Taipei, where relative equality and protective welfare arrangements rendered notions of 'urban renewal' palatable. Certainly, it is less congruent with currently fashionable notions of 'sustainable cities', if social dimensions of sustainability are to be taken seriously. Sustainable cities research, however, remains silent on this matter (for an exception see Imrie and Lees, 2014), as 'green (re)development' glosses over and legitimates gentrification, not unlike favela chic.

The research collected in this book, a landmark in the adventure of generic gentrification, affirms that the adventure continues as long as the notion allows us to connect such highly variegated socio-ecological processes. Each chapter confirms the relevance of gentrification in the questions it raises, as well as the limitations of a one-size-fits-all notion. Going beyond the philosophical issues of travelling theory, these case studies reveal the more meaningful limitations of gentrification to be the outcomes of socio-political struggles over the histories and geographies of these places. In this way, the book affirms the normative thrust of politics and social practices capable of removing the 'versus' between habitation and improvement. This, surely, is what the adventure is about: making the notion of gentrification irrelevant.

References

Davidson, M. (2009) 'Displacement, space and dwelling: placing gentrification debate', *Ethics, Place & Environment: A Journal of Philosophy & Geography*, vol 12, no 2, pp 219–34.

Fullilove, M. (2004) *Root shock: how tearing up city neighborhoods hurts America, and what we can do about it*, New York, NY: One World.

Glass, R. (1989) *Clichés of urban doom and other essays*, Oxford: Basil Blackwell.

Harvey, D. (1996) *Justice, nature and the geography of difference*, Oxford: Blackwell.

Hedin, K., Clark, E., Lundholm, E. and Malmberg, G. (2012) 'Neoliberalization of housing in Sweden: gentrification, filtering, and social polarization', *Annals of the Association of American Geographers*, vol 102, no 2, pp 443–63.

Imrie, R. and Lees, L. (eds) (2014) *Sustainable London? The future of a global city*, Bristol: Policy Press.

Jou, S.-C., Clark, E. and Chen, H.-W. (2014) 'Gentrification and revanchist urbanism in Taipei?', *Urban Studies*, first published on July 16, 2014 as doi:10.1177/0042098014541970

Lees, L. (2012) 'The geography of gentrification: thinking through comparative urbanism', *Progress in Human Geography*, vol 36, no 2, pp 155–71.

Lees, L. (2014) 'The urban injustices of new Labour's "new urban renewal": the case of the Aylesbury Estate in London', *Antipode*, vol 46, no 4, pp 921–47.

Ley, D. and Teo, S. (2014) 'Gentrification in Hong Kong? Epistemology vs. ontology', *International Journal of Urban and Regional Research*, vol 38, no 4, pp 1286–303.

Polanyi, K. (2001 [1944]) *The great transformation: the political and economic origins of our time*, Boston, MA: Beacon Press.

Porteous, J. and Smith, S. (2001) *Domicide: the global destruction of home*, Montreal: McGill-Queen's University Press.

Sayer, A. (2012) 'Facing the challenge of the return of the rich', in W. Atkinson, S. Roberts and M. Savage (eds) *Class inequality in austerity Britain*, Houndmills Basingstoke: Palgrave Macmillan, pp 163–79.

Schulman, S. (2012) *The gentrification of the mind: witness to a lost imagination*, Berkeley, CA: University of California Press.

Shao, Q. (2013) *Shanghai gone: domicide and defiance in a Chinese megacity*, Lanham, MD: Rowman & Littlefield.

Stengers, I. (2011) *Thinking with Whitehead: a free and wild creation of concepts*, Cambridge, MA: Harvard University Press.

Whitehead, A. (1925) *Science and the modern world*, New York, NY: The Free Press.

Whitehead, A. (1933) *Adventures of ideas*, New York, NY: The Free Press.

Whitehead, A. (1978 [1929]) *Process and reality* (corrected edn, ed D.R. Griffin and D.W. Sherburne), New York, NY: The Free Press.

Index

C

J

K

L

O

P

S

T

U

V